Disequilibrium, Growth and Labor Market Dynamics

Springer
Berlin
Heidelberg
New York
Barcelona
Hong Kong
London
Milan
Paris
Singapore
Tokyo

Carl Chiarella · Peter Flaschel
Gangolf Groh · Willi Semmler
with contributions by Carsten Köper

Disequilibrium, Growth and Labor Market Dynamics

Macro Perspectives

With 73 Figures
and 23 Tables

Springer

Prof. Dr. Carl Chiarella
University of Technology, Sydney
School of Finance and Economics
P.O. Box 123
Broadway, NSW 2007
Sydney
Australia
carl.chiarella@uts.edu.au

Prof. Dr. Peter Flaschel
University of Bielefeld
Faculty of Economics
Postfach 100131
33501 Bielefeld
Germany
pflaschel@wiwi.uni-bielefeld.de

Dr. Gangolf Groh
University of Magdeburg
Faculty of Economics
Postfach 4120
39016 Magdeburg
Germany

Prof. Dr. Willi Semmler
University of Bielefeld
Faculty of Economics
Postfach 100131
33501 Bielefeld
Germany

New School University
Department of Economics
65 Fifth Ave, New York
NY 10003
USA

ISBN 3-540-64909-3 Springer-Verlag Berlin Heidelberg New York

Library of Congress Cataloging-in-Publication Data
Die Deutsche Bibliothek - CIP-Einheitsaufnahme
Disequilibrium, growth and labor market dynamics: macro perspectives / Carl Chiarella; Peter Flaschel; Gangolf Groh; Willi Semmler. - Berlin; Heidelberg; New York; Barcelona; Hong Kong; London; Milan; Paris; Singapore; Tokyo: Springer, 2000
ISBN 3-540-64909-3

Springer-Verlag is a company in the specialist publishing group BertelsmannSpringer

Printed in Germany

Hardcover-Design: Erich Kirchner, Heidelberg

SPIN 10691081 42/2202-5 4 3 2 1 0 – Printed on acid-free paper

Preface

In this book on disequilibrium, growth and labor market dynamics we take predominantly a macroeconomic perspective. We present a working model that can easily be varied in different directions in order to subsume innovations in the literature on macroeconomics, old and new, and to contribute to important currently discussed macroeconomic issues. Our working model is set up in a way that there is a close relationship between our presented dynamic models and modern macroeconometric models with disequilibrium both in the labor and the goods markets. One of our objectives is, therefore, to narrow the gap between theoretical and applied structural macrodynamic model building.

We hope that the book will be a useful reference for all researchers, academic teachers and practitioners of macroeconomic and macroeconometric model building who are interested in economic dynamics, independently of whether they use equilibrium or disequilibrium methods in their own research. We base this hope on the fact that our approach contains a number of unique features. The emphasis on the identification and analysis of the basic feedback mechanisms at work in modern macroeconomies. A detailed study of the partial as well as integrated dynamic interaction between these feedback mechanisms that constitute the interdependence of markets and sectors of the modern macroeconomy. The relationship between the macroeconomic framework of our working model and the Walrasian, Non-Walrasian and New-Keynesian reformulations of macroeconomics. The development of a framework for the analysis of the dynamic structure of modern macroeconometric models. Finally the development of an approach to the theoretical investigations of large scale macrodynamic models that involves an appropriate blend of a range of analytical, diagrammatic and numerical tools and concepts. In our view, the primary objective of macroeconomics is to analyze the aforementioned basic feedback mechanisms and other types of economic interdependence, be it on the basis of the microfounded approaches currently prevailing (which however often severely restrict the range of interacting components) or on the basis of aggregates that are coherently formulated with respect to stock and flow conditions.

Various material of this book has been presented at different national and international conferences and workshops, in particular at meetings of the European Economic Association and European Econometric Society, the Annual Conferences of the Society for Computational Economics, the Annual Conference of Economists, Australia, the Annual Symposia of the Society for Nonlinear Dynamics and Econometrics, New York, the Conference of the Society of Economic Dynamics, the International Atlantic Economic Conference, the Annual Meetings of the 'Verein für Socialpolitik', the Workshops on Economics with Heterogeneous Interacting Agents, Italy, the Viennese Workshop on Optimal Control, Dynamic Games, Nonlinear Dynamics and Adaptive Systems, the Workshop of the International School of

Economic Research, Siena, the Conference on 'Bifurcations and Chaos in Economic and Social Systems' in Umea / Sweden, the workshop on Econometric Model Building, New York, and the Conference on Commerce, Complexity and Evolution at the University of New South Wales/ Sydney. Parts of the book have also been presented in particular at seminars at the University of Technology, Sydney, Monash University / Melbourne, the Reserve Bank of Australia, Sydney, the Free University of Berlin, the Universities of Konstanz, Bamberg, Mainz, and Bielefeld.

We want to thank the audiences of the above conferences, workshops and seminars and other scholars, colleagues and friends who have commented on our work at those various occasions. Thanks go in particular to Richard Day, Reiner Franke, Alfred Greiner, Cars Hommes, Klaus Jaeger, Stefan Mittnik, Reinhard Neck, Matthias Raith, Carsten Köper, Ingrid Kubin, Thomas Lux, Alan Powell, Hans Jürgen Ramser, James Ramsey, Michael Woodford, and Peiyuan Zhu.

October 1999

Carl Chiarella — University of Technology, Sydney, Australia

Peter Flaschel — University of Bielefeld, Bielefeld, Germany

Gangolf Groh — Otto-Von-Guericke University, Madgeburg, Germany

Willi Semmler — University of Bielefeld, Bielefeld, Germany
and New School University, New York, U.S.A

Contents

III The Perspective: Theoretical Aspects of Modern Macroeconometric Model Building

Chapter 1

Introduction: Integrated Macrodynamics

This book is about labor market dynamics and the macroeconomy and it continues the work by Flaschel, Franke and Semmler (1997) and Chiarella and Flaschel (1999b) on monetary macrodynamics and the macro foundations of Keynesian monetary growth. We extend a short-run Keynesian oriented monetary framework to include wage-price dynamics and economic growth because these are important factors affecting the medium- and long-run performance of the labor market. The term disequilibrium in the title refers to non-market clearing situations, namely to the fact that markets, specifically product or labor markets are not cleared at each instant of time. This requires a study of out-of-equilibrium dynamics and resulting feedback chains and other adjustment mechanisms of the economy. We do not consider microeconomic issues, economic policy and econometric issues here, since the book is mainly on extending integrated macrodynamic modeling with particular stress on the labor market. Microeconomic issues are however more or less implicitly present due to the theoretical history of the structural equations used (see in particular part III) and should receive further attention in future reconsiderations of the work here presented. Macroeconometric model building and policy issues are the perspective of the book, and thus will be addressed in future work by the authors, by extending the foundations laid for this type of analysis in part III of the book.

Recent Approaches
Recent labor market theories have dominantly taken a microeconomic perspective on the labor market by explaining unemployment solely as labor market dependent - dependent on wages and labor market rigidities. Variants of the latter type of theories that have been used to explain the persistence of unemployment in Europe include the bargaining model (McDonald and Solow (1981)), the efficiency wage and shirking theory (Shapiro and Stiglitz, 1984), the insider-outsider theory (Lindbeck and Snower (1989)), the hysteresis model (Blanchard and Summers, 1986) and the matching model (Pissarides and Mortensen (1997)). Unemployment has also been explained on the basis of macroeconomic theories, in particular:

- New Keynesians view unemployment dominantly as a result of a disequilibrium in the labor market. They mostly presume some rigidities in the product and/or labor markets. New Keynesians therefore rely less on the theory of perfectly competitive markets rather than theories of monopolistic or oligopolistic competition. Those theories allow for some stickiness of price and wage movements, so that labor market disequilibria are brought about by the reaction of quantities. Thus, price rigidity on product and labor markets can translate shocks into large employment fluctuations.[1]

- Another direction of macroeconomic theory, although more popular in Europe than in the U.S., has explicitly employed a disequilibrium and rationing approach to explain non-clearing product and labor markets. Here prices and wages are not only seen to be sluggish but rather fixed when quantities adjust whereby disequilibria with persistent unemployment can arise.[2]

- The currently widely used intertemporal general equilibrium theory, for example the real business cycle (RBC-) model, maintains that there is unemployment due to the employment-leisure choice. Here the decisions on consumption and the supply of labor respond optimally to shocks, for example, technology shocks. Prices and wages move infinitely fast to clear markets and expected wage and asset price changes will lead to variation in labor supply and thus to a variation of employment. [3]

In our book we also take an explicit macroeconomic perspective and we design a framework which will allow to consider the above three approaches as limit cases or extensions of our approach.

Feedback and Adjustment Mechanisms

In our modeling of the macro economy where there is an interaction of all major markets - the capital market, the product and the labor market - we allow for non-market clearing situations. In this way we are able to explore the destabilizing or stabilizing mechanisms in a macroeconomy. We do not deny that microeconomic foundations of the behavior of economic agents and forward looking behavior of households and firms, for example, are also important for a proper study of macroeconomics. Yet what truly seems to constitute macroeconomics are the macroeconomic adjustment and feedback mechanisms across the various markets and agents. These can only be properly understood when studied from a macroeconomic perspective. Such macroeconomic adjustment mechanisms represent a combination and interaction of the following elements:

- the Keynes effect (nominal price-interest rate comovements which lead to economic expansion if wages and prices are decreasing),

- the Pigou effect (real money – or wealth – holdings change with inflation: the real balance effect leads to economic expansion via consumption demand if wage and price deflation is occurring),

- the Mundell effect (a negative impact of the expected rate of inflation on the real interest rate which may lead to further economic expansion via investment or consumption behavior in an inflationary environment),

[1] For typical recent textbook representation, see Romer (1996)

[2] This approach is coherently presented in Malinvaud (1977, 1980)

[3] A book in this vain is Cooley (1995)

- Fisher debt effects (negative effects of price decreases on real debt and thus on investment behavior of firms or consumption behavior of debtor households),
- the Rose effect (the destabilizing / stabilizing role of real wage changes depending on wage and price flexibilities and marginal propensities to consume and invest),
- the Harrodian accelerator mechanism in fixed business investment (when there is a positive relationship between changes in capacity utilization and intended investment),
- the Metzler effect (the effect of expected sales on inventory holding and the inventory accelerator mechanism),
- the Dornbusch effect (external destabilizing nominal dynamics based on exchange rate flexibility and a positive feedback mechanism between expected and actual depreciation or appreciation),
- the effect of asset price inflation or deflation (long-term bonds or equities) on spending behavior (based on positive feedback effects between asset price changes, expected capital gains and spending behavior).

We know that not all of the above, and more, later to be mentioned, macroeconomic adjustment - mechanisms are uncontroversial with respect to empirical evidence of their strength and the extent to which they are stabilizing or destabilizing. Yet, in our view the study of these mechanisms and their interactions truly constitute the core of macroeconomics. Their relevance and their feedback effects will be studied in all three parts of this book.

The Macro Structure

Next, we survey some macro structures of our subsequent models. We shall consider three major markets: the money and financial market, the goods market and its inventory dynamics and the labor market. Our study of these markets builds on the work of Keynes (1936), Metzler (1941) and Goodwin (1967); thus we use the abbreviation KMG-model to denote our integrated model. Our model of disequilibrium and growth represents specifically reformulated and extended partial dynamic models of the IS-LM-PC approach of the textbook literature, whereby PC stands for the Phillips-curve, with goods markets in disequilibrium as in Metzler's approach, and with the interaction of capital accumulation and income distribution as in Goodwin's growth cycle analysis.

We extend our basic model in the direction of fairly detailed, high-dimensional macrotheoretic disequilibrium growth models. We also will extend our model to include growth in particular endogenous growth. We also will include considerations on an endogenous NAIRU which may vary over time and intend to go beyond LM representations of the money and financial markets. We show how our model can be used as a bench mark model to evaluate currently used structural macroeconometric models. Such models should be based on fully-specified budget identities. Consistency checks should be made through the computation of steady states and the various types of subdynamics studied in isolation as well as in their interaction.
In order to indicate the macrostructures that we want to pursue let us briefly consider the

following summary of the essential components of an integrated Keynesian disequilibrium macromodel. Figure 1.1 shows in shaded section in the middle what might be considered the backbone of Keynes's (1936) work. In the 'General Theory of Employment, Interest and Money' Keynes suggests the basic causal nexus that makes goods markets behavior, via the investment decisions of firms dependent on what occurs on money and financial markets. Labor markets in turn depend on the outcome on the goods markets with their determination of output depending on actual aggregate goods demand.

However there has been quite a different nexus of the macroeconomy at the center of the macroeconomic debate of the last two decades. In recent dynamic macro models it is mostly the supply side nexus that has been stressed, in particular the dynamic wage-price block. This block is shown as wage-price spiral bottom, here augmented by aspects of demand pressure in both the labor and the goods market, on the left hand side of figure 1.1 and it is surely no exaggeration to state that it has dominated the development of macrostatic and macrodynamic mainstream thinking in recent decades. Supply side effects have been integrated into Keynesian IS-LM models, which via rational expectations have been reduced subsequently to supply side dynamics without effective demand constraint, see Sargent (1987, Ch.5).[4]

One of the consequences of such a concentration on supply side issues has been that the relevance of the above considered causal nexus and the feedback structure we have added to it, see the arrows leading back to the shaded area in figure 1.1, have by and large been neglected.

Micro, Macro and Policy Issues

By emphasizing the macrostructure we do not want to neglect microfoundations and intertemporal behavior of agents. We do think that intertemporal and forward looking behavior is important in macroeconomics. Decisions of agents (households, firms) are made with a view of the future path of the variables, in short, expectations of the future affect current decisions. We also think that intertemporal budget constraints are important constraints for agents and agents spending decisions are in part affected by assets and current or expected future asset prices. We do not build, however, full fledged, intertemporal macro models by assuming dynamic optimization of households and firms, although at various places we will discuss those models. We are leaning more toward heterogeneous agent models where one fraction of agents may be optimizing, the other fraction following more adaptive or trendchasing behavior. Moreover, our emphasis is on macro modeling and the many stabilizing or destabilizing feedback mechanisms, known in the earlier literature on Keynesian macrodynamics. Those have almost entirely been absent in more recent macrodynamic model building with product market, money market and wage-price interactions.[5] The exception seems to be the stabilizing Keynes and Pigou effects, which have survived, but mostly simply serve the purpose of providing for the models at hand a shock-absorber mechanism on the basis of which impulse-propagation mechanisms can be set up and investigated. Even when Keynesian demand constraints are given some atten-

---

[4]For a critique of such results see Flaschel and Picard (1986), Flaschel (1993, 1994b) and Flaschel, Franke and Semmler (1997).

[5]See for example Romer (1996).

tion, those stabilizing mechanisms result in rapid convergence to full employment steady states unless shocks continue to hit the economy.

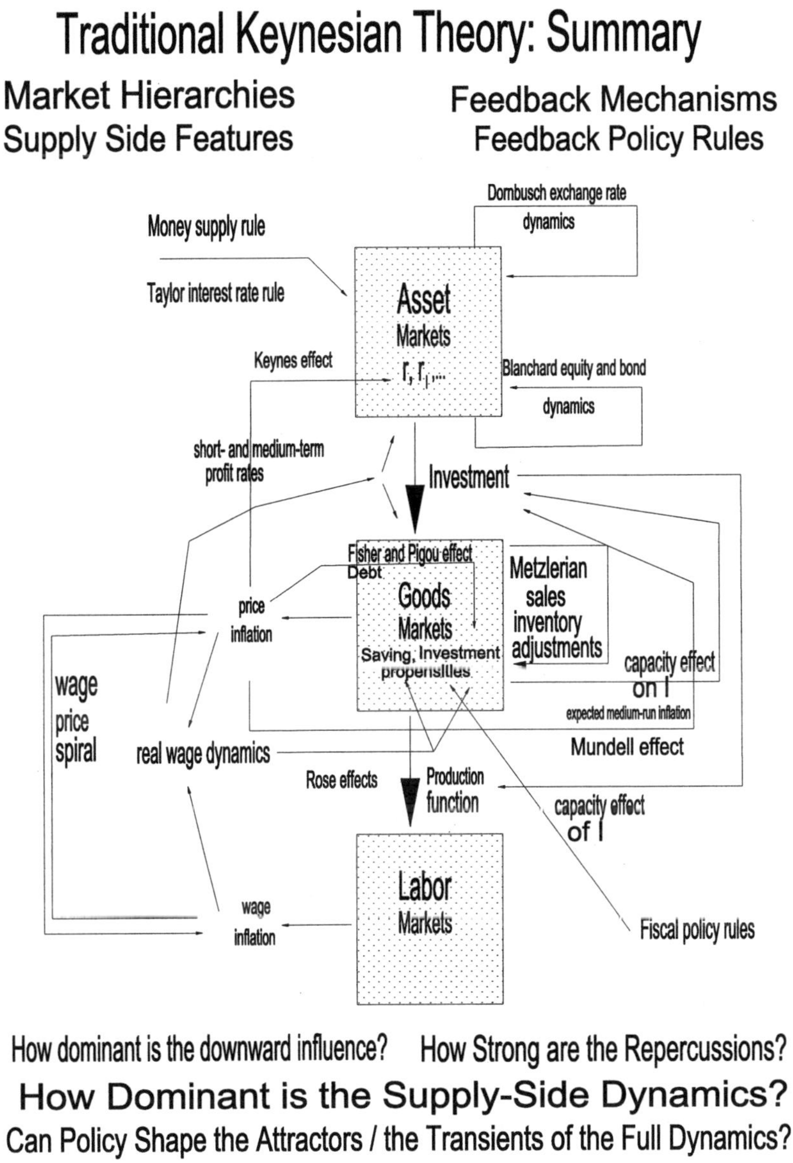

Figure 1.1: The scope of traditional Keynesian theory.

The micro founded supply-side approach ignores a number of important destabilizing feedback effects arising from the aforementioned macroeconomic mechanisms. In particular;

there are (locally) destabilizing effects of rising inflation and expected inflation (Mundell-effects); there are destabilizing Metzlerian inventory accelerator mechanisms; there is the implication, when aggregate demand depends on income distribution and the real wage that either price or wage flexibility must be destabilizing (normal or adverse Rose-effects); there are destabilizing Fisher debt deflation effects with respect to investment or consumption behavior in particular if there is high debt of firms or certain types of households. Finally, there are cumulative processes in exchange rate and asset market dynamics. The latter occurs if expected and actual rates of appreciation or depreciation do exert a positive feedback on each other. There are therefore a variety of reasons on the basis of which one might expect that steady states of economic models are more likely to be surrounded by centrifugal forces than by centripetal ones. The study of such growth and macro fluctuations - fluctuations endogenously arising from disequilibrium adjustment processes such as those mentioned above - should, in our view, remain on the agenda of macrodynamic theorizing. This should have important consequences on the understanding of economic policy issues as well. In our book, however, we deal with policy issues only in a very elementary way. In figure 1.1, for example, we additionally present, top-left and bottom-right, the policy feedback rules that can interact with market outcomes of the private sector. This does not presume that policy can just manipulate this sector from the outside, but that there may be interactions of the behavior assumed for the private sector and the type of policy considered to a more or less significant degree. Policy issues are, however, not yet extensively developed here. In this context the Lucas critique against traditional Keynesian macroeconomic or macroeconometric models, which do not allow for a response of private agents to policy changes would need to be taken into consideration, when we come to develop more fully the feedback loops. In fact, as Sargent (1993, 1998) has recently shown adaptive learning mechanisms may become useful again in macro economics. Since we do not stress policy issues in our book this will be the subject of future work.

Dynamic Techniques

In our book the dynamics of our models will be studied analytically and by computer simulations using modern numerical tools of the theory of nonlinear dynamical systems. Those tools are also applied to study the higher dimensional systems.[6] There is of course always the still fashionable possibility, to rely on full fledged rational expectation models and to model economic dynamics such that the jump variable technique can be applied, for example, when saddle path instability arises. We would, however, like to point out that in the present development of our models we endow our agents with neither the information of the model structure in which they play out their economic roles, nor the computational ability, that they would need to form expectations in a way that has been referred to as "rational" in a large body of literature in the last two decades. The reasons for adopting our approach are further detailed in Flaschel, Franke and Semmler (1997) and Chiarella and Flaschel (1999b,e).[7] In essence these reasons revolve around a critique of the jump–variable technique which the adoption of a "rational" expectations approach would necessitate. Hereby the criticism is not so much directed toward the computational aspect of rational

[6]See Chiarella, Flaschel and Khomin (1999a,b) for details in this respect and for two software packages by which part of the simulations shown in this paper were accomplished.

[7]See George and Oxley (1985), Chiarella (1986, 1990a,1991,1992b), Oxley and George (1994) and Chiarella and Khomin (1999c)) as well as a growing body of empirical evidence, e.g. Frankel and Froot (1987/1990)

expectations behavior - to compute stable branches of saddle paths - but rather toward the informational and behavioral assumptions involved. The recent criticism suggests that a more adaptive approach to expectations modeling may be more appropriate (see the above cited recent work by Sargent (1993, 1998). Rational expectations models employing the jump variable technique have, however, frequently stressed the importance of the treatment of anticipated future events, a topic that should also be considered and solved by the integrated disequilibrium growth dynamics we have in mind. Indeed, new computational techniques can help us nowadays to successfully undertake this effort. Finally, we want to stress that future research, as we have mentioned above, will also need to incorporate the effects of heterogeneity of expectations and of learning on the part of the various economic agents in the economy.

A Brief Outline

Part I of our book introduces, in chapter 2, the partial components of our macromodel and their features with special emphasis on the labor market and goods market disequilibrium and surveys, in chapter 3, the form and implications of the basic integrated working model for the closed economy from the theoretical as well as from the numerical point of view. It also provides perspectives for extending the working model towards small open economies as well as towards the theoretical processing of macroeconometric model building.

Part II of the book turns then to Walrasian, non-Walrasian and New Keynesian variants of our macroeconomic modeling procedure. It basically finds, in chapter 4, that advances of neoclassical growth theory, in particular the inclusion of endogenous growth can be integrated into our working model without much change in its basic philosophy and features. On the other hand, the (discontinuous) limiting situation of infinite adjustment speeds and thus full market clearing, combined with myopic perfect foresight, gives rise to a radically different behavior of the working model with nearly no relationships to the features to the disequilibrium KMG model of part I. Chapter 5, by contrast, provides necessary completions of our working model when fluctuations, generated endogenously or caused by large exogenous shocks, become so pronounced that certain supply bottlenecks are hit. However, in contrast to non-Walrasian theory this only rarely happens so that the Keynesian or KMG regime of this extended disequilibrium growth model remains the dominant one. Chapter 6 of part II, finally, shows that the two PC's approach of the KMG model can be reformulated in various ways from a New Keynesian perspective without altering the dynamics of the integrated KMG model very much, though enriching it now with respect to an endogenous determination of the NAIRU rate of employment on the labor market.

Part III contrasts our approach to disequilibrium and growth with applied macroeconometric models. We in particular focus on the Murphy model for the Australian economy and the Fair model for the US economy. We also briefly discuss the econometric models of McKibbin and Sachs (1991) and the IMF Multimod Mark III model, as presented in Laxton et al. (1998). Our theoretical reformulation of the Murphy model is presented on the extensive level in chapter 6 by building a bridge between our theoretical KMG approach to disequilibrium growth and the applied approach presented in Powell and Murphy (1997), whose relationship to the theoretical approach became apparent during the work of Chiarella and Flaschel (1999) on hierarchically structured Keynesian models of disequilibrium growth. Fair's (1984, 1994) work is, of course, better known than the Murphy model. It is very similar in spirit to our model of chapters 7 to 9 which motivates the discussion of his work at the close of chapter 9 of part III where we analyze a core case of our theoretical form of a macroeconometric model from the theoretical as well as from the numerical point of view which has many points in common with the Fair approach. The intermediate chapter 8 provides the general case of macroeconometric KMG model on the intensive form level and a discussion of its steady state reference path, and shows thereby the difficulties that have to be overcome in future work with respect to theoretical as well as numerical investigations of such a, from the theoretical point of view, large macrodynamic model of the short-, the medium- and the long-run behavior of advanced market economies.

Part I

An Overview on Foundations and Perspectives

Part I of the book presents our working model with some extensions and perspectives. We synthesize well-known partial macrodynamical systems into a coherent integrated labor and goods market disequilibrium growth model and develop a perspective for high order integrated macrodynamic model building. Our working model contrasts to current mainstream methodology with its stress on representative agent, microfoundations and rational expectations. We emphasize disequilibria in product and labor markets, macroeconomic feedback and adjustment mechanisms, and heterogeneity in the household sector and in expectations formation. We sketch a macroeconometric framework that is built on these principles and which will be further analyzed in part III, while part II is devoted to theoretical extensions of the basic working model of part I.

In section 2.1, we reconsider the textbook IS-LM-PC model, where PC denotes that IS-LM is augmented by wage-price dynamics, i.e., a Phillips Curve mechanism including inflationary expectations. We show that a correct analysis and slight extension of this model type gives rise fairly easily to persistent fluctuations in employment and inflation rates rather than to the shock absorbing behavior that is generally believed to be the outcome of such extended IS-LM analysis. Section 2.2 considers non-market clearing on the product market and quantity dynamics. We here employ the Metzler inventory adjustment process to study of how product market disequilibria move in time and may or may not converge to goods market equilibrium. Again there is the possibility for persistent fluctuations when appropriate assumptions on the Metzlerian accelerator mechanism are made. In section 2.3 we consider supply side dynamics in isolation, though not one of the Aggregate Supply (AS) type, but rather one that extends the basic approaches to the classical growth cycle model with an explicit labor market dynamics such as Goodwin (1967) and Rose (1967). We call this the PC-AC approach, since Phillips Curves now interact with capital accumulation or an Accumulation Curve which also allows for a refined treatment of wage-price dynamics, and also adverse adjustments of real wages and real debt (in the case of deflation). Section 2.4 represents a modern discussion of Phillips curves. In fact we will present here two Phillips-curves, the wage and the price Phillips-curve, and offer a unifying and very general framework for such discussions, later to be synthesized into our systematic presentation of integrated models of disequilibrium and growth. We also show how such wage-price dynamics can give rise to an endogenous NAIRU.

Chapter 3 pertains to the integration of our working model and its extensions. In section 3.1 we present and investigate our working model of integrated disequilibrium growth theory. We obtain this as integration of the nominal dynamics, the quantity dynamics and the accumulation dynamics considered in isolation in chapter 2 and present some theoretical results on the resulting six-dimensional dynamics. In addition we study numerical features of the model, allowing only for intrinsic (unavoidable) nonlinearities at first and then for an extrinsic nonlinearity of an institutional type. We here study destabilizing Rose-, Mundell- and Metzler-effects in their interaction and thus obtain, on the one hand, an already fairly advanced feedback structure between goods and labor markets, including the stabilizing Keynes-effect as short-cut to the full interaction with asset markets. We also extend our model to endogenize rates of natural growth as well as 'natural' unemployment. Section 3.2 generalizes the theoretical as well as numerical results to the case of open economies where the Dornbusch type exchange rate dynamics is also present. This section also points out interesting new dynamic features, in particular related to a new extrinsic nonlinearity in the relationship between currency depreciation (or appreciation) and expected interest rate differentials. As shown, a locally destabilizing adjustment mechanism may arise if exchange rates are very flexible, but will result in growth cycle scenario nevertheless when the mentioned nonlinearity is applied. We also investigate stabilizing influences of money wage behavior by a kinked PC as introduced in sections 2.1, 3.1.

With section 3.3 we come to perspectives of this type of integrated disequilibrium growth model building. Though we stress the importance of micro-foundations, we maintain and explain that macro-foundations are needed, first in order to know what is to be micro-founded and second since in our view macroeconomics' most important subject is the investigation of interdependence of markets when macroeconomic adjustment mechanisms are at work. Fully-specified macrodynamics are possible and sensible even in the case where statistical laws make heterogeneous individual behavior unimportant. However, micro-foundations are important in order to control as much as possible what is assumed on the macro-level. For this purposes, microfoundations have to be descriptively adequate to the situation under consideration and must take account of the degree of heterogeneity present in the area where factual macro-hypotheses are needed for the analysis of interdependence of actual market economies. The main purpose of this section therefore, is to discuss principles that properly formulated fully-specified disequilibrium growth macro-models should fulfill.

In section 3.4 finally we sketch a compact theoretical reformulation of a modern macroeconometric approach to disequilibrium and growth and show how such an approach can be subjected to theoretical as well as numerical analysis, giving rise to insights resembling our closed and open economy working models. We show that there is now indeed great need and also great potential to establish fully specified disequilibrium macro models, which are consistently formulated with respect to budget equations and steady state solutions, that can be analyzed from the theoretical, the numerical and the applied point of view on a level of generality characteristic for the modern macroeconometric models that are currently in use.

Chapter 2

Disequilibrium, Growth and Labor Market Dynamics: Foundations

2.1 Introduction

This chapter introduces the basic partial components of what in chapter 3 will become our integrated model of nominal adjustment processes, goods market disequilibrium dynamics, and growth and labor market dynamics. First, we consider the Keynesian analysis of the interaction of Keynes- and Mundell-effects by way of a proper formulation of IS-LM-PC analysis, where short-run goods and money market equilibrium is coupled with medium run sluggish wage adjustment by way of a money wage Phillips curve (the PC component), markup pricing and adaptively formed inflationary expectations. Second, the treatment of goods market disequilibrium and of sluggish quantity adjustment processes is introduced by way of a Metzlerian inventory adjustment mechanism that is closely related in its formal features to the dynamics generated by the classic Kaldorian model of the trade cycle. Third, the interaction of growth and income distribution is presented in an intuitive way referring to Goodwin's growth cycle model and extended in various ways, in particular by the consideration of nominal debt deflation in such a growth context. Integration of these three aspects of disequilibrium, growth and labor market dynamics thus gives rise to a model of Keynes-Metzler-Goodwin, or briefly KMG type, which will be introduced and investigated in its basic format in chapter 3.

2.2 Effective demand, employment and nominal adjustments

We will start our analysis, from the demand side, by means of the conventional IS-LM model, augmented by a Phillips-Curve (PC) dynamic. In this first step we presume that the product market clears, but not so the labor market which is represented by a Phillips-Curve. We include an adaptive expectations formation, as it has often been discussed in earlier literature and has recently come back into macroeconomic modeling, see Sargent (1999). We argue that this well-known dynamic model should by now be well-understood, yet we also obtain surprising results. We will reveal, on the one hand, the true power of the IS-LM-PC approach which can give rise to persistent fluctuations in the place of the generally assumed global asymptotic stability of the steady state of the model. On the other hand, we show that this approach is at least as limited with respect to a full understanding of the fundamental feedback mechanisms of macrodynamic systems, discussed in the introductory chapter 1, as is the case for the basic Accumulation-Phillips-Curve (AC-PC) dynamics, and their Rose (1967) type extensions, to be considered below. Both approaches are in fact complementary to each other, since IS-LM-PC analysis introduces interest rate flexibility, giving rise to the Keynes-effect, and inflationary expectations, giving rise to the Mundell-effect, also in the AC-PC framework. We will study their interaction with respect to the stability question in an integrated model in chapter 3 and will approach thereby the broad perspective outlined in the introduction.

2.2.1 Textbook IS-LM-PC modeling

Macroeconomic textbooks, including those on the advanced level, usually include sections which extend the IS-LM model to the medium run, where wage and price adjustments result from disequilibria in the labor market. Here generally expectations and NAIRU augmented PC dynamics are employed in order to show or indicate the stability of the 'full employment' or NAIRU-equilibrium. This is in particular true for the prominent textbook by Dornbusch and Fischer (1994, 1996) who make use of the following simple IS-LM-PC dynamics.[1] They discuss the effects of supply side and demand side shocks and the subsequent readjustments to the NAIRU rate of employment by means of the following model:[2]

$$\dot{Y} = a_1(\bar{\mu} - \pi) + a_0\bar{f}, \; \hat{M} = \bar{\mu} = const \tag{2.1}$$
$$\pi = \hat{p} = \hat{w} = \beta_w(Y - \bar{Y}) + \pi^e \tag{2.2}$$
$$\dot{\pi}^e = \beta_{\pi^e}(\pi - \pi^e) \tag{2.3}$$

This model is based on a dynamic theory of effective demand represented in eqn. (2.1) where the time rate of change $\dot{Y}$ of IS-LM equilibrium output Y is postulated to depend positively on the rate of change of real balances M/p for which we get $\hat{M} - \hat{p} = \bar{\mu} - \pi$, $\bar{\mu}$ the growth rate of the money supply. The rate of change $\dot{Y}$ results from the conventional Keynes-effect of static IS-LM theory but depends also on an exogenously given *dynamic* fiscal policy parameter $\bar{f}$. Eqn. (2.2) then adds a linear expectations augmented natural rate (money wage and price level) PC which is based on output levels instead of rates of unemployment, due to the assumption of fixed proportions in production.

Since this model is based on fixed proportions in production, a constant labor supply and a constant markup on average wage costs, equation (2.2) can easily be translated into one that along the line of the Phillips-Curve uses rates of unemployment (or employment) in place of Y, see below. Furthermore, the assumption on markup-pricing immediately implies that wage and price inflation can be identified and represented by a unique magnitude π.

[1]These authors employ a special discrete time presentation of the following model, a difference which however is not essential for our following discussion of their model.

[2]Note that the real wage is constant in this approach to economic dynamics, which therefore is clearly a complementary approach to the dynamical analysis performed in section 2.3.

Eqn. (2.3) finally is the conventional adaptive expectations mechanism used in elementary inertia theories of inflation and stagflation, with π^e denoting the expected rate of inflation. The above model can be reduced to the following form:

$$\begin{aligned}\dot{Y} &= a_1(\bar{\mu} - \pi) + a_0\bar{f} \\ \dot{\pi} &= \beta_w a_1(\bar{\mu} - \pi) + \beta_{\pi^e}\beta_w(Y - \bar{Y}) + \beta_w a_0\bar{f}\end{aligned}$$

which is a linear autonomous differential equations system of dimension 2 in the variables output and inflation.

These dynamics imply everything one would like to find in a basic model of monetarist wage-price dynamics with adaptive expectations, here however in the context of a system that is apparently of IS-LM-PC type. There is a unique and economically meaningful steady state $Y_o = \bar{Y}, \pi_o = \bar{\mu} + a_0\bar{f}/a_1$ which reduces to $Y_o = \bar{Y}, \pi_o = \bar{\mu}$ if fiscal policy is stationary. This steady state is globally asymptotically stable in the whole phase plane for all possible parameter values of the model and is of a cyclical nature when adjustment of inflationary expectations is fast and converges monotonically when the adjustment is slow. There hold the monetarist propositions on monetary policy, accelerating inflation, periods of inflation and stagflation, long-run neutrality, changing expectations mechanisms and the like in this framework of medium run IS-LM dynamics. A detailed discussion of all of this – which due to the linearity of the model is straightforward – is provided in Dornbusch and Fischer (1994, 1996) and Flaschel and Groh (1996a, Ch.4, 1998) and will not be repeated here. Moreover, one could argue that this model of Dornbusch and Fischer (1994, Ch.16) is not a valid extension of their linear IS-LM analysis[3] towards an inclusion of the dynamics of wages, prices and inflationary expectations.[4]

Two simple observations must here suffice to justify the claim that this type of analysis is an invalid one even when based on the assumptions that are made by Dornbusch and Fischer (1994, 1996). The first observation is that investment depends on the real rate of interest in their book: rising inflationary expectations π^e will move the IS-curve to the right and thus must enter the original $\dot{Y}$ equation as a mathematical necessity. The second observation is that the Phillips curve is a nonlinear dynamic equation, since it is based on the growth rate and not the time derivative of money wages. However, transformed, the dynamics to be analyzed is thus a (very simple) nonlinear one and thus cannot be represented by the above linear dynamics from the global point of view. These dynamics therefore do not represent a correct formalization of the Dornbusch and Fischer (1994, 1996) assumptions about the Keynesian short- and the monetarist medium-run and thus should be dismissed for these and other reasons, see the work we cited above.

2.2.2 Keynesian IS-LM-PC analysis

The first correction of the dynamics that must be made on the basis of the assumptions of Dornbusch and Fischer's (194, 1996) book, is that the outcome of their linear IS-LM

[3]This in principle should be well-known from Tobin (1975) and subsequent work, but which still seem to be unfamiliar, see Groth (1993) in this regard.

[4]Note that – though globally asymptotically stable – the model is still incomplete since the right half of the phase plane is not an invariant set of this dynamics, i.e., output can be become negative along trajectories that start in an economically meaningful domain.

model, reformulated in terms of the employment rate $V = (Y/x)/L$, should be represented as follows:[5]

$$V = a_0 + a_1 m + a_2 \pi^e, \quad a_1, a_2 > 0, \quad \bar{V} > a_o + a_2 \bar{\mu}$$

since an increase in real balances $m = M/p$ will increase IS-LM equilibrium output (the Keynes-effect) and an increase in inflationary expectations π^e will do the same (the so-called Mundell effect), due to the rightward shift of the IS curve that results from this parametric change. The PC dynamics, easily transformed to rates of change $\hat{m}$ of real balances due to the given growth rate $\bar{\mu}$ of the money supply, then read (when output data are transformed to rate of employment expressions):

$$\widehat{m} = \bar{\mu} - \beta_w(V - \bar{V}) - \pi^e \tag{2.4}$$

$$\dot{\pi}^e = \beta_{\pi^e}(\pi - \pi^e) = \beta_{\pi^e}\beta_w(V - \bar{V}) \tag{2.5}$$

There is of course again the assumption of adaptive expectations in order to make the model determinate. This is the complete model of the Dornbusch and Fischer (1994, 1996) approach to medium run wage-price dynamics. We shall see that this proper IS-LM-PC dynamics has little in common with the dynamics considered in the preceding subsection.

Proposition 2.1.

There are always two steady states of the dynamics (2.4) – (2.5), one that is interior to the right half of the phase plane and thus economically meaningful and one that lies on its boundary:

$$m_0 = (\bar{V} - a_0 - a_2\bar{\mu})/a_1 > 0, \; \pi_0^e = \bar{\mu} \quad \textit{and} \quad m_0 = 0, \; \pi_0^e = (\bar{V} - a_0)/a_2 > 0,$$

respectively. The dynamics around the border steady state are always of saddle-point type ($\det J < 0$*), while the dynamics around the interior steady state will be represented by a stable node, a stable focus, an unstable focus and an unstable node as the parameter β_{π^e}, the adjustment speed of inflationary expectations, is increase from close to zero to close to infinity.*

The proof of these results is simple and is provided in Flaschel and Groh (1998). They in particular state that the dynamics are *never* globally asymptotically stable and are also not locally asymptotically stable if inflationary expectations are adjusted with sufficient speed. The monetarist belief in the overall asymptotic stability of the private sector is therefore not justified in an IS-LM-PC framework, which at best allows for corridor stability (when the Keynes-effect is sufficiently strong relative to the Mundell-effect), but not for more, see also Groth (1993) on this matter. If the steady state is locally explosive it will be globally explosive. The dynamics therefore are not viable ones in this case and the question must be posed what can make them bounded in such an explosive situation.

Already Keynes (1936) in fact did provide the basic answer to this question when stating:

> Thus it is fortunate that workers, though unconsciously, are instinctively more reasonable economists than the classical school, inasmuch as they resist reductions of money-wages, which are seldom or never of an all-round character...(p.14). The chief result of this policy (of flexible wages, the authors) would

[5] $x = 1/l_y$ labor productivity. Note that we also make use of the labor coefficient l_y in the place of x in the following.

> be to cause a great instability of prices, so violent perhaps as to make business calculations futile ... (p.269)

We use the following stylized modification of the PC used so far in order to provide a mathematical expression for the institutional fact just quoted:

$$\widehat{w} = \max\{\beta_w(V - \bar{V}) + \pi^e, 0\}.$$

This Phillips curve says that money wages behave as in the preceding subsection if their growth rate is positive, but stay constant if they would be falling in the previous situations. There is thus no wage deflation possible now. Of course the assumed kink in the money wage PC could be smoothed or some wage deflation could be allowed for, but this will not alter the conclusions significantly. We consider this kinked Phillips curve as a much better description of reality than the one that is linear throughout.[6]

The immediate consequence of this new form of the Phillips curve is that system (2.4) – (2.5) now only applies when $\beta_w(V - \bar{V}) + \pi^e \geq 0$ holds while it must be replaced by

$$\widehat{m} = \bar{\mu} \tag{2.6}$$
$$\dot{\pi}^e = -\beta_{\pi^e}\pi^e \tag{2.7}$$

in the case $\beta_w(V - \bar{V}) + \pi^e < 0$.[7] We thus have a system of differential equations which is now only continuous, but which can be made a smooth system in an obvious way. We call this system the patched system while we refer to the earlier dynamics as the unpatched one.

There are a variety of propositions that can be formulated in the context of such patched dynamics, see Flaschel and Groh (1998) in particular, but due to space limitations we will consider here only one of them which describes the outcome of the explosive case of the Dornbusch and Fischer (1994, 1996) model in the patched situation when there is steady state inflation ($\bar{\mu} > 0$). This proposition refers to figure 2.1 which represents the considered dynamics in the m, π^e state space.

Proposition 2.2 (Viability Theorem)

1. *There exist exactly three steady states for the patched dynamics: S_o, S_1, W if $\bar{\mu} > 0$ holds. These steady states are connected by the $\dot{\pi}^e = 0$ isocline.*

2. *Consider the case when the interior steady state W is locally repelling (which occurs for values of β_{π^e} chosen sufficiently large). Then: Every trajectory in D_o converges to a persistent cycle around W (and in D_1).*

[6]See Laxton, Rose and Tambakis (1997) for a recent empirical discussion of the likelihood of this kind of nonlinearity in the integrated price level - rate of unemployment Phillips curve.

[7]The two systems are identical at the border line $\hat{w} = \beta_w(V - \bar{V}) + \pi^e = 0$.

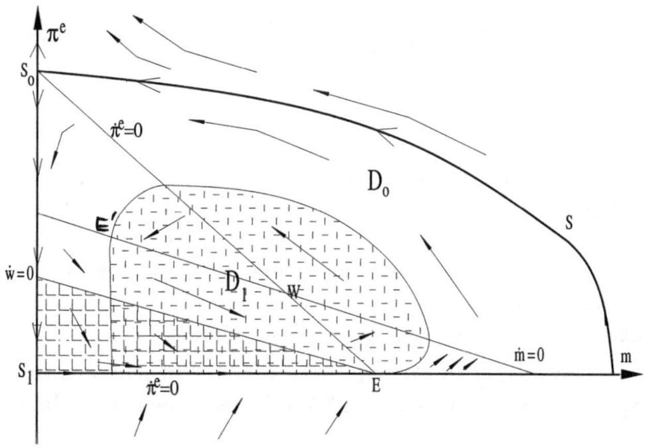

Figure 2.1:
Implications of the kinked Phillips curve in the case of steady state inflation.

As figure 2.1 shows the domain below the separatrix S of the saddlepoint S_0 in the nonnegative orthant is now an invariant domain D_o, i.e., no trajectory which starts in it can leave it. Note also that the domain below the $\dot{w} = 0$ isocline is governed by the above revised dynamics in the place of the one of the preceding section, which however only alters the direction of the dynamics qualitatively on the horizontal axes which is now also an isocline ($\dot{\pi}^e = 0$) of the patched dynamics (up to point E). Note furthermore that the trajectory which starts in E (horizontally), followed up to point E' and then vertically continued down to the m-axis, also defines an invariant domain D_1 of the patched dynamics which moreover is attracting for all trajectories in the interior of D_o. We thus have that all orbits in D_o (with the exception of the ones on the vertical axis) are either inside of D_1 or are entering the domain D_1 (from its left) at some point in time.

We do not go into the proof of this proposition or a deeper explanation of the phase diagram shown, but refer the reader to the above quoted work in this regard.[8] We simply close this subsection by stating that the depicted figure 2.1 is far away from anything that can be found on IS-LM-PC dynamics in the literature, and this is simply due to the fact that there is a Mundell effect (in IS-LM), a simple growth law (of wages) and a fundamental institutional asymmetry in the Phillips-curve, which makes the overall dynamics viable, abstracting from shocks in m or π^e that throw the dynamics beyond the separatrix S shown in figure 2.1.

2.2.3 Reinterpreting the IS-LM-PC dynamics

Let us here first recapitulate the results of the preceding subsection by means of a numerical example. Figures 2.2 shows the various situations considered in this subsection for the case

[8] An IS-LM-PC model that is formally identical to the one here considered will be investigated in detail in section 6.3.

of a stable or unstable steady state of the unpatched dynamics, with $\beta_{\pi^e} = 0.2$ in the latter case and with $a_0 = 0.75, a_1 = 1, a_2 = 1, \bar{V} = 0.95, \bar{\mu} = 0.05, \beta_w = 0.5$ throughout. We use white color to visualize starting points of the phase space which give rise (or are supposed to give rise) to convergence to the steady state and grey color for the unstable (explosive) situations. The figure 2.2 top left represents the situation asserted, but not proved by the textbook literature: asymptotic stability for all points of $\Re^2$ with a positive value of real balances m. We have seen that such an assertion cannot be true, in particular due to the existence of a further steady state (of saddlepoint type) of the correctly specified model. The figure 2.2 top right, by contrast, shows the true situation in the case of the unpatched system and inflationary expectations that are sufficiently sluggish and thus make the steady state locally stable (the white area), but not globally stable due to the stable separatrix that belongs to the border steady state. Next, the figure 2.2 bottom left shows the situation where inflationary expectations are sufficiently fast (but not really fast as the chosen value $\beta_{\pi^e} = 0.2$ shows). We see that all situations off the interior steady state will not lead us back to it and thus get total instability (all grey). Therefore, in the figure 2.2 bottom right, we have added the kink to these dynamics and get for the resulting patched system that the steady state, though locally unstable, is now surrounded by a periodic attractor or a stable persistent cycle which is attracting for all initial situations below the shown separatrix (the white area). Note finally, that the increase in the speed of adjustment of inflationary expectations that has been considered here reduces the size of the corridor where the system exhibits viability (based on the kink in the locally explosive case), as the presentations on the right hand side of figure 2.2 show.

Let us now proceed to a reformulation and reinterpretation of the structural equations underlying the dynamical system of the preceding subsection which do not alter its mathematical formulation and stability features, but which give the goods market in the place of the labor market the decisive role in the explanation of the stability and instability scenarios just discussed. In order to introduce this reformulation of IS-LM-PC analysis, we start from a stylized representation of empirical results testing the conventional NAIRU model provided by Fair (1997a), and extended in Fair (1997b). Fair's (1997a) reconsideration of the structural price and wage equation leads him to the, here simplified, result that it is in fact the price Phillips curve which determines the shape of the integrated Phillips curve of the literature (associating price inflation with labor market disequilibrium), while wage inflation is following price inflation more or less passively, which implies that the integrated Phillips curve now refers to demand pressure on the goods market and not, as is customarily assumed on the labor market. In fact, if we consider two Phillips curves, a wage and price Phillips curve, this leads to the following special reformulation (for full specifications of the two Phillips curves, see sections 2.3 and 2.4).

$$\hat{w} = \kappa_w \hat{p} + (1-\kappa_w)\pi^e, \quad \kappa_w \in (0,1) \tag{2.8}$$

$$\hat{p} = \beta_p(U_c - \bar{U}_c) + \kappa_p \hat{w} + (1-\kappa_p)\pi^e, \quad \kappa_p \in (0,1) \tag{2.9}$$

or, if solved and presuming a medium-run inflation rate this explicitly gives:

$$\hat{p} = \frac{1}{1-\kappa_w\kappa_p}\beta_p(U_c - \bar{U}_c) + \pi^e.$$

Here the rate of capacity utilization U_c is now used in place of the usual rate of employment as the measure of demand pressure that drives price inflation, $\bar{U}_c$ the target rate of capacity utilization. Formally seen this Phillips curve can even be represented exactly as in section 2.4, except that labor supply and capital stock growth are still excluded due to the medium run nature of our analysis, if one makes use of the following implications of our assumption of a fixed proportions technology (x, y^p the fixed labor and capital productivity ratios):

$$U_c = \frac{Y}{Y^p} = \frac{1}{l_y y^p}\frac{L^d}{K} = \frac{1}{l_y y^p}\frac{L}{K}\frac{L^d}{L} = \frac{1}{l_y y^p}\frac{L}{K}V = c_1 V$$

The price Phillips curve thereby becomes of the form:

$$\hat{p} = \frac{1}{1-\kappa_w \kappa_p}\beta_p c_1 (V - \bar{V}) + \pi^e$$

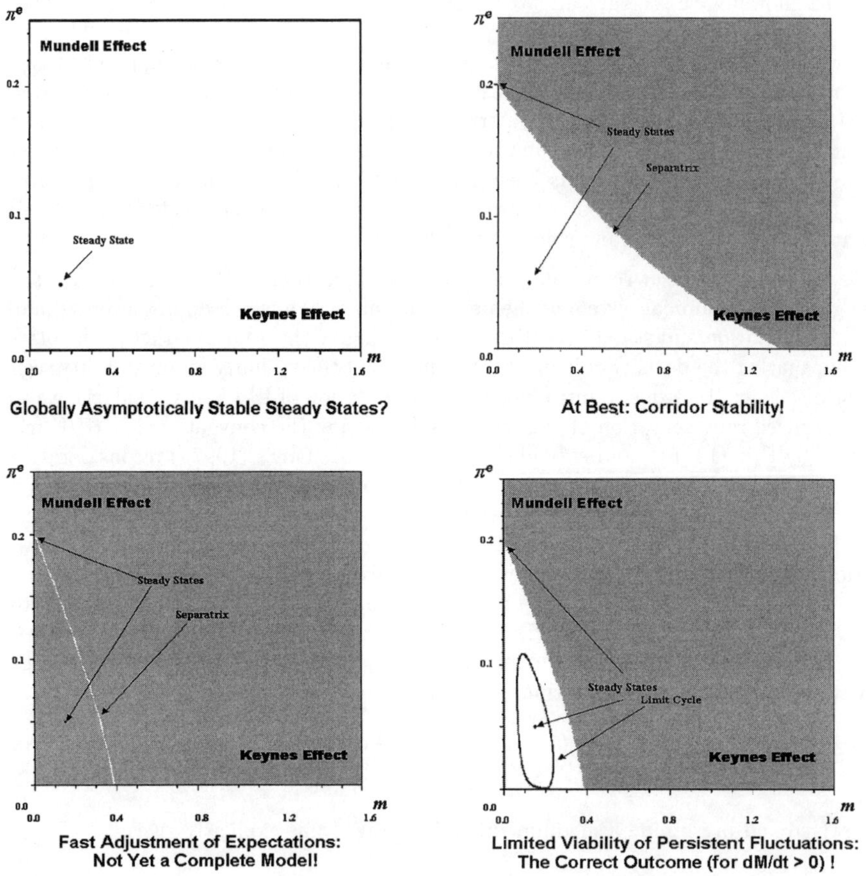

Figure 2.2: The different aspects of the Dornbusch/Fischer approach to IS-LM-PC analysis.

without implying that the demand pressure driving inflation is a labor market phenomenon. We also note that the NAIRU rate $\bar{V}$ implied by it is not at all related to labor market issues. In fact the above shows that it is the NAIRU rate of firms' capacity utilization, while there is in fact no labor market NAIRU at work in the present model. This shows that there is the possibility that the literature on the conventional type of integrated PC's might completely misinterpret the NAIRU phenomenon.[9]

On the basis of this reformulation of the (across markets) integrated Phillips curve the analysis of section 2.4 can be applied, with the interpretational differences just stressed, namely that $\bar{U}_c$ determines the steady state value of the rate of employment and that the destabilizing Mundell - effect is now solely due to the behavior of firms and not at all to the process of wage negotiations. This implies that price flexibility is now bad for economic stability via the so-called Mundell effect. This effect, adding to the Rose adverse real wage effect and the Fisher debt effect considered in section 2.3 below, says that there can be a positive (destabilizing) feedback mechanism leading from rising inflation to rising expected inflation. Then, via the real rate of interest, to rising aggregate demand and thus to further inflationary impulses if the negative Keynes feedback effect on aggregate demand based on a positive correlation of the nominal price level and the nominal interest rate is not strong enough to overcome this cumulative tendency in the interaction of expected and actual rates of price inflation. Price flexibility must therefore be regarded with suspicion, in particular when it occurs under deflationary pressure, as shown in subsection 2.1.2 and in later subsections on Rose and Fisher debt effects. Real floors to economic activity are not so easily established as ceilings. The latter are built into the system via supply bottlenecks or via monetary and fiscal policy, which may stop accelerating growth, but which not so easily can revive declining economic activity.[10]

A recent discussion concerning the core of practical macroeconomics, in the papers and proceedings issue of the American Economic Review 1997, provides numerous statements on pros and cons for the IS-LM framework. It is recognized that there still remains scope and relevance for traditional Keynesian dynamics, in particular in the applied area, with the cons generally referring to a lack of microfoundations[11] of Keynesian analyses. Nevertheless, from this discussion one encounters observations of the following kind:

> Right or wrong, the IS-LM model, and its intellectual cousins, the Mundell-Fleming model and the various incarnations of aggregate supply - aggregate demand models, have proved incredibly useful at analyzing fluctuations and the effects of policy. (Blanchard, 1997, p.245)

Yet, in view of the analysis presented in this subsection and the following ones, it can be claimed that traditional Keynesian analysis is in fact still poorly presented even on the textbook level, but also in more advanced types of analysis, if dynamic issues are addressed. There is no thorough discussion of the many scenarios even the simple IS-LM-PC model can give rise to, there is no investigation of the additional instabilities arising from Rose

[9]See also Fair (1997a,b) on this issue.

[10]See here also Flaschel (1994c) and Flaschel and Franke (1996,98).

[11]Generally meaning microfoundations based on the representative agent and intertemporal utility maximization paradigm. We do not enter here into the debate as to whether such a paradigm provides a useful basis for microfoundations of macroeconomics.

real wage and Fisher debt effects to be considered in the next sections, nor is there any far-reaching analysis of the full picture of traditional Keynesian dynamics as sketched in chapter 1. There is no well-documented general analysis of the wage-price spiral, based on demand pressure and cost-push terms, as we shall present it in the following sections, no detailed study of an integrated theoretical model with sluggish price as well as quantity adjustments and varying rates of capacity utilization for both labor and capital as we shall present it in section 2.3, no such model type with less than perfect exchange rate dynamics, see section 3.2, and no such model where endogenous growth, financial markets, policy feedback rules, and more, are systematically investigated as to their contribution of the overall behavior of the macroeconomy.

There are however integrated models which address many of these issues, but not all of them, from an applied perspective. Yet, these empirically motivated structural macroeconometric models have until recently[12] never been analyzed in detail from the theoretical perspective, since these models are filled with a lot of empirical details, often not complete with respect to long run aspects, and not represented in the form of a theoretical reference model in the literature which would have allowed the analysis of the existence of steady states, their stability and of mechanisms that ensure global boundedness should the steady state be surrounded by centrifugal forces. Recent structural macroeconometric models now tend to include long-run considerations, but they still continue to believe that the deterministic part of the dynamics they consider is behaving like a shock absorber, a dynamic scenario with a long tradition in dynamic economic theory, but nevertheless only one possibility among many others, in particular in the high order dynamical systems that any integrated macrodynamics will necessarily lead us to.

It can therefore not really be claimed that we do not have model types at our disposal which enrich the early Keynesian quantity dynamics by detailed price dynamics, asset market behavior, questions of open economies and more. But it is surely true that these models, or better, their common theoretical core (removing lags, special features and pure replication by disaggregation) are not presented and investigated to any satisfactory degree. In view of the above quotation from Blanchard (1997) it must therefore be added that the usefulness of dynamic IS-LM analysis is to be regarded as very limited and fragmented in its present state where there are only more or less isolated attempts available for this type of analysis, see for example Turnovsky (1977, 1995). Furthermore, there is still the confusion (see again the above quotation from Blanchard (1997)) that AS-AD dynamics, as for example presented in Sargent (1987, Ch.5), is the model of Keynesian medium and long run analysis. This, however, cannot be true simply due to the fact that capital is always fully employed in these approaches, while Keynesian dynamics should in principle study the reasons for the possible underemployment (or overemployment) of all factors of production.

We thus conclude that even those authors who are sympathetic to the traditional Keynesian way of analyzing the macroeconomy do not sufficiently describe what such analyses have been capable of achieving. As far as systematic explorations of the fluctuating growth patterns to which they can give rise are concerned, such analyses are still in a state of infancy. Barro (1994) comes a step closer to the true alternative in macrodynamic analysis when he states:

[12]See for example Barnett and He (1998) for an exception.

> We have available, at this time, two types of internally-consistent models that allow for cyclical interactions between monetary and real variables. The conventional IS/LM model achieves this interaction by assuming that the price level and the nominal wage rate are typically too high and adjust only gradually toward their market-clearing values. The market-clearing models with incomplete information get this interaction by assuming that people have imperfect knowledge about the general price level.

It is clearly stated here that both wage and price rigidity and imbalance in the labor and the goods market are the basic building blocks of the disequilibrium approach to macrodynamics, which cannot therefore be of the Aggregate Supply-Aggregate Demand (AS-AD) variety, but it is not made clear that the analysis of the 'cyclical interactions between monetary and real variables' is not yet very far developed. Certainly, it is admitted by Barro that disequilibrium approaches can be internally consistent, as we shall try to develop them below in a basic integrated format.

We conclude this section with the observation that much remains to be done even on the level of traditional Keynesian IS-LM growth dynamics in order to obtain a well-understood reference model against which the achievements of more recent studies of the dynamic implications of market imperfections, supply side bottlenecks, and also of perfect market clearing approaches, can be evaluated and put into perspective. To demonstrate this in more detail will be the topic of the remaining sections of Part I and will also concern us in part II and part III from the perspective of integrated models with Keynesian rationing in the markets for goods and labor.

2.3 Goods market disequilibrium and quantity adjustments

Next we turn to the study of quantity adjustment mechanisms on goods markets. The study of quantity adjustment processes on goods markets were popular in dynamical theories of output and growth in the period after the publication of Keynes' (1936) 'General Theory' until the beginning of the seventies. Shortly after Samuelson's (1939) study of multiplier - accelerator interaction with its four stability scenarios and Harrod's (1939) essay on instabilities in dynamic growth theory there appeared the trade cycle model of Kaldor (1940) and the growth analysis of Domar (1946). Hicks (1950) synthesized the trade cycle and growth analysis of the forties in a certain way and created the model type that was viewed as the prototype model of economic fluctuations including growth in the sixties, also widely used in macroeconometric model building, see Evans (1969) for a typical example and a detailed representation of theories of the multiplier - accelerator type. Goodwin (1951) laid foundations for a multiplier - accelerator model type that could generate complex dynamics, not unrelated to the early multiplier – accelerator approach with gestation lags of Kalecki (1935).

Accelerator mechanisms are present in models of economic growth or the business cycle when rates of capacity utilization (or output per capital) influence investment behavior and they are most effective in creating instability scenarios when they enter the investment function not only as a proportional term, but also in derivative form where investment is driven not so much by output levels, but rather by their rate of change. Such goods market accelerating mechanisms are no longer at the center of interest. Integrated models of monetary growth of theoretical or applied nature are built today without much reference to multiplier-accelerator analysis. In particular models of equilibrium growth have become the focus of interest now, which moreover are often believed to be attracting with respect to the steady state and the deterministic part they exhibit, so that their stochastic reformulation leads to the application of the Frisch paradigm of impulse and propagation of varying degrees of importance of these two cycle generating and propagating mechanisms. Local instability of steady states and the global boundedness of the dynamics that results from behavioral nonlinearities have also received some interest, but solely in theoretical work on nonlinear economic dynamics.

In this book we will generally use levels of capacity utilization as partial determinant of investment behavior and not their rate of change. We will leave the analysis of derivative effects of capacity utilization on investment for future investigations on the importance of growth theories of Harrod (1939) and Domar (1946) type. Furthermore, the generalization of the trade cycle approach of Kaldor (1940) to growing economies is not an easy matter, as Skott (1991) has observed in particular, see also the reconsideration of the Kaldor model below. The introduction of multiplier - accelerator mechanisms into the analysis of business fixed investment and capital stock growth is therefore to be approached in detail as a separate topic that has to investigate thoroughly the instability scenarios that are created for long run growth on this basis. Easier to integrate and to investigate from a partial as well as from an integrated perspective are multiplier - accelerator analyses that concern the shorter run and the role of inventory investment. Such study of goods market disequilibrium, in place of analyses of real growth dynamics, is in fact necessary in a Keynesian approach that attempts to model sluggish price as well as quantity dynamics. Prominent examples with goods market disequilibrium can be found in Kaldor (1940), Tobin (1975) and Blanchard (1981).

The seminal paper that laid the foundations for multiplier - accelerator modeling of inventory adjustment processes is Metzler (1941), see also Evans (1969). Franke and Lux (1993) and Franke (1996), among others, have recently revived this approach showing that it gives rise to Hopf-bifurcation and cyclical loss of stability if the accelerator mechanism becomes sufficiently strong and that the explosiveness that comes about for even stronger accelerating effects can be tamed by means of appropriate nonlinearities in the inventory adjustment behavior of firms. We will use this approach, to be presented in this section in isolation from growth and monetary dynamics, in order to provide a sound basis of integrated models of disequilibrium and growth dynamics.

In order to provide a thorough and nevertheless intuitive analysis of Metzlerian inventory adjustment mechanisms and the goods market disequilibrium dynamics, it is useful to start from Kaldor's (1940) trade cycle mechanism since this mechanism is of importance from a methodological point of view in many other partial disequilibrium approaches, besides inventory dynamics (to be considered here). For example in Cagan type models of inflationary dynamics or in Dornbusch type models of exchange rate dynamics. Kaldor's intuitive fast - slow dynamics of output and capital stock adjustment in fact is always applicable if expectations (the fast variable) interact with actual change (the slower variable), at least when disequilibrium adjustments are allowed for.

2.3.1 An early modeling of the trade cycle

Let us therefore start with the Kaldor (1940) model. The Kaldor model is one of the early nonlinear business cycle models which exhibits local dynamic multiplier instability at its steady state, but can be made globally bounded via a simple nonlinearity in demand behavior. As viability mechanism, for example, an investment function is conceived which becomes bounded as income passes through certain thresholds. This idea is also employed in Goodwin's (1951) multiplier-accelerator approach to the trade cycle as well as in other variants of this model type. We concentrate here on Kaldor's approach since it allows for a natural analog in the analysis of the inventory adjustment mechanism as conceived by Metzler (1941) and since it moreover can be applied to many situations where expectations produce local instability and on this basis global stability via the assumption of threshold behavior. In the following reformulation of the Kaldor trade cycle mechanism, these dynamics are based on the following two laws of motion and only one nonlinearity to be considered later on in the investment function:[13]

$$\dot{K} = I(Y,K), \quad I_Y > 0, I_K < 0, \tag{2.10}$$

$$\dot{Y} = \beta_y(\bar{C} + cY + I(Y,K) - Y) = \beta_y(I(Y,K) - sY + \bar{C}). \tag{2.11}$$

with the (by assumption) unique and strictly positive equilibrium $I(Y_o, K_o) = 0, Y_o = \bar{C}/s$, where $s = 1 - c \in (0,1)$ denotes the marginal propensity of households to save and $\bar{C}$ their autonomous consumption. The model therefore supplements a capital accumulation equation $\dot{K}$ based on the capital stock adjustment principle with a simple textbook version of the dynamic multiplier $\dot{Y}$ of Keynesian goods market disequilibrium analysis. It is posited that net investment is always realized. Note that this model exhibits negative net investment and savings in the depressions it gives rise to. This can be remedied by a growth cycle reformulation of it which we shall briefly consider later on.

The important innovation in this model, as compared to the IS-LM model of the preceding section, is the alternative type of investment behavior it assumes, which is now based on the so-called capital stock adjustment principle.[14] The second equation of this dynamic model is the dynamic multiplier process, which represents the simplest way to introduce sluggish output adjustment in a Keynesian approach to goods market disequilibrium.

Following Kaldor (1940) we assume with regard to this multiplier process that it is unstable at the stationary state of the economy ($\dot{K}_o = 0, \dot{Y}_o = 0$), i.e., the marginal propensity to spend $c + I_Y$ is assumed to be greater than 1 ($s < I_Y$) at this (medium run) equilibrium solution $K_o, Y_o = \bar{C}/s$. This instability condition is however, as Chang and Smyth (1971) have shown, not yet sufficient for instability. A stronger condition is in fact necessary to achieve this aim, namely $\beta_y(I_Y - s) + I_K > 0$. In this case, the Jacobian at the steady state of the above dynamical system will have a positive trace (and a determinant that is always

[13]See Flaschel (1993), Flaschel and Groh (1996b), Flaschel, Franke and Semmler (1997) for further investigations of this model type, also with respect to the related approach of Goodwin (1951).

[14]See Matthews (1970) for a detailed comparison of this principle with the accelerator principle employed in multiplier - accelerator explanations of business fluctuations.

positive). The stationary equilibrium is thus either an unstable node or an (unstable) source in this case.

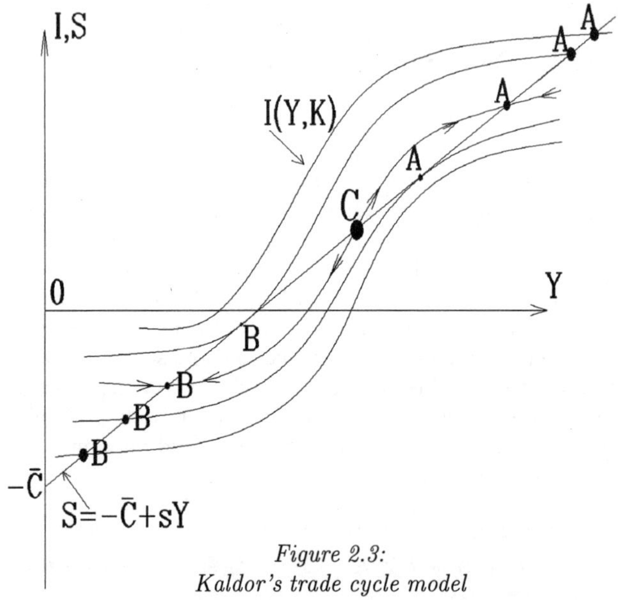

Figure 2.3:
Kaldor's trade cycle model
(A's, B's the stable and C's the unstable IS-equilibria).

The basic idea of Kaldor's approach to an explanation of the trade cycle as persistent deterministic fluctuations is that the investment function is a nonlinear (increasing) function of national income Y with investment being fairly insensitive to changes in Y for small as well for large values of income Y. The simplest representation of Kaldor's cycle mechanism is given by the situations of goods market equilibria as well as goods market disequilibria shown in figure 2.3:

Figure 2.3 shows that there can be three (or more[15]) IS-equilibria in such a model, two stable ones ($I_Y < s$) for high as well as low values of national income and an unstable one in between ($I_Y > s$). The economy will then, if the dynamic multiplier process works with sufficient strength, always be near either to a boom or a depressed situation, the unstable situation in between characterizing some sort of average situation. Yet, it was assumed above that the growth, or the decline, in the capital stock exerts a negative influence on the level of net investment. In the above boom situation we thus get that the I-curve shifts downwards, whereas in the depressed situation, where net investment is negative, we have a shrinking capital stock and thus an upward shifting I-curve. These shifts of the I-curve will continue until a point is reached where the upper IS-equilibrium (the case of a downward shifting I-curve) and the lower IS-equilibrium (the case of its upward shift) disappears (AC and BC, respectively).[16] In such a case the economy switches to the alternative stable

[15]If there is more than one point of inflection of the I-curve in the above diagram (which may give rise to more than only one limit cycle).

[16]See Evans (1969) and Lorenz and Gabisch (1989) for further analytical and graphical presentations of these assertions.

equilibrium, and thus falls into a depression in the initial case of a boom equilibrium and rises into a boom in the opposite situation. The model thus generates, under suitable further mathematical conditions, a succession of booms which all change into depressions after a while and vice versa. This is the intuitive idea behind Kaldor's model of the trade cycle.

This model therefore suggests that there should exist stable limit cycles in the evolution of the K,Y-dynamics from which all relevant trajectories are attracted. To show this by graphical means in an economically meaningful way we assume that the slope (now) of the $\dot{Y} = 0$-isocline ($sY = I(Y,K) + \bar{C}$)[17] is such that a box of the type shown in figure 2.4 can be drawn in an economically meaningful subdomain of the whole phase space. This box is normally chosen in the literature such that it contains parts of the boundary of the nonnegative orthant so that only $K > 0, Y > 0$ can be assured by it (see Chang and Smyth (1971) for example). This, however, is not a sensible procedure, since the forces which restrict the dynamics to a compact domain cannot be formulated by making use of the 'catastrophe values' $K = 0, Y = 0$, where savings and investment behavior will be no longer of a reliable nature. An economically meaningful procedure must restrict the dynamics to a compact domain that uses economically sensible limits for the possible fluctuations in net national income in particular.

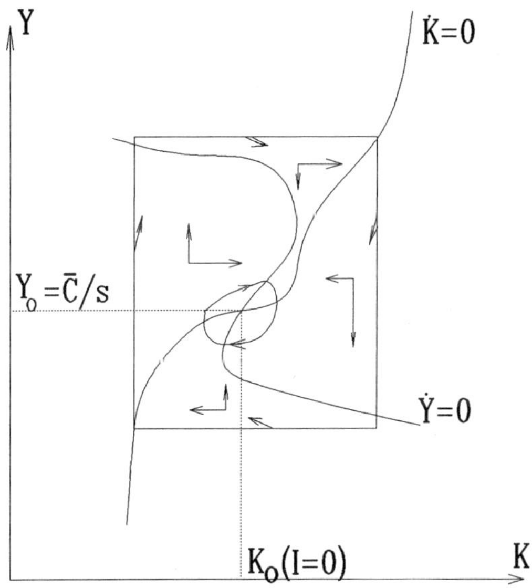

Figure 2.4:
The construction of a limit cycle for the Kaldor model.

To motivate the above graph a little bit further let us assume in addition that the investment function reads as follows:

$$I = \varphi(Y) - bK, \quad \varphi' > 0, b > 0,$$

[17]The other isocline is given by $I(Y,K) = 0$ and thus defines a strictly increasing function $Y(K)$ by means of the implicit function theorem.

where the graph of φ is of a shape as it is depicted in the figure 2.5:

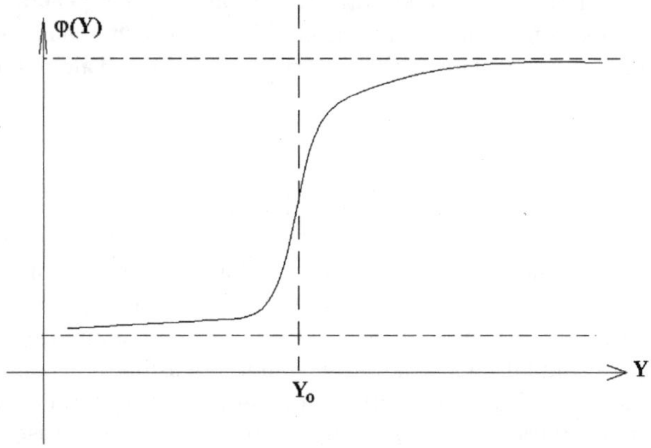

Figure 2.5: The Kaldor nonlinearity in the investment function

where it is expressed that net investment is always positive if the capital stock, and thus bK, are sufficiently small, and investment eventually ceases to increase if income continuously increases. This function can be justified in its shape by the observation that the marginal propensity to invest is low in situations where income Y has deviated from its normal (or average) level to a considerable degree (since a change in economic activity is then expected). The $\dot{K} = 0, \dot{Y} = 0$ isoclines are in this case given by

$$K = \frac{\varphi(Y)}{b} \text{ and } K = \frac{\varphi(Y) - sY + \bar{C}}{b}$$

and the steady state by $Y_o = \frac{1}{s}\bar{C}, K_o = \varphi(Y_o)/b$. The slope of the first isocline (as is already known) is positive throughout, while the slope of the second is positive by assumption in a neighborhood of the stationary state. Since the slope of the function φ is small far off the stationary state value Y_o, the slope of the second isocline must, however, become negative then in a way as shown above.

Varian (1979) has discussed Kaldor's trade cycle model from the perspective of catastrophe theory, which studies the singularities of potential functions like, e.g., the following one for the Kaldor model:

$$\begin{aligned} V_K(Y) &= -\int_{Y_o}^{Y} \beta_y(I(y,K) - sy + \bar{C})dy, \\ V_K' &= -\beta_y(I(Y,K) - sY + \bar{C}, \\ V_K'' &= -\beta_y(I_Y - s). \end{aligned}$$

The variable Y is called the state variable and the variable K the control variable in this context. The above one-parameter family of potential functions for the dynamic multiplier process reflects the stable cases of this adjustment process by minima ($I_Y - s < 0$) and the unstable ones by maxima ($I_Y - s > 0$) of the function V_K. The catastrophe manifold or the set of all singular points $V_K' = 0$ of this parameterized family of functions V_K is in this case given by the set of all IS-equilibria of the Kaldor model and it is described again by the curve $\dot{Y} = 0$ as in the following figure 2.6:

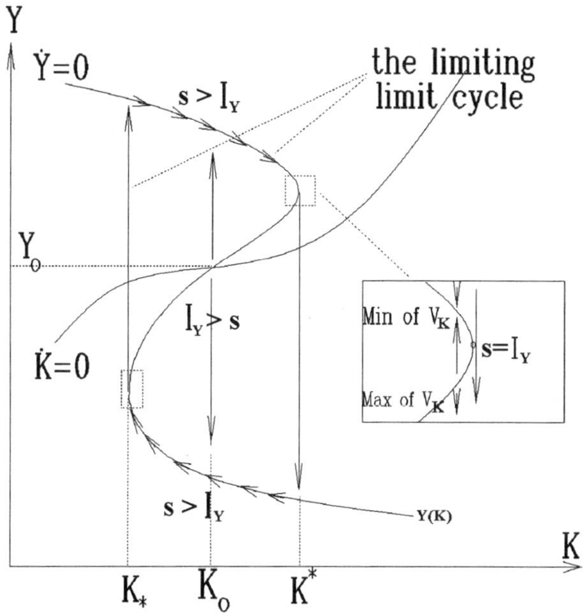

Figure 2.6: The limiting limit cycle of the Kaldor model from the 'viewpoint of catastrophe theory'.

The bifurcation set in the space of control variables K with regard to this catastrophe manifold is given by the two points K_* and K^* in the above diagram, i.e., by the two points where the multiplier turns from stability to instability with respect to a change in the level of income Y.

Catastrophe theory now investigates the type of singularity that occurs at such bifurcation points, which is here given by the simplest form that exists, the so-called fold catastrophe, at each of the two bifurcation points K_*, K^*.[18] It thus studies the above graph of $\dot{Y} = 0$ from a local perspective in order to determine the various shapes of the catastrophe manifolds at points which correspond to points in the bifurcation set. Due to its local character, such an analysis, however, does not contribute much to the study of the dynamics that is associated with the above phase diagram. It mainly says that the stability of positions on the upper leaf of this fold will get lost at the fold and that some sort of sudden change or jump must then occur. But since this analysis is restricted to a small box in the above phase space it cannot say anything more on what is occurring. The same thing, of course, applies to the lower leaf of the above goods-market equilibrium curve. The local analysis of the above catastrophe manifold is thus not very illuminating – due to the straightforward character of the fold catastrophe.[19]

[18]See Poston and Stewart (1978, Ch.9) for further details on the concepts of catastrophe theory in general and on the fold catastrophe in particular.

[19]This situation changes when the next type of catastrophe is considered, the so-called cusp, since this type will allow a meaningful type of local dynamic analysis, see Varian (1979) for an economic application of it.

Our interest in the above diagram lies in the global situation it represents and the intuitive story that may be related with it (as well as the formal means that may be applied to it). To this end we now assume that the adjustment speed in the above dynamic multiplier process is (close to) infinity. Adjustment in the vertical direction of the above diagram is therefore (nearly) instantaneous (as indicated by the above arrows). The motion of the system is consequently always close to the above two stable leaves of the graph of $\dot{Y} = 0$ – up to the two points represented by the bifurcation set where a large jump in the variable Y must occur from the upper part of the equilibrium manifold to the lower one or vice versa. Such a situation of very rapid change occurs at regular instances, since the capital stock is increasing in the upper stable part of this manifold and it is shrinking in the lower part according to the investment levels that are realized in these two cases.

A third perspective for an understanding of the trade cycle mechanism of the Kaldor (1940) model can therefore be proposed as follows. We analyze the local stability properties of the steady state of the laws of motion for Y and K by means of the Jacobian of this system first. This gives

$$\begin{aligned} \det J &= \det \begin{pmatrix} \beta_y(I_Y - s) & \beta_y I_K \\ I_Y & I_K \end{pmatrix} = \det \begin{pmatrix} -\beta_y s & 0 \\ I_Y & I_K \end{pmatrix} > 0 \quad \text{and} \\ \text{trace } J &= \beta_y(I_Y - s) + I_K > 0 \text{ iff } \beta_y > -I_K/(I_Y - s) \ \text{ and } I_Y > s\ (> 0) \end{aligned}$$

which thus describes the case of local instability. The above statement on instability is subsequently posited to hold. In fact, it denotes Kaldor's unstable dynamic multiplier based on an adjustment speed chosen sufficiently large. Rewrite the Y, K dynamics as follows

$$\frac{1}{\beta_y}\dot{Y} = I(Y,K) + \bar{C} - sY, \quad \dot{K} = I(Y,K).$$

To explore these dynamics for β_y sufficiently large, it may be of help to consider the following constrained system (the case $\beta_y = \infty$):

$$\begin{aligned} 0 &= I(Y,K) + \bar{C} - sY, \ \ i.e., \ \ K(Y) \ \text{ as in figure 2.6} && (2.12) \\ \dot{K} &= I(Y,K) = sY(K) - \bar{C} && (2.13) \end{aligned}$$

which replaces the above two-dimensional dynamics by a single dynamical equation defined on the graph of $Y(K)$. Geometrically, this means that the dynamics are confined to the $\dot{Y} = 0$ curve in the phase space for (Y, K), as shown in the following figure 2.7:

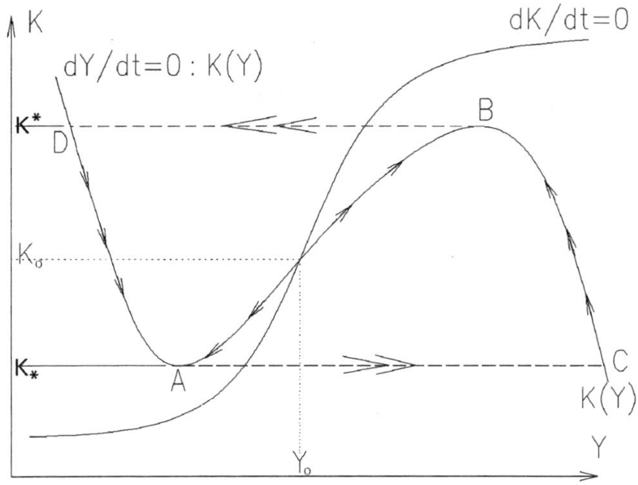

Figure 2.7:
The limiting limit cycle of the Kaldor model as relaxation oscillation.[20]

Equation (2.13) implies that $\dot{K}$ is negative to the left of $Y_o = \bar{C}/s$ and positive to its right which gives rise to the adjustments along $\dot{Y} = 0$ as shown in figure 2.7. For any starting point on $\dot{Y} = 0$, the state variable K therefore evolves to either point A or B. Due to $sY - \bar{C} < 0$ or $sY - \bar{C} > 0$ at these points, they cannot be fixed points of the dynamics. Without the unconstrained system $\dot{Y}$ and $\dot{K}$ it would be difficult to decide what happens when point A or B is reached. On the basis of the laws of motion of the unconstrained system one may, however, reasonably assume that the rate of output Y changes discontinuously, jumping to points C or D in figure 2.7, respectively (with a constant value of K during their jump). The dynamics are therefore characterized by so-called relaxation oscillations giving rise to a perpetual cycle DACB, a limit limit cycle as it is called in Chiarella (1990); for a similar model including the stock market, see Chiarella, Semmler and Mittnik (1998).

The constrained system (2.12) is thus asymptotically related to an unconstrained system of higher dimension, the so-called regularization of the constrained system which can be considered as a refinement of the constrained model. This refinement will produce limit cycles that are close to the limit limit cycle DACB if the parameter β_y (the speed of the dynamic multiplier) is sufficiently large.

In this simple geometrical way, we have developed a suggestive idea of the characteristics of the Kaldorian trade cycle (for β_y sufficiently large). Starting in point D, we can say that income Y is low there relative to the capital stock K and that disinvestment takes place slowly, while the dynamic multiplier keeps output close to the equilibrium output for each K: $I(Y, K) = sY - \bar{C}$. Due to the declining K we have an increasing $I(\cdot, K)$ and thus an increasing Y until the point A is reached, where $K = K_*$ holds, still exhibiting a fairly low level of equilibrium output Y. There is, however, no further goods market equilibrium

[20] Note that the axes have interchanged here in order to prepare the diagram for or later representation of the Metzler relaxation cycle.

of Y to the left of the steady level Y_o for values of K below A, yet there is a unique asymptotically stable equilibrium output at C for K_*, which then attracts disequilibrium output Y at a very high speed (or instantaneously, if $\beta_y = \infty$ holds). The system then jumps from a state of depression at A to a state of boom at C. From then on, output is high relative to the capital stock K generated by moving from D to A. Net investment therefore becomes positive and the capital stock starts to increase. These increases tend to diminish net investment and the highest attained value of output Y starts to fall slowly from then on. The system moves upward in this way until point B is reached, where rapid income movement from high to low occurs – the exact opposite of the movement that lead us from A to C. The Kaldorian trade cycle therefore exhibits (for fast multiplier dynamics) rapid upturns and downturns followed by very slow upturns and downturns which can be tailored to fairly different phase lengths and shapes of the cycle.

Kaldor's trade cycle result can thus also be explained by means of such a special case of adjustment speeds β_y. Equilibrium income is then either high and slowly declining due the increase it implies for the stock of capital – until there is an immediate (or very rapid) transition to a very low new equilibrium level for it – or it is low and slowly increasing due to the decline in the capital stock that then occurs – until it reaches a level where a rapid upturn sets in to bring it back to the high levels that prevailed before the downturn. This is the verbal description of a so-called relaxation oscillation which due to its global approach may provide a better means for studying the dynamics of the Kaldor model than is given by the above local approach of catastrophe theory. Relaxation oscillations come about when a time lag (or a speed of adjustment) in a dynamic model approaches 0 (∞). As shown above, one of the differential equations then collapses into an algebraic equation which decreases the dimension of the dynamics by one. It is tempting then to rationalize the limit case of infinite adjustment speeds by means of some kind of jumping hypothesis – as we have done it in the above Kaldor model. Yet, careful mathematical analysis is necessary here in order to really demonstrate the equivalence of the dynamics for high as well as infinite adjustment speeds. Examples of how to analyze such limiting discontinuous oscillations where one of the differential equations has become an equilibrium condition are given in Chiarella (1990, Chs. 2 and 3).

We have seen above that stagnant booms or slowly recovering depressions – with rapid changes in between – characterize the Kaldor trade cycle dynamics. A similar situation as the above twofold fold of the Kaldor model applies for the phase diagram of the Goodwin (1951) multiplier - accelerator cycle model, since the curve of goods market equilibria is a straight line in this case, the nonlinearity now being present in the other isocline of this model. The question arises whether the Goodwin model will also allow for a relaxation oscillation interpretation or whether it will differ in this respect from the Kaldor model. Chiarella (1990, Ch. 3.3) provides the formal details that such an interpretation is indeed possible if the phase space of the dynamics is reformulated in an appropriate way. A different method for calculating the function which characterizes the relaxation oscillation must therefore be applied in this case in order to determine from it again the limiting limit cycle as in the Kaldor model.

We remark that a discrete time version of the Kaldor model can generate chaos by a sufficient increase in the parameter β_y (see Dana and Malgrange, 1984). This is because the dynamic multiplier which is highly stabilizing in the continuous time case is overstretched in the discrete time case. It is also worthwhile noting that Dana and Malgrange (1984) have extended the Kaldor model to a growing economy, see also below.

In a growth context, Skott (1991) shows that it is reasonable to assume that the investment function is homogeneous of degree one in output and the capital stock, i.e., it is then of the form $I(Y,K) = KH(Y/K)$ where the function H is again of the type depicted in figure 2.5. The ratio $y = Y/K$ can be interpreted as the rate of capacity utilization of firms (when fixed proportions in production are given), which indeed can be considered as one decisive argument in investment behavior as assumed above. Setting $\bar{C}$ equal to zero (as is usual in growth theory) then gives rise to

$$\begin{aligned} \hat{Y} &= \beta_y(I(Y/K)/(Y/K) - s), \quad \hat{K} = I(Y/K), \text{ i.e.} \\ \hat{y} &= \beta_y(I(y) - sy) - I(y), \quad y = Y/K. \end{aligned}$$

The dynamics reduce in this case to a one-dimensional one, which for $I'(y_o) > s$ is explosive, at least locally, if the dynamic multiplier acts with sufficient strength. In the case of a form of the investment function as in figure 2.5, there will be again two outward equilibria which are attracting so that the dynamic settles down at one of them. However, since the investment is not shifting in this intensive form situation no further law of motion is present and thus no limit cycle behavior possible. It follows that a second state variable, seems to be needed to generalize the Kaldorian trade cycle to a model that allows for economic growth. This is a disadvantage of the Kaldor model that does not apply to its reformulation for the case of inventory investment to be considered below.

However, by assuming an exogenously growth trend g for autonomous expenditures, as in Dana and Malgrange (1984), it is possible to generalize the limit cycle of the stationary Kaldor economy to the case of a growing economy:

$$\dot{Y} = \beta_y(\bar{C}e^{gt} + cY + I(Y,K) - Y), \quad \dot{K} = I(Y,K)$$

Making use of the state variables $y = Ye^{-gt}, k = Ke^{-gt}$ this simple modification of the Kaldor model gives rise to[15]

$$\begin{aligned} \dot{y} &= \beta_y(I(y,k) - sy + \bar{C}) - gy \\ \dot{k} &= I(y,k) - gk \end{aligned}$$

This model allows for a Kaldorian growth cycle in the same way as in the stationary case we have considered above, see Dana and Malgrange (1984) for the necessary assumptions and derivations.[16] We shall not go into this analysis here, since the original Kaldor trade cycle approach is already sufficient for our following purposes and since the addition of exogenously driven growth is not too convincing from today's perspective.

2.3.2 Metzlerian inventory dynamics

In this subsection we shall apply the Kaldor trade cycle mechanism to quantity adjustments on the market for goods that only concern its shorter run aspects and no longer the process of capital accumulation. Unintended inventory accumulation in conjunction with disappointed sales expectations will now lead us to a situation of local explosiveness of stationary goods market equilibria, no longer dependent on excessive marginal propensities to spend, to be coupled now with nonlinearities in adjustment speeds far off the stationary state that here keep the dynamics bounded from the global point of view. The model obtained in this way will be used as an integral part of the fundamental KMG model of chapter 3, in conjunction with the nominal dynamics considered in the preceding section and the real growth dynamics to be considered in the next section. For the moment we however assume that nominal wages and prices are fixed and that fixed business investment does not depend on the rate of interest, but just as consumption solely on output and income Y.

To concentrate on the essential components that make up the Metzler (1941) inventory multiplier – accelerator mechanism we make use of the following simple textbook representation of aggregate demand

$$Y^d = \bar{C} + cY + \bar{I} + iY + \delta\bar{K} = d_1 Y + d_0. \tag{2.14}$$

We assume that the parameters in this equation are such that $d_0 > 0$ and $d_1 \in (0,1)$ holds true. On this basis, the partial model describing the interaction of expected sales Y^e, actual sales Y^d, output Y and intended as well as actual inventory adjustments, $\mathcal{I}, \dot{N}$, along Metzlerian lines, can be represented as follows:

$$\dot{Y}^e = \beta_{y^e}(Y^d - Y^e) = \beta_{y^e}(d_1 Y + d_0 - Y^e) \tag{2.15}$$

$$\dot{N} = Y - Y^d = (1 - d_1)Y - d_0 \tag{2.16}$$

where the output Y produced by firms is given by

$$Y = Y^e + \mathcal{I} = Y^e + \beta_n(\beta_{n^d} Y^e - N), \tag{2.17}$$

i.e. the sum of the expected sales and intended inventory changes. Note here that intended inventory changes $\beta_n(\beta_{n^d} Y^e - N)$ are based on the inventory adjustment speed β_n with which the discrepancy $\beta_{n^d} Y^e - N$ between desired inventories $\beta_{n^d} Y^e$ and actual ones, N, is translated into desired inventory changes (β_{n^d} denoting the given desired inventory / sales ratio). Note also that actual inventory changes $\dot{N}$ are simply given by $Y - Y^d$, i.e., by output that is not sold on the market place. These inventory dynamics dispense with the (inconsistent) dynamic multiplier story (which assumes that aggregate demand is always served, but does not consider all sources, or sinks, needed for this assumption, if the output of firms deviates from this demand), which is often used due its simplicity when a Keynesian goods market disequilibrium description is needed in macrodynamic analysis, see Blanchard (1981) for example.

Inserting the expression for output, equation (2.17), into the laws of motion for expected sales and inventory changes gives the following linear autonomous system of differential equations of dimension 2:

$$\dot{Y}^e = \beta_{y^e}(d_1 \beta_n(\beta_{n^d} Y^e - N) + d_0 - (1 - d_1)Y^e)$$

$$\dot{N} = (1 - d_1)(Y^e + \beta_n(\beta_{n^d} Y^e - N)) - d_0$$

The steady state of these dynamics is given by

$$Y_0^d = Y_0^e = Y_0 = \frac{d_0}{1 - d_1}, \qquad N_0 = \beta_{n^d} Y_0, \qquad \mathcal{I}_o = 0$$

One easily gets as linear part (or Jacobian) of this system of differential equations the following matrix J:

$$J = \begin{pmatrix} (d_1 - 1 + d_1\beta_n\beta_{n^d})\beta_{y^e} & -d_1\beta_n\beta_{y^e} \\ (1-d_1)(1+\beta_n\beta_{n^d}) & -(1-d_1)\beta_n \end{pmatrix}.$$

For the determinant of this matrix we get

$$|J| = (1-d_1)^2\beta_{y^e}\beta_n + (1-d_1)d_1\beta_{y^e}\beta_n > 0$$

and for the trace

$$\text{trace}J = -\beta_{y^e}(1 - d_1 - \beta_n\beta_{n^d}d_1) - \beta_n(1-d_1)$$

From these expressions we get that the dynamics (2.15), (2.16) can only be unstable if $1 - d_1 - \beta_n\beta_{n^d}d_1 < 0$ (or $\beta_{y^e}\beta_{n^d}d_1 - (1-d_1) > 0$) holds and then if and only if

$$\beta_{y^e} > \beta_{y^e}^H = -\frac{\beta_n(1-d_1)}{1 - d_1 - \beta_n\beta_{n^d}d_1} \quad (\text{or} \quad \beta_n > \beta_n^H = \frac{\beta_{y^e}(1-d_1)}{\beta_{y^e}\beta_{n^d}d_1 - (1-d_1)}).$$

At $\beta_{y^e}^H$ (or β_n^H) there occur degenerate Hopf - bifurcation where the system loses its stability in a cyclical fashion by way of passing through a center type dynamics at the bifurcation point. In contrast to the Kaldor (1940) trade cycle mechanism we here thus have that instability is basically dependent on the speeds of adjustments for inventories and sales expectations.

Since we want to show in this section the existence of persistent fluctuations and in particular relaxation oscillations for the inventory dynamics based primarily on the adjustment speed β_n of intended inventory changes, we assume in the following that $\beta_{y^e}\beta_{n^d}d_1 - (1-d_1) > 0$ holds and that the adjustments speed β_n for inventory changes satisfies

$$\beta_n > \beta_n^H = \frac{\beta_{y^e}(1-d_1)}{\beta_{y^e}\beta_{n^d}d_1 - (1-d_1)}$$

at the steady state of the dynamics, which means that the steady state is locally unstable. In this case, the dynamics (2.15), (2.16) would be totally unstable if the above linear approach to sales, sales expectations and inventory adjustment interactions would be maintained. In view of such a situation, Franke and Lux (1993) in particular assume that the inventory adjustment speed that firms choose is slowed down significantly the further the economy departs from the steady state (since firms become more cautious then). In their paper, Franke and Lux present a set of assumptions which in sum allow them to show that – despite local instability – such an inventory dynamics will be globally bounded or viable and give rise to persistent oscillations that will be turned into relaxation oscillations when expectations tend to become of the myopic perfect foresight variety.

A graphical representation of the type of nonlinearity assumed by Franke and Lux to obtain their result looks as shown in figure 2.8:

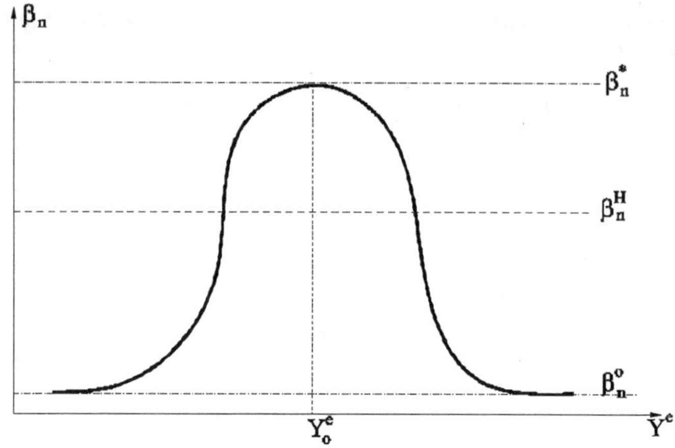

Figure 2.8:
Inventory adjustment speeds as a nonlinear function of sales expectations.

With this function we assume that firms expect a change in economic activity when their sales expectations depart very much from the stationary solution Y_o^e or the average behavior of the economy. Sales expectations nevertheless still follow the level of aggregate demand since firms still want to produce what they expect to sell. Yet, with respect to the building up (or running down) of inventories they see no need to adjust these inventories (which are already fairly high or low) further in a fast way to the observed high (low) levels of sales, since this would mean that they would quickly approach a stock of inventories that is clearly inadequate (much too high or too low) from the viewpoint of the average behavior of the economy. Hence they consider such inventories as already too much off the norm, abnormally high in the boom and abnormally low in the recession, and only slowly adjust them further into the direction of the observed expansion or contraction in goods demand. By contrast, situations where inventories and sales expectations are close to the steady state or average behavior of the economy, do not warn firms that their inventory policy can run into trouble soon and thus let them produce at levels that are based on sales expectations plus an inventory policy that attempts to bring inventories quickly back to their desired levels.

The result of this nonlinear inventory policy will be that firms are generally either in a boom situation (where sales and sales expectations are slowly falling and inventories still sluggishly adjusted upwards) or in a state of depression (where sales and sales expectations are slowly rising and inventories still sluggishly adjusted downwards). In order to show this by means of arguments used for the Kaldorian trade cycle mechanism we first of all show that the basic figure 2.3 underlying Kaldor's original presentation of his trade cycle can also be applied to the presently considered situation. This is shown in the following figure 2.9 which considers a specific decomposition of the sales expectations mechanism (concerning the fast variable), such that the role of the slow variable, now the level of inventories N in the place of the capital stock K, becomes clear.

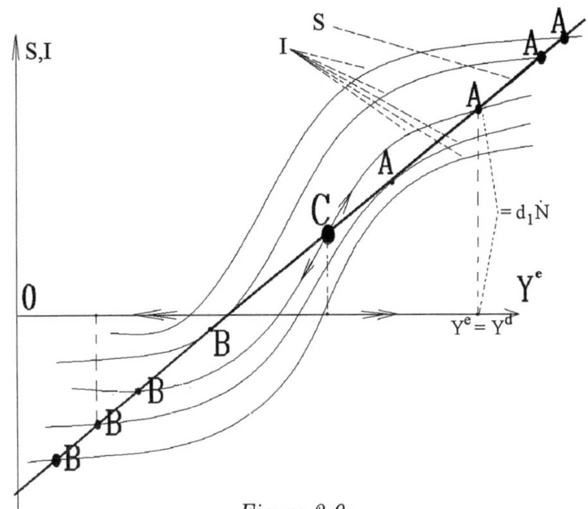

Figure 2.9:
A Metzlerian nonlinear inventory accelerator mechanism
(A's, B's the stable and C's the unstable $Y^e = Y^d$-equilibria).

The equation underlying this one-dimensional dynamical system is:

$$\dot{Y}^e = \beta_{y^e}(d_1 Y + d_o - Y^e) = \beta_{y^e}(d_1\beta_n(Y^e)(\beta_{n^d}Y^e - N) + d_0 - (1-d_1)Y^e)$$

where the variable N is now interpreted as the shift parameter with respect to one of the two curves shown in the above diagram (in the place of the former shift parameter K). Abbreviating the function $d_1\beta_n(\beta_{n^d}Y^e - N)$ by $\imath(Y^e)$ and $d_0 - (1-d_1)Y^e$ by $s(Y^e)$ shows the definition of the two functions $\imath, s$ employed in figure 2.9 in analogy to the Kaldorian diagram in figure 2.3 and on this basis the three equilibria or stationary points of the $\dot{Y}^e$ equation for a given parametric choice of the stock of inventories N. At the points where the $\imath, s$ curves intersect (and where myopic perfect foresight $Y^d = Y^e$ and $\dot{N} = \mathcal{I}$ holds) we in addition have as vertical distance from the horizontal axis the expressions $d_1\beta_n(\beta_{n^d}Y^e - N) = \mathcal{I} = \dot{N}$ which provide a measures for the direction of inventory adjustments that occurs at this equilibrium.

Figure 2.9 therefore shows that we have $\dot{N} > 0$ at the upper stable equilibrium and $\dot{N} < 0$ at the lower (stable) one. The slow variable N therefore shifts the $d_1\dot{N}$ curve downwards and thus the upper equilibrium position (when it prevails) to the left, until this equilibrium position gets indeed lost and is replaced by the lower stable equilibrium which is rapidly approached once the upper equilibrium has disappeared, when sales expectations work with sufficient speed. The opposite, of course, occurs again in the lower stable equilibrium, exactly in the spirit of the Kaldor (1940) trade cycle model. The model therefore generates again persistent fluctuations that can be further investigated from the viewpoint of the Poincaré - Bendixson theorem, from the viewpoint of catastrophe theory and the viewpoint of relaxation oscillations just as the Kaldor model.[21]

[21]Note that we could create the situation of corridor stability if the assumption on the strength of inventory adjustments is reversed, i.e., if inventories are adjusted sluggishly close to the steady state and quickly far away from it.

Let us here briefly mention that Powell and Murphy (1997) use the condition $Y^d = Y^e$ in their macroeconometric disequilibrium model of the Australian economy, i.e., they in fact assume that the economy is always at one of the stable perfect foresight equilibria shown in the figure 2.9 where output and sales are distinguished only by intended (= actual) inventory changes. Assuming a nonlinear accelerator principle as it underlies the figure 2.9 should therefore help to stabilize their dynamics in cases where the steady state is found to be unstable (which seems to be the case in certain situations their empirical approach allows for). However, considering only perfect foresight equilibria with respect to sales expectations does not yet reveal the dynamics that surround this limit case and is therefore to be supplemented by the 'unconstrained' dynamical system in order to get a full dynamical picture.

In the following, we will not reproduce the details of our Kaldor (1940) based reformulation of the Metzlerian inventory cycle mechanism, which would simply repeat the presentations of the preceding subsection, but only sketch them again in the intuitive way of fold catastrophes and the approximate relaxation oscillations surrounding them and then show a special example of the above nonlinearity in the adjustment speed of inventories and the resulting global stability of the dynamics and their limit cycle (or limit limit cycle in the limit case of pure relaxation oscillations) by way of a numerical simulation of these dynamics. From the perspective of fast / slow motions we have again the phase portrait shown in figure 2.10:

On the right leaf of the fold we have slowly declining sales expectations (following aggregate demand with a time delay) and slowly rising inventories, the latter due to the extraordinarily high levels of sales and the production plans based on their expected values and the cautious behavior of firms in such situations. This process continues until inventory additions have fallen to such a low level that the boom equilibrium position $Y^e = Y^d = d_o + d_1(Y^e + \mathcal{I})$ can no longer be maintained and disappears as a point of attraction. There is then fast or instantaneous adjustment to a position on the left leaf of the fold where we then have low levels of demand, output and sales expectations combined with a stock of inventories that is much too high for this depressed situation. Inventories then start falling while sales and thus expected sales are slowly increasing, giving rise to a type of dynamics that is the opposite of those applying to the right leaf of the fold and that will lead us back to the right leaf after the elapse of a certain time span. Note that this recovery is based on the assumption that firms do not quickly reduce their inventory overhead in view of the depressed level of actual and expected sales as far as the corresponding speed of adjustment is concerned, but that they think that the new target level $\beta_{n^d}Y^e$ is so much off the average that a slow adjustment to this level seems desirable.

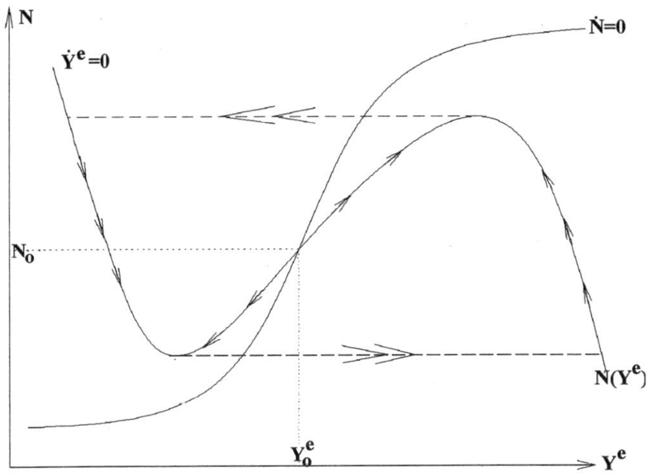

Figure 2.10: The limit limit cycle of the Metzlerian model from the viewpoint of fold catastrophes and surrounding relaxation oscillations.

In order to simulate the dynamics just considered, we choose for the adjustment speed β_n of inventories the following functional form of their dependence on sales expectations:

$$\beta_n = (\beta_n^* - \beta_n^0)\exp(-\beta_n^1(Y^e - Y_0^e)^2) + \beta_n^0,$$

where $\beta_n^* - \beta_n^0 > \frac{1-d_1}{d_1\beta_{n^d}}$ and $0 < \beta_n^0 < \frac{1-d_1}{d_1\beta_{n^d}}$ holds.

On the basis of this concrete choice, the dynamics (2.15), (2.16) can now be exemplified by means of the numerical simulation shown in figure 2.11.

The parameters used for the numerical example shown in figure 2.11 are:

$d_o = 0.2, d_1 = 0.8,\ \ \delta = .1,\ \ \beta_{n^d} = .3,\ \ \beta_n^o = .6,\ \ \beta_n^* = 10,\ \ \beta_n^1 - 20,\ \ \beta_{y^e} = 50.$

Table 2.1.

The figures 2.11 at the bottom show again the relaxation oscillation – now in sales expectations Y^e. Inventories N, on the other hand, exhibit no jump in their levels (as is reasonable), but of course their growth rate is subject to such jumps whenever a regime switch occurs in the perfect foresight regime from optimistic (nearly perfect) sales expectations to pessimistic ones and vice versa. The bottom right figure 2.11 however here reveals that such sales expectations are not always perfect, since aggregate demand may overshoot sales expectations during a regime switch – at least for the discretization we have chosen here to simulate this model.

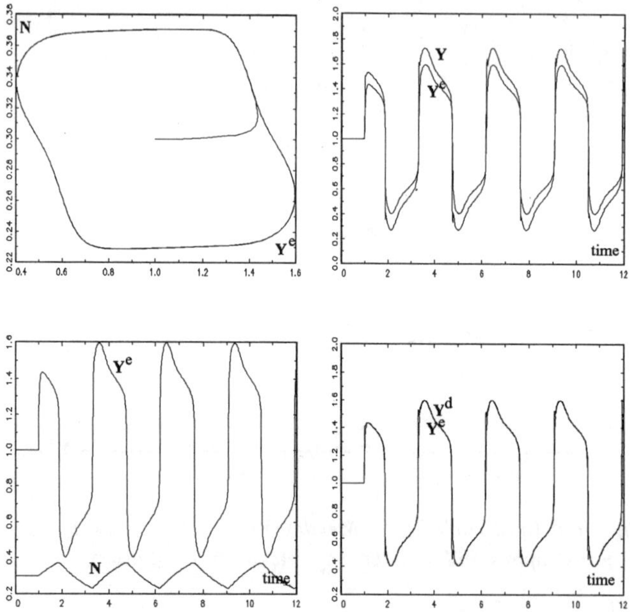

Figure 2.11:
A numerical representation of relaxation oscillations in the Metzlerian 2D dynamics.

The top-right figure 2.11 shows the development of output as compared to sales expectations (and aggregate demand). Of course, the path of output must depart in a systematic way from that of expected sales, since firms pursue an active inventory policy. Finally, the top-left figure 2.11 shows again the relaxation cycle in its phase space, thereby revealing again part of the $\dot{Y}^e = 0$-isocline as well as the nearly horizontal adjustments that occur in sales expectations when phases of boom give way to phases of recession or depression by way of a regime switch in sales expectations. The figures 2.11 also show that the cycle period is approximately 3 years. We note that the phase length of this cycle can be decreased if the parameter β_{n^d} is reduced in size. Of course, the amplitude of the cycle is completely determined by the shape of the nonlinearity that has been assumed for its generation.

We conclude that the Metzlerian inventory adjustment mechanism can imply interesting persistent fluctuations (also of chaotic type if discrete time analysis is applied, see Dana and Malgrange (1984)), even in still fairly simple formulations of the interaction of its fundamental variables, sales and expected sales, actual and desired inventory adjustments and the output decisions of firms in such a framework. This mechanism is in our view a constituent part of integrated macrodynamics, since it allows for the treatment of sluggish quantity adjustment besides the more generally accepted situation of sluggish wage and also price level adjustment.

2.4 Labor market and real wage dynamics

After having studied the quantity dynamics on the goods market, we now turn to the labor market and real wage adjustments. Here, for the most part, the supply side view is currently dominant. The central element on which analyses of supply side processes are founded is the assumption of the equality of real wages with the marginal product of labor, or of the price level with marginal nominal wage costs. Such analyses work by way of a conventional aggregate supply (AS-) curve as the competitive theory of the price level in a Keynesian setup, where firms are to be treated as quantity-takers and price-setters or, in a Walrasian setup, as a theory of labor demand, giving rise there to a Lucas type supply function in scenarios of price-taking firms.

Yet, as we would argue in a Keynesian environment with price setting firms, supply side processes should have an explicit and detailed representation. This could easily also be done in the case of fixed proportions in production, where marginal productivity theory is no longer applicable. This modeling of macroeconomic interaction should not depend on the assumption of so-called neoclassical production functions, though its implications might vary to some extent with the assumptions that are made with respect to available production technologies.

We shall show in this section that attempts to include the dynamics of supply in models with a Keynesian short-run give rise to an analysis of wage-price dynamics that can be usefully compared with the implications of the supply side dynamics of some variants of Goodwin's (1967) classical growth cycle model. Subsequently we will demonstrate that this claim indeed holds with respect to integrated Keynesian models of traditional type. We will also briefly indicate that similar outcomes can be expected for models of the neo-Keynesian or the new-Keynesian variety. Yet, in order to make clear the essential idea underpinning the nature of the dynamics we will present the classical growth cycle model here in much simpler terms than were used in the original work by Goodwin, the fundamental and prototypic nature of which has been stressed by Solow (1990) in particular.

After our brief representation of the model we will indicate what has to be added to it when integrated into a Keynesian framework as far as goods and asset markets are concerned. We then provide two extensions of the model, and their synthesis, which serve to indicate its potential for more advanced types of analyses. The first of these extensions is related to the goods-market analysis of Rose (1967), another early contribution to cyclical growth and employment fluctuations that at least in some respects is closely related to the Goodwin approach. The second integrates stocks and financial assets in a very elementary way in order to approach the topic of debt deflation when integrated with the price dynamics of the Rose approach.

2.4.1 The Goodwin growth cycle model

Figure 2.12 provides the basic elements needed to derive Goodwin's (1967) classical growth cycle model of labor market and the real wage. We see an overshooting mechanism in an environment where we still abstract from technical change, and are implicitly assuming again a fixed proportions technology. We have top left a real wage Phillips-Curve (PC), relating the rate of growth $\hat{\omega}$ of real wages with the state of the labor market, expressed by the rate of employment V, which has been drawn as strictly convex, but which as a minimum need fulfill only the following three conditions in order to obtain the conclusions of this prototype model:[22]

- there is a uniquely determined **N**on-**A**ccelerating-**I**nflation **R**ate of **U**tilization $\bar{V}$ of the labor force,[23]
- the PC curve exhibits negative values below this rate, and thus implies falling real wages in this domain,
- the PC shows positive values to the right of the NAIRU, implying rising real wages on this side.

We thus do not need in the following analysis that the real wage PC, as far as its dependence on the the rate of employment V is concerned, is monotonically increasing as is generally assumed in the literature and shown in the figure 2.12.[24]

Corresponding to this real wage Phillips Curve we assume as second building block of our model an Accumulation Curve (or AC) which postulates that the rate of change, $\hat{V}$, of the rate of employment is a function of the level of real wages, again with a benchmark value, a Non-Accelerating-Growth Rate of (real) Wages $\bar{\omega}$ (NAGRW), which separates regimes of rising from regimes of falling rates of employment, due to their impact on profitability and thus the rate of investment. As before, all conclusions of the classical growth cycle model hold under the above three conditions, and thus again we do not demand monotonicity of the curve shown top right in figure 2.12.

[22]Continuity of this curve is of course assumed in addition.

[23]Note that we reinterpret the NAIRU of the literature here in terms of the rate of employment (or utilization) V of the labor force, not in terms of unemployment.

[24]Note that a real wage PC is obtained from the conventional money wage PC (augmented by inflationary expectations of course) by assuming myopic perfect foresight with regard to the expected rate of inflation.

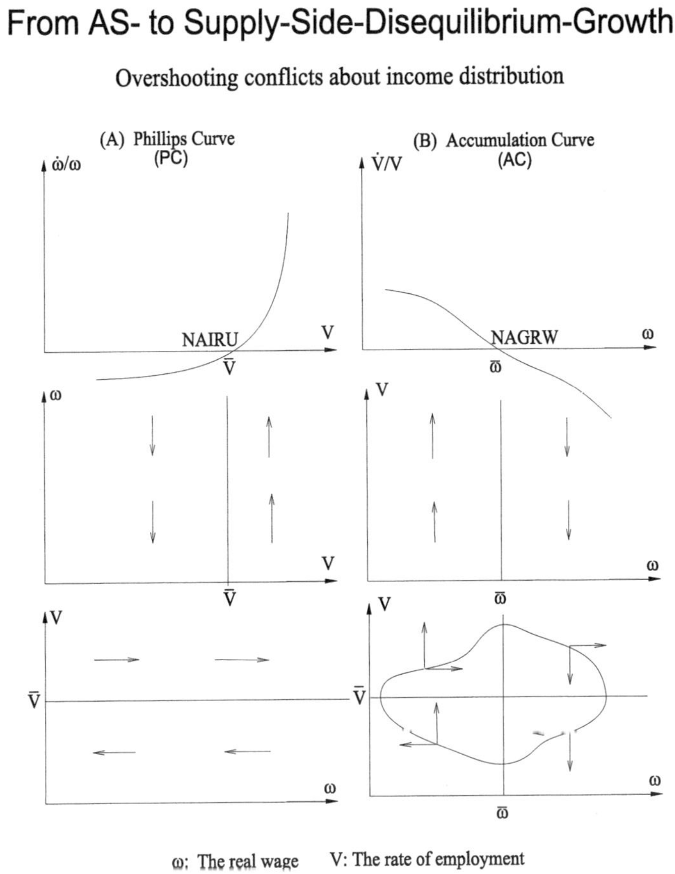

Figure 2.12: The classical growth cycle model.

On the basis of the two curves shown at the top of figure 2.12 one gets the adjustments of the rate of employment and of real wages as shown in the middle of this figure. In order to then obtain the dynamic consequences for the interaction of real wages with the rate of employment (bottom right) one has to mirror the implications of the PC part of the model along the 45° degree line (bottom left). The phase space bottom right then simply integrates the neighboring situations as shown by the arrows in this space. The further implication of this model, that all curves, in the positive part of the phase space shown, must be closed orbits, can of course not be proven by this simple graphical argument. In order to get this result in an intuitively understandable way, one has to consider the following type of function:

$$L(\omega, V) = \int_{\bar{V}}^{V} PC(\tilde{V})/\tilde{V}\, d\tilde{V} - \int_{\bar{\omega}}^{\omega} AC(\tilde{\omega})/\tilde{\omega}\, d\tilde{\omega}.$$

The graph of this function, called a Liapunov function, has the form of a global sink, under the assumptions made, with its minimum at $\bar{\omega}, \bar{V}$ and with all level curves (where the function assumes a given value) closed. Projected into the ω, V phase space the closed curves from the level curves are just the orbits of the considered dynamics since it is easily shown that L is constant along the trajectories of the investigated dynamical system. Figure 2.13 shows an example for such a situation:

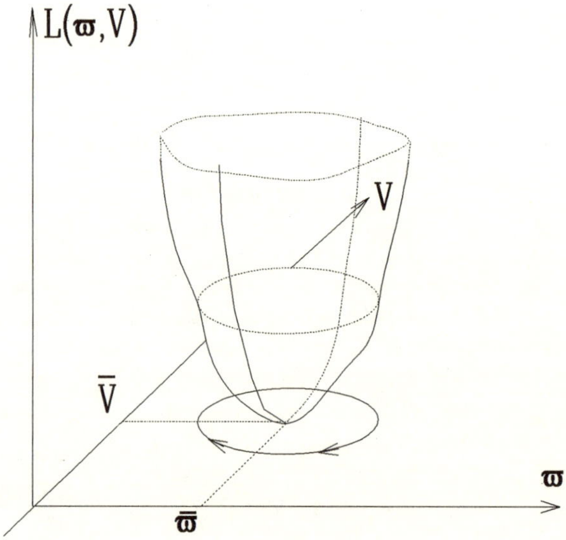

Figure 2.13:
The Liapunov function and the implied center type dynamics.

We add that this proof applies, to very general situations as far as functional shapes of the PC-AC curves are concerned, but some modification is required for systems which do not rely on the simple cross-dual nature of the AC-PC interaction shown in figure 2.12.[25]

We thus have the result that all trajectories generated by the interaction of PC and AC dynamics represent periodic motions of the real wage and the rate of employment as the one shown in figure 2.12, bottom right. We do not describe this overshooting dynamic in detail. This has been done many times already. The overshooting occurs in a growing economy if there is labor force growth or Harrod neutral technical change and it should also be applicable (not necessarily with periodic motions throughout) to modern representations of technical change, see Desai and Shah (1981) for an early attempt along Kennedy-Weizsäcker lines.

Desai (1973) has extended the classical growth cycle model by an explicit treatment of price level dynamics, through a delayed type of markup pricing.[26] Using in addition a money

[25]See Flaschel, Franke and Semmler (1997) for the consideration of cross-dual macrodynamics on various levels of generality.

[26]See also Flaschel (1984a) in this regard.

wage Phillips curve where price inflation enters additively with a factor η that can be less than, equal to or larger than one, one can show by means of the above Liapunov function L that the steady state $\bar{\omega}, \bar{V}$ of these extended dynamics becomes a global sink (a global source) if $\eta < 1$ ($\eta > 1$) holds true (while $\eta = 1$ gives the original Goodwin growth cycle). This is one among a variety of examples which shows that this growth cycle represents a border case between asymptotic stability and instability, of which one can thus say that its closed orbit structure is exceptional (structurally unstable), but that its message of overshooting conflicts about income distribution in a growing economy may nevertheless be found in many modules that rely on a dynamic interaction of wages, prices and factor utilization rates.[27]

Next we want to integrate goods market disequilibrium. Figure 2.14 indicates what complexities this might add to the classical growth cycle. We measure disequilibrium in the product market by capacity utilization $U_c = Y/Y^p$ and, on the other hand, by the rate of inventory disequilibrium $U_n = N/N^d$. Here, Y denotes actual output and Y^p potential output (for a fixed proportions technology), while N denotes actual and N^d desired inventories. Furthermore, we shall also use in figure 2.14 the measures V^w, the (inside) employment rate of the employed workforce (based on over- or under-time work of the employed), and $\rho_l, r_l - \pi^e$ the rate of profit and the real rate of interest, π^e the expected rate of inflation, everything here conceived as average over the longer run. Allowing for varying rates of capacity utilization of firms implies in addition that we now have to distinguish between the actual rate of employment, V, and the potential one, V^p, based on fully utilized capital stock and on a normal working-day of all members of the workforce. Note that these measures appear in the form of a proportional control here, and not yet in integral form (representing some sort of moving average) nor in form of a derivative control, i.e., in form of a time rate of change.

[27]See Flaschel and Krüger (1984, 1988), Flaschel(1993) and Flaschel and Sethi (1996) for further related extensions.

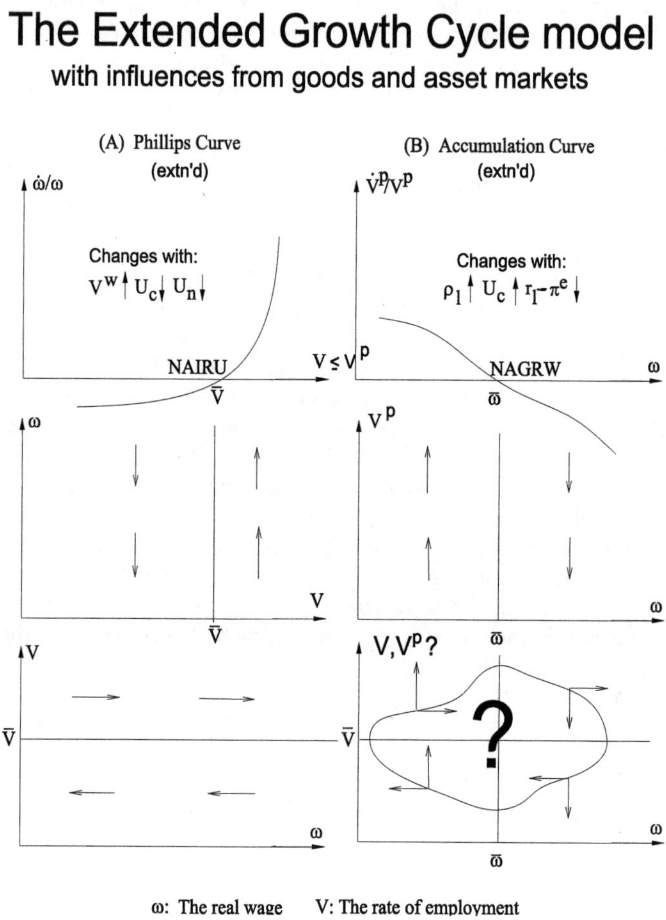

Figure 2.14: The classical growth cycle model in perspective.

Obviously, the AC dynamics now concerns the relationship between real wages and the growth rate of potential employment, via the resulting profitability conditions of firms and the investment decision based on them. Furthermore, rates of capacity utilization U_c and the real financing costs of firms as measured by $r_l - \pi^e$ may also influence their investment decision and thus the growth path of potential employment and must therefore be added as 'shift' terms to the AC dynamics as indicated in figure 2.14, top right. Note that we do not add the inventory measure here since we believe that this measure is related to short-run (pricing) decisions of firms solely. The PC dynamics top left, on the other hand, will be positively influenced by the internal employment rate of firms, and negatively, through positive changes in the price level, by the two rates that characterize the disequilibrium experienced by firms on the market for goods. We thus get that the two curves underlying the classical growth cycle mechanism are neither fixed nor do they give rise to a unique phase space diagram, bottom right, as was the case in figure 2.12. Instead actual and potential employment will in general differ in a model that adds the interaction of goods and asset markets, the real - financial interaction, so that higher dimensional representations may become unavoidable when these additions are considered.

The phase diagram bottom right in figure 2.14 indicates in simple terms that the outcome of an integrated treatment of income distribution, growth, goods market and asset market behavior may be difficult and may not lead to the result that figure 2.12 will continue to play a prominent role in such extended dynamics. We will return to this topic later.

Let us next investigate two fundamental extensions of the classical growth cycle model that integrate, on the one hand, financial assets and liabilities, and, on the other hand, aspects of fluctuating goods market behavior in a still very basic way, in order to show how the dynamics are changed by these modifications. We consider first the case where firms not only use retained profits to finance their investment, but also loans (from asset holding households), while worker households still spend what they receive as income. The following model is based on Keen (1999), investigated in detail in Chiarella and Flaschel (1999j,k,l) and Chiarella, Flaschel and Semmler (1999), and is only briefly considered here. For further details the reader is therefore referred to the cited papers.

Let us first consider the budget equation of firms. This equation simply states that the excess of nominal investment expenditures pI over pure profits of firms ρpK is to be financed by new loans as shown in the following equation where D is the stock of loans of firms:

$$\dot{D} = pI - \rho pK.$$

We presume a money wage PC of the type $\hat{w} = \beta_w(V - \bar{V})$, with w the money wage, and an investment equation of the type $I/K = \alpha(\rho - \rho_{min})$ with $\alpha > 1$. The definition of the pure rate of profits, ρ, net of interest payments rD on loans, is given by: $\frac{pY^p - rD - wl_yY^p}{pK}$. The price level p and the rate of interest r are considered as given for the time being, as well as the benchmark rate of return on capital ρ_{min}. The parameter l_y denotes the labor coefficient of the assumed fixed proportions technology, the other coefficient being given by the potential output capital ratio $y^p = Y^p/K$. Since this is still a supply side dynamics actual output will always equal potential output due to Say's law, which is assumed to prevail in this type of model.

These structural equations of the model give rise to:

$$\hat{u} = \beta_w(V - \bar{V}), \quad \text{the reformulated PC dynamics} \tag{2.18}$$

$$\hat{V} = \alpha(\rho - \rho_{min}) - n, \quad \text{the reformulated AC dynamics} \tag{2.19}$$

$$\dot{d} = \alpha(\rho - \rho_{min})(1 - d) - \rho, \quad \text{the reformulated budget equation} \tag{2.20}$$

where $u = w/p \cdot l_y$ denotes the share of wages, n is the rate of natural growth, d the debt to capital ratio $D/(pK)$ of firms, and $\rho = y^p(1 - u) - rd$ the rate of return on capital in this supply driven approach to economic growth. The dynamically endogenous variables are u, V as in the previous model and the ratio d.

Proposition 2.3:

1. Assume $0 < r < n$. *Then: The steady state*

$$V_o = \bar{V} + n/\beta_w \tag{2.21}$$
$$u_o = (y^p - \rho_o - rd_o)/y^p, \quad \rho_o = \rho_{min} + n/\alpha \tag{2.22}$$
$$d_o = 1 - \rho_o/n = (\alpha - 1)/\alpha - \rho_{min}/n \tag{2.23}$$

of the dynamics (2.18) – (2.20) is locally asymptotically stable.

2. This steady state is not globally asymptotically stable with respect to shocks of the debt capital ratio d, which, when sufficiently large, can lead to an explosive development of the debt ratio starting from economically meaningful values for this ratio d.

The details of this proposition and the proofs are provided in Chiarella and Flaschel (1999j) and will not be repeated here. We simply conclude here that debt financed investment makes the classical growth cycle convergent for small shocks in its state variable, but that sufficiently high debt per unit of capital can make these dynamics divergent, giving rise to corridor stability in the place of the purely closed orbit structure we established for the original model.

2.4.2 Debt deflation and adverse real wage adjustment

Due to the long run nature of the model it is of course necessary to add a theory of the price level to the above analysis. This will be done here by referring to demand pressure solely, with no supply side cost-push terms added. Such an extension demands the integration of goods market disequilibrium and fluctuating rates of capacity utilization. This will be achieved in the simplest way possible in a framework that stresses income distribution affected by the flows of profit, wage and interest.

Let us thus now extend the model (2.18) – (2.20) to include in a minimal way the possibility for price level deflation and thus the possibility for debt deflation (high levels of debt combined with declining profitability due to falling output prices) as well as the possibility of an adverse adjustment of real wages,[28] both leading to instability of the steady state of the model. This gives rise to the following type of nominal dynamics for wages w, prices p and the debt ratio d, coupled with an investment driven growth and employment path:[29]

$$\hat{w} = \frac{1}{1-\kappa_w\kappa_p}[\beta_w(V-\bar{V}) + \kappa_w\beta_p(U_c - \bar{U}_c)] \tag{2.24}$$
$$\hat{p} = \frac{1}{1-\kappa_w\kappa_p}[\kappa_p\beta_w(V-\bar{V}) + \beta_p(U_c - \bar{U}_c)] \tag{2.25}$$
$$\hat{V}^p = \alpha(\rho - \rho_{min}) - n \tag{2.26}$$
$$\dot{d} = \alpha(\rho - \rho_{min})(1-d) - \rho - \hat{p}d \tag{2.27}$$

These dynamics are based on the following static (and linearized) relationship representing Keynesian goods market equilibrium, here directly expressed in terms of the rate of capacity

[28]Meaning that real wages rise in the depression and vice versa.

[29]The details of which are explained below.

utilization U_c of firms:

$$U_c = \bar{U}_c + d_1(\frac{w}{p} - (\frac{w}{p})_o) + d_2(d - d_o), \qquad d_1, d_2 \leq 0.$$

This equation is used in the following as a shortcut for a delayed feedback chain on the market for goods. We have assumed in this equation that output and capacity utilization depend negatively on the real wage, based on the particular view that the negative real wage effect in investment dominates the positive one in consumption (the orthodox point of view), and have also assumed that output and capacity utilization depend negatively on the debt ratio d, again because investment depends negatively on it. We stress that this equation for U_c is a short-cut to a much more general situation investigated in detail in Chiarella and Flaschel (1999j). The above goods market representation allows for Rose (1967) type real wage effects of traditional type, where price flexibility will be destabilizing and for Fisher debt effects, where price flexibility will also be destabilizing, but it excludes Mundell-effects for example, based on inflationary expectations, considered in section 2.1. Finally we have $\rho = y - \frac{w}{p} l_y y - rd = y^p U_c(1 - \frac{w}{p} l_y) - rd$ for the rate of pure profits ρ.

The first two laws of motion for wages w and prices p can be easily derived, under one additional assumption stated below, from the following wage-price adjustment equations:

$$\hat{w} = \beta_w(V - \bar{V}) + \kappa_w \hat{p} + (1 - \kappa_w)\pi^e, \quad 0 < \kappa_w < 1 \tag{2.28}$$

$$\hat{p} = \beta_p(U_c - \bar{U}_c) + \kappa_p \hat{w} + (1 - \kappa_p)\pi^e, \quad 0 < \kappa_p < 1. \tag{2.29}$$

These equations represent two symmetrically formulated Phillips curves in the place of the hybrid single one that is usually considered in the literature, see Solow and Stiglitz (1968) for an early formulation of this type, Rose (1990) for a recent and more advanced one, and Fair (1997a,b) for an application of such an approach. These two equations which are more formally explored in the next section state that wage as well as price inflation depend positively on the demand pressure in the market for labor or goods, respectively, and on a weighted average of the relevant cost-push expression for each of these PC's, actual price inflation in the first and actual wage inflation in the second case both combined with an average rate of inflation π^e that is expected to hold over the medium run. This rate is set equal to zero in the present subsection for reasons of simplicity. Investigation of the role of expected inflation has been the subject of section 2.1.

The equations (2.24), (2.25), derived from (2.28), (2.29), are easily understood. They state that wage as well as price level dynamics can be expressed in terms of the two demand pressure variables solely, by an appropriate elimination of the cost-push terms contained in their original formulation (2.28), (2.29). Increasing demand pressure in one of the markets is therefore already sufficient to raise both wage and price inflation rates. Note in this regard also that there is a second Non-Accelerating-Inflation Rate of Utilization $\bar{U}_c$ now present in the model, for the goods market and the rate of capacity utilization of the capital stock in place of the stock of labor, which plays a similar benchmark role for price inflation as the rate $\bar{V}$ did for wage inflation. Demand pressure is therefore always measured relative to such benchmark rates, both assumed to be less than 1.

The other two equations (2.26), (2.27) are the same as before, with the exception that $\hat{p}d$ has now to be added to (2.27), due to the definition $d = D/(pK)$ of the ratio d, since the price level p is now a variable of the model. For simplicity we assume in the following that the minimum rate of profit ρ_{min} of investors is equal to r, the given rate of interest of the model.[30]

Note that the equation for the actual rate of employment V is related to the rate of capacity utilization U_c in the following way:

$$V = l_y Y/L = l_y(Y/Y^p)(Y^p/K)/(L/K) = l_y U_c y^p/l \quad (L \text{ labor supply, } \hat{L} = n)$$

where l_y, y^p are again the labor coefficient and the potential output capital ratio of the fixed proportions technology and where $l = L/K$ denotes the factor endowment ratio of the economy. Note also that the third equation (2.26) now concerns the evolution of the potential rate of employment $V^p = l_y Y^p/L$ as discussed in connection with figure 2.14. The dynamical system (2.24) – (2.27) therefore needs further reformulation in order to make it an autonomous system of dimension 4, since V now depends on U_c, l and since (2.26) can no longer be used to describe the actual evolution of the rate of employment as in the earlier treatments of cyclical growth (where there was always full capacity growth).

A simple reformulation of the dynamics (2.24) – (2.27) is in this regard provided by making use of the following relationship between the ratios V, V^p, U_c :

$$V = l_y Y/L = l_y Y^p/L \cdot Y/Y^p = V^p \cdot U_c$$

by which the rate of employment V can be removed from the above 4D dynamics which are then based on the state variables w, p, V^p, d, since U_c has been assumed to be a function of w, p, d.

The interior steady state of these dynamics in the state variables w, p, V^p, d is characterized by:

$$\begin{aligned}
d_o &= 1 - r/n && (2.30)\\
U_c^o &= \bar{U}_c && (2.31)\\
V_o^p &= U_c^o/\bar{V} && (2.32)\\
\rho_o &= y^p U_c(1 - \omega_o l_y) - r d_o = r, \quad \omega = w/p && (2.33)\\
\omega_o &= \frac{1 - (\rho_o + r d_o)/(U_c y^p)}{l_y} && (2.34)\\
p_o &= \text{determined by initial conditions} && (2.35)\\
w_o &= p_o \omega_o. && (2.36)
\end{aligned}$$

It is therefore in fact not uniquely determined as far as nominal magnitudes are concerned, since these dynamics can be further reduced to an autonomous system in the real variables ω, V^p, d due to the fact that equations (2.24), (2.25) can be transformed into the single law of motion for the real wage:

$$\hat{\omega} = \frac{1}{1 - \kappa_w \kappa_p}[(1 - \kappa_p)\beta_w(V - \bar{V}) - (1 - \kappa_w)\beta_p(U_c - \bar{U}_c)]. \quad (2.37)$$

All dynamical equations (2.24) – (2.27) therefore only depend on ω, V^p, d which means that the 4D system has a singular Jacobian at the steady state and thus exhibits zero root

[30] See again Chiarella and Flaschel (1999j) for a much more general treatment of such growth dynamics.

hysteresis[31] with respect to the nominal variables of the model which are thus determined in their long-run behavior also by historical conditions. The law of motion for nominal prices (and wages) can therefore be treated as appended to the real dynamics.

Proposition 2.4

1. *Assume* $0 < r < n$, $\kappa_p = 0$, *and that* β_p, d_2 *are both chosen sufficiently small. Assume furthermore that the investment parameter* α *is chosen such that* $\alpha r - n > 0$ *holds true. Then: The steady state (2.30) – (2.36) of the dynamics (2.24) – (2.27) is locally asymptotically stable.*
2. *The steady state (2.30) – (2.36) of the dynamics (2.24) – (2.27) is not locally asymptotically stable for all price adjustment speeds* β_p *chosen sufficiently large.*
3. *Assume that nominal wages are completely fixed* ($\beta_w, \kappa_w = 0$). *Then: The dynamics (2.24) – (2.27) is monotonically explosive, implying higher and higher nominal wages and debt to capital ratios, for initial debt capital ratios chosen sufficiently high and all real wage levels above their steady state value.*

Proof: See Chiarella and Flaschel (1999j) and note that their approach makes use of the state variable l in the place of V^p.

Sufficiently sluggish price level adjustments are thus favorable for local asymptotic stability, while sufficiently flexible price levels will definitely destroy it. This is due to the joint working of the destabilizing Rose (1967) real wage and Fisher (1933) debt deflation mechanisms. On the one hand, if prices are more flexible than real wages we get that depressions will increase the real wage, since prices fall faster than nominal wages in such a situation, deepening the depression already under way, a Rose-effect as in Rose (1967), but here no longer in a framework of Keynes-Wicksell type.[32] On the other hand, if prices are sufficiently flexible, downward in the case of a deflationary situation, they will raise real debt d significantly, see (2.27) and note that $\hat{p}$ will be negative in such a situation. This depresses economic activity further and thus leads to a deflationary spiral as was happening to some extent during the Great Depression of the thirties and as has again to some extent been the fear of policy makers in 1998.

We thus end up with a model type and its implications that has extended AC-PC analysis considerably, with regard to the range of PC-dynamics to be used and with respect to Keynesian demand pressure appearing in PC and now in AC-dynamics as well. Nevertheless, the PC discussion as well as the treatment of Keynesian demand problem must be further improved in the light of what has been shown. This will be done next, thereby continuing the discussion of the question mark in figure 2.14 of this section.

In closing this section we remark that the Goodwin (1967) growth cycle model has of course been extended in numerous other ways after its publication which cannot be surveyed here

[31] At least one eigenvalue of the Jacobian of the dynamics at the steady state is zero, here due to economically motivated linear dependencies between the laws of motion of the economy. Locally stable dynamical systems having zero eigenvalues will tend to a steady state dependent upon initial conditions. This is unlike locally stable systems with non-zero eigenvalues whose steady states are independent of initial conditions.

[32] See Flaschel (1993), Flaschel, Franke and Semmler (1997), Chiarella and Flaschel (1996a, 1999b) and Chiarella and Flaschel (1999j,k,l) for a variety of treatments of this model type that have much in common with the Goodwin (1967) and Rose (1967) analysis of growth or employment cycles.

due to lack of space. In this regard the reader is referred to Flaschel (1993), Flaschel (1995), Chiarella and Flaschel (1995), Flaschel, Franke and Semmler (1997), Chiarella and Flaschel (1999b), where also the question of global boundedness of locally diverging dynamics is pursued in detail.

2.5 Labor market, two Phillips-curves and nominal adjustments

We have already stressed the importance of the use of separate Phillips curves for wage and price dynamics in macroeconomics. Indeed, there exists a long, mainly non main-stream, tradition to make use of two such curves in economic theorizing, in particular in the growth cycle literature. We have already referred to this tradition in the previous sections. There is also an early article by Solow and Stiglitz (1968) where symmetrically formulated wage and price PC's are used, both with demand pressure and cost-push terms, to investigate medium run dynamics where regime switching occurs. In addition there is the related macroeconomic literature of non-Walrasian type, Malinvaud (1980), Benassy (1986, 1993), Picard (1983), Hénin and Michel (1982) and others, where such PC's have often been used in conjunction with both labor and goods market disequilibrium, see Malinvaud (1980) for a typical example. Rowthorn (1980) makes use of a dynamic price PC coupled with a static wage PC in order to show how the conflict over income distribution allows for an endogenous determination of the NAIRU rate of capacity utilization of both labor and capital, an approach that will be briefly reconsidered later. There is finally recent work by Rose (1990) where PC's of the type above were introduced. These curves have been used extensively in Chiarella and Flaschel (1999b) in a series of hierarchically structured models of monetary growth.

Turning to applied work on Phillips curves, we have already considered in simplified form the approach by Fair (1997a,b). Fair's (1997a) approach exhibits of course further arguments in the structural wage and price equations, such as labor productivity growth and import prices. Furthermore, he stresses, based on his earlier work, that these PC's are better specified in level form rather than in terms of rates of growth, as wage and as price equations and not as equations describing wage and price inflation rates immediately. Yet, in his structural macroeconometric models and their wage price block in particular, short- and medium-run aspects are dominant, which is a common feature in such applied structural models. Long-run aspects and in particular a full-fledged steady state analysis is not present and presented, just as in many other works of this type, see however Powell and Murphy (1997) and Laxton et al. (1998) for recent attempts to include steady state reference paths into such structural macroeconometric models.

Undertaking a steady state analysis in applied macroeconomic work is in our view very important, since it provides one with a consistency check of the employed model as far as the model formulation is concerned. Should the used model structure, in its deterministic part, not allow for a well-defined balanced growth path, the question of whether there is convergence to a point attractor in the long run cannot be sensibly addressed. By contrast, all macroeconometric model builders assume such convergence or shock absorber behavior as a non-questionable fact when building their models and try to incorporate it into them by making appropriate changes to the structure, if such convergence does not seem to hold initially. From this perspective it, therefore, seems natural to demand that all equations of the model must be formulated in a way such that they allow a specialization to situations of steady growth (or decline) of the real and the nominal magnitudes that are involved.

Therefore, returning to the wage and price equations of Fair (1997a,b), it should be possible to transform these equations into rates of change, unless they are explicitly designed for particular periods of unsteady growth and inflation (and thus may loose their relevance outside the particular period chosen). We start the brief discussion of Fair's (1997a) wage and price equations by also showing the terms referring to productivity growth and import prices. However, we remove all logarithms used in these equations and thus present them here in their original level form. The price and wage equations of Fair (1997a, p.6) then read in their discrete time formulation as follows:

$$p_t = c \cdot p_{t-1}^{\beta_1} (\frac{w_t(1+\tau_p)}{(1+\lambda)^t})^{\beta_2} (\frac{p_{mt}}{p_{t-1}})^{\beta_3} (\frac{1}{U_t - U_{min} + 0.02})^{\beta_4} (1+t)^{\beta_5} \tag{2.38}$$

$$w_t = c \cdot (\frac{w_{t-1}}{(1+\lambda)^{t-1}})^{\gamma_1} p_t^{\gamma_2} p_{t-1}^{\gamma_3} (1+t)^{\gamma_4} (1+\lambda)^t. \tag{2.39}$$

In these equations we denote, as usual, prices and wages by p_t, w_t (now in discrete time), by τ_p, λ the given rate of payroll taxes and of labor productivity growth (which are not necessarily constant in Fair's formulation of these equations), by p_{mt} import prices and by $U = 1 - V$ the rate of unemployment (of labor).[33] The time trend in these equations is meant by Fair to pick up any trend effects on nominal prices and wages not captured by the other variables and thus is 'void' of content from the present theoretical point of view and therefore suppressed in our following investigations of these equations. The $\beta's$ and $\gamma's$ are given parameters while the c- terms in front of these equations represent error terms in Fair's investigation, but are given magnitudes here for reasons of simplicity.

In equation (2.39), the current wage rate, measured in efficiency units, is a simple function of its past value at $t-1$, as well as past price levels, expressing Fair's empirical finding that wages are following the price level more or less passively. Concerning equation (2.38), a goods market measure for demand pressure (in the place of the rate of unemployment U) would of course have been preferable from the theoretical point of view, but is difficult to construct empirically, although Fair (1997a, p.6) mentions the potential level of output in the construction of his index of labor productivity and its rate of growth. As is obvious, the price equation contains demand pressure as well as cost-push terms, the wage term again being measured in efficiency units and the import price term relative to the current value of the domestic price level. When considering the real wage equation that results from the two equations shown above, Fair (1997a, p.8) adds the following parameter restriction to the wage and price equations in order to get a meaningful behavior of the real wage over time:

$$\gamma_3 = \frac{\beta_1}{1-\beta_2}(1-\gamma_2) - \gamma_1.$$

We shall see below that there should indeed be two parameter restrictions imposed on the two equations should these equations fulfill the requirement of allowing for steady wage and price inflation and that these restrictions will imply the one used by Fair.

[33]See in Fair (1997a, p.27) for the justification of the nonlinearity used with respect to this labor market based measure of demand pressure.

In order to show this we investigate what the above equations imply for steady price and wage inflation. In such a situation they can be reduced to the following growth rate expressions (by expressing them in logarithms and taking first differences):[34]

$$\hat{p}_t = \beta_1\hat{p}_{t-1} + \beta_2(\hat{w}_t - \lambda) + \beta_3(\hat{p}_{mt} - \hat{p}_{t-1}) \tag{2.40}$$
$$\hat{w}_t = \lambda + \gamma_1(\hat{w}_{t-1} - \lambda) + \gamma_2\hat{p}_t + \gamma_3\hat{p}_{t-1} \tag{2.41}$$

since the demand pressure variable is a constant in the steady state. There immediately follows that

$$\beta_1 + \beta_2 = 1, \quad \gamma_1 + \gamma_2 + \gamma_3 = 1$$

must hold in the steady state where all inflation rates must be equal to each other, wages of course measured in efficiency units. We thus get two restrictions for the wage price equations of Fair (1997a) should they be consistent with steady state analysis and also immediately get from them the one restriction that is used by Fair in their place. Imposing these restrictions on the original equations (with $\beta_5, \gamma_4 = 0$) however means that these equations are equivalent to their formulation in terms of rates of growth and that there is thus no necessity to make use of structural equations in level form in order to describe the wage price dynamics of structural macroeconometric model building.

We thus end up with the conclusions that specifying wage and price dynamics as two separate equations is highly desirable in theoretical as well as applied macroeconomic analyses. This makes explicit the reasons that may or may not lead to a single integrated Phillips curve later on that demand pressure variables should be specific to the price variable to be considered and only be substituted by measures referring to other markets if there is good reason to do so. Moreover, the theory based level form formulations of such wage and price equations should be reducible to rates of growth, possibly considering demand as well as cost pressure terms. This general perspective is important for macroeconometric model building.

As already stressed, Rose (1990) has revived the consideration of the two PC's approach, an approach taken up in Chiarella and Flaschel (1999b) in order to formulate the wage price module of a series of integrated models of monetary growth. In this work, however, the degree of generality chosen basically remained limited to the PC's (2.28), (2.29) Yet, these two equations are but the beginning of truly general PC's formulation and investigation.

In order to show this at least partially, the re-reading of the articles of Phillips is of great help. Phillips (1954) investigated three possible types of fiscal policies, proportional, derivative and integral feedback policy rules which change for example government expenditures, broadly speaking, in proportion to output gaps, in proportion to their time rate of change and in proportion to the accumulated differences of such gaps, of course with a negative feedback sign in order to counteract less than normal situations in particular. Similarly, inflation rates may be driven by factor utilization gaps, or, in the case of wage inflation specifically, by deviations of the rate of employment from its NAIRU level, but also by the rate of change of the employment rate or the accumulated differences (where positive and negative signs may occur) of the deviation of unemployment rates from normal levels, here again considered in continuous time.

[34]Where $\hat{x}_t$ is defined by $\frac{x_t - x_{t-1}}{x_{t-1}}$.

Though not framed in this type of language, all three possibilities are in fact taken into account in early or recent investigations of the PC approach, as we shall see in more detail below, the proportional control by the original approach of Phillips, the derivative control in form of the so-called Phillips loops discussion and in a paper by Kuh (1967) where the level of wages or of the wage share, and not its growth rate, was related to the rate of unemployment, and the integral control when it was claimed that the rate of unemployment is not in fact determining the rate of inflation itself, but rather its time rate of change. Marrying Phillips (1954) with Phillips (1958) with respect to a treatment of wage and price inflation thus provides a fairly general framework on the basis of which the various findings in the literature on 'the' Phillips curve can be evaluated and investigated in a unified way.[35]

Let us first extend our formulation of the wage and price PC's (2.28), (2.29) of section 2.1. by these additional measures of demand pressure and their influence on wage and price inflation, leaving aside here the issue for the cost-pressure terms which in principle could be treated in the same way. The wage and price PC's then read:

$$\hat{w} = \beta_{w_1}(V - \bar{V}) + \beta_{w_2}\hat{V} + \beta_{w_3}\int (V - \bar{V})dt + \kappa_w\hat{p} + (1-\kappa_w)\pi^e \quad (2.42)$$

$$\hat{p} = \beta_{p_1}(U_c - \bar{U}_c) + \beta_{p_2}\hat{U}_c + \beta_{p_3}\int (U_c - \bar{U}_c)dt + \kappa_p\hat{w} + (1-\kappa_p)\pi^e \quad (2.43)$$

Note here that dimensional homogeneity demands that we should express derivative control in terms of growth rates and not as time rates of change and that it may be preferable to use $V/\bar{V} - 1, U_c/\bar{U}_c - 1$ as measures of demand pressure, in the place of the simple differences shown above, which at present, however, only leads to proportional changes in the sizes of the parameters employed in these Phillips curves.

Next there exists another important extension of the considered PC's. This extension takes note of the fact that the labor and goods market disequilibrium in fact is reflected in at least two qualitatively different measures of such disequilibrium. In the case of the labor market, through the external rate of employment of the labor force and the internal rate of employment of the employed. In the case of the goods market through the rate of utilization of the capital stock and the rate of utilization of the stock of inventories measured through the ratio of actual inventories to the ones desired by firms. This leads us to the following alternative extension of the two PC's approach:

$$\hat{w} = \beta_{w_1}(V - \bar{V}) + \beta_{w_2}(V^w - 1) + \kappa_w\hat{p} + (1-\kappa_w)\pi^e \quad (2.44)$$

$$\hat{p} = \beta_{p_1}(U_c - \bar{U}_c) - \beta_{p_2}(U_n - 1) + \kappa_p\hat{w} + (1-\kappa_p)\pi^e \quad (2.45)$$

where $V = L^w/L, V^w = L^d/L^w$ denote the external and the internal rate of employment and $U_c = Y/Y^p, U_n = N/N^d$ the rate of capacity utilization and the inventory / desired inventory ratio (L^d actual employment in 'hours', L^w the employed part of the workforce, also representing the normal working day, and Y, Y^p actual and potential output, N, N^d actual and desired inventory levels). Note here that normal working hours may be diminished by some average rate of 'absenteeism' which would imply that the rate of employment of the employed is to be compared with a number smaller than one, in place of the 1 used above.

[35] See Flaschel (1991) for a quite different and very powerful application of derivative control mechanisms to economic dynamics.

Note also that equations (2.42), (2.43) as well as equations (2.44), (2.45) are of the general form

$$\begin{aligned}\hat{w} &= \beta_w(\cdot) + \kappa_w\hat{p} + (1-\kappa_w)\pi^e \\ \hat{p} &= \beta_p(\cdot) + \kappa_p\hat{w} + (1-\kappa_p)\pi^e\end{aligned}$$

and thus represent, when appropriately reordered, two linear equations in the unknowns $\hat{w} - \pi^e$, $\hat{p} - \pi^e$ that can be uniquely solved for $\hat{w} - \pi^e$, $\hat{p} - \pi^e$ when $\kappa_w, \kappa_p \in [0,1]$ fulfill $\kappa_w\kappa_p < 1$, giving rise then to:

$$\begin{aligned}\hat{w} - \pi^e &= \frac{1}{1-\kappa_w\kappa_p}[\beta_w(\cdot) + \kappa_w\beta_p(\cdot)] \\ \hat{p} - \pi^e &= \frac{1}{1-\kappa_w\kappa_p}[\beta_p(\cdot) + \kappa_p\beta_w(\cdot)].\end{aligned}$$

Integrating across markets for example the two PC's approach (2.44), (2.45) would thus imply that four qualitatively different measures for demand pressure in the markets for labor as well as for goods have to be used both for money wage and price level inflation for describing their deviation from expected inflation in the usual way by an expectations augmented PC, see Laxton et al. (1998) for a typical example, where, as is customary, only one measure of demand pressure, on the labor market, is considered. Making furthermore use of all of Phillips' (1954) three types of control the obtained integrated PC's will be further differentiated, leading to 12 types of expressions that may appear in the integrated, across markets, price level PC that dominates the mainstream literature. Furthermore, as before, two different types of NAIRU's will then be present in the integrated (wage and) price PC which in general cannot be identified with each other. Finally, as already mentioned, further differentiation may concern the cost pressure terms of the PC's shown above, but will not be considered here in its details.

The stage of money wage and price level Phillips curves discussion now reached thus exhibits in each case six different measures of demand pressure in the corresponding PC, which, when transformed into integrated PC's, spanning across markets, in the way just shown, leads us to the following fairly complex expressions for expectations augmented PC's:[36]

$$\begin{aligned}\hat{w} = \pi^e &+ \frac{1}{1-\kappa_w\kappa_p}[\beta_{w_1}(V-\bar{V}) + \beta_{w_2}\hat{V} + \beta_{w_3}\int(V-\bar{V})dt \\ &+ \beta_{w_4}(V^w-1) + \beta_{w_5}\hat{V}^w + \beta_{w_6}\int(V^w-1)dt \\ &+ \kappa_w(\beta_{p_1}(U_c-\bar{U}_c) + \beta_{p_2}\hat{U}_c + \beta_{p_{31}}\int(U_c-\bar{U}_c)dt \\ &+ \beta_{p_4}(U_n-1) + \beta_{p_5}\hat{U}_n + \beta_{p_6}\int(U_n-1)dt)] \qquad (2.46) \\ \hat{p} = \pi^e &+ \frac{1}{1-\kappa_w\kappa_p}[\kappa_p(\beta_{w_1}(V-\bar{V}) + \beta_{w_2}\hat{V} + \beta_{w_3}\int(V-\bar{V})dt \\ &+ \beta_{w_4}(V^w-1) + \beta_{w_5}\hat{V}^w + \beta_{w_6}\int(V^w-1)dt) \\ &+ \beta_{p_1}(U_c-\bar{U}_c) + \beta_{p_2}\hat{U}_c + \beta_{p_{31}}\int(U_c-\bar{U}_c)dt \\ &+ \beta_{p_4}(U_n-1) + \beta_{p_5}\hat{U}_n + \beta_{p_6}\int(U_n-1)dt] \qquad (2.47)\end{aligned}$$

[36]Note that π^e was set equal to zero in the models considered in section 2.

As should be obvious now, the second of these equations represents 'the' integrated price Phillips curve of this extended approach to wage and price inflation and its various measures of demand pressure, where the actual wage and price inflation cost-push cross reference has been removed by mathematical substitution. Obviously, this equation is much more complicated than the simple expectations augmented price Phillips curve of the theoretical literature or its Walrasian reinterpretation as a Lucas supply curve.

Let us briefly consider various applied approaches to PC measurements on the basis of the equations (2.46), (2.47). Fair (1997a,b), as already shown, provides one of the rare studies (disregarding structural macroeconometric model building for the moment) which starts from two PC's, though he makes use of $\beta_{p_1} \neq 0$ solely as far as demand pressure variables are concerned. In his view the price Phillips curve is therefore the important one.

Concerning modern macroeconometric model building, we find in Powell and Murphy (1997) a money wage Phillips curve with $\beta_{w_1}, \beta_{w_2} \neq 0$ and a price Phillips curve that appears to be based on cost-push terms solely, but which (when appropriately reformulated, see Chiarella, Flaschel, Groh, Köper and Semmler (1999a)) in fact also makes use of $\beta_{p_1} \neq 1$ implicitly. Furthermore, the parameter β_{w_2} is about 8 times larger than β_{w_1} when the nonlinear wage Phillips curve measured in this work is linearized at the steady state, which supports Kuh's (1967) assertion that the wage Phillips curve is a level relationship rather than one concerning rates of inflation, and which at the same time stresses the importance of Phillips loops as already observed by Phillips (1958) himself. Indeed, if $\hat{w} = \beta_{w_2}\hat{V}$ represents the dominant part of the money wage Phillips curve, we get by simple integration $w = constV^{\beta_{w_2}}$ and thus a wage curve as considered on the microlevel by Blanchflower and Oswald (1994) for example. In this view the wage Phillips curve, with derivative control solely, is therefore the important one.

Laxton et al. (1998) use for the Multimod Mark III model of the IMF an integrated, or hybrid, PC of the type (2.47) with only $\beta_{w_1} \neq 0$, and thus the most basic type of PC approach, but stress instead the strict convexity of this curve and the dynamic NAIRU considerations this may give rise to. In this view, therefore, the wage Phillips curve with proportional term only is the important one. Stock and Watson (1997) find evidence for a Phillips curve of the type $\dot{\pi} = \beta_{w_3}(V - \bar{V})$, $\pi = \hat{p}$, which by the choice of notation here used indicates that this view is in fact based on an integral control in the money wage Phillips curve (solely) and possibly also on a specific, implicit treatment of inflationary expectations in addition. Roberts (1997) derives a conventional expectations augmented price Phillips curve from regional wage curves as in Blanchflower and Oswald (1994) and thus argues that proportional control is relevant in the aggregate even if derivative control applies to the regional level.

We thus find in this brief discussion of applied approaches a variety of opinions. Yet there are few studies as regards the inside employment rates and inventory utilization rates. This is possibly due to the lack of data. Only Fair (1997a,b) takes account of the possibility that demand pressure on the goods market may be qualitatively and quantitatively different from demand pressure on the labor market. On the other hand, at least the possibility for proportional, derivative and integral control is taken into account by this literature, though not reflected and compared in these terms. It must, therefore, be noted that the discussion on Phillips curves is at present again a lively one, but also a still unsettled one. Of course, not all of the expressions shown in (2.47) must be relevant from the empirical point of view, at all times and in all countries. But this should be the outcome of a systematic investigation and not the result of more or less isolated views and investigations. Despite the recent approaches to PC analysis it therefore appears as if the analysis and investigation of these curves would be better approached from the extended perspective we have described above.

We mention in passing that also the theory of inflationary expectations may be developed further along the lines suggested by our analysis of Phillips curves. In this respect recall first that we have myopic perfect foresight in our wage - price dynamics of price and wage inflation respectively, but have also assumed that these rates of inflation enter wage and price formation processes only with a weight κ_w, κ_p, respectively. In addition we have employed a uniform measure of average inflation, expected to characterize the medium run, which enters these processes with weight $1-\kappa_w, 1-\kappa_p$, respectively. We are inclined to assume that the expectation of medium-run inflation cannot be perfect, but that it is based on some time series method, simple adaptive expectations schemes, or, humped shaped weighting schemes of past observation expressing some price inertia; for the latter see Gordon (1997). We have also the theory-based p-star concept of the German Bundesbank. Also it should be noted that medium run wage inflation may be different from medium run price inflation. There is thus also considerable scope to extend the discussion on the expectational terms in the Phillips curves which however is left here for future investigations, see Chiarella and Flaschel (1999a,c) for further discussions of these issues. Finally we want to note that some empirical estimates of the two Phillips curve approach for the US and Germany are, with some success, undertaken in Flaschel, Gong and Semmler (1999) and Gong, Flaschel and Semmler (1999).

Next, let us consider a theoretical approach by Rowthorn (1980) which makes use of a price Phillips curve with proportional control and a wage Phillips curve with derivative control in order to provide an IS-LM-PC model, in his case in fact a monetarist model of inflation and stagflation, which is formally of the same type as the ones considered in section 2.1, but which allows for an endogenous determination of the NAIRU rates $\bar{V}, \bar{U}_c$ in addition, based on the conflict over income distribution. This is an interesting extension of the IS-LM-PC dynamics considered in section 2.1 and it furthermore provides a theoretical example of how the use of various special types of Phillips curves, appropriately combined, can lead to quite different views of the interaction of unemployment and inflation as compared to the conventional one.[37]

The fundamental features and building blocks of Rowthorn's reformulation of this interaction, here augmented by IS-LM analysis in the place of his simpler quantity theoretic approach, are the following ones:

$$\hat{p} = \beta_p(\Pi^* - \Pi) + \pi^e \tag{2.48}$$
$$\Pi^* = \Pi^*(U_c) \tag{2.49}$$
$$\Pi = 1 - u, \quad u = (w/p)l_y \quad \text{the share of wages} \tag{2.50}$$
$$\hat{w} = \beta_w \hat{V} + \hat{p}. \tag{2.51}$$

We have a price Phillips curve of the proportional kind, based on a kind of self reference on price inflation expected to hold over the medium run and a wage Phillips curve of the

[37]See also Flaschel (1984b) and Flaschel and Groh (1996a) in this regard.

derivative type with myopic perfect foresight as far as price inflation is concerned. Price inflation is driven by the gap between the desired profit share Π^* and the actual one, Π, with the desired profit share being a positive function of the rate of capacity utilization U_c of firms. In the background of this model we have our fixed proportions technology with given labor productivity $1/l_y$ and thus get a strict proportionality between the rate of capacity utilization and the rate of employment, as a very simple form of Okun's law, $U_c = const{\cdot}V$. Furthermore, the money wage Phillips curve gives rise to (by its integration): $w/p = constV^{\beta_w}$, a functional form that then also applies to the wage share u in the place of the real wage w/p. Inserting all these expressions into the price Phillips curve $\hat{p} = \beta_p(\Pi^* - \Pi) + \pi^e$ then gives rise to

$$\hat{p} = \beta_p(\Pi^*(V) - (1 - u(V))) + \pi^e = \beta_p(\Pi^*(V) + u(V) - 1) + \pi^e$$

with both Π^*, u being strictly increasing functions of the rate of employment V. On the surface this is just an ordinary PC of the monetarist type, as we have employed it before, though now possibly a nonlinear one. Disregarding this latter possibility and assuming that the parameters of model are such that there is a solution $\bar{V} \in (0,1)$ where $\Pi^*(\bar{V}) + u(\bar{V}) = 1$ holds, which is then uniquely determined, we get from these alternative underpinnings of the formal IS-LM-PC model analyzed in section 2.1 an endogenous explanation of the NAIRU rate of employment, there given as a parameter. The issue of an endogenously changing NAIRU, or more specifically a time varying NAIRU has recently been discussed by Gordon (1997) and by other papers in the same journal. In our case the NAIRU rate, among others, depends on the relationship $\Pi^*(U_c)$, and thus negatively on the shape and steepness of this curve, which characterizes the strength with which capital owners defend their income shares, and also negatively on the parameter β_w which measures the strength by which labor defends its income share. Therefore, the stronger the conflict over income distribution, the lower is the NAIRU rate of employment at which the income shares demanded, $\Pi^*(V) + u(V)$, become compatible with what is available for distribution; thereby allowing for a steady behavior of wage and price inflation. This provides in simple terms a simultaneous interpretation of both the NAIRU rate of capacity utilization and the NAIRU rate of employment, surrounded by a dynamic that is of the same type as the one investigated in section 2.1. We stress again that this has become possible through a simple specialization of the very general type of PC's we have investigated above. Note however that Okun's law, which is based on a positive correlation between the rate of capacity utilization and the rate of employment, has been used here in order to derive this specific view on the explanation of steady rates of factor utilization.

We conclude with the observation that much remains to be done in the theoretical discussion of the form and the implications of PC approaches, where many more outcomes may be obtained than is generally believed. The same also holds true for empirical studies of Phillips curves, where there is a lack of systematic investigation of the wealth of possibilities to which we have referred above.

In the next chapter, we will put together what we have demonstrated in this chapter with respect to nominal adjustment processes, quantity adjustment processes, and the interaction of capital accumulation with income distribution and aggregate demand. We shall see that there is a still very basic working model type that represents the interaction of these partial mechanisms in a way that is coherent with respect to budget equations, steady state solutions and that shows that there are at least six laws of motion involved in a Keynesian formulation of real and financial market interactions with disequilibrium adjustment processes for wages, prices, quantities and expectations.

Chapter 3

Disequilibrium, Growth and Labor Market Dynamics: Synthesis and Perspectives

3.1 Introduction

In this chapter we integrate the Keynes-Metzler-Goodwin approaches of chapter 2 into a coherent whole, briefly called the KMG model from now on,[1] paying in particular attention to consistency checks such as the budget constraints for households, firms and the government[2] as well as the existence of interior steady solutions, which are indeed uniquely determined and stable under plausible parameter restrictions. These integrated dynamics, the KMG alternative to conventional AS-AD growth, are already of dimension 6, but do nevertheless only display the absolute minimum of dynamic variables needed to represent sluggish adjustment of wages, prices and quantities, and to some extent expectations, in the context of monetary growth. Section 3.1 introduces and explains the basic integrated model of this KMG type directly on the intensive form level and investigates its basic properties. In section 3.2 we extend this approach to growth in disequilibrium to open economies and briefly sketch basic results and numerical features for this Dornbusch (1976) type enlargement of the basic KMG dynamics through state variables representing exchange rate dynamics and expectations about currency de- or appreciation. On the basis of these most basic representations of integrated KMG growth for closed and open economies we then discuss in section 3.3 the popular stress on microfoundations as against the need for macrofoundations which should provide basic or more elaborate integrated pictures of the working of whole monetary economies. In particular the macrofounded view should contain all important mechanisms or feedback structures known from the macrostatic and macrodynamic literature in order to facilitate the discussion of their relative importance analytically, numerically and also empirically. We believe that full representation of the basic markets of the macroeconomy and the investigation of their full interdependence, including proper specifications of all budget equations, is at least as important as the need

[1] This KMG model, the working model of Chiarella and Flaschel (1999b, Ch.6), will be expanded in various ways in part II.

[2] See the appendix 3.6.2 to this chapter in this regard.

for proper microfoundations, which often provide only partial structures or special cases of the integrated macrodynamical systems which are the focus of this book. The ultimate aim of such integrated approaches should be theoretically sound macroeconometric model building. A basic theoretical approach to such still larger structures of monetary growth in disequilibrium is sketched and briefly investigated in section 3.4 and will be discussed in detail in part III of this book.

3.2 The working KMG model of fluctuating growth

Let us now start to put together what we have learned from IS-LM-PC analysis (the Keynes component), from the study of the goods market disequilibrium (the Metzler component), and from labor market dynamics and the classical growth cycle (the Goodwin subdynamics), and in addition also from our consideration of two PC's or wage-price adjustment mechanisms in the place of only one.

We shall use the wage price equations in the form (2.24), (2.25) and will thus considerably generalize the conventional representation of the aforementioned expectations augmented integrated price Phillips curve. We will add to our K(eynes)-M(etzler)-G(oodwin) model an investment function that now includes, besides a measure of the profitability of firms, the real rate of interest as in IS-LM-PC analysis and the rate of capacity utilization as in Malinvaud (1980), but not yet in derivative form as in Harrodian knife edge growth analysis. Furthermore, we will have two types of households in the following, workers who consume what they get and asset holders who consume and save (the latter in the form of money, government bonds and equities). Finally, we will reformulate and extend our synthesis by means of a Metzlerian inventory adjustment mechanism and thus allow in addition to sluggish wage and price adjustment also for sluggish quantity adjustment. In the place of IS-equilibrium we thus now have the interaction of sales expectations, output (including desired inventory changes) and actual aggregate demand and on this basis unintended inventory changes and an inventory adjustment mechanism.

Since this model is intended to be complete with respect to the interaction of all these elements we have, of course, to consider the capacity effects of investment in addition to the income effects of investment. We thus now again include growth which we here solely derive from the natural growth of the labor force in the usual way, and implicitly also from exogenous Harrod neutral technical change as in Chiarella and Flaschel (1999b, Ch.4). Making technical change explicit would not alter the presentation of the model, but would demand only that all labor and wage expressions have to reinterpreted in terms of efficiency units.[3]

The model we obtain in this way resembles the working model of Chiarella and Flaschel (1999b) which is there derived as a systematic extension of earlier traditional models of monetary growth of Tobin, Keynes-Wicksell and IS-LM type. This model can be extended to include, a more refined government sector, in particular with respect to income taxation, smooth factor substitution in place of the fixed proportions technology and more advanced modeling of expectation formation than was considered so far. These generalization are considered in their relevance and with respect to their implications in Chiarella and Flaschel

[3]With the parameter l_y^e in the place of l_y then.

(1999a,e) and will here be left aside for reasons of simplicity, since they do not alter the conclusions drawn in this section in a significant way.

The working model, the KMG model, which we reconsider below, represents in our view the basic format of Keynesian monetary growth analysis. We are of course aware that the Hicksian representation of the Keynes-component of this model type will not be considered as a proper Keynes-representation by a variety of macroeconomists. Nevertheless it is important to have such a traditional reference case, the KMG model, at our disposal in order to allow a precise presentation of where one could depart from it to get a better theory of fluctuating growth of deterministic or even of stochastic type. The problem in the literature on monetary growth, see Orphanides and Solow (1990) for example, was, that such a traditional integrated Keynesian prototype dynamics was completely missing as an explicitly spelled out model type, not to speak of the analysis of the dynamics this model type will give rise to.

Let us now start with an overview on the intensive form representation of 6D KMG-dynamics that we obtain from our above considerations. The extensive form of this KMG model is presented in appendix 3.6.2, in order to show that the intensive form results from a model type that is coherently formulated with respect to behavior and budget restrictions and thus does not allow for demand of agents that is not backed up by the supply of funds (or loans) that finance these expenditures. The first dynamical law of KMG growth concerns the real wage $\omega = w/p$ and is in fact a direct consequence of the integrated two PC's approach (2.24), (2.25), as it has been derived from the wage-price dynamics (2.28), (2.29). Subtracting (2.25) from (2.24) gives rise to

$$\begin{aligned} \hat{\omega} &= \hat{w} - \hat{p} \\ &= \frac{1}{1-\kappa_w\kappa_p}[(1-\kappa_p)\beta_w(V-\bar{V}) - (1-\kappa_w)\beta_p(U_c-\bar{U}_c)] \end{aligned} \tag{3.1}$$

which simply states that the adjustment of real wages depends positively on the demand pressure on the market for labor and negatively on that in the market for goods. We immediately realize that either wage or price flexibility should add instability to the dynamics of this section. These are normal or abnormal Rose effects, depending on whether real wage increases increase or decrease economic activity.

The next law of motion concerns the dynamics of the factor endowment ratio $l = L/K$, where it is assumed that labor supply L grows with the given natural rate n and the capital stock, in our Keynesian approach, with the rate of net investment, $\hat{K} = I/K$. The essential element in this law of motion is, therefore, given by the net investment function which is specified as follows:

$$I/K = i_1(\rho^e - (r - \pi^e)) + i_2(U_c - \bar{U}_c) + n.$$

This function, as all other behavioral equations, are assumed as linear, just as our simple production function $L^d = l_y Y, Y^p = y^p K$, with l_y, y^p given magnitudes. This is done in order to keep the initial version of the model as linear as is possible, which allows us to clearly see its intrinsic or unavoidable nonlinearities at the beginning of the analysis of the KMG dynamics. Note also that the trend term in this investment equation is given by the natural rate of growth. The interaction of natural growth with trend growth in investment will be considered at the end of this section.

Investment per unit of capital thus depends on the expected rate of profit ρ^e, the real rate of interest $r - \pi^e$ and the rate of capacity utilization U_c, representing Tobin's q and the capacity effect considered by Malinvaud (1980) and others. All these magnitudes are actual (short-run) values and should be replaced by medium run averages in applications of this model type, which increases the dimension of the dynamics without adding too much new structure to the model, see Flaschel, Gong, and Semmler (1999), Gong, Flaschel, and Semmler (1999) for such extensions and applications of the model. Here however, only the above simple formulation of investment behavior will be used, and it gives rise to the following law of motion for the labor intensity $l = L/K$:

$$\widehat{l} = -i_1(\rho^e - (r - \pi^e)) - i_2(U_c - \bar{U}_c). \tag{3.2}$$

The next dynamical law is basically taken from section 2.1., since it is based on the definitional equation for real balances (per unit of capital now): $m = M/(pK)$, implying $\hat{m} = \bar{\mu} + n - \hat{l} - \hat{p}$, where it is again assumed that the money supply M grows with a given rate $\bar{\mu}$, since policy questions are not yet of interest. Making use of the equation for $\hat{p}$ this gives:

$$\widehat{m} = \bar{\mu} - n + \hat{l} - \pi^e - \frac{1}{1 - \kappa_w \kappa_p}[\beta_p(U_c - \bar{U}_c) + \kappa_p \beta_w(V - \bar{V})] \tag{3.3}$$

We see that increased capacity utilization on both the labor and the goods market will speed up inflation and thus reduce the growth rate of real balances, leading to corresponding nominal interest rate changes due to the Keynes-effect as it derives from the simple LM-curve still present in this model type.

Next we have the law for inflationary expectations which is a simple extension of the one used before, since we now determine these expectations as an average of backward and forward looking behavior (time series methods and forecasts by means of small scale theoretical models). Time series methods can in principle be as complicated and refined as possible, however, only when numerical simulations of the model are intended. From the viewpoint of theory they should at first be chosen as simple as possible in order to allow for an analytical treatment of stability issues as we shall provide it below, i.e., they will of the simple adaptive type made use of in section 2.1 (they can be made a humped shaped average of past observations of inflation by means of nested adaptive expectation schemes in a next step for example). Forward looking expectations can be based on the p-star concept of the German Bundesbank for example, which states that inflation rates will converge to the difference of $\bar{\mu}$, the growth rate of the money supply, and $\hat{Y}^p$, the growth rate of potential output, as long as the velocity of money can be considered a given magnitude over the longer run. Again made as simple as possible this setup gives the result that such inflationary expectations assume that there is convergence of inflation rates back to the steady rate $\bar{\mu} - n$, giving rise to:

$$\dot{\pi}^e = \beta_{\pi^e}[\alpha(\hat{p} - \pi^e) + (1 - \alpha)(\bar{\mu} - n - \pi^e)] \tag{3.4}$$

$$= \beta_{\pi^e}[\alpha \frac{1}{1 - \kappa_w \kappa_p}(\beta_p(U_c - \bar{U}_c) + \kappa_p \beta_w(V - \bar{V})) + (1 - \alpha)(\bar{\mu} - n - \pi^e)] \tag{3.5}$$

where α denotes the weight attached to the backward looking type of expectations and $1 - \alpha$ the one for the forward looking type. The destabilizing role of the Mundell effect is clearly visible in this extended equation, since economic activity depends positively on expected inflation, due to the assumed investment behavior, and since an increase in economic activity, here measured by two rates of factor capacity utilization, speeds up the increase in inflationary expectations as shown by this equation.

There remains the quantity adjustment process on the market for goods which is composed of the adjustment of sales expectations and the changes in actual inventories, $y^e = Y^e/K$ and $\nu = N/K$, both already in per unit of capital form, see here section 2.2 and Metzler (1941) for the original approach. These two laws of motion read:[4]

$$\dot{y}^e = \beta_{y^e}(y^d - y^e) + \hat{l}y^e \tag{3.6}$$

$$\dot{\nu} = y - y^d + (\hat{l} - n)\nu \tag{3.7}$$

where the terms involving l are simply due to the fact that everything is expressed in per unit of capital terms. Sales expectations of firms, y^e, are here assumed to change in an adaptive fashion, following actual demand y^d with some time delay, while actual inventories changes are given by definition through the difference between actual output y and actual demand y^d, again corrected by a term that takes account of the intensive form under consideration.

This closes the description of the laws of motion of the state variables of our basic KMG dynamics which concern income distribution, relative factor growth, inflation as measured by the change of real balances, inflationary expectations, sales expectations and actual inventory changes. These dynamical laws do not yet form a complete system, but must be supplemented by some algebraic equations which define the statically endogenous magnitudes we used in the above differential equations. These equations are given by:

$$\begin{aligned}
y &= \beta_n(\beta_{n^d}y^e - \nu) + (1 + n\beta_{n^d})y^e \\
y^d &= \omega l_y y + (1 - s_c)(\rho^e - t^n) + i_1(\rho^e - (r - \pi^e)) + i_2(U_c - \bar{U}_c) + n + \delta + g \\
V &= l^d/l, \ U_c = y/y^p, \ l^d = L^d/K = l_y y, \\
\rho^e &= y^e - \delta - \omega l_y y, \ r = r_0 + (h_1 y - m)/h_2.
\end{aligned}$$

These equations describe output y equal to expected sales and voluntary inventory changes, which follow $\beta_{n^d}y^e - \nu$, the difference between desired inventories and the actual ones, with speed β_n, aggregate demand y^d which is composed of the real wage sum per unit of capital (since workers do not save), consumption of asset holders based on expected profits after taxes $\rho^e - t^n$, where taxes net of interest t^n are treated as a parameter of the model as in Sargent (1987, Ch.5), gross investment (δ the depreciation rate) and government expenditures g, again assumed a parameter of the model. The remaining equations then define the rate of employment V, the rate of capacity utilization U_c, the expected rate of profit, ρ^e, based on the sales expectations of firms, and the nominal rate of interest as defined by a linear form of money market equilibrium. These explanations must suffice here as a presentation of the static part of the working KMG model of Chiarella and Flaschel (1999b). For additional explanations and a detailed analysis of this model type the reader is referred to this cited work as well as to the appendix 3.6.2 where the model in its originally extensive form is presented.

[4]See Franke and Lux (1993) and Franke (1996) for contributions, demonstrating the existence of inventory cycles by means of appropriate extrinsic nonlinearities, from which our inclusion of this quantity adjustment process on the market for goods in section 2.2 took its point of departure.

Note with respect to the full structure of traditional Keynesian monetary growth presented in figure 1.1 we now employ an advanced description of the wage-price module, yet we still consider a closed economy (no Dornbusch exchange rate dynamics), and do not consider explicitly internal asset markets, except the static LM determination of the nominal rate of interest, as in Sargent (1987, Ch.1-5). Thus, we do not yet consider Blanchard (1981) type asset market dynamics, nor do we yet have Fisher debt effects as considered before and have also abstracted from wealth (Pigou) effects in consumption as well as money demand. The above disequilibrium growth model therefore just stresses sluggish wage, price and quantity dynamics (including expectations) and resulting capacity utilization problems for labor as well as capital. Thus it does not yet consider real-financial interactions in the proper sense.

Despite the linearity assumed for all behavioral equations the model is intrinsically nonlinear, due to its use of growth laws of motion and the unavoidable appearance of products and ratios of state variables in various places. The considered dynamics therefore should be capable of generating stable limit cycles in particular and also more complex attractors for its trajectories even on this basic level of its formulation. The following proposition, though not a trivial one due to the high dimension of the considered dynamics, does not yet show the existence of stable limit cycles, for example, since the occurrence of either super- or sub-critical Hopf-bifurcations, the complement of which is of exceptional nature, cannot be shown here explicitly, due to the well known enormous numerical difficulties that are involved in such a proof already for nonlinear systems of dimension 2.

Proposition 3.1

1. *Assume sufficiently sluggish adjustments for wages, prices, and inflationary expectations, and a strong Keynes-Effect (h_2 sufficiently small).*[5] *Then:*
   The interior steady state of the 6D dynamics (3.1) – (3.7), which is easily calculated and uniquely determined, is locally asymptotically stable for all adjustment speeds of sales expectations β_{y^e} chosen sufficiently large and speeds of adjustments of inventories, β_n, chosen sufficiently low .
2. *The 6D determinant of the Jacobian of the dynamics at the steady state is always positive.*
3. *If $\beta_{\pi^e}, \beta_n, h_2$ are chosen sufficiently large, the steady state equilibrium is locally repelling. The system therefore undergoes a (generally non degenerate) Hopf bifurcation at intermediate value of these (and other) parameters, which generates persistent fluctuations, attractors in the supercritical case and repellers in the subcritical one.*

The periodic fluctuations obtained in this way integrate the growth cycle analysis of section 2.3 with the inflationary dynamics of section 2.1, coupled with Metzlerian quantity adjustment in the market for goods considered in section 2.2 and they are generated independently of any kink in the money wage PC. Further details on this proposition and the partial models it encompasses are provided in Chiarella and Flaschel (1999b), where a proof is provided for the dynamic multiplier equivalent of the Metzlerian inventory adjustment

[5]Such that $y_y^d < 1$ holds in particular, i.e., the marginal propensity to spend is less than one.

process here used. We do not go into a proof of this proposition here, but simply add some explanations to the assertions made.[6]

The steady state of the system is asserted to be locally attracting for all price and quantity adjustment speeds, including the Metzlerian inventory accelerator, sufficiently low. The sales expectations which mirror the stable Keynesian multiplier dynamics then improve stability if chosen sufficiently large. In addition, we should have a fairly interest-inelastic money demand function which in such a case produces large positively correlated swings of the nominal rate of interest when the price level rises or falls. Partial insights into the stability of Keynesian dynamics, augmented with what we know of the Rose effects considered in section 2.3 or even static conclusions of Keynesian theory, appropriately combined, then allow here for a stability assertion for the full 6D dynamics of the integrated KMG growth model. Furthermore, since the determinant does not change sign when the parameters of the model are changed, we know that loss of stability can only occur in a cyclical fashion since eigenvalues must then cross the imaginary axis excluding 0 (and will generally do so with positive speed). The resulting situations of Hopf bifurcations then generally imply that this change in stability of the system is accompanied by either the 'birth' of a stable limit cycle (with increasing amplitude) to the right of the critical bifurcation value (where a pair of eigenvalues has become purely imaginary) or the death of an unstable limit cycle (via its shrinking amplitude) to the left of this critical point when this point is approached.

Figure 3.1 illustrate these situations and shows in particular the example of a stable limit cycle that has been created in this way. This figure shows on its left hand side the Hopf–bifurcation locus for the three parameter sets (β_p, β_w), (β_p, β_{π_1}) and (β_{y^e}, β_n), i.e., the locus where a supercritical, subcritical or degenerate Hopf–bifurcation occurs. A vertical line is used to separate sub from super–critical Hopf–bifurcations. The parameters for the limit cycle on the right hand side of figures 3.1 are provided in Chiarella and Flaschel (1999b, Ch.6) and they correspond to a point just above the Hopf loci in (β_p, β_w)–space as well as (β_p, β_{π_1})–space and just below the Hopf–curve in (β_{y^e}, β_n)–space (in the middle of the depicted supercritical domain).

Let us consider the (β_w, β_p)–parameter–space as an example. For any given β_p, increasing β_w from 0 to 1 means that the system will reach a point where it loses its local stability in a cyclical fashion. At a supercritical Hopf bifurcation this will happen via the birth of an attracting limit cycle which 'surrounds' the now unstable steady state. At a subcritical Hopf–bifurcation an unstable limit cycle will disappear as β_w approaches this bifurcation value, where the corridor of local asymptotic stability that existed beforehand has gone. At a degenerate Hopf bifurcation, this same loss of stability need not be accompanied by either the 'birth' of a stable limit cycle or the 'death' of an unstable limit cycle, but here purely implosive behavior may simply change into a purely explosive one. These various types of Hopf–bifurcations are treated and depicted in their details, for example, in Wiggins (1990) and Strogatz (1994). The (β_p, β_w)–diagram in the figure 3.1 thus basically shows that there

[6]See Flaschel, Gong and Semmler (1999) for details on the proof of this proposition.

is generally – up to very small parameter values of β_p – the birth of a stable limit cycle as β_w crosses the depicted Hopf locus.

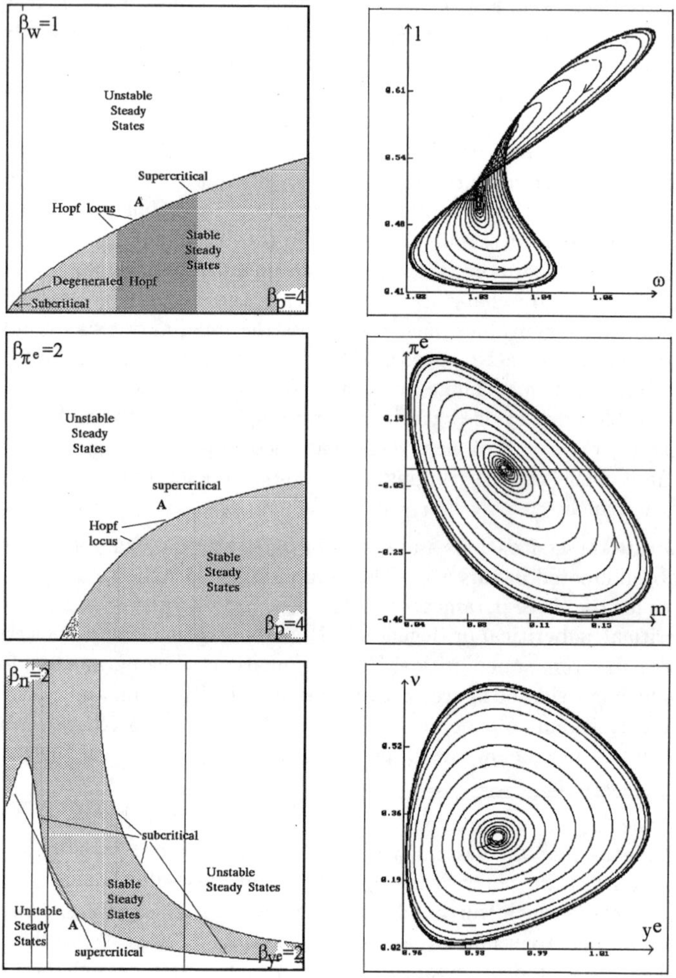

Figures 3.1: Hopf bifurcation curves and stable limit cycles.

The same occurs in the next bifurcation diagram for β_π, the adjustment speed of inflationary expectations in place of β_w, the adjustment speed of wages. The figure 3.1 in addition shows that a choice of the parameter β_p, the adjustment speed of prices, sufficiently small will make the six-dimensional dynamical system locally unstable. The two plots considered together suggest that flexible wages and inflationary expectations and very sluggish prices work against local asymptotic stability. We note that Tobin (1992,1993,1994) has recently stressed the role of price flexibility on output stability. However, he only considers inflationary expectations in their interaction with the conventional type of Phillips curve. Our analysis introduces additional destabilizing channels by the real wage Rose effect.

The last Hopf–bifurcation diagram is for the two adjustment speeds of the Metzlerian inventory mechanism, i.e., β_{y^e} and β_n, the speed of adjustment of sales expectations and of planned inventory adjustments towards desired inventory stocks. It shows that there here exists a band of stable steady states, limited by a region of unstable steady states for low values of β_{y^e} and β_n as well as for high values of these parameters (since the assumptions of the stability part of the proposition 3.1 are not yet fulfilled in the considered situation). Moreover, loss of stability via increased β_n is always 'subcritical', while loss of stability via a decreased β_n may be sub– or supercritical (as shown in the diagram). Again, sufficiently low or high adjustment speeds here work against local asymptotic stability, with respect to both β_{y^e} and β_n.

Hopf–bifurcations have generally been considered for two-dimensional and three-dimensional systems in the economic literature. Surely a six-dimensional system like the one above is much more demanding with respect to an analysis of the complete set of the Routh–Hurwitz stability conditions and at present out of reach for this system, apart from the statement of the above proposition 3.1 for adjustment speeds close to zero or infinity. Yet, even for two-dimensional systems, and even much more so for three-dimensional systems, it is generally a horrendous analytical task to investigate whether the Hopf–bifurcation is sub– or supercritical and an analytical proof of this is therefore generally missing in applications of the Hopf theorem in the economic literature (an exception to this rule is Lux (1993, 1995)). Numerical methods therefore have to be used in all such cases in order to decide on the important part of the Hopf–theorem, the existence of either *stable* limit cycles, describing persistent oscillations, or *unstable* ones (which are related to corridors of stability).

On the right–hand side of figure 3.1 we in addition show an example of a stable limit cycle, generated via a supercritical Hopf–bifurcation, via three projections into 2D representing the real (Goodwin/Rose), the monetary (Mundell/Tobin) and the Metzlerian subdynamics of the integrated 6D dynamics. Note that this stable limit cycle is generated by the intrinsic nonlinearities of our KMG growth model solely and not by nonlinearity assumptions on the behavioral or technical relationships of this model. The diagrams to the right in figure 3.1 show how the limit cycle, the simple closed curve surrounding the steady state (and the trajectories that depart from it) in the three projections of the considered 6D dynamics, is approached when the steady state of the model is disturbed via a small l–shock. We here show the (ω, l)–, (m, π)– and (y^e, ν)–projection of this limit cycle which in fact represent the real, the monetary and the inventory subdynamics of our 6D system.

Let us next consider changes in the adjustment speed β_w of wages (which was equal to 0.21 for the limit cycle shown in figures 3.1). The first thing we have to note here is that the only intrinsically nonlinear dynamics considered will soon become strongly explosive for further increases of this wage adjustment parameter which, as in the unbounded dynamics we exemplified in section 2.1, calls for additional (extrinsic) nonlinearities in order to regain viability. As before we therefore make use of a kinked money wage Phillips curve (which does not allow for falling money wages) in order to see whether this institutional nonlinearity also helps in a 6D case where the planar arguments used in section 2.1 no longer apply. This is indeed the case here and it leads us to viable or bounded dynamics even if wage adjustment speed is increased up to 26 per cent (a speed far beyond any empirically plausible value).

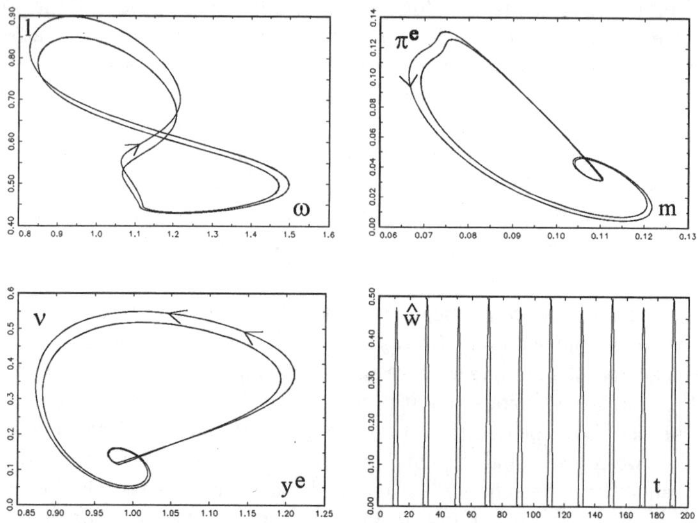

Figures 3.2:
Fast wage adjustment and period 2 limit cycles ($\beta_w = 5$).

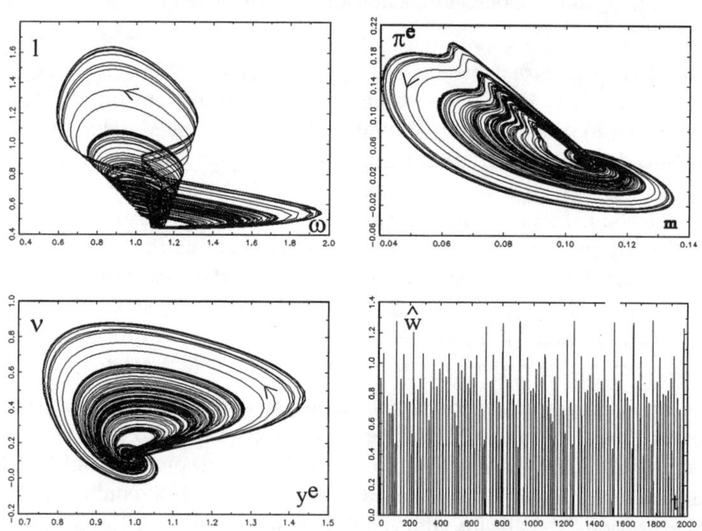

Figures 3.3:
Very fast wage adjustment and the emergence of complex dynamics ($\beta_w = 26$).

We here only show two different phase plots from a series of plots provided in Chiarella and Flaschel (1999b),[7] and also in Chiarella and Flaschel (1996b), to which the reader is referred for further details and the table of parameter values used in the considered situation (which without the kink in the wage PC would lead to immediate economic breakdown of the then only intrinsically nonlinear dynamics). We consider a situation where there is steady state inflation, due to the fact that the growth rate of the money supply exceeds the real rate of growth of the economy. This avoids the outcome in which the economy can get stuck in a stable depressed situation below the originally given interior steady state solution, since depression and downwardly rigid wages are then combined with growing real balances and thus an expansionary Keynes nominal interest rate effect. For low adjustment speeds of nominal wages one gets a stable and simple looking limit cycle, just as the one shown in the figures 3.1, but now obtained from a global nonlinearity, due to the purely explosive nature of the unrestricted original dynamics. Increasing the speed of adjustment of wages then leads at a certain point (and from the mathematical point of view) to a doubling of the period length of the cycle, as shown in the figure 3.2. This process repeats itself as the parameter β_w is further increased, leading to a cascade of period doublings (with period 4, 8, 16, 32, etc.) which we do not show here explicitly. It is known that such a sequence of period doublings will lead to complex dynamics eventually (here defined as convergence to an attractor which is not a point, a limit cycle or a quasi-periodic trajectory, see Parker and Chua (1989) for details). We thus get from this simple institutional nonlinearity not only an example for Keynes (1936) observation we quoted in section 2.1, but also the at first astonishing situation that not much is needed in higher dimensional macrodynamical systems in order to get complex attractors, conditional however on the situation that wage adjustment occurs with dramatic speed (which actually is not observed in real economies).

Note here that the figures 3.2 and 3.3 only show (projections of) the attractors of the underlying dynamical systems and not the transient behavior towards these attractors (as it was shown in figures 3.1). Note also that further simulations in Chiarella and Flaschel (1999b, Ch.6) have shown, in comparison to figure 3.1, that the 2D real, the monetary and the inventory subdynamical system, when appropriately isolated from each other, can exhibit quite different stability features. For example wage flexibility may be destabilizing in the full 6D dynamics, but is stabilizing in the 2D real dynamics, based on a normal Rose effect, implying that this Rose effect becomes reversed when the 2D dynamics is linked with the monetary and the Metzlerian dynamics. This is an interesting situation, since we cannot therefore in general claim that the insights of partial dynamical investigations will be preserved when integration with other important parts of the macroeconomy is performed. This observation, however, only concerns local stability analysis and thus precedes our above consideration of kinked PC's and the boundedness these kinks can add to locally cumulative forces.

In order to show that the above period doubling sequence indeed leads to complex dynamics one has to calculate Liapunov exponents in addition, as discussed in detail with respect to theoretical aspects and numerical computations in Parker and Chua (1989). Positive maximum Liapunov exponents imply complex dynamics, which is the case for the presently considered situation from approximately $\beta_w = 10.5$ onwards as figure 3.4 shows.

[7]Note that the cycle length, as characterized by successive periods of wage inflation is approximately 20 years, as shown by the figure 3.2 bottom-right.

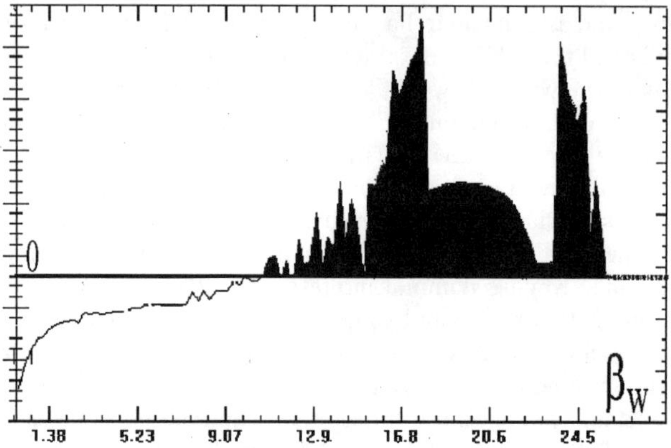

Figure 3.4:
The maximum Liapunov exponent for $\beta_w \in [0, 25]$, which is positive in the black area.

Finally, we consider the generalized situation where the three rates $\bar{V}, \gamma = n$, characterizing the steady rate of employment, the trend term in capital stock growth set equal to natural growth and natural growth itself, are considered as dynamic variables and are thus determined endogenously. Following Chiarella and Flaschel (1998) we here assume specifically that the NAIRU rate of employment is time varying. It follows the actual employment rate with some time delay, as does the natural rate of growth of the labor force with respect to the trend growth rate of the capital stock. This latter rate, like the NAIRU, is following actual capital stock growth with some time delay, which in sum gives three simple adjustment rules for these 'natural rates' of macroeconomic theory.[8]

[8]There is a further change in the model, see Chiarella and Flaschel (1999b), which concerns its quantity adjustment mechanism, which however is of secondary importance and does not disturb the qualitative conclusion drawn for this extension of the KMG model.

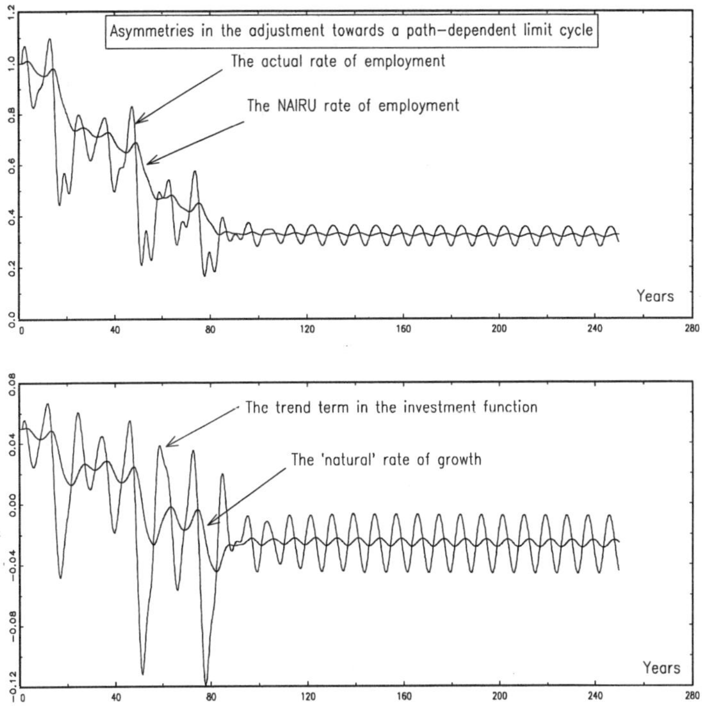

Figure 3.5: Endogenous 'natural' growth and employment: A depressed limit cycle in the case of high steady state inflation.

The new dynamic feature introduced by this lagged adjustments of 'natural' rates is called zero-root hysteresis in the literature, meaning that the dynamics has now at least one (here in general two) zero eigenvalues of its Jacobian at the steady state, here related to the fact that the steady state values of the NAIRU rate $\bar{V}$ and of natural growth n are no longer given magnitudes, but can in fact be any positive value. Dependent on historical conditions or on shocks that occur during the evolution of the dynamics, the system may therefore converge to different attractors, point attractors, limit cycles and more complicated ones. Let us attempt to describe what a kinked money wage Phillips curve combined with this type of zero root hysteresis may imply. Due to the kink, depressions tend to be longer and deeper than upswings, which means that on average the 'natural rates' of the economy tend to decline as there are more depression than boom situations at work. A first conclusion therefore could be that the economy will decline forever if such forces are at work and will thus be subject to breakdown in finite time (when for example the rate of employment has become sufficiently close to zero). Figure 3.5 shows that this need not be the case, since it shows that the economy in fact stops declining at some point in time and converges to a limit cycle thereafter. However, inspecting the numbers on the axes, shows that initial fluctuations produce significantly negative rates of growth and that the limit cycle occurs in a region where there are only negative rates of growth. Though interesting, the depicted situation is therefore surely of an exceptional type.

The parameter values of the situation shown in figure 3.5 are provided in Chiarella and Flaschel (1998), here however subject to the side condition that monetary growth is ten percent while real growth is only five percent in the interior steady state solution o the 6D dynamics. This means that monetary policy is very loose and explains to some extent why fluctuations are large and why there are persistent fluctuations present. A much more restrictive monetary policy which reduces the (constant) growth rate of the money supply by 3.4 percent instead leads to the result, shown in figure 3.6, which is quite surprising with respect to qualitative as well as quantitative features.

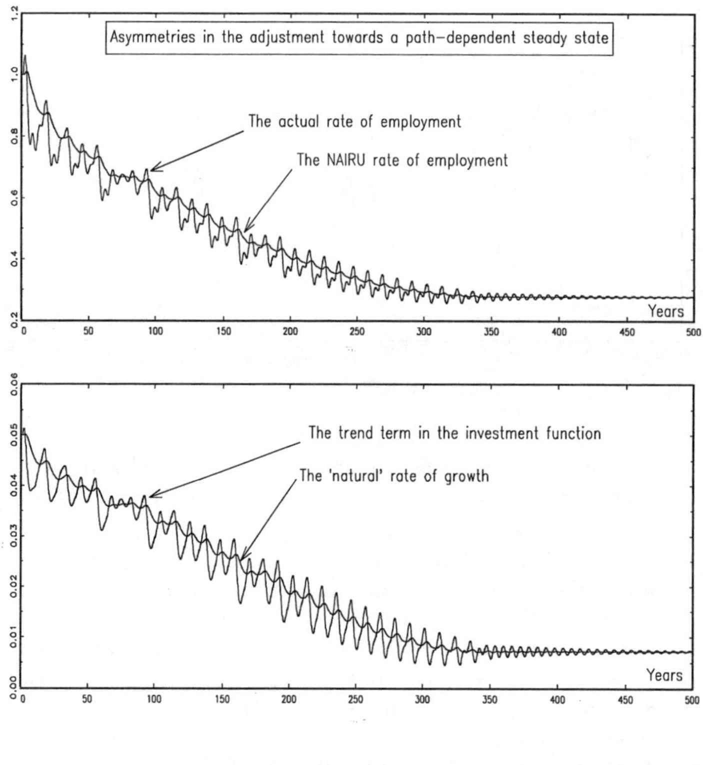

*Figure 3.6: Endogenous 'natural' growth and employment:
A depressed point attractor in the case of low steady state inflation.*

Here, too, we get a long, not unexpected even longer, period of asymmetric cyclical downturns which, however, as in the previous figure 3.15 come to a halt, now only after approximately 350 years, and now with fluctuations that die out when the floor in the movement of the rate $\bar{V}$ has been reached. We stress here that the long-run features of the dynamics are not yet close to empirically observed figures, but that it is nevertheless surprising to see how the employment situation (on an average monotonically) moves from 100 % to only 30 % and that the growth rates of capital and labor supply fall in a similar fashion from initially 5 % to steady 1 %. Figure 3.6 therefore drastically exemplifies how downturns that are longer than upturns, due to the institutional asymmetry in the money-wage Phillips-curve that is operative here in the downturns, can drag the rates of employment and the rates of growth down to levels that must be considered as highly problematic, if not catastrophic.

With these observations we conclude our discussion of integrated Keynesian dynamics in the case of closed economies.

3.3 Integrated macrodynamics in an open economy

Next we apply our modeling strategy to the case of open economies in order to survey briefly results we already have obtained elsewhere. We thus have to allow now for international trade and capital flows and also interest payments from international asset holdings. Due to the budget equations formulated for the three sectors of our economy, households (workers and asset holders), firms and the government, we have, also from the perspective of the small open economy, that net trade, net capital flows and net international interest payments sum to zero (all expressed in the domestic currency for example), even in the case of a sluggish adjustment of the exchange rate with respect to international interest rate differentials. Thus there is no need here for the central bank to intervene in the foreign exchange market, since supply of foreign currency will always be equal to demand for it. Of course, the central bank may nevertheless want to intervene in the case of undesirable exchange rate movements, in which case its reserve changes show up in the consolidated government budget constraint as well as in the balance of payments (which is again balanced through these additions).

With respect to trade flows we have now to distinguish between domestic and foreign commodities which are imperfect substitutes. In order to at first formulate the KMG model for small open economies as simply as possible we assume with respect to economic behavior in the rest of the world that it is restricted to steady rates of growth of prices and quantities and steady rates of interest, but that foreign consumption of domestic goods is nevertheless varying with the terms of trade $\eta = p/(ep^*)$, where e denotes the nominal exchange rate (the price of the foreign currency) and p^* the foreign price level. These special assumptions have to be removed later on by considering, for example, fully specified two-country models in the place of the partial situation given at present. We do not go into the details of the modeling of trade flows any further here, but simply state that it gives rise to net export and export equations, nx, x, per unit of domestic capital that both depend on η solely, with both net export nx and export x decreasing for increasing η. We observe that the export equation has to be added to the equation that so far described aggregate demand per unit of capital, y^d, while net imports (but only for consumption purposes) reduce domestic goods demand of domestic residents. Furthermore, the net export equation will enter the equation describing exchange rate dynamics as we shall see below. The reader is referred to Chiarella and Flaschel (1999c-e) for the details of this still preliminary treatment of the changes concerning the real side of the economy.

Concerning international capital flows, we assume that the interest rate parity condition does not hold in the ideal way it is usually formulated. Instead, there in general exist international interest rate differentials that drive capital flows in the world, which in this basic approach are not modeled explicitly. These in turn give rise to delayed nominal exchange rate changes that will – in our only intrinsically nonlinear setup – even tend to make prevailing differences in expected interest rates more pronounced. This is so, since high expected interest rate countries will attract capital inflows, their currency will appreciate and thus lead to still higher expected interest rates for foreigners when they revise their depreciation expectations correspondingly. There are thus, at least close to the steady state (where interest rates are equalized), cumulative forces at work which tend to increase expected interest rate differentials in the world, including gains from depreciation, if depreciation expectations are adaptively following observed currency depreciation. Of course, these cumulative processes cannot go on for ever which means that adjustment processes relating depreciation with expected depreciation must change further off the steady state when interest rate differentials pass certain threshold values. We will try to model such changes in exchange rate dynamics by extending the resulting (at first again only intrinsically nonlinear) dynamics by an extrinsic nonlinearity in the market for foreign exchange that will imply (as an example) how cumulative processes may be stopped and reversed, leading to persistent fluctuations in the place of the initially purely explosive behavior.

The rate of change of the exchange rate is therefore assumed to be (locally) of the same sign (but of different magnitude, depending on the degree of international capital mobility) as the expected interest rate differentials themselves (with expectations concerning de- or appreciation of the exchange rate). Note here however, that this assumption needs further discussion and improvement in future extensions of the model. The process by which domestic residents and the world economy accepts inferior rates of return, via domestic depreciation or appreciation, is not justified explicitly. However, since the KMG approach starts from the consideration of price-quantity adjustment processes in the real part of the economy, the scene is not yet ready for a full treatment of financial markets (which would require a full portfolio approach, as we will attempt to introduce it in future work) in order to allow for a systematic and stepwise extension of the KMG approach to growth and fluctuations.

This intermediate step to the modeling of international capital flows, based on exchange rate changes and expectations about them, leads us therefore to the following two new dynamic equations which increase the dimension of the KMG dynamics by 2 to 8D (where we of course then neglect the endogenous adjustments of 'natural' rates considered at the end of the preceding section).

$$\hat{e} = \beta_e(\beta(r_o^* + \epsilon - r) - nx(\eta)), \quad \eta = \frac{p}{ep^*}, nx'(\eta) < 0 \tag{3.8}$$

$$\dot{\epsilon} = \beta_\epsilon[\alpha_\epsilon(\hat{e} - \epsilon) + (1 - \alpha_\epsilon)(\hat{e}^+ - \epsilon)] \tag{3.9}$$

In these equations we denote by means of an 'asterisk' foreign country data. We assume from now on, for reasons of simplicity, that there is zero (steady) inflation in the world economy and that the steady state of the domestic economy is also inflation free (money supply and labor supply are growing at the same rate by assumption). We thus have a given foreign price level p^* and a constant nominal exchange rate e in the steady state of the domestic economy. This allows to make use of the nominal state variables e, p in the place of the ratios η, m when presenting the laws of motion of the economy in intensive form, which is sometimes convenient since these nominal dynamics are easier to interpret and to comment than the shown ratios.

Equation (3.8) gives the law of motion for the exchange rate e and assumes that its rate of growth depends on $\beta(r_o^* + \epsilon - r)$, representing the extent of international capital movements caused by the interest rate differential $r_o^* + \epsilon - r$, with r_o^* the given world rate of interest, ϵ the expected rate of depreciation and the parameter β as a measure of the degree of capital mobility (with $\beta = \infty$ representing the case of perfect capital mobility usually considered in the literature where $r_o^* + \epsilon = r$ holds true). We have added to this a term that measures the extent of foreign exchange market exchanges that are due to net exports nx, but abstract from interest payments and foreign exchange market operations in the formulation of exchange rate dynamics (3.8). The addition of the nx−term introduces a negative relationship between the growth rate of the exchange rate and its current level.

Equation (3.9) adds the law of motion for expected depreciation, $\epsilon = \hat{e}^e$. This law is formulated in the same way as the law for inflationary expectations and thus is also based on backward looking and forward looking components and justified in the same way as equation (3.5). With respect to the theory based expression $\hat{e}^+$ that guides the forward looking part of expectations formation we again assume that it is given in the simplest way possible by the steady rate of depreciation which has been assumed as zero above. It is again easy to provide less simplistic determinations of $\hat{e}^+$, for example by means of the PPP theorem, which however is not yet done in the following theoretical and numerical analysis of the 8D KMG dynamics of this section. We will even assume (to simplify presentations) that only backward looking expectations are present ($\alpha_\epsilon = 1$), which however is no real restriction as long as $\alpha_\epsilon > 0$ is assured.

The above extension of the 6D KMG dynamics for the closed economy is surely still a simple one, though of course mathematical complexity may increase considerably by the addition of two further laws of motion (not necessarily however with respect to local stability as we shall see below). We have the isolated interaction of depreciation and expected depreciation as long as the domestic rate of interest r and net exports nx are kept constant. Due to the implied changes in aggregate demand for the domestic good (which now depends on e via the terms of trade η) we get implied changes in the domestic rate r and in net exports nx which in turn influence the dynamics of the exchange rate e. These however are already all channels that relate the 6D dynamics of the real, the monetary and the Metzler part of the model with the Dornbusch (1976) type of exchange rate dynamics (based on somewhat sluggish adjustments in the exchange rate now).

In view of these 'simple' feedbacks between the KMG and the Dornbusch part of the considered dynamical system the following proposition does not come as unexpected:

Proposition 3.2

1. There is a unique (interior) steady–state solution or point of rest of the dynamics (3.1)–(3.9) fulfilling $\omega_0, l_0, p_0, e_o \neq 0$, *see Chiarella and Flaschel (1999e) for the detailed list of these steady state values.*

2. Assume that the corresponding interior steady state of the subdynamics (3.1)–(3.7) for the closed economy is locally asymptotically stable for e, ϵ *frozen at their steady state values* e_o, ϵ_o*, see the preceding section in this regard. Then: The interior steady state of the full 8D dynamics is locally asymptotically stable for all adjustment speeds* β_e, β_ϵ *that are sufficiently small.*

3. The determinant of the Jacobian of the dynamics (3.1) – (3.9) at the steady state is always positive.

4. By contrast, if β_e *(or* β*) and* β_ϵ *are sufficiently large, then the interior steady state equilibrium of (3.1) – (3.9) is locally repelling. The system therefore generally undergoes Hopf bifurcations at intermediate value of these adjustment parameters for the foreign sector, of the same type as considered in the preceding proposition 3.1.*

For a proof of this proposition, which is based on what is already known for the closed economy case, the reader is referred to Chiarella and Flaschel (1999c,d,e). We assume that the parameters of the model are chosen such that the steady state values for ω, l, m, ρ, r, e are all positive and thus meaningful. It is obvious that the statements on Hopf bifurcations made for the closed economy case all apply to the present situation as well and will thus not be repeated here. Such Hopf -bifurcations are a local phenomenon, in particular in the present case of only intrinsic nonlinearities, also in the Dornbusch part of the dynamics. Increasing the parameters β_e (or β) and β_ϵ sufficiently will thus give rise to strong explosiveness solely and thus to a situation that cannot at all considered as viable or economically sound. Again we need to refer to at least one extrinsic nonlinearity in order to get the result that the Dornbusch subdynamics and their interaction with the KMG structure allows for economic viability or boundedness in a meaningful range of the 8D state space.

Of course, we do not have at our disposal here an institutional nonlinearity as represented in stylized form by the kinked PC considered before (that helped there to tame the internal destabilizing Mundell effect of inflationary expectations). A simple, also very stylized situation can however be sketched here to show, or indicate, economic boundedness for the Dornbusch type external nominal instability just considered (which is qualitatively of the same type as the destabilizing Mundell feedback mechanism), by means of analytical methods for the isolated 2D dynamics (3.8)–(3.9) and by numerical simulations for the full 8D dynamics (3.1)–(3.9).

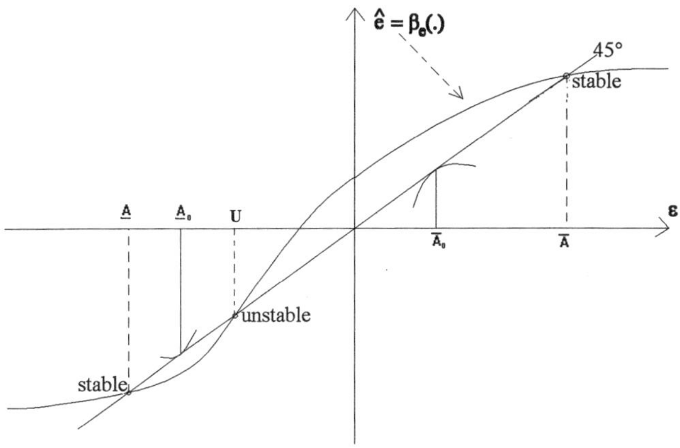

Figure 3.7:
Exchange rate dynamics and shifting myopic perfect foresight equilibria.

In order to demonstrate this briefly, consider the nonlinear relationship between actual and expected depreciation (or appreciation) shown in figure 3.7. This curve generalizes the situation given by equation (3.8) in that it assumes that the parameter value β, characterizing the extent of capital flows, is now changing with the size of the expected rate of return differential $r_o^* + \epsilon - r$ ($\beta(0) = 0$ still). We consider in figure 3.7 a situation where net exports are for the time being given, but where – due to the partial nature of the present consideration – the rate r is assumed to equal the rate r_o^*, which implies that only exchange rate expectations drive the rate of return differential on internationally traded bonds. We thus assume for the function $\beta(\epsilon)$ that its slope is larger than one at the steady state value $\epsilon = 0$ ($nx = 0$), and thus also a certain neighborhood of it, but becomes smaller than one if ϵ becomes sufficiently large in absolute terms.

Considering first point U in figure 3.7, we there have a perfect foresight equilibrium, where for example adaptively formed expectations are confirmed at a negative value of expected depreciation $\epsilon = U$, which however is unstable with respect to such adaptive (and other backward looking) expectations schemes. Adaptive expectation schemes, for example, will therefore imply, if β_ϵ is large, that expectations of appreciation decline rapidly to the left of U and increase rapidly to its right until the stable perfect foresight equilibria shown to the left and right of U are reached, respectively. Disregarding still changes in nx indeed implies that (3.9) is an autonomous differential equation in the single variable ϵ that produces exactly the stability results just stated.

Yet, $\hat{e}$ is negative in the left stable equilibrium and positive in the right one. This implies, since net exports nx per unit of capital are assumed to depend positively on the nominal exchange rate e, that net exports nx will be falling at the left and rising in the right hand stable equilibrium.The nonlinear curve shown in figure 3.7 therefore shifts upwards when the lower stable perfect foresight equilibrium prevails and downwards in the opposite case. The prevailing perfect foresight equilibrium and the unstable one thus move closer to each other during this adjustment process until a situation is reached where the carrier of this adjustment, the lower or the upper stable equilibrium disappears (at $\underline{A}_o, \overline{A}_o$, respectively) and the single remaining upper or lower stable equilibrium becomes the global attractor of the isolated actual and expected depreciation or appreciation dynamics. This situation repeats itself periodically and thus leads us again to stable limit cycle behavior in the case of a finite speed of adjustment of expected depreciation and to relaxation oscillations, characterized by immediate jumps to the alternative stable equilibrium if the other one disappears, if speeds of adjustment are infinite, see Chiarella and Flaschel (1999e) for proofs in the 2D $e, \dot{\epsilon}$ phase plane that corresponds to these verbal statements and Chiarella (1990b, 1992a) for the initial contribution of this type (also for the case of 3 state variables).[9]

Of course, the $\beta(\epsilon)$−curve need not be as regular and stable as it was assumed above. Furthermore the 2D situation just described is embedded into the whole 8D structure, since the nominal interest rate r and the price level p will move during these dynamic interactions of actual and expected depreciation. Important for the economic story to be told only is that economic agents are cautious for large interest rate differentials, thereby implementing a low value of β which makes the external nominal dynamics converge to a perfect foresight situation. In this situation however, the nominal exchange rate keeps falling or rising, though with less speed than in the uncautious case and also with a decelerating speed until a point is reached where the cautious behavior is indeed confirmed by a rapid change to a situation that is just the opposite of the one that so far prevailed. Cautious capital movements in the presence of large interest rate differentials (which expect significant changes in these differentials due to trend changes in exchange rates) therefore create situations in which such scenarios become more and more likely and sooner or later also a reality.

In the following numerical simulations of the 8D dynamics (in fact then slightly extended into 9D dynamics due to the addition of a sluggishly adjusting trade balance in view of the large and rapid swings that occur in the terms of trade) we will stick to the simple functional form shown in figure 3.7, but of course should keep in mind that this relationship is much more refined with respect to shifts and structural breaks than can be considered at present. Here we only show that extrinsic nonlinearities as shown in figure 3.7 can make an originally explosive dynamics an economically bounded one, even in its full interaction with the KMG part of the model, and that also further interesting features may result from such a nonlinearity, in particular when coupled with the kinked PC as discussed before.

The following simulation studies are taken from Chiarella and Flaschel (1999d) to which the reader is referred for further details and in particular the parameter values underlying the shown figures. Let us here first consider the nonlinearity in capital flows shown in figure 3.7 as the only extrinsic nonlinearity, but operating of course in the full open economy KMG dynamics. Due to the parameter choices for the exchange rate subdynamics, the integrated dynamics would rapidly explode without this nonlinearity, yet in its presence behaves instead in the way shown in figures 3.8, 3.9.

[9]Flaschel and Sethi (1999), based on Chiarella (1986, 1990), treat relaxation oscillations in the framework of the Cagan model of inflationary mechanisms, chosen by Chiarella (1986, 1990) initially to explain the importance of relaxation oscillations in economics, see also our treatment of Kaldor's (1940) trade cycle mechanism and Metzler's inventory mechanism in section 2.2. Chiarella (1991,1992b) also discusses rational expectation and perfect foresight dynamics, respectively, in continuous time stochastic and discrete time deterministic monetary models.

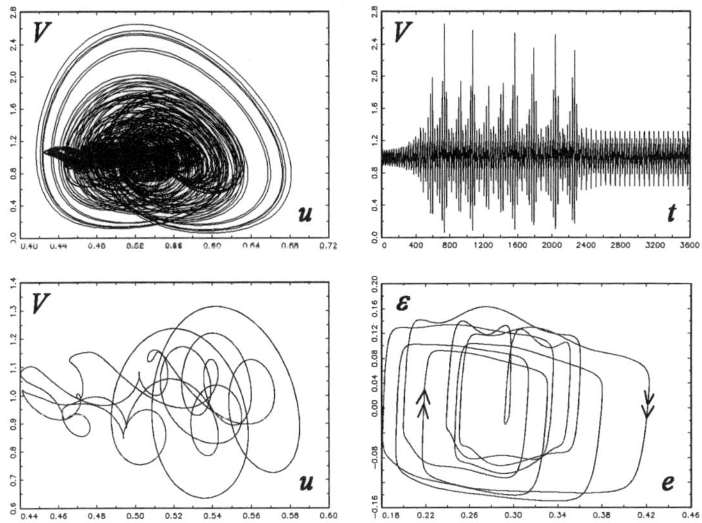

Figure 3.8: The 8D dynamics with perfect foresight relaxation oscillations and sluggishly adjusting international trade, transient and limit behavior ($u = \omega l_y^e$).

In figure 3.8 we see on the left hand side that the fundamental variables of the 2D PC-AC analysis of section 2.3 do not display the simple closed orbit structure of that growth cycle model. The phase plot top left shows however the transient behavior in the wage share / employment rate phase space which eventually settles down to the high order limit cycle (a 2D projection of the 9D dynamics) shown bottom left. Yet, there too, a simple inspection of the cycle does not reveal much since its shape is heavily dependent on the oscillations originating from the exchange rate dynamics, even if transferred to the real part of the economy via sluggishly adjusting trade with some time delay. The phase plot bottom right reveals (to some extent) what happens if the adjustment parameters of the c, ϵ subdynamics are chosen sufficiently high. There then occurs nearly instantaneous adjustment in the vertical direction followed by relatively slow upward or downward movements of the exchange rate and expected depreciation once a new near to perfect foresight situation is reestablished. The situation shown is thus close to a 2D relaxation oscillation though everything happens in the fully integrated system. The time series top right finally shows the evolution of the rate of employment, for a horizon of 3600 years! We can see that the movement in V is extreme and irregular in the first 2400 years, but that it then 'suddenly' settles down at the limit cycle indicated in the bottom figures 3.8. We thus get the result that transient behavior can be extremely long even in a mostly intrinsically nonlinear system. This raises of course the question whether the study of the attractors of such dynamics is of any use from the economic point of view and whether we should not rather focus our attention on a study of transient behavior in response to various shocks.

Let us next consider a situation where only the kink in the money wage PC is present, but where there is no extrinsic nonlinearity in the exchange rate dynamics (and where adjustment speeds in this sector have been reduced). However with respect to the kink we do not assume any more that wages are completely rigid downwards, but can fall instead, here at most at a minimum rate of −3 percent, as the parameter f in the subtitle to figure 3.9 indicates.

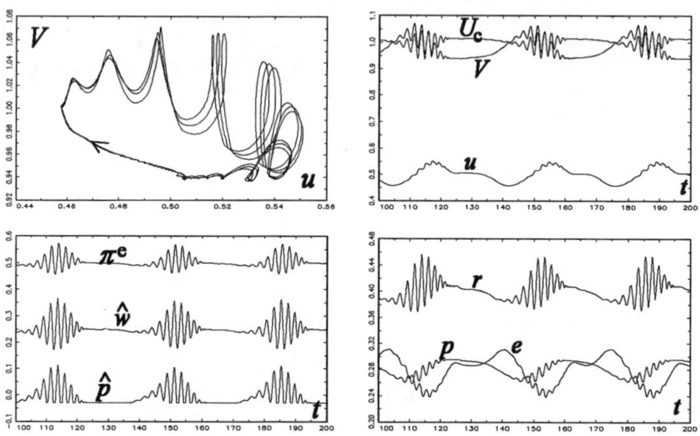

Figure 3.9:
The 8D dynamics with a kinked Phillips curve for $t \in [100, 200]$ ($f = -0.03$).

In figure 3.9 top left we can now recognize Goodwin (1967) type large fluctuations[10] (with a phase length of approximately 30 years) which however are subject to shorter fluctuating growth (with at first explosive behavior) in the upper part where there is NAIRU employment on an average. Due to the kink in the money wage PC the shape of the shorter cycle becomes however more and more asymmetric with recessions becoming longer and deeper and upswings shorter and weaker. This process continues until the economy gets stuck, for some time, in a nearly stationary depressed situation with a very high wage share u and a high unemployment rate $1 - V$. Yet, in this situation wages are falling at 3 percent while prices, due to normal conditions in the rate of capacity utilization of firms, are basically stationary with an insufficient growth rate of the capital stock and thus the employment rate, see the time series bottom left and top right. The real wage and the wage share are therefore slowly decreasing. Due to the fact that profitability considerations here dominate investment behavior, the growth rate of the capital stock thus is increasing again and with it the rate of employment until the situation of NAIRU-employment is reestablished, where the kink has become inoperative again and where therefore the short-term fluctuations come back into being and the process just described starts to repeat itself.

[10]Note however that the Goodwin approach is here redefined in the sense of Rose (1967), since the cycle is now unique and generated by local explosiveness coupled with global boundedness, a change in perspective which we believe to be in line with what Goodwin thought on this subject, when the simple cross-dual dynamics of his original growth cycle model are extended by Keynesian goods market features and more.

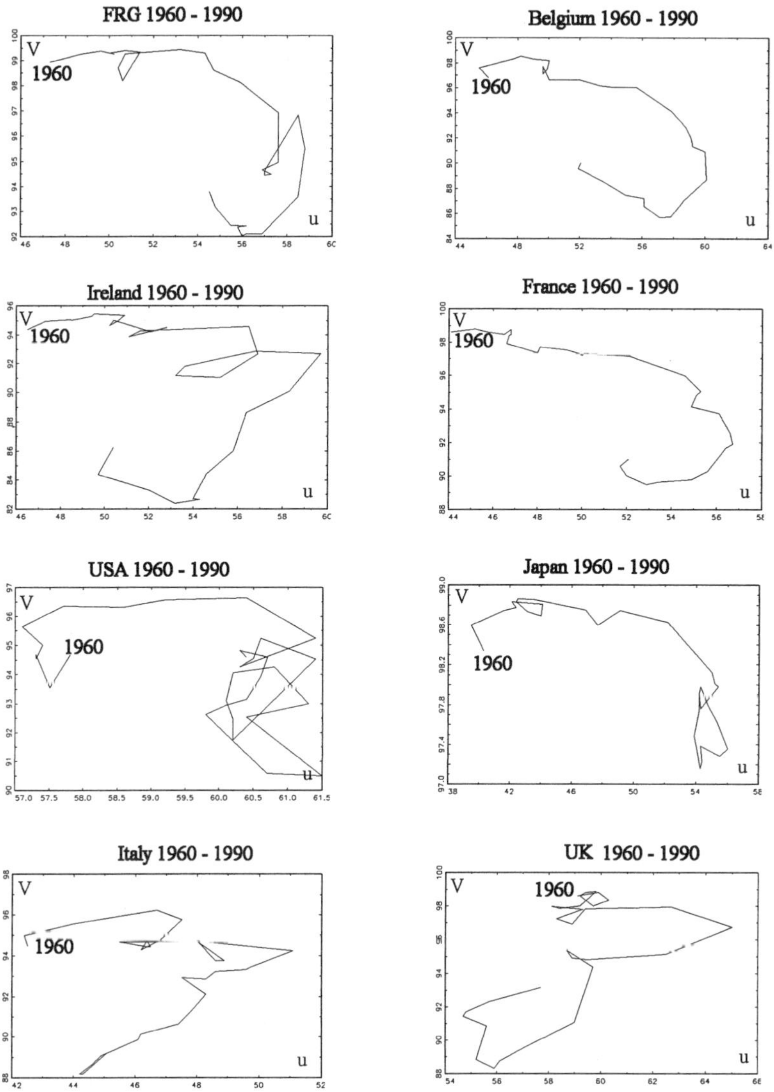

Figure 3.10: Growth cycles in 8 OECD countries?: Clockwise orientation! Closed orbits? Long Phase! Automatic recovery?
Horizontal axis: Wage share u; Vertical axis: Employment rate V.[11]

[11]See Flaschel and Groh (1995) for the details underlying these factual phase plots of the basic growth cycle variables and Desai (1984), Solow (1990) for related observations.

One may raise the question whether such a long swing in the wage share u and the employment rate V has anything to due with actually observed swings in these two magnitudes. Let us therefore briefly look at some data, shown in figure 3.10, here with particular stress on the case of Germany and Belgium:

We can see in the two phase plots for Germany and Belgium for the years 1960 to 1990 that there is indeed a clockwise movement in these diagrams and that the movement does at best represent three quarters of a full cycle meaning that the phase length of empirically observed cyclical patterns of this type (if they exist) might even be longer than the one of the simulated economy (see figure 3.9, where only crude estimates of parameter sizes have been performed). In the German economy the situation shown does not seem to have improved very much since 1990, but seems to have produced depressed cycles of the type shown in figure 3.9 (whose shorter fluctuations around normal employment are not present in the figures 3.10). In the USA by contrast, such depressed cycles already occurred in the seventies and eighties and appear to have been overcome in the mean time. However, these are only very basic observations meant to induce careful empirical investigations, since the existence of such a PC-AC growth cycle mechanism would be of enormous importance for the future development of the theory we are pursuing here.

Let us return to figure 3.9 again, which in fact exemplifies further important regularities, some in line and some not in line with empirical observations. First, it is visible that the rate of capacity utilization fluctuates heavily but moves in line with the rate of employment in periods of high average employment, confirming Okun's law in the form it was formulated in Okun (1970) In periods of depression however, both rates move in opposite directions, the rate of capacity utilization slowly declining due to declining aggregate demand and the rate of employment increasing due to increasing profitability and thus increasing investment behavior which however does not prevent the decline in aggregate demand due to falling real wages (equivalent here to a falling wage share). Nominal interest rates and the price level are obviously positively correlated, see the figure 3.9 bottom right, the so-called Gibson paradox (see Sargent (1973)), which however is not so paradoxical on the basis of the simple LM theory in this integrated dynamics. Finally, we have opposite movements in price levels (interest rates) and nominal exchange rates which shows exchange rate overshooting, since e is still rising when interest has already fallen below the world rate of interest.

Figures 3.11 show the integration of the occurrence of a kinked PC with relaxation oscillations in the market for foreign exchange. The relaxation oscillations in expected depreciation are clearly visible in the time series representation bottom right, which also shows their relationship to wage and price level fluctuations (where the latter are now much stronger than the former due to increased price flexibility). The time series bottom left in this regard show in more detail that wages are falling in depressions with a constant rate of one percent and price at a much larger rate now, leading to adverse real wage adjustments and thus weak recoveries as the phase plot top left shows. Since there is no comparable kink in the price PC, the rate of capacity utilization of firms is fluctuating around its normal level (here assumed to be one for simplicity). In the same way, through simple renormalization we have also assumed the NAIRU rate of employment to be equal to one, yet see top left as well as top right that the actual rate of employment is fluctuating in a corridor completely below the NAIRU rate $\bar{V} = 1$. From a 2D perspective this appears as impossible since a limit cycle then always encloses the steady state. This however is not necessarily true in higher dimensions as figure 3.11 exemplifies. We thus get the result that the long-run behavior of the economy has nothing to do with the NAIRU rate of employment or the so-called 'natural rate'. It can therefore be completely misleading to claim, as many economists do, that the normal rate of employment must be the long-run outcome of market economies if they are left to themselves. We stress again that this result is obtained since price flexibility appears to make upswings so weak that they cannot reach the state of normal employment again.

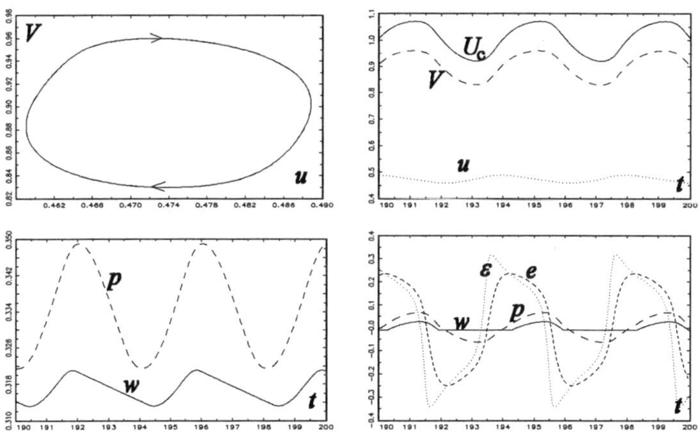

Figure 3.11:
A persistent depressed employment cycle $(f = -.01)$.[12]

In the figure 3.12 we show again, but now from a different perspective, the consequences of increased upward nominal wage flexibility, while preserving the assumption that wages cannot fall faster than by one percent a year. This figure 3.12 shows a bifurcation diagram for this parameter change where wage adjustment speeds are increased from 0.5 to 3.5 and where the resulting local maxima and minima of the real wage ω are plotted against this change of the parameter β_w along the attractor of the dynamics. It is obvious that the dynamics along the attractor become more and more complex, with increasing amplitude of the cycle, however, passing through windows of simple limit cycle behavior from time to time. Again it is demonstrated that the kink in the money wage PC adds considerable stability to the model even for fairly fast adjustment speed of money wages.

[12]Now with a phase length of 5 years solely.

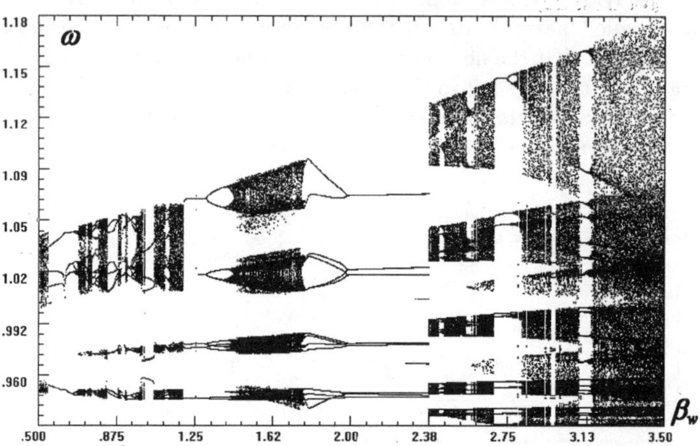

Figure 3.12: A bifurcation diagram for increasing wage flexibility in the presence of a kinked Phillips curve.[13]

This closes our numerical investigation of the open KMG dynamics with one or two extrinsic nonlinearities. In Chiarella and Flaschel (1999e) we formulate these dynamics also for the simpler 6D case of Keynes-Wicksell monetary growth models, which are close to supply side AS-AD growth dynamics. We then extend these simplified dynamics to the two country case (10D) and from there to two interacting economies of the KMG type (14D). As is shown in Chiarella and Flaschel (1999e) the dynamics then become still more complicated, since the results shown in this section are then relevant for two economies at possibly very different states of their dynamics, then coupled with each other through trade flows as well as capital flows. Further research is underway to determine the results we expect to hold for sluggish or for fast adjustments of prices. quantities and expectations.

3.4 Microfoundations and macromechanisms

It is time now to take stock and to consider what we have achieved by starting from textbook presentations of IS-LM-PC analysis, of Metzlerian quantity adjustment, and AC-PC growth cycle modeling, and by developing these partial pictures of cyclical growth and medium run aspects of IS-LM price-quantity dynamics further, finally synthesizing them into a coherent whole, the KMG model of fluctuating growth (and its open economy counterpart). This latter model type, see appendix 2 for its full presentation (including all

[13]This characterizes in a different way the occurrence of period doubling sequences to complex dynamics, see Chiarella and Flaschel (1999d) for details. Note that we need only mild nonlinearities here, due to the high dimensionality of the considered dynamics, in order to obtain complex attractors for truly economic systems in the place of the many somewhat artificial models used to obtain 'chaos' in 1D or 2D dimensional discrete time dynamics.

budget constraints) on the extensive form level, represents an economy with the range of markets and sectors as displayed in table 3.1. This economic structure shown in this table is basically of the same type as the one that was used by Sargent (1987, Ch. 1 – 5) for a systematic presentation of static and dynamic macroeconomics of traditional type.

	Labor market	Goods market	Money market	Bonds market	Equities market
Households	L	C	$M^d, \dot{M}^d$	$B^d, \dot{B}^d$	$E^d, \dot{E}^d$
Firms	L^d	$Y, I + \delta K$	–	–	$E, \dot{E}$
Government	–	G	$M, \dot{M}$	$B, \dot{B}$	–

Table 3.1: A basic market and sector framework for macroeconomics.

In table 3.1 we use the index d to denote 'quantities demanded' and no index in the case of 'quantities supplied'. Furthermore, since we use continuous-time models throughout we have to distinguish between flow and stock demand and supply since we here follow the macroeconomic tradition which distinguishes between stock and flow constraints in such a setup, see Turnovsky (1977) and Sargent (1987) for example. This said, the symbols in table 3.1 should be clear as to their economic meaning. As in Sargent (1987) firms use solely equities to finance their investment expenditures and to fulfill their budget restriction, while government can use bonds and money in this regard. Since we do not consider wealth effects in consumption and money demand, see also Sargent (1987, Ch. V), we do not have to treat equity and bond accumulation explicitly, as there is no feedback from them on goods, labor and the money market. Of course, this has to be regarded as preliminary, and must be replaced by a full treatment of financial markets later on.

Our modeling framework is therefore chosen, initially, as close as possible to the one that is employed in advanced textbook presentations of traditional macrodynamics, see also Turnovsky (1977, 1995). However it employs of course, due to its inclusion of PC-AC analysis, heterogeneous agents in the household sector, pure workers and pure asset holders at this stage of the investigation. In some respects the KMG model of the preceding sections may also be characterized as simply providing further dynamic extensions to the analysis that forms the core of Sargent's (1987) investigation of Keynesian dynamics in part I of his book,[14] by adding sluggish price adjustment and related to that unintended fluctuations in capital stock utilization U_c, by replacing goods market equilibrium through a delayed Metzlerian treatment of quantity adjustment processes on this market, by allowing for effects of income distribution on aggregate consumption in addition to their effect on aggregate investment, by making investment dependent on the new variable U_c in addition to Tobin's q as in Sargent (1987), and by allowing for heterogeneous backward and forward looking expectations in the place of only adaptive or only perfect foresight ones.

[14] Also in the case of neoclassical smooth factor substitution, as is shown in Chiarella and Flaschel (1999b).

The working KMG model is therefore nothing but a synthesis of basic ideas associated with Keynesian medium and long run dynamics. Such dynamics must at least exhibit gradually adjusting prices, wages and also quantities and based on that, disequilibrium rates of employment of both labor and capital in order to provide a true starting point for the Keynesian analysis of under- or over-utilized resources, and not to be restricted to labor market phenomena solely. This observation was also made recently by Barro (1994). Yet, the literature on Keynesian dynamics has concentrated on AS-AD growth models as in Sargent (1987), if economic growth was treated at all, and thus has generally made use of a hybrid model type where capital was always fully employed and were there is only disequilibrium on the labor market, see also Barro's (1994) critique of AS-AD analysis in this regard.

Our model is based on an IS-LM approach. The survey of Orphanides and Solow (1990) on models of monetary growth for example does not even mention IS-LM growth. This omission may be due to the fact that it appeared to be too complex in particular with respect to the minimum of six laws of motion that then are involved for a complete presentation of such price-quantity dynamics (4D in the case when IS equilibrium is assumed). A further reason may be due to the fact that the marginal productivity rule was generally used as a short-run theory, in the place of its correct position as a medium run approach to price dynamics (see Powell and Murphy (1997) and Chiarella and Flaschel (1999b)) thus preventing a discussion of short-run price and quantity adjustment processes around or towards this equilibrium condition where prices equal marginal wage costs. In AS-AD growth, firms appear to be price and quantity takers which is a mixture of Keynesian and Walrasian elements that cannot be regarded as being consistent and must be replaced by some type of price and quantity model of disequilibrium and growth.

In Chiarella and Flaschel (1999b) this argument is justified in detail. Starting from the Tobin model of neoclassical monetary growth where the theory of inflation is based on money market (dis)equilibrium, they move towards an integrated type of Keynes-Wicksell model by distinguishing between investment and savings behavior and by relating price inflation to IS-disequilibrium (in the place of money market disequilibrium) as was typical for the full capacity growth models of Keynes-Wicksell type of the sixties and seventies, see Orphanides and Solow (1990), Flaschel (1992, 1994a, 1999c,d), Flaschel, Franke and Semmler (1997) as well as Chiarella and Flaschel (1996a) for further details on this type of approach.

Yet, IS-disequilibrium (on the background of full capacity growth) is not a plausible measure of the true extent of actual goods market disequilibria, since firms are generally quite capable of adjusting their output to the current state of aggregate demand, while adjustments in their capital stock usually occupies a much longer time span. We therefore need to go beyond the Keynes-Wicksell approach to formulate a model of IS-LM growth where goods market disequilibrium appears in the form of an unintended capital stock utilization, coupled with a pricing behavior as considered before (with both demand and cost pressure components).

However, using IS equilibrium, i.e., an infinite speed of adjustment of output towards aggregate demand, gives rise to certain problematic implications of this model type, see Chiarella and Flaschel (1999b, Ch.4), which seem to be due to the fact that adjustment speeds of prices and quantities are treated in a radically different way. Therefore, at least the dynamic multiplier should be added to the goods market adjustment processes, implying the need to consider inventory changes, which finally leads us back to the modeling of the Metzlerian inventory adjustment process. Hereby we finally arrive at the working Keynes-Metzler model of Chiarella and Flaschel (1999b, Ch.6).

By such a hierarchical structured sequence of integrated disequilibrium models of monetary growth we therefore can develop a model type which allows for sluggish wage, price and quantity adjustments (including expectations) with fully specified sectors and markets as they are shown in table 3.1. We view the result of this effort as providing macrofoundations to non-market clearing macroeconomics, in the sense that a method is now available that allows us to go from first rough models of fully specified disequilibrium growth to more and more refined structural presentations of such treatments of monetary growth, by systematically removing the (most) problematic structures of such approaches, replacing them by more and more relevant ones from the theoretical as well as from the applied point of view.

Adding investment and removing Says' Law, introducing problems of capital stock utilization (also for neoclassical production functions), introducing inventory adjustment processes and more were the steps taken in Chiarella and Flaschel (1999b). In part II we add regime switching[15] when inventories are exhausted and the treatment of market imperfections as alternative to the Phillips curves we have considered above. Chiarella and Flaschel (1999e) integrates open economy issues, and work in progress improves the description of the output and investment decision of firms and the treatment of financial markets by replacing in particular delayed interest rate parity adjustment processes through a full description of portfolio choices in the presence of interest rate differentials along the lines set out in Franke and Semmler (1999).

Macrofoundations therefore attempt to provide the global perspective of how models of disequilibrium and growth can be formulated by starting from simple and well known, but nevertheless fully integrated pictures of growth dynamics. These are then developed into model types that become more and more coherent with respect to the building blocks needed for such complete, descriptively oriented disequilibrium and growth models; in particular with respect to fully specified budget restrictions on the macrolevel; with respect to the relevance of their steady state reference solutions as long-run restrictions of applied macroeconometric economic model building; and with respect to the fundamental feedback chains that are believed to interact on the macrolevel.

In this task, which will rapidly increase the dimension of the dynamics to be considered, descriptively oriented macroeconomics can proceed much faster than the completely microfounded one. This is due to the fact that models with intertemporal optimizing behavior are difficult to solve. It is also very difficult to treat aggregation in as detailed a way as would be necessary for an all embracing microfounded type of analysis. Those models would need to pay attention to heterogeneous agents, heterogeneous expectations, disequilibrium adjustment processes, monetary growth phenomena and more. Indeed the technical difficulty in handling all of these features (even numerically) provides a hard constraint on the degree of generality that can be handled by a micro-oriented approach.

As is obvious from this brief comparison of macrofounded and microfounded approaches, macrofoundations concentrate on providing an overall perspective that may or may not

[15]See also Flaschel (1999a,b) with respect to the treatment of regime switches in dynamic models of Keynesian or neoclassical type.

be microfounded, concentrate on describing and analyzing economic interdependence and the most important feedback structures that arise from it and compare dynamic features as macrodynamics becomes more and advanced in their structures. Microfoundations, by contrast, are important to control analytically what has been specified descriptively and to improve thereby the modules that make up the integrated macrodynamics. Microfoundation is important and complementary to macrofoundation, for example, the microfoundation of consumption and investment behavior, money holding and pricing processes. Yet one also needs macro perspectives (explicitly or implicitly) in order to have an idea of what is to be micro-founded, unless macroeconomics is considered just a special case of Walrasian general equilibrium theory. Indeed, a macro perspective is particularly needed if one wants to explore the effects of feedback mechanisms in models of monetary growth with disequilibrium in the real markets.

We are now ready to outline the main interacting economic feedback chains and implied economic interdependence that are present in our proposed modeling approach. Each chain in the following list is still considered in isolation (independent of the other adjustment processes) and thus shows their working with all other variable kept fixed. Essential macro economic feedback mechanisms, to name only the most basic ones which are all involved in the KMG growth model for open economies of section 3.2, are as follows.

1. The Rose Real Wage Adjustment Mechanism (4 Different Outcomes):

Real Wage $\uparrow$ $\Rightarrow$ Labor and Capital Utilization $\uparrow, \downarrow$, depending on marginal propensities to consume and to invest, $\Rightarrow$ Real Wage Growth $\uparrow, \downarrow$, depending on wage and price adjustment speeds

Real wage increases can increase or decrease economic activities (depending on their relative impact on consumption and investment behavior), which in turn determines their normal or adverse adjustment, depending on wage and price level adjustment speeds.

2. The Keynes Effect of Stabilizing Nominal Wage and Price Adjustments:

Price Level $\uparrow$ $\Rightarrow$ Nominal Interest Rate $\uparrow$ $\Rightarrow$ Labor and Capital Utilization Rates $\downarrow$ $\Rightarrow$ Inflation Rate $\downarrow$

The Keynes effect is the best known one (at least from the static point of view) and it is generally used in isolation (but also in combination with the also stabilizing Pigou effect) if scenarios of a stable adjustment towards the full employment position is aimed for.

3. The Internal Mundell Effect of Destabilizing Inflationary Expectations:

Expected Inflation $\uparrow \Rightarrow$ Real Interest Rate $\downarrow \Rightarrow$ Labor and Capital Utilization Rates $\uparrow \Rightarrow$ Inflation $\uparrow \Rightarrow$ Expected Inflation $\uparrow$

In general terms the Mundell effect is based on the fact that increases in expected inflation widen the gap between the real rate of profit and the real rate of interest and thus lead (via investment in this case) to increased economic activity and thus to a further stimulus to inflation and in this way also to increased expected inflation, giving rise to a process of cumulative instability (at least close to the steady state).

4. The Metzler Sales / Inventory Adjustment Process:

Expected Sales $\uparrow \Rightarrow$ Output $\uparrow \Rightarrow$ Goods Demand $\uparrow \Rightarrow$ Expected Sales $\uparrow$, for high inventory and sales expectations adjustment speeds

We stress with respect to the Metzlerian inventory adjustment mechanism that it will give rise to local instability when the inventory adjustment speed or the accelerator component of this mechanism is chosen sufficiently high (and coupled with a sufficiently fast adjustment of sales expectations).

5. The External Dornbusch Feedback Structure of Destabilizing Expectations of Depreciation:

Expected Depreciation $\uparrow \Rightarrow$ Exchange Rate Growth $\uparrow \Rightarrow$ Expected Depreciation $\uparrow$, depending on the degree of capital mobility and exchange rate expectations adjustment speed

This feedback structure is similar to the preceding one, but now refers to financial markets in the place of real markets. Increases in expected depreciation increase the gap between returns on foreign and domestic financial assets, thereby inducing further capital outflow, which leads to further depreciation and then to further increases in expected depreciation, also giving rise to a process of cumulative instability at least close to the steady state.

These feedback chains are all present in our macro models[16] of the preceding sections and they of course all interact in our fully integrated macrodynamics.[17]

More macroeconomic feedback mechanisms will be present and discussed in detail in the subsequent parts of the book, in particular in part III, where destabilizing Fisher debt effects reappear and also stabilizing wealth or Pigou effects in consumption behavior. Figure 3.13 summarizes the local stability properties of all these feedback chains, and also further ones, namely the destabilizing interaction of equity and long-term bond price dynamics and related capital gains, which can be treated similarly to the Dornbusch cumulative exchange

[16] The Dornbusch mechanism of course only in the open economy.

[17] See an example of their numerical analysis by means of eigenvalue diagrams in the next section.

rate dynamics,[18] and as stated the real wealth effects,[19] and the Fisher (1933) debt effects as treated previously in section 2.3.[20]

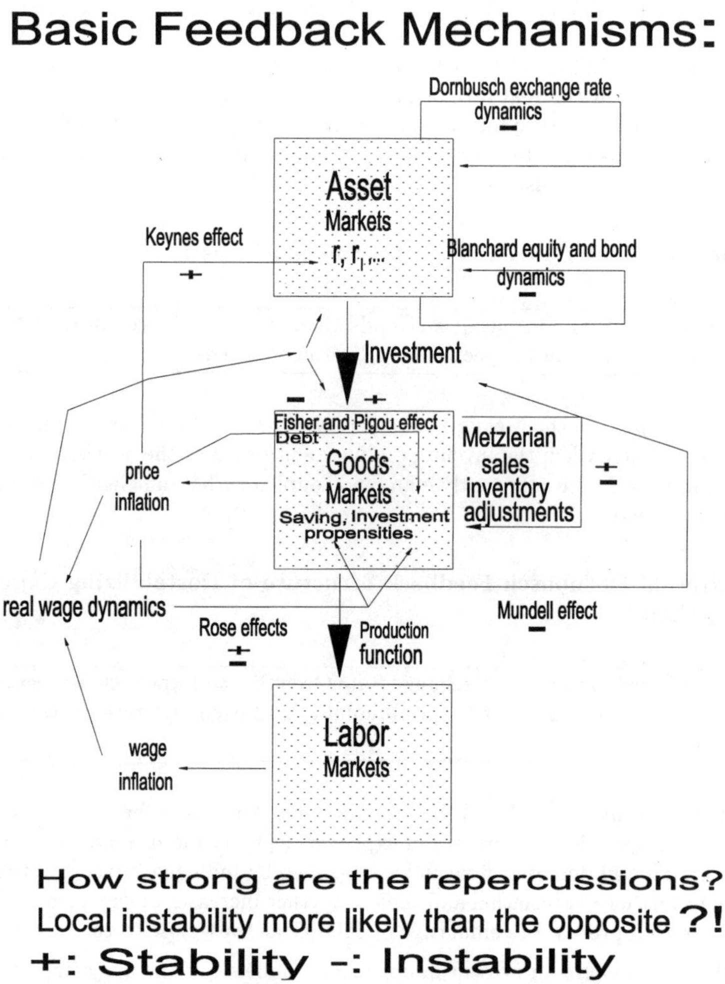

Figure 3.13: Feedback mechanisms in integrated models with short-run price rigidities and Keynesian quantity adjustment processes.

Our experience with this type of model of disequilibrium and growth suggests that in applied situations (for reasonable sizes of the parameters of the models) local stability will

[18]See Chiarella and Flaschel (1999e).

[19]See also Chiarella, Flaschel, Groh, Köper and Semmler (1999a).

[20]See also Chiarella, Flaschel and Semmler (1999) for a general model based on Fisher debt effects.

be more likely than the opposite in the intrinsically nonlinear situation which thus will again imply that additional extrinsic nonlinearities have to be introduced in order to get bounded dynamics, since the intrinsic nonlinearities will generally be too weak to make the dynamics globally bounded.

Furthermore, the feedback links shown in figure 3.13 provide a good idea of what parameters, in particular speeds of adjustment, have to be chosen in what way in order to generate an increase of local (in-)instability of the steady state solution.

Figure 3.13 also alludes to the question of whether the downward influence (depicted as shaded area in the middle of figure 3.13) is the dominant one, meaning that asset markets dominate the outcome on goods markets which in turn dominate the labor market situation or whether the feedbacks (shown as surrounding the shaded area) are so strong that it is more adequate to speak of a real-financial interaction than of a dominant feedback chain. At present, we cannot however provide an answer to this question, since financial market are not yet modeled in sufficient detail in their interaction with real markets in our approach as it is so far developed.

In order to approach such a situation from our modeling perspective the scenario of tables 3.1 - 3.3 might provide a framework with sufficient generality on the basis of which the figure 3.13 can be filled with mathematical detail and tested with respect to its stability and dominance propositions.

A Stylized General Framework for Macrodynamic Modeling Building:

	Workers	Asset Holders
Young	Labor supply	Time-consuming model-consistent expectations formation
Old	Retired workers	Rentier with a less perfect analysis of financial markets

Table 3.2: An OLG^2 approach to the Household Sector, combining intertemporal aspects and income distribution.

Given our framework we can propose to use as perspective for an advanced modeling of disequilibrium and growth a model with two basic types of agents, workers (who consume and save) and pure asset holders (who also consume and save), both exhibiting two types of generations so that their savings decisions might be approached via OLG analysis and the life cycle hypothesis, giving rise in sum to a certain type of OLG^2 analysis as in the matrix like representation used in table 3.2. Note that we for the moment have inserted a particular (life cycle) scheme of expectations formation into this table, which assumes that young asset holders (the ambitious ones) work hard (reducing their leisure time thereby) and arrive at myopic perfect foresight by means of their efforts, while old asset holders (retired ones) use less time-consuming methods (time series methods) for predicting the change in the asset prices of the assets they hold. The advantage of such an approach would be that it can draw on existing microfoundations of this type and that it can allow us to assess the relative importance of income distribution versus intertemporal substitution effects.

	Labor	Non traded Goods	Exports	Imports	Housing
Workers	+	+	-	-	+
Asset holders	-	+	-	-	+
Firms	+	+	+	+	+
Government	+	+	-	-	-
Prices Expectations		Medium run dynamics			
Stocks Growth		Long run dynamics			

Table 3.3: The real part of the economy.

	Money	Short-term Bonds	Long-term Bonds	Equities	Foreign Bonds
Workers	+	+	-	-	-
Asset holders	+	+	+	+	+
Firms	-	-	-	+	-
Government	+	+	+	-	-
Prices Expectations		Delayed interest rate dynamics			
Stocks Growth		Financial stock accumulation			

Table 3.4: The financial part of the economy.

On such a basis for household behavior one could again consider a small open economy where only domestic goods are traded domestically while imports are used as inputs by firms solely and exports are different from the domestically traded good, all put together in form of nested CES / CET production functions with three in the place of only two inputs now. The plus signs in the real and financial substructures of the economy in table 3.3 indicate activity in the corresponding cell of the economy, while minus signs are used to indicate that the model built on such a structure will not make use of an economic activity in this area. Concerning workers we therefore see that their income expenditures will concern consumption proper and the purchase of housing, the central element guiding their wealth accumulation decision, plus money and short-term bond accumulation (time and savings deposits basically) as outcome of their savings decision.

Asset holders make the same type of decisions, but in addition allocate their savings to long-term bonds, equity holdings and foreign bonds (and possibly also loans if the Fisher debt effect of section 2.3. is to be incorporated into the model). In order to keep the model still simple only long-term bonds are at first traded internationally (not for example equities as instrument of firms to obtain foreign sales branches for their economic activities). Firms use labor, capital and imports to produce domestically traded goods and exports, and they plan output and employment in the presence of a demand constraint on the domestic market in a cost-minimizing way, while investment and pricing decisions are made as previously discussed.

Government now also employs workers in the public consumption of domestic production, financing its deficit via new money or short- or long-term bonds. This allows the inclusion of aspects of the term structure of interest rates into the model beside the exchange rate dynamics already considered. If desired, loans of asset holders to firms may be added to the model to not only allow for a Fisher debt effect in consumption (which is there already), but also for one in investment of the type we considered in section 2.3.

The procedures surrounding such a framework for disequilibrium and growth models may be further explained and justified by means of the following (broadly speaking) methodological or consistency requirements for integrated disequilibrium growth theory (DGT):

> 1) A minimally complete set of markets: Five Real Markets, Five Financial Markets. 2) A minimally complete set of heterogeneous agents (households, Min=4?): Workers and Asset Holders, Young and Old (OLG^2). 3) Fully specified sets of budget equations for all agents of the economy (and consideration of the feedbacks they give rise to). 4) Dimensional homogeneity of all employed structural equations. 5) Fully specified set of steady state values. 6) Starting point as linear as is possible: Only intrinsic nonlinearities at first. 7) Systematic check of all the feedback chains of the model and of their stabilizing potential in isolation and in interaction: Local stability analysis. 8) Systematic addition of extrinsic nonlinearities later on: Kinked or strictly convex Phillips Curves, Nonlinearities in adjustment speeds, etc. 9) Consideration of global boundedness, role of transient behavior, types of attractors and more: Tailoring plausible extrinsic nonlinearities to achieve economic viability.

Let us add more on microfoundations here. Microfoundations, i.e., the basing of behavior on constrained optimization problems, are desirable, but not necessary for the fulfillment of the above research agenda. On the one hand, actual behavior (for example the application of cost-plus pricing rules) may be so diverse and filled with so many details that the derivation of price level adjustments may not only be very time consuming, but nearly impossible if average laws of motion are the focus of interest. Yet, whenever possible the insights of optimizing behavior, in the area of price formation in the present example, are of course important, in particular if the behavior of firms in an effort to avoid large optimization costs is properly taken into account.

By contrast, it is well known, in particular in Walrasian economics that nearly everything can be microfounded if sufficient heterogeneity is assumed to prevail. Microfoundations, if of help must therefore make the verbal justifications for particular behavioral rules more transparent and thus easier to defend, and are thus to be viewed as additional support and not as means of exclusion when macroeconomic interdependence is investigated. After all it is real economic interdependence in actual market economies which we want to understand by means of applicable economic theory and not so much the whole range of possibilities for individual behavior in more or less artificial circumstances of life.

It is our contention that the study of macroeconomic interdependence in models of disequilibrium and growth should occupy a central place in academic discussion on the evolution of the macroeconomy. Thus it should be regarded as complementary to the Walrasian understanding of the economy. The need for macroeconomists to be open minded to a range of approaches in their efforts to reach an understanding of the workings of modern economies is, we believe, implicit in the following quote from Turnovsky (1995):

"Macroeconomics has never reached a consensus and probably never will. The subject is too diverse and the approaches too varied for that to become likely." (S. Turnovsky, Methods of Macroeconomic Dynamics, MIT Press, 1995, Preface)

Current macroeconomics favors representative agent approaches, intertemporal utility and profit or cash flow maximization, market clearing and rational expectations. As is obvious from our discussion so far and also from the subsequent chapters of this book, we favor heterogeneous agent approaches (here still of a minimum type), disequilibrium as basis of labor and goods market adjustment processes, and also heterogeneous, boundedly rational expectations formation with respect to goods and also asset prices as the initial approach to integrated and applicable macrodynamics. Not debatable, however, is that intertemporal aspects of firms, households and government behavior are of great importance for the future development of such macrodynamics, which are not yet really present in the basic KMG framework we have discussed in this chapter. We will consider these topics further in the next parts of the book. Next we want to consider briefly the importance of our approach for understanding and improving structural macroeconometric model building, of modern as well as of traditional type.[21]

3.5 Macroeconometric model building

We mainly want to refer here to perspective core structures as we find them in presentations of modern macroeconometric model building with, as compared to earlier models, a low number of behavioral relationships and identities. Inspecting for example the Murphy model with its originally 100 equations reveals that many aspects of figures 3.1, 3.13, and not much more, are present in this model type, though sometimes somewhat hidden or integrated in a different way than we would propose, and still radically different in the treatment of expectations concerning financial decisions where saddlepoint situations prevail and jump variable techniques remain dominant.

We shall take the discrete time presentation of the macroeconometric model by Murphy, as provided in great detail in Powell and Murphy (1997), as point of departure. We shall seek to formulate on this basis continuous time versions of applicable integrated disequilibrium growth models, that extend our theoretical KMG approach significantly, and that try to synthesize into this framework as much as possible the macrostructures provided by the Powell and Murphy (1997) model.[22] Such modern macroeconometric models are therefore here taken as reference point or perspective for a systematic extension of the KMG approach to disequilibrium and growth that will combine structures rich enough to be applicable to the study of actual economies and compact enough (following the rules set out in the preceding section) to allow for theoretical as well as numerical analysis as sketched in sections 3.2, 3.3, see also subsection 3.4.4. Such a research program, in our view, will allow in important ways the further development of the type of investigation begun in Barnett

[21] A type of analysis that will reconsidered in detail in part III.

[22] See Chiarella and Flaschel (1999f-i), Chiarella, Flaschel and Zhu (1999a-c) and Chiarella, Flaschel, Groh, Köper and Semmler (1999a,b), and part III here, for the detailed formulation and investigation of such applicable disequilibrium growth models that are the focus of this section.

and He (1998). They study the Bergstrom, Nowman and Wymer (1994) continuous time macroeconometric model for the UK economy, which exhibits 14 second order differential equations, from the numerical perspective using modern tools from the theory of nonlinear dynamical systems.

Let us therefore now introduce the components on which our extension of KMG modeling towards applicable growth dynamics will be based. We here take the Murphy model as reference point, since it is one of the best documented macroeconometric models, with all of its 100 equations presented and explained in detail in Powell and Murphy (1997), and since it represents a full fledged disequilibrium growth model with detailed descriptions of a balanced growth reference path. A similar model type, yet one not allowing for disequilibrium adjustment processes in the goods market, see section 7.10, is given by the Multimod Mark III model of the IMF, as presented in Laxton et al. (1998). This model presentation is not as detailed as the one of Powell and Murphy (1997), however, but does offer instead a variety of further considerations (concerning in particular microfoundations and balanced growth analysis) from the theoretical as well as from the applied perspective. The recent emphasis on the long-run behavior of economies and on steady state solutions with respect to applied structural model building is indeed a notable feature of modern macroeconometric model building.

3.5.1 The national accounts of the model

In order to provide the reader with a short but complete overview of the sectors and their activities, we supply a closed national accounting system for the whole economy to be considered.[23] It shows the interactions between the sectors in our model and provides a check on the formal correctness of the system.[24]

Firms

The firms produce two kinds of output, the export good which only is tradeable on the world market and the domestic good which can only be sold in the domestic economy. The domestic good serves as the consumption good for the asset holders, the workforce, and the government. It can also be used for investments in inventories, in business fixed capital and in housing. Firms use three kinds of inputs for their production: imports, capital, and labor. Imports and labor have to be bought on their markets at prices including import and payroll taxes. The capital stock in the firms' sector depreciates by a given depreciation rate δ. The value added taxes, which only apply to trade in consumer goods, appear on the left side of the production account, because they have to be paid to the government. The balance is the profit of the firms' sector which can be viewed from an ex-ante perspective (as expected profit and intended inventory investment) as well as from an ex-post perspective (as realized profit plus actual inventory investment).

[23]Since we are following Powell and Murphy (1997) all amounts are valued in domestic currency, to be represented by the Australian dollars \$A in the present section.

[24]The following presentation of the system of national accounts of the considered economy has been taken from Chiarella, Flaschel, Groh, Köper and Semmler (1999a) and will be taken up again in part III of this book.

Production Account of Firms:

Uses	Resources
Imports $ep_m^* J^a$	Consumption $p_v C_w^g$ (workers)
Depreciation $p_y \delta K$	Consumption $p_v C_c$ (asset holders)
Value Added Taxes $\tau_v p_y (C_w^g + C_c + G)$	Consumption $p_v G$ (government)
Taxes on imports $\tau_m e p_m^* J^a$	Exports $p_x X^a$
Wages (excluding payroll taxes) wL_f^d	Gross Investment $p_y I$ (of firms)
Payroll Taxes $\tau_p w L_f^d$	Durables (Dwellings) $p_y I_h$ (sold to asset holders)
Profits $\Pi = \rho^e p_y K + p_y \mathcal{I} = \rho^a p_y K + p_y \dot{N}$	Inventory Investment $p_y \dot{N}$ (of firms)

Note that profits are not subject to any direct tax. By assumption, profits $\rho^e p_y K$, based on sales expectations, are used only to pay dividends to asset holders and then subject to capital income taxation. One can see this in the income account. Note that there are no subsidies paid to the firms' sector.

Income Account of Firms:

Uses	Resources
Dividends $\rho^e p_y K$	Profits Π
Savings $S_f^n = p_y \mathcal{I}$	

The accumulation account displays investments in business fixed capital and in inventories, representing the only stocks which can be accumulated by firms. There is therefore no possibility for the accumulation of financial stocks, i.e., no holding of money and bonds by firms. Investments that generally will exceed the savings and the depreciation funds of firms generate a financial deficit in this sector. Note that all investment occurs at producer prices p_y.

Accumulation Account of Firms:

Uses	Resources
Gross Investment $p_y I$	Depreciation $p_y \delta K$
Inventory Investment $p_y \dot{N}$	Savings S_f^n
	Financial Deficit FD

The financial deficit must be financed by selling new equities. This assumption is not very realistic, but is still used as in the KMG approach for simplicity. It will be reconsidered in further reformulations of the model which will develop a richer structure for the financial sector.

Financial Account of Firms:

Uses	Resources
Financial Deficit FD	Equity Financing $p_e \dot{E}$

Households (asset holders)

While firms produce and sell two types of goods (domestically traded goods Y, export commodities X), the sector of asset holders sells housing services to workers (who do not own houses by themselves in the present framework). Hence there is a production account for this sector as well.

Production Account of Households (Asset Owners/Housing Investment):

Uses	Resources
Depreciation $p_y \delta_h K_h$	Rent $p_h C_w^h$
Earnings Π_h	

The income of this sector consists of interest payments (long and short term bonds, the former also from abroad), dividends from the firms sector, and the profits from selling housing services. This income is diminished by capital income taxation at the rate τ_c and spent on domestic goods (consumption proper and housing). The remaining amount represents the savings of this sector.

Income Account of Households (Asset Owners):

Uses	Resources
Tax payment $\tau_c r B$	Interest payment rB (short-term bonds)
Tax payment $\tau_c B_1^l$	Interest payment B_1^l (long-term bonds)
Taxes $\tau_c(p_h C_w^h - p_y \delta_h K_h)$	Interest payment $e(1-\tau_c^*)B_2^l$ (from abroad)
Tax payment $\tau_c \rho^e p_y K$	Dividend payment $\rho^e p_y K$ (of firms)
Consumption $p_v C_c$	Earnings Π_h (from rent)
Savings S_c^n	

The savings S_c^n, in sum with the depreciation of the housing capital stock, is split into gross investment in housing and the financial surplus in the sector of asset holders.

Accumulation Account of Households (Asset Owners):

Uses	Resources
Gross Investment $p_y I_h$	Depreciation $p_y \delta_h K_h$
Financial Surplus FS	Savings S_c^n

The financial surplus is distributed to all financial assets contained in our model.

Financial Account of Households (Asset Owners):

Uses	Resources
Money $\dot{M}_c$	Financial Surplus FS
Short-term bonds $\dot{B}_c$	
Long-term bonds $\dot{B}_1^l/r_l$	
Foreign Bonds $e\dot{B}_2^l/r_l^*$	
Equities $p_e\dot{E}$	

Households (workers)

This sector produces nothing at all, but only supplies the labor services to firms. Therefore the production account remains empty. The income of workers includes wages, unemployment benefits, and pensions. It is used for tax payments and consumption. The remaining item, savings of workers, are not used for any type of real investment, but are held in two specific financial assets only: Money and saving-deposits (short-term bonds). Note that we apply the participation rate of workers in the working age group (16 to 65) also to the calculation of pension payments to the retired worker L_2 who therefore only get pension payments in an amount that is scaled down by this participation rate.

Production Account of Households (Workers):

Uses	Resources
–	–

Income Account of Households (Workers):

Uses	Resources
Taxes $\tau_w[wL^d + w^u(L - L^w) + w^r\alpha_l L_2]$	Wages $wL^d = wL_f^d + wL_g^d$
Consumption $p_v C_w^g + p_h C_w^h$	Unemployment benefits $w^u(L - L^w)$
Savings S_w^n	Pensions $w^r\alpha_l L_2$

Accumulation Account of Households (Workers):

Uses	Resources
Financial Surplus FS	Savings S_w^n

Financial Account of Households (Workers):

Uses	Resources
Money accumulation $\dot{M}_w$	
Bond accumulation $\dot{B}_w$	Financial Surplus FS

Government (fiscal and monetary authorities)

The government sector's production shows the costless provision of public goods which is considered as identical to the self consumption of the government. To provide the economy with these public goods the government has to buy the goods G on the domestic market and pay wages to the workers it employs for this purpose (L_g^w).

Production Account of Fiscal and Monetary Authorities:

Uses	Resources
Government expenditure for goods $p_v G$	Costless Provision of
Salaries $w^b L_g^d = wL_g^d + \tau_p wL_g^d$	public goods = self consumption

The only sources of income for the government are the various taxes. They are used for interest payments, pensions, unemployment benefits and salaries as well as public consumption. The balance of this account are the savings of the government. Mostly these savings are negative hence there is in general a financial deficit present in the accumulation account, rather than a financial surplus.

Income Account of Fiscal and Monetary Authorities:

Uses	Resources
Interest payment rB	Wage income taxes $\tau_w[wL^d + w^u(L - L^w) + w^r\alpha_l L_2]$
Interest payment $B^l = B_1^l + B_1^{l*}$	Profit and interest taxes $\tau_c\rho^e p_y K + \tau_c rB + \tau_c B_1^l + \tau_c B_1^{l*}$
Pensions $w^r\alpha_l L_2$	Rent income taxes $\tau_c(p_h C_w^h - p_y\delta_h K_h)$
Unemployment benefits $w^u(L - L^w)$	Payroll taxes $\tau_n wL_f^d + \tau_n wL_g^d$
Self consumption $p_v G + w^b L_g^d$	Value added tax $\tau_v p_y(C_w^g + C_c + G)$
Savings S_g^n	Import taxes $\tau_m e p_m^* J^a$

Accumulation Account of Fiscal and Monetary Authorities:

Uses	Resources
	Savings S_g^n
	Financial Deficit FD

In the financial account of the government one can see the sources, from which the deficit is financed: by issuing new money or new bonds (short- and long-term). Another item of this financial account may be given by changes in the stock of foreign reserves R. Such changes become necessary and have to be considered when interventions in the market for foreign exchange, designed to influence the exchange rate e, appear desirable to the monetary authority. In the present form the model will however imply $\dot{R} = 0$ on the basis of the savings decisions made by households, firms and the government.

Financial Account of Fiscal and Monetary Authorities:

Uses	Resources
Reserve changes $e\dot{R}$	Money supply changes $\dot{M} = \dot{M}_c + \dot{M}_w$
Financial deficit FD	Short-term debt $\dot{B}$
	Long-term debt $\dot{B}^l/r_l = \dot{B}_1^l/r_l + \dot{B}_1^{l*}/r_l$

International relationships

The balance of payments contains all transactions with foreign countries. It shows the amounts of goods, interest payments (on the basis of capital services), and flows of capital in domestic currency that cross the borders at the considered point in time.

Balance of Payments:

Debit	Credit
Imports $ep_m^* J^a$	Exports $ep_x^* X^a$
Factor Income to abroad $(1-\tau_c)B_1^{l*}$	Factor Income from Abroad $e(1-\tau_c^*)B_2^l$
Capital Exports $e\dot{B}_2^l/r_l^*$	Capital Imports $\dot{B}_1^{l*}/r_l$
Changes in reserves $e\dot{R}$	

This closes our ex-post presentation of the structure of a very general integrated disequilibrium macromodel which is considered in great detail in Chiarella, Flaschel, Groh, Köper and Semmler (1999a,b), Chiarella, Flaschel and Zhu (1999c) at the extensive form level, in intensive form, with respect to the steady state solution such a model type gives rise to and with respect to its local and global stability features, see here part III.

3.5.2 The implied CTD growth model

Next we briefly survey the new features of the Continuous Time Disequilibrium (CTD) growth model that is built on the structural details described before. Subsequently we will then discuss the core form of the implied dynamics in making a variety of assumptions that help to suppress feedbacks and structures that are of secondary importance in a first treatment of integrated macroeconometrically oriented CTD models. We conclude then with a brief survey of what can be done and has so far been done in the theoretical and numerical discussion of this CTD model. This includes brief notes on the methodology of switching on and off various subdynamics contained in the full dynamics and a survey of the tools that can be used in a detailed numerical investigation of the dynamic properties of the full dynamics as well as of their subsystems.

Starting with firms, we stress again that their technological basis is now of a fairly advanced nature, making use as far as production is concerned of a nested CES input and CET output technology with three factors (labor, imports and capital) and two outputs (domestically traded goods and exported commodities). Domestic output is demand constrained in the way we previously have formulated it, while output for the world market is not constrained and is subject to price taking behavior at (basically) given world market prices. Since the capital stock is also given at each moment in time, firms decide on labor and import input and export output in a cost-minimizing way in addition to their Metzlerian adjustment behavior with respect to domestically traded commodities.

In addition, medium run target levels of the firms for inputs and outputs, including domestic production, but excluding the capital stock, can be formulated, by removing the demand constraint on the domestic goods market and by deriving thereby potential values for domestic output, exports, imports and employment through profit maximizing behavior constrained by the existing stock of capital. The potential output level that results from this optimization will be used again as benchmark to describe the rate of capacity utilization as in our KMG approach to CTD growth. Investment behavior is similar to the one used in our KMG approach, but augmented now by a term that measures the tightness of monetary policy. There are furthermore various error correction mechanisms with respect to the medium run characteristics or targets of firms. Of course, there is a budget constraint for firms, here still based on equity financing of investment and unintended inventories.

We consider next the asset holder subsector of the household sector. There is a life cycle consumption function based on the sum of profit and interest income and on the real and financial wealth held in this subsector. Actual consumption follows desired consumption with a time delay and is the basis of a Cagan type money demand of this sector. Real wealth concerns houses rented to workers whose evolution in time is described by an investment behavior (now of asset holders, purchasing part of the domestic production of firms in this way) that is similar in spirit to the investment behavior of firms (now however of course referring to rents in the place of profit). The dynamics of rents is described by a Phillips curve of the type we have used so far for the price PC of firms. The remaining savings, determined by the budget restriction of this subsector, are distributed to the financial assets that exist in the chosen framework, with a rule that specifies the change in money holdings in a way that allows for a neutral distribution of the new money supply between asset holders and workers.

As obvious from our system of national accounts we now allow for savings of workers (in the form of money and saving deposits) and thus have to take note of their interest income now, in addition to wage income, unemployment benefits and pension payments that are also included. A life cycle hypothesis determines also workers' consumption, now consumption proper and housing services.[25] There are now three generations present in this part of the household sector, whose rates of growth are however treated in a fairly simplistic way.[26]

---

[25]In Chiarella and Flaschel (1999l) we add loan-funded housing investment of workers to the model and consider the Fisher debt effect that can be based on such a situation.

[26]See Powell and Murphy (1997) for a much more advanced demographic module of the model.

The savings, as determined by the budget restriction of this subsector, are distributed to new money holdings and saving deposits, as already stated, with a rule that specifies the change in money holdings in a way that allows for a neutral distribution of the new money supply in the household sector as a whole.

As is already obvious from the presented system of national accounts, there are numerous taxes and transfers now present in the government sector of the economy, and the government now uses up labor input besides domestic production through its activities. All this must of course appear in the government budget restriction, including the new supply of money due to a money supply rule based on deviations of inflation, capacity utilization and nominal interest from their targets levels. The resulting government deficit or surplus leads to corresponding changes in the short-term and long-term government bonds that are issued by this sector, giving rise to the government budget constraint of the model. Besides simple rules that determine the allocation of bonds to workers and asset holders (and also internationally) we have two further policy rules in the model, a wage taxation policy rules that attempts to move the government deficit to some target level and an import taxation rule that allows for balanced trade (including import taxation) in the steady state which greatly simplifies the calculation of the steady state of the model.

The quantity and price adjustment processes are of KMG type, now however including the over- and undertime work of the employed as a further expression in the money wage PC, and also a price index based on domestic goods and housing services, for the cost push term in this PC. We now again include adjustments in natural rates of growth and employment as considered before. Asset market price dynamics extends exchange rate dynamics methodology of section 2.5. to equities and long-term bonds, thus departing there too from the saddlepoint methodology in a specific way. Finally, the foreign sector is basically modeled as in section 3.2 , concerning trade, capital and interest flows in the world economy and the steady state characteristics of the rest of the world (which now include the international prices of the traded commodities). This concludes our brief survey on the general CTD growth to be used in the following in appropriately simplified form for a study of aspects of the core dynamics of such a model type. The reader is again referred to Chiarella, Flaschel, Groh, Köper and Semmler (1999a,b) and part III for a detailed presentation and investigation of this brief guide to the modeling of applicable CTD growth based on the KMG approach and on Powell and Murphy's (1997) formulation of a modern macroeconometric model.

3.5.3 The 18D core dynamics

Next we consider what is added to the KMG growth model of sections 3.1, 3.2 by the general approach we have sketched. There are of course now many details present in the static relationships underlying the laws of motion of the model, for example in the expression for aggregate demand, sectoral incomes and expenditures, and more, which we will not consider here in detail. We will instead concentrate here on the laws of motion that have to added to the 8D dynamics of the open KMG economy on the basis of what we have discussed above, subject to the list of the following specializing assumptions that make up our starting macroeconometric core model of CTD growth.

These assumptions are: 1) fixed proportions in production (which avoids nonlinear interdependence in the solution of the production block of the economy); 2) the elimination of lagged adjustment to target values for investment, consumption, trade patterns and also medium run rates of return and of inflation, where current values are now used in their place which reduces the number of the laws of motion significantly; 3) the exclusion of interest income from the consumption decision of workers (in order to decouple wealth accumulation from the rest of the economy) ; 4) the exclusion of wealth effects from consumption planning of workers (in order to decouple wealth accumulation from the rest of the economy); 5) the treatment of the consumption of asset holders by means of a simple trend term (which makes the steady state and the dynamics of the model independent of wealth accumulation in this subsector); 6) the elimination of pure cash holdings from the savings decisions of workers and asset holders by abstracting from pure cash management problems and the adoption of a Taylor type interest rate policy rule in the place of the money supply rule (which makes 'cash' supply for daily transactions endogenous, and its distribution between workers and asset holders irrelevant, and which replaces the conventional Keynes-effect by a direct steering of the nominal rate of interest on short-term bonds); 7) given magnitudes for all 'natural' rates of growth and employment (which removes some laws of motion from the model); 8) the use of only the rate of inflation of domestically traded goods in the money wage PC (which avoids the use of the price index); and, as already stated, the replacement of the LM curve by the adoption of an interest rate policy rule through the central bank.

Taken together we thus get a considerable difference to the full CTD growth model which in fact allows us to reduce its dynamic dimension from a 39D system of differential equations to an 18D system.[27] Sometimes this reduction does not lead to too much loss in mathematical complexity, as far as for example the use of lagged adjustment processes are concerned. Sometimes the reduction is a great help for making the model solvable with respect to intensive form and steady state calculations, as is in particular the case when going from smooth input and output substitution to fixed proportions in production. Nevertheless, the obtained dynamics remains much more general than those of the 8D KMG approach and thus can be considered as a useful intermediate case between the full dynamics and the KMG growth model.

What now are the new laws of motion that lead us from the 8D to the 18D case. There is first of all a new quantity adjustment rule involved, since we now have over- or under-time work of the employed and in view of this a lagged employment policy rule of firms which attempt to adjust their labor force such that this type of work is reduced to some extent. Next there is the Phillips curve for housing services, based on demand pressure around a normal rate of vacancies and cost pressure as represented by the domestic rate of inflation, and there is furthermore the growth law for the stock of houses (relative to the capital stock of firms) based on the housing investment decisions of asset holders.

Since government adjusts wage taxation in order to approach a certain target debt to GNP ratio, bond accumulation (short-term and long-term bonds) now feeds back into the core dynamics of the model, not yet through wealth effects, but rather due to this type of fiscal policy rule. There is furthermore the rule describing the dynamics of import

[27]See Chiarella and Flaschel (1999f,g,h) and Chiarella, Flaschel and Zhu (1999a) for detailed investigations of this model type on the extensive and the intensive level, with respect to the involved feedback mechanisms and for further numerical investigations of this model type.

taxation, needed to obtain a steady state solution of the model that is independent in its domestic aspects from international trade and the exchange rate (which is given by a complicated expression in the steady state). In the government sector there is finally the law of motion for the short term rate of interest now in the place of the law of motion for real balances. There remain the asset markets which, in the case of equities, due to missing wealth effects, do not feedback yet into the core dynamics of the model. In the case of long-term bonds and the resultant term structure of interest rates, the asset markets influence the core dynamics as long-term interest is compared to expected profitability both for fixed business investment and for the housing investment of asset holders. This is so since the interest spread between the long- and the short-term interest rates is used by investors to judge the tightness of monetary policy and its expected influence on the activity level of the economy. We thus need a law of motion for the price of long–term bonds a task that is solved similarly to the formulation of exchange rate dynamics in section 2.5., now of course by comparing expected returns of long-term bonds with the short-term rate of interest set by the central bank.

We add that we will assume here that the inflation target of the central bank is set equal to zero, which implies zero steady state inflation and which thus allows us to use nominal magnitudes as state variable of the dynamics to be considered without the need to reduce them to relative expressions (real balances, relative prices) as was the case in the KMG approach. In conjunction with the interest rate policy rule now adopted and the endogeneity of money supply that is associated with it this however implies that we will observe shock-dependent long run behavior of wages, prices and rents and thus zero-root hysteresis (of qualitatively the same type as in the case of the 'natural' rates dynamics considered in section 2.4.). We observe finally that we are still considering a small open economy, with the rest of the world in the steady state, which in particular implies that this economy is exposed to given international magnitudes concerning real growth rates and nominal interest rates (and also rates of inflation, which already have been assumed to be zero in the steady state).

Let us briefly comment now on an important methodology which allows us to switch on and off certain subdynamics of these 18D dynamics, as already made use of for the higher dimensional system surrounding these 18D dynamics. One can for example concentrate on the 9D real part of the economy by assuming that import taxation is always balancing nominal export and import volumes, in which case these items become irrelevant for the profit statements of firms and for their investment decisions. We assume in addition that there is no debt target approached by the government, which makes the evolution of government debt redundant, assume that the central bank fixes the short -term rate of interest at its steady state level and assume that adjustment speeds in the markets for foreign exchange and long-term bonds are zero. This in fact gives rise to a closed economy model of the KMG type, augmented by a housing sector (2D), and the employment policy rule for firms (both of which can also be removed from the dynamics which then leads us back to the model investigated in section 2.4.). Yet this full 9D situation represents an interesting extension of our KMG model and it can be used as a starting point in order to approach the 18D situation by switching on the policy rules of the model or the representation of the dynamics of financial markets here employed or both. In this way it becomes possible to learn systematically the new (or old) dynamic features of large (18D) dynamical systems from the features of appropriately chosen subdynamics and also vice versa.

3.5.4 Numerical investigations

We do not repeat in this section the numerical approaches applied to the study of the closed and the open KMG model of disequilibrium growth, which were given by time series representations, phase plots, the calculation of Hopf bifurcation loci (including the determination of the kind of a Hopf bifurcation), the detection of period doubling sequences towards complex dynamics, bifurcation diagrams and the calculation of Liapunov exponents. All these tools for considering the dynamic features of our high dimensional dynamical systems are of great interest, but are at present not yet applied carefully enough to the stage of complexity now reached , and thus must await future application.

We will, however, here present two further tools for the study of such systems. The first one being eigenvalue analysis by which the stability assertions of partial dynamic models on the feedback mechanisms shown in figure 3.13 can be checked as to their validity in truly interdependent labor, goods, bonds and housing markets and of course also in more generality. The second being the calculation of basins of attraction by which we can check what kind of shocks will be absorbed by the economically meaningful attractors of the dynamics and which ones will lead to behavior that leaves the range of economically acceptable values.

Let us first present some eigenvalue diagrams which plot the maximum real part of the eigenvalues of the Jacobian of the dynamic system calculated at the steady state. Due to the fact that we do not want to go here into a thorough discussion of the parameter set of the model and its many details, these are used for preliminary illustrative purposes solely, see chapter 9 for details. Figure 3.14 shows such eigenvalue diagrams in the case of an adverse working of the Rose effect from the 2D perspective, i.e., the case where consumption reacts much more (positively) to real wage increases than does investment (which of course reacts negatively).

We see top left that increasing exterior wage flexibility (as measured by the parameter β_{w1}) is destabilizing, in line with the intuition of the related 2D subdynamics, since real wage increases increase aggregate demand and thus favor further real wage increases as they come about by increasing wage flexibility sufficiently on the basis of a given price flexibility. Note that we have zero root hysteresis in the model, due to the treatment of the money market, which means that asymptotic stability is always represented by a zero, the then maximum real part of eigenvalues, giving rise to the horizontal lines in the above eigenvalue diagrams. Next, increasing price flexibility for a given degree of wage flexibility should of course increase local stability, which it does in the figure 3.14 top right if price flexibility is already sufficiently high. For sufficiently small values of the parameter β_p we however see that local asymptotic stability close to $\beta_p = 0$ is turned into local instability for increases in the speed of adjustment of prices, until the normal predictions of the existence of an adverse Rose effect come into being.

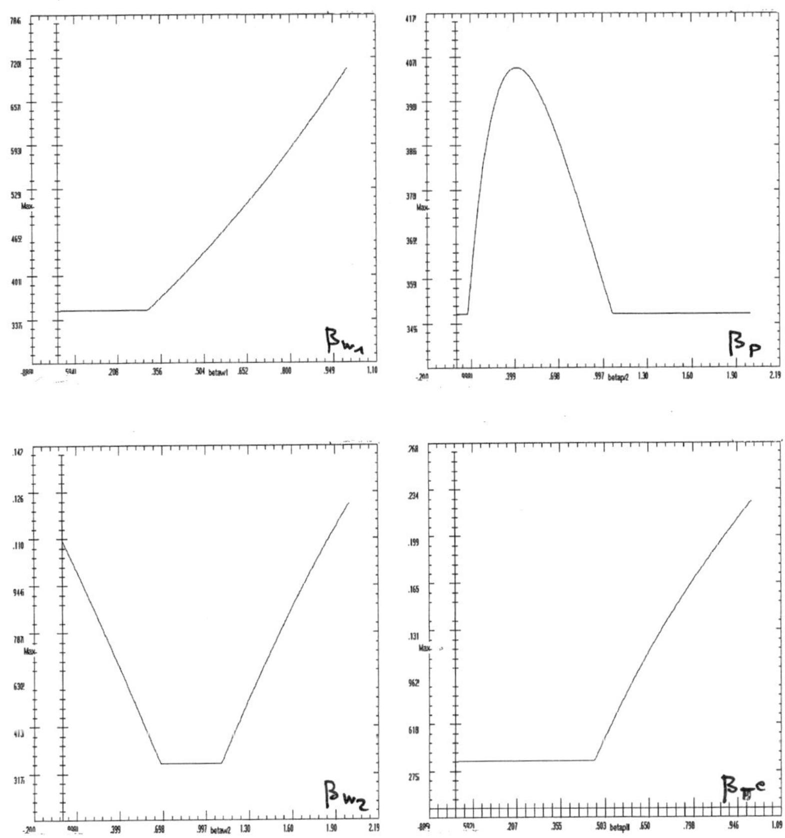

Figure 3.14: Eigenvalue diagrams for the parameters $\beta_{w1}, \beta_p, \beta_{w2}, \beta_{\pi^l}$, the adjustment speed of wages (due to exterior and interior employment), of prices and of inflationary expectations (purely adaptive ones).

The figure 3.14 bottom right by contrast show the normal working of the Mundell effect in the present 18D environment, just as in the simple 2D situation considered in section 2.1, i.e., increasing the speed of adjustment of adaptively formed inflationary expectations (all other parameters fixed) will lead to positive real parts of eigenvalues and thus to local instability of the steady state of the dynamics. Finally, and this represents a new phenomenon, from the perspective of sections 2.3. and 2.4. at least, having a derivative term in the money wage PC as in section 2.4. and as in Powell and Murphy (1997), which can be explained by the existence of over- and under-time work as it is present in the considered 18D model, leads to an interesting stability scenario. As we can see from the eigenvalue diagram bottom left, increasing the strength of the parameter that characterizes money wage adjustment due to over- or under-utilized workers within the firms (which determines their employment policy and thus the rate of change of the rate of employment) leads at first to an increase in local stability. But if this type of adjustment becomes too strong it leads to local instability that is increasing with the parameter β_{w2}.

Thus we see that eigenvalue diagrams are a very useful tool for checking the claims that are normally made with respect to the stabilizing features of Rose-, Mundell-, Keynes-, Metzler- and other effects or with respect to other isolated feedback chain arguments. Yet, such considerations are clearly local in nature and thus remain somewhat limited if global behavior is shaped by extrinsic nonlinearities far off the steady state. However a study of the systematic treatment of such extrinsic nonlinearities remains the object of future research. For this reason we again only treat one such nonlinearity which has proved to be very powerful from the analytical point of view with respect to 2D IS-LM-PC analysis and in numerical examples also for the 6D closed and 8D open economy models. We refer to the kinked Phillips curve introduced in section 2.2.

In the following further simulation study of the 18D model, see figure 3.15, we however make use of a kink that has a negative floor where there would be a constant rate of decline of money wages. A negative floor is necessitated by the fact that there is zero steady state inflation in the model. A zero floor kink due to the fact that there is no steady state inflation in the model, would give rise to a continuum of persistent underemployment situations (above the NAIRU). In figure 3.15 we have local instability of the steady state, but due to the intrinsic nonlinearities of the 18D dynamics, a stable limit cycle around the steady state is born by a supercritical Hopf bifurcation. This figure provides information as to what the mathematical and economic basins of attraction of this limit cycle will look like both with and without a kink in the money wage Phillips curve. Regions outside these basins lead to purely explosive behavior of the dynamics.

The darker shading outside shows the set of initial values from which the dynamics are purely explosive and thus not yet completely specified from the economic point of view. In the domain surrounded by white color we see the set of initial values from where the trajectories of the dynamics are attracted by the 'small' limit cycle shown in black in the middle of the small dark area. However, we do not yet always have a meaningful economic dynamics in this area since some variables of the model will there still assume meaningless values from the economic point of view, e.g., a negative nominal rate of interest. Only the small darkest area around the limit cycle is therefore of interest as far as the intrinsically nonlinear 18D dynamics is concerned, since from this set of initial values all trajectories remain economically meaningful and converge to the limit cycle shown. Our first conclusion is therefore that the dynamics is not always globally viable, neither from a purely mathematical nor from an economic point of view.

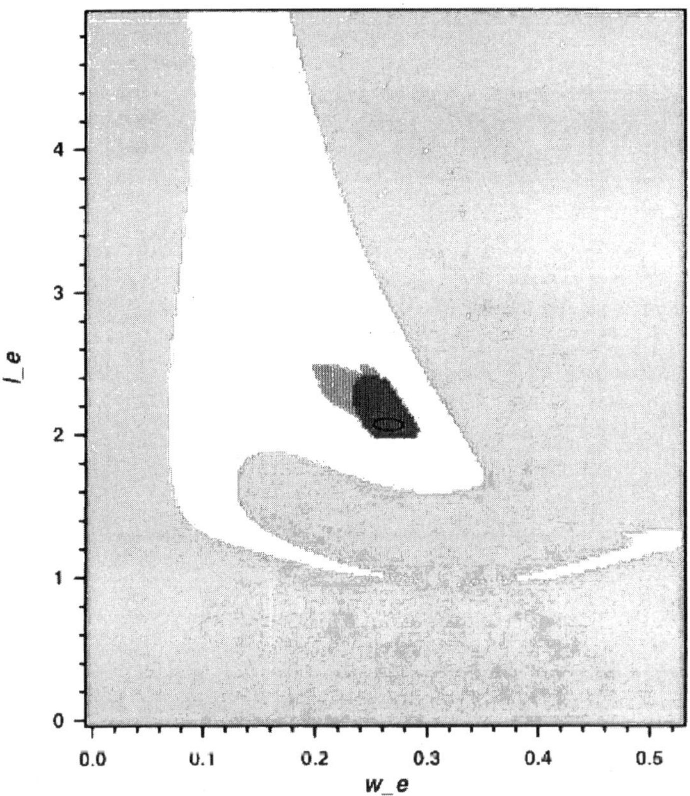

Figure 3.15: Economic and mathematical basins of attraction of a single persistent fluctuation around the steady state of the considered 18D dynamics, for shocks of the steady state values of nominal wages w^e and the factor endowment ratio l^e.

The question arises again whether a kink in the Phillips curve can improve the economic viability of the dynamics, by enlarging the 'small' basin of attraction of the limit cycle attractor of the dynamics. The resulting extension of the basin of attraction this augmented nonlinear situation is shown in grey to the left of the former basin of attraction and must of course overlap the dark area whenever the kink is not operative. By and large we see that larger negative shocks to the money wage than before will now not endanger the economic viability of the dynamics. We stress however that the depicted situation is a projection of an 18D system and should therefore not be interpreted from the 2D point of view. An example for such too narrow a view would be given if one would claim that the basins shown should represent connected sets, which of course is not true for a 2D representation of an 18D system. This in particular explains, at least to some extent, the fact that there are even very small isolated bright areas in the outside dark area of purely explosive situations (not visible, due to the lack of colors in this presentation) from which the systems converges to the limit cycle shown.

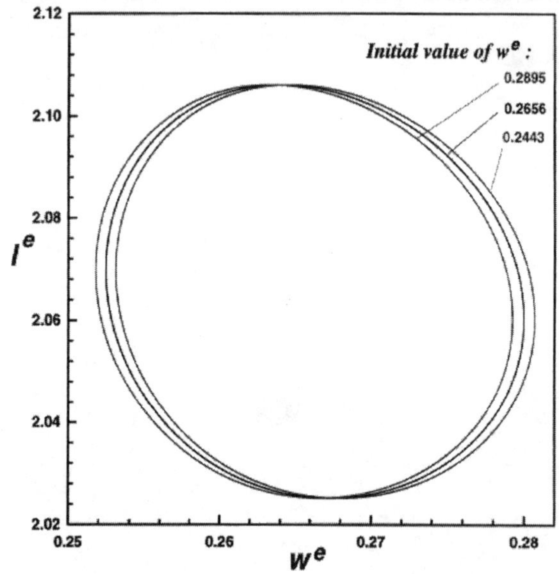

Figure 3.16: Hysteresis with respect to the nominal variables of the attractor of the 18D dynamics; the initial value of 0.2656 representing the unshocked situation.

In order to close this brief numerical investigation of a still largely uninvestigated 18D dynamics let us finally consider the obtained limit cycle in somewhat more detail. We shock the steady state solution of the dynamics (both positively and negatively) in order to see the behavior of the trajectories of the dynamics after the occurrence of such shocks. As a result we can gauge the dependency of the attractor of the dynamics on such shocks with respect to nominal magnitudes, such as the magnitude w^e, the nominal wage in efficiency units, shown on the horizontal axis of figures 3.15, 3.16, due to the hysteretical situations we stressed above. Indeed, consider the positive (negative) shock of the nominal wage (in efficiency units) as in figure 3.16, the initial value of 0.2895 (0.2443) being compared to the unshocked value of 0.2656. We find that such shocks worsen (improve) the nominal positions of wage earners in the long-run by displacing the limit cycle to the left (right), possibly due to the fact that such positive (negative) shocks induce the central bank to a restrictive (expansionary) monetary policy because of the assumed Taylor interest rate policy rule.

With this simulation study we close the preliminary numerical investigation of the 18D core dynamics of the general CTD growth model we have sketched in this section. Of course, much more remains to be done in order to get some feeling for the local and the global stability properties of such large (from the mathematical point of view) dynamical systems of disequilibrium and growth. The formulation and analysis of such macroeconometric version of the KMG model of sections 3.1, 3.2 will be continued in part III.

3.6 Summary and outlook

We have started the first part of the book with an IS-LM analysis augmented by inflation and expected inflation in the conventional way. We thus obtained what we here call the IS-LM-PC model and we were able to show that textbook presentations of this model type may be misleading and incomplete. When corrected and completed they give rise to persistent fluctuations of employment and inflation around the steady state position when adjustment of adaptively formed expectations is sufficiently fast. Thereafter we have more explicitly introduced the labor market and considered the interaction of real wage, employment and economic growth.

These two model types therefore provide us with a theory of medium-run as well as long-run employment cycles which due to their common PC element suggests that it should be possible to integrate them into larger dynamics with at least two cycle generating mechanisms.

We have supplemented this introductory discussion of growth and inflation with a reconsideration of theoretical and applied PC discussion and have found, that the former is still fairly underdeveloped with respect to a general treatment of wage-price dynamics and the demand pressure elements that may be involved in this interaction. We have also seen that applied approaches have generally been broader than the standard theoretical discussion of the PC,and we briefly treated the empirical investigations of Phillips curves.

We then derived a coherent core model of short-run Keynesian quantity dynamics, medium-run wage price dynamics and long-run growth cycle dynamics, based on fully specified budget equations for all sectors and a unique economic steady state reference path. This core model integrated the IS-LM-PC analysis (based on Keynes- and Mundell-effects) by making use in addition of Metzlerian quantity adjustment processes on the market for goods in the place of its infinitely fast adjustment to Keynesian goods market equilibrium. This model type of disequilibrium and monetary growth should since long have been the basic reference case of an integrated treatment of Keynesian macroeconomics. However, it has been neglected in the literature on monetary growth, see Orphanides and Solow (1990) for example, possibly due to the fact that AS-AD growth, as treated in Sargent (1987, Ch. 5) was generally considered as the Keynesian theory of monetary growth.

Another possible reason for this neglect is the fact that the analysis of nonlinear economic dynamics was usually restricted to dimension 3, whereas we have seen that an integrated model of Keynesian monetary growth, with sluggish price and quantity adjustment, including expectation formation on aggregate demand as well as inflation, and under- or over-utilized labor as well as capital requires a minimum of dimension 6 in order to capture all the dynamic feedback mechanisms that are at work then.

With the KMG model of sections 3.1, 3.2, a working model is set up for a fundamental and very general labor and goods market disequilibrium growth theory which can be investigated from the theoretical perspective allowing for a detailed treatment of the labor market dynamics extensions to an open economy, the treatment of the crucial role of macroeconomic feedback mechanisms and an empirical analysis. Furthermore, as shown in chapter 5, recent non-Walrasian macro-approaches with their regime switching methodology can easily be discussed in our model context, by adding to it supply side constraints whose impact turns out to be of a fairly secondary nature. Also the partial New Keynesian treatment of market imperfections can be integrated into our approach. Finally, setting adjustment speeds equal to infinity in such extended KMG approaches will lead to a market clearing limit case, yet such models do not look too appealing compared with the prototype disequilibrium approaches from which this limit has been obtained, see chapter 4.

Another topic still to be discussed is endogenous growth. Let us mention here that endogenous growth means much more in today's macro theories than we have embedded into our modeling approach so far. We have assumed a simple type of endogenous Harrod neutral technical change and also endogenous natural rates of growth.The discussion on endogenous technical change in the recent literature has pursued different routes, see McCallum (1996), and there is an urgent need to incorporate the advances there made into our integrated models of disequilibrium and growth, beyond the first attempts undertaken in Flaschel and Groh (1996a), Chiarella, Flaschel, Groh and Semmler (1999) and Flaschel, Groh and Semmler (1999). [28] This topic will be pursued further in chapter 4 of part II.

We have also treated endogenous 'natural' rates of (un-)employment or endogenous NAIRU rate of employment in various places of the first part of our book. We in particular have referred to the empirical work by Fair (1997 a,b). Other recent work on the NAIRU discussion should be incorporated and used to refine our treatment of an integrated macro approach. Let us point here to work published by Blanchard and Katz (1997), Cross (1987, 1995), Gordon (1997), Phelps and Zoega (1997), Murphy and Topel (1997), Staiger, Stock and Watson (1997), Stiglitz (1997) and Summers (1990) which may be very usefully incorporated into our framework.

We also have briefly touched upon the discussion on continuous time macroeconometric models. Such approaches are close to our compact representations of Continuous-Time Disequilibrium growth or CTD growth models. Such models are much easier to analyze with respect to stability features, attractors, and the like, since they are not married with the overshooting phenomena of discrete time dynamics right from the start. Applied CTD (growth) models are receiving new attention in the literature, see for example Allen and Hall (1997), Barnett and He (1998), Barnett, Gandolfo and Hillinger (1996), Bergstrom (1996), and Bergstrom, Nowman and Wandasiewicz (1994), for example. With respect to the latter, also the work by Garratt, Lee, Peseran and Shin (1998) should be mentioned, which though their approach is formulated as stochastic discrete time model, uses a detailed description of balanced growth long-run restrictions as a basis of this model type, but no short-run restrictions as in the structural macroeconometric approaches of Powell and Murphy (1997), Laxton et al. (1998) and others.

There finally remains the topic of the role of the financial market and macroeconomic dynamics. With respect to loans and debt deflation a treatment is given in Chiarella, Flaschel and Semmler (1999). Further treatments of some aspects of the above mentioned topics are undertaken in parts II and III.

[28]We there in particular show that the dynamics of the employed models of IS-LM or KMG growth are not changed significantly by the conventional additions used in the literature of endogenous growth if these additions are supplemented by appropriate assumption on investment behavior.

3.7 Appendices

In this section we list the notation used in the extensive and intensive form of the working KMG model and also present this 6D CTD growth model in its original form including comments on the various structural equations that are employed.

3.7.1 Notation

The closed economy KMG model of section 3.1 is based on the following basically standard macroeconomic notation:

A. Statically or dynamically endogenous variables:

Y	Output
Y^d	Aggregate demand $C + I + \delta K + G$
Y^e	Expected aggregate demand
N	Stock of inventories
N^d	Desired stock of inventories
$\mathcal{I}$	Desired inventory investment
L^d	Level of employment
C	Consumption
I	Fixed business investment
I^a	Actual total investment $= I + \dot{N}$ total investment)
r	Nominal rate of interest (price of bonds $p_b = 1$)
p_e	Price of Equities
S_p	Private savings
S_f	Savings of firms ($= Y_f$, the income of firms)
S_q	Government savings
$S = S_p + S_f + S_g$	Total savings
T	Real taxes
G	Government expenditure
ρ^e	Rate of profit (Expected rate of profit)
$V = L^d/L$	Rate of employment
Y^p	Potential output
$\Delta Y^e = Y^e - Y^d$	Sales expectations error
$U_c = Y/Y^p$	Rate of capacity utilization
K	Capital stock
w	Nominal wages
p	Price level
π^e	Expected rate of inflation (medium–run)
M	Money supply (index d: demand)
L	Normal labor supply
B	Bonds (index d: demand)
E	Equities (index d: demand)
W	Real Wealth
ω	Real wage ($u = \omega/x$ the wage share)
$\nu = N/K$	Inventory-capital ratio

B. Parameters

$\bar{V}$	1. NAIRU-type normal utilization rate concept (of labor)
$\bar{U}_c$	2. NAIRU-type normal utilization rate concept (of capital)
δ	Depreciation rate
$\bar{\mu}$	Steady growth rate of the money supply

n	Natural growth rate
$i_{1,2}$	Investment parameters
$h_{1,2}$	Money demand parameters
β_w	Wage adjustment parameter
β_p	Price adjustment parameter
β_π	Inflationary expectations adjustment parameter
α	Weights for forward and backward looking expectations
β_{n^d}	Desired Inventory output ratio
β_n	Inventory adjustment parameter
β_{y^e}	Demand expectations adjustment parameter
$\kappa_{w,p}$	Weights for short– and medium–run inflation
κ	$= (1-\kappa_w\kappa_p)^{-1}$
y^p	Potential output–capital ratio ($\neq y$, the actual ratio)
$x = 1/l_y^e$	Output–labor ratio
t^n	Lump sum taxes per unit of capital
g	Government expenditures per unit of capital
s_c	Savings–ratio (out of profits and interest)
s_w	Savings–ratio (out of wages, = 0 here)

C. Mathematical notation

$\dot{x}$	Time derivative of a variable x
$\widehat{x}$	Growth rate of x
l', l_w	Total and partial derivatives
$r_o, etc.$	Steady state values
$y = Y/K, etc.$	Real variables in intensive form
$m = M/(pK), etc.$	Nominal variables in intensive form

3.7.2 The working model in extensive form

The agents in the model consist of households (in their capacity as workers and asset holders), firms (which perform the role of production units and investors) and government (acting as the fiscal and monetary authority). These agents interact on markets for goods, labor and financial assets. A more detailed discussion of the economic underpinnings of the model as well as its significance in the literature on Keynesian monetary growth models is given in Chiarella and Flaschel (1999a,b).

The equations of this Metzlerian I/S–LM–growth model are as follows:

1. Definitions (remunerations and wealth):

$$\omega = w/p, \quad \rho^e = (Y^e - \delta K - \omega L^d)/K, \tag{3.10}$$

$$W = (M + B + p_e E)/p, \quad p_b = 1. \tag{3.11}$$

This set of equations introduces variables to be employed in the following structural equations of the model, namely the definition of real wages ω, the expected rate of profit on real capital ρ^e (based on expected sales Y^e) and the definition of real wealth W. Wealth is here composed of money M, fixed price bonds B ($p_b = 1$) and equities E as in Sargent (1987).

Household behavior is described next by the following set of equations:

2. Households (workers and asset-holders):

$$
\begin{aligned}
W &= (M^d + B^d + p_e E^d)/p, \ M^d = h_1 pY + h_2 pK(r_o - r), && (3.12)\\
C &= \omega L^d + (1 - s_c)[\rho^e K + rB/p - T], && (3.13)\\
S_p &= s_c[\rho^e K + rB/p - T] = (\dot{M}^d + \dot{B}^d + p_e \dot{E}^d)/p, && (3.14)\\
\hat{L} &= n = \text{const.} && (3.15)
\end{aligned}
$$

We here start from Walras' Law of Stocks which states that real wealth W, in equation (3.12), is the constraint for the stock demand for real money balances and real bond and equity holdings at each moment in time. Money demand is specified as a simple linear function of nominal income pY and interest r (r_o the steady state rate of interest) in the usual way. The form of this function is chosen in this way in order to allow for a simple formula for the rate of interest in the intensive form of the model, i.e. it is still chosen for mathematical convenience to some extent and not exclusively for economic reasons. Nonlinear money demand functions with real wealth in the place of the capital stock would be more appropriate and thus should replace this simple function in later extensions.

Consumption C, in equation (3.13), is based on classical saving habits with savings out of wages set equal to zero for simplicity. For the time being we assume that real taxes T are paid out of (expected) profit and interest income solely and in a lump sum fashion. Extending such tax payments to wage income does not make much difference to the model and is here bypassed to make this model comparable to the ones considered in Chiarella and Flaschel (1999b). Equation (3.14) provides the definition of real private savings S_p (here of wealth owners) which is then allocated to desired changes in the stock of money, bonds and equities held. Finally, in equation (3.15), workers are assumed to supply labor L inelastically at each moment in time with a rate of growth $\hat{L}$ given by n, the so-called natural rate of growth.

The behavior of the production sector of the economy is described by the following set of equations:

3. Firms (production-units and investors):

$$
\begin{aligned}
Y^p &= y^p K, \ y^p = \text{ const. }, \ U_c = Y/Y^p = y/y^p \ (y = Y/K), && (3.16)\\
L^d &= Y/x, \ x = \text{ const.}, \ V = L^d/L = Y/(xL), && (3.17)\\
I &= i_1(\rho^e - (r - \pi^e))K + i_2(U_c - \bar{U}_c)K + nK, && (3.18)\\
S_f &= Y_f = Y - Y^e = \mathcal{I}, && (3.19)\\
\Delta Y^e &= Y^e - \delta K - C - I - G = Y^e - Y^d, && (3.20)\\
p_e \dot{E}/p &= I + \Delta Y^e = I + (\dot{N} - \mathcal{I}), && (3.21)\\
I^a &= I + \dot{N} = I + \Delta Y^e + \mathcal{I} = p_e \dot{E}/p + \mathcal{I}, && (3.22)\\
\hat{K} &= I/K. && (3.23)
\end{aligned}
$$

According to equations (3.16), (3.17), firms produce commodities in amount Y in the technologically simplest way possible, via a fixed proportions technology characterized by the potential output/capital ratio $y^p = Y^p/K$ and a fixed ratio $x = 1/l_y^e$ between actual output Y and labor L^d needed to produce this output. This simple concept of technology allows for a straightforward definition of the rate of utilization U_c, V of capital as well as labor.[29]

In equation (3.18) investment per unit of capital I/K is driven by two forces, the rate of return differential between the expected rate of profit ρ^e and the real rate of interest $(r-\pi^e)$ and the deviation of actual capacity utilization U_c from the normal or non-accelerating - inflation rate of capacity utilization $\bar{U}_c$. There is also an exogenous trend term in the investment equation which is set equal to the natural rate of growth for reasons of simplicity. Savings of firms, eqn. (3.19), is equal to the excess of output over expected sales (caused by planned inventory changes), since we assume in this model that expected sales are the basis of firms' dividend payments (after deduction of capital depreciation δK and real wage payments ωL^d).

The next equation (3.20) defines the excess of expected demand over actual demand which here has to be financed by firms by issuing new equities. We assume, as in Sargent (1987), that firms issue no bonds and retain no expected earnings. It follows, as expressed in eqn. (3.21), that the total amount of new equities issued by firms must equal in value the sum of intended fixed capital investment and unexpected inventory changes, $\Delta Y^e = \dot{N} - \mathcal{I}$; compare our later formulation of the inventory adjustment mechanism. The next equation (3.22) describes on this basis actual investment I^a from various perspectives and here only serves to add some details about the accounting framework of the type of firms here considered. Finally, eqn. (3.23) states that (fixed business) investment plans of firms are always realized in this Keynesian (demand oriented) context by way of corresponding inventory changes.

We now turn to a brief description of the government sector:

4. Government (fiscal and monetary authority):

$$T = \text{lump sum such that } t^n = \frac{T - rB/p}{K} := \text{const.} \tag{3.24}$$

$$G = gK, \quad g = \text{const.} \tag{3.25}$$

$$S_g = T - rB/p - G \quad [= -(\dot{M} + \dot{B})/p, \text{ see below}], \tag{3.26}$$

$$\hat{M} = \bar{\mu}, \tag{3.27}$$

$$\dot{B} = pG + rB - pT - \dot{M}. \tag{3.28}$$

The government sector is here described in as simple a way as possible by way of policy rules such that the role of bond financing of government expenditures for the dynamics of the model, and of steady state inflation, can be discussed, yet by assumption still without feedback mechanism on the real part of the private sector of the economy, leaving the discussion of the proper role of fiscal and monetary policy rules for later investigations of the KMG approach to monetary growth. In equation (3.24), real taxes net of interest are assumed to be constant per unit of capital, as in Sargent (1987, part I). Similarly, in eqn. (3.25), real government expenditures are assumed to be constant per unit of capital, which in sum gives that fiscal policy is represented by simple parameters in the intensive form of the model. The definition of government savings, eqn. (3.26), S_g is an obvious one. Equation (3.27) states that money supply growth $\bar{\mu}$ is of a given magnitude which gives the

[29] Chiarella and Flaschel(1999b, Ch.5) show that such an approach can be extended to the case of smooth factor substitution without much change in its substance.

most neutral way the monetary authority can behave if this rate of growth is identified with the natural rate of growth which makes wages and prices stationary in the steady state. In view of these simple rules for government and central bank behavior the issue of new bonds by the government is then determined residually via equation (3.28) which states that money and bond financing must exactly cover the deficit in government expenditure financing.

We now describe the equilibrium conditions of the model:

5. <u>Equilibrium conditions (asset-markets):</u>

$$M = M^d = h_1 pY + h_2 pK(r_o - r) \quad [B = B^d, E = E^d], \tag{3.29}$$

$$p_e = \rho^e pK/[(r - \pi^e)E], \tag{3.30}$$

$$\dot{M} = \dot{M}^d, \; \dot{B} = \dot{B}^d \quad [\dot{E} = \dot{E}^d]. \tag{3.31}$$

Asset markets, see also Sargent (1987), are assumed to clear at all times. Equation (3.29) describes this assumption for the money market. Bonds and equities are assumed to be perfect substitutes (here still under static price expectations with respect to the price of equities as in Sargent (1987)), which is the content of equation (3.30) and which determines the price of shares in this model. This amounts to assuming, in the light of the assumed Walras's Law of stocks, that the clearing of the money market implies that the bond and equity market are then cleared as well. Finally, in eqn. (3.31), it is assumed that wealth owners accept the inflows of money and bonds issued by the government for the current period, reallocating them only in the next period by adjusting their portfolios in view of a new situation. It is easy to check by means of the considered saving relationships that the assumed consistency of money and bonds flow supply and flow demand implies the consistency of the flow supply and demand for equities, compare also the first equation of the next block of equations. These flow equalities represent ex-post conditions, implied by the budget constraints for households, firms and the government, but do not yet explain the forces that lead to their fulfillment on the primary or flow markets for financial assets. The working of these primary markets is thus not explained in the present approach to KMG growth.

The disequilibrium situation in the goods market is an important component driving the dynamics of the economy. This situation is described by the following equations:

6. <u>Disequilibrium situation (goods-market adjustments):</u>

$$S = S_p + S_g + S_f = p_e\dot{E}^d/p + \mathcal{I} = I + \dot{N} = I^a = p_e\dot{E}/p + \mathcal{I}, \tag{3.32}$$

$$Y^d = C + I + \delta K + G, \tag{3.33}$$

$$N^d = \beta_{n^d} Y^e, \; \mathcal{I} = nN^d + \beta_n(N^d - N), \tag{3.34}$$

$$Y = Y^e + \mathcal{I}, \tag{3.35}$$

$$\dot{Y}^e = nY^e + \beta_{y^e}(Y^d - Y^e), \tag{3.36}$$

$$\dot{N} = Y - Y^d = S - I \qquad [S - I^p = Y^e - Y^d]. \tag{3.37}$$

Equation (3.32) of this disequilibrium block of the model describes the various identities that can be related with the ex post identity of savings S and investment I^a for a closed economy. It is here added for accounting purposes solely. Equation (3.33) then defines aggregate demand Y^d which is never constrained in the present model. In equation (3.34) desired inventories N^d are assumed to be a constant proportion of expected sales Y^e. Furthermore intended inventory investment $\mathcal{I}$ is then determined on this basis via the adjustment speed β_n multiplied by the current gap between intended and actual inventories $(N^d - N)$ and augmented by a growth term that integrates in the simplest way the fact that this inventory adjustment rule is operating in a growing economy. Output of firms Y in equation (3.35) is the sum of expected sales and planned inventory adjustments. Sales expectations are here formed in a purely adaptive way, again augmented by a growth term as shown by equation (3.36). Finally, in eqn. (3.37), actual inventory changes are given by the discrepancy between output Y and actual sales Y^d equal to the difference between total savings S and fixed business investment I.

We now turn to the last sector of our model which is the wage-price module or the supply side of the model as it is often characterized in the literature.

7. Wage-Price-Sector (adjustment equations):

$$\hat{w} = \beta_w(V - \bar{V}) + \kappa_w \hat{p} + (1 - \kappa_w)\pi^e, \tag{3.38}$$

$$\hat{p} = \beta_p(U_c - \bar{U}_c) + \kappa_p \hat{w} + (1 - \kappa_p)\pi^e, \tag{3.39}$$

$$\dot{\pi}^e = \beta_{\pi^e}(\alpha\hat{p} + (1 - \alpha)(\bar{\mu} - n) - \pi^e). \tag{3.40}$$

This 'supply side' description is based on fairly symmetric assumptions on the causes of wage- and price-inflation. Wage inflation according to eqn. (3.38) is driven on the one hand by a demand pull component, given by the deviation of the actual rate of employment V from the NAIRU-rate $\bar{V}$, and on the other hand by a cost push term measured by a weighted average of the actual rate of price inflation $\hat{p}$ and a medium-run expected rate of inflation π^e. Similarly, in eqn. (3.39), price inflation is driven by the demand pull term (given by the deviation of the actual rate of capacity utilization U_c from the NAIRU rate $\bar{U}_c$) and the weighted average of the actual rate of wage inflation $\hat{w}$ and a medium-run expected rate of inflation π^e. This latter expected rate of inflation is in turn determined by a composition of backward-looking (adaptive) and forward-looking (regressive) expectations. This amounts, when appropriately simplified, to an inflationary expectations mechanism as in (3.40) where expectations are governed in an adaptive way by a weighted average of the actual and the steady state rate of inflation. It is also easy to extend this mechanism in a way such that price forecasting rules as for example used by the FED (so-called p^*-concepts) are explicitly introduced into the forward-looking component of this expectations mechanism.

This ends the description of the extensive form of the model used as basic synthesis of the AC-PC and IS-LM-PC (with Metzlerian inventory adjustments) models of this part of the book.

Part II

The Working Model: Walrasian, Non-Walrasian and New-Keynesian Reformulations

In part II of the book the relationship between our working model developed in part I and three important directions in the economic literature will be investigated, namely flex-price models in the neoclassical tradition, neo-keynesian fix-price approaches of the Non-Walrasian type and theories including market imperfections as pursued, e.g., by New Keynesians.

In chapter 4 we at first extend our working model with sluggishly adjusting prices and quantities to include endogenous technical change, and smooth factor substitution in production coupled with fluctuating rates of capacity utilization, and also wage income taxation. This extended working model is subsequently modified, following the Walrasian market-clearing approach, by assuming instantaneous adjustment of wages, prices and quantities, such that there is always full utilization of labor and of capital, which will lead us to dichotomizing real and nominal dynamics, with well known instability features in the evolution of nominal magnitudes, but stability in the real part of the model. In a next step we move further into the direction of the Walrasian approach to macroeconomics by using demand and supply functions for worker households that are obtained from constrained utility maximization, in the place of the classical saving habits so far assumed, and by remedying the nominal instability observed in the preceding section through the well-known jump variable technique, customarily applied in such (dichotomizing) real / nominal saddlepoint situations. It is demonstrated in a next section, which changes will occur in this equilibrium setup, if instead of the price level now real output adjusts to clear the goods market, while prices can then again be adjusted sluggishly without disturbing general equilibrium, here by a delayed adjustment towards marked up marginal wage costs. This reformulation no longer allows for the application of the jump variable technique, but does not remove the observed saddlepoint instability from the dynamics. In an outlook it will therefore finally be shown, by way of a smaller dynamical model with classical features, how the resulting local instability scenarios can be kept within economically reasonable bounds by adding appropriate extrinsic nonlinearities to the behavior of the dynamic model far off the steady state.

Chapter 5 highlights the connections between our working model and approaches of the Non-Walrasian type, which are indeed very close in spirit to our approach. In both cases temporary equilibria on the basis of temporarily fixed prices, in a broad sense, and their change in time are considered. The main difference between the two kinds of approaches can be seen in the fact, that regime switches, which are typical for Non-Walrasian theories, have not occurred with regard to the variants of our working model developed so far, where the dynamics does not escape the so-called "Keynesian regime", in which demand is never rationed. In this chapter it will therefore be shown on the one hand, how this model can be extended into this direction by the addition of appropriately formulated supply bottlenecks, which may become binding in situations far off the steady state. On the other hand, however, it is demonstrated, that due to the various buffers present in our model like inventories, the possibility of overtime work and over-utilization of capital, such situations of demand rationing will usually not last very long and in most cases will not occur at all. This important point will also be illustrated by a number of simulations at the end of the chapter.

A reformulation of the KMG model which aims to capture some key elements of modern theories of imperfect competition as concerns the product and labor markets is then provided in chapter 6. This is mainly done by replacing the dynamic rules for wage and price formation by the corresponding equations of the respective theoretical background. After giving a discrete-time reformulation of our approach, reformulations of the wage-price module are first given on the basis of a linear production function with a fixed markup factor, giving rise again to an endogenous explanation of the labor market NAIRU in particular which may however be surrounded by centrifugal forces. In this context the importance of a kinked money wage Phillips-curve for stabilizing the economy is considered and analyzed analytically as well as numerically. In a second step the fixed proportions in production are replaced by a neoclassical production function and a markup now based on marginal wage costs. In further subsections profit share targets of firms and a variable markup factor are also investigated. As will be shown, many important dynamic properties of our original working model will remain unchanged in spite of the changes in the analytical part brought about by the above modifications in the wage-price module.

We stress finally that this part of the book shows, on the one hand and in many respects, how the working model of part I can be significantly extended, without too much change in the qualitative properties of the dynamics as long as there is (somewhat) sluggish adjustment of prices and quantities. On the other hand, much remains to be done in the further improvement of the modules of the (extended) working model, concerning in particular the treatment of asset markets and the closedness of the economy.

Chapter 4

Flex-Price Approaches: Exceptional Limit Cases?

4.1 Introduction

In this chapter we will first consider some basic innovations and extensions of the KMG model introduced in Part I, which mainly concern the inclusion of wage taxation and exogenous Harrod-neutral technical change. This is done in section 4.2. In the last years, however, a growing part of the literature is concerned with an endogenization of technological progress, see e.g. the contributions of Romer (1986, 1990), Mankiw, Romer and Weil (1992), Lucas (1988) and others as well as the surveys in Schneider and Ziesemer (1994), Barro and Sala-i-Martin (1995), McCallum (1996) and Aghion and Howitt (1998). Therefore section 4.3 shows, how endogenous technical change can also be included into the KMG-framework developed so far. This is done by making use of the approach of Lucas (1988), which synthesizes a technology production function of the Uzawa (1965) type and an externality of the technology level on the production of goods in the tradition of Romer (1986). In a first step, the inclusion of these new aspects will be considered under the assumption of a fixed proportions technology; after this the changes are analyzed which come about by smooth factor substitution.

Section 4.4 then leads to the central issue of this chapter, namely a "classical" reformulation of the KMG model, i.e. a version with fully flexible wages, prices and interest rates and accordingly instantaneous market clearing at each point in time, similar to the Neoclassical synthesis of the basic IS-LM-model. The main result will be, that the real dynamics become completely independent of the nominal ones, which mirrors the well-known neutrality results of (neo-) classical economics.

This approach is developed further in section 4.5, where the model is enriched by Walrasian supply and demand functions as well as heterogeneity of agents and expectations. The main reason for this Walrasian reformulation, which allows for a dependence of the consumption and labor supply (of workers) on real wages and interest rates in a macroeconomic formulation as in Barro and Grilli (1994) is to make the KMG model easier comparable with modern market clearing approaches like the New Classical Macroeconomics, especially with regard to Real Business Cycle (RBC-) theories, pursued, among others, by Kydland

and Prescott (1982), Nelson and Plosser (1982), Long and Plosser (1983), Barro (1989) and, especially with regard to the introduction of the intertemporal labor substitution, by Lucas and Rapping (1969). In the context of the resulting saddle point dynamics then the jump variable technique as originally introduced by Sargent and Wallace (1973) and broadly applied thereafter will play an important role.

This technique, however, will no longer be applicable in another approach considered in section 4.6, where the price level is assumed to be statically exogenous and where the task of clearing the goods market is fulfilled by instantaneously adjusting output. The analysis here shows, that now local explosiveness may occur, and the fact, that the jump variable technique can now no longer be applied, underlines the necessity of establishing economic bounds on the dynamics in order to avoid global instability.

The appendix in section 4.7 finally shows how such global boundedness can be guaranteed by assuming an appropriate nonlinearity in the labor market in connection with an endogenous growth rate of the labor supply. This approach therefore demonstrates, that viability of such a classical version of the KMG model can also be constructed without referring to the jump variable technique.

4.2 Sluggish adjustments: An extended KMG reference case

We extend in this section the basic KMG model, considered in part I, Chapter 2 and the appendix to that part on the intensive as well as on the extensive level, to include into it technical change and wage taxation (besides property income taxation) and prove fundamental stability assertions which generalize the ones of section 2.2 in a straightforward way (where no proof of these assertions was provided). The present section also synthesizes extensions of the model of IS-LM growth and the Keynes-Metzler model investigated in Chiarella and Flaschel (1999b, Chs. 4 and 6) and it generalizes the proof of local asymptotic stability there provided for four and five dimensional models of IS-LM and Kaldor-Tobin type to the six dimensional dynamics that results in the present section. We thus enrich earlier approaches to integrated disequilibrium growth of the KMG variety by important aspects of factual economies, which are in particular needed when the model is estimated for actual economies as in Chapter 7 of this book, and which are nevertheless of a type that basically does not alter the dynamics of the simpler model types which are their point of departure.

Let us first consider Harrod-neutral technical progress that proceeds at a constant rate n_l. This extension of the KMG approach takes account of the fact that labor productivity x as well as capital intensity k^d exhibit, from a long run perspective, a positive trend in capitalist market economies. They thus cannot be treated as given constants in these model types when the aim of the investigation is to pay some attention to stylized facts and stylized magnitudes of growth patterns in their interaction with business fluctuations.

Harrod-neutral technical progress is in the case of a fixed (at each moment in time) proportions technology defined by a fixed potential output-capital ratio $y^p = Y^p/K$ and a growing output-employment ratio $x = Y/L^d$ with a given growth rate $\hat{x} = n_l$ of x which here in addition is assumed to be independent of the level of output that is actually produced. These assumptions imply that the actual ratios $k^d = K/L^d, l^d = L^d/K$ (describing actual capital and labor intensity) will change over time, not only because of fluctuations in the utilization rate of the capital stock, but also in the steady state where we will have $\hat{k}^d = n_l = -\hat{l}^d$.

These assumptions and implications are part of Kaldor's list of the stylized facts of growth theory, see Jones (1975, pp.7,8) for example, and they will imply others in the models considered here, namely: Continued growth in the aggregate volume of production, a steady rate of profit and a steady income distribution measured by the profit (or wage) share in national income [the latter if there is a steady share of investment in output]. To these facts we would here add, from the perspective of the monetarist critique of Keynesianism, the condition of a positive rate of unemployment as far as the features of steady growth are concerned. The addition of Harrod neutral technical change demands for the consideration of labor and wage magnitudes in terms of efficiency units which however only reinterprets the corresponding expressions of the model without technical change and does not at all alter the equations describing their interaction with the rest of the dynamical system.

The KMG model of part I is secondly changed by allowing now for a proportional wage income tax. This extension is also of a secondary nature as far as the mathematical structure of the dynamics is concerned, since we here still stick to the assumption that workers consume what they get,[1] which implies that aggregate consumption and demand remain unchanged when income is transferred from worker households to the government.

The above new characteristics of the technology of our economy imply the following changes in the models of chapter 2 (and the appendix of part I). Labor productivity $x = Y/L^d$ is now assumed to follow a growth trend with constant rate n_l, i.e., the variable x is now determined by the growth law $x = x_o \exp(n_l t)$. Trend growth in the output of the economy, with the rate of employment a fixed magnitude, will therefore occur at the rate $n + n_l$, i.e., the growth in labor supply plus that in labor productivity. This new 'natural' growth trend of the economy consequently has to be used as point of reference for money supply, for the trend component of the investment schedule in business fixed investment and inventories and in the formulation of expectations of aggregate sales and inflation, replacing the former natural growth rate n. Finally, the wage-price sector of our economy has also to reflect the growth in labor productivity, on the one hand, through an augmented target of workers that besides expected current and medium run inflation is now also to be based on the constant increase in labor productivity that they observe. On the other hand, the partial markup pricing objective assumed to underlie the term $\kappa_p \hat{w}$ in the price formation rule of firms now gives rise to the expression $\hat{w} - n_l$ as cost push reference for firms which thus has to be used in the place of $\hat{w}$ in the formation of the rate of price inflation.

Chiarella and Flaschel (1999b, Ch.4) consider two further changes in the dynamics of the considered Keynesian monetary growth model which concern the equation which describes the formation of inflationary expectations

$$\dot{\pi} = \beta_{\pi_1^e}(\hat{p} - \pi^e) + \beta_{\pi_2^e}(\bar{\mu} - (n + n_l) - \pi^e).$$

On the one hand, they replace the adaptive term in this adjustment equation by

$$\beta_{\pi_1^e}(\alpha\hat{p} + (1-\alpha)(\hat{w} - n_l) - \pi^e) = \beta_{\pi_1^e}(\alpha(\hat{p} - \pi^e) + (1-\alpha)(\hat{w} - n_l - \pi^e))$$

[1]See Ch. 8 for a relaxation of this assumption.

which states that adaptive expectations are now based on an average of price and wage inflation (the latter only insofar as this inflation rate deviates from the trend in labor productivity growth). Note here that the earlier situation is reproduced when $\alpha = 1$ is assumed and that we have departed from the corresponding equation for inflationary expectations in section 3.1 of part I by using $\beta_{\pi_1^e}, \beta_{\pi_2^e}$ in the place of the coefficients there employed. The rationale for the above extension of the expectations mechanism is that economic agents believe to some extent that wage inflation will become price inflation in the end (if it exceeds the rate of productivity growth) and that they therefore integrate aspects of wage inflation into their views on medium run inflation π^e.[2]

On the other hand, we assume as in Chiarella and Flaschel (1999b, Ch.4) with respect to the forward looking component in the formation of inflationary expectations that economic agents adopt the so-called p-star concept of certain monetary authorities in their calculation of future price changes. A basic version of this concept is as follows: Economic agents assume that the price level is determined in the longer run by the development of the quantity of money and of normal output as the quantity theory of money suggests, i.e. the moving attracting equilibrium of future price levels is assumed by agents at each moment in time to be given by:

$$p^* = \bar{v}M/(\bar{U}_c Y^p),$$

where $\bar{v}$ is the velocity of money (estimated/assumed as a constant). Since there is no inside money in the present model the magnitude M is fully under the control of the central bank. The only remaining problem for the bank as well as economic agents is to estimate the development of normal output which in our model is given by potential output times the desired rate of capacity utilization.

In terms of growth rates the above equation gives rise to

$$\hat{p}^* = \bar{\mu} - \hat{K},$$

due to our assumption of a fixed proportions technology. The monetary authority as well as the public therefore has only to obtain knowledge of the growth rate of the capital stock in order to calculate the present rate of growth of the center of gravity of the price level rightly or wrongly assumed to exist for the actual rate of inflation. We here assume that the actual rate of growth of the capital stock is common knowledge and thus end up with the following reformulation of the forward looking term in the above expectations equations:

$$\beta_{\pi_2^e}(\hat{p}^* - \pi^e) = \beta_{\pi_2^e}(\bar{\mu} - \hat{K} - \pi^e).$$

Note that this term reduces to our earlier formulation of forward looking inflationary expectations when it is assumed that potential output and the capital stock grow at their steady rates. Note also that this is only a second step towards a more advanced theory of future inflation. Further steps necessarily must use more elaborate models of price-forecasting than have been introduced here which take more of the present structure of the model into account than only the long run quantity theory of money to which it gives rise ($\bar{v} = 1/h_1!$).

These assumptions on the formation of inflationary expectations in contrast to the ones made on technical change and taxation, will alter the dynamical equations of the model

[2]It is also not difficult to formulate a separate equation for expected price and wage inflation. However, the dimension of the dynamics is thereby increased by one.

on the intensive form level. We only assert here that these alterations to the dynamics will however be of secondary importance still since they do not modify the employed dynamic equations and the feedback loops that derive from them towards qualitatively new expressions. In fact the average of wage and price inflation is qualitatively seen of the same form as the one for price inflation itself as we shall see below. In order not to overload the notation of the model and since we do not address policy issues in this part of the book we therefore do not add the above extended view on the formation of inflationary expectations to the equations of the KMG model presented below.

The equations of the extended KMG model thus are:

1. Definitions (remunerations and wealth):

$$u = \omega/x = wL^d/(pY), \quad \rho^e = (Y^e - \delta K - \omega L^d)/K \tag{4.1}$$

$$W = (M + B + p_e E)/p, \quad p_b = 1 \tag{4.2}$$

2. Households (workers and asset-holders):

$$W = (M^d + B^d + p_e E^d)/p, \; M^d = h_1 pY + h_2 pK(r_o - r) \tag{4.3}$$

$$C = \omega L^d - T_w + (1 - s_c)[\rho^e K + rB/p - T_c] \tag{4.4}$$

$$\begin{aligned} S_p &= Y^e - \delta K + rB/p - T_w - T_c - C = s_c[\rho^e K + rB/p - T_c] \\ &= (\dot{M}^d + \dot{B}^d + p_e \dot{E}^d)/p \end{aligned} \tag{4.5}$$

$$\hat{L} = n = \text{const} \tag{4.6}$$

3. Firms (production-units and investors):

$$Y^p = y^p K, \; y^p = \text{ const. }, \quad U_c = Y/Y^p = y/y^p, \quad y = Y/K \tag{4.7}$$

$$L^d = Y/x, \quad x = x_o \exp(n_l t) \;\; \hat{x} = n_l, \quad V = L^d/L = Y/(xL) \tag{4.8}$$

$$I/K = i_1(\rho^e - (r - \pi^e)) + i_2(U_c - \bar{U}_c) + \gamma, \; \gamma = n + n_l \tag{4.9}$$

$$S_f = Y_f = Y - Y^e = \mathcal{I} \tag{4.10}$$

$$\Delta Y^e = Y^e - \delta K - C - I - G = Y^e - Y^d \tag{4.11}$$

$$p_e \dot{E}/p = I + \Delta Y^e = I + (\dot{N} - \mathcal{I}) \tag{4.12}$$

$$I^a = I + \dot{N} = I + \mathcal{I} + \Delta Y^e = I^p + \Delta Y^e = p_e \dot{E}/p + \mathcal{I} \tag{4.13}$$

$$\hat{K} = I/K \tag{4.14}$$

4. Government (fiscal and monetary authority):

$$T = T_w + T_c, \; T_w = \tau_w \omega L^d, \; T_c \text{ s.t. } t_c^n = (T_c - rB/p)/K = \text{ const} \tag{4.15}$$

$$G = T_w + gK, \quad g = const \tag{4.16}$$

$$S_g = T - rB/p - G \;\; [= -(\dot{M} + \dot{B})/p \text{ see (4.19)}] \tag{4.17}$$

$$\hat{M} = \bar{\mu} \tag{4.18}$$

$$\dot{B} = pG + rB - pT - \dot{M} \tag{4.19}$$

5. Equilibrium conditions (asset-markets):

$$M = M^d = h_1 pY + h_2 pK(r_o - r), \quad [B = B^d, E = E^d] \tag{4.20}$$

$$r = \frac{\rho^e pK + \dot{p}_e E}{p_e E} \tag{4.21}$$

$$\dot{M} = \dot{M}^d, \; \dot{B} = \dot{B}^d \;\; [\dot{E} = \dot{E}^d] \tag{4.22}$$

6. Disequilibrium situation (goods-market adjustments):

$$S = S_p + S_g + S_f = p_e\dot{E}^d/p + \mathcal{I} = I + \dot{N} = I^a = p_e\dot{E}/p + \mathcal{I} \quad (4.23)$$

$$Y^d = C + I + \delta K + G \quad (4.24)$$

$$N^d = \beta_{n^d}Y^e \quad (4.25)$$

$$\mathcal{I} = \beta_n(N^d - N) + \gamma N^d, \ \gamma = n + n_l \quad (4.26)$$

$$Y = Y^e + \mathcal{I} \quad (4.27)$$

$$\dot{Y}^e = \beta_{y^e}(Y^d - Y^e) + \gamma Y^e, \ \gamma = n + n_l \quad (4.28)$$

$$\dot{N} = Y - Y^d = S - I \qquad [S - I^p = Y^e - Y^d] \quad (4.29)$$

7. Wage-Price-Sector (adjustment equations):

$$\hat{w} = \beta_w(V - \bar{V}) + \kappa_w(\hat{p} + n_l) + (1 - \kappa_w)(\pi^e + n_l) \quad (4.30)$$

$$\hat{p} = \beta_p(U_c - \bar{U}_c) + \kappa_p(\hat{w} - n_l) + (1 - \kappa_p)\pi^e \quad (4.31)$$

$$\dot{\pi}^e = \beta_{\pi^e_1}(\hat{p} - \pi^e) + \beta_{\pi^e_2}(\bar{\mu} - \gamma - \pi^e), \ \gamma = n + n_l. \quad (4.32)$$

In block 1 the wage share u, the (expected) profit rate ρ^e of the firms and the real wealth of the households are defined. The latter consists of money holdings, bonds (of government) and equities (issued by firms); the bonds are of the fix price type with price $p_b = 1$. Block 2 characterizes the household sector consisting of workers and asset holders. Equation (4.3) describes their desired real wealth in terms of its components. Bonds and equities are assumed to be perfect substitutes. The desired division of total wealth between these two assets on the one hand and money on the other hand is described by the money demand function, which, as usual, depends positively on real income and negatively on the nominal rate of interest. The latter fact is captured by the difference between the actual rate of interest and its steady state value. Due to the assumption, that workers spend their entire disposable income whereas asset holders save a part from it, the consumption function (4.4) results with T_w and T_c denoting taxes for workers and asset holders, respectively. The difference between the disposable income of the whole household sector $Y^e - \delta K + rB/p - T_w - T_c$ and consumption then defines private savings, which are reflected by the corresponding desired changes in money, bond and equity holdings as described by equation (4.5). Equation (4.6) finally states, that labor supply is growing by a constant rate n.

The next block concerns the behavior of firms. Equations (4.7) and (4.8) describe their linear production technology with fixed proportions, with y representing the capital productivity (which is constant over time) and x denoting labor productivity, which grows over time by a constant rate n_l, according to the assumption of Harrod-neutral technical progress. Y^p denotes potential output, U_c the rate of utilization of real fixed capital and V, as before, the rate of employment. Equation (4.9) then describes the investment behavior of the firms, which depends on the one hand positively on the difference between the (expected) profit rate and the (expected) real rate of interest; on the other hand, investment is driven by the rate of capacity utilization U_c, which is compared to a reference level $\bar{U}_c$, which may be referred to as the natural rate of utilization. The third factor γ influencing investment is the real growth rate of the economy (consisting of the growth rate of the labor supply n and the rate of technical change n_l), which ensures an appropriate rate of investment also in the steady state, where the first two terms are zero. Whereas equation (4.9) referred to investment in fixed capital, the next equation, (4.10), defines desired inventory investments $\mathcal{I}$, which firms finance by detaining an appropriate part of their profits; thus,

$\mathcal{I}$ represents the savings of the firms, denoted by S_f. In contrast to this, equation (4.11) describes the non-desired changes in inventories coming about by the difference between expected output Y^e and aggregate demand Y^d. In order to understand the next equation, (4.12), correctly, the concrete "timing" of the single decisions and transactions is important. Thinking for the moment in discrete time, firms decide "at the end of period $t-1$" on their production in t, based on their demand expectation Y^e and their desired inventory investments (see equation (4.27) below). On this basis also income payments to the private households are determined, which in turn are correctly anticipated by the latter. At "the beginning of period t", however, firms realize the difference between their expectation Y^e and actual demand Y^d, but having already decided upon production a revision is not possible any more. On the other hand, they feel obliged to fulfill the income expectations of the households in any case, so that they have to finance the gap by issuing additional equities. Thus, the total sum of new equities is determined not only by the investment plans of firms but also by the difference between Y^e and Y^d. (Note, that this concerns not only the case $Y^e > Y^d$ but also the opposite one, where inventories are being reduced, so that there are additional revenues to finance investment in fixed capital which in turn diminishes the amount of new equities that have to be issued.) $\dot{E}/p$ therefore represents a "Clower supply", formulated by firms under the impression of a deviation of aggregate demand from their production. Equation (4.13) then gives the identity for actual total investment I^a, both in fixed capital and in inventories, where $\dot{N} = \mathcal{I} + \Delta Y^e$ denotes the entire change in inventories.

Block 4 provides the accounting identities for the government. According to equation (4.15) taxes are raised from workers proportional to their income and from asset holders in a way that (capital) taxes net of interest payments are a constant fraction of the stock of real capital; this assumption has the advantage of simplifying the subsequent formulation of the model in intensive form. In equation (4.16) and (4.18) the assumptions concerning government expenditures G and the growth rate of money supply M are laid down; while the first evolves according to the sum of the taxes on labor income and a constant fraction of the capital stock, the latter is assumed to grow by a constant rate μ. In order to fulfill the government's budget constraint, the emission of new bonds $\dot{B}$ then has to follow equation (4.19).

The equilibrium conditions for the asset-markets are depicted in block 5. Equation (4.20) repeats the functional form of the money demand as already described and determines equilibrium on the money market. Note, that due to the temporarily given values for Y, p and M this equation determines the nominal rate of interest r. The next equation is a no-arbitrage condition for the market of equities. As equities and bonds are assumed to be perfect substitutes and can both be resold in each point of time, their short run rates of return have to be equal. The right hand side of (4.21) describes the (nominal) rate of return on equities as consisting of dividend payments $\rho^e pK$ and the rate of change of the equity price times the number of equities ($\dot{p}_e E$), both divided by the nominal value of the existing equity stock $p_e E$. This equation therefore provides a differential equation for p_e, the price for equities, which however does not feed back into the dynamics of the real part of the economy, because there is no real wealth effect in the consumption function. The clearing of the money-, the bond- and the equity-market is then expressed by equation (4.22). Note again in this context, that disequilibrium on the market for goods ($Y^e \neq Y^d$) is nevertheless possible, because firms perfectly perceive this already at the very beginning of the "time period" considered, and that still before markets open, i.e. still before the disequilibrium actually occurs. So they immediately adjust their emission of new equities to this situation in order to be able to fulfill in any case the income expectations of the private households. Thus, e.g., in the case of insufficient demand, that part of income, which households effectively keep back from the demand for goods, finds expression in the demand for the additional equities that firms have already issued in advance due to their perfect anticipation of the disequilibrium on the market for goods. In this way it is ensured, that the budget restrictions of the agents considered remain fulfilled.

This situation on the goods-market is then described by block 6, where the first equation expresses the item just discussed in terms of aggregate savings. Equation (4.24) lists the components of aggregate demand and by equation (4.25) the desired stock of inventories N^d is assumed to depend in a linear way on the expected demand Y^e. The desired investment in inventories $\mathcal{I}$, however, follows this target with a delay as expressed by the next equation, (4.26); by the second term, γN^d, it is furthermore ensured, that inventories will grow in the steady state (where $N^d = N$) with the growth rate of the economy, $\gamma = n + n_l$. As already discussed, actual production Y is determined by the sum of expected demand Y^e and intended inventory investment $\mathcal{I}$ as shown by equation (4.27). Expected demand Y^e adjusts in time according to the gap on the goods market and the constant growth term, which is expressed by the next equation. Block 6 is concluded by the identity of the actual change in inventories (consisting both of intended and unintended changes), which has to equal the difference between aggregate savings and investment in fixed capital.

Block 7 finally describes the dynamic adjustments in the wage-price-sector, where the first two equations describe the two Phillips curves already known from Part I: Nominal wages are driven by the situation on the labor market, the rate of technical change and the rate of inflation, which enters here via a convex combination of the actual and the expected rate, where the latter represents expectations concerning the medium run. The development of the price level, on the other hand, is determined by the rate of capacity utilization, a term representing (wage) cost pressure and the inflationary climate. The last equation defines the formation of expectations which consist of a backward and a forward looking part as already discussed above.

This KMG model with Harrod-neutral technical change is formally identical to the KMG model without technical progress as can be seen as follows: Equations (4.30),(4.31) can be rearranged in the usual way, now giving rise to

$$\begin{aligned}\hat{w} - \pi^e - n_l &= \beta_w(V - \bar{V}) + \kappa_w(\hat{p} - \pi^e),\\ \hat{p} - \pi^e &= \beta_p(U_c - \bar{U}_c) + \kappa_p(\hat{w} - \pi^e - n_l).\end{aligned}$$

Solving for the two variables $\hat{w} - \pi^e - n_l$, $\hat{p} - \pi^e$ these two equations imply

$$\begin{aligned}\hat{w} - \pi^e - n_l &= \kappa[\beta_w(V - \bar{V}) + \kappa_w\beta_p(U_c - \bar{U}_c)], \quad \kappa = (1 - \kappa_w\kappa_p)^{-1}\\ \hat{p} - \pi^e &= \kappa[\beta_p(U_c - \bar{U}_c) + \kappa_p\beta_w(V - \bar{V})], \quad \kappa = (1 - \kappa_w\kappa_p)^{-1}.\end{aligned}$$

Subtracting the second from the first equation furthermore implies

$$\hat{u} = \hat{w} - \hat{p} - n_l \;=\; \kappa[(1 - \kappa_p)\beta_w(V - \bar{V}) + (\kappa_w - 1)\beta_p(U_c - \bar{U}_c)],$$

which gives the first of the differential equations to be employed in the following in the same form as in the earlier models without technical change (where $\hat{\omega} = \hat{u}$ held).

We denote by L^e, L^{de} labor supply and employment measured in efficiency units, i.e., $L^e = L\exp(n_2 t), L^{de} = L^d \exp(n_2 t)$ denote effective labor supply and effective employment as distinct from labor supply and employment in 'natural' units. Straightforward calculations then allow to express the above dynamical model (4.1) – (4.32) in the following compact intensive form representation as a six–dimensional dynamical system in the variables $u = \omega/x$, the share of wages in national gross output, $l^e = L^e/K$, the full employment labor intensity of the economy measured in efficiency units, $m = M/(pK)$, real balances per unit of capital, π^e, inflationary expectations, y^e, expected sales per unit of capital, and ν, actual inventory holdings per unit of capital.[3] Note, that the dynamics of B and E are not considered here, because they do not feed back into the real dynamics here due to the exclusion of real wealth effects.

$$\begin{aligned}
\widehat{u} &= \kappa[(1-\kappa_p)\beta_w(\frac{y}{x_o l^e}-1)+(\kappa_w-1)\beta_p(y/y^p-1)] && (4.33)\\
\widehat{l^e} &= -(i_1(\rho^e-(r-\pi^e))+i_2(y/y^p-1)) && (4.34)\\
\widehat{m} &= \bar{\mu}-\pi^e-(n+n_l)-\kappa[\beta_p(y/y^p-1)+\kappa_p\beta_w(\frac{y}{x_o l^e}-1)]+\widehat{l^e} && (4.35)\\
\dot{\pi}^e &= \beta_{\pi_1^e}\kappa[\beta_p(y/y^p-1)+\kappa_p\beta_w(\frac{y}{x_o l^e}-1)]+\beta_{\pi_2^e}(\bar{\mu}-(n+n_l)-\pi^e) && (4.36)\\
\dot{y}^e &= \beta_{y^e}(y^d-y^e)+\hat{l}^e y^e && (4.37)\\
\dot{\nu} &= y-y^d+(\hat{l}^e-(n+n_l))\nu && (4.38)
\end{aligned}$$

with the following algebraic equations supplementing these six laws of motion:

$$\begin{aligned}
y &= \beta_n(\beta_{n^d}y^e-\nu)+(1+(n+n_l)\beta_{n^d})y^e\\
y^d &= uy+(1-s_c)(\rho^e-t_c^n)+i_1(\rho^e-(r-\pi^e))+i_2(y/y^p-1)+n+n_l+\delta+g\\
\rho^e &= y^e-\delta-uy\\
r &= r_0+(h_1 y-m)/h_2.
\end{aligned}$$

In view of these equations it is again obvious that this dynamical system is mathematically of the same type as the one of the KMG model without technical change and wage taxation. The model is thus closer to reality than the one in part I, but nevertheless, due to its construction, has a structure of basically the same intensive form. This is in particular true with respect to the inclusion of wage taxation which, on the one hand, is necessary due to the empirical magnitudes that are here involved, but which, on the other hand, here only means a redistribution of income between the same marginal(=average) propensity to consume. Concerning technical change the use of Harrod neutral technical progress, as is well known, needs nothing more than a reinterpretation of the magnitudes we have employed so far in part I, in order to include the stylized fact of positive trend in labor productivity into this disequilibrium model of monetary growth.

[3]For notational simplicity we renormalize $\bar{V}, \bar{U}_c$ by 1; this is done by an appropriate reinterpretation of the adjustment speeds β_w, β_p and i_2 and of the production parameters x and y^p.

Proposition 4.1:

There exists a uniquely determined interior steady–state *of the dynamics (4.33) – (4.38) (where $u_0, l_0, m_0 \neq 0$ holds) which is given by*

$$\begin{aligned} y_0 &= y^p, \quad l_0^e = y_o/x_o, \quad y_0^e = y_0^d = y_0/(1+(n+n_l)\beta_{n^d}), \quad \nu_0 = \beta_{n^d} y_0^e \\ \rho_0^e &= t_c^n + (n+n_l+g-t_c^n)/s_c, \quad u_0 = (y_0^e - \delta - \rho_0^e)/y_0 \\ \pi_0^e &= \bar{\mu} - (n+n_l) \ (= \hat{p}_o = \hat{w}_o - n_l), \quad m_0 = h_1 y_0, \quad r_0 = \rho_0^e + \pi_0^e \end{aligned}$$

Proof: Setting the equations of (4.33) – (4.38) equal to zero (based on the assumption that no steady state value is zero) implies by means of (4.33), (4.35), (4.36) through appropriate linear combinations of these equations that $V = \frac{y}{x_o l^e} = 1, U_c = y/y^p = 1$ must hold. Furthermore, we get from (4.34), (4.37) that $y^d = y^e$ holds true in the steady state. The equation for y^d then implies: $s_c(\rho^e - t_c^n) + t_c^n - g = n + n_l$. It is then easy to obtain the above steady state values from these three equalities. ∎

We assume that the parameters of the model are chosen such that the steady state values of u_o, r_o are both positive. Note that the steady state is in addition characterized by

$$\hat{K}_0 = \hat{Y}_0 = n + n_l, \quad \hat{\omega}_0 = \hat{w}_0 - \hat{p}_0 = n_l, \quad \hat{L}_0^d = \hat{L}_o = n, \quad \hat{p}_0 = \pi_0^e = \bar{\mu} - n - n_l.$$

Note also that the long-run (steady state) behavior of the economy is basically supply side based with superneutrality of money in addition. Concerning income distribution we have the generalized Cambridge type equation $s_c(\rho^e - t_c^n) = n + n_l$ which in particular implies that a rising savings rate s_c will depress the net rate of profit (all other parameters unchanged).

Proposition 4.2

Assume $\beta_n = 0$. Then: The 6 dimensional dynamical system (4.33)–(4.38) is locally asymptotically stable at the above steady state if the parameters $h_2, \beta_{\pi_1^e}, \beta_p, \beta_w$ are all sufficiently small and the parameter β_{y^e} sufficiently large.

Proof: Assuming $\beta_n = 0$ implies that the dynamics (4.33)–(4.37) does not depend on the law of motion for ν. Furthermore, these reduced dynamics are of the same mathematical type as the Kaldor-Tobin dynamics considered in Chiarella and Flaschel (1999b, Ch.6), since y is then strictly proportional to y^e : $y = (1 + (n+n_l)\beta_{n^d})y^e$ (which reduces the quantity dynamics to a multiplier dynamics basically). However, these reduced dynamics have been proved there to exhibit a locally asymptotically interior steady state under the conditions stated in the above proposition 4.2. Finally, the Jacobian J of the dynamics (4.33)–(4.38) at the steady state is obtained from the Jacobian $\bar{J}$ of the reduced dynamics (4.33)–(4.37) by the addition of the column $(0,0,0,0,0,J_{66})$, and of course a sixth row which also exhibits the entry J_{66}, which moreover is easily shown to be negative. Therefore, the real parts of the eigenvalues of J are all negative if and only if the real parts of the eigenvalues of $\bar{J}$ fulfill this condition. This proves the assertion and it also implies that the assertions (made in Chiarella and Flaschel (1999b, Ch.6)) on the Kaldor-Tobin type dynamics will hold true for the dynamics (4.33)–(4.38) as well, as long as $\beta_n = 0$ is given.
∎

Proposition 4.3

The 6 dimensional dynamical system (4.33)–(4.38) is locally asymptotically stable at the above steady state if the parameters $h_2, \beta_{\pi_1^e}, \beta_p, \beta_w, \beta_n$ *are all sufficiently small and the parameter* β_{y^e} *sufficiently large.*

Proof: Assuming β_n sufficiently small implies that the real parts of the eigenvalues of the Jacobian J considered in the preceding proof must all be negative, since these real parts depend continuously on the parameters of the model. ∎

Proposition 4.4

Consider the Jacobian J of the dynamical system (4.33)–(4.38) at the steady state. The determinant of this $6\star 6$*-matrix* $\det J$*, is always positive. The system can therefore lose or gain asymptotic stability by way of Hopf-bifurcations solely (if eigenvalues cross the imaginary axis with positive speed).*

Proof: The dynamics of the present 6D KMG model are of the same mathematical type as the Keynes-Metzler dynamics considered in Chiarella and Flaschel (1999b, Ch.6), since the addition of wage taxation and Harrod neutral technical change have not changed the mathematical form of the equations compared to the Keynes-Metzler model type. The assertion of proposition 4.4 therefore follows immediately from proposition 6.4 in Chiarella and Flaschel (1999b, Ch.6). ∎

Experience with the KMG model type obtained in Chiarella and Flaschel (1999b, Ch.6) with respect to the basically identical model of Keynes-Metzler type suggests that Hopf-bifurcations (leading to unstable steady states) will occur when the speeds of adjustments $\beta_n, \beta_{\pi^e}, \beta_p$ or β_w are increased and if the parameter h_2 is made large enough. Concerning β_{y^e} the system will lose stability by way of a Hopf-bifurcation if β_n is given as sufficiently large and β_{y^e} made sufficiently small. There are, of course, many further possibilities of these types concerning the other parameters of the dynamics. All these situations can be tested numerically in the various ways we have summarized in part I of the book, in particular by means of eigenvalue diagrams and bifurcation diagrams.

We have obtained in this section the fundamental insight that the KMG dynamics will imply convergence to the steady state in cases of a sluggish adjustment of prices, quantities and adaptive inflationary expectations, supported by a fast adjustment of sales expectations (the dynamic multiplier effect) and a Keynes-effect that is sufficiently strong (h_2 small). Furthermore, there exist definite ways in which the system will lose this convergence property in a cyclical fashion thereby providing the basis for the theory of the business cycle by means of endogenously generated fluctuations. Integrated disequilibrium growth models of KMG type, which due to their high dimensionality exhibit already considerable complexity, therefore imply in a convincing way fundamental results as they are intuitively expected to emerge from such model types. Of course, the obtained results only represent the beginning of a detailed analysis of KMG growth theory. This topic is extended in the following section by adding endogenously generated growth to this model type before the attempt is made to do the same for the flex-price approach, the neoclassical border case of the KMG model type considered in this and the following section.

4.3 Substitution and endogenous technical change

We now extend the model of the preceding section further and include smooth factor substitution as well as endogenous technical change and growth into its equations in order to show that these two typical ingredients of the neoclassical theory of economic growth again do not alter the structure of the basic KMG approach to economic growth in a significant way concerning its origin in the Keynesian theory of IS-LM growth.

There exist various possibilities in the literature to model endogenous technical change starting from neoclassical production functions with no technical change included, see Barro and Sala-i-Martin (1995), Aghion and Howitt (1998), Schneider and Ziesemer (1994) for examples. We here follow Barro and Sala-i-Martin (1995, Ch.4) and use as representation of such technical change an approach based on Uzawa (1965) and Romer (1986), synthesized by Lucas (1988), called the URL approach in the following. Other representations of endogenous change will not significantly alter the conclusions of this section which therefore serves the purpose of illustrating the implications of an integration of the production of technological change into the KMG model of the preceding section.

The URL approach to endogenous technical change is generally presented by means of the following two equations, characterizing the productive activities of firms:

$$\dot{A} = \eta L_2^d / L^d A, \quad \eta > 0, \quad \text{the research unit,} \tag{4.39}$$
$$Y = K^\beta (A L_1^d)^{1-\beta} A^\xi, \quad \xi > 0, \quad \text{the production unit.} \tag{4.40}$$

The activities of the employed workforce $L^d = L_1^d + L_2^d$ are here split between the production of output (4.40), based on the employment L_1^d, here described by means of a Cobb-Douglas production function augmented by the productivity measure A and further augmented by the Romer externality A^ξ, and the production of labor productivity growth as described by equation (4.39), which assumes that the growth rate of the productivity measure A inside the Cobb-Douglas production function is proportional to the ratio between workers employed in the research unit and workers employed in the production unit. The production of productivity growth by the individual firms furthermore has an additional effect on aggregate productivity growth as measured by the Romer externality A^ξ in the equation (4.40).

The production function (4.40) is easily reformulated as follows:

$$Y = K^\beta (A^{\frac{1-\beta+\xi}{1-\beta}} L_1^d)^{1-\beta} = K^\beta (n_l L_1^d)^{1-\beta}$$

and shows in this way that it is of the usual type (Harrod neutral technical change in the presence of smooth factor substitution), yet with a growth rate $\hat{n}_l$ of aggregate labor productivity n_l that exceeds the growth rate $\hat{A}$ produced by the firms (due to the Romer externality): $\hat{n}_l = (1+\xi/(1-\beta))\hat{A}$. This approach to the production of technological change is considered in detail in Barro and Sala-i-Martin (1995, Ch.4). We will reformulate this approach here for a general neoclassical production with the usual properties.

The equations of the extended KMG model with smooth factor substitution are:

1. <u>Definitions (remunerations and wealth):</u>

$$u = \omega/x = wL^d/(pY), \quad \rho^e = (Y^e - \delta K - \omega L^d)/K \tag{4.41}$$

$$
\begin{array}{rcll}
W & = & (M + B + p_e E)/p, \ \ p_b = 1 & (4.42) \\
 & & & (4.43) \\
 & 2. & \underline{\text{Households (workers and asset-holders):}} & \\
W & = & (M^d + B^d + p_e E^d)/p, \ M^d = h_1 pY + h_2 pK(r_o - r) & (4.44) \\
C & = & \omega L^d - T_w + (1 - s_c)[\rho^e K + rB/p - T_c] & (4.45) \\
S_p & = & Y^e - \delta K + rB/p - T_w - T_c - C = s_c[\rho^e K + rB/p - T_c] & \\
 & = & (\dot{M}^d + \dot{B}^d + p_e \dot{E}^d)/p & (4.46) \\
\hat{L} & = & n = \text{const} & (4.47) \\
 & 3. & \underline{\text{Firms (production-units and investors):}} & \\
L_1^p & \text{det'd} & \text{via} \quad \omega = F_L(K, \exp(n_l t)L) & (4.48) \\
Y^p & = & F(K, \exp(n_l t)L_1^p), \ \ U_c = Y/Y^p = y/y^p, \ \ y = Y/K & (4.49) \\
L_1^d & \text{det'd} & \text{via} \quad Y = F(K, \exp(n_l t)L_1^d), \ \ V_1 = L_1^d/L & (4.50) \\
n_l & = & \hat{A}(1 + \xi), \quad \hat{A} = \eta L_2^d/L^d = \eta h & (4.51) \\
L^d & = & L_1^d + L_2^d, \quad V = L^d/L & (4.52) \\
I & = & i_1(\rho^e - (r - \pi^e))K + i_2(U_c - \bar{U}_c)K + \gamma K, \ \gamma = n + n_l & (4.53) \\
S_f & = & Y_f = Y - Y^e = \mathcal{I} & (4.54) \\
\Delta Y^e & = & Y^e - \delta K - C - I - G = Y^e - Y^d & (4.55) \\
p_e \dot{E}/p & = & I + \Delta Y^e = I + (\dot{N} - \mathcal{I}) & (4.56) \\
I^a & = & I + \dot{N} = I + \mathcal{I} + \Delta Y^e = I^p + \Delta Y^e = p_e \dot{E}/p + \mathcal{I} & (4.57) \\
\hat{K} & = & I/K & (4.58) \\
 & 4. & \underline{\text{Government (fiscal and monetary authority):}} & \\
T & = & T_w + T_c, \ T_w = \tau_w \omega L^d, \ T_c \ \text{s.t.} \ t_c^n = \dfrac{T_c - rB/p}{K} = \text{const} & (4.59) \\
G & = & T_w + gK, \quad g = const & (4.60) \\
S_g & = & T - rB/p - G \ \ [= -(\dot{M} + \dot{B})/p \ \text{see (4.63)}] & (4.61) \\
M & = & \bar{\mu} & (4.62) \\
\dot{B} & = & pG + rB - pT - \dot{M} & (4.63) \\
 & 5. & \underline{\text{Equilibrium conditions (asset-markets):}} & \\
M & = & M^d = h_1 pY + h_2 pK(r_o - r), \quad [B = B^d, E = E^d] & (4.64) \\
r & = & \dfrac{\rho^e pK + \dot{p}_e E}{p_e E} & (4.65) \\
\dot{M} & = & \dot{M}^d, \ \dot{B} = \dot{B}^d \quad [\dot{E} = \dot{E}^d] & (4.66) \\
 & 6. & \underline{\text{Disequilibrium situation (goods-market adjustments):}} & \\
S & = & S_p + S_g + S_f = p_e \dot{E}^d/p + \mathcal{I} = I + \dot{N} = I^a = p_e \dot{E}/p + \mathcal{I} & (4.67) \\
Y^d & = & C + I + \delta K + G & (4.68) \\
N^d & = & \beta_{n^d} Y^e & (4.69) \\
\mathcal{I} & = & \beta_n(N^d - N) + \gamma N^d, \ \gamma = n + n_l & (4.70) \\
Y & = & Y^e + \mathcal{I} & (4.71)
\end{array}
$$

$$\begin{array}{rcll}
\dot{Y}^e & = & \beta_{y^e}(Y^d - Y^e) + \gamma Y^e,\ \gamma = n + n_l & (4.72)\\
\dot{N} & = & Y - Y^d = S - I \qquad [S - I^p = Y^e - Y^d] & (4.73)\\
 & 7. & \underline{\text{Wage-Price-Sector (adjustment equations):}} & \\
\hat{w} & = & \beta_w(V - \bar{V}) + \kappa_w(\hat{p} + n_l) + (1 - \kappa_w)(\pi^e + n_l) & (4.74)\\
\hat{p} & = & \beta_p(U_c - \bar{U}_c) + \kappa_p(\hat{w} - n_l) + (1 - \kappa_p)\pi^e & (4.75)\\
\dot{\pi}^e & = & \beta_{\pi_1^e}(\hat{p} - \pi^e) + \beta_{\pi_2^e}(\bar{\mu} - \gamma - \pi^e),\ \gamma = n + n_l. & (4.76)
\end{array}$$

Up to the inclusion of smooth factor substitution this KMG model is of the same type as the one considered in the preceding section as long as h, η, ξ, characterizing the production of technical change on the individual as well as on the aggregate level, are given magnitudes. This is easily obtained from the expressions

$$V = V_1/(1-h), \quad V_1 = L_1^d/L = y/(x_o l^e), \quad n_l = \eta h(1+\xi)$$

and by inserting these expressions into (4.33) – (4.38). Due to this straightforward equivalence we shall consider below the case of fixed proportions in production first. The case of smooth factor substitution is then considered briefly at the end of this section in combination with URL technical change and in the further sections of this chapter without endogenous technical change, which as we show below is not essential for the understanding of the dynamics of KMG growth in disequilibrium as well as in equilibrium. In the case of fixed proportions in production, the URL approach is to be represented by:

$$\begin{array}{rcl}
\hat{A} & = & \eta L_2^d/L^d, \quad \eta > 0\\
Y & = & \min\{y^p K, A L_1^d A^\xi\} = \min\{y^p K, A^{1+\xi} L_1^d\} = \min\{y^p K, x L_1^d\}
\end{array}$$

which then gives rise to the following dynamical system (with fixed proportions in production in the place smooth factor substitution). For notational simplicity we again renormalize $\bar{V}, \bar{U}_c$ by 1.

$$\begin{array}{rcll}
\widehat{u} & = & \kappa[(1-\kappa_p)\beta_w(\frac{y}{x_o l^e(1-h)} - 1) + (\kappa_w - 1)\beta_p(\frac{y}{y^p} - 1)] & (4.77)\\
\widehat{l^e} & = & -(i_1(\rho^e - (r - \pi^e)) + i_2(\frac{y}{y^p} - 1)) & (4.78)\\
\widehat{m} & = & \bar{\mu} - \pi^e - (n + \eta h(1+\xi)) - \kappa[\beta_p(\frac{y}{y^p} - 1) + \kappa_p\beta_w(\frac{y}{x_o l^e(1-h)} - 1)] + \widehat{l^e} & (4.79)\\
\dot{\pi}^e & = & \beta_{\pi_1^e}\kappa[\beta_p(\frac{y}{y^p} - 1) + \kappa_p\beta_w(\frac{y}{x_o l^e(1-h)} - 1)] + \beta_{\pi_2^e}(\bar{\mu} - n - \eta h(1+\xi)) - \pi^e) & \\
 & & & (4.80)\\
\dot{y}^e & = & \beta_{y^e}(y^d - y^e) + \widehat{l^e} y^e & (4.81)\\
\dot{\nu} & = & y - y^d + (\widehat{l^e} - (n + \eta h(1+\xi)))\nu & (4.82)
\end{array}$$

with:

$$\begin{array}{rcl}
y & = & \beta_n(\beta_{n^d} y^e - \nu) + (1 + (n + \eta h(1+\xi))\beta_{n^d}) y^e\\
y^d & = & uy + (1 - s_c)(\rho^e - t_c^n) + i_1(\rho^e - (r - \pi^e)) + i_2(\frac{y}{y^p} - 1) + n + \eta h(1+\xi) + \delta + g\\
\rho^e & = & y^e - \delta - uy, \quad r = r_0 + (h_1 y - m)/h_2.
\end{array}$$

In view of these equations it is obvious that this dynamical system is mathematically of the same type as the one of section 4.2, since $n_l = \eta h(1+\xi)$ is then a given magnitude. The model is thus again closer to reality without any change in the analytical difficulties of its mathematical treatment and without change in the propositions stated and proved in the preceding section. The *unique interior steady–state* configuration of the dynamics (4.77) – (4.82) (with $u_0, l_0, m_0 \neq 0$) in particular reads as before and thus needs not be repeated here.

Labor productivity x of the fixed propositions case of section 4.2 is however now based on the relationship

$$x = A^{1+\xi}, \ i.e., \ n_l = \hat{x} = (1+\xi)\hat{A} = (1+\xi)\eta h,$$

with $h = L_2^d/L^d$ the proportion of employed workers devoted to the production of technological change. The next natural step of course is to allow for variations of the ratio h and thus for varying labor productivity growth in the place of the so far given growth rate n_l.

In order to allow, in a first step towards endogenous technical change, for a simple formulation of h-changes we assume that the growth term γ in investment demand, inventory adjustments and sales expectations[4] is no longer given by $n + n_l$, which now becomes an endogenously determined magnitude, but given independently from this expression as the exogenous long-run demand growth expectations of firms. On the basis of this distinction between $\gamma, n + n_l$ we then assume as law of motion for the labor allocation ratio h of firms:

$$\dot{h} \ = \ \beta_{h_1}((\gamma - \hat{x}) - n) + \beta_{h_2}(V-1), \ V = L^d/L, \hat{x} = (1+\xi)\eta h$$

where we interpret the expression $\gamma - \hat{x}$ as trend growth rate of labor demand, viewed by firms to come about on the basis of their investment decisions and their produced productivity increases, contrasted with the growth rate of labor supply available to fill this gap between capital stock and productivity growth. Firms therefore increase their efforts in raising labor productivity in the case of insufficient growth in the labor supply and vice versa. Furthermore the state of the labor market itself should also matter here, since it signals how much buffer is available should for example the trend growth in labor demand exceed the growth rate of labor supply, where tight labor markets of course will induce firms to more increases in h and thus $\hat{x}$ than is the case in the opposite situation.

Similarly, we assume for n, the growth rate of labor supply, to be motivated from the perspective of the potential workforce, as law of motion:

$$\dot{n} \ = \ \beta_{n_1}((\gamma - \hat{x}) - n) + \beta_{n_2}(V-1), \ V = L^d/L, \hat{x} = (1+\xi)\eta h$$

where we again interpret the expression $\gamma - \hat{x}$ as trend growth rate of labor demand now influencing the decision of potential workers to join or leave the actual workforce. The state of the labor market should again play a role here, since it signals how much competition the new entrants into the labor markets have to face. We basically assume by this equation that their exists, besides the active component in the labor market, also a latent part of people attracted by the labor market in good times, and repelled from the labor market in bad times, returning to some sort of subsistence sector in such situations. It is not difficult to see that actual market economies are surrounded by such a latent labor supply ranging

[4] And also in the forward looking component of inflationary expectations, see eqns. (4.53), (4.70), (4.72), (4.76).

from migration and return migration from and to subsistence economies to segments of the potential workforce concerning students, housewives, pensioners, etc. The above only postulates that the growth rate of labor supply responds to the conditions that prevail or will prevail in the future on the labor market, maybe in a next step in an asymmetric way, since strong increases in periods of lasting expansions are easier to monitor than decreases in lasting states of depressions.

In the steady state we must of course have again

$$\gamma = n + n_l = n + (1+\xi)\eta h, \quad \xi, \eta \text{ given magnitudes}$$

which means that the two rates n, n_l must in sum adjust to the given trend growth assumed for the investment behavior of firms. We thus have endogenous growth in the model as far as labor productivity and labor supply growth is concerned, but not yet endogenous output growth (which would demand for an endogenization of the term γ).

$$\begin{aligned}
\widehat{u} &= \kappa[(1-\kappa_p)\beta_w(\frac{y}{x_o l^e(1-h)}-1)+(\kappa_w-1)\beta_p(\frac{y}{y^p}-1)] && (4.83)\\
\widehat{l^e} &= n+\eta h(1+\xi)-(i_1(\rho^e-(r-\pi^e))+i_2(\frac{y}{y^p}-1))-\gamma && (4.84)\\
\widehat{m} &= \bar{\mu}-(\pi^e+\kappa[\beta_p(\frac{y}{y^p}-1)+\kappa_p\beta_w(\frac{y}{x_o l^e(1-h)}-1)]) \\
&- (i_1(\rho^e-(r-\pi^e))+i_2(\frac{y}{y^p}-1)+\gamma) && (4.85)\\
\dot{\pi}^e &= \beta_{\pi_1^e}\kappa[\beta_p(\frac{y}{y^p}-1)+\kappa_p\beta_w(\frac{y}{x_o l^e(1-h)}-1)]+\beta_{\pi_2^e}(\bar{\mu}-\gamma-\pi^e) && (4.86)\\
\dot{y}^e &= \beta_{y^e}(y^d-y^e)-(i_1(\rho^e-(r-\pi^e))+i_2(\frac{y}{y^p}-1))y^e && (4.87)\\
\dot{\nu} &= y-y^d-(i_1(\rho^e-(r-\pi^e))+i_2(\frac{y}{y^p}-1)+\gamma)\nu && (4.88)\\
\dot{h} &= \beta_{h_1}(\gamma-\eta h(1+\xi)-n)+\beta_{h_2}(\frac{y}{x_o l^e(1-h)}-1) && (4.89)\\
\dot{n} &= \beta_{n_1}(\gamma-\eta h(1+\xi)-n)+\beta_{n_2}(\frac{y}{x_o l^e(1-h)}-1) && (4.90)
\end{aligned}$$

with :

$$\begin{aligned}
y &= \beta_n(\beta_{n^d}y^e-\nu)+(1+\gamma\beta_{n^d})y^e\\
y^d &= uy+(1-s_c)(\rho^e-t_c^n)+i_1(\rho^e-(r-\pi^e))+i_2(\frac{y}{y^p}-1)+\gamma+\delta+g\\
\rho^e &= y^e-\delta-uy, \quad r = r_0+(h_1 y-m)/h_2
\end{aligned}$$

The first impression is that the dynamics have become considerably more complex by the addition of endogenous technical change, generated by part of the workforce of firms, and by the law of motion assumed for the ratio h, despite the fact that the wage price block gives rise to the same formal expressions as in the case of no technical change. A second look however reveals that the state variable h, though it enters the initially considered dynamical system in various places, does so only via $V, \hat{x}$ and ρ^e while the state variable n only affects the law of motion for l^e. Furthermore, the rate of employment V is the only variable of the initial dynamical system that affects the new dynamical laws for h, n.

The interior steady state solution for the above dynamics is no longer uniquely determined, since the Jacobian at the steady state of the full 8D dynamics cannot have rank 8, due to the fact that an appropriate combination of the expressions on the right hand side of the shown dynamics sum to zero. This steady state solution is given by the following equations:

$$y_0 = y^p, \ l_{10}^{de} = y_0, \ l_0^e = l_0^{de} = l_{10}^{de}/(1-h_0) \tag{4.91}$$

$$y_0^e = y_0^d = y_0/(1+\gamma\beta_{n^d}), \quad \gamma = n_o + \hat{x}_o = n_o + (1+\xi)\eta h_0 \tag{4.92}$$

$$m_0 = h_1 y_0, \ \pi_0^e = \mu - i_o, \quad r_0 = \rho_0^e + \pi_o^e, \quad \nu_0 = \beta_{n^d} y_0^e \tag{4.93}$$

$$\rho_0^e = t_c^n + \frac{\gamma + g - t_c^n}{s_c}, \quad \omega_0 = \frac{y_o^e - \delta - \rho_o^e}{l_o^d} \tag{4.94}$$

which is a system of equations with one degree of freedom implying that the variable $h_o \in (0,1)$ can be chosen arbitrarily.

An important new result here is what we would like to call the productivity paradox (related to the savings paradox of the simple IS analysis of goods market equilibrium). This paradox is based on the fact that policies that attempt to increase the Romer externality ξ may reduce the rate of productivity increases $\hat{A}$ that firms produce, without any change of aggregate productivity, and are then doomed to failure. This is of course caused by the given trend term γ that fixes output growth in the steady state, similar to the role played by a given level of investment in the formulation of the savings paradox of IS analysis. Note that the productivity paradox will arise by necessity if the natural rate n is a given magnitude in which case h and the interior steady state are again uniquely determined, due to the formula that relates γ, h, n in the steady state.[5]

Closer inspection of the laws of motion that make up the above 8D dynamical system reveals that there is indeed a basic possibility by which the original 6D dynamics of section 4.2 can be regained, at least from the mathematical point of view, though now of course with a different interpretation of the state variable l^e in particular. This situation is obtained when one assumes $\beta_{n1} = \infty$ implying $n = \gamma - \hat{x}$, i.e., labor force growth is adjusted with infinite speed to the gap between trend capital stock growth and productivity growth at all points in time, coupled with the assumption $\beta_{h_2} = 0$, i.e., firms do not alter their labor force composition in response to fluctuating states of the labor market. In this case we have that any given ratio of research employment h will not be altered by firms during the evolution of the dynamics of the model. Since h is constant in this case and $\gamma = n + \eta(1+\xi)h$ we have reduced the dynamics again to (4.77) – (4.82) and thus to the one considered in the preceding section, whose propositions then again apply. Let us therefore next consider the case where $\beta_{h_2} > 0$ holds (supplemented by $\beta_{n1} = \infty$ still). We then have as laws of motion of the system:

[5] The $\dot{h}$-dynamic is then no longer a linear combination of the other dynamic equations.

$$\widehat{u} = \kappa[(1-\kappa_p)\beta_w(\frac{y}{x_o l^e(1-h)} - 1) + (\kappa_w - 1)\beta_p(\frac{y}{y^p} - 1)] \tag{4.95}$$

$$\widehat{l^e} = -(i_1(\rho^e - (r - \pi^e)) + i_2(\frac{y}{y^p} - 1)) \tag{4.96}$$

$$\begin{aligned} \widehat{m} &= \bar{\mu} - (\pi^e + \kappa[\beta_p(\frac{y}{y^p} - 1) + \kappa_p\beta_w(\frac{y}{x_o l^e(1-h)} - 1)]) \\ &- (i_1(\rho^e - (r - \pi^e)) + i_2(\frac{y}{y^p} - 1) + \gamma) \end{aligned} \tag{4.97}$$

$$\dot{\pi}^e = \beta_{\pi_1^e}\kappa[\beta_p(\frac{y}{y^p} - 1) + \kappa_p\beta_w(\frac{y}{x_o l^e(1-h)} - 1)] + \beta_{\pi_2^e}(\bar{\mu} - \gamma - \pi^e) \tag{4.98}$$

$$\dot{y}^e = \beta_{y^e}(y^d - y^e) - (i_1(\rho^e - (r - \pi^e)) + i_2(\frac{y}{y^p} - 1))y^e \tag{4.99}$$

$$\dot{\nu} = y - y^d - (i_1(\rho^e - (r - \pi^e)) + i_2(\frac{y}{y^p} - 1) + \gamma)\nu \tag{4.100}$$

$$\dot{h} = \beta_{h_2}(\frac{y}{x_o l^e(1-h)} - 1) \tag{4.101}$$

with:

$$\begin{aligned} y &= \beta_n(\beta_{n^d}y^e - \nu) + (1 + \gamma\beta_{n^d})y^e \\ y^d &= uy + (1 - s_c)(\rho^e - t_c^n) + i_1(\rho^e - (r - \pi^e)) + i_2(\frac{y}{y^p} - 1) + \gamma + \delta + g \\ \rho^e &= y^e - \delta - uy, \quad r = r_0 + (h_1 y - m)/h_2. \end{aligned}$$

Note with respect to these dynamics that the variable h, but not the resulting productivity growth rate $\hat{x}$, here feeds back into the rest of the dynamics. We thus have endogenous productivity change, but not yet endogenous growth in the considered economy. With respect to this intermediate situation between section 4.2 and the full 8D dynamics with sluggishly adjusting labor supply growth we now prove the following propositions:

Proposition 4.5

> *There is an interval of* interior steady–state solutions *or point of rests of the dynamics (4.95)–(4.100) which is given by the expressions (4.91) – (4.94) parameterized by an arbitrary choice of* $h \in (0,1)$.

This proposition follows directly from (4.91) – (4.94) by observing again that the state variable h can be chosen there in an arbitrary way, in order to determine the steady state values of $l^e = l^{de}, n$ and $\hat{x}$, on which the other steady state solutions do not depend. Should there be convergence to steady states it will be a path-dependent one, where history and shocks do matter.

Proposition 4.6

> *This steady–state is locally asymptotically stable for all adjustment speeds* β_{h_2} *and parameter values* η *chosen sufficiently low in all cases where the 6D sub-dynamics of section 4.2 (and its immediate generalizations of this section) are locally asymptotically stable.*

Sufficiently sluggish wage, price and inflationary expectations adjustments coupled with fast sales expectations and a weak inventory accelerator mechanism, now also combined with slow technical change and slow shifts of employment between the production and research units of firms, will therefore be favorable for local asymptotic stability. Note however that such stability assertions are here coupled with the situation of shock dependent convergence towards a continuum of steady states as the attractors of the dynamics. A further analytical treatment of proposition 4.6 would derive a static functional relationship, as in de Klundert and Schaik (1990), between h and other state variables of the system on the basis of which the variable h can be removed by substitution from the remaining dynamics.

Proposition 4.7

Consider the Jacobian J of the dynamics (4.95)–(4.100) at the steady state. The determinant of this $7 \star 7$-matrix, $\det J$, is always zero, while the upper $6 \star 6$ principal minor is always positive (as in the 6D case of the preceding section). It follows that the system can only lose or gain asymptotic stability by way of a Hopf-bifurcation (if eigenvalues cross the imaginary axis with positive speed).

Note for the considered situation that one eigenvalue must always be equal to zero here, while no further eigenvalue can become zero in addition. Loss of stability therefore always takes place by the occurrence of two purely imaginary eigenvalues when the bifurcation value is reached. As before we get close to this situation either shrinking unstable limit cycles before the bifurcation point is reached or stable expanding ones after it has been passed.

Proposition 4.8

The system will lose its local asymptotic stability if β_{h_2} is made sufficiently large.

This proposition is proved in the same way as related ones for the system without endogenous technical change by showing that the parameter β_{h_2} appears in the trace of the Jacobian J of the dynamics at the steady state only once and there with a positive coefficient (due to the law of motion $\dot{h} = \beta_{h_2}(\frac{y}{x_o l^e(1-h)} - 1$ for the ratio h) which can be made arbitrarily large by means of the parameter β_{h_2} without change in the other elements in the trace of J.

The proofs for propositions 4.5 – 4.8 are thus not difficult to provide, since they are closely related to the ones for the propositions of section 4.2. We add here that there is again a linear combination of the expressions on the right hand side of (4.95)–(4.100) which adds to zero, while the assertion on the $6 \star 6$ subdeterminant that belongs to the originally 6D dynamics is obtained as in Chiarella and Flaschel (1999b, Ch.6). Choosing $\beta_{h_2}, \eta = 0$ gives the dynamics of the preceding section, which when asymptotically stable (only negative real parts of the eigenvalues of the Jacobian of this system) remains asymptotically stable (now with one zero eigenvalue and thus zero root hysteresis) for small variations of the parameters $\beta_{h_2}, \eta = 0$, since eigenvalues depend continuously on the parameters of the system.

We thus in sum have that the attractors of the dynamics (4.95)–(4.100) are shock dependent, including the stable limit cycles that may be generated by the asserted existence of

Hopf bifurcations, which means that the rate of productivity change of the economy will depend on average or in the limit on the history of the evolution of this economy. We stress however once again that the steady growth rate of output is still given exogenously in the present approach to disequilibrium growth which therefore does not yet contribute to an endogenous explanation of observed growth rate differences in the world economy, but does this only for observed productivity growth differentials.

We now add smooth factor substitution to the model and see that this modifies the considered dynamical model significantly. The parameter y^p of the model with fixed proportions in production becomes an endogenous magnitude of the model then, due to the following standard implications of the production block in module 3. of the model (4.41) – (4.76), representing in intensive form the production decisions of firms in the case of substitution:

$$\begin{aligned}
\omega^e &= F_2(1, l_1^{pe}) = f'(l_1^{pe}), \quad l_1^{pe} = \exp(n_l t)L_1^p/K, \; \omega^e = \omega/\exp(n_l t)\\
y^p &= F(1, l_1^{pe}) = f(l_1^{pe}) = f((f')^{-1}(\omega^e))\\
y &= F(1, l_1^{de}) = f(l_1^{de}), \; i.e., \; l_1^{de} = f^{-1}(y), \quad l_1^{de} = \exp(n_l t)L_1^d/K.
\end{aligned}$$

We denote in these equations by F_2 the second partial derivative of the function F, while F_L was used in block 3. to denote the derivative of the composed function $F(K, \exp(n_l t)L_1^d)$ with respect to the variable L_1^d. Note also that we represent in the above equations by f the production function in intensive form, here reduced to efficiency unit expressions in addition. Note finally that we use ω^e, the real wage in terms of efficiency units, in the place of u, the wage share, in the representation of the 6D core dynamics of the model. These equations now replace the expressions $l_1^{de} = y/x_o$ and $y^p = const$ of the fixed proportions case. The dynamical equations thus read in the case of substitution, here for simplicity with given parameters $n, n_l, \gamma = n + n_l, h$ (and thus no laws of motion for n, h):

$$\begin{aligned}
\widehat{\omega}^e &= \kappa[(1-\kappa_p)\beta_w(V-1) + (\kappa_w - 1)\beta_p(U_c - 1)] && (4.102)\\
\widehat{l}^e &= -(i_1(\rho^e - (r - \pi^e)) + i_2(U_c - 1)) && (4.103)\\
\widehat{m} &= \bar{\mu} - (\pi^e + \kappa[\beta_p(U_c - 1) + \kappa_p\beta_w(V-1)]) && (4.104)\\
&- (i_1(\rho^e - (r - \pi^e)) + i_2(U_c - 1) + \gamma) && (4.105)\\
\dot{\pi}^e &= \beta_{\pi_1^e}\kappa[\beta_p(U_c - 1) + \kappa_p\beta_w(V-1)] + \beta_{\pi_2^e}(\bar{\mu} - \gamma - \pi^e) && (4.106)\\
\dot{y}^e &= \beta_{y^e}(y^d - y^e) - (i_1(\rho^e - (r - \pi^e)) + i_2(U_c - 1))y^e && (4.107)\\
\dot{\nu} &= y - y^d - (i_1(\rho^e - (r - \pi^e)) + i_2(U_c - 1) + \gamma)\nu && (4.108)
\end{aligned}$$

with:

$$\begin{aligned}
y &= \beta_n(\beta_{n^d} y^e - \nu) + (1 + \gamma\beta_{n^d})y^e\\
y^d &= \omega^e f^{-1}(y) + (1 - s_c)(\rho^e - t_c^n)\\
&+ i_1(\rho^e - (r - \pi^e)) + i_2(U_c - 1) + \gamma + \delta + g\\
\rho^e &= y^e - \delta - \omega^e f^{-1}(y), \quad r = r_0 + (h_1 y - m)/h_2\\
V &= \frac{f^{-1}(y)}{l^e(1-h)}, \quad U_c = \frac{y}{f((f')^{-1}(\omega^e))}.
\end{aligned}$$

As the system is represented we can easily see that its crucial difference from the various 6D dynamics considered in this and the preceding section is given by the term $U_c = \frac{y}{f((f')^{-1}(\omega^e))}$, since the other change $V = \frac{f^{-1}(y)}{l^e(1-h)}$ solely replaces a linear relationship by a nonlinear one which does not matter with respect to local stability analysis. We here only assert, but do not prove that propositions 4.2 – 4.4 of the preceding section also apply to the above dynamical system, whose unique interior steady state is determined as in Chiarella and Flaschel (1999b, Ch.5), see also the next section for its presentation in the case of no productivity growth ($h = 0$) and no inventory adjustment mechanism.

The proofs of the assertion 4.2 – 4.4 for smooth factor substitution follow the methodology applied in the preceding section in the case of fixed propositions in production. The Routh-Hurwitz conditions for local asymptotic stability of the interior steady state of the dynamics are thereby shown to apply for an appropriately chosen subdynamics (with the state variables l^e, m, y^e), while appropriate (small) extensions of this core dynamics to 4D, 5D, and the 6D case guarantee that real parts of the original eigenvalues remain negative and that the new ones must be negative due the signs of determinants obtained by these extensions. We thus again find that the core KMG dynamics considered in the preceding section already provides a good representation of what happens when endogenous technical change and now substitution are added to the model.

However, we do not go into a unifying discussion here, when endogenous h and endogenous n are coupled with smooth factor substitution. In this general case the full 8D dynamics (4.83) – (4.90) has to be treated, augmented by the two nonlinearities introduced by substitution into the expressions V, U_c as shown above. On the basis of what has been presented in sections 4.2 and 4.3 it is however not implausible that we will get through this most general case a dynamical system that marries the stability assertions of propositions 4.3, 4.4 with those provided by propositions 4.6 – 4.8. We thereby get that the KMG dynamics with and without endogenous technical change and neoclassical smooth factor substitution has intuitively appealing properties from a Keynesian perspective with respect to stability, business fluctuations and growth in a monetary economy. These properties will now be contrasted with the special KMG dynamics that comes about when perfect market clearing is assumed on all markets of the economy, and even more when combined with perfect inflationary expectations. Since technical change, of exogenous or endogenous type, did not significantly modify the results achieved in sections 4.2 and 4.3, we will abstract from it again in the following sections, which however have to make use of smooth factor substitution besides the other flexibilities already mentioned in order to provide a proper starting point for an analysis of the dynamics of models of monetary growth and fluctuations of Walrasian type.

4.4 Market clearing: Classical real and dichotomizing nominal dynamics?

In this section we investigate the KMG model of the preceding sections, with smooth factor substitution (but no technical change), now for fully flexible price levels (wage, price, interest) by which all markets are assumed to clear instantaneously. We want to investigate how the model of section 4.2 is modified in such a limiting situation and what the static and dynamic consequences of such an ideal behavior of the economy are. Our findings will be that the real dynamics then become independent of the nominal dynamics and of a radically simplified Solovian type, while the theory of inflation becomes a very indirect and complicated one, based on IS-LM equilibrium that is completely separated from the real dynamics. Instead of interacting sluggish price - quantity adjustment processes and their high order real and nominal dynamic interaction we here get a dynamical system of dimension 2 that is dichotomizing and basically trivial to analyze from the mathematical point of view, with a nominal and static part that is based, from the economic perspective, on complicated expressions for the level of prices and the resulting rate of inflation. These findings should raise doubts on whether perfect price and wage flexibilities are really meaningful assumptions on the macroeconomic level, where interdependence of aggregate prices and quantities should be investigated from the viewpoint of real economic structures and their evolution.

The obtained special model of KMG equilibrium growth is developed further towards a Walrasian representation of the macroeconomy in section 4.5 where we combine perfect market clearing with basic Walrasian demand and supply functions of flexprice macroeconomic model building, there with heterogeneous agents and heterogeneous expectations, the joint occurrence of adaptive expectations and myopic perfect foresight, considered separately in the present section. This Walrasian reformulation of the statics and the dynamics of KMG equilibrium growth with two representative agents makes the theory of inflation more transparent, but basically confirms the results of section 4.4 on nominal instabilities, now in a framework that is no longer dichotomizing. Since the price level is considered a statically endogenous variable in such models, the observed local saddle point instability is reinterpreted as saddle point stability by the application of the so-called jump variable technique. Our findings are that the obtained representation of real-nominal interaction is again not a convincing approach to the modeling of macroeconomic interdependence of labor, goods and money markets.

In section 4.6 we therefore present a third approach to monetary growth in equilibrium of which the just considered one is a limit case. We radically simplify here the theory of inflation by basing it on firms' behavior in a simple dynamic way leaving no room for price level jumps by assumption. Local stability remains a critical issue however also in this approach to equilibrium growth. Yet, due to the clear separation into statically and dynamically endogenous variables in this section one can argue that nonlinearity and boundedness of the dynamics are the crucial issues and questions to be addressed in cases of local explosiveness. Such global boundedness (in a classical world) is briefly considered in the closing section of this chapter.

To ease the presentation and the analysis of KMG growth with general equilibrium on all markets we assume in the remainder of this chapter that $\mu = n = const$ holds, so that there is no inflation or deflation in the steady state of the model. This allows us to use the price level as a state variable in the dynamic analysis of the model and the rate of inflation in the place of the law of motion for real balances per unit of capital we have employed so far. Assuming full equilibrium obtained from setting $\beta_w, \beta_p = \infty$, and since there is no need to discuss an inventory adjustment mechanism in such a situation, we get as border case of the KMG model of section 4.2 the following set of equations, describing full capacity growth with respect to labor and capital and market clearing wage - price determination.

1. Definitions (remunerations and wealth):

$$\omega = w/p, \quad \rho = (Y^p - \delta K - \omega L)/K \tag{4.109}$$

$$W = (M + B + p_e E)/p, \quad p_b = 1 \tag{4.110}$$

2. Households (workers and asset-holders):

$$W = (M^d + B^d + p_e E^d)/p, \quad \text{see (4.127)} \tag{4.111}$$

$$C = \omega L - T_w + (1 - s_c)[\rho K + rB/p - T_c], \quad s_w = 0 \tag{4.112}$$

$$S_p = s_c[\rho K + rB/p - T_c] = (\dot{M} + \dot{B} + p_e \dot{E})/p \tag{4.113}$$

$$\hat{L} = n = const \tag{4.114}$$

3a. Firms: Production and Investment: (4.115)

$$Y^p = F(K, L^p), \quad \omega = F_L(K, L^p) \tag{4.116}$$

$$I = i_1(\rho - (r - \pi^e))K + nK \tag{4.117}$$

$$I = p_e \dot{E}/p \tag{4.118}$$

$$\hat{K} = I/K \tag{4.119}$$

4. Government (fiscal and monetary authority):

$$T = T_w + T_c \tag{4.120}$$

$$T_w = \tau_w \omega L \tag{4.121}$$

$$T_c = t_c^n K + rB, \quad t_c^n = (T_c - rB)/K = \text{ const} \tag{4.122}$$

$$G = T_w + gK, \quad g = const \tag{4.123}$$

$$S_g = T - rB/p - G \tag{4.124}$$

$$\hat{M} = \bar{\mu} = const \tag{4.125}$$

$$\dot{B} = pG + rB - pT - \dot{M} \tag{4.126}$$

5. Equilibrium conditions (asset-markets):

$$M = M^d = h_1 pY + h_2 pK(r_o - r), \quad [B = B^d, E = E^d] \tag{4.127}$$

$$r = \frac{\rho p k + \dot{p}_e E}{p_e E} \tag{4.128}$$

6. Equilibrium situation (goods-market):

$$Y^p = C + I + \delta K + G, \quad \text{due to } \beta_p = \infty \tag{4.129}$$

7. Equilibrium situation (labor-market):

$$L^p = L, \quad \text{due to } \beta_w = \infty \tag{4.130}$$

8. Inflationary Expectations:

$$\dot{\pi}^e = \beta_{\pi^e}(\hat{p} - \pi^e), \quad \bar{\mu} = n, \beta_{\pi^e} \leq \infty. \tag{4.131}$$

Perfect wage flexibility is here viewed to generate labor market equilibrium $L^d = L^p = L$ and perfect price flexibility goods market equilibrium $Y^p = Y^d = Y$ at all points in time, while the Metzlerian inventory adjustment process appears to be redundant now as there is no real need for inventory holdings in this equilibrium approach to monetary growth.[6] For notational simplicity, we will use Y in the place of Y^p for representing goods market

[6] See however section 4.6 for another formulation of such equilibrium growth that is closer in spirit (and in mechanism assignment) to the market adjustment processes envisaged by the KMG model type and

equilibrium. Up to the use of a neoclassical production function (with the usual properties, see section 4.3), the model is just a limit case of the model of section 4.2. We therefore need not explain its equations once again, but only note that we have simplified the model slightly, since we no longer consider heterogeneous expectations formation, but will instead contrast purely adaptive ones ($\beta_{\pi^e} < \infty$) with myopic perfect foresight ($\beta_{\pi^e} = \infty$) in our following investigations of the model. Furthermore, the sector of firms is simplified, where investment now only depends on the difference between the real rate of profit and the real rate of interest (see equation (4.117)), because due to the assumption of market clearing in each point of time there are now no utilization problems. For the same reason, there are no unintended inventory investments any more, so that the emission of new equities now equals the nominal value of investments in fixed capital as expressed by equation (4.118). This presentation of the structural form of KMG equilibrium growth (and the laws of motion that we will derive from it below) shows that the model has become a much more compact one now. As the above equations show, this moving equilibrium model of monetary growth gives rise to only two laws of motion for the state variables $l = L/K, \pi^e$, the full employment labor intensity and expected inflation, which can be written as follows:

$$\hat{l} = -i_1(\rho - (r - \pi^e)) = n + g - t_c^n - s_c(\rho - t_c^n), \quad l = L/K \tag{4.132}$$

$$\dot{\pi}^e = \beta_{\pi^e}(\hat{p}(l, \pi) - \pi^e), \quad \beta_{\pi^e} \leq \infty \tag{4.133}$$

In order to obtain an autonomous system of differential equations from these two equations, we have to determine the temporary equilibrium values of the rate of profit ρ and the rate of interest r as well as the rate of growth of the equilibrium price level p as functions of the state variables l, π^e of the dynamics. We have $\rho = F(1,l) - \delta - F_L(1,l)l$ by definition and $(M/L)l = p(h_1 f(l) + h_2(r_o - r))$ as representation of money market equilibrium and thus equation for the determination of the nominal rate of interest. The rate of inflation is here assumed (but not yet shown) to be a function $\hat{p} = h(l, \pi^e)$ of the state variables l, π^e as well. Expressed in this way, the system thus appears to be much simpler than the one investigated in section 4.2. However, we have three statically endogenous variables now, w, p, r, which clear the labor, the goods and the money market, with one of them, the price level p, also needed in derivative form by the adaptive expectational mechanism. We stress that the KMG growth model is radically simplified with respect to the number of the employed laws of motion when temporary equilibrium is assumed to hold on all markets of the economy (in the place of only the asset markets). By contrast, the rate of inflation $\hat{p}$, which we need (in expected form) in the investment function of the model and only there, will be shown to be a complicated function of the state variables of the model, due to its high degree of static interdependence.

---

note also that the following solution of the temporary equilibrium part could be interpreted to suggest that it is the nominal rate of interest that clears the goods market and the role of the price level to clear the money market, while money wages adjust such that the revenue of firms equal their nominal wage costs at the margin at the full employment level, which thereby becomes compatible with the profit maximizing employment decision of firms.

As in the Solow model of real growth, we have the functional relationships of the marginal productivity theory of income distribution:

$$\omega(l) = F_L(K,L) = F_L(1,L/K) = f'(l), \quad y(l) = F(1,L/K) = f(l), \quad \rho(l) = f(l) - f'(l)l - \delta$$

which as usual imply that l is a decreasing function of ω: $l = (f')^{-1}(\omega)$, $y = f(l)$ an increasing function of l and ρ an increasing function of $l : \rho = \rho(l)$, since we have $\rho'(l) = -f''(l)l > 0$. We thus face no difficulties as far as the supply side of the economy is concerned, since output, real wages and the rate of profit depend in simple ways on the dynamical variable l, the full employment labor intensity, solely. On the demand side, which now determines as in Friedman (1970, 1971) the nominal rate of interest r and the price level p from IS and LM equations on the basis of the supply side expressions just determined, we have the equations:

$$\begin{aligned} y(l) &= \omega(l)l + (1-s_c)(\rho(l) - t_c^n) + i_1(\rho(l) - r + \pi^e) + n + \delta + g \quad \text{or} \\ 0 &\overset{IS}{=} i_1(\rho(l) - r + \pi^e) + n + g - t_c^n - s_c(\rho(l) - t_c^n) \quad \text{and} \\ \bar{m}l &\overset{LM}{=} p(h_1 y(l) + h_2(r_o - r)), \quad \bar{m} = M/L = const. \end{aligned}$$

These equations give rise to:

$$\begin{aligned} r &= r(l,\pi^e) = \rho(l) + \pi^e + \frac{n - s_c(\rho(l) - t_c^n) - (t_c^n - g)}{i_1} \\ p &= p(l,r) = \bar{m}l/(h_1 f(l) + h_2(r_o - r)), \quad \bar{m} = M/L = const. \end{aligned}$$

We see that r-adjustment clears the goods market (from the mathematical point of view) and p-adjustment (on the basis of a predetermined r) the money market, which represents a classical description of the role of these two variables. The obtained results are still simple and explicit, but they demand that the r, ρ, y-equations are to be inserted into the p-equation (and the r-equation) in order to arrive at an expression for the price level p that depends on the state variables l, π^e solely:

$$p = g(l,\pi^e) = \frac{\bar{m}l}{h_1 f(l) + h_2(r_o - \rho(l) - \pi^e - (n - s_c(\rho(l) - t_c^n) - (t_c^n - g))/i_1)}.$$

Note that the dependence of p on l is ambiguous, depending in particular on the comparison of investment and saving propensities i_1, s_c, implying that the rate of interest r depends positively on l if $i_1 > s_c$ holds and negatively in the opposite case. Note furthermore that the function g[7] is obviously an increasing function of the expected rate of inflation, due to a direct combination of the Keynes and the Mundell effect in this flexprice IS-LM temporary equilibrium model.

Differentiating the functional relationship $p = g(l,\pi^e)$ with respect to time gives:

$$\dot{p} = g_1\dot{l} + g_2\dot{\pi}^e \quad \text{or} \quad \hat{p} = \frac{g_1}{g}\dot{l} + \frac{g_2}{g}\dot{\pi}^e$$

and thus on the basis of the law of motion for the variable π^e :

$$\hat{p}(1 - \frac{g_2}{g}\beta_{\pi^e}) = \frac{g_1}{g}\dot{l} - \frac{g_2}{g}\beta_{\pi^e}\pi^e.$$

This expression implies as theory of inflation of the general equilibrium reformulation of the KMG growth model the equation:

[7] To be distinguished from the government policy parameter g.

$$\hat{p} \;=\; h(l,\pi^e) = \frac{\frac{g_1(l,\pi^e)}{g(l,\pi^e)}l(n+g-t_c^n-s_c(\rho(l)-t_c^n)) - \frac{g_2(l,\pi^e)}{g(l,\pi^e)}\beta_{\pi^e}\pi^e}{1-\frac{g_2(l,\pi^e)}{g(l,\pi^e)}\beta_{\pi^e}} \quad (4.134)$$

This finally provides us with the relationship $\hat{p}(l,\pi^e) = h(l,\pi^e)$ we postulated in equation (4.133). We can see from this expression that the rate of inflation is not always a well defined function of the state variables l, π^e of the model and that – ignoring this problem – its law of motion is a complicated nonlinear function of the state variables of the model. This is in striking contrast to the law of motion for the rate of inflation of the KMG model of section 4.2 with its sluggish wage and price adjustment of Phillips curve type, which are replaced by an IS-LM theory of the price and wage level in particular. Note also that the rate of inflation becomes infinite by definition when the system is shocked (not shown by its above after-shock representation), since the price level is a statically endogenous variable in the present equilibrium approach to monetary growth.

The stability analysis of the dynamics (4.132), (4.133) is much less demanding than the one of sections 4.2 and 4.3 with their two Phillips curves representation of the wage-price module. Inserting the equation $\rho = \rho(l), \rho'(l) > 0$ into the law of motion for l gives rise to:

$$\hat{l} \;=\; n+g-t_c^n - s_c(\rho(l)-t_c^n) \quad (4.135)$$

which obviously describes a globally stable and monotonic adjustment of the full employment labor intensity towards its unique interior steady state value $l_o = \rho^{-1}(n/s_c+\delta+t_c^n)$.[8] The model therefore does no longer allow for a theory of business fluctuations in its present deterministic setup and inflationary expectations, though determining investment behavior, do not matter for the real dynamics which are completely supply driven. Since the derivative of this dynamic equation with respect to other state variable π^e is zero, it suffices to calculate the corresponding partial derivative of equation (4.133) at the steady state in order to judge the asymptotic stability of system (4.132), (4.133). For local asymptotic stability it indeed suffices to consider the following reduced dynamic equation where the real part of the economy is already in its steady state

$$\dot{\pi}^e \;=\; \beta_{\pi^e}\hat{p}(l_o,\pi^e).$$

This dynamic implies the explicit law of motion

$$\dot{\pi}^e \;=\; q(\pi^e) = \beta_{\pi^e}\frac{\beta_{\pi^e}\pi^e}{\frac{g_2(l_o,\pi^e)}{g(l_o,\pi^e)}\beta_{\pi^e}-1}\pi^e \quad (4.136)$$

due to

$$\hat{p}-\pi^e \;=\; -\left(\frac{\frac{g_2(l_o,\pi^e)}{g(l_o,\pi^e)}\beta_{\pi^e}\pi^e}{1-\frac{g_2(l_o,\pi^e)}{g(l_o,\pi^e)}\beta_{\pi^e}}+\pi^e\right).$$

[8]Which is well defined under the usual assumptions on neoclassical production functions $y = f(l)$.

We get from

$$g(l_o, \pi^e) = \frac{\bar{m} l_o}{h_1 f(l_o) + h_2(-\pi^e)}$$
$$g_2(l_o, \pi^e) = \frac{\bar{m} l_o h_2}{(h_1 f(l_o) + h_2(-\pi^e))^2}$$

for the fraction g_2/g the expression

$$\tilde{g}(\pi^e) = \frac{g_2(l_o, \pi^e)}{g(l_o, \pi^e)} = \frac{h_2}{h_1 f(l_o) + h_2(-\pi^e)}$$

and for the derivative of this expression the simple relationship: $\tilde{g}'(\pi^e) = \tilde{g}(\pi^e)^2$.

For the derivative of the function $q(\pi^e)$ defined one then gets at $\pi^e = 0$ the expression

$$q'(0) = \frac{\beta_{\pi^e}}{\frac{h_2}{h_1 f(l_o)} \beta_{\pi^e} - 1}$$

which is positive if $\beta_{\pi^e} > \frac{h_1 f(l_o)}{h_2}$ holds. Furthermore, since $\pi^e = 0$ is the only point of rest of the law of motion $\dot{\pi}^e = q(\pi^e)$, we get that this dynamic must be unstable in the large, where in the large means the largest domain where the function $q(\pi^e)$ is well-defined.

Proposition 4.9

1. *There exists* a uniquely determined interior steady–state *of the dynamics (4.109) – (4.131) (where* $u_0, l_0, m_0 \neq 0$ *holds) which is given by*[9]

$$\rho_o = t_c^n + (n + g - t_c^n)/s_c, \quad \rho(l_o) = \rho_o$$
$$y_0 = y^p(0) = f(l_0), \quad \omega_0 = f'(l_0)$$
$$\pi_0^e = \bar{\mu} - n = 0 \ (= \hat{p}_o = \hat{w}_o), \quad m_0 = h_1 y_0, \quad r_0 = \rho_0.$$

2. *Assume that* $\beta_{\pi^e} > \frac{h_1 f(l_o)}{h_2}$ *holds. The Jacobian of the dynamics (4.132), (4.133) at the steady state is characterized by the following sign structure:*

$$J = \begin{pmatrix} - & 0 \\ ? & + \end{pmatrix}$$

implying one positive and one negative eigenvalue and thus saddle point dynamics around the steady state.

Proof: 1. Straightforward, since the function $\rho(l) = f(l) - \delta - f'(l)l$ represents a bijective mapping of $\Re_+$ onto itself.

2. The sign structure for the Jacobian has already been shown above, while the assertion on the eigenvalues follows from the fact that the determinant of J is equal to the product of the eigenvalues. ∎

[9] Note that there are no inventories in the present model type.

The considered dynamics are thus of the type as represented in the figure 4.1 (since eigenvectors here coincide with the coordinate axes of $\Re^2$). Increasing the parameter β_{π^e} towards infinity in addition implies that one eigenvalue stays negative at a fixed location while the other one approaches $+\infty$, since the trace (the sum of the eigenvalues) approaches $+\infty$ in this case (while $\det J$ approaches $-\infty$). We thus have in this case a saddle point dynamics that gets more and more explosive in its nominal part, with a real sector that is completely independent of such inflationary dynamics. We note however that the system is locally asymptotically stable for adjustment speeds of inflationary expectations below $\frac{h_1 f(l_o)}{h_2}$. Stability problems therefore only arise when inflationary expectations are adjusted with sufficient speed. The resulting situation then does not represent a complete dynamical model from the economic point of view. The KMG system thus is of a very peculiar type when general market clearing is assumed to prevail in the structure underlying the model (and if inflationary expectations are revised with sufficient speed).

Let us contrast this result with the KMG growth dynamics with only finite adjustment speeds of prices, wages and quantities. In the case of no technical change the KMG dynamics with neoclassical factor substitution reads according to what we have shown in section 4.3 (with only adaptive expectation formation now):

$$\begin{aligned}
\widehat{\omega} &= \kappa[(1-\kappa_p)\beta_w(V-1)+(\kappa_w-1)\beta_p(U_c-1)] && (4.137)\\
\widehat{l} &= -(i_1(\rho^e-(r-\pi^e))+i_2(U_c-1)) && (4.138)\\
\widehat{m} &= \bar{\mu}-(\pi^e+\kappa[\beta_p(U_c-1)+\kappa_p\beta_w(V-1)]) && (4.139)\\
&- (i_1(\rho^e-(r-\pi^e))+i_2(U_c-1)+n) && (4.140)\\
\dot{\pi}^e &= \beta_{\pi^e}\kappa[\beta_p(U_c-1)+\kappa_p\beta_w(V-1)] && (4.141)\\
\dot{y}^e &= \beta_{y^e}(y^d-y^e)-(i_1(\rho^e-(r-\pi^e))+i_2(U_c-1))y^e && (4.142)\\
\dot{\nu} &= y-y^d-(i_1(\rho^e-(r-\pi^e))+i_2(U_c-1)+n)\nu && (4.143)
\end{aligned}$$

with:

$$\begin{aligned}
y &= \beta_n(\beta_{n^d}y^e-\nu)+(1+\gamma\beta_{n^d})y^e\\
y^d &= \omega f^{-1}(y)+(1-s_c)(\rho^e-t_c^n)\\
&+ i_1(\rho^e-(r-\pi^e))+i_2(U_c-1)+n+\delta+g\\
\rho^e &= y^e-\delta-\omega f^{-1}(y), \quad r=r_0+(h_1y-m)/h_2\\
V &= \frac{f^{-1}(y)}{l}, \quad U_c=\frac{y}{f((f')^{-1}(\omega))}.
\end{aligned}$$

In this case we have the basic results:

Proposition 4.10

1. *There exists* a uniquely determined interior steady–state *of the dynamics (4.137) – (4.143) (where $u_0, l_0, m_0 \neq 0$ holds) which is given by*

$$\rho_o = t_c^n+(n+g-t_c^n)/s_c, \quad \rho(l_o)=\rho_o$$

$$
\begin{aligned}
y_0 &= y^p(0) = f(l_0), \quad \omega_0 = f'(l_0) \\
y_o^e &= y_o^d = y_o/(1+n\beta_{n^d}), \quad \nu_o = \beta_{n^d} y_o^e \\
\pi_0^e &= \bar{\mu} - n = 0 \ (= \hat{p}_o = \hat{w}_o), \quad m_0 = h_1 y_0, \quad r_0 = \rho_0.
\end{aligned}
$$

2. The determinant of the Jacobian of the dynamics (4.137) - (4.143) at the steady state is always positive.

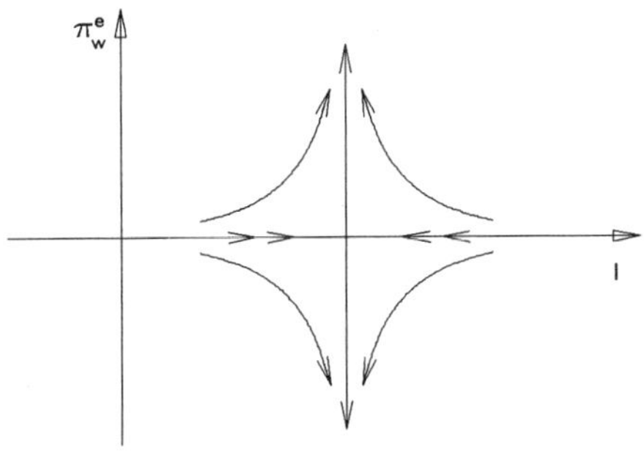

Figure 4.1:
Nominal saddle point dynamics with stable real growth

Proof: 1. The only change in the steady state values is here due to the inventories that are now held by firms in the steady state and which grow with the real growth rate n. This addition to the steady state calculations gives rise to further expressions (for expected sales and inventories per unit of capital) as in sections 4.2 and 3.

2. See Chiarella and Flaschel (1999b, Ch.6) for the proof in the case of fixed proportions in production which can be easily transferred to the situation here under consideration. ∎

We thus obtain that there is a striking contrast between the KMG growth model with finite vs. infinite adjustment speeds of prices and wages. The most remarkable differences are the following ones:

- Dynamical dimension: 6D vs. 2D.
- Static complexity: Linear wage price adjustment rules vs. a complicated nonlinear expression (4.134) for the actual rate of inflation.
- Local stability for sluggish adjustment of prices and quantities (up to sales expectations) with a full interaction of real and nominal expressions vs. dichotomizing nominal dynamics which is always unstable.
- Discontinuous change in the determinant of the Jacobian of the dynamics at the steady state at $\beta_w = \beta_p = \infty$.
- Determinant $\to +\infty$ for $\beta_{\pi^e} \to +\infty$ in the 6D case and $\to -\infty$ for $\beta_{\pi^e} \to +\infty$ in the 2D case.

We conclude that the limit case of perfect price and wage flexibility of the KMG approach to monetary growth is of extremely different type compared to the situation where disequilibria drive wages and prices in the economy with only finite speed. In the considered situation there is thus no possibility of building a bridge between market clearing and non market clearing approaches. However, while the latter one give rise to results that can be considered as plausible from the perspective of traditional Keynesian thinking, the ones for the discontinuous limit case cannot be considered as satisfying in the form they have been presented so far. The next section will show in this respect how KMG growth may be modified further from the perspective of the market clearing paradigm in order to arrive at a dynamic structure that can be considered a model of monetary growth.

The basic problem with the considered equilibrium growth version of the KMG model is that the theory of the rate of inflation it implies looks very cumbersome from the perspective of sections 4.2 and 4.3 and their two Phillips curve approach to wage and price dynamics, due to the high degree of static interdependence that is now involved in the model. We here have only one law of motion for the real part of the dynamics, which is independent of the nominal dynamics, and which just represents the dynamics of the Solow growth model in the case of differentiated saving habits: $s_w = 0, s_c \in (0,1)$. Assuming that the real part has found its point of rest then shows that the price level dynamics is purely explosive (for adjustments of adaptive inflationary expectations that are sufficiently fast), in stark contrast to the behavior of the real part of the economy, based on a static interaction of the Keynes-effect as derived from money demand, the Mundell-effect as it derives from investment demand and the inflationary expectations mechanism. Solving this interaction gives that forecasting errors with respect to inflation depend positively on the expected rate of inflation ($\beta_{\pi^e} > h_1 f(l_o)/h_2$) which implements a positive feedback loop of the expected rate of inflation onto its rate of change leading to the cumulative instability in the nominal part of the model shown in figure 4.1. Surely this is a drastic change in the behavior of the dynamics as compared to the case of sluggish adjustments of wages and prices. It raises the question whether this dichotomizing limit case can really be considered a meaningful representation of equilibrium KMG growth.

The impression of the extreme nature of equilibrium KMG growth is further confirmed when the limit case of perfect foresight ($\beta_{\pi^e} = \infty : \hat{p} = \pi^e$) is considered. In this case we get from IS-equilibrium as equation for the rate of inflation the following expression

$$\hat{p} = r - \rho(l) + \frac{s_c(\rho(l) - t_c^n) + t_c^n - g - n}{i_1}.$$

From LM-equilibrium we furthermore get again

$$r = r_o + (h_1 f(l) - \bar{m}(l/p))/h_2.$$

This immediately shows that r depends positively on p, the Keynes-effect, and thus $\hat{p}$ positively on p via the IS condition and the Mundell effect present in it. Not unexpectedly from the perspective of fast adaptive expectations, we thus again find that the nominal dynamics are purely explosive throughout. This instability scenario is closely related to the one of the simple Cagan monetary model with myopic perfect foresight, from which the so-called jump-variable technique was obtained by Sargent and Wallace (1973) which allowed them to turn such instability into stability. We will return to this instability result and its reformulation by the jump-variable technique in the following sections of this chapter.

Summing up we get in the case of myopic perfect foresight ($\beta_{\pi^e} = \infty$) *as full representation* of the model (4.109) – (4.131) on the intensive form level the autonomous dynamical system:

$$\begin{aligned} \hat{l} &= n + g - t_c^n - s_c(\rho(l) - t_c^n) \\ \hat{p} &= r_o + (h_1 f(l) - \bar{m}(l/p))/h_2 - \rho(l) + \frac{s_c(\rho(l) - t_c^n) + (t_c^n - g) - n}{i_1}. \end{aligned}$$

These dichotomizing dynamics provide a full description of the left-overs of KMG growth theory under full market-clearing and myopic perfect foresight, Solovian growth dynamics coupled with IS-LM based knife-edge type inflation theory, here in a world with heterogeneous agents. Note here that disequilibrium KMG growth was also based on myopic perfect foresight, see section 4.2, there concerning both wage and price inflation, but with a coefficient of less than unity in at least one of the two equations describing such wage and price dynamics, due to the addition of medium-run inflationary expectations which there were not of the perfect foresight variety. We thus have now two very different growth dynamics at our disposal, one with a number of delayed feedback mechanism and heterogeneous expectations leading to high order growth dynamics and a number of still basic propositions concerning convergence, persistent fluctuations and explosive cyclical growth and a very perfect structure with only poor dynamic properties.

These findings are in line with results obtained in Franke (1992), Flaschel (1993) and Flaschel, Franke and Semmler (1997) in the case of AS-AD growth theory. In our view they pose the question of how to choose between competing macrodynamic theories of traditional disequilibrium type showing traditional stability properties and their general equilibrium limit case with very special dynamic implications. The choice in the literature often, explicitly or implicitly, favors the second possibility by combining Walrasian market clearing with rational expectations in a Walrasian representative agents setup and thus is prepared to turn saddle point instability into saddle point stability (by use of the jump variable technique) in order to get economies with real and nominal adjustment processes that, after shocks, converge back (often monotonically) to long-run balanced growth positions. In view of such a choice we will consider in the next section a further revision of KMG growth dynamics which moves it closer to the Walrasian approach to monetary growth, while retaining its heterogeneous agents framework (now with heterogeneous expectations in addition), providing a more interesting type of dynamics than the one of the present section and also a detailed characterization of the jump-variable technique that we have only mentioned so far.

4.5 Market clearing: Walrasian reformulation and saddle point stability

We provide in this section a reformulation of the KMG equilibrium growth model now directly with myopic perfect foresight of investors (and asset holders) considered at the end of section 4.4 that gets away from its Kaldorian savings assumptions, that introduces in a basic way intertemporal aspects into the consumption and savings decisions of worker households and that also removes the assumption of inelastic labor supply from the temporary equilibrium block of the model. We thereby move closer to the type of behavioral assumptions that are made for households' behavior in general in the intertemporal market-clearing approaches to fluctuations and growth, here in the basic format underlying Barro and Grilli's (1994) macroeconomic analysis. We stay however in the heterogeneous household approach of our KMG framework, but reformulate the behavioral assumptions on consumption demand (and labor supply) of workers as well as asset holders, the former as stated in the spirit of the Walrasian approach to macrodynamics.

In the context of the following considerations the so called "jump variable technique" will play an important role. We shall therefore firstly briefly review its origin as well as consider an application of it in the context of a simple version of the Ramsey model. After presenting some criteria for the jump variable technique to guarantee stability in linear dynamic systems we will then return to the Walrasian reformulation of the KMG model.

The main idea behind this technique builds on the fact, that the instability results of economic models with perfect foresight can be overcome, if some of the dynamic variables are allowed to adjust instantaneously, i.e. to jump. This principle was first introduced and justified in a well-known article by Sargent and Wallace (1973), where they removed the explosiveness of the price level in Cagan's model of hyperinflation, which results from the original model in the case of perfect foresight on the rate of inflation. The key to overcoming this result was to make the price level a statically endogenous variable and to replace the initial condition for it (i.e. the assumption of a statically predetermined price level) by an appropriate terminal condition, derived from an imposed boundedness of the price level for time converging to infinity. On this basis the necessary jump of the price level after a shock (in the money supply) as well as its smooth development thereafter could be computed.[10]

The appropriateness of this procedure, however, has remained controversial in the literature. So, e.g., Turnovsky (1995) points out, that even in the Cagan model with rational expectations the assumption of a sluggish price level adjustment can be meaningfully retained, if it is combined with an explicit treatment of temporary disequilibrium on the money market.[11] Flaschel, Franke and Semmler (1997) and Chiarella and Flaschel (1999b) show, based on original work by Chiarella (1986,1990a) which was reconsidered in Flaschel (1993, pp.304ff.), that by introduction of an appropriate nonlinearity into the functional dependence of the real money demand on the expected rate of inflation the global explosiveness of the Cagan model can be avoided also without the application of the jump variable technique, which makes the conventional justification of the impositions of such jumps inapplicable.[12] Moreover, the picture may change considerably, when the assumption, that *all* agents have rational expectations, is not satisfied. If, e.g., some of the agents in the economy considered form their expectations in another way, this will also alter the time path according to which the economy actually evolves.[13]

[10]For a more detailed description of the application of this technique see, besides the original article by Sargent and Wallace, Turnovsky (1995, pp.69ff.).

[11]See Turnovsky (1995, p.76).

[12]See Flaschel, Franke and Semmler (1997, pp.79ff.) and Chiarella and Flaschel (1999b, 1.6) in particular, and also Flaschel and Sethi (1998).

[13]Another argument points to the difficulties connected with the analytical determination of a saddle path solution (to be considered below) and thus of the point, to which the jump has to be directed. In

Furthermore, there is no microfoundation available for the Cagan macromodel by which the necessity of a nonexplosive behavior of the economy could be rationalized. Note again, that although Sargent and Wallace give a verbal justification in this direction for the instantaneous adjustment of the price level, its boundedness in the long run (in the case of a money supply remaining at a constant level after the shock considered) is only based on an appropriate assumption on the expectations of the public.[14] This, however, is a crucial point, as e.g. Blanchard (1979) points out in a context formally similar to the Cagan model, because the general solution for the price level consists of a linear combination of the forward and the backward looking solution (with pure forward and pure backward looking behavior as polar cases).[15] He shows that, in a framework without any optimality requirements, it is already difficult to give a convincing reason for stationarity of the expectational variable(s) and that, even if this could be done, the solution may not be unique.

Thus, in the last consequence, the meaningfulness of the jump variable technique will depend on the concrete model context to which it is applied. As just discussed, for the Cagan model, as well as many other macrodynamical models, alternative treatments are now available and suggest that the conventional justification of the jump variable technique is not at all convincing once the local perspective of linear dynamic models is overcome. On the other hand, there are the microfounded approaches like, e.g., microfounded neoclassical growth models, where due to the optimizing behavior of (representative) agents, combined with rational expectations, the application of the jump variable technique is not only justified but unavoidable. The question there however is whether the implied jump variable already represents a convincing choice from the perspective of actual market economies or whether the proposed optimization procedure should be extended towards a delayed adjustment of the variable in question, due e.g. to adjustment costs.

An illustrative example for the microfounded approach is given by the well-known Ramsey model, which shall be presented here in a very simple form. Suppose, there is a (large) number of identical households[16] $h = 1, .., H$, each of them wishing to maximize the present value of his consumption utility:[17]

$$\max \mathcal{U} = \int_0^\infty U(C_t^h) \exp(-\theta t) dt = \int_0^\infty \ln(C_t^h) \exp(-\theta t) dt \tag{4.144}$$

under the constraints

$$\begin{aligned} \dot{K}^h(t) &= r(t)K^h(t) + \omega(t)L^h(t) - C^h(t) && (4.145) \\ \lim_{t\to\infty} K^h(t) \exp\left(-\int_0^t r(s)ds\right) &\leq 0 && (4.146) \\ K^h(0) &= K_0^h && (4.147) \end{aligned}$$

---

the meantime, however, there exist techniques by which such a solution can be obtained, see Semmler and Sieveking (1997), so that this critique is no longer of great importance.

[14]See Sargent and Wallace (1973, p.1045) and note that today's macro-applications of the jump variable technique generally do not even supply such a verbal justification of the trajectories they single out as the actual ones, which represents a crucial omission in nonlinear macrodynamical models.

[15]See Blanchard (1979, p.115).

[16]Note, however, that the model is not confined to this. Heterogeneity of households, e.g. with regard to their wealth, can be easily embodied into this model structure.

[17]A more general approach would, e.g., still include the utility of leisure or of government consumption. See, e.g., Turnovsky (1995, pp.233ff.).

with $C^h(t)$ being the real consumption of household h at time t, $K^h(t)$ his real wealth, $L^h(t)$ his labor supply (which is not constrained from the demand side by assuming perfect market clearing at all points of time), $r(t)$ the real rate of interest and $\omega(t)$ the real wage rate. The utility function U and the rate of time preference θ are assumed to be equal for all households. K_0^h finally is the initial value of wealth of household h, which is given at time 0 and can, on principle, also be negative. As the only purpose of this exposition is a short demonstration of the jump-variable technique, we have chosen in equation (4.144) for sake of simplicity a very special case, namely a logarithmic utility function, which will ease the subsequent computations considerably. Furthermore, we assume here a constant labor supply $L^h(t) = \bar{L}^h \; \forall t$ and abstract from economic growth.

The first constraint, (4.145), represents the flow budget constraint and states, that the change in real wealth in time is defined by the difference between labor and capital income and real consumption. The second condition, (4.146), sometimes called a No-Ponzi-game-condition,[18] states that the present value of indebtedness of a single household has to be zero. This condition has to be postulated, because otherwise it would be optimal for a household to borrow at each point of time as much as is necessary to drive marginal utility of consumption to zero and to finance interest payments in the subsequent periods by further credits. The question, however, is, by which means the No-Ponzi-game condition is enforced. There are at least two ways one can think of.[19] The first one appeals to the assumption of perfect foresight with the consequence, that nobody will be inclined to lend to a person, who is known to intend to play a Ponzi-game. In this context one can additionally imagine some kind of monitoring concerning the borrowers. Another possibility can be seen in the fact, that playing a "Ponzi scheme" will sooner or later lead to a situation, where the indebtedness of the borrower is so large, that the size of loanable funds of the economy considered will not suffice to provide him with the necessary means to pay the interest on his debt. At latest then the cheat will become obvious with consequences easy to imagine. If these are sufficiently unpleasant, this will prevent the household from choosing such a path.

Deriving now the optimality conditions from the corresponding Hamiltonian yields:[20]

$$\dot{C}^h(t) = (r(t) - \theta)C^h(t) \tag{4.148}$$

$$\lim_{t\to\infty} K^h(t)U'(C^h(t))\exp(-\theta t) = 0. \tag{4.149}$$

Equation (4.148) represents the Euler condition for the case of the a logarithmic utility function. The transversality condition (4.149) imposes – in addition to the No-Ponzi-game condition (4.146), which ruled out too large degrees of indebtedness – a limit on the accumulation of positive wealth. As pointed out by Blanchard and Fischer (1989), the rationale behind this condition can be demonstrated by looking at the optimization problem (4.144)–(4.147) with a finite time horizon,[21] T. Then at this last point in time it is optimal for the considered household to consume not only his entire income but also his entire wealth, at least as long as the marginal utility of consumption is strictly positive, as

[18] See Blanchard and Fischer (1989, p.49).

[19] A further one is given by Blanchard and Fischer (1989, p.84).

[20] See Blanchard and Fischer (1989, pp.39ff.).

[21] Blanchard and Fischer (1989, p.43).

shall be assumed. This fact can be expressed by the following equation:

$$K^h(T)U'(C^h(T))\exp(-\theta T) = 0$$

For $T \to \infty$ this condition converges to the transversality condition (4.149).[22]

Together with this condition the Euler equation (4.148) in connection with the budget constraint (4.145) can be shown[23] to lead to the following unique solution for $C^h(0)$, i.e. the optimal real consumption[24] of household h in $t = 0$:

$$C^h(0) = \theta\left[K_0^h + \int_0^\infty \omega(t)L^h(t)\exp\left(-\int_0^t r(s)ds\right)dt\right]. \tag{4.150}$$

Thus, given the initial wealth K_0^h as well as the – perfectly anticipated – actual and future values for real wages and interest rates, each household is able to determine on this basis his optimal consumption in $t = 0$ (provided the present value of labor income is finite).

This, of course, immediately raises the question, how the path of real wages and interest rates is determined, and this, in turn, leads to the question about the aggregative behavior of the economy as a whole. Assuming a neoclassical production function $F(K(t), L(t))$ with homogeneity of degree one (with $K(t) = \sum_{h=1}^H K^h(t)$ and $L(t) = \sum_{h=1}^H \bar{L}^h =: \bar{L}$ representing aggregate capital and labor input, respectively), applying marginal productivity theory and using the intensive form of the production function ($f(k(t)) := F(K(t), \bar{L})/\bar{L}$ with $k(t) = K(t)/\bar{L}$) yields for $r(t)$ and $\omega(t)$:

$$r(t) = f'(k(t)) \quad \text{and} \quad \omega(t) = f(k(t)) - f'(k(t))k(t) \tag{4.151}$$

which – due to the constant labor supply – can be interpreted as functions of the aggregate capital stock $K(t)$. Aggregating (4.148) and (4.145) over all households and dividing by $\bar{L}$, immediately the following dynamical system emerges:

$$\dot{c}(t) = (f'(k(t)) - \theta)c(t) \quad \text{with} \quad c(t) := (1/\bar{L})\sum_{h=1}^H C^h(t) \tag{4.152}$$

$$\dot{k}(t) = f(k(t)) - c(t). \tag{4.153}$$

As can be easily shown, the resulting dynamics is of the saddlepoint type, so that we get a phase plot as in figure 4.2.

[22]Note, that it is a common practice to solve problems with infinite time horizon first by consideration of its finite-time counterpart, leading to a solution in dependence of the time horizon T; thereafter, the limit of the solution for $T \to \infty$ is determined. Although the obtained result is in general indeed a solution of the infinite-horizon problem, it is, however, not in all cases the only one (see, e.g. Brock (1974, pp.757ff.). for an example in this direction, however in another context than the present one). A prominent example can be seen in the case of a dynamic dyopoly, where the Bertrand solution, which is the unique solution for the finite-time model, represents only one of (continuously) many solutions for the infinite horizon case, due to the Folk theorem, see e.g. Tirole (1988, pp.245ff.).

[23]For the technical details to obtain this result see e.g. Blanchard and Fischer (1989, Ch.2), there with the No-Ponzi-game condition (with strict equality) instead of the transversality condition.

[24]Note again, that the subsequent expression is valid only for the concrete assumptions made here, which concerns especially the logarithmic utility function.

If now $c(t)$ and $k(t)$ were both predetermined at each point in time, i.e. if they were both statically exogenous variables, the steady state would be clearly unstable, because the initial value vector (k_0, c_0) would usually not lie on the stable manifold. In the present case, however, only the capital intensity k is predetermined, whereas consumption c is statically endogenous. Furthermore, the dynamic system (4.152) and (4.153) represents only a necessary condition for an optimal solution but not a sufficient one. Thus, trajectories defined by this system represent only candidates for an optimal time path, nothing more. Another requirement for optimality represents the transversality condition[25] (4.149) mentioned above (appropriately redefined with regard to c and k). It can now be shown,[26] that the stable manifold of the steady state is the only trajectory, which satisfies the necessary conditions (4.152) and (4.153) as well as the transversality condition (4.149) (and the No-Ponzi-game condition (4.146)). To put it in another way: For any given initial wealth and any given sequence of real wages and interest rates any household is able to determine his optimal consumption at a given point of time according to equation (4.150). But only on the stable manifold is this decision of the households – with regard to the aggregate accumulation equation (4.153) – consistent with the path, that actually evolves; only in this case do the consumption decisions of the households lead in the aggregate to a time path of the capital stock, that in turn generates real wages and interest rates which exactly coincide with the households' expectations, on the basis of which they determined their consumption.

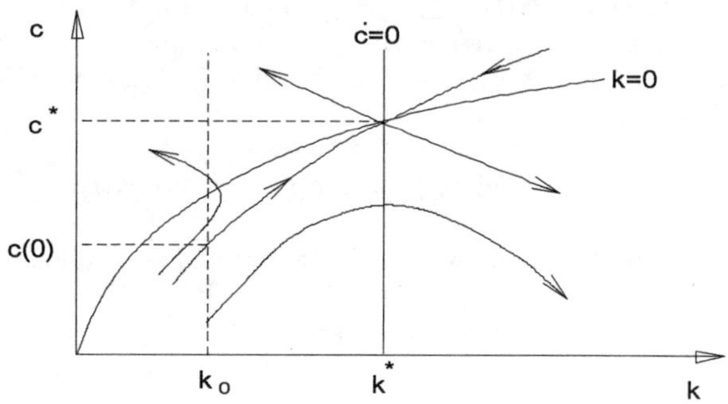

Figure 4.2:
Saddlepoint stability in the Ramsey model

Suppose now, an economy evolves along such a path or finds itself in the steady state. If now a change in the parameters of the model occurs, the steady state and its stable manifold will change their location in the phase space with the consequence, that the initial point now lies outside the (new) stable manifold. The agents of the model, however, will realize the parameter change and – due to the assumption of perfect foresight – adjust their expectations concerning the future evolution of the economy and the corresponding future wages and interest rates accordingly. At this point, now, the fact, that real consumption is statically endogenous, becomes important. For now, consumption will be immediately adjusted to these new expectations, so that it "jumps" onto the new stable manifold of the

[25]Note however, that this is not always true. An example for an optimization problem, where the optimal solution does not fulfill the transversality condition, is given in Feichtinger and Hartl (1986, pp.40ff.).

[26]See Blanchard and Fischer (1989, p.75).

new steady state. In the present framework, characterized by optimizing agents with perfect foresight, the jump variable technique therefore is not based on an arbitrary assumption in order to enforce stability but is rather a cogent consequence of the underlying assumptions of the intertemporal optimization procedure, i.e., the jump is explained by the model. On the other hand, as mentioned above, it might be less convincing in models where these prerequisites are not given, both from the mathematical and the economic point of view.

The ability of a statically endogenous variable like consumption to adjust immediately to a new situation and thus to reduce apparently higher dimensional dynamics to its stable branch leads to a more general analysis. As Blanchard and Kahn (1980) have pointed out for the case of a linear dynamical system describing the evolution of an economy, there is a connection between the stability properties of this system on the one hand and the relation between the number of its unstable roots and the number of statically endogenous variables on the other hand. The main results can be summarized as follows:[27]

- If the number of unstable roots equals the number of jump variables, then there exists a unique stable (nonexplosive) solution that can be used for describing the evolution of the economy.
- If the number of unstable roots is less than the number of jump variables, there are an infinite number of such stable solutions.
- If the number of unstable roots exceeds the number of jump variables, there is no solution that is nonexplosive.

These observations indicate that there may be mathematical problems for the application of the jump variable technique in the construction of macrodynamic models that are not micro-founded. In the case of nonlinear macro-dynamic systems these problems are further enhanced, since all trajectories may then be economically bounded ones, fluctuating around or converging to a particular steady state[28] with unstable as well as stable roots. The economic (macro ad hoc) motivation that people will always choose to be on the stable manifold (of a particular steady state) by a particular type of jump of a particularly chosen variable will then not at all be as simple as in the original Sargent and Wallace (1973) approach, since the situations that may here arise (in higher dimensional systems) cannot be classified and discussed from the global point of view to a satisfactory degree.

The main point of the foregoing analysis has been to emphasize that the jump onto the stable manifold by the initial value of the control variable ($c(0)$) in intertemporal optimizing models is not at all arbitrarily imposed. Rather it is part and parcel of soundly based optimization theory. However, in descriptive dynamic models (of the type analyzed in this book) no such theoretical rationale exists for the application of the jump variable technique for situations in which local saddle point dynamics emerge. In surveying the history of the development of the application of this technique to descriptive dynamic models we have gained the impression that in the back of the minds of its strongest advocates was some kind of false analogy with the analysis of saddle point behavior in intertemporal optimizing models.

[27]See also Turnovsky (1995, p.131).

[28]Which moreover may not be uniquely determined then, see Hirsch and Smale (1974, p.240) for a typical example in 2D space.

With these results in mind we can now return to the Walrasian reformulation of our KMG approach. The following discussion of the revised model is concentrated on the changes made to the model and does not repeat the equations of the model of section 4.4 that have remained unaltered here.

2*a*. Households (workers):

$$C_w = c_w((1-\tau_w)\omega, r-\pi^e_w)L, \quad c_{w1a}>0, c_{w2a}<0, \quad \hat{L}=n \tag{4.154}$$

$$L^s = \ell((1-\tau_w)\omega, r-\pi^e_w)L, \quad \ell_1>0, \ell_2>0, \quad \hat{L}=n \tag{4.155}$$

$$S_w = (1-\tau_w)\omega L^s + rB_w/p - T_{wc} - C_w = \dot{B}_w/p. \tag{4.156}$$

We again assume that the number of workers L (and their normal labor supply) grows with a constant rate n, the natural rate of growth of the economy. On this basis we however now have in addition instantaneously variable labor supply $\ell(\cdot)$ per unit of household, which depends positively on the real wage net of taxes $(1-\tau_w)\omega$ and also on the real rate of interest $r-\pi^e_w$ on bonds as it is perceived by workers (capital taxes are lump-sum, see below). Similarly, current real consumption of workers c_w per unit of household depends positively on real wages (after taxes), but negatively on their expectation of the real rate of interest.[29] Workers' real savings S_w follow by definition, including wage and capital income taxation, and these savings are totally spent on the acquisition of government fixed price bonds which exhibit a variable nominal interest rate r.

For the consumption of asset owners we assume that it is not changed when their income, interest rates and wealth change, since their consumption is determined by fixed habits (and is basically not constrained) and thus independent of fluctuations in their income and wealth. Similarly to the case of for government expenditures, see the model of section 4.4, we here make the simplest assumption possible and assume that the consumption of asset owners per unit of capital is constant (and thus a parameter for the analysis of the model in per unit of capital form):

2*b*. Households (asset holders):

$$C_c = c_cK, \quad c_c = const \tag{4.157}$$

$$S_c = \rho K + rB_c/p - T_{cc} - c_cK = (\dot{M} + \dot{B}_c + p_e\dot{E})/p. \tag{4.158}$$

The government sector, block 4. of the earlier models, is again formulated in a way as neutral as possible as far as the laws of motion of the economy are concerned and is now of the following form:

4. Government (fiscal and monetary authority):

$$\begin{aligned}
T &= T_w + T_{wc} + T_{cc} \\
T_w &= \tau_w \omega L^s \\
T_{wc} &= t^n_{wc}K + rB_w, \quad t^n_{wc} = (T_{wc} - rB_w)/K = \text{ const} \\
T_{cc} &= t^n_{cc}K + rB_c, \quad t^n_{cc} = (T_{cc} - rB_c)/K = \text{ const} \\
G &= T_w + gK, \quad g = const \\
S_g &= T - rB/p - G \\
\hat{M} &= \bar{\mu} = const \\
\dot{B} &= pG + rB - pT - \dot{M}.
\end{aligned}$$

[29]See Barro and Grilli (1994) for details.

The assumptions on T_{wc}, T_{cc} imply the following expressions for the savings of workers and asset holders per unit of capital:

$$S_w/K = (1-\tau_w)\omega l^s - t^n_{wc} - c_w, \quad S_c/K = \rho - t^n_{cc} - c_c$$

which shows that these expressions are independent of asset accumulation due to the assumptions made above on the collection of taxes with respect to capital income. Of course, such assumption only serve the purpose of simplifying the analysis temporarily, by making as many policy instruments as possible exogenous for the present investigation of the dynamics of the private sector with its partly Walrasian structure. Such a procedure however implies that much is going on in the bond dynamics of the model, since new bond issuing $\dot{B}$ must of course be such that the government budget constraint is always fulfilled in the presence of all these exogenous parameters characterizing the behavior of the fiscal and the monetary authority.

Money is held by asset holders solely and is demanded (as far as stock demand is concerned) by assuming now the usual Cagan type form of money demand (often used in theoretical as well as applied work):

5. Equilibrium conditions (asset-markets):

$$M = M^d = h_1 pY \exp(-h_2(r - r_o)), \quad \hat{M} = \bar{\mu} = n, \quad \bar{m} = M/L = const \quad (4.159)$$

This again suffices to describe the allocation of financial wealth between money, interest bearing (fixed price) bonds and equities in a world where, as in the preceding section, bonds and equities are perfect substitutes from the viewpoint of asset holders (now with myopic perfect expectations).

Finally we come to inflationary expectations, now of firms and workers separately, which are given as follows:

8. Inflationary expectations:

$$\dot{\pi}^e_w = \beta_{\pi^e_w}(\hat{p} - \pi^e_w), \quad \pi^e_f = \hat{p} \quad (4.160)$$

i.e., we assume backward looking expectations in the case of workers (adaptive expectations) and myopic perfect foresight in the case of firms (and implicitly also for asset holders) as the institutions that determine the investment in the capital stock. This closes the description of the alterations made to the model of section 4.4.

As differential equations we get from the above reformulation of a moving equilibrium model of monetary growth of section 4.4 the equations:

$$\begin{aligned}
\hat{l} &= n - (y - c_w((1-\tau_w)\omega, r - \pi^e_w)l - c_c - \delta - \tau_w\omega\ell((1-\tau_w)\omega, r - \pi^e_w)l - g) \\
&= -i_1(\rho + \hat{p} - r), \quad l = L/K && (4.161) \\
\hat{p} &\overset{IS}{=} (y - c_w((1-\tau_w)\omega, r - \pi^e_w)l - c_c \\
&- i_1(\rho - r) - n - \delta - \tau_w\omega\ell((1-\tau_w)\omega, r - \pi^e_w)l - g)/i_1 && (4.162) \\
\dot{\pi}^e_w &= \beta_{\pi^e_w}(\hat{p} - \pi^e_w) && (4.163)
\end{aligned}$$

on the basis of the statically endogenous variables y, ρ, ω, r to be determined below. These equations show as new aspects of the dynamics endogenously determined savings rates and heterogeneous expectations, which in particular now provide a direct expression for the rate of inflation via goods market equilibrium, due to myopic perfect foresight in the markets that determine investment decisions. Note that we have used the IS-curve as determining the actual rate of inflation via investment behavior that adjusts to the supply side of the model, and that the price level p is nevertheless considered a statically endogenous variable of the model that is capable of performing jumps if required by postulated equilibrium conditions. Despite this understanding of its role the model nevertheless only establishes a dynamic law for price level movements that will be exploited in two different ways in the following. The remaining statically endogenous variables are determined, basically as in the preceding section, by the following nonlinear equation system on the basis of temporarily state variable l, π_w and, as just discussed, the price level p:

$$\omega = f'(l^s),\ f''(l^s) < 0 \quad l^s = \ell((1-\tau_w)\omega, r - \pi_w^e)l \tag{4.164}$$
$$\rho(l^s) = f(l^s) - f'(l^s)l^s - \delta, \quad \rho'(l^s) > 0 \tag{4.165}$$
$$y = f(l^s), \quad f'(l^s) > 0 \tag{4.166}$$
$$\ln(\bar{m}l) = \ln(h_1 p) + \ln y + h_2(r_o - r), \quad h_1, h_2, \bar{m} > 0 \tag{4.167}$$

representing in particular labor market and money market equilibrium. Solving the last equation for the rate of interest r gives:

$$r = r_o + \frac{\ln(f(l^s)/l) + \ln p + \ln h_1 - \ln \bar{m}}{h_2}.$$

The rate of interest therefore in particular depends on the 'state variable' p, representing the Keynes-effect in the usual way.

We stress that the above theory of the rate of inflation is a consequence of the myopic perfect foresight assumption made for firms and the assumed goods market equilibrium condition

$$y = c_w(\cdot,\cdot)l + c_c + i_1(\cdot) + n + \delta + \tau_w\omega\ell(\cdot,\cdot)l + g$$

which, as is known from the many applications of the jump variable technique, only determines a relationship between the rate of inflation $\hat{p}$ and the price level p, a relationship that will be exploited in a particular way by jump variable technique to be considered below. Furthermore, this expression has to be inserted, alongside with the expressions for the statically endogenous variables, into the first and third law of motion of the system (4.161) – (4.163) in order to get representations of them that only depend on the state variables of the system, then providing an autonomous system of three nonlinear differential equations in the variables l, p, π_w^e. This system (4.161)–(4.163) is now well defined at all points of its phase space, in contrast to the dynamics we have investigated in the preceding section. Note finally, that the assumed consumption behavior and the now variable labor supply together with the general equilibrium structure of the considered model imply an interdependent temporary equilibrium position of a somewhat complicated nature, in contrast to the situation of the disequilibrium KMG growth model with its sluggishly adjusting wages, prices, quantities and expectations of section 4.2 of this chapter.

Proposition 4.11

Assume $\ell \equiv 1$ and $\tau_w = 0$ for reasons of simplicity.[30] *Assume furthermore that $\epsilon = \frac{(dc_w(.,.)/dl_o)l_o}{c_w(.,.)} > 1$ is fulfilled (compare for a similar assumption proposition 4.14) with the consequence that $\frac{d}{dl_o}(c_w(f'(l_o), \rho(l_o))l_o) = \frac{(dc_w(.,.)}{dl_o)}l_o + c_w(.,.) < 0$ holds true. Let further l_o exceed a value $\tilde{l}_o$ which is defined by $\rho(\tilde{l}_o) = 0$. In addition, the condition $\lim_{l_o \to \tilde{l}_o^+} c_w(.,.) = \infty$ shall be fulfilled. Let furthermore the production function satisfy $\lim_{l_o \to \infty} f(l_o) = \infty$. Then: The dynamical system (4.161) - (4.163) exhibits a unique (economical meaningful) interior steady state represented by:*

$$\begin{aligned} f(l_o) &= c_w(f'(l_o), \rho(l_o))l_o + c_c + n + \delta + g \\ \hat{p}_o &= \pi^e_{wo} = \pi^e_{fo} = 0, \quad p_o = \frac{\bar{m}l_o}{h_1 f(l_o)}, \quad r = r_o = \rho(l_o). \end{aligned}$$

Proof: Straightforward, if one takes into account that from an economic point of view only such values for l_o come into question, for which $\rho(l_o) = f(l_o) - f'(l_o)l_o - \delta > 0$ is satisfied, because otherwise firms would produce losses which hardly can be thought of as representing a steady state situation. If now in addition $\epsilon > 1$ is fulfilled, the function $c_w(f'(l_o), \rho(l_o))l_o$ is strictly monotonically decreasing in l_o for all $l_o > \tilde{l}_o$. For l_o approaching $\tilde{l}_o$ from the right, $c_w(.,.)l_o$ goes to infinity due to the corresponding assumption made. As, on the other hand, $f(l_o)$ is a rising function in l_o without any upper bound, there must be a unique intersection between these two curves at a value for l_o associated with $\rho(l_o) > 0$. ∎

We assume in the following that the choice of the production and consumption functions is such that the required conditions are fulfilled.[31]

Proposition 4.12

Assume in addition to the assumptions of proposition 4.11 that $\beta_{\pi^e_w} = 0$ holds and that π^e_w is fixed at its steady state value 0. Then:

1. The dynamics (4.161), (4.162) are locally of saddle point type, i.e., we have $\det J < 0$ and thus two real eigenvalues of opposite sign for the Jacobian of this reduced dynamical system at the steady state.

[30] See Romer (1996, p.161) for the justification of the first assumption. A simple institutional constraint may also be assumed here to justify such an assumption. Moreover, although it is difficult to obtain the result of a constant labor supply in general (especially if real wages are very low and if households have wealth at their disposal), it might be well defendable in a certain range of wages and interest rates (current and future ones). Note in this context, that there are not only possible offsetting effects between wage and interest rate movements on the amount of labor supplied, but that also for each of these both factors (holding constant the other one) income effect and substitution effect often work into opposite directions. If one now assumes, that the dynamics of the economy never leaves a region, where the reaction of the labor supply on (current) wages and interest rates is at best weak, the assumption of a constant labor supply there can be considered as an admissible approximation.

[31] An example where these assumptions are valid is given by the following production and consumption functions: $f(l) = l^\alpha$, $0 < \alpha < 1$ and $c_w(\omega, r) = a\frac{\omega}{r}$, $a > 0$. (Note, that as far as only the steady state is considered, the ratio $\frac{\omega}{r}$ represents the present value of future labor income; thus, such a relationship for real consumption could be derived from intertemporal optimization, if in addition one neglects real wealth as a further determinant for consumption). Inserting now $f'(l_o)$ for ω_o and $\rho(l_o) = f(l_o) - f'(l_o)l_o - \delta$ for r_o leads to a situation as described above for all values l_o exceeding $\tilde{l}_o$ and thus to a uniquely determined steady state.

2. The dynamics (4.161) – (4.163) are locally also of saddle point type if $\beta_{\pi_w^e} \sim 0$ holds, in which case there will one positive and two negative eigenvalues for the Jacobian at the steady state of the dynamics.

Proof: 1. In order to show that $\det J < 0$ holds true we remove all expressions from the law of motions (4.161), (4.162) that produce linear dependencies in this Jacobian J. The dynamical equations can therefore be reduced to the following non equivalent dynamics without any change in the sign of $\det J$.

$$\begin{aligned} \dot{l} &= i_1(r(l,p) - \rho(l)) \\ \dot{p} &= f(l) - c_w(f'(l), r(l,p))l. \end{aligned}$$

The Jacobian of this reduced system reads at the steady state:

$$J = \begin{pmatrix} i_1 r_l - i_1 \rho' & i_1 r_p \\ f' - c_w - c_{w1a} f'' l - c_{w2a} r_l l & -c_{w2a} r_p l \end{pmatrix}.$$

For $\det J$ we therefore get the expression:

$$J = \begin{vmatrix} -i_1 \rho' & i_1 r_p \\ f' - c_w - c_{w1a} f'' l & -c_{w2a} r_p \end{vmatrix} = \begin{vmatrix} - & + \\ + & + \end{vmatrix}$$

since $f(l) - c_w(f'(l), r(l, p_o))$ is positively sloped at the steady state.

2. We show that the determinant of the Jacobian of the dynamics (4.161) – (4.163) at the steady state is (always) positive, if $\beta_{\pi_w^e} > 0$ holds. This implies that the two eigenvalues considered in part 1. of the proposition (where $\beta_{\pi_w^e} = 0$), which keep their sign for small variations in the parameter $\beta_{\pi_w^e}$ will be augmented by a third eigenvalue of negative sign, since the determinant of J is always the product of its eigenvalues, which proves the assertion 2.

In order to calculate the sign of the determinant of J it suffices to note that the partial derivatives of the $\hat{p}$-equation can be removed from the third row of J without change in sign of $\det J$ by subtracting the second row of J from it. For $\det J$ we therefore get in the 3D case the qualitative expression:

$$J = \begin{vmatrix} - & + & ? \\ + & + & ? \\ 0 & 0 & - \end{vmatrix} > 0$$

due to what has been shown in the first part of the proposition. ∎

The following proposition states that the same situation is given when the adjustment speed of inflationary expectations is sufficiently high.

Proposition 4.13

Assume again $\ell \equiv 1$ and $\tau_w = 0$. Then: The dynamics (4.161) – (4.163) are locally also of saddle point type if $\beta_{\pi_w^e} > 0$ is sufficiently large, in which case there will also be one positive and two negative eigenvalues for the Jacobian at the steady state of the dynamics.

Proof: The determinant of the Jacobian of the dynamics (4.161) – (4.163) remains positive at the steady state for all choices of the adjustment parameter β_{π^e}, due to arguments used in the proof of the preceding proposition: The third law of motion can again be reduced to $\dot{\pi}^e_w = \beta_{\pi^e_w}(-\pi^e_w)$ without change in the sign of the determinant of the Jacobian of the 3D dynamics at the steady state. Furthermore, the trace of J is negative for all β_{π^e} sufficiently large, since $\hat{p}_p = -c_{w2a}r_pl < 0$ which implies that the entry J_{33} of the Jacobian of the full dynamics at the steady state is always negative and can be made arbitrarily large by increasing the adjustment speed of inflationary expectations of workers sufficiently.

Taken together these two conditions on J imply that there are either two negative and one positive eigenvalue of J or two conjugate complex ones with negative real part coupled with a positive real eigenvalue, since the determinant of J is the product of the three eigenvalues of J. There are only two further situations in which there is a positive determinant, namely three real and positive eigenvalues and two conjugate complex ones with nonnegative real part coupled with a positive real eigenvalue. In these situations we have however trace $J > 0$, since trace is the sum of eigenvalues, in contradiction to what has been shown above. ■

We thus in sum have that the dynamics (4.161) – (4.163) is locally of saddle point type (with a one-dimensional unstable manifold) for small as well as for large adjustment parameters β_{π^e}. At present it is however not clear what happens at intermediate values of this adjustment parameter, since $\hat{l}_l$ is ambiguous in its sign and since $\hat{p}_p > o$ holds true as representation of an inverse Keynes-effect in the present model.

The now conventional way of making use of the proven saddle point instability, is by way of the jump variable technique, with the intent of getting saddle point stability from saddle point instability and on this basis a meaningful theory of monetary growth. We will illustrate this methodology by means of a further specialization of the dynamic model underlying propositions 4.12, 4.13.

The situation considered in proposition 4.12.1. represents a good starting point for discussing the (in-)stability of Walrasian general equilibrium models of monetary growth, if one wants to concentrate on the implications of myopic perfect foresight in the system (4.161) – (4.163). For the purpose of illustrating the jump variable technique we shall however consider yet another subdynamics of the general dynamics (4.161) – (4.163) that concentrates on the interaction of inflation and expected inflation in such a setup with heterogeneous expectations formation, and which thus neglects the capacity effect of fluctuations in investment and savings (as if $i_1 = 0$ in this respect).

For this purpose we assume in addition to the assumptions of proposition 4.13 that $c_{w2a} = 0$ holds true in a neighborhood of the steady state of the dynamics. This implies that the first law of motion, for l, does no longer depend on the other two state variables of the dynamics (4.161) – (4.163). This law of motion then reads

$$\hat{l} = n - (f(l) - c_w(f'(l))l - c_c - \delta - g).$$

We assume now in addition that this equation allows for a steady state solution l_o as the 3D dynamics in proposition 4.11 and that l is fixed at this steady state position.

Assuming that labor intensity stays in the steady state implies of course $\omega = \omega_o, \rho = \rho_o$ in addition, i.e., a frozen real dynamics. For the remaining laws of motion of the economy we then simply have:

$$\hat{p} = r - \rho_o \tag{4.168}$$

$$\dot{\pi}^e_w = \beta_{\pi^e_w}(\hat{p} - \pi^e_w) \tag{4.169}$$

with the money market equilibrium equation reading in this case

$$r = r_o + \frac{\ln(f(l_o)/l_o) + \ln p + \ln h_1 - \ln \bar{m})}{h_2}.$$

Making use of the variable transformation $z = \ln p$ then gives rise to a linear dynamical system in the variables z, π^e_w of the form

$$\begin{aligned} \dot{z} &= r(z) - \rho_o, \; r'(z) > 0 \\ \dot{\pi}^e_w &= \beta_{\pi^e_w}(\dot{z} - \pi^e_w). \end{aligned}$$

The determinant of the system matrix of these dynamics is obviously negative which again adds insights into the saddle point structure of full dynamics from this partial perspective. For the isoclines of this planar system in the state variables z, π^e_w we have the expressions:

$$\begin{aligned} \dot{z} = 0: &\quad r(z) = \rho_o, \quad i.e. \quad z = z_o \\ \dot{\pi}^e_w = 0: &\quad \pi^e_w = r(z) - \rho_o. \end{aligned}$$

Taken together, this gives rise to the following standard phase portrait of saddle point dynamics in the theory of monetary growth:

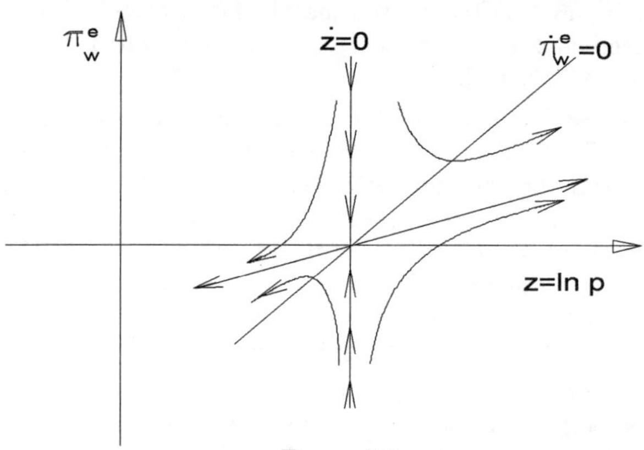

Figure 4.3:
Monetary saddle point dynamics with real steady growth

Shocks in the money supply and other shocks shift the isoclines of this system to a new steady state position where they again intersect. The jump variable technique then maintains that the statically endogenous price level of the present model would jump in such a situation such that it poses the system again on the stable branch of the new phase portrait of the dynamics. From there the laws of motion of the dynamics are operating again and lead the state variables back to their steady state values in a continuous fashion as discussed at the beginning of this section; see furthermore Blanchard and Kahn (1980), Gray and Turnovsky (1982) and Turnovsky (1995) for detailed analyses of this type of jump variable technique. In this way it is achieved that the system is always (monotonically) converging to its steady state after being hit and displaced from it by some shock.

Figure 4.3 shows that there is perpetual inflation to the right of the $\dot{z} = 0, z = \ln p$ isocline and everlasting deflation to the left of it, both with no possibility for a turning point. This situation is again due to the positive relationship between the price level p and the rate of inflation $\hat{p}$ that is generated by the IS-LM equilibrium part of the model and its classical adjustment mechanism. We in particular have that both p and $\hat{p}$ adjust at one and the same time (like statically endogenous variables) in order to achieve both goods market equilibrium and to get situated on the stable branch of the saddle point dynamics generated by the model. Note that these jumps are not explained by a more complete type of dynamics, but simply imposed on the model from the outside.[32]

We stress again that the present book does not suggest that this jump variable technique, here exemplified for a Walrasian modification of KMG growth, is really meaningful on the macro-level, since local analysis is an insufficient tool to discuss such issues and since global results are often difficult to obtain and may lead to a wealth of different situations where mathematical solutions are not easily imposed, and economically justified, that guarantee that the economy converges back to a steady state if thrown out of it. These topics are treated in depth in Chiarella (1990a,b, 1992a,b), Chiarella and Khomin (1999), Flaschel, Franke and Semmler (1997) and Flaschel and Sethi (1998) and will therefore not be reconsidered here.

Summing up, the main purpose of this section was to provide a Walrasian reformulation of the household sector for a KMG type model with perfectly flexible prices and quantities and to demonstrate the application of the jump variable technique in such a setup, which nowadays appears to be a well-established tool in analyzing models with local saddle point dynamics. On the other hand, as discussed in various places of this section, this procedure is not necessarily an appropriate tool to overcome the problems connected with an unstable steady state solution. As shown, the meaningfulness of this approach depends heavily on the concrete economic background of the model in question. Thus, e.g., its applicability in intertemporal optimization models such as neoclassical growth models of the Ramsey type is implied by the theoretical underpinnings of the optimizing behavior of agents with rational expectations. On the other hand, in completely specified descriptive models of actual economies (like the nonlinear KMG models of this book), where sluggish adjustments of wages and prices are of importance, there seems to be no cogent theoretical basis for the use of the jump variable technique. But even with full market clearing the jump variable technique will not necessarily represent an appropriate solution technique in this model type as will be shown in the next section.

[32]A model where jumps – in expectations! – can occur and can be explained from the perspective of fast, but not infinitely fast adjustments of expectations has been considered in section 2.3.2. There the jumps occur due to the model's structure and not at a point in time where the model is temporarily set aside or 'switched off'.

4.6 KMG equilibrium growth

We have so far not really discussed the conditions used to go from our starting reference case of KMG growth of section 4.2 with its sluggish price and quantity adjustment processes to the limit situation of perfect market clearing on the labor market as well as on the market for goods we considered in section 4.4. In fact considering the adjustment processes of KMG disequilibrium growth of sections 4.2, 4.3 shows that the assumptions enumerated in the following list should be used to go from disequilibrium growth to equilibrium growth on the basis of the KMG model of sections 4.2, 4.3 if the spirit of their types of adjustments is to be preserved.

- Setting $\beta_w = \infty$ in (4.30) implies $V = \bar{V}(= 1), l = f^{-1}(y)$ by way of instantaneously adjusting nominal wages w.
- Setting $\beta_{n^d} = \beta_n = 0, \beta_{y^e} = \infty$ implies $Y = Y^d = Y^e$ (and $\mathcal{I} = N = 0$ by block 6 of the model of section 4.2), that is goods market equilibrium by way of infinitely fast adjusting sales expectations and output towards aggregate demand Y^d with no intention to hold or add to inventories.
- Setting $\beta_p = \infty$ in (4.75) implies $U_c = \bar{U}_c(= 1), y = y^p$ by way of instantaneously adjusting price levels p which adjusts the price level p to marginal wage costs $w/F_L(K, L)$ due to the consideration of substitution in the extended module 3. of the KMG model of section 4.3.

The role of perfect price flexibility in the KMG approach is therefore not to clear the goods market (which due to the Keynesian character of the model happens by instantaneous quantity adjustments), but to adjust prices instantaneously to marginal wage costs, instead of only sluggishly as in the KMG approach of section 4.3.

These are basic observations that in essence only restructure the equilibrium growth dynamics of the sections 4.4 and 4.5 from a Keynesian perspective, without dismissing neither the chosen market clearing approach nor the Walrasian formulation of the sector of worker households. Yet, since quantity adjustments clear the market for goods, we do not need perfect price flexibility in addition. It is plausible from the empirical perspective that the rate of output of firms can be adjusted instantaneously should new conditions demand for such a change, but it is equally implausible from this perspective (and intended to overcome the logic and the type of jump variable technique just discussed) that aggregate price levels double instantaneously should a shock demand this from the perspective of sections 4.4 and 4.5. Empirical observations in fact suggest the following

- There are two instruments by which firms can react to goods market disequilibrium: by adjusting prices or by adjusting output until goods market equilibrium is obtained.
- There are now many partial studies that suggest that it is much easier for firms to adjust output than it is to adjust prices, in particular since output only concerns intrafirm decisions, while prices are set to influence customers' behavior.
- If firms adjust output to clear the goods market, they have to be treated as price setters for reasons of economic consistency, for example by assuming delayed markup pricing with respect to normal operating costs.

- Taking the variables w, Y, r as equilibrating variables with respect to labor, goods and money market in the place of w, p, r seems more adequate from a Keynesian perspective (discussed above) and also allows for temporary full equilibrium. Note that the indicated adjustment processes need not imply that the equilibrium values of w, Y, r itself are to be determined from their market clearing equations in this strict sense.

From a Keynesian perspective we would therefore argue that the variables w, Y, r (Y the rate of output!) should be used as statically endogenous variables that adjust instantaneously to clear the markets for labor, output and money, if full temporary equilibrium is considered as a useful modeling strategy, while the remaining variables of the model, now also prices besides stocks of labor and capital and inflationary expectations of workers are dynamically endogenous variables (the latter two as in the preceding section). Instantaneous output adjustment in fact gives the degree of freedom that allows for sluggish price level adjustment, as the empirically more plausible configuration, without having to depart from the market clearing paradigm. Viewed from the perspective of a purely Walrasian reasoning there is thus surely now some sort of imperfection in the behavior of firms, representing a first step into Keynesian dynamical analysis of monetary growth, which however does not exclude at all the possibility of complete market clearing at each moment in time as long as wages, output and interest rates are indeed capable of adjusting to their market clearing values at each moment. If infinitely fast adjustment of prices and quantities is possible at all, it should concern (from a Keynesian perspective) the rate of output set by firms and not the price level that results from their many faceted pricing decisions. This simple change in perspective will now be applied to the model of the preceding section with its Walrasian consumption demand and labor supply schedules in the case of worker households and will modify its static and dynamic analysis considerably.

The following set of equations represent the model analyzed in the preceding section with the change in perspective concerning the equilibrating variables just considered. Note that not all equations of the former model are repeated here, but only those that are essential for the understanding of the working of the new model of equilibrium growth:

1. Definitions (remunerations):

$$\omega = w/p, \quad \rho = (Y - \delta K - \omega L^d)/K \tag{4.170}$$

2. Households (workers and asset-holders):

$$C = c_w((1-\tau_w)\omega, r - \pi_w^e)L + c_c K, \tag{4.171}$$

$$\hat{L} = n, \quad L^s = \ell((1-\tau_w)\omega, r - \pi_w^e)L \tag{4.172}$$

3. Firms (production, pricing and investment):

$$Y = F(K, L^d), \tag{4.173}$$

$$\dot{p} = \beta_p((1+a)w/F_L(K,L) - p), \quad a > 0 \tag{4.174}$$

$$I = i_1(\rho - (r - \hat{p}))K + nK, \tag{4.175}$$

$$\hat{K} = I/K. \tag{4.176}$$

4. Government (fiscal and monetary authority):

$$T = T_w + T_{wc} + T_{cc} \tag{4.177}$$

$$T_w = \tau_w \omega L^s \tag{4.178}$$

$$
\begin{aligned}
T_{wc} &= t^n_{wc}K + rB_w, \quad t^n_{wc} = (T_{wc} - rB_w)/K = \text{ const} && (4.179)\\
T_{cc} &= t^n_{cc}K + rB_c, \quad t^n_{cc} = (T_{cc} - rB_c)/K = \text{ const} && (4.180)\\
G &= T_w + gK, \quad g = const && (4.181)\\
\hat{M} &= \bar{\mu} = const && (4.182)\\
& \text{5. } \underline{\text{Equilibrium condition (asset-markets):}} &&\\
M &= M^d = h_1 pY \exp(-h_2(r - r_o)) : \ \rightarrow r && (4.183)\\
& \text{6. } \underline{\text{Equilibrium condition (goods-market):}} &&\\
Y &= C + I + \delta K + G : \ \rightarrow Y && (4.184)\\
& \text{7. } \underline{\text{Equilibrium condition (labor-market):}} &&\\
L^d &= L^s : \ \rightarrow w && (4.185)\\
& \text{8. } \underline{\text{Inflationary expectations (of workers):}} &&\\
\dot{\pi}^e_w &= \beta_{\pi^e_w}(\hat{p} - \pi^e_w) && (4.186)
\end{aligned}
$$

Note first that the above model is the one of the preceding section if we assume $\beta_p = \infty$ and $a = 0$ in which case firms adjust their price to marginal wage costs with infinite speed. This earlier model is therefore a limit case of the above extended model, but not necessarily a continuous one (since the price level is then regulated by an algebraic condition in the place of a differential equation). It may therefore be that perfect price flexibility does not mirror situations of a very fast adjustment of the price level towards marginal wage costs, in our view a problem for the use of the algebraic condition in the place of the adjustment process here considered.

Note with respect to this model too, that we have reduced its presentation to its structural equations, leaving out here the identities for savings and the financing of investment plans. Note furthermore, that capital income taxation as well as the distribution of assets does again not matter here very much, due to the assumption made on tax collection and the consumption of asset holders. The static part of the model determines, as already explained above, through general market equilibrium the variables w, Y, r on the basis of a temporarily given price level p in particular. The investment decision of firms (and the financial decision of asset holders) is again based on myopic perfect foresight on the rate of inflation (which in fact is determined by firms and not by the market), while workers continue to have an adaptive revision of their inflationary expectations used in their consumption and labor supply decision.

We thus have as the essential and only new equation of the model the rule for the price setting behavior of firms, where we assume that the target price level of firms is given by marked up normal marginal wage costs $(1 + a)w\frac{dL}{dY}$, the measure for 'normal' being provided by the normal employment (the normal working day period) L of the employed labor force. The level L generally differs from the actual employment L^s of the labor force L, due to its over- or underemployment caused by the level of equilibrium goods demand Y and their labor supply schedule in particular. Actual price level changes are assumed now to occur with a lag with respect to the difference that exists between the target price level $p^* = (1 + a)w/F_L(K, L)$ and the actual one, p.[33] The price level is thus

[33]This simple extension of the marginal cost rule of perfectly competitive prices in particular claims that the price level is subject to upward forces and thus starts moving upwards before its equality with marginal wage costs has been reached (from below).

unambiguously described as a dynamically endogenous variable now, and not allowed to jump (by assumption), while output Y or demand Y^d are assumed to adjust with infinite speed in order to clear the market for goods. Up to this essential difference the model is exactly the same as in the preceding section. Of course, also other markup pricing rules can be used in the place of the above one, for example one based on normal average costs. One then has to assume in addition that the markup is large enough so that the price level generally stays above the competitive one.

Goods market equilibrium in per unit of capital form is now described by:

$$y = f(l^d) = c_w((1-\tau_w)\omega, r - \pi_w^e)l + c_c + i_1(\rho - r + \hat{p}) + n + \delta + \tau_w \omega l^s + g$$

with the rate of inflation $\hat{p}$ and the rate of profit ρ being defined by:

$$\hat{p} = \beta_p((1+a)\omega/f'(l) - 1), \quad \rho = y(l^d) - \delta - \omega l^d.$$

Labor market equilibrium is represented by:

$$l^d = f^{-1}(y) = l^s = \ell((1-\tau_w)\omega, r - \pi_w^e))l.$$

In these equations, the nominal rate of interest is again given by money market equilibrium, i.e., when solved by the equation:

$$r = r_o + \frac{\ln(y(l^d)/l) + \ln p + \ln h_1 - \ln(\bar{m}))}{h_2}.$$

This gives three nonlinear equations for the determination of the three statically endogenous variables y, w, r, and of $l^s = l^d = f^{-1}(y)$, which can thereby be expressed as functions of the dynamically endogenous variables l, p, π_w^e, and thus be removed from the presentation of the laws of motion of the considered model of equilibrium growth. The state variables obey the following laws of motion:

$$\begin{aligned} \hat{l} &= n - (y - c_w((1-\tau_w)\omega, r - \pi_w^e)l - c_c - \delta - \tau_w \omega \ell((1-\tau_w)\omega, r - \pi_w^e)l - g) \\ &= -i_1(\rho - r + \hat{p})) && (4.187) \\ \hat{p} &= \beta_p((1+a)\omega/f'(l) - 1) && (4.188) \\ \dot{\pi}_w^e &= \beta_{\pi_w^e}(\hat{p} - \pi_w^e) && (4.189) \end{aligned}$$

which now group the price level p unambiguously among the dynamically endogenous variables. Note, that they are all predetermined now at each point in time[34] with consequences to be discussed below. This closes the intensive form description of the equilibrium model of monetary growth to be analyzed in this section.

To see the difference to the growth model of the preceding section in as clear a way as possible we shall again make the following simplifying assumptions:

- $\tau_w = 0$, which simplifies the presentation of the equations to be used for comparative statics and dynamic analysis, and

[34] Even in the limit of myopic perfect foresight.

- $\ell \equiv 1$, which significantly simplifies the feedback structure of the equilibrium part and the steady state calculations to be performed below.

We define $\omega(l) = f'(l)/(1+a)$ and $\rho(l) = f(l)-\delta-\omega(l)l$. Furthermore, the function $c(l)$ is defined by $c(\omega(l), \rho(l))$. This function $c(l)$ has the derivative $c'(l) = c_{w1a}f''(l)/(1+a)+c_{w2a}\rho'(l)$ which is unambiguously negative, since $c_{w1a} > 0, c_{w2a} < 0, \rho' > 0$ holds true. The elasticity of this function $c(l)$ is given by $\epsilon(l) = -c'(l)l/c(l) > 0$.

Proposition 4.14

Assume $\epsilon(l) > 1$ at all values of the labor intensity l. Then: The dynamical system (4.187) – (4.189) has a unique interior steady state given by the solution of

$$f(l_o) = c(l_o)l_o + c_c + n + \delta + g$$

and by

$$\begin{aligned} y_o &= f(l_o) \\ \omega_o &= f'(l_o)/(1+a) \\ r_o &= \rho(l_o) \\ \hat{p}_o &= \pi^e_{wo} = 0 \\ p_o &= l_o\bar{m}/(h_1 y_o). \end{aligned}$$

Proof: Due to the assumption $\epsilon(l) = -c'(l)l/c(l) > 1$ we get that the right hand side of the following equation

$$f(l_o) = c(l_o)l_o + c_c + n + \delta + g$$

is a decreasing function of the steady state value l_o on the positive domain of $\Re$. With respect to the left hand side of this equation we have as usual the Inada conditions which immediately implies that there is a unique intersection in the positive domain of $\Re$ of the curves that represent the right and left hand side of the above equations. The remaining steady state values of the dynamics are then obtained in a recursive fashion from this steady state level of the full employment labor intensity. ■

The interior steady state solution l_o, p_o, π^e_{wo} is, up to the markup factor a, the same as the one considered in proposition 4.11 in the preceding section. There is thus basically no change in the perspective on such long-run characteristics of the dynamics. The essential difference therefore must be found in the comparative statics of its temporary equilibrium positions and in the dynamical adjustments that are in operation off the steady state position.

The temporary equilibrium of the model is now given by:

$$y = f(l) = c_w(\omega, r - \pi^e_w)l + c_c + i_1(\rho - r + \hat{p}) + n + \delta + g \qquad (4.190)$$

$$r = r_o + \frac{\ln(f(l)/l) + \ln p + \ln h_1 - \ln \bar{m}}{h_2} \qquad (4.191)$$

where

$$\rho = f(l) - \delta - \omega l \quad \text{and} \quad \hat{p} = \beta_p((1+a)\omega/f'(l) - 1).$$

These equations constitute a system of two equations in the two unknowns ω, r, since $y = f(l)$ is a given magnitude under the assumption of an inelastic labor supply. Inserting the $r, \rho, \hat{p}$ - equations into the equation (4.190) provides us with a single equation in the unknown ω which thereby is made implicitly dependent on the state variables l, p, π_w^e of the revised dynamics of this section. Note, that although ω is thus a statically endogenous variable, it does not give rise to the application of the jump variable technique, since there is no dynamic equation for ω. Furthermore, the three dynamic variables l, p and π_w^e are all assumed to be predetermined, or statically exogenous, at every point in time, so that there is no possibility of applying the root criterion mentioned in section 4.5.

Consider now the demand side in equation (4.190) with all functions just considered inserted into it, i.e.

$$y^d(\omega; l, p, \pi_w^e) = c_w(\omega, r(l,p) - \pi_w^e)l + c_c + i_1(\rho(\omega, l) - r(l,p) + \hat{p}(\omega, l)) + n + \delta + g.$$

From the expressions constituting $r, \rho, \hat{p}$ we know that

$$r_l < 0, r_p > 0, \rho_l > 0, \rho_\omega < 0, \hat{p}_\omega > 0, \hat{p}_l > 0$$

holds true. Assume now for the time being $\beta_p = 0$. There then follows

$$y_\omega^d = (c_{w1a} - i_1)l \gtreqless 0, \quad y_l^d > 0, \quad y_p^d < 0, \quad y_{\pi_w^e}^d > 0.$$

Proposition 4.15

Assume $y_l^d > f'(l)$ at the steady state and $\beta_p = 0$. Then: The temporary equilibrium (4.190), (4.191) is characterized, in a neighborhood of the steady state, by the following comparative static properties

$$\begin{array}{llll} \omega_l < 0, & \omega_p > 0, & \omega_{\pi_e} < 0, & \text{if } c_{w1a} > i_1 \quad [r_l < 0, r_p > 0, r_{\pi_w^e} = 0] \\ \omega_l > 0, & \omega_p < 0, & \omega_{\pi_e} > 0, & \text{if } c_{w1a} < i_1 \quad [r_l < 0, r_p > 0, r_{\pi_w^e} = 0]. \end{array}$$

Note that the situation $i_1 < c_{w1a}$ represents the case where the so-called mass purchasing power effect outweighs the cost effect of real wage increases at the steady state, while the opposite is true in the case $i_1 > c_{w1a}$. It is therefore easy to understand why ω_p is positive in the first case and negative in the second one, since we have $r_p > 0$ and thus a reduction of aggregate demand via the interest rate effect which must be compensated by an increase of ω in the first case and a decrease of the real wage in the second one.

Proof: Goods market and money market equilibrium is according to the above characterized by

$$H(\omega; l, p, \pi_w^e) = f(l) - y^d(\omega, l, p, \pi_w^e) \equiv 0.$$

This function is zero at the steady state determined in proposition 4.14 and fulfills the assumptions of the implicit function theorem at this point of the phase space. By this theorem we therefore get from this identity in a neighborhood of the steady state:

$$\begin{aligned}\omega_l &= -\frac{H_l}{H_\omega} = \frac{f'(l) - y_l^d}{y_\omega^d} = \frac{f'(l) - y_l^d}{(c_{w1a} - i_1)l} > 0\\ \omega_p &= -\frac{H_p}{H_\omega} = \frac{i_1 r_p - c_{w2a} r_p l}{(c_{w1a} - i_1)l} < 0\\ \omega_{\pi_w^e} &= -\frac{H_{\pi_w^e}}{H_\omega} = \frac{c_{w2a} l}{(c_{w1a} - i_1)l} > 0\end{aligned}$$

which proves the proposition. ■

Note that the real wage cannot be determined as a function of the state variables of the dynamics if $c_{w1a} = i_1, \beta_p = 0$ holds, since the equation system (4.190), (4.191) does not exhibit a solution ω, r in this case. Note furthermore, that assuming $\beta_p > 0$ gives rise to

$$H_l = f'(l) - y_l^d + i_1\beta_p(1+a)\omega f''(l)f'(l)^{-2}, \quad H_\omega = (i_1 - c_{w1a})l - i_1\beta_p(1+a)f'(l)^{-1}.$$

This extension adds power to the relevance of the case $i_1 < c_{w1a}$ as the typical situation that determines the comparative static properties of the equilibrium part of the model, in particular if the parameter β_p is made large enough, in which case the sign of ω_l however becomes positive. The dependence of real wages ω on the price level is therefore then always a positive one, which surely establishes a destabilizing feedback chain between real wage and price increases via the assumed markup pricing behavior.

Proposition 4.16

Assume $\ell \equiv 1$ and $\tau_w = 0$ and that $\beta_{\pi_w^e} = 0$ holds so that π_w^e can be fixed at its steady state value 0*. Then:*

1. The dynamics (4.187), (4.188) are locally of saddle point type, i.e., we have $\det J < 0$ *and thus two real eigenvalues of opposite sign for the Jacobian of this reduced dynamical system at the steady state, if β_p is chosen sufficiently large.*

2. The dynamics (4.187) – (4.189) are locally also of saddle point type if $\beta_{\pi_w^e} \approx$ 0*, and β_p sufficiently large, holds in which case there will one positive and two negative eigenvalues for the Jacobian at the steady state of the dynamics.*

Proof: 1. In order to show that $\det J < 0$ holds true we remove all expressions from the law of motions (4.187), (4.188) that produce linear dependencies in this Jacobian J. The dynamical equations can in this way be reduced to the following non equivalent dynamics without any change in the sign of $\det J$.

$$\begin{aligned}\dot{l} &= r(l,p) - f(l) + \omega l\\ \dot{p} &= \omega/f'(l)\end{aligned}$$

The Jacobian of this reduced system reads at the steady state:

$$J = \begin{pmatrix} r_l - f' + \omega + \omega f''/(f')^2 & r_p \\ \omega_l/f' - \omega f''/(f')^2 & \omega_p/f' \end{pmatrix}.$$

For det J we therefore get the expression:

$$J = \begin{vmatrix} - & + \\ + & + \end{vmatrix}$$

if β_p is sufficiently large.

2. In order to calculate the sign of the determinant of J it suffices to note that the partial derivatives of the $\hat{p}$-equation can be removed from the third row of J without change in sign of det J by subtracting the second row of J from it. For det J we therefore get in the 3D case the qualitative expression:

$$J = \begin{vmatrix} - & + & ? \\ + & + & ? \\ 0 & 0 & - \end{vmatrix} > 0$$

due to what has been shown in the first part of the proposition. ■

What is different in the situation considered in proposition 4.16 as compared to the preceding section?

Proposition 4.17

Assume again $\ell \equiv 1$ and $\tau_w = 0$. Then: The dynamics (4.187) – (4.189) are locally also of saddle point type if both $\beta_{\pi^e_w}, \beta_p$ are sufficiently large, in which case there will be one positive and two negative eigenvalues for the Jacobian at the steady state of the dynamics.

Proof: The determinant of the Jacobian of the dynamics (4.187) – (4.189) remains positive at the steady state for all choices of the adjustment parameter β_{π^e}, due to arguments used in the proof of the preceding proposition: The third law of motion can again be reduced to $\dot{\pi}^e_w = \beta_{\pi^e_w}(-\pi^e_w)$ without change in the sign of the determinant of the Jacobian of the 2D dynamics at the steady state. Furthermore, the trace of J is negative for all β_{π^e}, β_p sufficiently large, since $\hat{p}_{\pi^e_w} = \beta_p(1+a)\omega_{\pi^e_w}/f'(l)$ is negative which implies that the entry J_{33} of the Jacobian of the full dynamics at the steady state is always negative and can be made arbitrarily large by increasing the adjustment speed of inflationary expectations of workers sufficiently in the assumed situation.

Taken together these two conditions on J imply that there are either two negative and one positive eigenvalue of J or two conjugate complex ones with negative real part coupled with a positive real eigenvalue, since the determinant of J is the product of the three eigenvalues of J. There are only two further situations in which there is a positive determinant, namely three real and positive eigenvalues and two conjugate complex ones with nonnegative real part coupled with a positive real eigenvalue. In these situations we have however trace $J > 0$, since trace is the sum of eigenvalues, in contradiction to what has been shown above. ■

We thus in sum have that the dynamics (4.187) – (4.189) is locally of saddle point type (with a one-dimensional unstable manifold) for small as well as for large adjustment parameters β_{π^e} (assuming that β_p is sufficiently large). This shows that the situation in the

Keynesian formulation of equilibrium growth is not fundamentally different from the one in the Walrasian setup if fast adjustment of prices to (marked up) marginal cost pricing occurs. The huge difference however now is that the price level is no longer allowed to jump, which means that other means than those supplied by the jump variable technique have to be found in order to make the considered dynamics economically meaningful ones.

Note however that the trace of the Jacobian J of the dynamics (4.187) – (4.189) at the steady state can always be made positive by a sufficient increase of the parameter β_p relative to the other parameters of the model. This situation that is established thereby might be called a Harrod type instability in the wage price interaction of the model, which is subject to centrifugal forces when the mass purchasing power argument is valid or the adjustment speed of the price level sufficiently high.

The model will therefore produce in such, as well in many other, situations local explosiveness without having at its disposal statically endogenous variables that may be assumed to jump such that convergence is obtained from situations of initial divergence. This is independent of the further problem of whether the dynamics are at all of appropriate saddle point type in order to allow for the application of the jump variable technique. Instead of looking for solutions to the noted stability problems in this direction, in order to lead us back to situations considered in the preceding sections, a possible alternative solution in fact now is to establish economic boundedness of the considered dynamics which if given would make the analysis of local saddle point stability redundant.

The question therefore arises again which forces may keep the economy viable should it depart significantly from its steady state solution. We conjecture, but cannot prove this here that the dynamics as presently formulated does not yet guarantee such economic boundedness. Further modifications are therefore needed in order to achieve such an aim.

Flexible labor supply

Let us assume for the following that $i_1 = 0, \tau_w = 0$ holds, but that $\ell(\omega, r - \pi_w^e)$ is varying ($\ell(\omega_o, r_o) = 1$ now solely). Furthermore, the state variable l is kept fixed at its steady state position based on the assumed investment behavior.[35] The then remaining state variables p, π_w^e obey the laws of motion:

$$\hat{p} = \beta_p((1+a)\omega/f'(l_o) - 1) \quad (4.192)$$

$$\dot{\pi}_w^e = \beta_{\pi_w^e}(\hat{p} - \pi_w^e). \quad (4.193)$$

We know from the above that $c_{w1a}, -c_{w2a}, \ell_1, \ell_2 > 0$ holds and also $r_y, r_p > 0, \rho_y > 0, \rho_\omega < 0$, since the rate of profit is an increasing function of the variable y (close to the steady state). Note that we now have variable y, but fixed l_o which is possible since labor supply is a statically endogenous variable despite the fact that l_o is given. We thus have now the variables y, ω, r to be determined from goods, labor and money market equilibrium.

Proposition 4.18

Assume $l_1(1 - c_2 r_1)/c_1 + l_2 r_1 > g' > l_2 r_1$ at the interior steady state of the dynamics.

[35] Note that this will imply in the following that the rate of interest need not adjust to the rate of profit in the considered situation.

1. The dynamical system (4.192) – (4.193) has a unique interior steady state given by:

$$\begin{aligned} \omega_o &= f'(l_o)/(1+a) \\ \rho_o &= f(l_o) - \delta - \omega_o l_o \\ y_o &= f(l_o) = c(\omega_o, r_o)l_o + c_c + n + \delta + g \\ f^{-1}(y_o) &= \ell(\omega_o, r_o)l_o = l_o, \quad \textit{by assumption} \\ p_o &= \frac{l_o \bar{m}}{h_1 y_o}, \quad \pi^e_{wo} = 0 \end{aligned}$$

2. For the comparative statics of the temporary equilibrium position or the short-run we have in the considered case close to the steady state:

$$y_p < 0, y_{\pi^e_w} > 0, \omega_p < 0, \omega_{\pi^e_w} > 0,$$

i.e., we get effects on output that correspond to the Keynes- and the Mundell-effect of traditional IS-LM analysis and effects on real wages that are also of conventional type.

3. This steady state is locally asymptotically stable for all parameter values $\beta_{\pi^e_w}$ chosen sufficiently small.

4. The steady state loses its stability by way of a Hopf bifurcation at a uniquely determined value $\beta^H_{\pi^e_w}$ of $\beta_{\pi^e_w}$ if the parameter β_p is chosen such that $(\beta_p(1+a)/f'(l_o))\omega_{\pi^e_w} > 1$ holds true.

5. The steady state of the system is locally asymptotically stable for all $\beta_{\pi^e_w} < -p_o\omega_p/\omega_{\pi^e_w} > 0$ independently of the size of the price adjustment parameter β_p.

In the situation considered in assertion 5, the model of the preceding section and the jump variable technique employed for its solution are not approached when $\beta_p \to \infty, a \to 0$ is assumed. The Sargent and Wallace (1973) solution to the modeling of monetary growth thus represents a discontinuity as far as the role of price flexibility, represented by the parameter β_p, is concerned, at least in the case of a sluggish adjustment of workers' expectations of inflationary expectations.

Proof: 1. A direct consequence of setting the laws of motion of the considered system equal to zero due to the recursive nature of the calculation of the steady state values in this situation.

2. The temporary equilibrium position of (4.192)–(4.193) is defined by:

$$y - c(\omega, r(y,p) - \pi^e_w) - const = 0, \quad f^{-1}(y) - \ell(\omega, r(y,p) - \pi^e_w) = 0.$$

This system of equation defines implicitly two functions $y(p, \pi^e_w), \omega(p, \pi^e_w)$ whose derivatives are given by the implicit function theorem as follows:

$$\begin{pmatrix} y_p & y_{\pi^e_w} \\ \omega_p & \omega_{\pi^e_w} \end{pmatrix} = \frac{1}{-\ell_1(1-c_2r_1) + (g' - \ell_2 r_1)c_1} \begin{pmatrix} -\ell_1 & c_1 \\ \ell_2 r_1 - g' & 1 - c_2 r_1 \end{pmatrix} \begin{pmatrix} c_2 r_2 & -c_2 \\ \ell_2 r_2 & -\ell_2 \end{pmatrix}.$$

The assumptions made on partial derivatives then imply the stated comparative static effects for the temporary equilibrium positions.

3. The Jacobian of the dynamics (4.192) – (4.193) reads at the steady state:

$$J = \begin{pmatrix} (\beta_p(1+a)p_o/f'(l_o))\omega_p & (\beta_p(1+a)p_o/f'(l_o))\omega_{\pi_w^e} \\ (\beta_p(1+a)\beta_{\pi_w^e}/f'(l_o))\omega_p & (\beta_p(1+a)\beta_{\pi_w^e}/f'(l_o))\omega_{\pi_w^e} - \beta_{\pi_w^e} \end{pmatrix}.$$

This implies that $\det J = -\beta_p(1+a)p_o/f'(l_o))\omega_p\beta_{\pi_w^e}$ is positive throughout, since its sign is dependent on the sign of $\omega_p < 0$ solely. For trace J we get the expression:

$$(\beta_p(1+a)p_o/f'(l_o))\omega_p + (\beta_p(1+a)/f'(l_o))\omega_{\pi_w^e}$$

which is negative if $\beta_{\pi_w^e}$ is chosen sufficiently small (due to $\omega_p < 0$). This implies the local asymptotic stability of the steady state via the Routh Hurwitz theorem.

4. The assumption on the parameter β_p implies that $J_{22} > 0$ must hold true (due to $\omega_{\pi_w^e} > 0$). Choosing $\beta_{\pi_w^e}$ sufficiently large thus makes the trace of J zero and positive thereafter. Furthermore, the real parts of the eigenvalues of J depend positively on the parameter $\beta_{\pi_w^e}$ of the system and thus cross the imaginary axis with positive speed at the point where the Hopf bifurcation occurs.

5. A direct consequence of the formula for the trace of the Jacobian J. ■

We stress that the above results also hold in the case of average markup pricing (with a markup that is sufficiently large) and a lagged adjustment of prices again, of course. In a world where technologies are complex and optimization actions costly this may be the adequate response of firms in order to solve the problem of the pricing decision for their commodities.

4.7 Summary

We have shown in this chapter, on the one hand, that an important innovation of neoclassical macrodynamic theory, the consideration of endogenously generated growth in labor productivity and output can be easily transferred to our working model of disequilibrium and growth without much change in the qualitative structure of the dynamics and their stability features. Furthermore, also neoclassical smooth factor substitution was easily added to this type of dynamics with their fluctuating rates of employment of the labor force and of capacity utilization of the capital stock of firms. This in particular demonstrated that fixed proportions in production and endogenous technical change are unessential for the derivation of basic Keynesian propositions on instability and fluctuating growth.

On the other hand, we have also shown, that the limit case of infinite adjustment speeds of prices, quantities and expectations and thus of full market clearing, alters the dynamic structure of our Keynesian formulation of the interaction of labor, goods and asset markets dramatically, leading to a specific type of real - nominal dichotomy and to saddlepoint instability in the nominal adjustment processes unless the jump variable technique is applied to remove cumulative nominal processes by way of appropriate terminal conditions on the evolution of the price level. This is true independently of the specific formulation of the sector of worker households, by way of classical savings assumptions or a Walrasian derivation of their consumption and savings behavior (and their labor supply). As another version of such equilibrium growth, we have finally considered a Keynesian variant where goods, labor and asset markets are cleared by instantaneous adjustments of output, nominal wages and the nominal rate of interest, but where firms do no longer behave competitively in the presence of a Keynesian goods market equilibrium, but implement a delayed adjustment of prices towards their target value, given by marked up marginal wage costs. This version therefore combines general market clearing with delayed price setting behavior that departs from competitive conditions. In this way we could show that the jump variable technique is no longer applicable to such KMG equilibrium growth which however becomes locally unstable for high adjustment speeds of the price level to its target value. Global arguments are therefore needed in order to show that such equilibrium growth dynamics remains bounded or viable. Such arguments are provided as a perspective for future work for an appropriately simplified classical reformulation of KMG growth, that allows for a three dimensional representation of the implied dynamics, in the appendix 4.8 below.

4.8 Appendix: Labor market dynamics and classical viability

Starting from extended KMG disequilibrium growth in section 4.2, with factor substitution and endogenous technical change added in section 4.3, we have investigated in this chapter then how three variants of this model type behave when equilibrium levels of wages, prices and quantities replace their sluggish disequilibrium adjustment processes. The findings were that instability of saddlepoint type will then predominantly prevail in the neighborhood of the interior steady state of the dynamics which may, however, be turned into saddlepoint stability and thus after-shock convergence back to the steady state if the price level is capable of adjusting instantaneously in the special way demanded by the jump variable technique. This possibility was given in section 4.4 and 4.5, but by assumption absent in section 4.6, since there was no jump variable among the dynamic variables of the model of this section.

The problem with the model of section 4.6 and its often cumulative instability in price level dynamics, however, is that it may not be characterized by unbounded dynamics from the economic point of view and thus not yet be a completely specified model, despite various intrinsic nonlinearities already contained in it. It is our conjecture here that these nonlinearities are too weak still in order to suppress the considered explosiveness of price level dynamics far off the steady state. To achieve global boundedness or viability in dynamic models of dimension 3, as the one of section 4.6, is not an easy issue, since one has to address the question what the essential intrinsic or what further extrinsic nonlinearities far off the steady state are that prevent that local instability from being carried over into global instability. Lack of availability of the jump variable technique in a model as in the preceding section thus demands that this model is developed further in order to obtain the required economic viability or boundedness, in which case there is no necessity to employ the jump variable technique any more.

Having grouped the price level among the dynamically endogenous variables and the wage level among the statically endogenous ones in the preceding section helped to formulate a model of Keynesian monetary growth with general equilibrium at each moment in time, but surely one that is problematic from an empirical point of view, from which the opposite arrangement (concerning the role of wage and price flexibility) may be the more convincing one. We therefore return in this final section, with the chapter 5 already in perspective, to the assumption of sluggishly adjusting nominal wages and thus to labor market disequilibrium, in order to address the issue of economic boundedness from the perspective of labor market dynamics. Due to the analytical difficulties then involved we however simplify the behavior on the goods market radically, by assuming that a Keynesian coordination of investment and savings decisions is not yet present on this market. Having found that the dynamics of KMG growth under full market clearing becomes a supply driven one, with the IS-LM block concerning the dynamics of the price level solely (in the Walrasian setup) or instantaneously adjusting nominal wages and nominal interest (in the Keynesian setup), we thus suppress IS in this concluding section altogether and simplify the theory of the price level accordingly, in order to get as starting point for addressing viability issues a dynamic model of dimension 3 that can be handled analytically.

The final variant of KMG growth considered in this chapter therefore becomes one of classical disequilibrium growth with nonlinearities in labor market dynamics that make the dynamics globally bounded, irrespective of what is valid at and around the interior steady state of them, where local or global asymptotic stability, saddle point instability or pure local explosiveness may prevail, which will remain unnoticed by economic agents in the latter two cases. The Keynesian aspects of such dynamics will be taken up again in the next chapter where the question of global bounds arising from the supply side of the KMG growth model will complete the KMG structure used so far and be investigated in its details. At present we will however study the general KMG disequilibrium growth model of section 4.3 in the following classical supply side format, now at last from the global point of view.[36]

The equations of our classical reformulation of KMG growth with smooth factor substitution and endogenous technical change are:

1. Definitions (remunerations and wealth):

$$\omega = w/p, \quad \rho = (Y - \delta K - \omega L^d)/K, \quad W = M/p + K \tag{4.194}$$

2. Households (workers and asset-holders):

$$C = \omega L^d - T_w + (1 - s_c)[\rho K - T_c] \tag{4.195}$$

$$S_p = Y - \delta K - T_w - T_c - C = s_c[\rho K - T_c] = (\dot{M}/p + \dot{K}) \tag{4.196}$$

$$n = \hat{L} = n(V^w), \quad n' \geq 0, \; n(1) = \bar{n}, n(2) = \infty \tag{4.197}$$

3. Firms (production, research and investment):

$$L_1^d \text{ det'd via } \omega = F_L(K, \exp(n_l t)L) \tag{4.198}$$

$$Y = F(K, \exp(n_l t)L_1^d) \tag{4.199}$$

$$n_l = \hat{A}(1+\xi) \tag{4.200}$$

$$\hat{A} = \eta L_2^w / L_1^d = \eta h, \quad h = L_2^w / L_1^d \tag{4.201}$$

$$\hat{L}_1^w = \beta_l(V_1^w - 1) + n, \quad V_1^w = \frac{L_1^d}{L_1^w} \tag{4.202}$$

$$V = \frac{L_1^w + L_2^w}{L} = (1+h)V_1 \leq 1 \quad V_1 = \frac{L_1^w}{L} \tag{4.203}$$

$$h = h(V^w), \quad h' \geq 0, \; (1+\xi)\eta h(1) = \bar{n}_l \tag{4.204}$$

$$\tag{4.205}$$

4. Government (fiscal and monetary authority):

$$T = T_w + T_c, \quad T_w = \tau_w \omega L^d, \quad T_c = t_c^n K, \; t_c^n = \text{const} \tag{4.206}$$

$$\hat{M} = \bar{n} + \bar{n}_l \tag{4.207}$$

$$G = T + \dot{M}/p \tag{4.208}$$

$$S_g = T - G \tag{4.209}$$

5. Equilibrium conditions (asset-markets):

$$W = M^d/p + K^d \tag{4.210}$$

$$M = M^d = h_1 pY, \quad [K = K^d] \tag{4.211}$$

$$\hat{K} = (S_p + S_g)/K \quad [= S/K] \tag{4.212}$$

[36] See Flaschel (1999b) for further details on the following investigation.

$$
\begin{array}{rcll}
 & 6. & \underline{\text{Nominal wage dynamics (adjustment equation):}} & \\
\hat{w} & = & \beta_{w_1}(V-\bar{V})+\beta_{w_2}(V_1^w-1)+\hat{p}+n_l & (4.213)
\end{array}
$$

We assume for simplicity in the following the functions n, h of V_1^w are constant to the left of the normal level 1 of this rate of employment.

Since we have purely supply driven dynamics now we need not distinguish expected profit from actual profit here, but simply define in block 1 real wages ω and the rate of profit ρ in actual terms as two important variables that drive the economy. Real wealth W by contrast is here only needed for the full presentation of the budget restrictions of the model, but not in their dynamics, since there are no wealth effects in demand in the present formulation of the model. Consumption and the source of savings are formulated as in the KMG model of section 4.2, 4.3, but savings now only concern the accumulation of money and real capital as there are no other assets in this classical version of KMG growth. The growth rate of the supply of labor is now made an endogenous variable of the model and is in particular assumed to rise with sufficient speed as the rate of employment V_1^w of those employed in the production sector of the economy is approaching 200 %. The number here chosen only serves the purpose of illustrating the argument made below.

Firms use a neoclassical production technology with smooth factor substitution and URL type technical change as in section 4.3 of this chapter and employ labor L_1^d in the production sector up to the point where the marginal product of production workers equals the uniform real wage in the economy. An essential innovation of the present model is that it now allows for over- and underemployment in the production sector by distinguishing between workers employed in this sector, L_1^w, and the labor time they actually work, L_1^d which is determined by the marginal productivity theory of employment as just stated. Workers L_2^w in the research sector, by contrast, are assumed for simplicity, to have a normal working day solely, that is we here assume $L_2^d = L_2^w$. As in section 4.3, the amount of workers working in the research for productivity increases is assumed to be given by hL_1^d, where h is now assumed to be a non decreasing function of the employment $V_1^w = L_1^d/L_1^w$ of production workers. Due to the possibility of over- and undertime work, we have now to describe the employment policy of firms in addition, which is here simply done by assuming that firms change their workforce L_1^w in the production sector in proportion to the deviation of the internal rate of employment in this sector from the normal rate of employment of the employed, given by 1, plus a trend term given by the 'natural' rate of growth. It is important to note that this trend term can vary in periods of high internal employment rates of productive workers, then representing the fact that firms are in this case actively recruiting laborers from 'across the border'. As ratios we will need in the following the total rate of employment V on the external labor market, which is proportional to the one for production workers, and the internal rate of employment V_1^w of the latter group.

Taxation schemes are as in sections 4.2 and 4.3 and money supply is again growing at a constant rate, the interior steady state rate of the model. Since there are now no government bonds we have an endogenous determination of government expenditures G then, given by the government budget constraint. Asset markets are thus now very simple and are assumed to clear by price level adjustment according to the strict form of the quantity theory of money. Finally, there remains to describe how wages are now adjusted in the light of external and internal labor market disequilibria. We here assume that both disequilibria have influence on the rate of change of money wages, which in addition incorporate, via myopic perfect foresight, the actual change in the price level p and the actual rate of Harrod neutral technical change caused by the research activities of firms and the Romer externality as in section 4.3.

In order to derive the laws of motion of the economy in state variable form we need the following intermediate dynamical considerations. Calculating the rate of growth of the capital stock from the above gives:

$$\hat{K} = s_c(\rho - t_c^n) - \dot{M}/(pK) = s_c(\rho - t_c^n) - \hat{M} \cdot h_1 f(l_1^{de}), \quad \hat{M} = \bar{n} + \bar{n}_l$$

where

$$\rho = f(l_1^{de}) - \delta - f'(l_1^{de})l^{de}, \; l_1^{de} = \exp(n_l t)L_1^d/K, l^{de} = \exp(n_l t)(L_1^d + L_2^w)/K, l^{de} = (1+h)l_1^{de}$$

due to the assumed marginal productivity theory of employment in the production sector of the economy in particular. By marginal productivity theory we also know that the rate of employment of production workers per unit of capital, l_1^{de}, is subject to the condition $\omega^e = f'(l_1^{de}), f'' < 0$. We thus have $l_1^{de} = g(\omega^e), g' < 0$ as theory of the rate of employment of production workers on the basis of temporarily given real wages in efficiency units, $\omega^e = \omega / \exp(n_l t)$, due to equation (4.198) of the model. This implies

$$\hat{l}_1^{de} = \frac{g'(\omega^e)\dot{\omega}^e}{g(\omega^e)} = \frac{g'(\omega^e)\omega^e}{g(\omega^e)}\hat{\omega}^e = \epsilon(\omega^e)\hat{\omega}^e, \quad \omega^e > 0$$

with $\epsilon(\omega^e) = g'(\omega^e)\omega^e/g(\omega^e) < 0$. The final intermediate step is then given by taking note of the definitional relationship:

$$\hat{L}_1^d = \hat{K} + \hat{l}_1^{de} - n_l$$

which will allow us to calculate the growth rate of the employment of the production workers by means of the above model equations.

Using these formulae the model (4.194) – (4.213) gives rise to the following laws of motion:

$$\begin{aligned}
\hat{\omega}^e &= \beta_{w_1}(V - \bar{V}) + \beta_{w_2}(V_1^w - 1), \quad V = (1 + h(V_1^w)V_1^w)V_1 && (4.214)\\
\hat{V}_1^w &= \hat{K} + \hat{l}_1^{de} - n_l - \hat{L}_1^w && (4.215)\\
&= s_c(\rho - t_c^n) - (\bar{n} + \bar{n}_l)h_1 f(l_1^{de}) + \epsilon(\omega^e)\hat{\omega}^e - n_l(V_1^w) - \beta_l(V_1^w - 1) - n(V_1^w)\\
\hat{V}_1 &= \beta_l(V_1^w - 1) && (4.216)
\end{aligned}$$

in the case where all state variables are positive (in the case of zero levels the corresponding growth rates must be resolved into the time derivatives on the left hand side of these laws of motion and their levels multiplied to their right hand sides). Note again that ρ is defined by

$$\rho = f(l_1^{de}) - \delta - f'(l_1^{de})l^{de} = f(l_1^{de}) - \delta - f'(l_1^{de})(1 + h(V_1^w))l_1^{de}$$

where $l_1^{de} = g(\omega^e)$ due to the marginal productivity theory of employment.

Proposition 4.19

Assume that the equation

$$s_c(\rho(l_1^{de} - t_c^n) - (\bar{n} + \bar{n}_l)h_1 f(l_1^{de}) - (\bar{n} + \bar{n}_l) = 0$$

has exactly one solution $l_{1o}^{de} > 0$ (at $V_1^w = 1$). Then: There exists a uniquely determined interior steady–state *of the dynamics (4.214) – (4.216) (where $\omega^e, V_1^w, V_1 \neq 0$ holds) which is given by*

$$V_{1o}^w = 1; V_o = \bar{V}; V_{1o} = \bar{V}/(1 + h(1)); \quad \omega_o^e = f'(l_{1o}^{de})$$

Proof: A direct consequence of setting the right hand sides of (4.214) – (4.216) equal to zero and of considering only positive outcomes as solutions to this problem. ■

We observe that this steady state will be locally unstable if the parameter β_{w_1} is sufficiently large. The proof of this assertion is not obvious, but demands the tedious calculation of the $a_1a_2 - a_3$ term from the set of the Routh-Hurwitz conditions which can be shown to be negative if β_{w_1} is sufficiently large, see Flaschel (1999b) for details.

Proposition 4.20

The steady state is locally asymptotically stable if $\beta_{w_2} - (\beta_{w_1}\overline{V} - \delta) > 0$ holds for some suitably chosen $\delta > 0$. The size of δ can be chosen the larger, the larger the terms $\epsilon(\omega), \beta_l, \beta_{w_2}$ become.

Proof: See Flaschel (1999b). ■

Proposition 4.21

Assume that $f(l_1^{de})$ is an upward bounded function (of the state variables of the model) and that $s_c - (\bar{n} + \bar{n}_l)h_1 > 0, \beta_l > (\bar{n} + \bar{n}_l) + s_c(\delta + t_c^n)$ holds true. Then: The point in $\Re^3$:

$$V_1^w = 0; V_1 = 0; \omega_o^e = 0$$

is a steady–state of the dynamics (4.214) – (4.216) and of saddle point type.

Proof: The assertion on the steady state solution is obvious, since (4.214) – (4.216), rewritten as a system of differential equations, is obviously zero at this point in $\Re^3$. Furthermore, taking partial derivatives of the differential equations at this particular steady state means that (4.214) – (4.216) just have to be evaluated at this steady state in order to obtain the diagonal of the Jacobian at this steady state while all other entries in this Jacobian must be zero then. For J we therefore get in the expression:

$$J = \begin{pmatrix} -\beta_{w_1}\bar{V} - \beta_{w_2} & 0 & 0 \\ 0 & s_c f(l_1^{de}) - s_c(\delta + t_c^n) - (\bar{n} + \bar{n}_l)h_1 f(l_1^{de}) - (n(0) + n_l(0)) + \beta_l & 0 \\ 0 & 0 & -\beta_l \end{pmatrix}$$

The assertion on the saddle point character of the considered steady state then follows from what has been assumed, since J_{22} is positive then, while J_{11}, J_{33} are obviously negative. ■

It is easy to see that the hyper planes of $\Re^3$ defined by $\omega^e = 0, V_1 = 0$ and $V_1^w = 0$ are invariant subsets of R^3 of the dynamics (4.214) – (4.216), that is they cannot be left when the motion starts in them, and that they contain respectively the stable and the unstable manifold of the saddle point steady state at zero. It follows that no orbit of the dynamics that starts in the positive orthant of $\Re^3$ can approach this saddle steady state, since it would then have to be on the invariant stable manifold already.

The question arises whether there are further steady states of the dynamics (to which their orbits might then converge to). We briefly attempt to show here that there are indeed no further steady states in the nonnegative orthant of $\Re^3$. Assume first that $V_{1o}^w = 0$ holds at such a steady state. Then $V = 0$ by (4.216), rewritten as differential equation. By (4.214) we then also get $\omega^e = 0$, i.e., the zero in $\Re^3$ is the only steady state that fulfills $V_{1o}^w = 0$. Consider therefore next the case $V_{1o}^w = 1$ together with $\dot{V}_1, \dot{\omega}^e = 0$. In this case we get from (4.215) that l_{1o}^{de} must be the solution of this steady state condition, where $l_{1o}^{de} > 0$ is determined as in proposition 4.19. Thus $\omega_o^e = f'(l_{1o}^{de}) > 0$ and therefore $V = \bar{V}$ by (4.214), i.e., assuming $V_{1o}^w = 1$ gives rise to the interior solution considered in proposition 4.19.

There remains $V_{1o}^w \neq 0, 1$ to be considered. Equation (4.216) then implies $V_{1o} = 0$ and thus $V = 0$ which by equation (4.214) gives $\beta_{w_1}(-\bar{V}) + \beta_{w_2}(V_1^w - 1) = 0$ should $\omega^e \neq 0$ obtain and by (4.215)

$$s_c(\rho - t_c^n) - (\bar{n} + \bar{n}_l)h_1 f(l_1^{de}) - n_l(V_1^w) - n(V_1^w).$$

The last equation has the unique solution considered in proposition 4.19 in which case however $V_1^w \leq 1$ was assumed to hold. All other solutions must be based on having $V_1^w > 1$ which however implies that $V_1 = 0$ can not be attracting then. Similarly, $V_1^w > 0$ by the first equation which in sum means that further steady states, should they exist, will not be attractors of the dynamics. They can therefore be ignored in the global considerations that now follow.

Proposition 4.22

Assume that $f(l_1^{de})$ is an upward bounded function (of the state variables of the model). Then: The domain D in $\Re^3$ given by:

$$D = \{\omega^e, V_1^w, V / \omega^e \in (0, \infty), V_1^w \in (0, 2), V \in (0, 1]\}$$

is an invariant set of the dynamics (4.214) – (4.216) which therefore cannot be left by their orbits.

Proof: When formulating the model in this section we have already assumed the hard constraint $V \leq 1$ which simply says that the labor market has become exhausted (though of course new entrants appear according to $n = n(V_1^w)$, the employment situation within the firms). A hard constraint on the external labor market does not mean however that firms cannot produce according to the marginal productivity rule and the profit maximum this rule represents. As long as $V_1^w < 2$, which is our assumed bound on the overtime work performed by the employed they are not limited by the existing labor supply and thus continue to produce in the considered profit maximizing way. However at $V_1^w = 2$ we have

$$\hat{V}_1^w = s_c(\rho - t_c^n) - (\bar{n} + \bar{n}_l)h_1 f(l_1^{de}) + \epsilon(\omega^e)\hat{\omega}^e - n_l(2) - \beta_l - n(2)$$

since ρ is bounded if $f(l_1^{de})$ is bounded from above and since $n(2) = \infty$ has been assumed. This upper bound on overtime work cannot therefore be reached, according to the recruiting efforts of firms 'across the border' of the considered economy in situations close to this bound which means that the economy will turn before this bound can be reached. ■

Of course, due to the equality of real wages with the marginal product of labor gross profits will remain positive in the considered dynamics, if the capital productivity y does not fall below the rate of depreciation δ. We shall however not go into a consideration of this possibility here, which would also demand a consideration of the net rate of profit $\rho - t_c^n$.

We have the result that a simple recruiting hypothesis for periods of significant overtime work can keep the economy working at full capacity growth with no constraint in supplied labor hours, but probably one (sooner or later) on the external labor market, which makes the dynamics a system of differential inequalities then. The overall picture is, we conjecture, one in which orbits and their attractors (simple or complex ones) will be bounded from below and from above with respect to the state variables of the model and thus produce a theory of business fluctuations in the case where the interior steady state is a repeller. We thus close this chapter with a dynamic perspective that keeps the classical regime of profit maximizing firms in operation at all points in time, and which gives rise to bounded regular or irregular endogenous fluctuations if the interior steady state is an unstable node, focus or a saddle point, situations that are of no interest then for the actual working of the economy. We have again integrated here endogenous growth, which may help to stabilize the economy, but is not of central importance for the working of the dynamics as should be equally obvious from the above.

We have not yet considered the inflation rate implied by the operation of the laws of motion for the real part of the economy. Due to the assumed strict quantity theory of money we have of course:

$$\hat{p} = \hat{M} - \hat{Y} = \bar{n} + \bar{n}_l - \hat{y} - \hat{K}, y = f(l_1^{de}).$$

This implies the expression

$$\hat{p} = \bar{n} + \bar{n}_l - \epsilon(l_1^{de})\epsilon(\omega^e)\hat{\omega}^e - s_c(\rho - t_c^n) - (\bar{n} + \bar{n}_l)h_1 f(l_1^{de})$$

where the elasticity $\epsilon(\omega^e)$ is defined as above and where $\epsilon(l_1^{de})$ is the elasticity of the production function at l_1^{de}. We thus get that the rate of inflation is a somewhat complicated expression obtained from the real dynamics, which however remains bounded when the real dynamics remains bounded, as was shown above. In the present formulation of the model, where this inflation rate is perfectly foreseen by workers, there is thus nothing problematic to be obtained from the nominal side of the economy. Of course this is due to the fact that the real side is, as in section 4.4, but for different reasons, independent of the nominal side.

This situation does not change if money demand is made dependent on the relative return of money as compared to capital, which would only make the nominal side look more complicated than before. However, such an extension is in the tradition of the Tobin type models of monetary growth, which might in addition suggest that the concept of disposable income of asset holders should be revised then too, giving rise to $\rho K - \frac{M}{p}\pi^e - t_c^n K$ in the place of only $\rho K - t_c^n K$ as the measure of disposable income that keeps real wealth intact. We here only observe, but do not go into this question any further, that this will make the real and the nominal dynamics interdependent and thus may lead to complications that are not easily handled by the above approach to economic viability.[37]

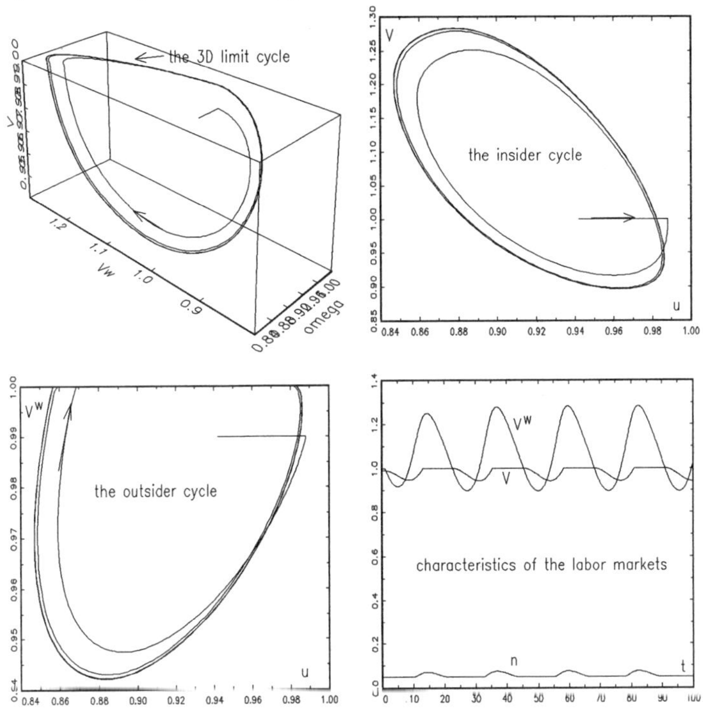

Figure 4.4:
A limit cycle of the dynamics and the full employment ceiling.

Let us finally have a look at a simulation run of the model just discussed. The parameter values on which the simulation in figure 4.4 is based are the following ones: $\beta_{w_1} = 0.5, \beta_{w_2} = 0.05, n = 0.05, \bar{V} = 0.99, s_c = 0.9, \beta_l = 0.1, \eta = 50, a = 0.5$.

The first plot in figure 4.4 shows the three dimensional dynamics in the variables V, V^w and ω as a whole, thereby clearly demonstrating the existence of a limit cycle as well as the development of the economy along the full employment ceiling during a certain phase of the cycle. The next two plots (top right and bottom left) then show the interaction between the wage share u and V^w, the employment of the employed (therefore called the "insider cycle"), and between u and the employment rate V (the "outsider cycle"). These two pictures illustrate in a clear way, that in phases, where the full employment constraint $V \leq 1$ is already binding, firms are nevertheless able to realize their desired labor demand by making use of overtime work. Note however, that although an upper bound exists also for overtime hours (200 %), it is not reached in the present case. The last plot finally displays the time series for V^w, V and the growth rate of labor supply n. That the last

[37]See Chiarella and Flaschel (1999b) for a detailed treatment of the Tobin type monetary growth models and of the Tobin effect these models are subject to.

is not constant over time mirrors the fact, that according to equation (4.197) this trend term (positively) depends on V^w, the employment of the employed, which comes about by migration.

Chapter 5

Fix-Price Approaches: Regime Switching Overstated

5.1 Introduction

In this chapter we reconsider the microfounded approaches to macro-statics and -dynamics that started from the so-called fix-price models (with quantity adjustments in the place of price adjustments) for their determination of temporary equilibrium positions. We shall reconsider these approaches here purely on the macrolevel and from the perspective of descriptive macrodynamics in order to investigate the contributions of these approaches to macrodynamics to a further improvement of our general KMG model of monetary growth.

Non-Walrasian macroeconomics has provided many significant contributions to macrostatics as reviewed recently in Benassy (1993). Important approaches in this regard are the models of Clower (1965), Barro and Grossman (1971), Benassy (1977, 1984, 1986) and Malinvaud (1977, 1980, 1984), to mention only a few of them. The common starting point of these theories can be seen in a critique of the main assumption of Walrasian market-clearing models, that transactions do not occur before the market clearing price vector has been found. If, however, in contrast to this, transactions at "wrong prices" are taken into account, they are typically connected with rationing on different markets. The crucial point is now, that supply and demand on a single market depend no longer only on the price vector (including not only goods prices but also wages, interest rates etc.), but also on the rationing, that agents have experienced on other markets. This type of demand, originally formulated by Clower (1965) and thus usually referred to as "Clower demand",[1] already appeared in our KMG model, where firms reacted with regard to their emission of new equities on the disequilibrium perfectly perceived by them at the beginning of each period. On this basis many approaches like, e.g. the one of Malinvaud (1980), came to a division of the state space of the economy into different regimes in dependence on the short side of the goods market and the labor market. Thus, if the temporarily given wage-price constellation led to aggregate demand being the binding constraint on the goods market and the resulting demand for labor being the short side on the labor market, the corresponding regime was called "Keynesian". On the other hand, if supply constraints due to capacity

[1]This designation was introduced by Benassy (1977).

or profitability constraints represented the short side on the goods as well as on the labor market, the economy found itself in a "Classical" regime. A situation with excess demand on both markets finally was called a regime of "repressed inflation". Malinvaud (1980) – as many other approaches in this respect – now formulated laws of motion for the temporarily fixed wages and prices in order to study the dynamic adjustment processes of the economy considered. In addition, however, he also took explicitly into account the dependence of investment on profitability as well as on capacity utilization and thus elements also playing an important role in our KMG framework. On this basis, a business cycle could be derived which, however, got stuck in the Keynesian regime with a stable depression, the size of which furthermore depended on the initial point, at which the dynamics took its point of departure.

Thus, although non-Walrasian theories considerably improved the description of the short-run, when prices are temporarily fixed, there are however far less contributions of this approach to the theory of business fluctuations and only very few to the theory of economic growth (in real or monetary economies). There is indeed only one footnote in Benassy (1993) with respect to these important subjects of macrodynamics, which (though not mentioning all contributions in this area) nevertheless provides the correct impression that there is not much to say about the non-Walrasian modeling of monetary growth. The explanation for this theoretical deficit in non-Walrasian macrodynamics is not difficult to provide if one looks at the papers in Hénin and Michel (1982) for example: Regime switching scenarios, as they are investigated thoroughly in the non-Walrasian statical analyses of general economic interdependence and spill-over of disequilibria between markets, can be managed in the static context. However, they become nearly untractable in the analysis of macroeconomic fluctuations and growth in monetary economies, in particular if the considered dynamics is no longer planar, due to laws of motion for real wages, real money balances, factor endowments, and more.

In this respect the paper by Picard (1983) has made significant progress since it provides a monetary growth model of non-Walrasian type with its typical switches of regimes (Keynesian or classical unemployment and repressed inflation), giving rise to a three-dimensional dynamics in the above named variables, which, however, is not easy to analyze (as the long appendices containing the proofs of Picard's (1983) propositions show).

In section 5.2 we will reconsider a slightly modified version of the original Picard model. Section 5.3 shows for the Picard approach to monetary growth that this analysis – and the model formulation on which it is based – can be considerably simplified if some basic aspects in the formulation of wage-price dynamics in the macrodynamic literature are taken into account, i.e., the facts (for which various rationalizations may be offered) that wages and prices start rising before the level of absolute full employment in the labor market and absolute capacity utilization within firms has been reached. These simple additions to the wage-price module (which are used here as an example solely) suffice to show that the environment of the steady state of such models of monetary growth is completely Keynesian (with no regime switching to classical unemployment or repressed inflation). The dynamics around the steady state is thereby radically simplified and propositions as in Picard (1983) are now easily proved and extended.

With this background the KMG model of chapter 4 is reconsidered in section 5.4, where now various boundaries concerning the supply side of the economy are included. As will be shown there, however, the explicit modeling of inventories and other buffers like overtime work prevent the economy from leaving the Keynesian regime (where demand is never rationed) for quite a large region around the steady state, although there are several subregimes within the Keynesian one, which have to be regarded. On the other hand, a switch out of the Keynesian regime can occur, when inventories become exhausted. This case and the resulting rationing of demand is also considered in section 5.4 which is closed by a number of simulation runs to investigate the stabilizing and destabilizing effects of different parameter constellations. In this context, a further important nonlinearity in form of a kinked Phillips-curve, which prevents nominal wages from falling when unemployment is high, is taken into account. After a summing up of the main results in section 5.5 the subsequent appendix shows, that one of the earliest contributions to models exhibiting regime switching, namely the one of Solow and Stiglitz (1968) can be interpreted as a special case of the KMG model.

We conclude that macroeconomic applications of the non market-clearing approach are predominantly Keynesian in nature and thus do not need the heavy machinery of nonlinear differential inequalities for most of its propositions.

5.2 A Non-Walrasian model of monetary growth

To demonstrate the working of a typical and already comparatively elaborated model of the non-Walrasian variety, the model of Picard (1983) shall be considered in this section. Picard (1983) distinguishes three commodities and four agents. Since however the banking sector and the rate of interest ascribed to it play no explicit role in the static or dynamic part of the model, it suffices for our purposes to assume as framework the following set of markets and sectors:

The commodities: goods, labor, money.
The sectors: households, firms, government.

The adoption of this framework changes the interpretation of the growth model of Picard (1983), but it does so without changing the temporary equilibrium positions nor the assumed laws of motion, but instead provides an interesting alternative view on the contents of these constituent parts of the model.

The Households: Households are represented as a single aggregate agent with their planned consumption given by

$$C = c(1-\tau)Y + dM/p, \quad c \in (0,1), d > 0$$

and an inelastic labor supply L that grows with the natural rate $n = \text{const} > 0$ over time. The income Y (before taxes τY) will be determined later on. The budget constraint of the household sector is

$$C + S = (1-\tau)Y + \dot{M}/p, \quad S = \dot{M}^d/p.$$

The Government: The government sector exhibits the following budget constraint

$$pI + pG = \tau pY + \dot{M}$$

i.e. the state finances real investment I and real public consumption G via real taxes τY and the real change in money supply $\dot{M}/p$. It is assumed that all income of the firms (wages and profits) is distributed to households (and then taxed) and that firms are organizing production as well as formulating investment plans. The amount of public consumption then adjusts so that the above budget constraint is fulfilled.

The Firms: Firms have a linear production technology of the form

$$\begin{aligned} Y^p &= y^p K, \quad y^p = \text{ const} \quad (U_c = Y/Y^p) \\ Y &= xL^d, \quad x = \text{ const} \quad (V = L^d/L) \end{aligned}$$

where as usual Y^p denotes potential output and Y actual output and thus $L^d = Y/x$ actual employment.

In order to determine actual output Y several intermediate concepts for the description of the supply and demand of goods are needed. We denote by $\widetilde{Y}^d$ the unconstrained demand for goods

$$\widetilde{Y}^d = C + I + G.$$

Furthermore

$$\widetilde{L}^d = \min\{\widetilde{Y}^d/x, Y^p/x\}, \quad \check{Y} = \min\{Y^p, xL\}$$

denote the minimum labor demand (when aggregate demand $\widetilde{Y}^d$ and potential output Y^p are taken into account as constraining labor demand) and the minimum production when potential output and the full employment output act as constraints on production [for $\omega = w/p < x$]. The above two magnitudes are called effective labor demand and the effective supply of goods in Picard (1983).

Finally, desired production $\overline{Y}$ is defined by Picard (1983) by

$$\overline{Y} = \min\{\widetilde{Y}^d, xL\}$$

and used as an argument in the investment behavior of firms which in its qualitative form is determined by

$$I/K = i_1\overline{Y}/K + i_2(x - w/p)$$

as long as real wages do not exceed labor productivity: $w/p < x$ (I/K is zero otherwise). This type of investment function (which allows for positive investment in the face of excess capacity) is justified in Picard (1983) in two different ways.

Note finally that we do not have to specify a budget restraint for firms since all profits are distributed to households and all investment is financed by the government.

Fix price equilibria: We have already defined effective demands and supplies on the labor market: $\widetilde{L}^d, L$ as well as on the market for goods: $\widetilde{Y}^d, \check{Y}$. We now assume that realized transactions on each of the two markets are given by the minimum of demand and supply:

$$Y = \min\{\widetilde{Y}^d, \check{Y}\}, \quad L^d = \min\{\widetilde{L}^d, L\} = Y/x.$$

These two magnitudes thus describe actual output and actual employment and are the basis of wage payments and profit transfers. They describe the temporary equilibrium position of the economy as far as output and employment are concerned. This temporary equilibrium position can be of one of the following three types:

$$\begin{aligned} \text{Keynesian unemployment (KU)} : Y &= \widetilde{Y}^d \leq \check{Y} \qquad (\widetilde{L}^d \leq L) \\ \text{Classical unemployment (CU)} : Y &= y^p K \leq \widetilde{Y}^d \qquad (\widetilde{L}^d \leq L) \\ \text{Repressed inflation (RI)} : Y &= xL \leq \widetilde{Y}^d \qquad (L \leq \widetilde{L}^d). \end{aligned}$$

In the Keynesian case there is excess supply in both the labor and the goods market, in the Classical case there is excess demand in the market for goods and excess supply in the market for labor and under repressed inflation there is excess demand in both the market for labor and the market for goods.[2]

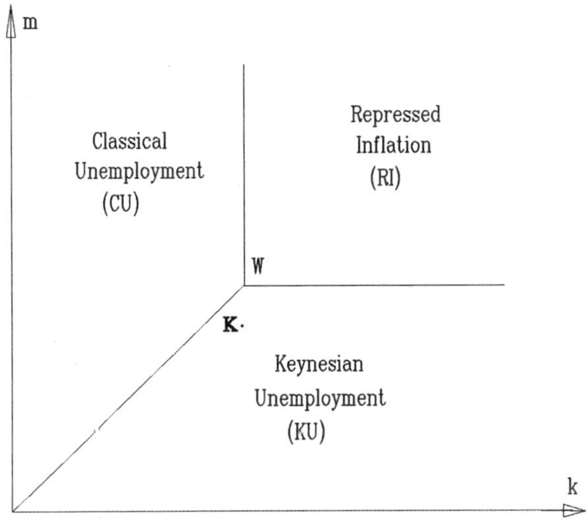

Figure 5.1:
The three regimes in the k, m state space.

Using the intensive form variables $k = K/L$ and $m = M/(pL)$ we can represent the domains of the validity of the three regimes as shown in figure 5.1, see Picard (1983, pp.272ff.) for details.

Under classical unemployment real balances m and thus effective demand are high and capital per unit of labor low, while the opposite is the case under Keynesian unemployment. Repressed inflation occurs in the economy if both magnitudes are high, leading to excess demand for goods as well as for labor.

If one now assumes that firms and the government are never rationed in the market for goods, so that this rationing only concerns the household sector, one can immediately progress from the given description of temporary equilibrium positions to dynamics, since the magnitudes I and G then describe realized magnitudes that can be used in conjunction with Y, L^d (and $\widetilde{L}^d, \widetilde{L}, \check{Y}$) to formulate the laws of motion of such an economy.

[2]The fourth possible combination of such market constellations is not available in the present type of model.

<u>The laws of motion of the economy:</u> Picard (1983) here assumes two specific types of Phillips curves, one for money wages w and one for the price level p, based on demand–pull as well as cost–push considerations of the following form ($\omega = w/p, \tilde{\omega}$ the given target real wage of workers):

$$\hat{w} = \beta_{w_1}\left(\frac{\tilde{L}^d - L}{\tilde{L}^d}\right) + \beta_{w_2}(\tilde{\omega} - \omega) + \kappa_w \pi^e, \quad \hat{p} = \beta_p\left(\frac{\tilde{Y}^d - \check{Y}}{\tilde{Y}^d}\right) + \kappa_p \pi^e$$

with positive β's as adjustment speeds and both κ_w and κ_p in the interval $[0,1]$. And for capital stock growth we of course have:

$$\widehat{K} = i_1 \overline{Y}/K + i_2(x - \omega)$$

or $\dot{K} = 0$ for $\omega \geq x$. These three laws of motion imply the following nonlinear autonomous dynamical system in the intensive form variables $\omega = w/p, m = M/(pL)$ and $k = K/L$ if we assume as in Picard (1983) that $\mu = \dot{M}/M =$ const holds and if expected inflation $\pi^e = \mu - n = \widehat{M} - \widehat{L}$ is fixed at the steady state value of the rate inflation $\mu - n$. For simplicity we assume $\mu = n$ in the following:

$$\widehat{\omega} = \beta_{w_1}\left(\frac{\tilde{L}^d - L}{\tilde{L}^d}\right) + \beta_{w_2}(\tilde{\omega} - \omega) - \beta_p\left(\frac{\tilde{Y}^d - \check{Y}}{\tilde{Y}^d}\right) \tag{5.1}$$

$$\widehat{m} = -\beta_p\left(\frac{\tilde{Y}^d - \check{Y}}{\tilde{Y}^d}\right) \tag{5.2}$$

$$\widehat{k} = i_1 \overline{Y}/K + i_2(x - \omega) - n \tag{5.3}$$

with

$$\frac{\tilde{L}^d - L}{\tilde{L}^d} = \frac{\tilde{l}^d - 1}{\tilde{l}^d}, \qquad \frac{\tilde{Y}^d - \check{Y}}{\tilde{Y}^d} = \frac{\tilde{y}^d - \check{y}}{\tilde{y}^d}, \qquad \frac{\overline{Y}}{K} = \frac{\overline{y}}{k}$$

where all variables have been transformed to intensive form by dividing through labor supply L.

Since $\check{y} = \min\{y^p k, x\}, \overline{y} = \min\{\tilde{y}^d, x\}, \tilde{l}^d = \min\{\tilde{y}^d/x, y^p k/x\}$ and $y = \min\{\tilde{y}^d, \check{y}\}$, $l^d = y/x$ there remains $\tilde{y}^d$ to be calculated. In the Keynesian regime one gets for this variable:

$$\tilde{y}^d = \frac{1}{1 - c(1-\tau) - \tau}(d + \mu)m = f^1(m) \tag{5.4}$$

which can be interpreted as a Keynesian multiplier, while $\tilde{y}^d$ is given in the Classical regime by

$$\tilde{y}^d = (c(1-\tau) + \tau)y^p k + (d + \mu)m = f^2(k, m) \tag{5.5}$$

and in the regime of repressed inflation by

$$\tilde{y}^d = (c(1-\tau) + \tau)x + (d + \mu)m = f^3(m). \tag{5.6}$$

This shows that the above dynamical system can indeed be reduced to the three state variables ω, m and k.

<u>Steady states and stability:</u> We define $\overline{\omega}$ by the condition

$$I/K = i_1 y^p + i_2(x - \overline{\omega}) = n, \quad \overline{\omega} < x$$

i.e. the wage rate that equalizes capital stock growth with natural growth at (desired) full capacity growth ($i_1 y^p < n!$). With respect to this expression the following proposition then holds, see Picard (1983, p.278):

Proposition 5.1

If $\tilde{\omega}$, the target real wage, belongs to an appropriately chosen neighborhood U_1 of $\overline{\omega}$, the above dynamical system has a unique stationary point (ω_0, m_0, k_0) which coincides with the Walrasian equilibrium (ω, W), see figure 5.1, when $\tilde{\omega} = \overline{\omega}$. Furthermore, when $\tilde{\omega} > \overline{\omega}$ $[\tilde{\omega} < \overline{\omega}]$ we have for the steady state (m_0, k_0) in the projected phase plane of figure 5.1: $(m_0, k_0) \in KU \cap CU$ $[(m_0, k_0) \in KU \cap RI]$, respectively.

Proof of Proposition 5.1 [For $\overline{\omega} = \tilde{\omega}$]:

1. $\dot{m} = 0 \quad (m \neq 0)$ implies $\widetilde{Y}^d = \check{Y} = \min\{Y^p, xL\}$.
2. In the case $\widetilde{Y}^d = Y^p \leq xL$ we then get $\overline{Y} = Y^p = \widetilde{Y}^d$, i.e., $\omega_0 = \tilde{\omega} = \overline{\omega}$. Therefore: $L = \min\{\widetilde{Y}^d/x, Y^p/x\}$ because of $\dot{\omega} = 0 \quad (\omega \neq 0)$, i.e., $\widetilde{Y}^d = xL$, i.e. we are in the situation W of figure 5.1, the Walrasian general equilibrium.

   We then get from the expressions for $\tilde{y}^d$ first

   $$x = \tilde{y}_0^d = \frac{1}{1 - c(1-\tau) - \tau}(d+\mu)m_0,$$

   the steady state value of real balances m_0, and from the expression for $\tilde{y}^d$ of the classical equilibrium

   $$x = (c(1-\tau) + \tau)y^p k_0 + (d+\mu)m_0,$$

   the steady state value of the capital intensity k_0.
3. In the case $\widetilde{Y}^d = xL = \bar{Y} \leq Y^p$ we, on the other hand, have that we are on the borderline between KU and RI, so that $\tilde{y}^d = x \leq y^p$ must hold true. Therefore:

   $$m_0 = (1 - c(1-\tau) - \tau)x/(d+\mu)$$

   and $\omega_o \leq \bar{\omega} = \tilde{\omega}$ due to $\dot{k} = 0 \quad (k \neq 0)$. We thus have $\beta_{w_2}(\tilde{\omega} - \omega) > 0$ and due to $\dot{\omega} = 0: \quad \widetilde{L}^d \leq L$ or $\min\{\widetilde{Y}^d/x, Y^p/x\} \leq L$ which again implies $\widetilde{Y}^d = Y^p = xL$. The remaining calculations are then as in the preceding case. ■

There are further steady state calculations in Picard (1983) and also one proposition on the local asymptotic stability of steady states in situations of interior steady states (where no minimum operator is operative, so that the dynamical system is then not only continuous, but also continuously differentiable). Since we are, however, in this chapter concerned mainly with the structure of non–Walrasian monetary growth models and not so much with the results that can be obtained from them, we can stop at this point.

Summing up the preceding presentation of this type of disequilibrium monetary growth theory we can state that

- its behavioral equations are simpler, but not unrelated to the Keynes–Metzler model of chapter 2 (with a stabilizing Pigou–effect in place of the stabilizing Keynes–effect of the latter model)
- it describes a situation that is closer to a description of a planned than of a market economy
- its richness of implication is based on the numerous regimes it allows for (in fact there are two further subregimes in each of three regimes we have considered in this section)
- it represents a complete model of monetary growth with a very complicated dynamical structure due to the various differential inequalities that have to be considered in general.

In view of this we shall demonstrate in the following section that a much richer structural form of Keynesian monetary growth (which is much closer to the description of a market economy than the model of this section) will be much simpler to treat from the viewpoint of dynamical systems (steady state and stability analysis) due to the fact that this flexible model of monetary growth of a market economy rarely undergoes switching of regimes and even much less often will allow for the establishment of Classical unemployment or repressed inflation in the sense of a rationing of the aggregate demand $\widetilde{Y}^d = C + I + G$. Therefore much of the effort that has gone into the analysis of laws of motions based on differential inequalities can simply be avoided by paying attention to the fact that market economies have a variety of mechanisms and flexibilities that allow them to avoid the rationing of consumers, or investors or the government on the macroeconomic level.

5.3 From Non-Walrasian to Keynesian modeling of monetary growth

The most basic critique of the non–Walrasian dynamics of section 5.2 is that its two Phillips–curves for money wages and the price level are misspecified with respect to the actual working of market economies. This is due to their neglect of NAIRU levels of rates of employment and also of rates of capacity utilization which may be difficult to rationalize from a microeconomic perspective, but which are surely relevant on the macroeconomic level.[3]

Whatever motivation is offered for the NAIRU rate of employment $\bar{V}$, it is generally agreed that money wages are subject to an upward pressure before everybody in the workforce is employed. The obvious and necessary change in the money wage PC thus is

$$\widehat{w} = \beta_w \left(\frac{\tilde{\tilde{L}}^d - \bar{V}L}{\tilde{\tilde{L}}^d} \right) + \beta_{w_2}(\widetilde{\omega} - \omega), \quad \bar{V} \in (0,1), \tilde{\tilde{L}}^d = \min\{\widetilde{Y}^d/x, \bar{U}_c Y^p/x\}$$

[3]See also Flaschel (1999a) with respect to the following reformulation of Non-Walrasian rationing regimes.

Likewise, the price level starts rising before either the capacity constraint or the labor supply constraint becomes binding, i.e., the law for price dynamics should be modified as follows

$$\widehat{p} = \beta_p \left(\frac{\widetilde{Y}^d - \check{\check{Y}}}{\widetilde{Y}^d} \right), \quad \check{\check{Y}} = \min\{\bar{U}_c Y^p, \bar{V} L x\}, \quad \bar{U}_c \in (0,1),$$

where $\bar{U}_c$ represents a normal degree of capacity utilization below 100%. Finally, firms should now use $\bar{\bar{Y}} = \min\{\widetilde{Y}^d, \bar{V} L x\}$ in the place of $\bar{Y} = \min\{\widetilde{Y}^d, Lx\}$ as the capacity constraint for their investment decisions which gives $\widehat{k} = i_1(\bar{\bar{Y}}/K) + i_2(x - \omega) - n$ as the third law of motion.

Up to the use of $\check{\check{Y}}, \bar{\bar{Y}}, \bar{V}L$ in the place of $\check{Y}, \bar{Y}$ and L in the dynamical system (5.1) - (5.3) the model is the same as before.

Proposition 5.2

The unique interior steady state of the revised dynamical system

$$\widehat{\omega} = \beta_{w_1} \left(\frac{\widetilde{L}^d - L\bar{V}}{\widetilde{L}^d} \right) + \beta_{w_2} (\tilde{\omega} - \omega) - \beta_p \left(\frac{\widetilde{Y}^d - \check{\check{Y}}}{\widetilde{Y}^d} \right) \tag{5.7}$$

$$\widehat{m} = -\beta_p \left(\frac{\widetilde{Y}^d - \check{\check{Y}}}{\widetilde{Y}^d} \right) \tag{5.8}$$

$$\widehat{k} = i_1 \left(\bar{\bar{Y}}/K \right) + i_2 (x - \omega) - n \tag{5.9}$$

is given by

$$\omega_0 = \tilde{\omega}, \quad m_0 = (1 - c(1-\tau) - \tau) x \bar{V}/(d+\mu), \quad k_0 = \frac{x\bar{V}}{y^p \bar{U}_c},$$

if we assume that $\tilde{\omega} = \bar{\omega}$ holds, $\bar{\omega}$ given by $i_1 \bar{U}_c y^p + i_2(x - \bar{\omega}) = n$. At this steady state we have

$$\widetilde{Y}^d = \bar{U}_c Y^p = \bar{V} L x < \min\{Y^p, xL\},$$

i.e., this steady state K, see figure 5.1, belongs to the region of Keynesian unemployment (which also holds true for all steady states belonging to a target real wage $\tilde{\omega}$ in a neighborhood of $\bar{\omega}$).

Proof: The proof of this proposition is based on the following simple observations:

1. $\dot{m} = 0 \quad (m \neq 0)$ implies $\widetilde{Y}^d = \check{\check{Y}} = \min\{\bar{U}_c Y^p, \bar{V} L x\}$.
2. In the case $\widetilde{Y}^d = \bar{U}_c Y^p \le \bar{V} L x$ we then get $\bar{\bar{Y}} = \bar{U}_c Y^p = \widetilde{Y}^d$, i.e., $\omega_0 = \bar{\omega} = \tilde{\omega}$. Therefore: $\bar{V} L = \min\{\widetilde{Y}^d/x, Y^p/x\}$ because of $\dot{\omega} = 0 \quad (\omega \neq 0)$, i.e., $\widetilde{Y}^d = x\bar{V}L$ or in sum

$$\widetilde{Y}^d = x\bar{V}L = \bar{U}_c Y^p.$$

Since we are thus always in the Keynesian regime we have

$$\tilde{y}^d = x\bar{V} = \frac{1}{1 - c(1-\tau) - \tau}(d+\mu) = m_0$$

as equation for m_0 and

$$x\bar{V} = \bar{U}_c y^p k_0$$

as equation for k_0 $[= x\bar{V}/(\bar{U}_c y^p)]$.

3. In the other case $\widetilde{Y}^d = \bar{V}Lx = \bar{\bar{Y}} \leq \bar{U}_c Y^p$ (see 1.), we have $\widetilde{y}^d = x\bar{V} \leq \bar{U}_c y^p$. We therefore again get $\omega_0 \leq \bar{\omega}$ and thus $\widetilde{L}^d \leq L\bar{V}$ or $\min\{\widetilde{Y}^d/x, \bar{U}_c Y^p/x\} \leq L\bar{V}$. Thus

$$\widetilde{y}^d = x\bar{V} = \bar{U}_c y^p.$$

Therefore $\omega_0 = \bar{\omega}$ and m_0, k_0 are determined as in the preceding case 2. ■

We thus get that $Y = \widetilde{Y}^d$ holds always in the neighborhood of the steady state and $L^d = \widetilde{Y}^d/x$, i.e., employment is always demand determined sufficiently close to the steady state. The KU-regime is therefore the only relevant one at least in the vicinity of the steady state solution of the dynamical system (5.7) – (5.9).

Remark: This result on the dominance of the Keynesian regime can be made much stronger if overtime work of insiders, smooth factor substitution, excessive production (with respect to the profit maximizing output) in order to satisfy customers' demand and inventories are taken into account as in Flaschel (1999a,b).

Instead of pursuing this line of approach further, let us reexamine here the dynamical laws for $\widehat{w}$ and $\widehat{p}$ with respect to their meaningfulness. Since we have the Keynesian demand regime ($Y = \widetilde{Y}^d$) close to the steady state we get for $\widetilde{\widetilde{L}}^d/L$ the expression $\min\{V, \bar{U}_c y^p k/x\}$ with $V = L^d/L = Y/(xL)$ the actual rate of employment. But how does the expression $\bar{U}_c y^p k/x$ influence money wage dynamics as proposed by the expression

$$\beta_{w_1}\left(\frac{\widetilde{\widetilde{L}}^d - \bar{V}L}{\widetilde{\widetilde{L}}^d}\right)$$

in the above money wage Phillips-curve? Furthermore, why this choice of a denominator? In our view it is sufficient to use (as is customary):

$$\beta_{w_1}\left(\frac{V-\bar{V}}{\bar{V}}\right) = \beta_{w_1}\left(V/\bar{V} - 1\right), V = L^d/L$$

in place of the above expression in order to describe (the demand pull component of) the dynamics of money-wages. Similarly (because of $\widetilde{Y}^d = Y$):

$$\beta_p\left(\frac{\widetilde{Y}^d - \min\{\bar{U}_c Y^p, \bar{V}Lx\}}{\widetilde{Y}^d}\right) = \beta_p\left(\frac{U_c - \min\{\bar{U}_c, \bar{V}x/(y^p k)\}}{U_c}\right).$$

But why $\bar{V}x/(y^p k)$ and U_c in the denominator of this expression? Again the term

$$\beta_p\left(\frac{U_c - \bar{U}_c}{\bar{U}_c}\right) = \beta_p\left(\frac{U_c}{\bar{U}_c} - 1\right)$$

is fully sufficient to express the demand pull component, now in the market for goods. Taken together, the dynamical system (5.7) – (5.9) should therefore be rewritten as

$$\widehat{\omega} = \beta_{w_1}\left(V/\bar{V} - 1\right) + \beta_{w_2}(\bar{\omega} - \omega) - \beta_p\left(U_c/\bar{U}_c - 1\right) \tag{5.10}$$

$$\widehat{m} = -\beta_p\left(U_c/\bar{U}_c - 1\right) \tag{5.11}$$

$$\widehat{k} = i_1 y_p U_c + i_2(x - \omega) \tag{5.12}$$

since $Y^d = Y, L^d = Y/x$ are the relevant expressions for the actual position of the economy, below or above $\bar{V}L$ and $\bar{U}_c Y^p$, but below L and Y^p.

Remark: The interior steady-state of the system (5.10) – (5.12) is the same as for the system (5.7) – (5.9).

Proposition 5.3

1. *The steady-state of the dynamical system (5.10) – (5.12) is locally asymptotically stable if $\beta_{w_1} < \beta_p$ holds true.*[4]
2. *The steady-state of the dynamical system (5.10) – (5.12) loses its stability in a cyclical fashion at the unique Hopf-bifurcation point:*

$$\beta_{w_1}^H = \frac{a_1 a_2}{\beta_p i_2 (V'/\bar{V})(-U_{ck}/\bar{U}_c)\omega_o m_o k_o}$$

through the birth of a stable limit cycle or the death of a stable corridor.[5]

Proof: 1. Due to the prevalence of the Keynesian regime around the steady-state we have

$$\tilde{y}^d(m) = y = \frac{1}{1 - c(1-\tau) - \tau}(d + \mu)m$$

for $V = L^d/L = Y/(xL) = y/x$ and $U_c = Y/Y^p = y/(y^p k)$. Hence, $V = V(m), V' > 0$ and $U_c = U_c(m, k)$, $U_{cm} > 0, U_{ck} < 0$.

According to the Routh–Hurwitz conditions, see Benhabib and Miyao (1981), one has to show

$$a_1 = -\text{trace}\, J > 0, \quad a_3 = \det J > 0, \quad a_1 a_2 - a_3 > 0 \quad (a_2 > 0)$$

where J is the Jacobian of the above dynamical system at the steady-state and where a_2 is given by the sum of principal minors of this matrix.

It is easy to show that $\det J < 0$ must hold, since linearly dependent expressions can be removed from J without altering its determinant which simplifies the calculation of this determinant significantly. Thus:

$$a_3 = -\det J = \beta_{w_1}\beta_p i_2 (V'/\bar{V})(-U_{ck}/\bar{U}_c)\omega_o m_o k_o > 0.$$

Quite obviously, also

$$a_1 = -\text{trace}\, J = \beta_{w_2}\omega_0 + \beta_p (U_{cm}/\bar{U}_c) m_0 + i_1 y_p (-U_{ck}) k_0 > 0.$$

Furthermore, we also immediately get:

$$a_2 = \beta_{w_2}\beta_p (U_{cm}/\bar{U}_c)\omega_o m_o + \beta_{w_2} i_2 y^p (-U_{ck})\omega_o k_o + \beta_p i_2 (-U_{ck}/\bar{U}_c)\omega_o k_o$$

Due to $V(m) = \tilde{y}^d(m)/x, U_c(m,k) = \tilde{y}^d(m)/(y^p k)$ we finally get (by setting the positive β_{w_2}–terms all equal to zero)

$$a_1 a_2 - a_3 > \beta_p i_2 (-U_c/\bar{U}_c)\omega_o m_o k_o \tilde{y}^{d'}(m_o)(\beta_p - \beta_{w_1}),$$

[4] This assertion is similar to one in Picard (1983, p.279), but does not allow for alternative regimes in the present framework.

[5] See the proof for the expressions that define $a_1 a_2$.

since $i_1 y^p(-U_{ck})k_o > 0$ and $y^p \bar{U}_c k_o = x\bar{V} \quad [\bar{U}_c Y^p = x\bar{V}L]$ at the steady state.

2. Since the parameter β_{w_1} only appears in the determinant of the Jacobian J the calculation of the Hopf-bifurcation point is an easy task, since it is characterized by $b = a_1 a_2 - a_3 = 0$, the only stability condition which can change its sign in the present situation. Furthermore, the value of b is a linear (negatively sloped) function of the parameter β_{w_1} which implies as in Benhabib and Miyao (1981) that the eigenvalues cross the imaginary axis with positive speed and thus allows the application of the Hopf-bifurcation theorem. ■

We thus have that price flexibility that is larger (with respect to its demand pull component) than wage flexibility (with respect to the demand pull component) is good for economic stability, which is not too surprising due to the assumed Pigou- or real balance-effect on aggregate demand. Furthermore, this stability is increased through increases in the parameter β_{w_2}, since this adjustment parameter only appears in $a_1 a_2$ and there always with positive signs as the above calculations have shown. We therefore have definite reasons to expect that the local asymptotic stability result holds also for $\beta_p << \beta_{w_1}$ if (e.g.) β_{w_2} is chosen sufficiently high. Nevertheless, there is a limit to this stability result if the parameter β_{w_1} is made sufficiently large (all others held constant), where the stability of the system gets lost in a cyclical fashion.

We conclude that the non-Walrasian approach to monetary growth of section 5.2 can be made a (very) special case of our general Keynes-Metzler model with only minor or – if less secondary – very improbable possibilities of a change in the generally Keynesian regime that governs its evolution. Regime switches and rationing arbitrarily close or even less close to the steady state of market economies is neither empirically plausible nor analytically convincing, since it is based on too strict inequalities in contrast to the many flexible adjustment procedures that are imaginable for developed market economies.

Thus, for example, the situation of repressed inflation will only happen far off the steady state if overtime work of the workforce of firms is taken into account, see section 5.1. The classical regime furthermore is much less likely if account is taken of smooth factor substitution and of the fact that firms will temporarily serve their customers in a Keynesian environment (where firms are not price-takers), beyond the point where prices equal marginal costs – should their inventories be exhausted, see section 5.3. The barriers to serving aggregate demand for goods are thus much less rigid than assumed in non-Walrasian macroeconomics which invests high technical competence in analyzing complicated growth dynamics which have not much in common with the macrodynamics of market economies. Reworking their structural equations in view of this not only will improve the model's relevance, but also simplifies its analysis radically as we hope to have shown in this chapter.

These results are in line with Benassy's (1984) model of a Keynesian limit cycle, where also an appropriate form of the Phillips-curve, that led (nominal) wages converge to infinity as the employment rate converged to one, ensured that the dynamics could not leave the boundaries of the Keynesian regime. The same is valid for the KMG model of the preceding chapter, which will be further extended in this regard in the following with the consequence, that switches away from the Keynesian regime, though possible in principle, will not occur for a large range of parameter values.

In general, we assume that the model's dynamics stays in domains where $\rho^e, M^d, I+\delta K, (1-\tau_c)r - \pi^e$ and all stock variables remain positive and where moreover the share of wages

$u = \omega L^d/Y$ remains below 1. To ensure these side conditions it may be necessary to introduce further and extrinsic nonlinearities into our dynamic model which so far rests on unavoidable or intrinsic nonlinearities solely. These are the only side-conditions for the variables of the model that have to be checked in this regard, since all other variables automatically remain restricted to economically meaningful values in finite time. We return to these side-conditions later on in this chapter.[6]

Non-Walrasian theory made us aware of the fact that all side-conditions of models of fluctuating growth must be specified and proved to hold but it vastly overstated the importance and actual relevance of these side conditions for the ordinary working of market economies.

5.4 Regime switching in KMG growth

In the following we now want to apply the Non-Walrasian methodology just discussed to the KMG model of chapter 4 in order to describe possible regime switches also in this context and to evaluate their relevance. As will be shown, supply bottlenecks can indeed occur in situations, when inventories become exhausted. On the other hand, the various buffers available in the economy as well as the fact mentioned above, that wages begin to rise already before full employment is reached, will make such situations quite exceptional and let them appear only far off the steady state. The next subsection shows, that as a consequence of the introduction of two upper bounds for production some changes due to the supply side already take place within the Keynesian regime without however changing its main characteristic, i.e. the full satisfaction of aggregate demand. Thus, even if actual production falls short of demand, inventories will prevent demand from being rationed. This constellation will not change before inventories become exhausted, a situation which is then analyzed in subsection 5.4.2. A numerical analysis of different scenarios of the whole model (with and without rationing) will be considered at the end of this section; there, the model will be enriched by a further extrinsic nonlinearity, i.e. a kinked Phillips-curve for nominal wages, which will have the effect of stabilizing the economy even for such parameter constellations, which would otherwise lead to explosiveness and regime switching.

5.4.1 Supply bottlenecks with positive inventories

In this subsection we consider the reference KMG growth model of the preceding chapter, now for sluggishly adjusting prices, wages and quantities throughout, and as basis for a general analysis of the Non-Walrasian regime switching approach to economic growth, which we presented in section 5.2 in its basic format. Since it is of importance for the evaluation of the role of supply side bottlenecks (classical regimes or regimes of repressed inflation) we shall include into the KMG model neoclassical smooth factor substitution, overtime work of the employed coupled with a sluggish employment policy of firms, and also endogenous natural growth, building on the presentation of these additions considered in chapter 4, sections 4.3 and 4.7. However, in order not to overload the presentation we

[6]Note here however, that the conditions $\rho^e > 0, u < 1$ can be ensured simultaneously in the following completions of the above version of the model (with smooth factor substitution) when there is no difference between expected demand Y^e and actual demand Y^d and when intended inventories are neglected as in the usual IS-LM approach of the traditional Keynesian macrodynamics.

shall not consider here technical change (neither endogenous nor exogenous one), since this has been treated extensively in the preceding chapter and is not of central interest in the consideration of the relevance of supply side constraints, which are in the center of interest of the present chapter. This section therefore marries aspects of disequilibrium KMG growth with the classical viability investigation of section 4.7, but leaves the integration of endogenous technical change for later reconsiderations of the employed model.

Before we start with the presentation of the model we have to define the two (here fairly soft) upper bounds for the productive activities of firms (arising from labor supply and profitability considerations) that are the basis of the regime switching approach in the KMG framework considered below. Such bounds are here introduced in a way as simple as possible in order to demonstrate in a basic way that there exist important buffers created by the behavior of firms that generally allow to avoid the rationing of *aggregate* goods demand in market economies even for larger deviations from their steady state growth path. These assumed bounds to production can be described in formal terms as follows:

$$\bar{Y}^w = F(K,(1+\bar{o})L^w) > 0 \quad \text{if } L^w > 0 \tag{5.13}$$

$$\bar{Y}^p = F(K,\bar{L}^p) = \omega\bar{L}^p + \delta K > 0. \tag{5.14}$$

Note that there is a unique solution $\bar{L}^p$ to the second condition for neoclassical production functions with the usual properties.

Equation (5.13) states (in slightly more general terms than in section 4.7) that there is a fixed limit to overtime work supplied by the employed workforce L^w of firms, given by the ratio term $\bar{o}$, which may be justified by legal restraints for example, but which in the end should of course be modeled as a flexible barrier. Normal hours worked, L^w, can therefore be at most augmented by $100\cdot\bar{o}$ percent of overtime work of the workforce L^w of firms, where the latter magnitude is fixed at each moment in time, since the employment of additional workers follows the path of overtime work only with a time delay. This is a limitation on labor supply within firms which already indicates that the regime of repressed inflation, in the form it was described in section 5.2, will here only be established as a hard constraint in periods of heavily booming economies.

Equation (5.14) adds the constraint that arises from the current size of the capital stock, which when operative gives rise to the so-called classical regime of Non-Walrasian economics. We here go to the extreme that firms extend their production in periods of high aggregate goods demand up to the point where profits become zero, i.e., where the real wage cost line ωL^d (augmented by capital stock depreciation δK) intersects the production function for a given value of K. Again this is only a first example for such an economic limit to the output of firms, which from the technological perspective could even be infinite in the case of a standard neoclassical production function. Non-Walrasian economics generally assumes that this limit is given by the profit maximizing output of firms and thus is very narrowly determined. However, from the perspective of descriptive macrodynamics, it is acceptable to assume that firms will go beyond the point where given output prices equal marginal wage costs by a variety of reasons that have to do with market shares, customer satisfaction and the like. Of course, the behavior of firms, in particular their pricing decision, may change significantly (in a nonlinear way) when the profit maximizing output is crossed from below. Such change in behavior is however not yet considered here, due to our general methodological approach of considering such behavioral nonlinearities only after the basic form of the model has been developed and investigated.

Equation (5.14) may of course be based also on any other magnitude between Y^p, the profit maximizing output at current wages and prices, and $\bar{Y}^p$ the zero profit output, that can be supplied as a systematic equation based on profitability considerations internal to the firm or external profitability comparisons. A possible procedure could be to assume that employment of the actual labor force is at most extended to the level where firms would use their potential (= profit-maximizing) output Y^p just for paying this employment of the presently employed workforce (which at this point produce more than just Y^p). Yet, in order to be at first as generous as possible regarding the production decisions of firms we will stick to the above very soft constraint on the behavior of firms. In order to defend their market shares and to satisfy their customers as far as possible it is thus assumed in the following that firms expand production beyond the point where prices are equalized to marginal wage costs up to the situation where prices equal average wage costs (based on net output). Such situations indeed characterize actual firm behavior in booming economies. The only question here is the determination of the limit to this type of behavior which of course must be less than ∞ since total profits would be $-\infty$ then.

The following set of equations describes the working of the economy in situations for all cases of constrained production of firms where inventories are positive and where aggregate goods demand can therefore be fulfilled by firms and is indeed fulfilled by assumption. Note, however, that there are now several subregimes within the Keynesian regime. So, e.g., there is a region, where actual production suffices to serve demand, so that no reduction of inventories is required for this purpose. On the other hand, there is a subregime where exactly this is necessary, because production is limited for some reason, i.e. there is an upper bound to production due to $Y^e + \mathcal{I}$, $\bar{Y}^p$ or $\bar{Y}^w$, so that demand can only be satisfied by selling additional goods from inventories; note, that the three possible boundaries to production just mentioned also provide a basis for a classification of further subregimes. The case, however, where no inventories are available any more to fill the gap between production and demand, represents another main regime, which will be analyzed in the next subsection. At this stage, we only want to point to the fact, that dividend payments now depend on the respective subregime and approach their lower bound zero in cases, where production costs of Y^e and $\mathcal{I}$ exceed expected (real) revenues Y^e of firms.

1. Definitions (remunerations and wealth):

$$\omega = w/p, \quad \tilde{\rho}^e = \max\{(Y^e - \delta K - \omega L^d)/K, 0\} \tag{5.15}$$

$$W = (M + B + p_e E)/p, \quad p_b = 1 \tag{5.16}$$

2. Households (workers and asset-holders):

$$W = (M^d + B^d + p_e E^d)/p \tag{5.17}$$

$$C = \omega L^d - T_w + (1 - s_c)[\tilde{\rho}^e K + rB/p - T_c], \quad s_w = 0 \tag{5.18}$$

$$T = T_w + T_c \tag{5.19}$$

$$\begin{aligned} S_p &= \omega L^d + \tilde{\rho}^e K + rB/p - T - C = s_c[\tilde{\rho}^e K + rB/p - T_c] \\ &= (\dot{M} + \dot{B} + p_e \dot{E})/p \end{aligned} \tag{5.20}$$

$$\hat{L} = n = \bar{n}_o + n_1(V^w - 1) + n_2(V - \bar{V}), n_1, n_2 > 0 \tag{5.21}$$

3. Firms (production-units and investors):

$$\omega = F_L(K, L^p), \quad Y^p = F(K, L^p), \quad \rho^p = (Y^p - \delta K - \omega L^p)/K \tag{5.22}$$

$$U_c = Y/Y^p, \quad U_c^e = (Y^e + \mathcal{I})/Y^p \tag{5.23}$$

$$L^d \quad \text{via } Y = F(K, L^d), \ V = L^w/L \leq 1, \ V^w = L^d/L^w, \tag{5.24}$$

$$\dot{L}^w = \beta_v(L^d - L^w) + \gamma L^w \gamma = n \tag{5.25}$$

$$I/K = i_1(\rho^p - (r - \pi^e)) + i_2(U_c^e - \bar{U}_c) + \gamma, \ \gamma = n, \ I + \delta K \geq 0 \tag{5.26}$$

$$S_f = Y - \tilde{\rho}^e K - \delta K - \omega L^d = I + \dot{N} - p_e \dot{E}/p \tag{5.27}$$

$$I = Y^d - \max\{Y^e, \delta K + \omega L^d\} + p_e \dot{E}/p \tag{5.28}$$

$$I^a = I + \dot{N} \tag{5.29}$$

$$\hat{K} = I/K \tag{5.30}$$

4. Government (fiscal and monetary authority):

$$T = T_w + T_c, \quad T_w = \tau_w \omega L^d, \ t_c^n = (T_c - rB/p)/K = const < 0 \tag{5.31}$$

$$G = \tau_w \omega L^d + \bar{g}K, \ \bar{g} \geq 0 \tag{5.32}$$

$$S_g = T - rB/p - G \ \ [= (t_c^n - \bar{g})K = -(\dot{M} + \dot{B})/p] \tag{5.33}$$

$$\hat{M} = \bar{\mu} = n \tag{5.34}$$

$$\dot{B} = pG + rB - pT - \dot{M} \tag{5.35}$$

5. Equilibrium conditions (asset-markets):

$$M = M^d = h_1 pY + h_2 pK(r_o - r), \ \ [B = B^d, E = E^d], \ B, E \geq 0, \ r > 0 \tag{5.36}$$

$$r = \frac{\tilde{\rho}^e pK + \dot{p}_e E}{p_e E} \tag{5.37}$$

6. Disequilibrium situation (goods-market adjustments):

$$S = S_p + S_g + S_f = Y - \delta K - (C + G) = I + \dot{N} = I^a \tag{5.38}$$

$$Y^d = C + I + \delta K + G \tag{5.39}$$

$$\dot{Y}^e = \beta_{y^e}(Y^d - Y^e) + \gamma Y^e, \ \gamma = n \tag{5.40}$$

$$N^d = \beta_{n^d} Y^e \tag{5.41}$$

$$\mathcal{I} = \beta_n(N^d - N) + \gamma N^d, \ \gamma = n \tag{5.42}$$

$$Y = \min\{Y^e + \mathcal{I}, \bar{Y}^p, \bar{Y}^w\}, \quad Y^e + \mathcal{I} > 0 \tag{5.43}$$

$$\dot{N} = Y - Y^d, \quad N > 0 \tag{5.44}$$

7. Wage-Price-Sector (adjustment equations):

$$\hat{w} = \beta_{w_1}(V - \bar{V}) + \beta_{w_2}(V^w - 1) + \kappa_w \hat{p} + (1 - \kappa_w)\pi^e \tag{5.45}$$

$$\hat{p} = \beta_{p_1}(U_c^e - \bar{U}_c) + \beta_{p_2} U_n + \kappa_p \hat{w} + (1 - \kappa_p)\pi^e, \quad U_n = (N^d - N)/K \tag{5.46}$$

$$\dot{\pi}^e = \beta_{\pi_1^e}(\hat{p} - \pi^e) + \beta_{\pi_2^e}(\bar{\mu} - n - \pi^e). \tag{5.47}$$

Note that the two assumed limits to production depend on the current state (variables) of the economy and are only needed in equation (5.43) of the model. Note further that aggregate demand Y^d is always served from production or from inventories $N > 0$ in the presently considered case. However, there are further changes necessary to the model concerning the dividend policy of firms, the choice of a measure of capacity utilization directing investment and pricing decisions of firms, and a few further changes concerning in particular investment and asset market behavior. All these changes will now be justified in detail by going through the above equations of the model step by step.

Concerning block 1. of the model we have as necessary change here, as compared to sections 4.2, 4.3 and 4.7 of the preceding chapter, that the rate of return used to characterize dividend payments to asset holders must of course always stay nonnegative, since there are no negative dividend payments. This constraint has been neglected so far due to the local character of the analysis supplied in the preceding chapter. Dividend payments are still based here on expected sales and current production costs (which generally include the production of inventories), that is on the expected level for the current cash flow of firms. Due to the assumed positive level of inventories expected sales can always be fulfilled by firms and thus can still be assumed as basis of their dividend policy, up to, for example, the exceptional case where

$$Y^e < \bar{Y}^p < \min\{\bar{Y}^w, Y^e + \mathcal{I}\}$$

holds or more generally where inventory production is so large that actual production is so much higher than expected sales that expected sales do not cover production costs. These examples show that the situation $\tilde{\rho}^e = 0$ is not likely to be met in simulation runs of the dynamics implied by the model. Of course this completed characterization of the dividend payments of firms has now to be applied when the income of asset holders, underlying their consumption and savings decision, is specified.

Considering next block 3 of the model, the sector of firms as far as their employment and investment decisions are concerned, we have to introduce specific measures now which underlie their investment decision and which modify the investment function to some extent, compared to the one of chapter 4. We define in (5.22) again potential output and employment, Y^p, L^p, by the profit maximizing levels and now also consider the rate of return ρ^p that corresponds to these levels (disregarding inventory production here).[7] Beyond this rate of return, rates of profits are falling. Excessive and still further increasing expected demand Y^e therefore would lead in such cases via falling rates of return to reductions in investment if this rate would determine the relative profitability measure so far used in the investment function. We therefore propose now to base this measure on the target rate of profit of firms, which for given wages and prices is measured by ρ^p.[8] Furthermore we have two measures of capacity utilization now, the actual one, U_c, and the one that is based on desired output levels of firms derived from their sales expectations and intended inventory changes. We consider the latter measure as the more appropriate one for representing demand pressure and use it for the investment and the pricing decisions of firms. Actual employment L^d is determined by actual production Y which is defined in equation (5.43) based on the three constraints that firms face with respect to goods demand, labor supply and a profitable use of the capital stock in existence. Hiring and firing of workers is again based on the comparison of actual hours worked with normal working conditions L^w and is thus not made dependent on expected sales in a direct way as in the case of investment.

[7] Making use of $\tilde{\rho}^p = y^p\bar{U}_c/(1+\gamma\beta_{n^d}) - \delta - \omega l^p$ would be more appropriate here, since we have so far neglected inventory holdings and excess capacity in rate of return calculations, see the definition of the rate ρ^e in chapter 4. We will circumvent this problem in the following investigation of the model, by assuming $\bar{U}_c = 1, \gamma = 0$ for reasons of simplicity.

[8] Inventories, though a necessity, are considered as a secondary issue and thus neglected in this expression, i.e., are not added to the capital stock of firms when their desired or other rates of profits are calculated.

The budget constraint of firms now reads $Y^d - \max\{Y^e, \delta K + \omega L^d\} + p_e\dot{E}/p = I$ where the first term denotes the income of firms based on their wage payments and their dividend policy and which is of the type of windfall profits and the second term represents again the issuing of new equities in order to close the gap between this income and the intended fixed business investment expenditures of firms. Note that this budget equation can be rewritten as

$$Y - \max\{Y^e, \delta K + \omega L^d\} + p_e\dot{E}/p = Y - Y^d + Y^d - \max\{Y^e, \delta K + \omega L^d\} + p_e\dot{E}/p = I + \dot{N}$$

which represents an accounting budget equation of firms that now also includes actual inventory changes $\dot{N}$ as the other factual investment activity of firms.

There is no change in the government sector of the model which again is played down as much as possible, since we want to concentrate on the private sector in this part of the book. The asset market equilibrium is also the same as before (see eqn. (5.37)). Note, that the capital gains captured by the term $\dot{p}_eE$ ensure, that the assumption of perfect substitutability between equities and bonds can be maintained also in such cases, where dividend payments are zero.[9]

We have already taken notice of the production decision of firms which is given by the minimum of intended production $Y^e + \mathcal{I}$, of maximum production $\bar{Y}^w$ of the workforce employed by firms, and of $\bar{Y}^p$ zero profit output as the absolute limit to firms willingness to supply their customers with goods in the case of a booming economy. Up to this modification, the inventory adjustment mechanism remains the same as before, since aggregate demand is never rationed in the present subdynamics of the complete model where actual inventory changes are of course again given by the excess of actual production Y over actual demand Y^d. Finally, the pricing decision is now based on two measures for disequilibrium within firms, the deviation of desired output $Y^e + \mathcal{I}$ from the normal level $\bar{U}_cY^p$ and the deviation of desired inventories from their actual level, measured relative to the size of the capital stock.

Taken together we therefore have as changes revised budget restrictions of asset holders and firms, certain revisions in the behavioral assumptions for firms which only to some extent generalize earlier presentations of them, an improved price Phillips curve and of course a supply decision of firms that now takes into account further limits to production than only the aggregate level of goods demand. As the model is currently formulated there are however further economic side conditions that may be violated which are:

1. A nonnegative amount of gross investment $I + \delta K$ (only checked numerically)
2. A positive nominal interest rate r (only checked numerically)
3. Nonnegative stocks of financial assets $(B, E \geq 0)$ (only checked numerically)
4. Levels of desired production $Y^e + \mathcal{I}$ that are bounded by a positive magnitude from below (only checked numerically)
5. Rates of employment $V \leq 1$ (imposed)

[9] We continue to use actual output of firms as measure for transactions in the money demand equation, though Y^d, the actual sales, might be a better measure for this purpose in the considered situation.

6. Nonnegative inventories $N \geq 0$ (imposed)

The first two conditions demand for nonlinearities in investment and money demand which will not be considered here (these side conditions therefore have to be checked in all simulations that are performed in order to exclude from consideration all trajectories where they are violated). Condition 3 will generally not be endangered in practicable applications of the model, but should of course also be checked for validity in actual simulation runs of the model. The same holds true for condition 4. Note here that expected sales Y^e must remain positive if actual sales Y^d remain positive throughout, which we shall show to be the case in the next paragraph. Condition 4 is therefore only violated when stocks of inventories are so high that desired inventory reductions exceed expected sales. Condition 5 is simply imposed onto the dynamics of the model, just as in the model considered in section 4.7. As in this earlier model it does not prevent further increases of the output of firms as long as the constraint $\bar{Y}^w$ is not yet operative. Note in this respect that our approach does not demand that the capacity rates U^c, U^e_c must be smaller or equal to 1 since firms will go up to the limit $\bar{Y}^p$ in their use of their productive capacity, which generally is much more than the desired capacity output Y^p on which their measuring of rates of capacity utilizations are based.

From the side conditions just considered we get that actual output Y must always be positive, if the number of employed persons L^w remains positive. This latter number cannot however approach zero, since the constraint $\bar{Y}^w$ would then become binding which would imply $L^d = (1+\bar{o})L^w > L^w$ and thus $\dot{L}^w > 0$ before $L^w = 0$ can be reached. Next, aggregate demand Y^d is bounded by a positive number from below, since this holds true for employment L^d and thus for wage income and the consumption of wage earners, while the consumption of asset holders remains positive, since their income remains positive due to the assumption $t^n_c < 0$ and since gross investment and government expenditures must remain nonnegative by assumption. If Y^d remains positive we get that Y^e remains positive, due to the assumed adaptive mechanism for the formation of sales expectations. The expected real rate of interest, however, in contrast to the other magnitudes considered, may become negative in which case capital losses $\hat{p}_e < 0$ must be such that the dividend rate of return becomes equalized through their addition with this negative rate of return on government bonds.

Condition 6, finally, could be weakened if backlog orders are allowed for. We will however consider it as a strict condition and investigate in the next section how the model's structure has to be changed when this floor in inventory holdings is reached. The model will therefore be made complete in this respect, in contrast to our present treatment of nominal interest, gross investment and desired production levels. We thus have to check in numerical simulations of the model's dynamics that these latter magnitudes stay in domains of economic relevance. Note here that all other variables, not explicitly considered here, automatically remain restricted to economically meaningful values in finite time, due to the employed growth law formulations and other types of adjustment rules. With respect to dividend payments and the rate $\tilde{\rho}^e$ on which they are based we expect furthermore for relevant trajectories of the dynamics that the situation:

$$Y^e < \bar{Y}^p \leq Y^e + \mathcal{I}$$

where they are zero does not occur for such high activity levels of the economy which generally should not be approached even approximately.

Summing up we assert that there is essentially only one significant change in the model, namely that production may now also be limited by the amount of overtime work that is available to firms or by the additional level of production that price-setting producers are willing to supply to their customers in situations of a booming economy at costs that exceed proceeds and that thus diminishes their profit sum. Despite these additional constraints on the level of production far off the steady state, actual sales are, in the presently considered situation, always equal to aggregate demand which also continues to determine expected demand and on this basis by and large the dividend payments that are made by firms. In short, the Keynesian regime here remains in full power with respect to the results that are achieved on the market place – up to the situation where aggregate demand exceeds intended or constrained production levels coupled with inventory changes that lead to zero inventories. This situation will be considered in the following section.

Note finally that the above model formulations imply that the Keynesian regime prevails around the steady state of the economy even if there were no possibilities for overtime work and for production at prices lower than marginal wage costs (and also if there were no increasing natural rate of growth (of the labor supply) for high levels of the employment rate). This is true since we have assumed in line with most of the macroeconomic literature that there is a NAIRU-level of the rate of employment $\bar{V}$ less than one and also a NAIRU-level of the rate of capacity utilization $\bar{U}_c$ less than one at which prices can become stationary and to which the economy will converge (if locally asymptotically stable).

Equations (5.45),(5.46) can be rearranged in the usual way, now giving rise to

$$\begin{aligned}\hat{w} - \pi^e &= \beta_{w_1}(V - \bar{V}) + \beta_{w_2}(V^w - 1) + \kappa_w(\hat{p} - \pi^e),\\ \hat{p} - \pi^e &= \beta_{p_1}(U_c^e - \bar{U}_c) + \beta_{p_2}U_n + \kappa_p(\hat{w} - \pi^e).\end{aligned}$$

Solving for the two variables $\hat{w} - \pi^e$, $\hat{p} - \pi^e$ these two equations then in turn imply

$$\begin{aligned}\hat{w} - \pi^e &= \kappa[\beta_{w_1}(V - \bar{V}) + \beta_{w_2}(V^w - 1) + \kappa_w(\beta_{p_1}(U_c^e - \bar{U}_c) + \beta_{p_2}U_n)], \quad \kappa = (1 - \kappa_w\kappa_p)^{-1}\\ \hat{p} - \pi^e &= \kappa[\beta_{p_1}(U_c^e - \bar{U}_c) + \beta_{p_2}U_n + \kappa_p(\beta_{w_1}(V - \bar{V}) + \beta_{w_2}(V^w - 1))], \quad \kappa = (1 - \kappa_w\kappa_p)^{-1}\end{aligned}$$

Subtracting the second from the first equation finally again provides the law of motion for the real wage

$$\hat{\omega} = \kappa[(1 - \kappa_p)(\beta_{w_1}(V - \bar{V}) + \beta_{w_2}(V^w - 1)) + (\kappa_w - 1)(\beta_{p_1}(U_c^e - \bar{U}_c) + \beta_{p_2}U_n)] \tag{5.48}$$

which gives the first of the differential equations to be employed in the following in qualitatively the same form as in the earlier models without supply side bottlenecks.

The law of motion for the full employment labor intensity L/K reads in the present model:

$$\hat{l} = -(i_1(\rho^p - (r - \pi^e)) + i_2(U_c^e - \bar{U}_c)) \tag{5.49}$$

and thus solely reflects the slightly changed type of investment behavior of this section.

The next two laws of motion for real balances $m = M/(pK)$ per unit of capital and inflationary expectations π^e are obtained from the expressions:

$$\hat{m} = -(\hat{p} - \pi^e) - \pi^e - (i_1(\rho^p - (r - \pi^e)) + i_2(U_c^e - \bar{U}_c)) \tag{5.50}$$

$$\dot{\pi}^e = \beta_{\pi_1^e}(\hat{p} - \pi^e) + \beta_{\pi_2^e}(\bar{\mu} - n - \pi^e) \tag{5.51}$$

by inserting the expression we obtained for $\hat{p}-\pi^e$ above (note that we have assumed $\bar{\mu}=n$ for reasons of simplicity).

The laws of motion for expected sales and inventories per unit of capital are as in the KMG models of chapter 4 and thus read in qualitative terms:

$$\dot{y}^e = \beta_{y^e}(y^d - y^e) + \hat{l}y^e \tag{5.52}$$

$$\dot{\nu} = y - y^d + (\hat{l} - n)\nu, \qquad \nu > 0 \tag{5.53}$$

Finally, we now have a further law of motion as in section 4.7, concerning the employment policy of firms, which in the present situation is given by the following differential equation for the workforce - capital ratio $l^w = L^w/K$:

$$\hat{l}^w = \beta_v(V^w - 1) - (i_1(\rho^p - (r - \pi^e)) + i_2(U_c^e - \bar{U}_c)). \tag{5.54}$$

In order to obtain an autonomous system of differential equations from the above laws of motion one has to supply the definitions for $V, V^w, U_c^e, U_n, \rho^p, r, y^d, y$ and their components in addition. For these expressions we obtain from the above model (5.15) – (5.46) the following set of equations (where f as usual denotes the given production function on the intensive form level):[10]

$$\begin{aligned}
V &= l^w/l \\
V^w &= l^d/l^w, \quad f(l^d) = y \\
U_c^e &= (y^e + \beta_n(\beta_{n^d}y^e - \nu) + n\beta_{n^d}y^e)/y^p \\
U_n &= \beta_{n^d}y^e - \nu \\
\rho^p &= f(l^p) - \delta - f'(l^p)l^p, \quad f'(l^p) = \omega \\
r &= r_o + (h_1 y + m)/h_2 \\
y^d &= \omega l^d + (1 - s_c)(\tilde{\rho}^e - t_c^n) + i_1(\rho^p - (r - \pi^e)) + i_2(U_c^e - \bar{U}_c) + n + \delta + \bar{g} \\
y &= \min\{y^e + \beta_n(\beta_{n^d}y^e - \nu) + n\beta_{n^d}y^e, \bar{y}^p, \bar{y}^w\} \\
y^p &= f(l^p), \quad l^p = (f')^{-1}(\omega) \\
\bar{y}^p &= f(\bar{l}^p) = \omega\bar{l}^p + \delta \\
\bar{y}^w &= f((1 + \bar{o})l^w) \\
\tilde{\rho}^e &= \max\{y^e - \delta - \omega l^d, 0\} \\
n &= \bar{n}_o + n_1(V^w - 1) + n_2(V - \bar{V}).
\end{aligned}$$

This dynamical system describes the evolution of the KMG growth dynamics with supply bottlenecks as long as $\nu > 0$ remains true, with no regime switching caused due to the varying size of aggregate demand y^d until inventories get exhausted.

Proposition 5.4

Assume (for notational simplicity) that $\bar{U}_c = 1, n = 0$ holds true. Then: There is a uniquely determined interior steady state solution of the dynamics of this

[10]Note here that the measure U_n is closely linked to the measure U_c^e and thus does not add something that is qualitatively very different from the effects of the rate of capacity utilization on the evolution of price inflation.

subsection which is given by:

$$\begin{aligned}
\tilde{\rho}^e &= \rho^p = \bar{g}/s_c - (1-s_c)t_c^n/s_c > 0 \\
y^e &> 0 \quad \textit{given by the solution to} \quad \rho^p = y^e - \delta - f'(f^{-1}(y^e))f^{-1}(y^e) \\
y^e &= y^d = y = y^p \\
\omega &= f'(f^{-1}(y^e)) \\
l^p &= f^{-1}(y^e) = l^d = l^w, \quad l = l^w/\bar{V} \\
r &= r_o = \rho^p \\
m &= h_1 y^e \\
\pi^e &= \hat{p} = \hat{w} = \hat{p}_e = \bar{\mu} - n = 0 \\
\nu &= \beta_{n^d} y^e > 0
\end{aligned}$$

Note with respect to this proposition that the steady state lies in the interior of the phase space of the dynamics considered in this subsection. Note furthermore that aggregate savings (and net investment) $S/K(= I/K)$ has to be zero in the steady state which is guaranteed by the following equation:

$$s_c(\rho^p - t_c^n) = g - t_c^n > 0$$

stating the equality between private savings and government dissavings in the steady state. Note finally that the equation $\tilde{\rho}^e = (n+\bar{g})/s_c - (1-s_c)t_c^n/s_c$ also holds true in the general case, and is obtained from goods market equilibrium in both cases, which thus determines the dividend rate of return of asset holders ($p_e E = pK$ in the steady state) as based on the size of natural growth, government expenditure and capital taxation rules, and the savings propensity of asset holders. This rate of return can therefore in particular be increased by increasing government expenditures per unit of capital and is completely independent from the marginal productivity theory of income distribution (which however determines the real wage in the steady state).

Proof: To be based on the steady state relationships $V = V^w = U_c^e = 1, U_n = 0, \rho^p = r_o, \pi^e = 0, y = y^d = y^p = y^e$ that can be obtained by setting the differential equations of this section equal to zero. ■

We conjecture, but cannot prove this in this subsection, that the system will be locally asymptotically stable for all adjustment speed parameters $\beta_x's$ chosen sufficiently low (up to the adjustment speed of sales expectations, which must be chosen sufficiently high and up to one exception to be considered below). The basis for this conjecture is that the system is basically of the type considered in sections 4.2, 4.3, since the constraints that were added to it are not in operation close to the steady state. However, we have now a seventh law of motion, the employment policy of firms, and have also added a second demand pressure term in the wage as well as in the price inflation equation the role of which has not yet been investigated. Furthermore the case of smooth factor substitution has not yet been considered very carefully so far. Due to the high dimension of the considered dynamics we cannot offer any proven proposition at this stage of the investigation.

The same holds true with respect to the assertion that the determinant of the system at the steady state will always be negative, so that the system can only gain or lose stability by way of Hopf-bifurcations. Stability losses will come about if either wage or price flexibility is chosen sufficiently high, if adaptively formed inflationary expectations are moving with sufficient speed, and if inventories are adjusted with sufficient speed. Again, this is but a conjecture based on the experience gained with closely related, but lower dimensional dynamic systems in the last chapter and in particular in Chiarella and Flaschel (1999b). We also expect that the adjustment parameter in the employment policy of firms will be destabilizing when chosen sufficiently high, but have to leave all these conjectures for numerical investigations for the time being. Note that the instability assertions made are not easy to prove as they will not operate through the trace of the Jacobian of the dynamics at the steady state, but only via higher principal minors of this Jacobian, the calculation of which however can be approached via the numerous linear dependencies that characterize components of the rows of this Jacobian. The following proposition provides an example for such a calculation.

Proposition 5.5

The dynamics of this subsection will be unstable at their interior steady state if the parameters $\beta_{\pi_1^e}, \beta_{y^e}$ are chosen sufficiently high.

Proof: Considering the interaction of the state variables in isolation gives rise to the following subdynamics of the full 7d dynamics as far as the parameters $\beta_{\pi_1^e}, \beta_{y^e}$ are concerned:

$$\dot{\pi}^e = \beta_{\pi_1^e}(\hat{p} - \pi^e) + \beta_{\pi_2^e}(\bar{\mu} - n - \pi^e) \tag{5.55}$$

$$\dot{y}^e = \beta_{y^e}(y^d - y^e) + \hat{l}y^e \tag{5.56}$$

It is easy to see that

$$\hat{p} - \pi^e = \kappa[\beta_{p_1}(U_c^e - \bar{U}_c) + \beta_{p_2}U_n + \kappa_p(\beta_{w_1}(V - \bar{V}) + \beta_{w_2}(V^w - 1))]$$

depends positively on y^e, since the expressions U_c^e, U_n, V^w all depend positively on y^e, while there is no direct influence of π^e on this equation, which drives inflationary expectations as far as the adaptive component is concerned as is shown above. The rate of change $\dot{y}^e$ in addition depends positively on inflationary expectations π^e, since y^d depends on them in this way. This gives for the corresponding $2 \star 2$ submatrix J(2,2) of the full Jacobian J the qualitative result:

$$J(2,2) = \begin{vmatrix} J_{44} & J_{45} \\ J_{54} & J_{55} \end{vmatrix} = \begin{vmatrix} 0 & +const\ \beta_{\pi_1^e} \\ +const\ \beta_{y^e} & ? \end{vmatrix} = -const\ \beta_{\pi_1^e}\beta_{y^e}$$

The sum of all principal minors of dimension two can thereby made negative by choosing the parameter pair $\beta_{\pi_1^e}, \beta_{y^e}$ jointly sufficiently large, since this pair does only appear together in the submatrix here considered. Therefore one of the conditions of the Routh-Hurwitz theorem that are sufficient for local asymptotic stability is violated in a way that implies the existence of at least one eigenvalue with positive real part. ■

We thus have local divergence with respect to at least a submanifold of dimension one which raises the question what the forces are that may nevertheless make the considered dynamics bounded in a domain that is of economic relevance. In order to investigate this question we have however first of all to complete the description of the dynamics for the case where inventories have been run down to zero. This task will be solved in the now following subsection.

5.4.2 Exhausted inventories and excessive aggregate demand

With respect to the notation of the KMG model of the preceding section we now have the situation that

$$Y^d = C_w + C_c + I + \delta K + G > Y = \min\{Y^e + \mathcal{I}, \bar{Y}^p, \bar{Y}^w\}, \quad N = 0$$

hold simultaneously, i.e., aggregate demand Y^d can no longer be fulfilled from the production decisions made by firms and from their inventory holdings.

In order to show how the model needs change in such a situation we measure the extent of rationing that will then occur with respect to the planned demands of economic agents by the coefficient $\alpha \in (0,1)$ defined by:

$$\omega L^d + \delta K + \alpha(C_c + I + \bar{g}K) = Y.$$

Thus, we assume that rationing concerns the consumption of asset owners, net investment in fixed capital and a part from government consumption, whereas investment compensating for depreciation δK as well as the consumption of workers ($C_w = (1-\tau)\omega L^d$) and the part of government expenditures equal to $\tau\omega L^d$ remain unaffected by the supply shortage.[11] In this context it is important to note the (downward) jump in dividend payments that will occur, when production is limited due to the boundary $\bar{Y}^w$ or $\bar{Y}^p$ and inventories become exhausted, so that the part of planned revenues Y^e, that was realized by sells from inventories before, vanishes. As, on the other hand, dividend payments represent a part of the income of asset holders, effective demand and thus also the value for α has to be calculated after this jump in dividend payments has appeared.[12] Note furthermore that $\alpha > 0$ is indeed guaranteed in the considered model, since we have $Y \leq \bar{Y}^p$ by assumption and thus $Y - \delta K - \omega L^d \geq 0$, leading to $Y - \delta K - C_w > 0$ due to $C_w = (1-\tau_w)\omega L^d < \omega L^d$. Note here also that actual inventory investment $\dot{N} = Y - Y^d > 0$ will lead us back to the situation of the preceding section. We here assume however that $\alpha \leq 1$ holds in the following modification of the preceding less restricted model.

The following set of equations describe the working of the economy in such extreme situations of a booming economy.

1. Definitions (remunerations and wealth):

$$\omega = w/p, \quad \tilde{\rho}^e = \max\{(\min\{Y^e, Y\} - \delta K - \omega L^d)/K, 0\} \tag{5.57}$$

$$W = (M + B + p_e E)/p \tag{5.58}$$

2. Households (workers and asset-holders):

$$W = (M^d + B^d + p_e E^d)/p \tag{5.59}$$

$$C = \omega L^d - T_w + (1 - s_c)[\tilde{\rho}^e K + rB/p - T_c] \tag{5.60}$$

$$C^a = \omega L^d - T_w + \alpha(1 - s_c)[\tilde{\rho}^e K + rB/p - T_c] \tag{5.61}$$

[11] Wage earners are here excluded from this proportional reduction of the demand plans of economic agents in order to avoid unnecessary complications for a first presentation of the case of rationing (since one would have to consider their forced savings in such a situation and thus add money holdings of workers for example).

[12] In general, it can not be excluded, that at least in some cases the jump in dividend payments just described is large enough to push aggregate demand again below the level of production, so that the economy immediately returns to the former regime after inventories have become exhausted.

$$
\begin{aligned}
S_p &= \omega L^d + \tilde{\rho}^e K + rB/p - T - C^a = (s_c + (1-\alpha)(1-s_c))[\tilde{\rho}^e K + rB/p - T_c] \\
&= (\dot{M} + \dot{B} + p_e \dot{E})/p, \quad T = T_w + T_c & (5.62) \\
\hat{L} &= n = \bar{n}_o + n_1(V^w - 1) + n_2(V - \bar{V}), \quad n_1, n_2 > 0 & (5.63)
\end{aligned}
$$

3. Firms (production-units and investors):

$$
\begin{aligned}
\omega &= F_L(K, L^p), \;\; Y^p = F(K, L^p), \;\; \rho^p = (Y^p - \delta K - \omega L^p)/K & (5.64) \\
U_c^e &= (Y^e + \mathcal{I})/Y^p & (5.65) \\
L^d & \quad \text{via } Y = F(K, L^d), \;\; V = L^w/L \leq 1, \;\; V^w = L^d/L^w & (5.66) \\
\dot{L}^w &= \beta_v(L^d - L^w) + \gamma L^w, \quad \gamma = n & (5.67) \\
I/K &= i_1(\rho^p - (r - \pi^e)) + i_2(U_c^e - \bar{U}_c) + \gamma, \; \gamma = n & (5.68) \\
I^a/K &= \alpha(i_1(\rho^p - (r - \pi^e)) + i_2(U_c^e - \bar{U}_c) + \gamma), \; \gamma = n, \; I^a + \delta K \geq 0 & (5.69) \\
I^a &= Y - \tilde{\rho}^e K - \delta K - \omega L^d + p_e \dot{E}/p = S_f + p_e \dot{E}/p & (5.70) \\
\hat{K} &= I^a/K & (5.71)
\end{aligned}
$$

4. Government (fiscal and monetary authority):

$$
\begin{aligned}
T &= T_w + T_c, \quad T_w = \tau_w \omega L^d, \; t_c^n = (T_c - rB/p)/K = const < 0 & (5.72) \\
G &= \tau_w \omega L^d + \bar{g} K, \quad \bar{g} \geq 0 & (5.73) \\
G^a &= \tau_w \omega L^d + \alpha \bar{g} K & (5.74) \\
S_g &= T - rB/p - G^a & (5.75) \\
\hat{M} &= \bar{\mu} = n & (5.76) \\
\dot{B} &= pG^a + rB - pT - \dot{M} & (5.77)
\end{aligned}
$$

5. Equilibrium conditions (asset-markets):

$$
\begin{aligned}
M &= M^d = h_1 pY + h_2 pK(r_o - r), \quad [B = B^d, E = E^d], \quad B, E \geq 0, \; r > 0 & (5.78) \\
r &= \frac{\tilde{\rho}^e pK + \dot{p}_e E}{p_e E} & (5.79)
\end{aligned}
$$

6. Disequilibrium situation (goods-market adjustments):

$$
\begin{aligned}
S &= S_p + S_g + S_f = Y - \delta K - (C^a + G^a) = I^a & (5.80) \\
Y^d &= C + I + \delta K + G & (5.81) \\
\dot{Y}^e &= \beta_{y^e}(Y^d - Y^e) + \gamma Y^e, \; \gamma = n & (5.82) \\
N^d &= \beta_{n^d} Y^e & (5.83) \\
\mathcal{I} &= \beta_n(N^d - N) + \gamma N^d, \; \gamma = n & (5.84) \\
Y &= \min\{Y^e + \mathcal{I}, \bar{Y}^p \bar{Y}^w\}, \quad Y^e + \mathcal{I} > 0 & (5.85) \\
\dot{N} &= \max\{Y - Y^d, 0\} \geq 0 \quad [> 0, \quad \text{if regime switching takes place}] & (5.86)
\end{aligned}
$$

7. Wage-Price-Sector (adjustment equations):

$$
\begin{aligned}
\hat{w} &= \beta_{w_1}(V - \bar{V}) + \beta_{w_2}(V^w - 1) + \kappa_w \hat{p} + (1 - \kappa_w)\pi^e & (5.87) \\
\hat{p} &= \beta_{p_1}(U_c^e - \bar{U}_c) + \beta_{p_2} U_n + \kappa_p \hat{w} + (1 - \kappa_p)\pi^e, \quad U_n = (N^d - N)/K & (5.88) \\
\dot{\pi}^e &= \beta_{\pi_1^e}(\hat{p} - \pi^e) + \beta_{\pi_2^e}(\bar{\mu} - n - \pi^e). & (5.89)
\end{aligned}
$$

As already described above, the fundamental change that has taken place now consists in the formulation of situations, where demand is larger than actual production and where at a certain point in time there are no inventory stocks available any more, by which the difference between Y^d and Y could be bridged. Before commenting on these changes in more detail we want to stress that the economy switches back to Regime 1 (considered in the preceding subsection) if and only if $\dot{N} = \max\{Y - Y^d, 0\}$ becomes positive again. Conversely, regime 1 is left and gives way to the regime considered in the present subsection if and only if the situation $Y^d > Y(\dot{N} < 0)$ is given and $N = 0$ is reached. We thus have in this extension of the KMG growth model by means of relevant macroeconomic supply bottlenecks only two regimes, a Keynesian (Regime 1) one where aggregate demand is always fulfilled and a Non-Keynesian one (Regime 2) where aggregate demand is rationed and where this rationing may be due to too low sales expectations and intended inventory changes or to exhausted possibilities for overtime work or to the zero profit bound on production. Therefore, in this latter case of exhausted inventories, the three regimes of Non-Walrasian macroeconomics reappear so to speak en miniature, but now as an event that will rarely occur in the investigated economy.

Turning now to the changes that differentiate regime 2 from regime 1, we have to note first that actual dividend payments are now formulated in a narrower way in equation (5.57), since firms will not pay dividends according to expected sales when they know that their actual production will be lower than expected sales, in which case only the amount $Y - \delta K - \omega L^d$ will be distributed. There are also the obvious changes due to rationed goods demand of asset holders, the firms and the government, which also modifies their savings which are now based on disposable income flows of type $\tilde{\rho}^e K + rB/p - T$ for asset holders, $Y - \tilde{\rho}^e K - \delta K - \omega L^d$ of firms and of $T - rB/p$ for the government. These are however already all changes when we go from regime 1 to regime 2 implying that there will only be few changes to the laws of motion of the preceding subsection when such a regime switch occurs. The following provides a list of these changes without presenting again the equations of the model in intensive form that have remained unchanged between the two regimes. The law of motion for the full employment labor intensity L/K now reads:

$$\hat{l} = n - \alpha(i_1(\rho^p - (r - \pi^e)) + i_2(U_c^e - \bar{U}_c) + n) \tag{5.90}$$

and the one for real balances $m = M/(pK)$ per unit of capital is changed by the same reason as follows

$$\hat{m} = \bar{\mu} - (\hat{p} - \pi^e) + \pi^e - \alpha(i_1(\rho^p - (r - \pi^e)) + i_2(U_c^e - \bar{U}_c) + n) \tag{5.91}$$

as is the one for the workforce - capital ratio $l^w = L^w/K$:

$$\hat{l^w} = \beta_v(V^w - 1) + n - \alpha(i_1(\rho^p - (r - \pi^e)) + i_2(U_c^e - \bar{U}_c) + n). \tag{5.92}$$

Since $\hat{l}$ is to be inserted into the law of motion for y^e there is therefore also an implicit change there, while we have $\nu = 0$ as long as regime 2 applies (in which case $U_n = \beta_{n^d} y^e$ holds). Concerning the static equations of the model we only have to note that aggregate demand is implicitly changed, since disposable income is different in regime 2:

$$\begin{aligned} y^d &= \omega l^d + (1 - s_c)(\tilde{\rho}^e - t_c^n) + i_1(\rho^p - (r - \pi^e)) + i_2(U_c^e - \bar{U}_c) + n + \delta + \bar{g} \\ \tilde{\rho}^e &= \max\{\min\{y^e, y\} - \delta - \omega l^d, 0\}. \end{aligned}$$

All other static expressions remain the same which in sum means that the formal change to the model is a very limited one.

We expect that the case of an economy-wide or global rationing[13] does play no role at all or only occurs under rare circumstances in the KMG model of this chapter, see our later numerical investigations of this model. Introducing in addition flexible wage, price, employment and labor supply adjustments, and also flexible investment and inventory adjustment mechanisms when aggregate demand becomes rationed will make such a case even more unlikely in a market economy. A simple model where exactly such situations are excluded from occurring is provided through a nonlinear Phillips curve mechanism in Benassy (1984), an approach which is easily generalized to the high-dimensional dynamics here under consideration (but not easy to be analyzed here, where there are many buffers and adjustment mechanisms available in order guarantee the general prevalence of the Keynesian regime).

As described above the case of empty inventories is characterized by three different possibilities for the constraint that acts on aggregate demand, leading to its rationing of the type

$$\omega L^d + \alpha C_c + \alpha I + \delta K + \alpha \bar{g} K = Y = \min\{Y^e + \mathcal{I}, \bar{Y}^p, \bar{Y}^w\}$$

with $\alpha \in (0,1)$. As in the Non-Walrasian approach considered in section 5.2, but now only for zero inventory stocks, we have a "Keynesian" regime[14] $Y^e + \mathcal{I} = \min\{Y^e + \mathcal{I}, \bar{Y}^p, \bar{Y}^w\}$, a classical regime $\bar{Y}^p = \min\{Y^e + \mathcal{I}, \bar{Y}^p, \bar{Y}^w\}$ and a regime of repressed inflation $\bar{Y}^w = \min\{Y^e + \mathcal{I}, \bar{Y}^p, \bar{Y}^w\}$ which of course overlap with each other at their boundaries.

The first of these regimes is characterized by the situation where desired output $Y^e + \mathcal{I}$ is restricting actual production and is below aggregate demand Y^d. It is to be expected then that sales expectations will be faster and faster adjusted towards actual aggregate demand (by way of a nonlinearity in the adjustment mechanism not considered in the above model) and that inventories are also adjusted faster than in the way given by the model so that the situation where desired production is the cause of demand rationing should soon be overcome by such flexibilities in actual market economies.

In the next regime, where $\bar{Y}^p$ and thus zero profitability due to excessive use of productive capacity is the cause of demand rationing, one would expect and add to the model strong nonlinearities in the price adjustment mechanism (much earlier than this barrier is in fact reached) which speed up the rate of increase in the price level by so much that the resulting fall in real wages (since labor markets are not yet too tight) will increase this barrier $\bar{Y}^p$ so strongly that it will no longer represent the limiting item. Of course, this is only a partial description of the whole dynamics and may not always hold in the phase space in this straightforward way, but may interact with tight labor in certain situations in a more complicated way.

In the third regime, where the limit to overtime work is the barrier for serving aggregate demand, we should expect that the parameter characterizing the employment policy of firms, β_l, is increased significantly. If, however, the labor market is in the state of absolute full employment with respect to the currently available labor force, the rate of growth of labor supply will be increased, in particular by active search of firms for laborers across the border of the considered economy so that this limit for serving aggregate demand can be

[13]This describes a situation, where all shops and factories have nothing left after each trading period

[14]This designation should not be taken too literally and not be confused with our regime 1. While in regime 1 demand is always served, its rationing is the main characteristic of regime 2 and thus also of the so-called "Keynesian" subregime just mentioned.

overcome. There are of course also real wage increases to be expected in such a situation which however will not help in the case where aggregate demand depends positively on real wages, yet it is to be expected that such real wage increases will have larger and larger effects on investment behavior leading to a negative dependence of aggregate demand on real wages eventually (by parameter changes not considered in the model).

All these observations suggest that the regime 2 introduced and considered in the present subsection will not last very long. We expect this to be true even in the framework of the model itself, an assertion which at present can only be confirmed by means of numerical simulations which are the topic of the next subsection.

At this stage, our model has already reached a high degree of completeness, as supply bottlenecks due to exhausted inventories are now explicitly taken into account. On the other hand, there are still a number of items to be checked numerically, especially the nonnegativity constraints on gross investment, interest rates, stocks in bonds, equities and output.[15] Furthermore, it should be checked, for which parameter constellations there is convergence to the (Keynesian) steady state and how, on the other hand, ceilings as $Y \leq 1$ and buffers like the possibility of overtime word help to keep the economy in meaningful bounds in the case of local explosiveness. The simulations to be considered in the next subsection will also treat the inclusion of a further nonlinearity, namely a kink in the Phillips-curve, by which a downward rigidity of money wages is described. As will be shown, for quite a large set of parameter values this leads to stable depressions with $V < \bar{V}$ instead of limit cycles, which would occur otherwise.

5.4.3 Numerical analysis

In this section we provide some numerical illustrations in particular with respect to proposition 5.5 on the destabilizing role of adaptively formed expectations if the speed of adjustment of these expectations is increased. We will see that the system's dynamics is indeed a converging one for low adjustment speed parameters, which becomes locally divergent already for relatively low speeds of adjustments of inflationary expectations. This local instability gives rise to global limit cycle behavior for a certain range of this adjustment speed beyond the region of local asymptotic stability and gives way to pure explosiveness and economic breakdown thereafter. The issue of economic viability is therefore not completely resolved by the supply side constraints we have added to the KMG model in this chapter. We therefore will add another extrinsic nonlinearity to the model at the end of this subsection which is of a very fundamental nature and which will indeed guarantee economic viability for a range of adjustment speeds that is significantly larger than the one without it.

In order to simulate the dynamics for both regime 1 and 2 of the preceding subsections we have to integrate these two subsections into a single dynamical model and have to make use of specific production functions in addition. We shall make use of a Cobb-Douglas production function where we have to keep in mind that marginal productivity theory will be valid in our model only in the steady state, i.e., the model allows for fluctuations in the share of wages despite the assumption of a production technology with elasticity of substitution equal to one. For reasons of simplicity we shall also assume in the following

[15]Compare in this respect also the treatment of these problems in Laxton et al. (1998).

that the natural rate of growth is zero and that the normal rate of capacity utilization of firms is given by one. Based on the assumptions

$$Y = F(K, L^d) = K^{1-a}(L^d)^a, a \in (0,1), \quad n \equiv 0 (= \bar{\mu}) \; (L = const, \hat{l} = -\hat{K}), \quad \bar{U}_c = 1.$$

the dynamical system to be investigated in this subsection is therefore the following one:

$$\begin{aligned}
\hat{\omega} &= \kappa[(1-\kappa_p)(\beta_{w_1}(V-\bar{V}) + \beta_{w_2}(V^w - 1)) \\
&+ (\kappa_w - 1)(\beta_{p_1}(U_c^e - 1) + \beta_{p_2}U_n)] && (5.93)\\
\hat{l} &= -g_k && (5.94)\\
\hat{m} &= -(\hat{p} - \pi^e) - \pi^e - g_k && (5.95)\\
\dot{\pi}^e &= \beta_{\pi_1^e}(\hat{p} - \pi^e) + \beta_{\pi_2^e}(-\pi^e) && (5.96)\\
\dot{y}^e &= \beta_{y^e}(y^d - y^e) - g_k y^e && (5.97)\\
\dot{\nu} &= y - y^d - g_k \nu && (5.98)\\
\hat{l}^w &= \beta_v(V^w - 1) - g_k && (5.99)
\end{aligned}$$

now supplemented by the following algebraic equations and regime switching conditions:[16]

$$\begin{aligned}
\hat{p} &= \kappa[\beta_{p_1}(U_c^e - 1) + \beta_{p_2}U_n \\
&+ \kappa_p(\beta_{w_1}(V - \bar{V}) + \beta_{w_2}(V^w - 1))] + \pi^e && (5.100)\\
V &= l^w/l \le 1 && (5.101)\\
V^w &= l^d/l^w, \quad y = f(l^d) = (l^d)^a, \quad l^d = y^{1/a} && (5.102)\\
U_c^e &= (y^e + \beta_n(\beta_{n^d}y^e - \nu))/y^p && (5.103)\\
U_n &= \beta_{n^d}y^e - \nu && (5.104)\\
\omega &= f'(l^p) = a(l^p)^{a-1}, \quad l^p = (a/\omega)^{\frac{1}{1-a}} && (5.105)\\
\rho^p &= f(l^p) - \delta - f'(l^p)l^p = (1-a)y^p - \delta, \quad y^p = (l^p)^a && (5.106)\\
r &= r_o + (h_1 y + m)/h_2 > 0 && (5.107)\\
y &= \min\{y^e + \beta_n(\beta_{n^d}y^e - \nu), \bar{y}^p, \bar{y}^w\} && (5.108)\\
\bar{y}^p &= (\bar{l}^p)^a = \omega \bar{l}^p \to \bar{l}^p = (1/\omega)^{\frac{1}{1-a}} > l^p = (a/\omega)^{\frac{1}{1-a}} && (5.109)\\
y^w &= ((1+\bar{o})l^w)^a && (5.110)\\
\tilde{\rho}^e &= \max\{y^e - \delta - \omega l^d, 0\}, \quad \text{if} \quad \nu > 0 && (5.111)\\
\tilde{\rho}^e &= \max\{\min[y^e, y] - \delta - \omega l^d, 0\}, \quad \text{if} \quad \nu = 0 && (5.112)\\
y^d &= \omega l^d + (1 - s_c)(\tilde{\rho}^e - t_c^n) \\
&+ i_1(\rho^p - (r - \pi^e)) + i_2(U_c^e - 1) + \delta + \bar{g} && (5.113)\\
\alpha &= \min\{\frac{y - \omega l^d}{(1-s_c)(\tilde{\rho}^e - t_c^n) + I/K + \delta + \bar{g}}, 1\} && (5.114)\\
I/K &= i_1(\rho^p - (r - \pi^e)) + i_2(U_c^e - 1) \ge 0 && (5.115)\\
g_k &= i_1(\rho^p - (r - \pi^e)) + i_2(U_c^e - 1), \quad \text{if} \quad \nu > 0 && (5.116)\\
g_k &= \alpha(i_1(\rho^p - (r - \pi^e)) + i_2(U_c^e - 1)), \quad \text{if} \quad \nu = 0. && (5.117)
\end{aligned}$$

[16]The steady state level of output, demand and sales expectations is given by $y = y^d = y^e = (\rho^p + \delta)/(1-\alpha)$.

As the model is specified now it represents a complete dynamic model as long as the side conditions $r > 0, I/K \geq \delta, y^e + \beta_n(\beta_{n^d} y^e - \nu) > 0$ (and also $B, E \geq 0$) are not violated during the fluctuations its dynamics will generally generate. These side conditions are always checked in the following simulation studies. Should they become violated the model must be developed further, by introducing further extrinsic nonlinearities, which avoid negative nominal rates of interest and the like. Surely the model is still much too linear in this respect in order to allow the expectation that the stated side conditions will be guaranteed for reasonable parameter ranges. We add that the rationing coefficient α will always be positive as long as gross investment stays nonnegative, due to the assumptions made on the parameters $\bar{g}, t_c^n$. Furthermore, $\alpha = 1$ will always imply that $y^d \leq y$ must hold true.

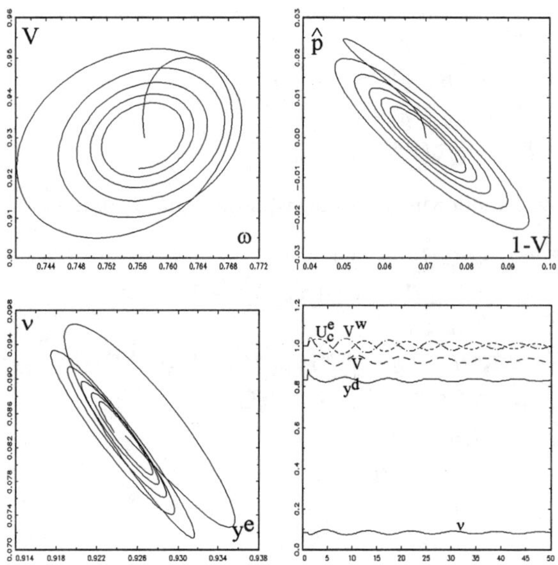

Figure 5.2: Convergence for sluggish adjustment speeds of inflationary expectations

Note next that when inventories get exhausted we may have a discontinuity (a downward jump) in dividend payments to asset holders if

$$y = \min\{\bar{y}^p, \bar{y}^w\}$$

holds, since sales expectations y^e may be larger than y in such a situation. However the bound $\bar{y}^w$, where overtime work gets exhausted, will rarely become operative and even more so the bound $\bar{y}^p$ where gross profits are zero. Therefore we will generally have $y = y^e + \beta_n(\beta_{n^d} y^e - \nu)$, and of course $y^d > y$, when a zero inventory level is reached[17] in which case $\beta_n(\beta_{n^d} y^e - \nu)$ will be positive and therefore $y^e < y$. In this case there is thus no discontinuity in dividend payments, but just a continuous switch in the measure

[17]The same holds when inventories return to positive levels by way of an aggregate demand that does not absorb total production.

on which the dividend policy of firms rests. As already mentioned above, in case of a discontinuous switch there will be a downward jump in aggregate demand as well (due to the consumption function of asset holders) which may in extreme situations be so large that demand rationing is completely avoided and therefore a return to positive inventory levels immediately. If this description does not apply we however have to use the factor α (based on reduced consumption demand of asset holders) to scale down actual investment, the only rationed goods demand that influences the real dynamics of the model in its present form.

The simulations of the dynamics in the figures 5.2ff., with the possibility of supply side restrictions, are based on the following base parameter set:

$s_c = 0.8,\quad \delta = 0.1,\quad t_c^n = -0.1,\quad \bar{g} = 0.1,\quad \bar{o} = 0.6$
$h_1 = 0.1,\quad h_2 = 0.05,\quad i_1 = 1,\quad i_2 = 0.2$
$\beta_{w_1} = 1,\quad \beta_{w_2} = 0,\quad \beta_{p_1} = 0.2,\quad \beta_{p_2} = 0\quad \kappa_w = 0.5,\quad \kappa_p = 0.5$
$\beta_{\pi_1} = 0.09,\quad \beta_{\pi_2} = 0,\quad \beta_{n^d} = 0.1,\quad \beta_n = 0.5,\quad \beta_y^e = 2,\quad \beta_v = 0.5$
$a = 0.7,\quad \bar{V} = 0.93,\quad \bar{\mu} = n = 0$

Table 5.1

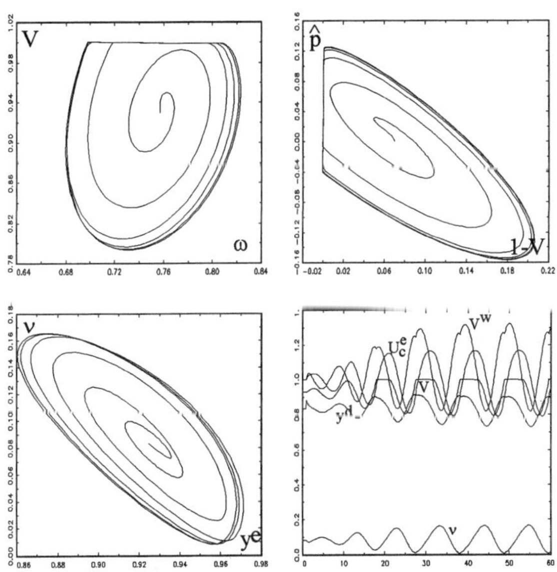

Figure 5.3: Destabilizing inflationary expectations and a supply side generated limit cycle: $\beta_{\pi_1} = 0.3$ (only $V \leq 1$).

We have a 3 % money supply shock at t=1 and a horizon of 50 years. Note that the consumption and investment parameters have been chosen such that the cost effect of real wage increases is the dominant effect in aggregate demand, because otherwise an upper turning point in the boom would not be necessarily guaranteed. Figure 5.2 now displays a situation, where the steady state is local asymptotically stable due to low adjustment speeds, especially concerning the expected rate of inflation. Note, that the choice of a $\beta_{w_2} > 0$ would enlarge the region of parameter values, for which asymptotic stability prevails.

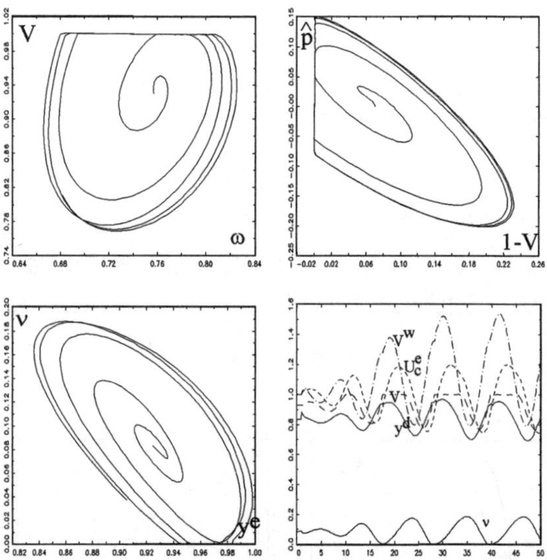

Figure 5.4: Increased local instability and regime 2 switches: $\beta_{\pi_1} = 0.37$

The next simulation run, shown in figure 5.3, now with a larger adjustment speed of inflationary expectations ($\beta_{\pi_1} = 0.3$), results in a Keynesian limit cycle, with similarities to what we have shown in figure 4.4. In this case, the full employment ceiling is reached in the boom phase of the business cycle without however representing a limit to production due to the possibility of overtime work, which clearly can be seen when looking at the time series for V^w in the lower right picture of figure 5.3. The lower left picture of figure 5.3 shows furthermore, that the whole dynamics takes place in regime 1, i.e. inventories are positive throughout and demand is never rationed here.

The situation in figure 5.3 is easily extended to include periods of demand rationing, when β_{π_1} is increased further, as figure 5.4 shows. For $\beta_{\pi_1} = 0.37$ inventories now reach their lower bound zero in the boom, so that supply bottlenecks become effective and demand rationing occurs. Furthermore, there is then also a downward jump of dividend payments in this upper region, as can be guessed from the corresponding kinks in the y^d–curve at $t \approx 27$ and $t \approx 39$, i.e., at those points in time, where inventories have approached zero. Note, that without the bounds on employment and inventories the development of the economy considered would be much more explosive in its deviation from its interior steady state. Notice also that the slump is now characterized by significantly higher deflation compared to the situation considered in figure 5.3.

The next simulation, shown in figure 5.5, now makes use of a new element which has not been taken account of so far. With regard to reality it is now assumed, that downward flexibility of the nominal wage is a phenomenon that usually cannot be observed, so that the corresponding part of the nominal wage Phillips curve is now replaced by a horizontal line. Formally, the equations for wage and price inflation now read:

$$\hat{p} = \beta_{p_1}(.) + \beta_{p_2}(.) + (1 - \kappa_p)\pi^e + 0$$

$$\hat{\omega} = -(\beta_{p_1}(.) + \beta_{p_2}(.)) - (1 - \kappa_p)\pi^e.$$

The consequences of this change in the wage-price sector are dramatical, as figure 5.5 illustrates. Instead of a limit cycle now convergence to a stable depression occurs with an employment rate V below the natural one $\bar{V}$. Although this is indeed the most important consequence, another one should also be regarded, namely the fact that now the economy again stays within the limits of regime 1, so that the supply bottlenecks of figure 5.4 do not appear any more. This might be surprising at the first look, as the downward rigidity of wages in the first place prevents a severe deflation as considered in figure 5.4. On the other hand, however, not only the phase of deflation is avoided, but also the whole business cycle and thus phases of an overheated economy, too.

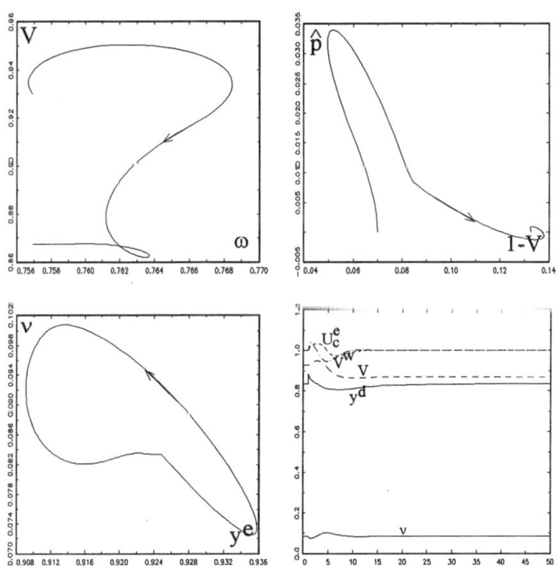

Figure 5.5: Reestablishing convergence, but stable depressions by absolute downward rigidity of nominal wages

In the figure 5.6, finally, we consider a situation with a less severe rigidity on wage adjustment. We assume now, that downward flexibility of nominal wages is possible, but that there is still a lower boundary for wage cuts. In other words: the floor for wage changes is no longer zero but given by a certain negative number, which we have chosen in the simulation underlying figure 5.6 as 0.01. Thus, nominal wages can fall as a reaction to high unemployment, but by not more than 1 % per period.

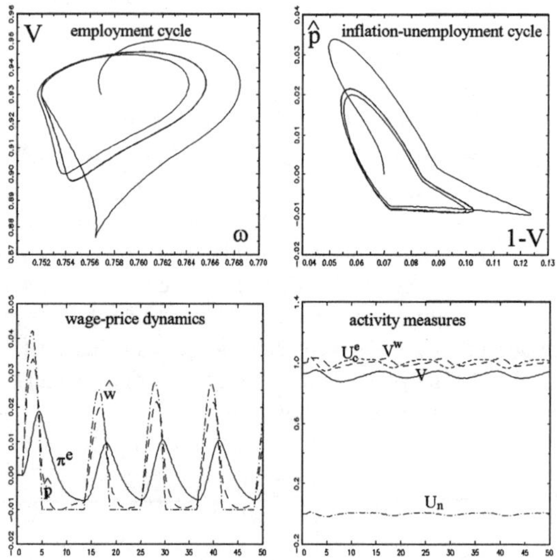

Figure 5.6: Mild limit cycle fluctuations for sluggishly decreasing nominal wages

As a result, the stable depressions of the preceding case now disappear, and again a limit cycle occurs, yet diminished in size in comparison to figure 5.3 or 5.4. Furthermore, the Keynesian regime 1 is never left. This example demonstrates, how additional nonlinearities, inserted into the model at appropriate places, can help to avoid instability scenarios like the one of figure 5.4, which are unlikely to provide a satisfactory description of the economy from an empirical point of view, if one takes into account, that situation of demand rationing rarely are observed in developed market economies. In contrast to this figure 5.6 already yields, e.g., a relationship between unemployment and inflation which is not too far from empirical patterns.

5.5 Summary

In this chapter we have shown, how the KMG model discussed so far could be appropriately extended in order to take account of possible regime switches as they are well-known from non-Walrasian disequilibrium theories. On the other hand, the question was raised, how relevant these regime switches actually are. Starting with Picard's (1983) model we have shown, that already in this context the importance of actual regime switches will be significantly reduced, if one takes into account, that wages and prices begin to rise much earlier than full employment of the labor force and full capacity utilization are reached.

This result was further underlined by the consideration of inventory changes and buffers like overtime work or overuse of productive capacity as they are now in the KMG model.

Here, the possibility for firms to serve their demand by selling from inventory stocks, or by going temporarily beyond the point where prices equal marginal wage costs, considerably enlarged the region, in which supply bottlenecks and demand rationing do not occur. On the other hand, at least from a more theoretical point of view, the possibility of regime switches cannot a priori be excluded and thus has to be modeled carefully, especially with regard to the interdependencies between the single markets concerned. This was done in section 5.3, where the case of exhausted inventories and resulting demand rationing as well as the possible feedbacks on dividend payments were explicitly considered. A number of simulation runs finally demonstrated, under which conditions regime switches become relevant. Furthermore, the stabilizing potential coming about by a kinked Phillips-curve, leading to a constant nominal wage in regions of high unemployment, has again been added and evaluated numerically.

This last point will again be taken up in the next chapter, where the importance of market imperfections on the labor market as well as on the goods market and their role for wage and price formation will be investigated. Before however turning to this point, we shortly want to consider in the subsequent appendix one of the earliest contributions made to Non-Walrasian disequilibrium theory, namely the model of Solow and Stiglitz (1968).

5.6 Solow and Stiglitz (1968): An early Non-Walrasian contribution

There is a seminal paper by Solow and Stiglitz (1968) entitled 'Output, employment, and wages in the short run', which considered regime switching even before the appearance of Barro and Grossman's (1971) 'A general disequilibrium model of income and employment' and in this respect not only the short run determination of output and employment, but also the (in our view) medium run consequences of these two variables for price and wage dynamics. This model has many things in common with our Keynes-Metzler model of chapter 2 and the present chapter, though it is far less complete than the latter model. Through appropriate modifications (as they have been suggested in section 3.3 of chapter 3) the Solow-Stiglitz model can indeed be made (nearly) a special case of our general Keynes-Metzler model with its rationing possibilities.

The equations of the Solow and Stiglitz (1968) model are (in our notation):[18]

$$
\begin{aligned}
Y^p &= F(L^p), \quad \omega = F'(L^p), \quad \omega = w/p && (5.118)\\
Y^w &= F(L^w) && (5.119)\\
\dot{L}^w &= \beta_l(F^{-1}(\min\{Y^p, Y^d\}) - L^w) && (5.120)\\
Y^d &= (1-s_w)\omega L^w + (1-s_c)(Y^d - \omega L^w) + I && (5.121)\\
Y &= \min\{Y^w, Y^d\} && (5.122)\\
\widehat{p} &= \beta_p(Y^d/Y^p) + \kappa_p\widehat{w} = \beta_p(U_c) + \kappa_p\widehat{w}, \quad \kappa_p \in (0,1) && (5.123)\\
\widehat{w} &= \beta_w(L^w/L) + \kappa_w\widehat{p} = \beta_w(V) + \kappa_w\widehat{p}, \quad \kappa_w \in (0,1) && (5.124)
\end{aligned}
$$

[18] $F(L^p) = Y^p$ the production function with K omitted.

$$L \;=\; const \tag{5.125}$$

There are only two min-operators in the model, in equation (5.120) which describes the dynamics of the employed workforce and in (5.122) which describes actual output. This latter equation states that firms are only limited in their output decision by the amount of workers they employ, L^w, and the state of effective demand, Y^d. The capacity constraint Y^p plays no role here, since it is assumed that firms will also produce at marginal wage costs that exceed the current price level in order to satisfy their customers' demand.[19] The above model is reduced to a dynamical system of dimension 2 in the state variables ω, L^w in Solow and Stiglitz (1968) and discussed extensively with respect to the many types of phase portraits such a dynamical model can give rise to, including regime switches to states of full employment where effective demand is no longer effective, but of a notional type only. We shall see that the latter is not true in a more flexible type of the Solow-Stiglitz model where as in section 5.4 of this chapter overtime work of insiders allows to satisfy effective demand even when the external labor market is completely exhausted.

In order to show this we now modify the Solow-Stiglitz model step by step into this direction. In view of our discussion of the Keynes-Metzler model in section 5.4 of this chapter we first of all replace equation (5.122) by

$$Y = \min\{Y^d, \bar{Y}^w, \bar{Y}^p\}$$

where again $\bar{Y}^w = F(2L^w)$ due to the possibility of overtime work (and $\bar{Y}^p = F(\bar{L}^p)$ defined by $\omega \bar{L}^p = \bar{Y}^p$ as in the Keynes-Metzler model with its possible (though rare) switches of regimes). Actual employment L^d of the employed workforce, L^w, is then given by $L^d = F^{-1}(Y)$, i.e. equation (5.120) reduces to

$$\dot{L}^w = \beta_l(L^d - L^w).$$

In view of this, equation (5.121) needs also reformulation. This equation suggests that expected sales Y^e are identical with aggregate demand Y^d $(\beta_{y^e} = \infty!)$ and that this magnitude is the basis for the dividend policy of the firm. This implies for the budget constraint of the firm (with pure equity financing):

$$p(Y^d - Y) + pI = p_e\dot{E}$$

which might be somewhat strange an assumption on dividend policies of firms. An alternative would be to use Y in the place of Y^d on the right hand side of equation (5.121) which would imply $pI = p_e\dot{E}$ as the budget constraint of firms.[20]

Be that as it may, taking overtime work into account implies that only the Keynesian regime is again possible around the steady state which gives rise to the following dynamical system[21]

$$Y^d \;=\; (1-s_w)\omega L^d + (1-s_c)(Y^d - \omega L^d) + I$$

[19]See pp.542/3 in Solow and Stiglitz (1968).

[20]See Solow and Stiglitz (1968, p.544) for a discussion of this alternative and note that the above equations of the Solow-Stiglitz model would then allow output Y to feedback into the rest of the model which it does not in the present formulation of it. Note also that this problematic feature of the original version of the Solow-Stiglitz model will not exist in our Keynesian reformulation of the model that follows below.

[21]We assume in the following for reasons of simplicity a linear production function without substitution and thus $Y^d = xL^d, Y^p = y^pK, x, y^p = $ const as in the formulation of the Keynes-Metzler model of chapter 2.

$$\begin{aligned} L^d &= F^{-1}(Y^d) = Y^d/x, \quad x = \text{const}^{22} \\ \dot{L}^w &= \beta_l(L^d - L^w) \\ \widehat{p} &= \beta_p(Y^d/Y^p) + \kappa_p\widehat{w}, \quad Y^p = y^pK, K = const \\ \widehat{w} &= \beta_w(L^w/L^d) + \kappa_w\widehat{p}, \quad L = const \end{aligned}$$

Due to the possibility of over- (and under-)time work $L^d \gtreqless L^w$ the Keynesian regime remains in power as long as $L^d \leq 2L^w, \omega \leq x$ holds true (with the additional restriction $L^w \leq L$ which however does not induce supply constraints on output Y). Note that $\dot{L}^w$ is only important here as determinant of the constraint $\bar{Y}^w$ (which is not considered at present, see however below).

The equation for effective demand can be solved for Y^d and gives:

$$(1 - (1 - s_w)\omega/x - (1 - s_c)(1 - \omega/x))Y^d = I$$

or

$$\begin{aligned} Y^d &= \frac{1}{s_w\omega/x + s_c(1 - \omega/x)} \cdot I \\ &= \frac{1}{s_w + (s_c - s_w)(1 - \omega/x)} \cdot I \;=\; Y^d(\omega), \quad Y^{d'} > 0 \end{aligned}$$

as Keynesian multiplier expression.[23]

The wage-price dynamics, on the other hand, can be considered as a system of two linear equations in the two unknowns $\widehat{w}, \widehat{p}$, which can be solved and gives [24]

$$\begin{pmatrix} \widehat{p} \\ \widehat{w} \end{pmatrix} = \begin{pmatrix} 1 & -\kappa_p \\ -\kappa_w & 1 \end{pmatrix}^{-1} \begin{pmatrix} \beta_p(\cdot) \\ \beta_w(\cdot) \end{pmatrix} = \frac{1}{1 - \kappa_p\kappa_w} \begin{pmatrix} 1 & \kappa_p \\ \kappa_w & 1 \end{pmatrix} \begin{pmatrix} \beta_p(\cdot) \\ \beta_w(\cdot) \end{pmatrix}$$

that is

$$\widehat{\omega} = \widehat{w} - \widehat{p} = \frac{1}{1 - \kappa_p\kappa_w}\left[(1 - \kappa_p)\beta_w(L^d/L) - (1 - \kappa_w)\beta_p(Y^d/Y^p)\right]$$

with $Y^p = const$ and $L^d = Y^d/x$. In brief this gives (for $s_c \geq s_w$)

$$\widehat{\omega} = \widetilde{\beta}_w(\omega) - \widetilde{\beta}_p(\omega), \quad \widetilde{\beta}'_w, \widetilde{\beta}'_p > 0$$

as the only law of motion for the economy, saying that sufficient wage flexibility will be destabilizing (β_p given) and a sufficient degree of price flexibility will be stabilizing (for β_w given). This is the typical (local) result of the Rose (1967) employment cycle mechanism and it must be accompanied by global considerations in the case of local instability.[25]

[22] $Y^p = y^pK = const$ and $\beta_p(\bar{U}_c) = 0$ for $0 < \bar{U}_c < 1$ as in the Keynes-Metzler model (and similar for $\beta_w(\cdot)$).

[23] Note that this representation of the product market, of Solow and Stiglitz (1968), is based on Kaldor's treatment of differential saving habits and not on the one by Pasinetti.

[24] For $\kappa_p\kappa_w < 1$ as in Solow and Stiglitz (1968).

[25] See Chiarella and Flaschel (1999b, Ch.3/4) for further considerations of such situations. We thank H.J. Ramser for making us aware of the similarities between Solow and Stiglitz (1968) and our treatments of the wage price module.

Assuming flexible worktime within the firm has been sufficient in our above reformulation of the Solow and Stiglitz model to remove supply constraints from a (fairly large) neighborhood of the steady state of the model. Taking note of this possibility however implies one further modification of the model, since the demand pull variable L^d/L is now to be decomposed into two components (and their independent operation): L^d/L^w, the employment rate of the workforce of firms or the inside employment rate and L^w/L, the employment rate on the labor market or the outside employment rate. These two variables should both be assumed to influence the wage bargain, for example in the way we have already made use of in section 5.4 of this chapter. The final form of the Solow-Stiglitz model thereby becomes in terms of its two state variables ω, L^w:[26]

$$\begin{aligned} \hat{\omega} &= \beta_{w_1}(L^w - \bar{V}) + \beta_{w_2}(Y^d(\omega)/L^w - 1) - \beta_p(Y^d(\omega) - \bar{V}), \\ & \quad \omega \le 1, \ \ \beta_{w_1}(0) = \beta_{w_2}(0) = \beta_p(0) = 0 \qquad (5.126) \\ \dot{L}^w &= \beta_l(Y^d(\omega) - L^w), \ \ L^w \le 1, Y^d \le 2L^w. \qquad (5.127) \end{aligned}$$

Due to the assumption $xL = y^p K (= 1)$ we have efficient factor endowments underlying this dynamical model (which does not consider capital accumulation and thus cannot be used to explain this assumption) and we have made explicit now the steady state values of the normal utilization of inside and outside labor and capital (the latter two are here related by a simple form of Okun's law based fixed proportions in production and efficient factor endowments).

The dynamical system (5.126) – (5.127) – though looking simple – is not at all easy to treat since it maps the many phase portraits (and their isoclines) considered in Solow and Stiglitz (1968) into one regime, the Keynesian regime now. In order to provide an impression of this complexity we propose one modification and simplification of it which allows the explicit calculation of the $\dot{\omega} = 0$–isocline:

$$\begin{aligned} \hat{\omega} &= \beta_{w_1}(L^w - \bar{V}) + \beta_{w_2}(Y^d(\omega) - L^w) - \beta_p(Y^d(\omega) - \bar{V}), \\ & \quad \omega \le 1, \ \ \beta_{w_1}, \beta_{w_2}, \beta_p > 0 \qquad (5.128) \\ \dot{L}^w &= \beta_l(Y^d(\omega) - L^w), \ \ L^w \le 1, Y^d \le 2L^w. \qquad (5.129) \end{aligned}$$

Introducing linearity into the adjustment for real wages (but not into the dependence of effective demand on them) gives as isoclines of the dynamical system (5.128) – (5.129):

$$\begin{aligned} \dot{\omega} &= 0: \quad \frac{(\beta_p - \beta_{w_2})Y^d(\omega) - (\beta_p - \beta_{w_1})\bar{V}}{\beta_{w_1} - \beta_{w_2}} \\ \dot{L}^w &= 0: \quad L^w = Y^d(\omega) = \frac{I}{s_c - (s_w - s_c)\omega}. \end{aligned}$$

On the basis of these expressions we now assume for the parameters of the model:

$$I/s_c < \bar{V} < I/s_w < 2(= 2L), \quad \beta_p(\omega) \to \infty \text{ as } \omega \to 1 (= x)$$

which determines the intersections of the $\dot{L}^w$–isocline with the vertical axis at $\omega = 0$ and $\omega = 1$ and which says that the price adjustment speed approaches infinity when real wages

[26]We here suppress for simplicity the positive constants: x, y^p, L, K, by setting them all equal to 1 and also suppress the various κ–expressions which of course cannot be equal to one, but which only matter with respect to the signs they imply for the considered dynamics.

approach output per worker from below (we assume that this reaction of β_p only happens close to $\omega = 1$).

On the basis of these assumptions the following phase portraits (a partial one and a specific one) of the dynamics (5.128) – (5.129) can be drawn:

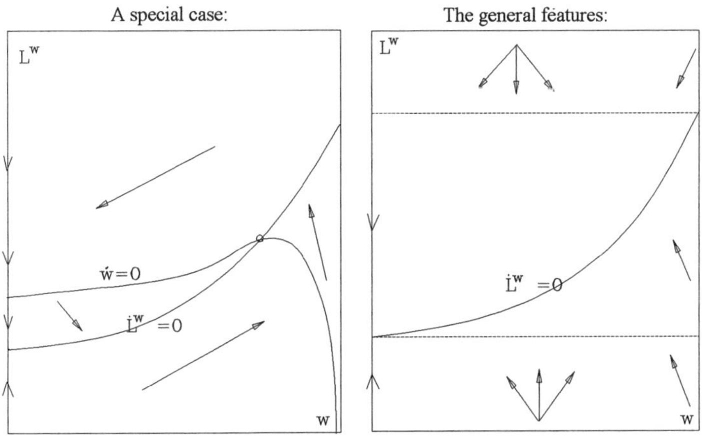

Figure 5.7:
Phase portraits of the modified Solow-Stiglitz model
(to the left: $\beta_{w_1} < \beta_p < \beta_{w_2}$).

It is easily proved that the dynamics (5.128) – (5.129) exhibits exactly two steady state solutions,[27] one interior and one on the vertical axis, as shown in left phase portrait. Furthermore the determinant of the Jacobian at the interior steady state is always positive, i.e., stability will generally be lost in a cyclical fashion by way of so-called Hopf bifurcation.

But this is all that can be said in general. Beyond that the $\dot{\omega} = 0$–isocline can be – if positively sloped – steeper or flatter than the $\dot{L}^w = 0$–isocline (or be negatively sloped or be identical with $\dot{L}^w = 0$–isocline). The real wage can fall or rise above (or below) the $\dot{\omega} = 0$–isocline which may also be vertical.

This gives rise to a multiplicity of qualitatively different phase portraits exhibiting global asymptotic stability, stable limit cycles, economic collapse due convergence to the second steady state and more – but all this is happening within the Keynesian regime solely and confined to the box shown at the right of figure 5.7 (which is an invariant set of the dynamics). In the left hand figure 5.7 we have chosen as parameter constellation the situation $\beta_{w_1} < \beta_p < \beta_{w_2}$ and β_l sufficiently small so that the interior steady state is locally unstable and thus gives rise to a stable limit cycle as shown in the following numerical simulation based on the qualitative features of the left hand figure 5.7:

[27] If $\beta_{w_1} \neq \beta_p(\omega)$, otherwise a third steady state solution might be created.

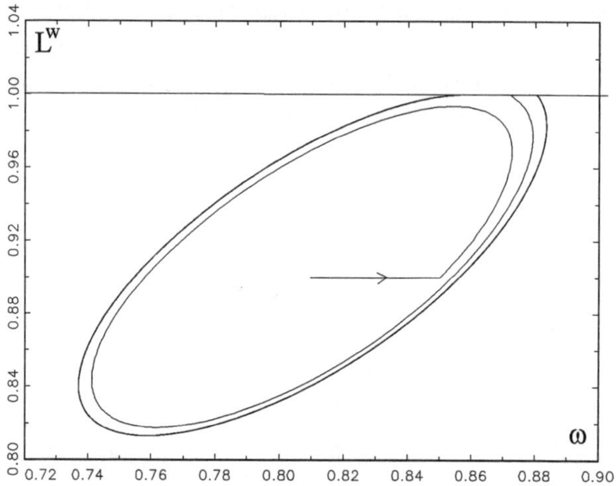

Figure 5.8:
A purely Keynesian limit cycle for the modified Solow-Stiglitz model
$(\beta_{w_1} = 0.3, \beta_{w_2} = 0.7, \beta_p = 0.5, \beta_l = 0.3, s_w = 0.2, s_c = 0.9, I = 0.3, \bar{V} = 0.9)$.

The outcome of this reconsideration of the Solow and Stiglitz (1968) model of wage/price dynamics thus is that it gives rise to many different dynamics even in a fairly simple Keynesian setup (where absolute full employment is possible, but does not lead to regime switches as in non-Walrasian theory, see the figure 5.8). These statements also hold true in the original version (5.126) – (5.127) of the dynamics (though then with still more complications as far as the phase portraits are concerned). Furthermore, returning to a neoclassical production function will not alter the findings on the general validity of the Keynesian regime in this model type – if account is taken of the fact that marginal wage costs do not represent an absolute upper limit to production in a Keynesian framework (where firms cannot be assumed to be price-takers), see also Solow and Stiglitz (1968, p.542). This implies that circular flow of income, and not the marginal productivity theory of wages, determines macroeconomic income distribution in general.

Due to the special nature of the above model (5.126) – (5.127) - which still neglects too many things of our general Keynes-Metzler approach to economic dynamics (with or without rationing) - we do not go any further into such a discussion here. In closing their dynamical investigations Solow and Stiglitz (1968, pp.559ff.) state that the next steps of extending the model should be the inclusion of money market phenomena, growth, variable investment, inventories and inflationary expectations. Our Keynes-Metzler model of this chapter can be considered as having done just this (and more) in a framework that basically allows for the Keynesian regime solely.

Chapter 6

Market Imperfections: Basic Integration and Comparison

6.1 Introduction

Whereas the non-Walrasian approaches considered in the preceding chapter were mainly concerned with a correct description of short-run rationing equilibria on the basis of temporarily given wages and prices, they usually left open the question, how these wages and prices are actually formed and why they are temporarily fixed. Partly as a reaction to this unsatisfactory situation a large number of theories emerged, that tried to give some foundation for these assumptions by explicit consideration of imperfections on the markets for labor or for goods (or both). Although theories of price formation under imperfect competition on the one hand and macroeconomic models based on price setting or non-market clearing prices both have a long tradition, attempts to integrate both lines have occupied a larger part in economic literature only recently during recent decades. They resulted in a variety of mainly microfounded models of general equilibrium, in which prices were derived from optimizing behavior of agents endowed with some market power. In the following some of these approaches[1] shall be briefly sketched, because they provide the background for the aggregative equations employed by Carlin and Soskice (1990) in their basic imperfect competition model, that will later be integrated into the KMG framework. As one main element of the latter is the existence of involuntary unemployment, the question arises, how the non-market-clearing wages, which are mainly responsible for this, are generated. On the other hand, the formation of the prices for goods plays an important role when judging the potential effect of changes of aggregate demand on output. A strict division into models of labor market imperfections on the one hand and imperfect competition on the product market on the other hand, however, is not applicable to all theories of this type. Thus, e.g., the seminal papers by Hart (1982), Blanchard and Kiyotaki (1987), Dixon (1987) and Benassy (1995) investigate economies which are characterized by market power on both markets. The resulting involuntary unemployment, however, is entirely caused by the labor market imperfections, because oligopolistic or monopolistic pricing on the goods market by itself would not be able to prevent full employment in the case of

[1]For good surveys and collections of important contributions to this theme see e.g. Mankiw and Romer (1991), Dixon and Rankin (1995), especially chapter 2, and Silvestre (1993, 1995).

a competitive labor market. Some approaches, however, also consider the possibility of "unemployment at all wages", that comes about by goods market imperfections solely due to demand functions on the single markets, whose price elasticity becomes smaller than 1 for prices sufficiently small, in connection with a constant labor supply.[2]

With regard to imperfections on the labor market a number of theories have been developed, the main representatives of which can be classified into efficiency wage approaches, insider-outsider theories and models of the wage bargain between employers and unions. The first group of the efficiency wage variety assumes, that the actual working effort of an employee depends positively on the real wage he or she gets. In a well-known approach of this kind, the so-called "shirking model" of Shapiro and Stiglitz (1984), the single firm has no opportunity of perfectly monitoring the working effort of its employees, so that the latter would have an incentive to shirk unless the wage is so high, that, compared to the outside option, they would have too much to lose, if they were detected while shirking and then dismissed. The equilibrium generated by the whole model is then characterized by an economy-wide rate of unemployment, that is high enough to lower the workers' outside option (via the probability of getting a new job after being fired) sufficiently to prevent them from shirking.

Another line of research, pursued mainly by Lindbeck and Snower (1989), pointed to the fact, that already employed workers, the so-called insiders, have specific knowledge and training with regard to the tasks they have to fulfill. This gives them the opportunity to carry through higher wages, because it would be costly for the firm to replace them by outsiders, i.e. new workers, who do not have the necessary experience so that costs would arise for instructing them. Furthermore, the insiders have the possibility not to cooperate with new workers, which still increases their bargaining power. Thus, also in this type of model a real wage emerges, which is too high to clear the labor market.

In models concerned with the wage bargain between unions and firms finally unemployment usually comes about as a result of some degree of monopoly power of the unions. As long as firms can determine employment according to their labor demand curve, which is assumed in the so-called "right-to-manage" approaches, the union in an industry can choose a point on this curve, that maximizes its objective function. As a high degree of employment is usually not the only aim of the union, the outcome will be a real wage above the market clearing competitive one. The difference between them (and thus the size of the resulting rate of unemployment) is positively dependent on the union's bargaining power. This result only changes, if one assumes so-called "efficient bargains", which not only concern the wage rate but also the level of employment, as done by McDonald and Solow (1981). In this case, a higher bargaining power of the unions can lead not only to a higher wage but also to a higher employment rate, which may even exceed the competitive one. The question, however arises, whether this type of negotiation is still efficient, if side effects are taken into account as e.g. (negative) effects on the profitability of real capital and thus on the rate of capital accumulation. Furthermore, the empirical relevance seems not to be completely convincing.[3]

---

[2]See, e.g., Dehez (1985), D'Aspremont, Dos Santos Ferreira and Gérard-Varet (1989, 1990, 1991, 1995) or Silvestre (1990) for models in this direction.

[3]Compare in this regard also Carlin and Soskice (1990, p.400).

With regard to high and persistent rates of unemployment in many countries some new approaches to labor market theory have appeared in recent years that have tried to endogenize the NAIRU. These models then exhibit hysteresis, i.e. the steady state level of unemployment is not unique but depends on the time path from which the economy starts or onto which it is thrown after a shock. As this element will also be present in some subsequent reformulations of the KMG model, a brief look shall be given here to the two main explanations of this phenomenon. The first one points to the fact, that a higher level of actual unemployment also increases the number of long-term unemployed, who eventually lose skills and thus become more and more unattractive to a potential employer. As a consequence, they cannot exert any downward pressure on wages any more, so that unions can bargain higher wages than they would be able to if these long-term unemployed were still be able to compete with the other workers. The result is a higher natural rate of unemployment.[4] The other reason for a path-dependent NAIRU comes about by a diminishing stigmatization and higher unemployment benefits in times of high unemployment, with the consequence, that an increasing part of the unemployed is no longer interested in getting a job again.[5] Note however, that this latter type of reasoning concerns no longer involuntary unemployment.

Besides these theories of non market clearing wages, a second class of models concerns imperfect competition on the market for goods. A part of these approaches can be divided into models of oligopoly in a one-good-world (as, e.g., the model of Hart (1982) mentioned above) and models with monopolistic competition in a multi-good-economy (like, e.g., the approaches of Dixit and Stiglitz (1977) or Blanchard and Kiyotaki (1987)). Some recent approaches, however, already combine both scenarios by assuming an economy with differentiated goods and an oligopoly on each single market.[6] A broad application of the methodology of imperfect competition on the goods markets has meanwhile also taken place in the RBC literature, as, e.g., the articles of Devereux, Head and Lapham (1993), Hairault and Portier (1993), Hornstein (1993), Rotemberg and Woodford (1992, 1993) or Galí (1994a,b) show. These models already possess an elaborate microeconomic structure including aspects like fixed costs in production, technical progress, material inputs from other firms, the feedbacks of the elasticity of investment demand on the demand curve for a single monopolist and more. On the other hand, goods market imperfections also play an important role in New Keynesian theories, which aim at giving an explanation for sluggish price adjustments. Thus, e.g., the well-known PAYM-insight[7] states, that under monopolistic price setting already small menu costs of price adjustment are sufficient to generate significant price rigidities. Thus, fluctuations in aggregate demand find their expression mainly in corresponding output fluctuations rather than in price changes. The same outcome, however, can also be generated without menu costs, if one, e.g., assumes labor productivity and demand elasticity as being constant, as is done by Carlin and Soskice (1990). Their basic imperfect competition model will be considered later on.

[4]See and Cross (1995, p.187) and Blanchard (1997, pp.419–420).

[5]See Blanchard (1997, p. 418).

[6]Compare in this respect e.g. Rotemberg and Woodford (1992), where, however, also the goods supplied by the oligopolists on a single market are near but not perfect substitutes. Another example is the model of D'Aspremont, Dos Santos Ferreira and Gérard-Varet (1995).

[7]This designation was chosen by Rotemberg (1987) and refers to the initials of the authors of the most important contributions in this respect, namely Parkin (1986), Akerlof and Yellen (1985) and Mankiw (1985).

The aim of the present chapter now consists in an integration of the main aspects and insights that can be obtained from imperfect competition approaches into the KMG model analyzed in the previous chapters. For this purpose the KMG model is first reformulated in discrete time in section 6.2 in order to ease the comparison with the existing literature. In section 6.3 then two key elements concerning non-competitive wage and price formation as they are formulated by Carlin and Soskice (1990) are built in into the KMG framework, thereby substituting earlier formulations of the corresponding laws of motion. Furthermore, the kink in the Phillips-curve which has been considered with respect to its consequences only numerically so far in section 5.4 of the preceding chapter, is now regarded in great detail also analytically. Whereas in section 6.3, due to the assumption of constant labor productivity and a constant markup, these considerations are based on a constant wage share, the latter is variable in section 6.4, where a neoclassical production function in connection with a markup on marginal wage costs is employed. In addition to this, variations of the model including profit share targets in the tradition of Rowthorn (1980) as well as a variable markup factor are considered. Section 6.5 finally summarizes the main results and makes some proposals for further research.

6.2 A discrete-time KMG reference case

We have investigated in chapters 4 and 5 a variety of extensions of the basic KMG growth model introduced and discussed in detail in part I of the book. These extensions concerned wage taxation, substitution, endogenous growth (also with respect to labor supply), overtime work, inventories and pricing decisions of firms, lagged employment adjustments in view of expected aggregate demand, lower and upper bounds to dividend payments, zero profitability constraints, labor market constraints and nonnegativity of inventories. We have mentioned further restrictions on the variables of the model, namely nonnegative gross investment, a positive nominal rate of interest, nonnegative stocks of government bonds and equities, and output decisions (based on expected demand and planned inventory changes) that are bounded away from zero. These latter restrictions are always checked with respect to their validity in simulation runs of the dynamics, but we have not and will not supply endogenous reasons (nonlinearities in economic behavior) that will prevent economically non-viable results with respect to these variables.

Furthermore, since the role of substitution and endogenous growth has been discussed extensively in chapters 5 and 4, respectively, we will not consider these issues in this chapter again in this detail (but will only provide some perspectives in this regard). We will use here however the consistency requirements that the rate of employment not be larger than one in the assumed situation of a temporarily given labor supply. However, negative inventories are now allowed for and interpreted as paid orders of consumption goods that will be served on a first in first out basis when actual aggregate demand is again below output and when there is therefore output going into inventories. We have to assume here that such delayed delivery does not change the consumption habits of workers, asset holders and the government and that the underlying supply constraints are not so large that also investment becomes rationed, the only goods demand which would alter the real growth path of the economy in the assumed situation. In short we therefore assume in this chapter that the Keynesian regime, regime 1 in the preceding chapter, can hold throughout due to the size of the fluctuations in economic activity that are here only allowed for. Of course, a switch to regime 2 can always be added to the model again as in chapter 5. We thus allow for constraints on dividends, employment rates and output as in chapter 5, but not for switches in the Keynesian regime. This regime thus drives the system at all points in time.

In order to allow comparison with models in the literature on market imperfections it is finally desirable to have a discrete time version of the KMG growth model implied by the assumptions just discussed. We therefore depart here from the continuous time presentations so far used and present the model on the extensive level in period form (with the length of the time period set equal to one). Whenever possible we shall however supply on the intensive form level a continuous time version of the implied dynamics since continuous-time dynamics is easier to treat and does not allow for dynamic complexities that are solely due to overshooting caused by the period length and the assumed strength of adjustments. An advantage of period analysis however is that it makes the assumed time structure of the originally continuous-time models much more transparent (for example when rates of profit and of interest are compared, since there is the choice between left and right hand derivatives in continuous time) and it also improves the treatment of budget restraints since flows can now be added to stocks instead of leading to formulae based on integration . We will use the resulting KMG growth model in the remainder to incorporate into it in particular the microfounded analysis of wage and price setting behavior and their short and medium run implications investigated in Carlin and Soskice (1990, Part II). The equations of the KMG growth model to be used as reference case in this regard are as follows:

1. Definitions (remunerations and wealth):

$$\omega_t = w_t/p_t, \quad \rho_t^e = (Y_t^e - \delta K_{t-1} - \omega_t L_t^d)/K_{t-1} \tag{6.1}$$

$$W_t = (M_{t-1} + B_{t-1} + p_{et}E_{t-1})/p_t, \quad p_b = 1. \tag{6.2}$$

$$\hat{z}_t = (z_t - z_{t-1})/z_{t-1} \quad \text{growth rate of a variable } z. \tag{6.3}$$

This set of equations introduces again variables to be employed in the structural equations of the model, the definition of real wages ω_t, of the expected rate of profit on real capital ρ_t^e,[8] based on sales expectations at $t-1$ for the present point in time t and the definition of current stock of real wealth W_t. Note that stocks that exist at time t are indexed by $t-1$, while their actual reallocation and revaluation happens in t and is thus indexed by t. Note also that this secondary market component of our financial markets must be integrated with the primary one (new issue and new demand for such assets), since there is no separation between primary and secondary markets (new issues and resale) needed in our discrete time approach to financial markets. Current real wealth held by asset owning households in t is composed of money M_{t-1}, fixed price bonds B_{t-1} ($p_b = 1$) and equities E_{t-1} as in Sargent (1987, Ch.1) and is determined on the basis of the current market prices for equities, p_{et}, and for output p_t. We stress that the real wealth given at t is based on assets bought at $t-1$, but valued at current prices for equities and goods. Furthermore, current output is produced with the capital stock given at $t-1$ and with labor that is paid in t. Note finally that the definition of growth rates $\hat{z}$ is indexed forward in order to ease the presentation of the intensive form of the model later on.

[8]We shall numerically only investigate situations where this rate of profit is positive which implies that dividend payments will stay positive along the considered trajectories.

Household behavior (with heterogeneous agents) is described next by the following set of equations.

2. Households (workers and asset-holders):

$$C_t = (1-\tau_w)\omega_t L_t^d + (1-s_c)[\rho_t^e K_{t-1} + r_t B_{t-1}/p_t - T_{ct}], \tag{6.4}$$

$$S_{pt} = s_c[\rho_t^e K_{t-1} + r_t B_{t-1}/p_t - T_{ct}] \tag{6.5}$$

$$\hat{L}_{t+1} = n = \text{const.} \tag{6.6}$$

$$W_t + S_{pt} = (M_t^d + B_t^d + p_{et}E_t^d)/p_t, \quad \text{cf. the asset market module below.} \tag{6.7}$$

Aggregate consumption of households, C_t, is based on classical saving habits with savings out of wages (after taxes) set equal to zero for simplicity. We again assume that capital taxes T_{ct} concerning (expected) profit and interest income are paid in a lump sum fashion (see module 4.). The next equation provides the definition of real private savings S_{pt} (here only of wealth owners) which is allocated to the actual changes in the stock of money, in bonds and in equities in the last equation of this module of the model. Next, workers are assumed to supply labor L_t inelastically at each moment in time with a rate of growth $\hat{L}_{t+1}$ given by n, the natural rate of growth. Note here again that we use end of period indices to characterize growth rates of quantities and prices. Finally, equation (6.7) states how real wealth and real savings act as budget restriction for the sum of the stock demand for real money balances and real bond and equities holdings of asset owners at time t (Walras' Law of Stocks and Flows).

The behavior of the sector of firms of the economy is described by the following set of equations:

3. Firms (production-units and investors):

$$Y_t^p = y^p K_{t-1},\ y^p = \text{ const. },\ U_{ct} = Y_t/Y_t^p = y_t/y^p\ \ (y_t = Y_t/K_{t-1}) \tag{6.8}$$

$$L_t^d = Y_t/x_t,\ \hat{x}_t = n_l = \text{ const.},\ V_t = L_t^w/L_t \le 1,\quad V_t^w = L_t^d/L_t^w \tag{6.9}$$

$$L_{t+1}^w = (1+\gamma)L_t^w + \beta_v(L_t^d - L_t^w),\quad \gamma = n + n_l \tag{6.10}$$

$$I_t = i_1(\rho_t^e - (r_t - \pi_t^e))K_{t-1} + i_2(U_{ct} - \bar{U}_c)K_{t-1} + \gamma K_{t-1}, \gamma = n + n_l \tag{6.11}$$

$$S_{ft} = Y_{ft} = Y_t - Y_t^e = \mathcal{I}_t, \tag{6.12}$$

$$\Delta Y_t^e = Y_t^e - \delta K_{t-1} - C_t - I_t - G_t = Y_t^e - Y_t^d \tag{6.13}$$

$$\frac{p_{et}\Delta E_t}{p_t} = I_t + \Delta Y_t^e = I_t + (N_t - N_{t-1} - \mathcal{I}_t), \tag{6.14}$$

$$I_t^a = I_t + N_t - N_{t-1} = I_t + \Delta Y_t^e + \mathcal{I}_t = p_{et}\Delta E_t/p_t + \mathcal{I}_t, \tag{6.15}$$

$$\hat{K}_t = (K_t - K_{t-1})/K_{t-1} = I_t/K_{t-1}. \tag{6.16}$$

According to eqns. (6.8),(6.9), firms produce commodities in amount Y_t via a fixed proportions technology characterized by the potential output-capital ratio $y^p = Y_t^p/K_{t-1}$ and a temporarily fixed ratio x between actual output Y_t and labor L_t^d needed to produce this output. This labor productivity ratio grows at the given rate n_l in time, i.e., we have returned to the assumption of exogenous Harrod neutral technical change. This simple concept of technology allows for a straightforward definition of the rate of utilization U_{ct}, V_t of capital as well as of labor. Note that current investment I_t will not have a capacity effect in the current point in time t which restricts the use of capital to K_{t-1}, and that labor is paid ex post, at t from the proceeds obtained from current output Y_t. The employment policy of firms, concerning their workforce L^w, is described next as in chapter 5. In eqn. (6.11) investment per unit of capital I_t/K_{t-1} is driven by two forces, the rate of return differential between the currently expected rate of profit ρ_t^e, concerning the time interval $[t-1,t]$ for which the capital stock, but not labor has been advanced, and the current real rate of interest $(r_t - \pi_t^e)$, where the nominal rate of interest (just as rates of inflation) is also indexed by the endpoint of the time interval it concerns, and the deviation of actual capacity utilization U_{ct} from the normal or non-accelerating -inflation rate of capacity utilization $\bar{U}_c$. Note that the expected rate π_t^e refers to the medium-run (see the wage-price module below) and thus not to the time interval $[t-1,t]$ as the two rates of return that are here being compared on its basis (see the remark below for an improvement of this situation). There is also an unexplained trend term in the investment equation which is set equal to the natural rate of growth for reasons of simplicity. Savings of firms, eqn. (6.12), is equal to the excess of output over expected sales (and caused by planned inventory changes), since we assume in this model for simplicity that expected sales are the basis of firms' dividend payments (after deduction of capital depreciation δK_{t-1} and real wage payments $\omega_t L_t^d$).

The next equation (6.13) defines the excess of expected demand over actual demand which – as just explained – has to be financed by firms by issuing new equities in the present version of the model. It follows, as expressed in eqn. (6.14), that the total amount of new equities issued by firms must equal in value the sum of intended fixed capital investment and unexpected inventory changes, $\Delta Y_t^e = N_t - N_{t-1} - \mathcal{I}_t$; compare our formulation of the inventory adjustment mechanism below. The next equation (6.15) describes on this basis actual investment I_t^a from various perspectives and here only serves to add some details about the accounting framework of the type of firms here considered. Finally, eqn. (6.16) states that (fixed business) investment plans of firms are always realized in this Keynesian (demand oriented) context, if needed by way of corresponding inventory changes.

We now turn to a brief description of the government sector:

4. Government (fiscal and monetary authority):

$$T_t = \tau_w \omega_t L_t^d + T_{ct}, \quad t_c^n = (T_{ct} - r_t B_{t-1}/p_t)/K_{t-1} = const < 0 \tag{6.17}$$

$$G_t = \tau_w \omega_t L_t^d + \bar{g} K_{t-1}, \; \bar{g} \geq 0 \tag{6.18}$$

$$S_{gt} = T_t - r_t B_{t-1}/p_t - G_t \; [= (t_c^n - \bar{g}) K_{t-1}] \tag{6.19}$$

$$M_t = (1+\bar{\mu}) M_{t-1}, \quad \bar{\mu} \neq n + n_l \text{ in general} \tag{6.20}$$

$$B_t = B_{t-1} + p_t G_t + r_t B_{t-1} - p_t T_t - (M_t - M_{t-1}). \tag{6.21}$$

(6.22)

The government sector is again described as simply as possible such that the role of bond financing of government expenditures appears explicitly, but does not yet feed back into the dynamics of the private sector of the model. In view of these various rules for government and central bank behavior the issue of new bonds by the government (net of open market operations by the central bank) is then determined residually via equation (6.21) which states that money and bond financing must exactly cover the deficit in government expenditure financing.

We now describe the asset market equilibrium conditions of the model:

5. <u>Equilibrium conditions (asset-markets):</u>

$$
\begin{aligned}
W_t + S_{pt} &= (M_t^d + B_t^d + p_{et}E_t^d)/p_t, && (6.23)\\
M_t &= M_t^d = h_1 p_t Y_t + h_2 p_t K_{t-1}(r_o - r_{t+1}) && (6.24)\\
p_{et}E_t &= (\rho_{t+1}^e p_{t+1} K_t + (p_{et} - p_{e,t-1})E_t)/r_{t+1}, && (6.25)\\
& [B_t = B_t^d, E_t = E_t^d]
\end{aligned}
$$

The source of the stock demands for financial assets is again shown in eqn. (6.23) as the aggregate value of the existing stock at current market prices plus the savings of asset owning households. Money demand is specified as a linear function of nominal income $p_t Y_t$ and interest r_{t+1} (r_o the steady state rate of interest) in the usual way. Note here that this interest rate r_{t+1} is determined in t, with interest paid in $t+1$ which gives the index to this rate. This convention conforms with the definition of ρ_{t+1}^e we use in the determination of share prices below. Asset markets are assumed to clear at all times. Equation (6.24) describes this assumption for the money market thereby providing the equation for the current market rate of interest to be used for the payments of interest in the next point in time. Bonds and equities are assumed to be perfect substitutes (on the basis of expected or actual rates of return, including capital gains, in $t+1$ which are formed in t on the basis of the information known in t) when the trade on the stock market is performed, see equation (6.25), which amounts to assuming, in the light of the assumed Walras's Law of stocks, that the clearing of the money market implies that the bond and equity market are then cleared as well (with wealth holders accepting any subdivision of their wealth with respect to bonds and equities).

The disequilibrium situation in the goods market is an important component driving the dynamics of the economy. This situation is described by the following equations:

6. <u>Disequilibrium situation (goods-market adjustments):</u>

$$
\begin{aligned}
S_t &= S_{pt} + S_{gt} + S_{ft} = p_{et}(E_t - E_{t-1})/p_t + \mathcal{I}_t = I_t + N_t - N_{t-1} = I_t^a && (6.26)\\
Y_t^d &= C_t + I_t + \delta K_{t-1} + G_t && (6.27)\\
N_t^d &= \beta_{n^d} Y_t^e && (6.28)\\
\mathcal{I}_t &= \gamma N_t^d + \beta_n (N_t^d - N_{t-1}), \quad \gamma = n + n_l && (6.29)\\
Y_t &= Y_t^e + \mathcal{I}_t, && (6.30)\\
Y_{t+1}^e &= (1+\gamma)Y_t^e + \beta_{y^e}(Y_t^d - Y_t^e), \quad \gamma = n + n_l && (6.31)\\
N_t &= N_{t-1} + Y_t - Y_t^d = S_t - I_t && (6.32)\\
U_{nt} &= (N_t^d - N_t)/K_{t-1} && (6.33)
\end{aligned}
$$

It is easy to check by means of the presented budget equations and savings relationships that the consistency of new money and new bonds flow supply and flow demand implies the consistency of the flow supply and demand for equities. Equation (6.26) of this disequilibrium block of the model describes on this basis simple identities that can be related with the ex post identity of total savings S_t and total investment I_t^a for a closed economy. It is here added for accounting purposes solely. Equation (6.27) then defines aggregate demand Y_t^d which is assumed to be never constrained in the present model. In eqn. (6.29) desired inventories N_t^d are assumed to be a constant fraction of expected sales Y_t^e and intended inventory investment $\mathcal{I}_t$ is determined on this basis via the adjustment speed β_n multiplied by the current gap between intended and actual inventories $(N_t^d - N_t)$, augmented by a growth term that integrates in the simplest way the fact that this inventory adjustment rule is operating in a growing economy. Output of firms Y_t in equation (6.30) is the sum of expected sales and planned inventory adjustments. Sales expectations are formed in a purely adaptive way, augmented by a simple term that accounts for growth; see equation (6.31). Finally, in eqn. (6.32), actual inventory changes are given by the discrepancy between actual output Y_t and actual sales Y_t^d, equal to the difference between total savings S_t and fixed business investment I_t. As in the preceding chapter we denote by U_{nt} the disequilibrium in desired inventory holdings relative to the capital stock that is in operation.

We now turn to the last module of our model which is the wage-price module or the supply side of the model (as it is often characterized in the literature).

7. Wage-Price-Sector (adjustment equations):

$$\begin{aligned}
\hat{w}_{t+1} = \frac{w_{t+1} - w_t}{w_t} &= \beta_{w_1}(V_t - \bar{V}) + \beta_{w_2}(V_t^w - 1) \\
&+ \kappa_w(\hat{p}_{t+1} + n_l) + (1 - \kappa_w)(\pi_t^e + n_l), \quad V_t^w = L_t^d / L_t^w \qquad (6.34) \\
\hat{p}_{t+1} = \frac{p_{t+1} - p_t}{p_t} &= \beta_{p_1}(U_{ct} - \bar{U}_c) + \beta_{p_2} U_{nt} \\
&+ \kappa_p(\hat{w}_{t+1} - n_l) + (1 - \kappa_p)\pi_t^e, \quad U_{nt} = (N^d - N)/K \qquad (6.35) \\
\pi_{t+1}^e = \pi_t^e &+ \beta_{\pi^e}(\alpha \hat{p}_{t+1} + (1 - \alpha)(\bar{\mu} - n - n_l) - \pi_t^e), \quad \bar{\mu} = n + n_l \qquad (6.36)
\end{aligned}$$

This 'supply side' description is still based on fairly symmetric assumptions on the causes of wage- and price-inflation. Wage inflation for $[t, t+1]$ according to eqn. (6.34) is driven, on the one hand, by a demand pull component, given by the deviation of the actual rate of employment V_t from the NAIRU-rate $\bar{V}$, and, on the other hand, by a cost push term measured by a weighted average of the short-run future rate of price inflation $\hat{p}_{t+1}$ (representing myopic perfect foresight) and a medium-run expected rate of inflation π_t^e. Similarly, in eqn. (6.35), price inflation is driven by the demand pull term, $(U_{ct} - \bar{U}_c)$, $\bar{U}_c$ the NAIRU rate of capacity utilization, and the weighted average of the short-run future rate of wage inflation $\hat{w}_{t+1}$ (representing myopic perfect foresight) and again the medium-run expected rate of inflation π_t^e. This latter expected rate of inflation is in turn determined by assuming that it follows a weighted average of short-run (perfect) and medium-run (regressive) expectations, leading to an inflationary expectations mechanism as in eqn. (6.36).

A final remark: We have assumed in the investment function (6.11) as expression for the expected rate of inflation the medium-run one we defined in eqn. (6.36), π_t^e, but use this rate there in conjunction with the short-run rate of interest and of profit. This asymmetric treatment of time horizons in investment behavior can be overcome in two ways: Either by using the (perfectly expected) short-run rate of inflation $\hat{p}_{t+1}$ in the place of π_t^e to define the real rate of interest used for investment calculations or to refer to medium-run concepts of interest and profitability in the i_1–term in the investment also, e.g. in the following simple way:

$$I_t = i_1(\rho_t^m - (r_t^m - \pi_t^e))K_{t-1} + i_2(U_{ct} - \bar{U}_c)K_{t-1}$$

$$\begin{aligned}
\rho_{t+1}^m &= \rho_t^m + \beta_\rho(\rho_{t+1}^e - \rho_t^m) \\
r_{t+1}^m &= r_t^m + \beta_r(r_{t+1} - r_t^m).
\end{aligned}$$

In the latter case it may also be appropriate to relabel the variable π_t^e, by π_t^{em}, to clearly show where we use concepts that refer to the medium run development of the economy.

Let us now derive the intensive form of the model of this section. The wage and price equations of block 7 of the model can again be reformulated as two linear equations in the unknowns $\hat{w}_{t+1} - \pi_t^e - n_l, \hat{p}_{t+1} - \pi_t^e$ giving rise to the following expressions for these two magnitudes:

$$\begin{aligned}
\hat{w}_{t+1} - \pi_t^e - n_l &= \kappa[\beta_{w_1}(V_t - \bar{V}) + \beta_{w_2}(V_t^w - 1) + \kappa_w(\beta_{p_1}(U_{ct} - \bar{U}_c) + \beta_{p_2}U_{nt})] \quad (6.37) \\
\hat{p}_{t+1} - \pi_t^e &= \kappa[\kappa_p(\beta_{w_1}(V_t - \bar{V}) + \beta_{w_2}(V_t^w - 1)) + \beta_{p_1}(U_{ct} - \bar{U}_c) + \beta_{p_2}U_{nt}] \quad (6.38)
\end{aligned}$$

These equations in turn imply for the dynamics of the share of wages $u_{t+1} = w_{t+1}/(p_{t+1}x_{t+1})$ the law of motion:

$$\begin{aligned}
\hat{u}_{t+1} = \hat{w}_{t+1} - \hat{p}_{t+1} - n_l &= \kappa[(1-\kappa_p)(\beta_{w_1}(V_t - \bar{V}) + \beta_{w_2}(V_t^w - 1)) \\
&- (1-\kappa_w)(\beta_{p_1}(U_{ct} - \bar{U}_c) + \beta_{p_2}U_{nt})]. \quad (6.39)
\end{aligned}$$

This statement, however, is only true when one neglects the second order term $\omega_{t+1}p_{t+1}$ in the formula that relates the nominal rates of wage and price inflation with the growth law for the real wage. Such second order terms are repeatedly neglected in all following calculations of the intensive form of the model with the above law providing the first dynamical equation of this intensive form. Note also, that the formula for $\hat{p}_{t+1} - \pi_t^e$ is repeatedly used in the following laws of motion of the intensive form of the model.

Neglecting second order terms in the calculation of rates of change we then get from the model (6.1) – (6.36) the following autonomous seven-dimensional dynamical system in the variables $u_t = w_t/(p_t x_t), l_t = x_t L_t/K_{t-1}, m_t = M_t/(p_t K_{t-1}), \pi_t^e, y_t^e = Y_t^e/K_{t-1}$, $\nu_t = N_{t-1}/K_{t-1}$, and $V_t^w = L_t^d/L_t^w$ which describe the laws of motion of the private sector of the model.[9]

$$\begin{aligned}
u_{t+1} &= u_t + u_t\kappa[(1-\kappa_p)(\beta_{w_1}(V_t - \bar{V}) + \beta_{w_2}(V_t^w - 1)) \\
&- (1-\kappa_w)(\beta_{p_1}(U_{ct} - \bar{U}_c) + \beta_{p_2}U_{nt})] \quad (6.40) \\
l_{t+1} &= l_t + l_t(-i_1(\rho_t^e - r_t + \pi_t^e) - i_2(U_{ct} - \bar{U}_c)), \quad (6.41) \\
m_{t+1} &= m_t + m_t(\bar{\mu} - (n + n_l) - (\hat{p}_{t+1} - \pi_t^e - \pi_t^e) \\
&- (i_1(\rho_t^e - r_t + \pi_t^e) + i_2(U_{ct} - \bar{U}_c))) \quad (6.42) \\
\pi_{t+1}^e &= \pi_t^e + \beta_{\pi_1^e}(\hat{p}_{t+1} - \pi_t^e) + \beta_{\pi_2^e}(\Delta\mu - \pi_t^e) \quad (6.43) \\
y_{t+1}^e &= y_t^e + \beta_{y^e}(y_t^d - y_t^e) - (i_1(\rho_t^e - r_t + \pi_t^e) + i_2(U_{ct} - \bar{U}_c))y_t^e \quad (6.44) \\
\nu_{t+1} &= \nu_t + y_t - y_t^d - (i_1(\rho_t^e - r_t + \pi_t^e) + i_2(U_{ct} - \bar{U}_c) + n + n_l)\nu_t \quad (6.45) \\
V_{t+1} &= V_t + V_t\beta_v(V_t^w - 1), \quad V_t \le 1 \quad (6.46)
\end{aligned}$$

[9]We assume again $\kappa_w\kappa_p \neq 1$ and use as abbreviations $\kappa = (1-\kappa_w\kappa_p)^{-1}, \beta_{\pi_1^e} = \beta_{\pi^e}\alpha, \beta_{\pi_2^e} = \beta_{\pi^e}(1-\alpha)$. Note that there are two further difference equations in this model (for $B_t/K_{t-1}, E_t/K_{t-1}$ which however do not feed back into the dynamics (6.40) – (6.46).

For output per capital $y_t = Y_t/K_{t-1}$ and aggregate demand per capital $y_t^d = Y_t^d/K_{t-1}$ we have the following expressions:

$$\begin{aligned} y_t &= (1+(n+n_l)\beta_{n^d})y_t^e + \beta_n(\beta_{n^d}y_t^e - \nu_t) && (6.47)\\ y_t^d &= u_t y_t + (1-s_c)(\rho_t^e - t_c^n) + i_1(\rho_t^e - r_t + \pi_t^e) + i_2(U_{ct} - \bar{U}_c) + n + n_l + \delta + \bar{g} \\ &= y_t^e + (i_1 - s_c)\rho_t^e - i_1(r_t - \pi_t^e) + i_2 U_{ct} + const. && (6.48)\end{aligned}$$

Here we make use of the abbreviations:

$$\begin{aligned} V_t^w &= L_t^d/L_t^w = l_t^d/l_t^w = y_t^d/(V_t l_t), \;\; U_{ct} = y_t/y^p, \;\; U_{nt} = \beta_{n^d}y_t^e - \nu_t && (6.49)\\ \rho_t^e &= y_t^e - \delta - u_t y_t && (6.50)\\ r_{t+1} &= r_0 + (h_1 y_t - m_t)/h_2. && (6.51)\end{aligned}$$

The dynamic model considered above is, except that it is a discrete time presentation that includes Harrod neutral technical change at the given rate n_l and excludes smooth factor substitution, identical to the regime 1 model of KMG growth considered in subsection 5.3.1. In chapter 5 care is taken to ensure that the profitability and labor supply bounds on production and the possibility for negative expected profits remain excluded from the considered orbits of these dynamics (just as negative gross investment, negative nominal interest rates, etc., see the corresponding list in section 5.3.1).

Proposition 6.1

There is a unique steady–state solution *or point of rest of the dynamics (6.40)–(6.46) fulfilling* $u_0, l_0, m_0, V_0 \neq 0$ *given by the following expressions:*[10]

$$\begin{aligned} y_0 &= \bar{U}_c y^p, \qquad y_0^e = y_0^d = \frac{y_0}{1+(n+n_l)\beta_{n^d}}, \;\; \nu_0 = \beta_{n^d}y_0^e \\ V &= \bar{V}, \;\; l_0^d = l_o^w = y_o, \;\; l_o = l_o^d/\bar{V}, \;\; V_0^w = 1 \\ \rho_0^e &= t_c^n + \frac{\bar{g} - t_c^n + n + n_l}{s_c}, \qquad u_0 = \frac{y_o^e - \delta - \rho_o^e}{y_o} \\ r_0 &= \rho_0^e + \bar{\mu} - (n+n_l) = \rho_0^e, \;\; m_0 = h_1 y_0, \;\; \pi_0^e = \bar{\mu} - (n+n_l) = 0. \end{aligned}$$

This steady state lies entirely in the Keynesian domain of the dynamics implying that regime switches as considered in section 5.3.2 are of the secondary type there investigated.

Proof: Combining equations (6.41) and (6.42), set equal to zero, reduces the latter equation to an expression for $\hat{p}_t$ which can then be used to remove the β_p–terms from the wage share equation. Equations (6.40), (6.46), set equal to zero, then imply $V^w = 1$ and $V = \bar{V}$. Equation (6.42) furthermore gives $\hat{p} = 0$ and equation (6.43) on this basis $\pi^e = 0$. From equations (6.44),(6.45), set equal to zero, we get $y^d = y^e$ and $\beta_{n^d}y^e = \nu$. This implies $U_n = 0$ and thus $\bar{U}_c = 1$. The growth for l, set equal to zero, then gives $\rho^e = r$ where the value of ρ^e can be obtained from the goods market equilibrium condition $y^d = y^e$ as shown in the proposition. Since r_o is set equal to the obtained value of ρ^e we finally get $m = h_1 y$ which proves the proposition. ■

[10]Note here again that the expressions for l have been defined by means of xL/K in order to measure labor in efficiency units, here equal to their output performance.

When parameterizing and iterating the continuous time dynamics of chapter 5 we have used the simple Euler method in this chapter (all differential quotients are replaced by difference quotients) with a step length of $h = 0.01$ in general. A step length of 1 in the discrete time model (6.40) – (6.46) of the present section, still assumed here to represent one year due to our choice of output-capital ratios and related magnitudes, in particular speeds of adjustment, is then of course far from good enough to get good approximations of the continuous time dynamics and even more importantly, to get dynamics that can be considered as meaningful from the economic point of view. Market periods at such rare points in time should not, when iterated, give a good approximation of real dynamics if parameter sizes are chosen to correspond to the time interval in question. Of course, the model (6.40) – (6.46) could be reinterpreted to represent a period model with quarterly or weekly data and parameter sizes would need to be adjusted accordingly. Choosing $h = 1/52$, i.e., choosing one week as period length is normally sufficient in our KMG model type with somewhat realistic parameter sizes to get results as in the continuous time dynamics (in particular when attractors are still simply points or closed curves) or to get results that are as reliable as the ones obtained from Runge-Kutta or still more refined numerical integration procedures for differential equations. The subdivision into 52 iteration steps per year of the considered continuous time model based on parameters values with the year as reference is thus often sufficient to get good approximations of the orbits of the continuous time dynamics.

These observations should be kept in mind when going economically from continuous time analysis to period analysis where the period length is given by 1 for reasons of notational simplicity, if one wants to get dynamical results for the discrete time case that resemble those of the continuous time one. In order to do this in an appropriate way starting from continuous time models with parameters that exhibit the year as reference period, we propose therefore the following modification of the above discrete time dynamical system in order to get results of the same kind as they are obtained from the continuous time model ($h = 1/52$) for example.

$$
\begin{aligned}
u_{t+1} &= u_t + u_t\kappa[(1-\kappa_p)(h\beta_{w_1}(V_t - \bar{V}) + h\beta_{w_2}(V_t^w - 1)) \\
&- (1-\kappa_w)(h\beta_{p_1}(U_{ct} - \bar{U}_c) + h\beta_{p_2}U_{nt})] && (6.52)\\
l_{t+1} &= l_t + l_t(-hi_1(\rho_t^e - r_t + \pi_t^e) - hi_2(U_{ct} - \bar{U}_c)), && (6.53)\\
m_{t+1} &= m_t + m_t(\bar{\mu} - (n + n_l) - (\hat{p}_{t+1} - \pi_t^e - \pi_t^e) \\
&- (hi_1(\rho_t^e - r_t + \pi_t^e) + hi_2(U_{ct} - \bar{U}_c))) && (6.54)\\
\pi_{t+1}^e &= \pi_t^e + h\beta_{\pi_1^e}(\hat{p}_{t+1} - \pi_t^e) + h\beta_{\pi_2^e}(\Delta\mu - \pi_t^e) && (6.55)\\
y_{t+1}^e &= y_t^e + \beta_{y^e}h(y_t^d - y_t^e) - (hi_1(\rho_t^e - r_t + \pi_t^e) + hi_2(U_{ct} - \bar{U}_c))y_t^e && (6.56)\\
\nu_{t+1} &= \nu_t + h(y_t - y_t^d) - (hi_1(\rho_t^e - r_t + \pi_t^e) + hi_2(U_{ct} - \bar{U}_c) + hn + hn_l)\nu_t && (6.57)\\
V_{t+1} &= V_t + V_t h\beta_v(V_t^w - 1), \quad V_t \le 1 && (6.58)
\end{aligned}
$$

For output per capital $y_t = Y_t/K_{t-1}$ and aggregate demand per capital $y_t^d = Y_t^d/K_{t-1}$ we have:

$$y_t = (1 + (n + n_l)\beta_{n^d})y_t^e + \beta_n(\beta_{n^d}y_t^e - \nu_t)$$

$$\begin{aligned} y_t^d &= u_t y_t + (1-s_c)(\rho_t^e - t_c^n) + i_1(\rho_t^e - r_t + \pi_t^e) + i_2(U_{ct} - \bar{U}_c) + n + n_l + \delta + \bar{g} \\ &= y_t^e + (i_1 - s_c)\rho_t^e - i_1(r_t - \pi_t^e) + i_2 U_{ct} + const. \end{aligned}$$

making again use of the abbreviations:

$$\begin{aligned} V_t^w &= L_t^d/L_t^w = l_t^d/l_t^w = y_t^d/(V_t l_t), \quad U_{ct} = y_t/y^p, \quad U_{nt} = \beta_{n^d} y^e - \nu \\ \rho_t^e &= y_t^e - \delta - u_t y_t \\ r_{t+1} &= r_0 + (h_1 y_t - m_t)/h_2 \end{aligned}$$

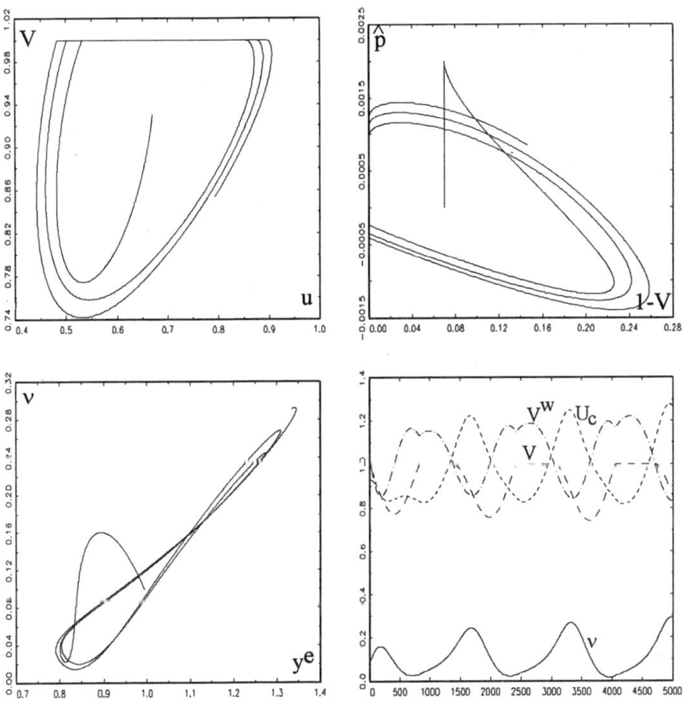

Figure 6.1: Slightly explosive cycles in purely demand driven KMG growth, compare also figure 5.4

These modifications of the dynamics (6.40) – (6.46) allow all parameters sizes still to be interpreted as yearly magnitudes if they depend on the length of the production period of the model. Changes of stocks, flows, and prices, however are now assumed to occur on a weekly basis, since the model (6.40) – (6.46) will not be workable when based on market coordinations only once a year. Changes are thus now scaled down by $h = 1/52$, starting from magnitudes representing yearly production, interest rates and the like. The above reformulation of the equations of the dynamics therefore shows weekly changes of output levels , interest rate , inflation rates etc. per year and they provide the basis for the following simulation run of the discrete time model. In order to get results that can be compared with the continuous time dynamics we have to scale down all price adjustment speeds by $h = 1/52$, the flow of investment as far as capital stock growth is concerned (but not as a component of the yearly level of aggregate demand), and also the adjustment speed in the employment policy of firms. Finally, the magnitudes $y^d - y^e$ in the expected sales mechanism and $y - y^d$ in the actual inventory adjustment must be divided by 52 in order to get the weekly changes in sales expectations per year and of inventory changes from these yearly measures of demand, sales expectations and output.

We thus now make use of the parameters shown in table 6.1, for the model (6.52) – (6.58), in order to get a simulation run of similar type as the one shown in figure 5.4 of chapter 5 (where however a Cobb-Douglas production technology was used in the place of the fixed proportions technology of the present subsection).

Note with respect to this parameter set that technology parameters must be different from those underlying figure 5.4 and that the model tends to be more unstable than the one of figure 5.4 due to the lack of substitution. We thus have increased here the parameter β_{w_1} from 0 to 0.5, which due to chapters 4 and 5 should increase stability and here indeed does, in order to get a viable situation of the type shown in figure 5.4 of chapter 5.

$$\begin{array}{|llllll|}\hline s_c = 0.8, & \delta = 0.1, & t_c^n = -0.1, & \bar{g} = 0.1, & y^p = 1, & \bar{V} = 0.93, \\ h_1 = 0.1, & h_2 = 0.05, & i_1 = 1, & i_2 = 0.2, & \bar{\mu} = n + n_l = 0.06, & \\ \beta_{w_1} = 1, & \beta_{w_2} = 0.3, & \beta_{p_1} = 0.2, & \beta_{p_2} = 0 & \kappa_w = 0.5, & \kappa_p = 0.5, \\ \beta_{\pi_1} = 0.37, & \beta_{\pi_2} = 0, & \beta_{n^d} = 0.1, & \beta_n = 0.5, & \beta_y^e = 2, & \beta_v = 0.5. \\ \hline\end{array}$$

Table 6.1

The figure 6.1 will be used as reference case for the models with market imperfections that are the subject of the following sections of this chapter. Note that inventories as well as the rate of profit (cf. the sizes for the share of wages) stay positive in this simulation example, that V, the rate of employment reaches again the full employment ceiling (while overtime work does not exceed 20 %) and that the wage share employment rate interaction (top left) as well as the phase plot for the rate of unemployment vs. the rate of inflation show the clockwise orientation that is known to characterize actual phase plots of these data. Note also that overtime work is already declining when the rate of employment reaches its maximum 1 and that this reverses the decline in overtime work for some time. In addition the rate of capacity utilization is not at all moving in line with the rates of employment shown (as Okun's law would suggest), but is instead moving in line with inventory levels, indicating sales expectations lag considerably behind the actual development of aggregate demand (see also the phase plot bottom left). This example of (projections of) an orbit of the considered dynamics shows therefore interesting features and details of a demand led theory of monetary growth and business fluctuations.

Let us finally formulate a general proposition on the here considered dynamics which is based on the theoretical experience gained for related model types and on further experience from simulation runs of the dynamics, but which will not be proved here. A proof of the assertions made in this proposition should follow the method of proof used for similar assertions made in chapter 4 on the KMG growth model with fixed proportions and exogenous Harrod neutral technical change, where however overtime work, lagged employment policies of firms and the like were not yet taken into account.

Proposition 6.2 (Conjecture)

Assume a period length h of the discrete time model (reformulated as indicated earlier for period length h) that is sufficiently small. Then:

1. The unique interior steady–state solution of the dynamics (6.40)–(6.46) is locally asymptotically stable for adjustment speeds $\beta_{w_1}, \beta_{p_1}, \beta_{\pi_1^e}, \beta_n$ *sufficiently low (weak Rose-, Mundell- and Metzler-effects), for* h_2 *sufficiently small (a strong Keynes-effect) and* β_{y^e}, β_{w_2}, β_v *sufficiently large (fast multiplier dynamics, a strong derivative term in the money wage Phillips curve*[11]*).*

2. The determinant of the Jacobian of the dynamics at the steady state is negative if all parameters are strictly positive, which excludes the possibility of zero characteristic roots for the considered dynamics.

3. The dynamics loses its local asymptotic stability by way of a Hopf bifurcation if the parameter $\beta_{\pi_1^e}$ *becomes sufficiently large (where the Mundell-effect outweighs the stabilizing Keynes-effect in particular, see also section 6.3).*

Once the system loses its local asymptotic stability property by way of such a Hopf-bifurcation there exist (in the supercritical case) stable limit cycles close to the situation of stability loss. In general however the nonlinearities present in the considered dynamics are too weak to generate global boundedness for a larger range of such parameter values. Nonlinearities as used in chapter 5 (substitution, more ceilings to economic activity than just the external rate of employment, a kink in the money wage Phillips curve and others) have therefore to be added again if economic viability is to be achieved in such situations. In section 6.3 we will consider again in this respect the powerful stabilizing role of a floor, there in a new form of money wage Phillips curve, on various levels of generality including a low dimensional case where the stabilizing role of a kink in the Phillips curve in the deflationary part of its originally linear shape can be investigated analytically.

The following sections will reconsider the KMG growth model of this section from the viewpoint of the theory of (microfounded) market imperfections in both the labor and the goods market. This will now modify the wage price module of the model and this in a way that in particular gives rise to an endogenous determination of both the NAIRU rate of employment and of capacity utilization, which have been considered as exogenously determined magnitudes in this part of the book so far. When sketching the basic KMG growth model in part I of the book we have however already indicated how natural rates of employment and of growth can be endogenized and how they might evolve in time, there too in an environment where there is a floor to falling wages should both of these rates become very insufficient.

From the descriptive point of view basic possibilities for getting low NAIRU rates of employment, in particular from government policy choosing the wrong 'natural' rate of employment, have been considered and discussed in Heap (1980). There the conventional

[11]The derivative term here referred to is obtained by inserting the employment policy rule, solved for $V_t^w - 1$, into the money wage Phillips curve.

Phillips curve inflation accelerator mechanism is augmented by a difference equation describing the evolution of the 'natural' rate of unemployment in situations of changing actual employment rates. The equation used by Heap (1980, p.612) is

$$U_t^* = U_{t-1}^* + c(U_{t-1} - U_{t-1}^*), \quad c > 0.$$

This equation says in descriptive terms, see Heap (1980), that the 'natural' rate of employment increases in periods where (for example) government policy chooses a rate of unemployment U_{t-1} above the current 'natural' one (and vice versa). In terms of our notation we have to rewrite this equation as

$$\bar{V}_t = \bar{V}_{t-1} + \beta_{\bar{v}}(\bar{V}_{t-1} - V_{t-1}), \quad \beta_{\bar{v}} > 0.$$

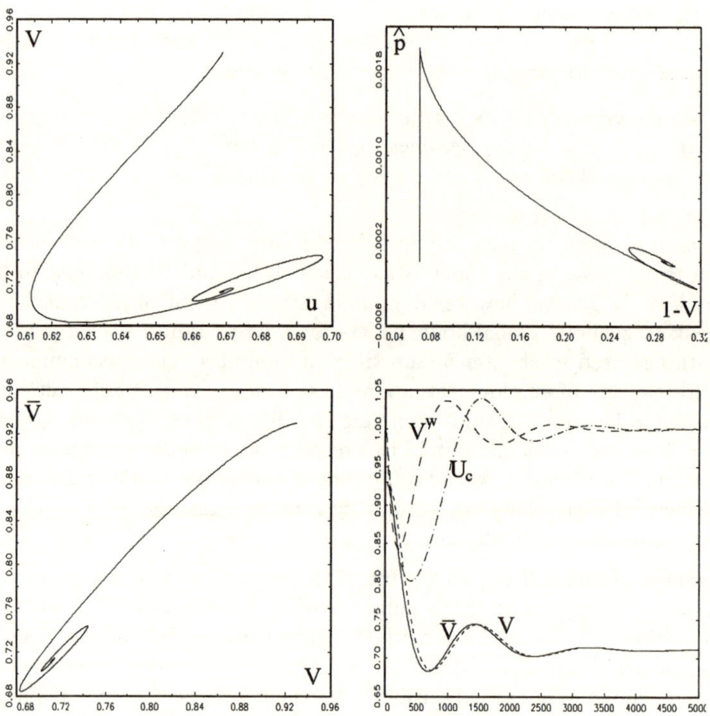

Figure 6.1a: Endogenous NAIRU: Consequences of an inflationary shock ($\beta_{\bar{v}} = 2$ per year)

Heap (1980, p.617) calls this dynamic law 'deceleration hypothesis', since its operation implies that a government that chooses and holds a 'natural' rate of employment above the currently prevailing one (since it considers current unemployment as unacceptably high) will according to the accelerator hypotheses cause the inflation rate to increase, yet here in combination with increasing 'natural' rates of employment. These increases will take inflationary pressure from the labor market, leading to smaller and smaller increases in the rate of inflation, until the rate of inflation stabilizes and the chosen level of employment becomes the 'natural' one. There is thus a long-run trade-off between inflation and (un)employment, which is here brought into being by an exogenous government policy concerning the actually prevailing rate of employment. These observations also imply that there is now hysteresis in the dynamics in the sense that the long run outcome now depends on the history of the economy and the shocks it was subject to. Formally this is due to the fact that the added law of motion can be obtained as a linear combination of the other ones, which implies a zero determinant of the Jacobian of the dynamics at the steady state and thus a characteristic root which is zero.

By contrast, if a depression is allowed to run its course it is then conceivable that declining actual rates of employment tear down the NAIRU rate of employment, leading (in the case of a linear Phillips curve) to wage and price deflation, which (for example) due to the Mundell-effect discussed above (but more importantly due to the Fisher-debt effect considered in part I of the book) leads to declining economic activity and thus deeper into the depression. The question is of course again which forces might stop such a decline in real and nominal magnitudes, favored from the monetarist perspective as a cure to inflation, but here already perhaps gone too far to justify such a view. A money wage policy that stops the decline in nominal magnitudes (or that does not allow for it right from the start) here seems to be the cure to (or prevents) this joint occurrence of depression and deflation, maybe also supported by a government policy of the type described above.

We therefore close this section by a simulation study of these assertions when the above law of motion is added to the KMG growth dynamics so far considered and when therefore the NAIRU rate of employment follows the actual rate of employment with some time delay. This adds the issue of hysteresis in employment and unemployment to the model of this section providing a scenario that can be compared with the imperfect competition situations and their endogenous determinations of NAIRU rates of employment (and capacity utilization) to be considered in the following sections of this chapter.

In figure 6.1a we see top right the positive shock in the inflation rate and a subsequent increase in the unemployment rate combined with decreasing rates of inflation back to zero inflation. The parameter values are those of figure 6.1 with the addition of a strong response of the NAIRU to the actual development of the rate of employment. We have in the place of the explosive cycle of figure 6.1 now nearly monotonic convergence of employment (and the other state variables of the dynamics) to a very low long-run rate of employment. Even small shocks thus have in the plots shown a very large effect on the long run position of the economy though the initial nearly monotonic decline in the rate of employment is stopped and becomes reversed at around 70 %, but only in a weak way that does not admit a return to the initial level of the NAIRU which was 7 %. The addition of a strong adjustment of the NAIRU rate of employment towards the actual employment rate here therefore makes the economy asymptotically stable, but at the cost of a high long run rate of unemployment, and has therefore dramatic consequences for the working of the dynamics.

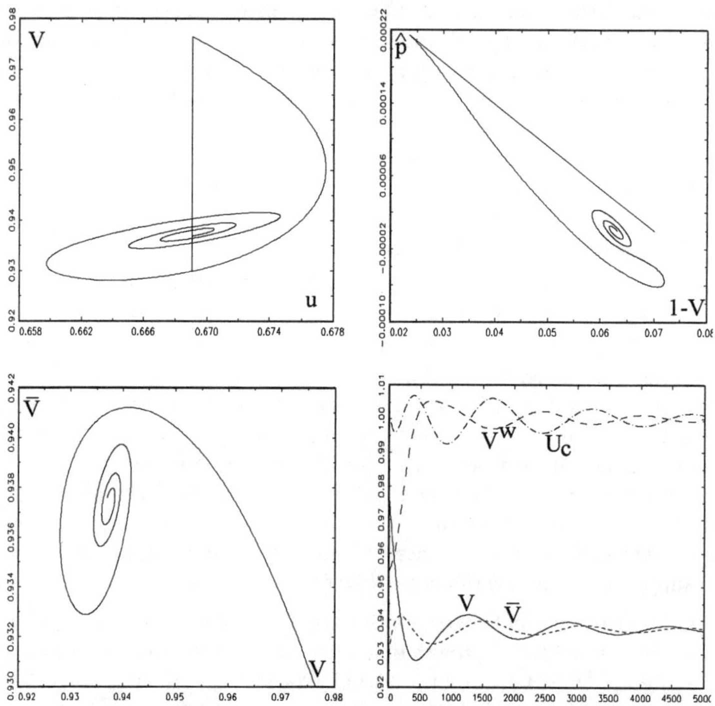

Figure 6.1b: Endogenous NAIRU: Consequences of a positive employment shock ($\beta_{\bar{v}} = 0.3$)

In figure 6.1b we consider finally a single positive shock to the rate of employment (not yet a pegging of this rate at a certain desired level) and a response of the NAIRU rate of employment of 1/3 % for every percent change in the actual rate of employment. We can see that the opposite of the situation just considered comes about in this case, now with more pronounced cyclical features and a much less dramatic long run effect on the steady state rate of employment. There is a steep increase in employment as well as in inflation at first, which thereafter converges back to zero inflation and an employment rate approximately 0.5 % higher than the originally given level. As the law of motion for the NAIRU is formulated we would expect from what is shown that there is convergence to zero inflation and 98 % employment should the government be prepared to not only shock actual employment by five percent, but to peg this high rate of employment at this level. Yet, the modification of the dynamics towards endogenous NAIRU movements is surely much too simple and one sided still in order to allow firm policy conclusions. Nevertheless, considering adjustments in the long-run behavior of the labor market is an important topic which deserves further investigation. Further (small) steps into such a direction from the perspective of integrated disequilibrium growth dynamics will be made in the subsequent sections of this chapter.

6.3 Imperfect competition: Given income distribution

The starting point of the following considerations is the basic imperfect competition model of Carlin and Soskice (1990). This model consists of two basic equations, each of them capturing in a compact way imperfections on the labor and the goods market, respectively. The first equation concerns the wage setting, for which a bargaining process between firms and unions is assumed that takes place in each industry. The outcome is the following dependence of the bargained real wage (BRW) ω^B on the expected price level p^e and the rate of unemployment U:

$$\omega^B = B(1-V), \quad B' < 0 \quad \Longleftrightarrow w^B = p^e B(1-V). \tag{6.59}$$

Although different approaches, which are described in the introduction to this chapter and extensively discussed in part IV of Carlin and Soskice, could now be used to derive the above result, we will concentrate here on a simple right-to-manage model of a monopolistic union in each industry.[12] The union in industry i is assumed to maximize the expected utility v_i of a representative member which is given by

$$v_i = (L_i^d/L_i)v(w_i/p) + (1 - L_i^d/L_i)v(z) \tag{6.60}$$

where L_i^d denotes employment in industry i and L_i the corresponding part of the labor force there, w_i the nominal wage in industry i, p the overall price level and v a utility function equal for all individuals. The variable z stands for the outside option which is determined by

$$z = (V)\omega^* + (1-V)b. \tag{6.61}$$

Thus, given an (economy-wide) unemployment rate $(1 - V)$, an unemployed worker in industry i can get a job elsewhere at a real wage ω^* with probability $1 - U$. Otherwise he will get the unemployment benefit b. If now the nominal wage w_i in industry i is raised, while it is kept constant in all the other industries, also the price for goods of industry i, p_i, will rise in comparison to the overall price level p, so that demand and as a consequence also employment L_i^d in this industry will decline. On the other hand, given a certain level for the real wage $\omega_i := w_i/p$ (which mirrors the relative price of industry i in comparison to p), employment L_i^d will positively depend on the level of aggregate demand, y^d. Holding the latter constant, assuming risk neutrality for the representative union member and denoting L_i^d as $L^d(\omega_i)$, the union in industry i sets the real wage ω_i such as to maximize

$$L^d(\omega_i)\omega_i + (1 - L^d(\omega_i))z.$$

Differentiation with respect to ω_i, setting the resulting expression equal to zero and dividing by $L^{d'}(\omega_i)$ yields

$$\omega_i + L^d(\omega_i)/L^{d'}(\omega_i).$$

[12]The following is a short-cut of the model that Carlin and Soskice (1990) present on pp.388ff.

Inserting the expression for z according to (6.61) and assuming a uniform behavior in all industries (so that $\omega_i = \omega^* = \omega$ is fulfilled) finally leads to

$$\omega^B = \left(\frac{1-V}{1-V-1/\eta} \right) b$$

with η denoting the absolute value of the elasticity of labor demand with respect to the real wage, $|L^{d'}(\omega)\omega/L^d(\omega)|$, which, for sake of simplicity, is held constant. As pointed out in Carlin and Soskice (1990, p.391), the real wage is a markup on the reservation wage z which in turn depends negatively on the economy-wide rate of unemployment. Thus, the above negative relationship between the bargained real wage (BRW) and the rate of unemployment (or, conversely, the positive dependence of the BRW and the rate of employment V as expressed by equation (6.59)) results. Reformulating this equation now in growth rates yields

$$\hat{w}_t = \hat{p}_t^e + \frac{\omega_t^B - \omega_{t-1}}{\omega_{t-1}}, \tag{6.62}$$

ω_{t-1} thereby denoting the value of the previous period. Thus, money wages have to rise in order to compensate expected inflation and to move the real wage of the last period to ω^B. In this context it is important to note, that the bargained real wage is not necessarily the one which is actually realized. The reason for this consists in the fact, that price expectations p^e, on which the negotiations concerning the nominal wage are based, need not coincide with the price level, that afterwards occurs.

The second fundamental equation used by Carlin and Soskice is derived from imperfect competition on the market for goods and reads:

$$p = \frac{1}{1-1/\epsilon} MC = \frac{1}{1-1/\epsilon} \frac{w}{MPL} \tag{6.63}$$

with p, as before, denoting the price level, ϵ the price elasticity of demand, MC marginal (wage) costs and MPL the marginal productivity of labor. Both, ϵ and MPL are assumed by Carlin and Soskice to be constant. This equation represents a standard formulation of monopolistic price setting and can directly be derived from a monopolist's maximization problem. The constant MPL can thereby be obtained by a linear production function. Also the assumption of a constant value for ϵ can be found even in many fully fledged microfounded models of imperfect competition, there usually arising from the assumption of a CES-utility function concerning the consumption demand of private households in connection with the somewhat problematic assumption, that the price setting of a single firm has only a negligible effect on the aggregate price level.[13] On the other hand, it is possible to imagine, that although ϵ and MPL are both changing with output, the same need not necessarily be true for the quotient of the markup factor $1 + \mu := 1/(1 - 1/\epsilon)$ and the marginal productivity of labor. Thus, Carlin and Soskice argue, that also in the case of a MPL declining with output (as generated by a neoclassical production function) a countercyclical markup may be sufficient to leave this quotient widely unaffected.[14] As

[13]See Dixit and Stiglitz (1977), Blanchard and Kiyotaki (1987) or Weitzman (1985) in this regard, to mention only a few.

[14]Note, however, that the empirical evidence on this is far from being clear-cut. So, e.g., a number of studies have also come to the result of a procyclical markup; a similar controversy exists also about the behavior of the marginal costs, see Layard, Nickell and Jackman (1991, pp.339 ff.

a consequence, the so-called price determined real wage (PRW) $\omega^P = MLP/(1+\mu)$ is a relatively flat function of output and thus employment.

At this point it is now possible to depict both curves, the BRW-curve reflecting imperfections on the labor market and the PRW-curve derived from imperfect competition on the markets for goods, in their dependence on the employment rate in a single figure:[15]

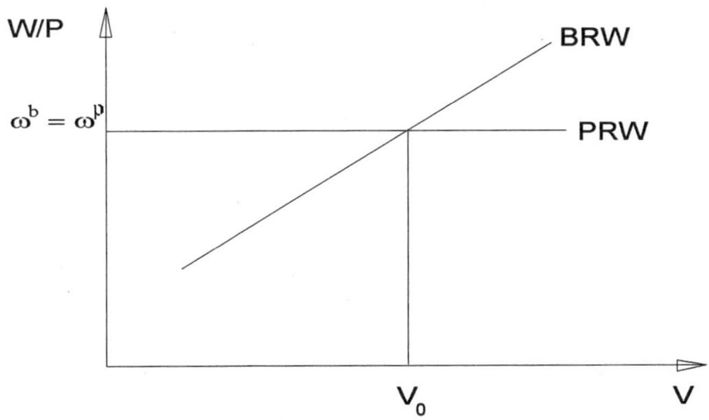

Figure 6.2: Bargained real wage (BRW), price determined real wage (PRW) and equilibrium rate of employment V_0 of the basic imperfect competition model of Carlin and Soskice (1990).

The intersection between the two curves defines the unique equilibrium rate of employment. If actual employment is larger, inflation will occur which (if not accommodated by monetary expansion) reduces aggregate demand and employment until the equilibrium rate is reached again. In contrast to this, an employment rate below the equilibrium one will cause deflation and thereby raise employment again. Note in this regard, that apart from the equilibrium rate of employment it is always the PRW which is actually realized due to the assumption, that nominal wages are formed on the basis of an *expected* price level, whereas firms determine their price afterwards when the nominal wage is already given.

Consequently, the question arises, if situations off the equilibrium rate of unemployment are not sustainable and if this rate is high, by which means this equilibrium rate can be influenced. Obviously, this can be done only by shifting at least one of the two curves, BRW, PRW. In their chapter 7, Carlin and Soskice discuss some of the measures at the disposal of the government, which are suitable to lower equilibrium unemployment by this way. One measure is e.g. to lower wage-taxation, so that post-tax real consumption wages rise, so that unions can agree to a lower gross real wage. As a consequence, the BRW curve shifts downward giving rise to a higher rate of employment. Another possibility is to raise government expenditures on training, which works into two directions. First, the better training of the workforce might lead to increasing productivity of labor, which causes an upward shift of the PRW-curve. On the other hand, better training, especially if it is provided to the unemployed, raises the abilities of the outsiders and thus reduces insider power which in turn leads to a downward shift of the BRW-curve. Both effects clearly increase the equilibrium rate of employment. Further measures discussed by Carlin and

[15]Similar expositions can be found, e.g., in Layard, Nickell and Jackman (1991), see their chs. 1 and 8.

Soskice are so-called income policies or a cut in unemployment benefits. Both will raise equilibrium employment by a downward shift of the BRW-curve.

In the following, the two central building blocks discussed above, i.e. the BRW- and PRW-equation, shall be integrated into the KMG framework of the previous chapters, thereby replacing the former laws of motion for nominal wages and prices.

6.3.1 Revising the wage-price module of KMG growth

The KMG growth model of the preceding section will now be modified in order to take account of the innovations of Carlin and Soskice (1990, Part II) with respect to the interaction in the wage / price module of the model. Adopting the basic description of the wage and price dynamics of these two authors we arrive at the following reformulation of the module 7 of the discrete time KMG growth model of section 6.2:

Wage-price adjustment equations.

$$\hat{w}_t = (\omega^*(V_t) - \omega_{t-1})/\omega_{t-1} + \pi_t^e, \quad (\omega^*)'(V_t) > 0 \tag{6.64}$$

$$\hat{p}_t = \hat{w}_t, \tag{6.65}$$

$$\pi_{t+1}^e = \pi_t^e + \beta_{\pi^e}(\hat{p}_t - \pi_t^e). \tag{6.66}$$

The equation for money wage dynamics (6.64): $\hat{w}_t = \frac{w_t - w_{t-1}}{w_{t-1}}$, is directly taken from Carlin and Soskice (1990, p.148) and it is based on a bargain real wage curve $\omega^*(V_t)$ that is derived from various perspectives in chapter 17 of their book. There also other determinants of the bargain real wage are presented, besides the (positive) influence of the current rate of employment V_t on the real wage target used in the above wage equation (6.64). Note the specific and new time structure involved in this equation for money wage determination which says that money wages today are set by comparing yesterday's real wage with the real wage target to be bargained for today, whose size is dependent on today's labor market performance, and which is to be augmented by the expectations of workers of the inflation rate concerning the time interval $[t-1, t]$ in order to arrive at a money wage claim which corresponds to their target $\omega^*(V_t)$. Carlin and Soskice (1990, p.149) then assume that prices are set immediately after wages have been set and this on the basis of a simple markup procedure based on average wage costs:[16]

$$p_t = (1+a)w_t/x, \quad a = const. > 0 \text{ the markup.}$$

We thus have in the present case a very simple cost basis for the target pricing of firms, a fixed markup for obtaining this target level, and no delay in the adjustment of actual prices towards their target levels, three basic aspects that all demand for generalizations later on. We have turned this markup equation into a derivative form in the above formulation of price setting behavior (6.65) which immediately implies as price Phillips curve for the economy the integrated equation

$$\hat{p}_t = \frac{p_t - p_{t-1}}{p_{t-1}} = (\omega^*(V_t) - \omega_{t-1})/\omega_{t-1} + \pi_t^e.$$

Finally, we have assumed in (6.66), as in Carlin and Soskice (1990, p.148), adaptive inflationary expectations as supplementing these new rules for wage and price setting behavior.

[16]With labor productivity $x = Y/L^d$ determined as in the preceding subsection.

Here π^e_{t+1} denotes the inflation rate expected by workers for the time interval from t to $t+1$. It may be more appropriate at a later stage of the discussion to discriminate between workers' and investors' (firms') expectations in this setup. Since workers (and their unions), by assumption, do not anticipate the price setting behavior of firms in their wage negotiations assuming adaptive expectations π^e_t there seems to be appropriate in such a first revision of the KMG reference model of section 6.2. By contrast, investors (firms) may have myopic perfect foresight and may thus use the true real rate of interest $r_{t-1} - \hat{p}_t$ in their profitability comparisons concerning their production in the interval $[t-1, t]$, see also Carlin and Soskice (1990, Ch.8) in this regard.

Adding exogenous Harrod neutral technical change to the description of this new wage price module modifies it as follows:

$$\hat{w}_t = (u^*(V_t) - u_{t-1})/u_{t-1} + \pi^e_t + n_l, \quad \hat{p}_t = \hat{w}_t - n_l \quad [(u^*)'(V_t) > 0]$$

with a target wage share u^* replacing the target real wage ω^* of workers. Following Carlin and Soskice (1990) we shall assume a linear target share function in the following given by

$$(u^*(V_t) - u_{t-1})/u_{t-1} = b_o + b_1 V_t$$

which is possible as long as the actual wage share can be considered as a given magnitude, on which the coefficients $b_o < 0, b_1 > 0$ depend.

The above revision of the wage price module of the KMG growth model is all that is needed in order to include the basic imperfect competition model of Carlin and Soskice (1990, Ch.6) into this disequilibrium approach to monetary growth. This provides still another example how the modules of the model can be revised in view of alternatives offered in the recent literature without losing sight of the need to supply integrated frameworks as the general reference point behind detailed, at first often only partial investigations of the resulting dynamical structure. A delayed form of markup pricing might be considered a more appropriate choice for such an integration in view of the point sales expectations assumed in the Metzlerian quantity adjustment module of the model, a topic to which we will return later on. Alternatively one might use a subjective aggregate demand schedule (which tries to extract the essence of the dynamic interaction between Keynesian aggregate demand and expected sales in KMG growth in terms of a static price-level goods-demand relationship) and allow imperfectly competitive firms to reflect and optimize their price - output decisions in terms of the demand changes they imply.

For the moment however we just implant the above module of the imperfect competition approach to labor and goods market interactions into the KMG model of the preceding section. It is interesting to note here that such an implantation is in fact not really a new thing for this model type (at least from a formal point of view), since there is a set of assumptions for the model of section 6.2 which indeed just generates this new view of the labor and the goods market interrelationships as a border case of the dynamics considered in the preceding section. These assumptions are given by the following list of parameter choices:

$$\beta_{w_1} = 0 \ [\beta_{w_2} > 0, \beta_v > 0], \kappa_w = 0, \beta_{p_1} = 0, \beta_{p_2} = 0, \kappa_p = 1, \beta_{\pi_2} = 0.$$

Inserting the employment policy equation of firms, equation (6.46), in reverted form into the law of motion (6.37) for nominal wages based on the above assumptions gives rise to the equation:

$$\hat{u}^e_{t+1} = \hat{w}_{t+1} - \pi^e_{t+1} - n_l = (\beta_{w_2}/\beta_v)\hat{V}_{t+1}$$

for the rate of growth of the target wage share of worker households. This dynamic equation is equivalent to the following level relationship between the wage share target and the rate of employment V_t

$$u^e_t = const(V_t)^{\beta_{w_2}/\beta_v}.$$

In order to realize this target wage share workers have to use the definitional money wage adjustment principle

$$\hat{w}_t = (u^e_t - u_{t-1})/u_{t-1} + \pi^e_t + n_l,$$

based on their inflationary expectations, that sets the rate of money wages changes such that the target wage share u^* is expected by workers to come about. A limit case of the model of section 6.2 therefore generates the bargaining relationship of the Carlin and Soskice (1990) approach.

We consider the following revised KMG model of monetary growth as a first attempt to formulate imperfect competition macroeconomics and their views on labor market dynamics as in Carlin and Soskice (1990, Part II) in an integrated framework with a complete set of markets and sectors, a Keynesian goods market disequilibrium adjustment process, and with all sectoral budget restrictions specified. Reformulating section 6.2 from this perspective gives rise to following intensive form representation of the six-dimensional dynamics in the place of the 7D dynamics investigated in section 6.2. The state variables now to be used are given by $u_t = w_t/(p_t x_t) = const, l_t = x_t L_t/K_{t-1}, m_t = M_t/(p_{t-1}K_{t-1}), \pi^e_t, y^e_t = Y^e_t/K_{t-1}$, $\nu_t = N_{t-1}/K_{t-1}$, and $V_t = L^d_t/L^w_t$.

$$\begin{aligned}
u &= u_t = 1/(1+a) = const && (6.67)\\
l_{t+1} &= l_t + l_t(-i_1(\rho^e_t - r_t + \pi^e_t) - i_2(U_{ct} - \bar{U}_c)), && (6.68)\\
m_{t+1} &= m_t + m_t[\bar{\mu} - (n+n_l) - (u^*(V_t) - u)/u - \pi^e_t\\
&- i_1(\rho^e_t - r_t + \pi^e_t) - i_2(U_{ct} - \bar{U}_c)] && (6.69)\\
\pi^e_{t+1} &= \pi^e_t + \beta_{\pi^e_1}(\hat{p}_t - \pi^e_t) && (6.70)\\
y^e_{t+1} &= y^e_t + \beta_{y^e}(y^d_t - y^e_t) - (i_1(\rho^e_t - r_t + \pi^e_t) + i_2(U_{ct} - \bar{U}_c))y^e_t && (6.71)\\
\nu_{t+1} &= \nu_t + y_t - y^d_t - (i_1(\rho^e_t - r_t + \pi^e_t) + i_2(U_{ct} - \bar{U}_c) + n + n_l)\nu_t && (6.72)\\
V_{t+1} &= V_t + V_t\beta_v(V^w_t - 1), \quad V_t \le 1 && (6.73)
\end{aligned}$$

For output per capital $y_t = Y_t/K_{t-1}$ and aggregate demand per unit of capital $y^d_t = Y^d_t/K_{t-1}$ we have again the following expressions:

$$\begin{aligned}
y_t &= (1 + (n+n_l)\beta_{n^d})y^e_t + \beta_n(\beta_{n^d}y^e_t - \nu_t) && (6.74)\\
y^d_t &= uy_t + (1-s_c)(\rho^e_t - t^n_c) + i_1(\rho^e_t - r_t + \pi^e_t) + i_2(U_{ct} - \bar{U}_c) + n + n_l + \delta + g && (6.75)
\end{aligned}$$

making use of the definitions and equilibrium conditions:

$$\begin{aligned}
V^w_t &= L^d_t/L^w_t = y^d_t/(V_t l_t), \quad U_{ct} = y_t/y^p, \quad U_{nt} = \beta_{n^d}y^e_t - \nu_t && (6.76)\\
\rho^e_t &= y^e_t - \delta - uy_t && (6.77)\\
r_t &= r_0 + (h_1 y_t - m_t)/h_2, \quad m_t = \frac{M_t}{p_{t-1}K_{t-1}}. && (6.78)
\end{aligned}$$

Note that the actual wage share is constant due to the pricing behavior of firms (which makes the Rose real wage effect disappear from the model) and that currently supplied real money balances per unit of capital are now measured in yesterdays prices. Corresponding to this the money market equilibrium condition is thus now given by

$$M_t = h_1 p_{t-1} Y_{t-1} + h_2 p_{t-1} K_{t-1}(r_o - r_{t+1}),$$

i.e., the money market clears before new prices are set by firms, just as new money wages are arrived at before the new price level becomes to be known. Recall also that profits ρ_t^e concern the production period $[t-1,t]$ and are based on operating capital K_{t-1}, with output decisions given by $Y_t = Y_t^e + \mathcal{I}_t$ and labor input L_t^d, paid at the end of the production period at money wage w_t. This profit rate is therefore compared with the real rate of interest of type $r_t - \pi_t^e$ (with r_t set at $t-1$) which is thus also based on the time interval $[t-1,t]$.

There is thus now a given wage share coupled with the dynamics of real balances as they are caused by the money wage setting behavior of workers and their unions. All other laws of motion are as in section 6.2 and thus simply supplement the new type of labor market dynamics by an inflationary expectations mechanism, Metzlerian quantity adjustments on the market for goods, and the growth law for the full employment labor intensity. There is however an important reinterpretation and change concerning inflationary expectations in the model. In section 6.2 we had myopic perfect foresight with respect to wage and price inflation, there coupled with expectations of inflation over the medium run which basically were following an average of currently generated inflation and the steady state level of price and wage inflation. Now however, inflationary expectations of workers π_t^e concern the short run evolution of the price level $\hat{p}_t$ and thus refer to the time interval $[t-1,t]$ on which this measure of inflation is based. There is thus no information concerning p_{t+1} and resulting inflation in the present model, but only expectations π_{t+1}^e based on past observations.

Proposition 6.3

Assume for notational simplicity (by appropriate normalization) that $\bar{U}_c = 1$ holds. There is a unique steady–state solution *or point of rest of the dynamics (6.67)–(6.73) fulfilling $l_0, m_0 \neq 0$ which is given by the following expressions:*

$$\begin{aligned}
u_o &= 1/(1+a), \quad V_o \;\; \textit{from} \;\; u_o = u^*(V_o): \; V_o = \frac{-b_o}{b_1} > 0 && (6.79)\\
\rho_o^e &= \frac{g - t_c^n + n + n_l}{s_c} + t_c^n && (6.80)\\
y_o &= \frac{\rho_o^e + \delta}{\frac{1}{1+(n+n_l)\beta_{n^d}} - u_o}: \quad U_c^o = y_o/y^p && (6.81)\\
y_o^e &= y_o^d = \frac{y_0}{1+(n+n_l)\beta_{n^d}}, \quad \nu_o = \beta_{n^d} y_o^e && (6.82)\\
\pi_o^e &= \hat{p}_o = \hat{w}_o - n_l = \bar{\mu} - (n+n_l) = \Delta\mu && (6.83)\\
r_o &\neq \rho_o^e \;\; \textit{from} \;\; i_1(\rho_o^e - r_o) + i_2(U_c^o - 1) = 0, \quad m_o = h_1 y_o && (6.84)\\
l_o^d &= y_o, \quad l_o = l_o^d/V_o. && (6.85)
\end{aligned}$$

We thus get as an important new result that the steady state rates of employment on the external labor market and of the rate of capacity utilization of firms are now endogenously determined and that the steady state rates of profit and real interest need no longer coincide. This is a striking difference to the features of KMG growth considered so far. The explanation for these new results are first that firms, through their pricing behavior, determine and fix the actual wage share at a given level whereby a certain rate of employment is implied in order to make the real wage claims of workers compatible with this given share of wages and the given rate of productivity increase. The higher the target real wage rate of workers for each given level of employment, and the higher the markup factor of firms, the lower is therefore the NAIRU rate of employment in the steady state. Note that the model implies accelerating inflation above this NAIRU and accelerating deflation below this level, as it is suggested by the phrase that underlies this abbreviation.

Next goods market equilibrium determines the steady state rate of profit of firms as in the other models of KMG growth which therefore depends on the trend terms in the investment equation (the natural rates of growth and technical change here by assumption), the savings propensities of asset holders and the two fiscal policy parameters of the government sector. This rate of profit now however determines a certain activity level y_o per unit of capital, since the wage share is no longer adjusting in order to allow for normal capacity growth at this given rate of profit. Factors increasing profitability will therefore now increase the rate of capacity utilization that prevails in the steady state. This rate is however no longer of the type of a NAIRU as there is no longer an impact of the rate of capacity utilization of firms on their pricing decision.

The next new implication of the model of this section is that the rate of interest must adjust in the steady state in order to equalize the growth rate of the capital stock with the natural growth rate $n + n_l$. In the case $i_2 = 0$ this will again equalize the rate of interest with the rate of profit. In the case $i_2 > 0$ firms however would disinvest at a constant rate due the excess in capacity they are facing and this must be balanced by a rate of interest that is lower than the rate of profit in order to get balanced growth. All remaining steady state expressions are as in the model of section 6.2 (and earlier ones) and thus need not be commented here.

The presently considered dynamics thus exhibits an ordinary type of Phillips curve for the short-run and the usual vertical one for the long run, but now with a steady state rate of employment that can be modified by influencing the pricing behavior of firms or the real wage bargaining solution of workers and unions. These interactions are here completely separated from the reasons that determine profitability and the rate of capacity utilization of firms in the steady state, which can be influenced by government fiscal policy and savings behavior. Apart from the very different outlook of steady state analysis we expect however that the medium run dynamics of the model will not be very different from those of section 6.2, our KMG reference case, though of course the Rose real wage effects, concerning the stabilizing or destabilizing role of wage and price flexibility are no longer active in this growth model with sluggish quantity adjustments concerning output and employment and its fairly standard (from the formal point of view) wage and price Phillips curve.

In order to get analytical results for the imperfect competition KMG model we have transferred the model back to continuous time. The dynamical model (6.67)–(6.73) then reads due to the new wage price block

$$\hat{p} = \hat{w} - n_l = (u^*(V) - u)/u + \pi^e = b_0 + b_1 V + \pi^e$$

as follows ($\Delta\mu = \bar{\mu} - (n + n_l), b_o < 0$):

$$\begin{aligned}
\hat{l} &= -i_1(\rho^e - r + \pi^e) - i_2(U_c - 1) && (6.86)\\
\hat{m} &= \Delta\mu - [(u^*(V) - u)/u + \pi^e] - i_1(\rho^e - r + \pi^e) - i_2(U_c - 1) && (6.87)\\
\dot{\pi}^e &= \beta_{\pi_1^e}(u^*(V) - u)/u) && (6.88)\\
\dot{y}^e &= \beta_{y^e}(y^d - y^e) - (i_1(\rho^e - r + \pi^e) + i_2(U_c - 1))y^e && (6.89)\\
\dot{\nu} &= y - y^d - (i_1(\rho^e - r + \pi^e) + i_2(U_c - 1) + n + n_l)\nu && (6.90)\\
\hat{V} &= \beta_v(V^w - 1), \quad V \leq 1 && (6.91)
\end{aligned}$$

with

$$\begin{aligned}
y &= (1 + (n + n_l)\beta_{n^d})y^e + \beta_n(\beta_{n^d}y^e - \nu)\\
y^d &= uy + (1 - s_c)(\rho^e - t_c^n) + i_1(\rho^e - r + \pi^e) + i_2(U_c - 1) + n + n_l + \delta + \bar{g}\\
V^w &= = y^d/(Vl), \quad U_c = y/y^p\\
\rho^e &= y^e - \delta - uy\\
r &= r_0 + (h_1 y - m)/h_2.
\end{aligned}$$

This dynamic model will now be investigated from various levels of generality in the following subsections of this section.

6.3.2 The 2D stagflation subdynamics: Local analysis

In order to understand the features of the dynamics with imperfect competition let us first consider the basic situation where

- growth is absent by ignoring the capacity effects (but not the goods market effects) of the investment terms based on the profit rate differential and on the rate of capacity utilization, i.e., by assuming that $l = L/K$ is frozen at its steady state value despite fluctuations in the rate of investment,
- $\beta_v = \infty$ holds, i.e., we have that $V^w = 1$ holds at all points in time and that the rate of external employment is adjusting with infinite speed towards the level needed by the current state aggregate goods demand.
- the Metzlerian quantity adjustment mechanism works with infinite speed such that $y = y^d = y^e$ holds at all times (inventories are neglected by assuming $\beta_{n^d} = 0$ in addition),
- regressive expectations are ignored by setting the parameter β_{pi_2} equal to zero.

In this case we have linear IS and LM curves, representing goods and money market equilibrium, of basically textbook type. Solving for goods market equilibrium (per unit of capital) then gives the following expression in terms of the parameters of the model:

$$y = y(m, \pi^e) = \frac{(i_1/h_2)m + i_1\pi^e + n + n_l + \bar{g} - t_c^n + (i_1 - s_c)\delta - i_1 r_o - i_2}{(s_c - i_1)(1-u) + i_1 h_1/h_2 - i_2 y^p}.$$

We assume that the parameters characterizing goods and money markets are such that the denominator in this expression is positive. We then get that the linear function $y = y(m, \pi^e) = a_1 m + a_2\pi^e + a_o$ is characterized by $a_1, a_2 > 0$ as in textbook IS-LM theory where increasing real balances shift the LM curve to the right and thus increase output and where increasing inflationary expectations shift the IS-curve to the right thereby also increasing the level of output (relative to the temporarily given level of the capital stock). The above continuous time dynamics can thus now be reduced to

$$\hat{m} = \bar{\mu} - (n + n_l) - [(u^*(V) - u)/u + \pi^e] = \Delta\mu - b_o - b_1 V - \pi^e \quad (6.92)$$

$$\dot{\pi}^e = \beta_{\pi_1^e}(u^*(V) - u)/u) \quad (6.93)$$

with $V = l^d/l = y/l = (a_1 m + a_2\pi^e + a_o)/l$ and both u and l given magnitudes (we set l equal to 1 in the following for notational simplicity). Note that we allow in this chapters for rates of growth of money supply, $\bar{\mu}$ that differ from natural growth $n + n_l$ and thus for steady state inflation in contrast to chapters 4 and 5 and that we have assumed as in Carlin and Soskice (1990, Ch.6) for simplicity and for methodological reasons a linear bargained real wage curve and thus use for $u^*(V)/u - 1$ the expressions

$$b_o + b_1 V = b_1(V - V_o), V_o = -b_o/b_1, b_o < 0, b_1 > 0$$

in the following derivations and calculations ($V_o = -b_o/b_1$ the endogenous NAIRU rate of employment of proposition 6.3).

There are two important characteristics of this Keynesian basic model of inflation:

- the model is nonlinear in the most basic way that is possible, and
- the model is based on $a_2 > 0$: a positive Mundell-effect besides $a_1 > 0$, the Keynes effect of falling wages here expressed in terms of rising real balances.

Of course, the V equation has to be inserted into eqns. (6.92) – (6.93) in order to get an autonomous differential equations system, now of only dimension 2.

In this subsection we summarize some local properties of the dynamics (6.92) – (6.93) which are not difficult to obtain and which are therefore not proved here:[17]

Proposition 6.4

There are two steady states of the dynamics (6.92) – (6.93), one that is interior to the right half of the phase plane and thus economically meaningful and one that lies on its boundary:

$$m_0 = (V_o - a_0 - a_2\Delta\mu)/a_1 > 0, \ \pi_0^e = \Delta\mu \quad \textit{and} \quad m_0 = 0, \ \pi_0^e = (V_o - a_0)/a_2 > 0.$$

[17]We assume for the remainder of the chapter $a_0 < V_o$. This assumption is not difficult to justify from the parameters of the underlying IS-LM model.

Proposition 6.5

1. The Jacobian of the dynamics at the interior steady state is given by

$$J = \begin{pmatrix} -ba_1 m_0 & -(ba_2+1)m_0 \\ \beta_{\pi_1^e} ba_1 & \beta_{\pi_1^e} ba_2 \end{pmatrix}$$

which implies $\det J = \beta_{\pi_1^e} ba_1 m_o > 0$ *(no saddle) and trace* $J = b(\beta_{\pi_1^e} a_2 - a_1 m_o)$.
2. The dynamics around the border steady state is of saddlepoint type ($\det J < 0$).

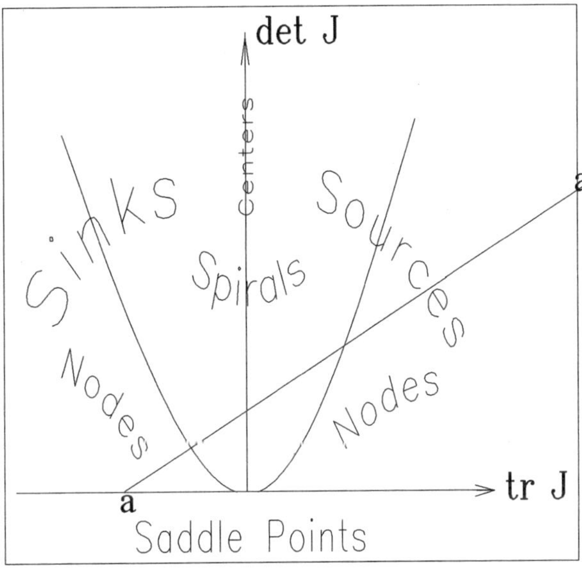

Figure 6.3:
The set of local stability features of the dynamics (6.92) – (6.93).

The local results of this proposition for the interior steady state can be summarized graphically in the trace$J$ – det J space as shown in figure 6.3,[18] where the half line aa is given by

$$(traceJ(\beta_{\pi_1^e}), \det J(\beta_{\pi_1^e})), \quad \beta_{\pi_1^e} \in [0, \infty).$$

The figure 6.3 shows that the local dynamics will be characterized (in this order) by stable nodes, stable foci, unstable foci and unstable nodes as the parameter $\beta_{\pi_1^e}$ is increased from zero to ∞. These results are due to the so-called Mundell-effect which in contrast to the stabilizing Keynes-effect is destabilizing: increases in inflationary expectations stimulate the economy (ceteris paribus) and thus give a further push to already existing inflation, since they decrease the real rate of interest and thus increase effective demand. For fast inflationary expectations this positive feedback mechanism then overcomes the negative

[18]The parabola separates cyclical (above) from monotonic behavior (below).

feedback provided by the Keynes-effect (see proposition 6.5 and the figure 6.3 accompanying it).

Proposition 6.6

The dynamics is subject to a degenerate Hopf-bifurcation (with a zero Liapunov coefficient) at the critical adjustment speed $\beta^H_{\pi^e_1} = a_1 m_o / a_2$ of inflationary expectations.

This proposition can easily be shown by means of the (complicated) formula for Liapunov coefficients supplied in Lux (1995) for dynamical systems of dimension 2, due to the very simple nonlinearity in the considered dynamics. These dynamics therefore do not fulfill the sufficient criteria for so-called super- or subcritical Hopf-bifurcation. We do not go into the details of this calculation here as this result only says that we have to use other tools to get information on possible limit cycle behavior of the trajectories of this dynamics. Nevertheless it is important to know that the present very basic type of nonlinearity of the model does give rise to border type local bifurcations solely.

These are the local results that can be obtained for the dynamical system (6.92) – (6.93) and which show that this system is already locally far more complex than the model treated in section 2.

6.3.3 Global characteristics of the 2D case

We approach the global features of our dynamical system by means of its phase diagram. The isoclines of system (6.92) – (6.93) are given by:

$$\dot{m} = 0: \quad \pi^e = \frac{V_o + \Delta\mu/b - a_0 - a_1 m}{1/b + a_2} \tag{6.94}$$

$$\dot{\pi}^e = 0: \quad \pi^e = \frac{V_o - a_0 - a_1 m}{a_2} \tag{6.95}$$

plus the vertical axis of the phase plane which is an invariant domain of the dynamics. On this basis the phase portrait can be drawn as follows (if one takes note of the fact that the intersection of the $\dot{\pi}^e = 0$ isocline with the vertical axis provides a second steady state of the dynamics):

Note that the saddle point S_o of the dynamics gives rise to a separatrix S to the right of it (as shown). The depicted phase portrait – and numerical simulations of the dynamical system, see figure 6.5 – suggest the following proposition.

Proposition 6.7

1. *The dynamics are never globally stable.*

2. *If locally stable (at the interior steady state) the dynamics exhibit corridor stability (which generally seems to end with the separatrix S shown in the figure 6.4).*

3. *If locally unstable the system is (always) totally unstable (that is all trajectories either approach $(0, +\infty)$ via the saddle path dynamics shown (a process of accelerating inflation) or give rise to a deflationary spiral which never ends.*

4. If $a_1 = 0$ holds (no Keynes-effect due to the liquidity trap) the system is explosive on both sides of the $\dot{\pi}^e = 0$ isocline and thus exhibits a never ending deflationary process in particular.

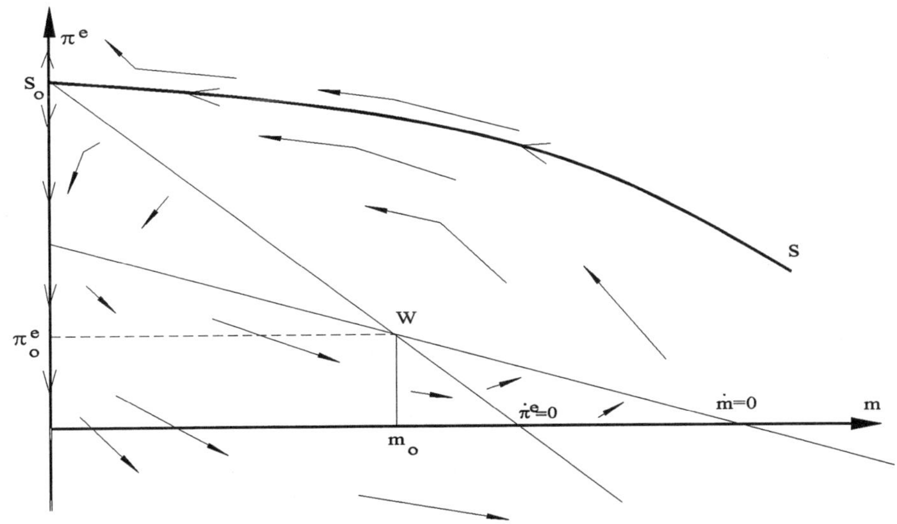

Figure 6.4:
The phase diagram of the dynamics (6.92) – (6.93) .

We do not prove the assertions of this proposition here which to some extent are obvious, but which with respect to the size of the corridor and with respect to the total instability asserted under 3. are not so obvious. The justification for this is that the model is not really a viable one and thus not yet of economic interest. Furthermore, the treatment of processes of inflation and deflation is still far too symmetric to be convincing with respect to actual economic dynamics. Finally, the situation of corridor stability is analyzed in detail and from a different angle (with more nonlinearities involved) in Groth (1992) and thus is already a known phenomenon in medium run IS-LM dynamics.

Figure 6.5 shows for the case of an unstable steady state (for $\beta_{\pi_1^e} = 0.2 > \beta_{\pi_1^e}^H$) that the separatrix in this case – as well as in all other cases of this type – connects the interior steady state W with the border steady state S_o, see the figure 6.5, and this for the parameter values $a_0 = 0.75, a_1 = 1, a_2 = 1, V_o = 0.95, \Delta\mu = 0.05, b = 0.5$:[19] This figure 6.5 suggests, as already asserted in proposition 6.7 – that the dynamics is globally unstable in all these cases, since each trajectory that locally departs from the steady state (and which exhibits a lower turning point) will have the same format as the shown stable manifold S of the point S_o, but will wind around it and the point W until it is above this separatrix S for all times (where it then 'converges' to $(0, +\infty)$). The dynamics is therefore – for $\beta_{\pi_1^e} > \beta_{\pi_1^e}^H$ – never a bounded or viable one and must be augmented then by forces that will keep the trajectories in an economically meaningful range.

[19]Note that the Hopf bifurcation value is in this situation given by $\beta_{\pi_1^e}^H = 0.15$.

Note that the dynamics need not be cyclical around the steady state as has been shown in the preceding subsection. Note also that the separatrix will be strictly falling throughout in the cases where the steady state is locally asymptotically stable in which case it cannot bend backwards as in the unstable situation considered in figure 6.5.

Further simulations of the dynamics have shown that orbits will be closed at the Hopf-bifurcation point below the separatrix S and that the system has a large potential to recover from deflationary processes and accompanying depressions (if a_1 is not close to zero) which however may be very deep. Yet, the next section will show that we need not worry about the possibility of no lower turning point of the dynamics since there is an important institutional constraint in actual economies which is here still missing and which prevents downward instability when added to the considered dynamics. Astonishingly, this simple institutional fact will also provide upward stability to situations that were previously explosive (as the one in figure 6.5).

6.3.4 Kinked Phillips curves: 2D analysis

Empirical observations, for example already in Phillips (1958), suggest that the conventional type of Phillips curve cannot be linear. We shall consider here an extreme, but not implausible example for those observations, namely a kinked money wage Phillips curve. That is we assume that the bargained real wage never results in downward money wage adjustments, so that the wage adjustment mechanism is modified as follows:

$$\boxed{\hat{w} = \max\{b(V - V_o) + \pi^e, 0\}.}$$

This Phillips curve says that money wages behave as in the preceding subsection if their growth rate is positive, but stay constant if they would be falling in the previous situations. There is thus no wage deflation possible now. Of course the kink could be smoothed or some wage deflation could be allowed for, but this will not alter the conclusions of this section significantly. We consider this kinked Phillips curve as a much better description of reality than the one that is linear throughout.

The immediate consequence of this new form of the Phillips curve is that system (6.92) – (6.93) now only applies when $b(V - V_o) + \pi^e \geq 0$ holds while it must be replaced by

$$\widehat{m} = \Delta\mu \tag{6.96}$$

$$\dot{\pi}^e = -\beta_{\pi_1^e}\pi^e \tag{6.97}$$

in the case of $b(V - V_o) + \pi^e < 0$.[20] We thus have now a system of differential equations which is only continuous (C^o), but which can be made a smooth system in an obvious

[20]The two systems are identical at the border line $\hat{w} = b(V - V_o) + \pi^e = 0$.

way. We call this system the patched system while we refer to the earlier dynamics as the unpatched one.

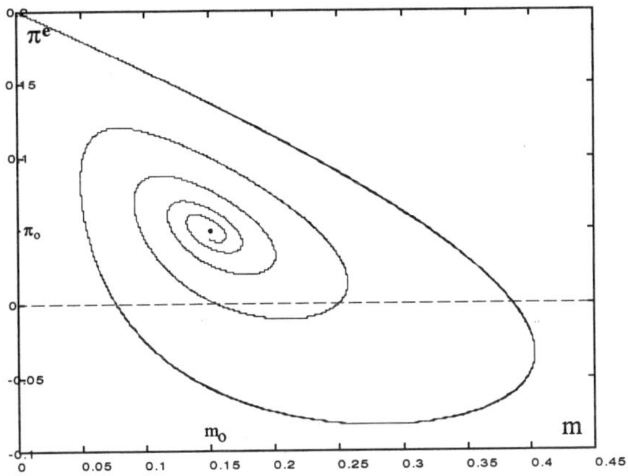

Figure 6.5: The separatrix S of the dynamics (6.92) – (6.93) in the case of local instability.[21]

To explore the difference to the previous unpatched dynamics let us consider the case $\Delta\mu = 0$ first. In this case there is the following simple, but radical modification of the dynamics (6.92) – (6.93) which now exhibits a continuum of depressed steady states as shown in figure 6.6.[22]

Depending on the size of the cycle in the inflationary region we end up (if we start below the separatrix S) in a stable depressed situation of less than 'natural' employment where wages and prices and inflationary expectations have become stationary and where there is no possibility of recovery since money wages do not fall by assumption in such a case. Downward money wage rigidity therefore causes stable depressions (of any possible size), but excludes of course now the possibility of deflationary spirals and economic collapse.

[21]We thank Thorsten Göke for the calculation of figure 6.5 as an application of a program he has developed for the numerical determination of stable manifolds of fixed points and more general situations.

[22]Note that there now exists a third steady state solution S_1 and that all points between W and S_1 are now steady states too – due to the form of the lower part of our patched dynamical system for $\Delta\mu = 0$.

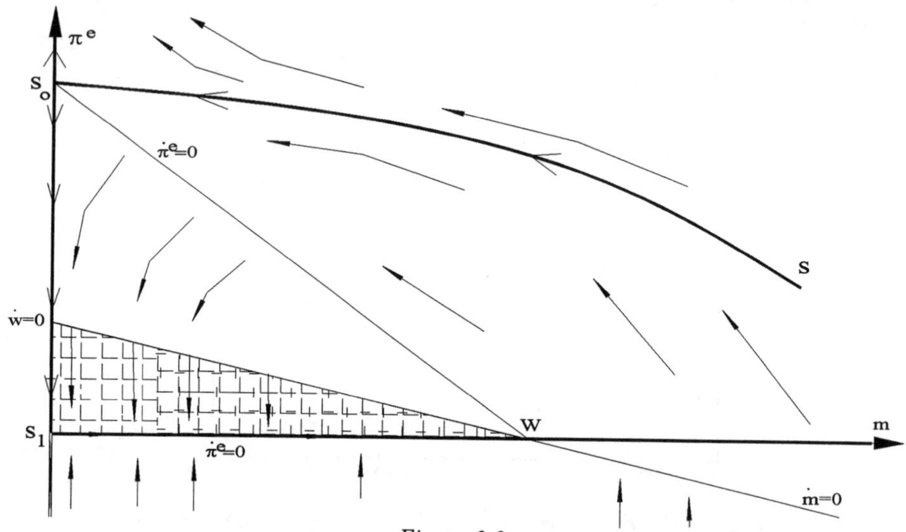

Figure 6.6:
The kinked Phillips curve with no steady state inflation.

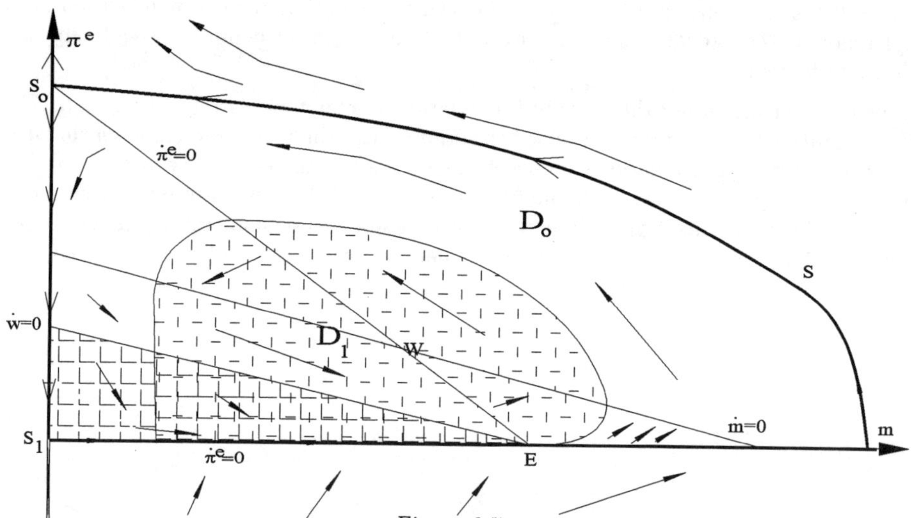

Figure 6.7:
The kinked Phillips curve with steady state inflation.

Is there anything that can improve the depicted situation and lead us back to normal employment (or beyond)? The simple answer to this question is that government should allow for (some) steady state inflation by allowing for a positive growth rate of the money supply in such an economy with a stationary steady state. This lifts the $\dot{m} = 0$ isocline above the $\dot{w} = 0$ locus and alters figure 6.6 as shown in figure 6.7 (if the depicted assumption on the separatrix S holds).

As the figure 6.7 shows the domain below the separatrix S (in the nonnegative orthant) is now an invariant domain D_o, i.e., no trajectory which starts in it can leave it. Note also that the domain below the $\dot{w} = 0$ isocline is governed by the above dynamics in the place of the one of the preceding section, which however only alters the direction of the dynamics on the horizontal axes which is now also an isocline ($\dot{\pi}^e = 0$) of the patched dynamics (up to point E). Note furthermore that the trajectory which starts in E (horizontally), followed up to point E' and then vertically continued up to the m-axis, also defines an invariant domain D_1 of the patched dynamics which moreover is attracting for all trajectories in the interior of D_o. We thus have that all orbits in D_o (with the exception of the ones on the vertical axis) are either inside of D_1 or are entering the domain D_1 (from its left). This implies the following proposition:

Proposition 6.8 (Viability Theorem)[23]

1. *There exist exactly three steady states for the patched dynamics:* S_o, S_1, W *if* $\Delta\mu > 0$ *holds. These steady states are connected by the* $\dot{\pi}^e = 0$ *isocline.*

2. *Assume that the interior steady state* W *is locally repelling (high values of* $\beta_{\pi_1^e}$*). Then: Every trajectory starting in* D_o *converges to a persistent cycle around* W *(and in* D_1*).*

3. *Assume that the interior steady state* W *is locally attracting (low values of* $\beta_{\pi_1^e}$*). Then: Every trajectory starting in* D_o *either converges to the steady state* W *or a persistent cycle around it.*

Proof: An immediate implication of the Poincaré -Bendixson theorem, see Hirsch and Smale (1974), if one makes the kink in the Phillips curve smooth. ∎

Remark: We expect that the limit cycle of case 2. is uniquely determined and that all trajectories of situation 3. will in fact converge to the steady state (but cannot prove this here).

Note that the above proposition also holds if the separatrix S does not cut the horizontal axis at all as long as it does not bend backward.[24] There are however situations where the above proposition does not apply and they are of the type shown in figure 6.8:

---

[23]We add here that output and employment will stay positive along this dynamics if for example $a_0 > 0$ is assumed and that the underlying IS-LM model can be specified in such a way that the nominal rate of interest will stay positive, too.

[24]The observation from numerical simulations is that the separatrix S will connect the points S_o, W in a cyclical or monotonic way in the case of local instability.

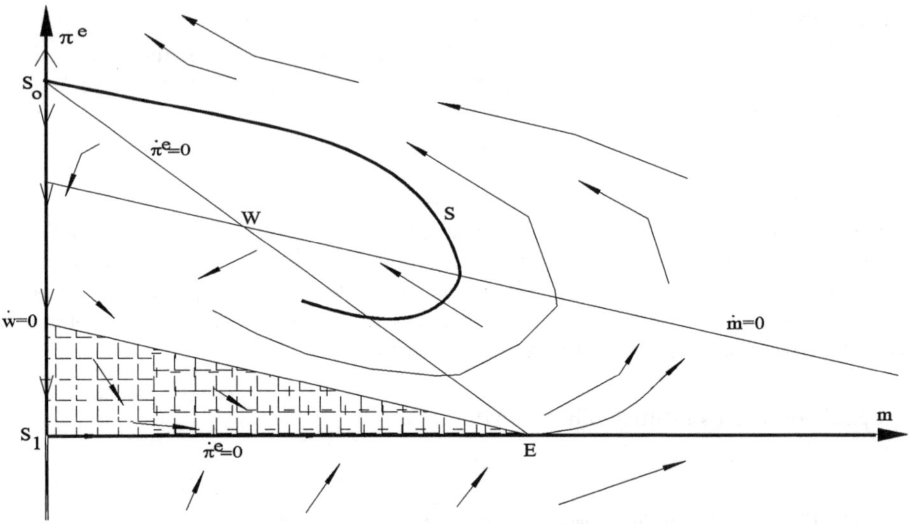

Figure 6.8:
Strong monetary growth and fast inflationary expectations.

In the figure 6.8 the separatrix of the unpatched system cycles around W before it approaches point S_o in a monotonic fashion, but it does not cut the horizontal axis on its way.[25] This situation is the more likely the larger the policy parameter $\Delta\mu$ becomes. Increasing the speed of adjustment of inflationary expectations sufficiently (which makes them approach the horizontal axis below $\dot{w} = 0$ nearly vertically) then produces a situation where trajectories can escape from below S and thus end up in an inflationary spiral as in the unpatched system.

Proposition 6.9 (Escape Theorem)

> *Consider a situation where the separatrix S that connects the points W and S_o in the unpatched system does not cut the horizontal axis (based on a growth rate of the money supply that is sufficiently high). Then: There exist adjustment speeds of inflationary expectations, chosen sufficiently high, where there is again no bound to inflation in the present specification of the model.*

This situation implies that expansionary monetary policy used to overcome the stable depressions shown in figure 6.6 must be exercised with care if it should not end up in such an inflationary boom. Note that the possibility of such an occurrence implies that the model is still incomplete in this case and should be further revised in order to allow for the existence of absolute full employment ceilings.

[25]Note that the separatrix not exists in the domain where the kink in the Phillips curve is operative.

6.3.5 4D and 6D extensions of the 2D stagflation dynamics

In this subsection we continue to disregard the contributions of fluctuating investment to capacity growth by assuming that their capacity effect is only given by $\hat{K} = n + n_l$ so that $l = xL/K$, the full employment - capital ratio in efficiency units, can remain fixed at its steady state value. Disregarding unbalanced factor growth does however not mean here that investment as a component of aggregate demand is diminished in the same way, but is in fact kept intact in the following. Therefore one might simply say that unbalanced factor growth is simply removed from the model by keeping the ratio l fixed at its steady state value.

We extend however the 2D stagflation dynamics of the preceding section now by quantity adjustments on the labor market as well as on the market for goods, by adding on the one hand again the sluggish adjustment of the workforce of firms in view of the over- or undertime work performed in the firm, i.e., equation (6.10) in the continuous time format:

$$\dot{L}^w = \beta_v(L^d - L^w) + \gamma L^w, \quad \gamma = n + n_l.$$

On the other hand we make use of Metzlerian output and inventory adjustment in the simplified way of the dynamic multiplier story (where inventory adjustments are in fact disregarded and where aggregate demand directs output adjustments immediately):

$$\dot{Y} = \beta_y(Y^d - Y) + \gamma Y, \quad \gamma = n + n_l.$$

This simplification of the goods market quantity adjustment process helps to save one law of motion so that the resulting inflationary dynamics are now of dimension 4 and are given by:

$$\begin{aligned}
\dot{m} &= [\Delta\mu - b_1(V - V_o) + \pi^e]m, \quad m = M/(pK), V_o = -b_o/b_1 && (6.98)\\
\dot{\pi}^e &= \beta_{\pi_1^e} b_1(V - V_o) && (6.99)\\
\dot{V} &= \beta_v(y - V), \quad V \leq 1, \quad y - V^w V = xL^d/L = y/l,\ l = 1 && (6.100)\\
\dot{y} &= \beta_y(y^d - y), \quad y = Y/K && (6.101)
\end{aligned}$$

with

$$\begin{aligned}
u &= 1/(1+a) \quad \text{a given magnitude}\\
y^d &= uy + (1 - s_c)(\rho - t_c^n) + i_1(\rho - r + \pi^e) + i_2(y/y^p - 1) + n + n_l + \delta + \bar{g}\\
\rho &= y - \delta - uy = y(1-u) - \delta\\
r &= r_0 + (h_1 y - m)/h_2, \quad r_o \text{ from proposition 6.4.}
\end{aligned}$$

Note here that we have inserted the new approach to price inflation. namely,

$$\hat{p} = \hat{w} - n_l = \frac{u*(V) - u}{u} + \pi^e = b_1(V - V_o) + \pi^e, \quad u^*(V) = u + ub_1(V - V_o)$$

into the first two laws of motion shown. Up to the multiplicative form in the first law of motion (caused by its growth law origin) we continue to have a linear dynamics here which is obviously closely related to the 2D dynamics investigated in the preceding section, but now exhibits delayed adjustment of output and employment towards their moving target, the level of aggregate goods demand. This goods demand can here be expressed as a linear relationship in the variables y, m, π^e as follows ($u = 1/(1+a)$):

$$\begin{aligned} y^d = y(y,m,\pi^e) &= [1 + i_2/y^p - (s_c - i_1)(1-u) - i_1 h_1/h_2]y \\ &+ i_1/h_2 m + i_1\pi^e + n + n_l + \bar{g} - t_c^n + (i_1 - s_c)\delta - i_1 r_o - i_2. \end{aligned}$$

We assume that the expression in square brackets, the marginal propensity to spend out of income, lies in the interval $(0,1)$ so that the multiplier theory is given in its basic format here, though with a lot of background behind this marginal propensity to spend. Note that this assumption can always be satisfied by assuming s_c sufficiently close to i_1 and by choosing the parameter h_2 sufficiently small (thereby increasing the strength of the Keynes effect in the inflationary cycle here considered).

Proposition 6.10

There is a unique interior steady–state solution *or point of rest of the dynamics (6.98)–(6.101) which is given by the following expressions:*

$$\begin{aligned} \rho_0 &= \frac{g - t_c^n + n + n_l}{s_c} + t_c^n \\ y_o &= (\rho_0 + \delta)/(1-u), \quad y_o^d = V_o = y_o \\ \pi_o^e &= \Delta\mu = \hat{p}_o = \hat{w}_o - n_l \\ m_0 &= h_1 y_0, \quad r_o \text{ from } i_1(\rho_o - r_o + \Delta\mu) + i_2(y_o/y^p - 1) = 0. \end{aligned}$$

Note again that the rate of interest need no longer be equal to $\rho_o + \pi_o^e$. The proof of the proposition is obvious from the laws of motion of these 4D dynamics and from what has been stated for the general case considered in proposition 6.3.

Proposition 6.11

1. The unique interior steady–state solution of the dynamics (6.98)–(6.101) is locally asymptotically stable for all adjustment speeds β_v, β_y sufficiently large (or a parameter b sufficiently small) and $\beta_{\pi_1^e}$ sufficiently low.

2. The determinant of the Jacobian of the dynamics at the steady state is negative if all adjustment speed parameters are strictly positive.

3. The dynamics loses its local asymptotic stability by way of a Hopf bifurcation if the parameter $\beta_{\pi_1^e}$ becomes sufficiently large.

When the Hopf bifurcation point has been passed we again will face pure explosiveness of the dynamics for most values of $\beta_{\pi_1^e}$ thereafter. We thus need again additional (extrinsic) nonlinearities in order to make the dynamics bounded in an economically meaningful domain. Again the kink in the Phillips curve considered in the preceding subsection will be used below in order to get such boundedness of the dynamics.

Proof of Proposition 6.11 1. Let us first investigate the case where $\beta_{\pi_1^e} = 0$ holds and where π^e is fixed at its steady state value. In this case it is easy to show for the Jacobian of the remaining 3D dynamics at the steady state the following qualitative characterization

$$J = \begin{pmatrix} J_{11} & J_{12} & J_{13} \\ J_{21} & J_{22} & J_{23} \\ J_{31} & J_{32} & J_{33} \end{pmatrix} = \begin{pmatrix} 0 & - & 0 \\ 0 & - & + \\ + & 0 & - \end{pmatrix}.$$

This sign structure immediately implies for the Routh-Hurwitz conditions $a_1(= -trace J) > 0, a_2 > 0, a_3(= -\det J) > 0, a_1a_2 - a_3 > 0$ that the first three sign restrictions will always hold true. Furthermore, the expression for $a_1a_2 - a_3$ is in the present situation given by:

$$a_1a_2 - a_3 = -(J_{22} + J_{33})J_{22}J_{33} + J_{21}J_{23}J_{31}.$$

In terms of adjustment speeds and the parameter b this gives rise to an expression which in its sign is of the type:

$$a_1a_2 - a_3 = (\beta_v + \beta_y)\beta_v\beta_y - b\beta_v\beta_y$$

This expression is positive under the assumptions of proposition 6.5.1 which in sum implies the asserted local asymptotic stability for the case $\beta_{\pi_1^e} = 0$. The case $\beta_{\pi_1^e} > 0$ will be considered below.

2. Due to the linear dependency between row 1 and row 2 of the Jacobian of the full dynamics (6.98)–(6.101) (at the steady state) we have that the determinant of this Jacobian can be reduced to an expression of the type:

$$J = \begin{vmatrix} 0 & ? & - & 0 \\ 0 & - & 0 & 0 \\ 0 & ? & - & + \\ + & ? & 0 & - \end{vmatrix}$$

which immediately gives that this determinant has the asserted positive sign. This fact then also implies that the dynamics must be locally asymptotically stable for all $\beta_{\pi_1^e} > 0$ sufficiently small if it is of this type for the reduced 3D case considered in 1., since eigenvalues depend continuously on the parameters of the model and since $\det J > 0$ implies that the fourth eigenvalue must be negative for small $\beta_{\pi_1^e} > 0$ if the first three (belonging to the considered 3D case) have negative real parts. These conclusions are very similar to earlier ones for dynamical systems of the KMG variety and they also imply assertion 3. as in these earlier propositions. ∎

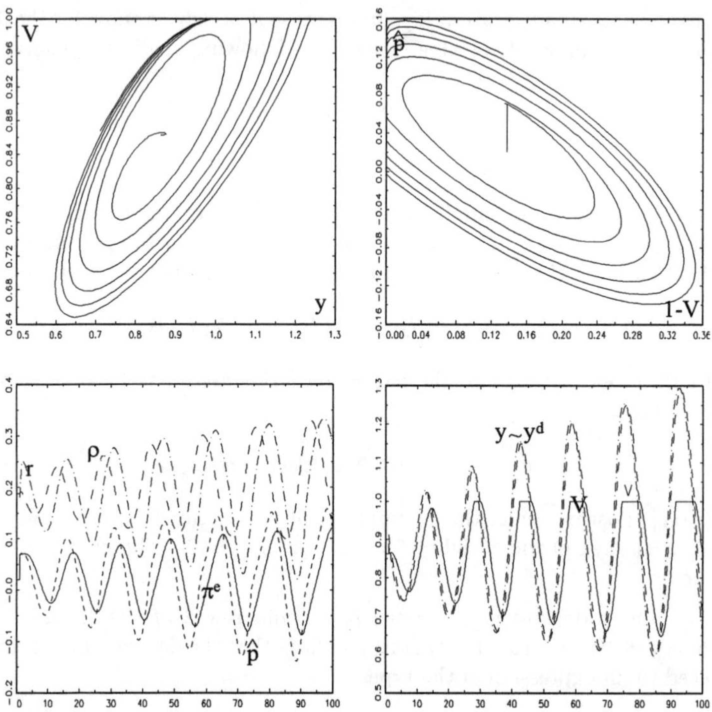

Figure 6.9: A slightly explosive 4D dynamics with sluggish quantity adjustments added

Figure 6.9 provides a simulation run for the dynamics just considered. We use as parameter set the set underlying figure 6.1 as far as it is still applicable and of course additional values for the parameters that are new to the model, as shown in table 6.2.

$s_c = 0.8,$	$\delta = 0.1,$	$t_c^n = -0.1,$	$\bar{g} = 0.1$
$h_1 = 0.1,$	$h_2 = 0.05,$	$i_1 = 1,$	$i_2 = 0.2$
$b_1 = 0.5,$	$\beta_{\pi_1} = 0.37,$	$\beta_y = 2,$	$\beta_v = 0.5$
$y^p = 1,$	$V_o = 0.8625,$	$\bar{\mu} = 0.05$	$n + n_l = 0.03$

Table 6.2

We have assumed a markup factor $a = 0.5$ in the figures 6.9ff., implying a steady state rate of employment and of capacity utilization of 86.25 %. The plot in figure 6.9 top right (concerning the unemployment inflation cycle) is not significantly different from the one shown in figure 6.1 if one takes note of the fact that we have used a 50 years horizon in 6.1 and a 100 years horizon in the present figure 6.9. The cycles shown are comparable in size and they have both the clockwise orientation expected from what is known empirically for such phase plots. The phase plot top left now furthermore shows that output y leads the evolution of the rate of employment as is to be expected from the formulation of the model. We see again the full employment ceiling in both the plots top left and bottom right. Finally, the time series bottom left show evolutions of the nominal variables of the dynamics, as compared to the evolution of activity level measures bottom right.

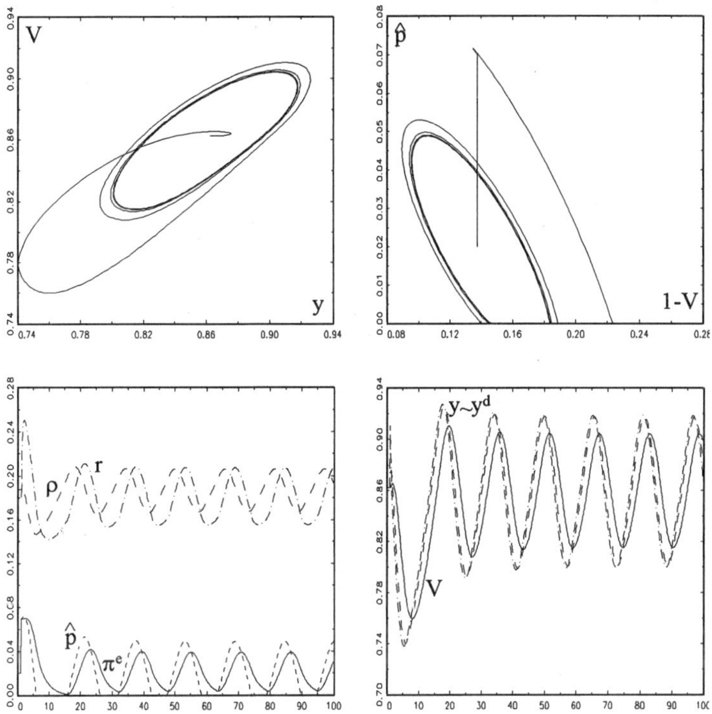

Figure 6.10: Viability via asymmetries in labor market dynamics

As long as the orbits of the dynamics are shown they represent an economically meaningful evolution of the economy. Yet explosiveness is visible and continues to prevail, leading to economically meaningless variables from some point in time onwards. Therefore extrinsic nonlinearities that imply viability or boundedness of the dynamics for all points in time have to be added. In view of what has been discussed for the 2D subdynamics of the 4d case here considered it is of course natural to consider nonlinearities in the money wage behavior first in order to see whether this is still a successful strategy of overcoming the destabilizing forces operating behind figure 6.9. Inspecting the 4D dynamics we can see that it is basically the Mundell effect of inflationary expectations that should still be responsible for the observed instability. Therefore, a kink in the money wage Phillips curve should again be sufficient to obtain the viability of the dynamics in the considered situation.

Let us therefore now add again a kink in the money wage behavior to the new view on money wage dynamics based on a bargained real wage curve, which now represents a floor to what can be achieved in such bargaining situations. This modifies the equation for price inflation to be inserted into the laws of motion for real balances and inflationary expectations as follows:

$$\hat{p} = \hat{w} - n_l = \max\{b(V - V_o) + \pi^e, -n_l + f\}$$

where $f \leq 0$ represents the floor to money wage behavior. This floor is to be augmented by $-n_l$ when going from wage to price inflation. Figure 6.10 shows the change caused in the preceding simulation if a strict floor to money wages is assumed to exist: $f = 0$.

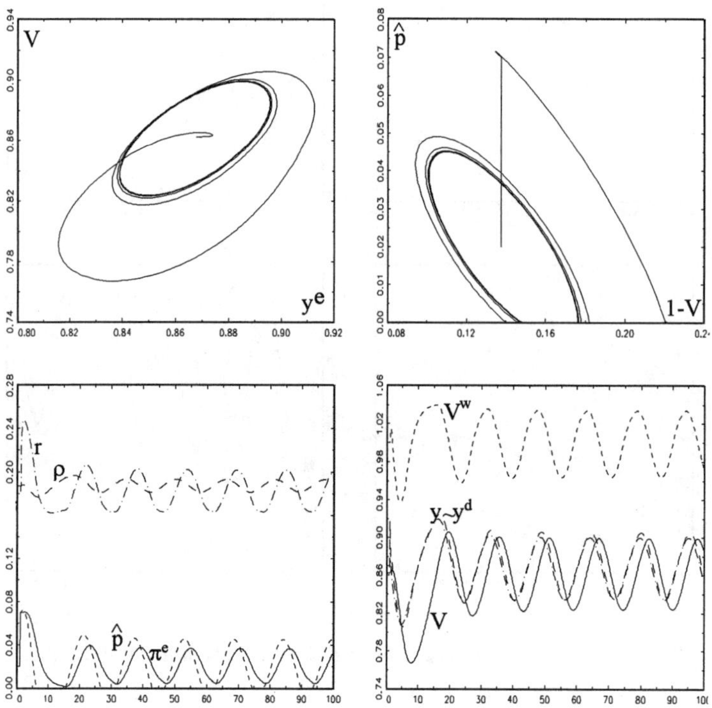

Figure 6.11: The full 6D dynamics: Viability and limit cycle behavior

The phase plot top right shows the kink in operation preventing the occurrence of negative rates of price inflation (due to the assumption $n_l = 0$ in the presently considered case). We see that the unemployment vs. inflation cycle is considerably reduced in size and now in fact characterized by convergence to a unique period motion in the full 4D state space. Furthermore the full employment ceiling is no longer reached and thus no longer limiting the evolution of the economy as the phase plot top left shows. We thus have that in the present example the kink in the Phillips curve (combined with steady state inflation) is as successful as in the 2D case in obtaining boundedness and stable periodic attractors in the case of locally explosive price quantity dynamics.

We finally briefly show that the conclusions reached for the 4D extension of the 2D stagflation cycle model may also be expected to hold in the general 6D imperfect competition model as long as the Metzlerian inventory adjustment mechanism is based on a low accelerator and a high adjustment speed of sales expectations (and thus close to the dynamic multiplier story) and at least as long as the parameters i_1, i_2 characterizing the fluctuating components in investment behavior are sufficiently low. In the following simulation run we assume the same investment parameters as in the two preceding ones, but now for the capacity effects of fluctuating rates of investment (by adding the law of motion for the full employment labor intensity) and by assuming $\beta_{n^d} = 0.1, \beta_n = 0.5, \beta_{y^e} = 2$ in the place of the single multiplier adjustment speed $\beta_y = 2$. All other parameter values remain as before. For the resulting 6D dynamical system we then get in this situation a phase plot that is nearly identical to the one shown in figure 6.10 despite the fact that quantity adjustment is now occurring in a much more complex way and fluctuating growth has now been added to the model.

6.4 Imperfect competition: Adjusting income distribution

The imperfect competition KMG growth model of the preceding section with its rigid determination of the share of wages through firms' pricing policy will now be modified in order to take account of smooth factor substitution and imperfect competition pricing rules as well as other pricing mechanisms that may help to understand the role of price inflation in the determination of income distribution and the NAIRU from a more advanced point of view. We continue however to make use of the Metzlerian expected sales / inventory adjustment mechanism and will do this in all models considered in this section on the basis of temporarily given prices and thus a given subjective demand expectation of firms. This demand expectation is revised in an adaptive way following observed realizations of aggregate demand with some time delay. In all cases we will however continue to use the money wage dynamics of the preceding section, based on a target real wage and expected price inflation. The new aspects considered thus solely concern the pricing behavior of firms and its implications for steady state analysis and the dynamics off the steady state (without and with kinks in the money wage Phillips curve).

Concerning pricing behavior and inflation we will always use two constituent elements (in varying formulations) in the following in order to arrive at an expression for price inflation that goes beyond the popular assumption that price inflation is just wage inflation (as in the preceding section). These two elements are:

- the formulation of a price target of price setting firms based on their cost schedules and given demand expectations and thus output decisions,
- the assumption of a delayed adjustment towards such target prices with perhaps asymmetries in upward and downward adjustment behavior.

In this respect we will provide in the next three subsections of this section three different procedures for the pricing decisions of firms with interesting steady state implications, but with basically the same dynamical features as in our KMG growth model of traditional Keynesian type.

6.4.1 Marked up marginal wage costs

In this subsection we assume as given a neoclassical production function with the usual properties, but not subject to technical change, and now complete the dynamics (6.86) – (6.91) with the following wage - price module:[26] Since the real wage ω is now allowed to vary due to the pricing policy of firms, the money wage adjustment equation, see (6.102) below, will no longer be given by a linear curve based on parameters b_o, b_1 as in the preceding sections.

Wage - price adjustment equations

$$\hat{w} = (\omega^*(V) - \omega)/\omega + \pi^e, \quad \omega^{*'}(V) > 0 \tag{6.102}$$

$$\hat{p} = \beta_p((1+a)w/pF_L(K, L^d) - 1) + \pi^e \tag{6.103}$$

$$\dot{\pi}^e = \beta_{\pi^e}(\hat{p} - \pi^e). \tag{6.104}$$

Due to the neglect of technical change, the money wage dynamics is based again on the bargained real wage function as in Carlin and Soskice (1990, Part II), now supplemented by marked up marginal cost pricing in the place of the average one used in the preceding section. Carlin and Soskice (1990, p.149) assume instantaneous adjustment of the price level to its target level, which in the above equation for price inflation is obtained by assuming $\beta_p = \infty$. Note that in the model we are using there is a choice between actual and normal marginal wage costs, $w/pF_L(K, L^d)$ vs. $w/pF_L(K, L^w)$ which we have settled by choosing marginal wage costs actually in operation as the basis of the price target of firms. Workers and firms here share adaptive expectations of the same type, which in the case of firms are justified as some form of self-reference (expected price inflation drives actual price inflation) by assuming that actual inflation depends on the inflationary climate it is operating in, in contrast to the hetero-reference in the money wage Phillips curve. Distinguishing between inflationary expectations of workers and firms, π_w^e, π_f^e, would add the difference $\pi_w^e - \pi_f^e$ to the dynamic system to be considered below and of course a further law of motion, determining the inflationary expectations of firms.

Since wage and price inflation are now distinguished from each other we get a law of motion for the real wage (and the wage share) now in addition to the equation for price inflation needed for the evolution of money balances as shown below. The dynamics (6.86) – (6.91) thereby become of the following now seven dimensional form:

[26]Note that we use as markup factor the expression $1 + a$ in the place of the micro oriented use of $\frac{1}{1-m}$ which reflects a given demand schedule for firms, see Carlin and Soskice (1990) for details on this latter approach.

$$\begin{aligned}
\hat{\omega} &= (\omega^*(V) - \omega)/\omega - \beta_p((1+a)\omega/f'(l^d) - 1) && (6.105)\\
\hat{l} &= -i_1(\rho^e - r + \pi^e) - i_2(U_c - \bar{U}_c) && (6.106)\\
\hat{m} &= \Delta\mu - \pi^e - \beta_p((1+a)\omega/f'(l^d) - 1) && \\
&- \; i_1(\rho^e - r + \pi^e) - i_2(U_c - \bar{U}_c) && (6.107)\\
\dot{\pi}^e &= \beta_{\pi_1^e}(\beta_p((1+a)\omega/f'(l^d) - 1)) && (6.108)\\
\dot{y}^e &= \beta_{y^e}(y^d - y^e) - (i_1(\rho^e - r + \pi^e) + i_2(U_c - \bar{U}_c))y^e && (6.109)\\
\dot{\nu} &= y - y^d - (i_1(\rho^e - r + \pi^e) + i_2(U_c - \bar{U}_c) + n)\nu && (6.110)\\
\hat{V} &= \beta_v(V^w - 1), \quad V \leq 1 && (6.111)
\end{aligned}$$

These laws of motion make use of the following algebraic equations

$$\begin{aligned}
y &= (1 + n\beta_{n^d})y^e + \beta_n(\beta_{n^d}y^e - \nu)\\
y^d &= \omega l^d + (1 - s_c)(\rho^e - t_c^n) + i_1(\rho^e - r + \pi^e) + i_2(U_c - \bar{U}_c) + n + \delta + \bar{g}\\
l^d &= f^{-1}(y)\\
V^w &= = l^d/(Vl) \;\; [l^w = Vl], \;\; U_c = y/y^p\\
\rho^e &= y^e - \delta - \omega l^d\\
r &= r_0 + (h_1 y - m)/h_2\\
y^p &= f(l^p), \quad \omega = f'(l^p).
\end{aligned}$$

Substitution and marginal wage cost pricing therefore enter the dynamics in specific and clearly defined ways, allowing for an easy interpretation of the shown revisions of the dynamics (6.106) – (6.111). As we can see from the laws of motion (6.106)–(6.111), the new price adjustment rule is involved in the dynamics of the real wage, the law of motion for real balances (the intensive form substitute for price inflation) and the dynamics of inflationary expectations. The fundamental change in the dynamics is that the real wage (and the wage share) has become a state variable of the model again in a way that appears to be quite different from the standard two Phillips curve approach and its real wage dynamics of the KMG reference case of section 2 of this chapter.

Proposition 6.12

Assume that $g \geq t^n$ holds and that $\omega^*(\cdot), i_1, i_2$ are such that $r_o > 0, V_o \in (0.1)$ is assured. There is a unique interior steady–state solution of the dynamics (6.105) – (6.111) which is given by the following expressions:

$$\begin{aligned}
\rho_o^e &= \frac{g - t_c^n + n}{s_c} + t_c^n && (6.112)\\
l_o^d \;\; &\textit{from} \;\; \rho_o^e = \frac{f(l_o^d)}{1 + n\beta_{n^d}} - \delta - \frac{f'(l_o^d)}{(1+a)} l_o^d && (6.113)\\
y_o &= f(l_o^d) && (6.114)\\
\omega_o &= f'(l_o^d)/(1+a) && (6.115)\\
y_o^e &= y_o^d = \frac{y_0}{1 + n\beta_{n^d}}, \quad \nu_o = \beta_{n^d} y_o^e && (6.116)
\end{aligned}$$

$$\begin{array}{rcll} V_o & from & \omega_o = \omega^*(V_o), \quad V_o^w = 1 & (6.117) \\ U_{co} & = & y_o/f(l_o^p) \neq \bar{U}_c, \quad f'(l_o^p) = \omega_o & (6.118) \\ \pi_o^e & = & \hat{p}_o = \hat{w}_o = \bar{\mu} - n = \Delta\mu & (6.119) \\ r_o & \neq & \rho_o^e \;\; from \;\; i_1(\rho_o^e - r_o) + i_2(U_c^o - \bar{U}_c) = 0 & (6.120) \\ m_o & = & h_1 y_o & (6.121) \\ l_o & = & l_o^d/V_o. & (6.122) \end{array}$$

This steady state solution is again based on a rate of profit that is obtained from goods market equilibrium (a rate which now differs from the real rate of interest to an extent that balances the deviation of the desired rate of capacity utilization from the steady state value of this rate). This rate of profit given then allows the determination of the level of employment per unit of capital l^d that is compatible with this rate of profit, by substituting y^e and ω_o through this employment magnitude in the expression that defines the rate of profit. The resulting nonlinear equation has a unique positive solution under the usual assumptions on neoclassical production functions. From the solution to this equation we then get the accompanying steady state expressions for y, y^e, ω and also for y^d and ν.

Next, the bargained real wage curve determines as in the preceding section the NAIRU level of the employment rate which can here be represented by $V_o = (\omega_o - \tilde{b}_o)/\tilde{b}_1$ if a linear approach to this curve is assumed ($\omega^*(V) = -\tilde{b}_o + \tilde{b}_1 V, \quad \tilde{b}_o < \omega_o, \tilde{b}_1 > 0$).[27] As new conclusion we therefore now get that fiscal policy, savings rates, trend investment, the markup and other parameters of the model influence the level of NAIRU rate of employment which thus is here a complex resultant of the structure of the model and not simply a consequence of the wage - price module as in section 2, see proposition 6.3. Similar observations apply to the steady state rate of capacity utilization which again is not equalized to the normal rate of capacity utilization desired by firms in combination with a interest and profit rate differential that is just sufficient to balance the investment caused by unbalanced capacity utilization, giving rise in sum to a volume of net investment equal to its trend value n.

Assuming that $1 + n\beta_{n^d} < 1 + a$ holds (which is plausible from the empirical point of view, since n, β_{n^d} can both be considered as small), we get that the slope of the (ρ_o^e, l_o^d) schedule,

$$\frac{f'(l_o^d)}{1 + n\beta_{n^d}} - \frac{f''(l_o^d)}{(1 + a)} l_o^d - \frac{f'(l_o^d)}{1 + a},$$

must be positive. This implies as comparative dynamic result that an increase in the markup a (which does not alter the steady state rate of profits) must be balanced by a decrease in the actual value of the labor intensity which implies decreases in $y_o, \omega_o, V_o, U_c^o, r_o, m_o$ and thus in particular in both the NAIRU rate of capacity utilization for labor and for capital (the reaction of l_o is indeterminate). An increase in government expenditures as represented by the term g by contrast implies an increase in the rate of profit ρ_o^e which increases l_o^d, y_o and decreases ω_o which increases the NAIRU rate of employment, but not necessarily the NAIRU rate of capacity utilization, since falling real wages increase the capacity limit of firms. Increasing the savings rate of asset owning households by contrast decreases the steady rate of profit and thus leads to the opposite conclusions

[27] Note the difference to the linear curve $b_o + b_1 V$ derived from the bargained real wage curve which we have used so far.

with respect to output, real wages and the NAIRU rate of employment and thus in particular to a Keynesian savings paradox since the activity level of firms as measured by output per unit of capital (and the rate of employment) will be depressed by a policy that intends to stimulate savings out of profits.

Finally, it is not difficult to calculate that the steady state debt to capital ratio b_o is given by $(g - t_c^n)/\bar{\mu} - h_1 y_o$ which implies that this debt ratio must decrease (and also the ratio $d_o = (B/Y)_o$) if the rate of growth $\bar{\mu}$ of the money supply is increased (since this increases the portion of the deficit that is money-financed). The reaction of these debt ratios with respect to an increase in government expenditures g or a decrease in the government tax ratio t_c^n is however less obvious though a detailed and more specific analysis will generally imply here that government debt as expressed by the considered ratios will rise in such situations.

Though we have represented the theory of price inflation at the beginning of this subsection as being of the cost-push variety it is not difficult to demonstrate that a reinterpretation of this rule for price level adjustment as demand pressure inflation, as in section 2 of the paper, is possible. Starting from the cost-push expression $\beta_p((1+a)\frac{\omega}{F_L(K,L^d)} - 1)$ we can reformulate this expression in the following way

$$\beta_p((1+a)\frac{\omega}{f'(l^d)} - 1) = \beta_p(1+a)(\frac{f'(l^p)}{f'(l^d)} - \frac{1}{1+a}).$$

Making use of a Cobb-Douglas production function $Y = K^\beta L^{1-\beta}$ it is easy to show that

$$\frac{f'(l^p)}{f'(l^d)} = \frac{(1-\beta)K^\beta (L^p)^{-\beta}}{(1-\beta)K^\beta (L^d)^{-\beta}} = (\frac{L^d}{L^p})^\beta = (\frac{Y}{Y^p})^{\beta/(1-\beta)}$$

must hold true then, which implies the demand pressure term

$$\beta_p((1+a)(\frac{Y}{Y^p})^{\beta/(1-\beta)} - \frac{1}{1+a}) = \beta_p(1+a)(U_c^{\beta/(1-\beta)} - \bar{U}_c)$$

for the price Phillips curve considered in equation (6.103) in the place of the term that was used there originally. Assuming $a = 0.1$ (which is not an unreasonable markup value in the case of marked up marginal wage costs) then gives $\bar{U}_c \approx 0.9$ and thus a reasonable value for a rate of capacity utilization that can be considered as 'normal'. The consequence of this brief reconsideration of the price Phillips curve of this subsection is that there may be two possible interpretations applicable to one and the same approach to price level dynamics. Furthermore this reinterpretation also shows that the dynamical structure of the presently considered imperfect competition variant of the KMG growth dynamics may be considered a special case of the KMG growth dynamics of traditional type which we recapitulated in this chapter from a discrete time perspective in section 2, since the real wage and price level dynamics are not very different from each other when viewed from a purely mathematical perspective. We therefore conjecture (but do not prove this here) that the stability features of traditional KMG growth will also hold true for the presently considered model type, concerning the stabilizing role of sluggish adjustment speeds, the existence of Hopf-bifurcations and also the globally stabilizing role of downwardly rigid money wages as they were considered at various places in this book. The dynamics of integrated growth models of imperfect competition on the market for labor and for goods are therefore in its basic format still of the KMG type, though now around a new and interesting steady state solution and with nonlinearities in both the wage and the price Phillips curve right from the start.

The core 2D analysis of the preceding section (where Rose effects were suppressed by complete real wage rigidity) is now extended to a 3D dynamical investigation right from the start, since the real wage is now a dynamic variable. This of course adds Rose-effects to the 2D stagflation cycle analysis of the preceding section, though these effects will here only appear in a special format as we shall see below.

Let us assume again that the quantity adjustment processes work with infinite speed and that the capacity effect of the fluctuating part in the investment function can be ignored so that the labor - capital ratio l can be considered a given magnitude (that is fixed to its steady state value). In such a situation we expect that employment (per unit of capital) l^d is a function of the remaining state variables of the dynamics, which are ω, m, π^e. We therefore assume the functional relationship

$$l^d = l^d(\omega, m, \pi^e), \quad l^d_\omega \gtreqless 0, l^d_m > 0, l^d_{\pi^e} > 0, \quad l^d_o = l^d(\omega_o, m_o, \pi^e_o)$$

where the steady state values employed are those determined in proposition 6.12. The first partial derivative as usual means that output and demand can depend positively on the real wage (if the profitability effect in the investment function is weak) or negatively (if the profitability effect in the investment function is strong), while the positivity of the remaining partial derivatives represent the Keynes and the Mundell effect, respectively. Note that these features also immediately hold with respect to the rate of employment V in the place of l^d, since the ratio l is a given magnitude in the present context.

The differential equations that remain to be considered are:

$$\hat{\omega} = (\omega^*(V) - \omega)/\omega - \beta_p((1+a)\omega/f'(l^d) - 1) \tag{6.123}$$
$$\hat{m} = \Delta\mu - \beta_p((1+a)\omega/f'(l^d) - 1) - \pi^e \tag{6.124}$$
$$\dot{\pi}^e = \beta_{\pi^e_1}(\beta_p((1+a)\omega/f'(l^d) - 1)) \tag{6.125}$$

with l^d, V as functions of the state variables of these dynamics as described above.

Proposition 6.13

Assume that the now constant value of l is given by the steady state value l_o calculated in proposition 6.12. Then:

1. There is a unique interior steady–state solution *of the dynamics (6.123) – (6.125) given by*

$$\omega_o = f'(l^d_o)/(1+a) = \omega^*(l^d_o/l_o), m_o = h_1 y_o, \pi^e_o = \bar{\mu} - n = \Delta\mu$$

where l^d_o, y_o, l_o are all determined as in proposition 6.12.

2. This steady state is locally asymptotically stable if $l^d_\omega > 0$ holds true and if the adjustment speed of the price level β_p is chosen sufficiently large or the speed of adjustment of inflationary expectations β_{π^e} sufficiently low.

3. The steady state loses its stability by way of a Hopf bifurcation if in the situation considered in assertion 2. price adjustment speed is decreased to a sufficient extent and inflationary expectations are adjusted sufficiently fast.

4. In the case $l^d_\omega < 0$, the role of the speed of adjustment of the price level is the reverse of the situations just considered.

The proof represents a routine exercise in view of the many similar situations already considered in this book.

6.4.2 Profit share targets

In this section we follow Rowthorn (1980) and assume that there is a desired profit share target of firms Π^* that depends positively on the rate of capacity utilization U_c that firms experience and that prices are revised with speed β_p according to the gap that exists between the desired and the actual profit share $\Pi^*, \Pi = 1 - \omega/x$. We here assume a given productivity of labor $x = Y/L^d$ and thus return to the case of a fixed proportions technology (again with no technical change) in this subsection on the role of imperfect competition on both the labor market and the market for goods.

Wage-price adjustment equations:

$$\hat{w} = (\omega^*(V) - \omega)/\omega + \pi^e, \quad \omega^{*'}(V) > 0 \tag{6.126}$$

$$\hat{p} = \beta_p(\Pi^*(U_c) - \Pi) + \pi^e, \quad \Pi^{*'} > 0, \; \Pi = 1 - \omega/x \tag{6.127}$$

$$\dot{\pi}^e = \beta_{\pi^e}(\hat{p} - \pi^e). \tag{6.128}$$

The new element is again the theory of price inflation which as said is based on a target share Π^* of firms which depends positively on the rate of capacity utilization they realize in this demand driven extension of the Rowthorn (1980) approach, see also chapter 2. The difference between the target profit share and the actual profit share drives price inflation, embedded into the inflationary climate of expected inflation which is changing in view of actual inflation in an adaptive way once again. The laws of motion are thereby changed in the three instances already discussed in the preceding subsection.

$$\hat{\omega} = (\omega^*(V) - \omega)/\omega - \beta_p(\Pi^*(U_c) - (1 - \omega/x)) \tag{6.129}$$

$$\hat{l} = -i_1(\rho^e - r + \pi^e) - i_2(U_c - \bar{U}_c) \tag{6.130}$$

$$\begin{aligned} \hat{m} &= \Delta\mu - \pi^e - \beta_p(\Pi^*(U_c) - (1 - \frac{\omega}{x})) \\ &- i_1(\rho^e - r + \pi^e) - i_2(U_c - \bar{U}_c) \end{aligned} \tag{6.131}$$

$$\dot{\pi}^e = \beta_{\pi^e_1}\beta_p(\Pi^*(U_c) - (1 - \omega/x)) \tag{6.132}$$

$$\dot{y}^e = \beta_{y^e}(y^d - y^e) - (i_1(\rho^e - r + \pi^e) + i_2(U_c - \bar{U}_c))y^e \tag{6.133}$$

$$\dot{\nu} = y - y^d - (i_1(\rho^e - r + \pi^e) + i_2(U_c - \bar{U}_c) + n)\nu \tag{6.134}$$

$$\hat{V} = \beta_v(V^w - 1), \quad V \leq 1 \tag{6.135}$$

with

$$\begin{aligned}
y &= (1+n\beta_{n^d})y^e + \beta_n(\beta_{n^d}y^e - \nu) \\
y^d &= \omega l^d + (1-s_c)(\rho^e - t_c^n) + i_1(\rho^e - r + \pi^e) + i_2(U_c - \bar{U}_c) + n + \delta + \bar{g} \\
l^d &= y/x \\
V^w &= = l^d/(Vl), \ \ Vl = l^w, \ \ U_c = y/y^p \\
\rho^e &= y^e - \delta - \omega l^d \\
r &= r_0 + (h_1 y - m)/h_2
\end{aligned}$$

Note that the real wage dynamics does not depend on the adjustment speed of wages as in the original KMG growth model and that the NAIRU rate of capacity utilization $\bar{U}_c$ does play no role in this equation, but now appears only in the expressions that represent capital stock growth. The considered real wage dynamics is now driven by income targets by workers as well as firms which have to be made compatible with each other in order to allow for steady growth of the economy. The economically meaningful steady state of the dynamics is again uniquely determined and given by:

Proposition 6.14

Assume that $\Pi^*(1) > \frac{\rho^e+\delta}{y^p} + \frac{n\beta_{n^d}}{1+n\beta_{n^d}}$ *holds (and again* $g \geq t^n$*). Assume furthermore that* $\omega^*(0) = 0, \omega^*(\infty)/x = 1$ *holds with respect to the function* ω^**. Then: There is* a unique interior steady–state solution *of the dynamics (6.129) – (6.135) given by the following expressions:*

$$\rho_o^e = \frac{g - t_c^n + n}{s_c} + t_c^n \tag{6.136}$$

$$y_o^e = y_o^d = \frac{y_o}{1+n\beta_{n^d}}, \quad \nu_o = \beta_{n^d} y_o^e \tag{6.137}$$

$$y_o, l_o \ \ \textit{from} \ \ \rho_o^e = \frac{y_o}{1+n\beta_{n^d}} - \delta - \omega^*(y_o/(xl_o))y_o/x \tag{6.138}$$

$$\textit{and} \ \ 1 = \Pi^*(y_o/y^p) + \omega^*(y_o/(xl_o))/x \tag{6.139}$$

$$l_o^d = y_o/x \tag{6.140}$$

$$\omega_o = \omega^*(y_o/(xl_o)) \tag{6.141}$$

$$V_o = y_o/(xl_o), \quad V_o^w = 1 \tag{6.142}$$

$$U_c^o = y_o/y^p \neq \bar{U}_c \tag{6.143}$$

$$\pi_o^e = \hat{p}_o = \hat{w}_o = \bar{\mu} - n = \Delta\mu \tag{6.144}$$

$$r_o \neq \rho_o^e \ \ \textit{from} \ \ i_1(\rho_o^e - r_o) + i_2(U_c^o - \bar{U}_c) = 0 \tag{6.145}$$

$$m_o = h_1 y_o. \tag{6.146}$$

The above steady state solution is basically of the same qualitative type as the one in the preceding subsection, though now more complicated to determine (on the basis of the rate of profit ρ^e as determined by goods market equilibrium as in the preceding subsection), since now based on a system of two nonlinear equations for the variables l, y based on the definition of this rate of profit and the condition that the target share of workers and firms have to sum to one in order to allow for steady growth of real and nominal magnitudes.

There are again endogenously determined NAIRU levels for the rate of employment and the rate of capacity utilization which in the latter case deviate from the desired rate of capacity utilization of firms.

Proof: In order to show that there is a uniquely determined positive solution of the considered dynamics when all time derivatives are set equal to zero it suffices to show that the two equations that determine y, l in proposition 6.14 allow for such a solution.[28] Multiplying the second of these equations by y_o and adding it to the first gives

$$\Pi^*(\frac{y_o}{y^p}) = \frac{\rho^e+\delta}{y_o} + \frac{n\beta_{n^d}}{1+n\beta_{n^d}}.$$

The right hand side of this equation is strictly increasing in y_o while the left hand side is strictly decreasing on the interval $[0, y^p]$ with values between ∞ and $\frac{\rho^e+\delta}{y^p} + \frac{n\beta_{n^d}}{1+n\beta_{n^d}}$. Due to the assumption $\Pi^*(1) > \frac{\rho^e+\delta}{y^p} + \frac{n\beta_{n^d}}{1+n\beta_{n^d}}$ we thus get that there is a unique positive solution y_o which moreover fulfills $y_o < y^p$.[29]

Inserting the obtained value for y_o into the equation $1 = \Pi^*(y_o/y^p)+\omega^*(y_o/(xl_o))/x$ provides us with one equation in the one remaining unknown l_o which can be uniquely solved for a positive value of l_o if $\omega^*(0) = 0, \omega^*(\infty)/x = 1$ holds true.[30] ∎

The proof of proposition 6.14 also shows that y_o must decrease if the function Π^* shifts upwards, i.e., if firms become more aggressive in pursuing their target share in income distribution (which they then distribute to asset holders in the form of dividends on the basis of their sales expectations). Note that the decrease in y_o, and consequently in $\bar{U}_c^o$, counteracts the increase in Π^* to some extent, but not by so much that there can be actually a fall in the target share of firms due to their increased effort to increase prices in the pursuit of a higher target share. Furthermore, since the share of workers has to fall in this situation there will be a decrease in the steady state rate of their employment as well so that utilization rates both worsen in the presence of a more aggressive pricing policy of firms.

By contrast there is no change in the utilization rate of the capital stock if workers pursue their real wage targets with more aggressiveness, i.e., if their $\omega^*(\cdot)$ schedule shifts upwards. In such a situation we only get that l_o must increase and V_o therefore decrease in order to get workers incomes claims again back in line with a profit share that has remained unchanged.

The core 2D analysis of the preceding section (where Rose effects were suppressed by complete real wage rigidity) is again extended to a 3D dynamical investigation right from the start, since the real wage is a dynamic variable now. Let us now make again the same simplifying assumptions as in the preceding subsection, i.e. regarding the labor - capital ratio l as a given magnitude due to an infinitely fast quantity adjustment process. Then output again can be expressed as a function of the three state variables ω, m and π^e:

$$y = y(\omega, m, \pi^e), \quad y_\omega \gtreqless 0, y_m > 0, y_{\pi^e} > 0, \quad l^d = y/x.$$

[28]We of course as always assume that parameters are chosen such that ρ^e, r are both positive in the steady state.

[29]Note here that the function $\Pi^*(\cdot)$ is a mapping into $[0,1]$ in order to be economically meaningful.

[30]We assume that this function is determined such that $V_o = y_o/(xl_o)$ holds true.

The differential equations that remain to be considered are then

$$\hat{\omega} = (\omega^*(V) - \omega)/\omega - \beta_p(\Pi^*(U_c) - (1 - \omega/x)) \quad (6.147)$$

$$\hat{m} = \Delta\mu - \pi^e - \beta_p(\Pi^*(U_c) - (1 - \frac{\omega}{x})) \quad (6.148)$$

$$\dot{\pi}^e = \beta_{\pi_1^e}\beta_p(\Pi^*(U_c) - (1 - \omega/x)) \quad (6.149)$$

with U_c, V as functions of the state variables of these dynamics as described above.

Proposition 6.15

Assume that the function $y = y(\omega, m, \pi^e)$ defined above fulfills $y_o = y(\omega_o, m_o, \pi_o^e)$ with respect to the steady state values defined in proposition 6.14. Assume furthermore that the now constant value of l is given by the steady state value l_o calculated in proposition 6.14. Then:

1. *There is* a unique interior steady–state solution *of the dynamics (6.147) – (6.149) which is given by the steady state values for the state variables of these dynamics determined in proposition 6.14.*

2. *This steady state is locally asymptotically stable if $l_\omega^d > 0$ holds true and if the price adjustment speed β_p is chosen sufficiently large and the speed of adjustment of inflationary expectations β_{π^e} sufficiently low.*

3. *The steady state loses its stability by way of a Hopf bifurcation if in the situation considered in assertion 2. The price adjustment speed is decreased to a sufficient extent or inflationary expectations are adjusted sufficiently fast.*

4. *If the case $l_\omega^d < 0$ holds, the role of the speed of adjustment of the price level is the reverse of the situations just considered.*

Proof: Assertion 1 is an obvious consequence of the steady state calculations provided in proposition 6.14 while the remaining stability assertions are a routine exercise in view of the many similar situations already considered in this book. ■

Note here also that the only change in these dynamics with respect to the preceding subsection concerns the price level adjustment rule (to be employed in all three equations of these dynamics) which is now given by

$$\beta_p(\Pi^*(l^d/(xy^p)) + \omega/x - 1)$$

in the place of the formerly used rule

$$\beta_p((1+a)\omega/f'(l^d) - 1).$$

This change is however only of a quantitative nature, since the qualitative dependence on the function l^d is the same in both cases.

6.4.3 Markup adjustments

As in the preceding subsection we here assume that production exhibits fixed proportions with no technical change and thus consider again the given ratios x, y^p as far as capacity utilization and employment functions are concerned. We now reintroduce demand pressure (on the market for goods) into the dynamics of the price level, yet here in the indirect way that firms apply a given markup a at each moment in time, which is subject to revision in view of the state of the goods market as measured by the rate of capacity utilization of firms in its deviation from the desired rate of capacity utilization.

Wage-price adjustment equations.

$$\begin{aligned} \hat{w} &= (\omega^*(V)-\omega)/\omega+\pi^e, \quad \omega^{*'}(V)>0 && (6.150)\\ p &= (1+a)w/x, \quad \widehat{1+a}=\beta_a(U_c-\bar{U}_c), \quad U_c=y/y^p && (6.151)\\ \dot{\pi}^e &= \beta_{\pi^e}(\hat{p}-\pi^e) && (6.152) \end{aligned}$$

Expected inflation has now been completely removed from the adjustment equation concerning the price level, so that only adaptive expectations of workers are now present in the model as far as rates of inflation are concerned. The equations shown give rise to the following types of real wage and price level dynamics:

$$\begin{aligned} \hat{\omega} &= -\widehat{(1+a)} = -\beta_a(U_c-\bar{U}_c)\\ \hat{p} &= \hat{w}+\widehat{(1+a)} = (\omega^*(V)-\omega)/\omega+\pi^e+\beta_a(U_c-\bar{U}_c). \end{aligned}$$

The integrated growth dynamics that results in this case reads:

$$\begin{aligned} \hat{\omega} &= -\beta_a(U_c-\bar{U}_c) && (6.153)\\ \hat{l} &= -i_1(\rho^e-r+\pi^e)-i_2(U_c-\bar{U}_c) && (6.154)\\ \hat{m} &= \Delta\mu-((\omega^*(V)-\omega)/\omega+\pi^e\\ &+ \beta_a(U_c-\bar{U}_c))-i_1(\rho^e-r+\pi^e)-i_2(U_c-\bar{U}_c) && (6.155)\\ \dot{\pi}^e &= \beta_{\pi_1^e}((\omega^*(V)-\omega)/\omega+\pi^e+\beta_a(U_c-\bar{U}_c)) && (6.156)\\ \dot{y}^e &= \beta_{y^e}(y^d-y^e)-(i_1(\rho^e-r+\pi^e)+i_2(U_c-\bar{U}_c))y^e && (6.157)\\ \dot{\nu} &= y-y^d-(i_1(\rho^e-r+\pi^e)+i_2(U_c-\bar{U}_c)+n)\nu && (6.158)\\ \hat{V} &= \beta_v(V^w-1), \quad V\le 1 && (6.159) \end{aligned}$$

with

$$\begin{aligned} y &= (1+n\beta_{n^d})y^e+\beta_n(\beta_{n^d}y^e-\nu)\\ y^d &= \omega l^d+(1-s_c)(\rho^e-t_c^n)+i_1(\rho^e-r+\pi^e)+i_2(U_c-\bar{U}_c)+n+\delta+\bar{g}\\ l^d &= y/x\\ V^w &= = l^d/(Vl), \ V=l^w/l, \ U_c=y/y^p\\ \rho^e &= y^e-\delta-\omega l^d\\ r &= r_0+(h_1y-m)/h_2. \end{aligned}$$

The equation describing the dynamics of real wages is now considerably simplified, as it now depends on the state of the goods market solely (while conventional Phillips curves tend to give the labor market the central role in this law of motion). As the following proposition shows there is no zero root hysteresis present in the current dynamical model, despite the impression that may be created by the formulation of the markup dynamics.

Proposition 6.16

Assume $g \geq t^n$. Then: There is a unique interior steady–state solution *of the dynamics (6.153) – (6.159) which is given by the following expressions:*

$$\begin{aligned}
\rho_o^e &= \frac{g - t_c^n + n}{s_c} + t_c^n && (6.160)\\
y_o &= \bar{U}_c y^p, \quad l_o^d = y_o/x, \quad U_c^o = \bar{U}_c && (6.161)\\
y_o^e &= y_o^d = \frac{y_0}{1 + n\beta_{n^d}}, \quad \nu_o = \beta_{n^d} y_o^e && (6.162)\\
\omega_o &= (y_o^e - \delta - \rho_o^e)/l_o^d && (6.163)\\
a_o &= x/\omega_o - 1 && (6.164)\\
V_o \ \textit{from} \ & \omega_o = \omega^*(V_o) && (6.165)\\
\pi_o^e &= \hat{p}_o = \hat{w}_o = \bar{\mu} - n = \Delta\mu && (6.166)\\
r_o &= \rho_o^e, \quad m_o = h_1 y_o && (6.167)\\
l_o &= l_o^d/V_o, \quad V_o^w = 1 && (6.168)
\end{aligned}$$

These steady state calculations reveal that we are now nearly back at the steady state characterizations of the traditional KMG growth model, up to the determination of the NAIRU level for the rate of employment which remains to be determined by the bargained real wage equation, indeed closer than to the imperfect competition model with a given income distribution. With respect to dynamic analysis we again only consider the basic 3D extension of the 2D stagflation model type which adds Rose type real wage dynamics to the consideration of the interaction of the Keynes and the Mundell effect.

Again, we have now a three-dimensional system instead of the two-dimensional one of the preceding section, where Rose effects were suppressed by complete real wage rigidity. As in the preceding two subsections we now can write real output as a function of ω, m and π^e due to the assumption of an infinite speed of the quantity adjustment processes:

$$y = y(\omega, m, \pi^e), \quad y_\omega \gtreqless 0, y_m > 0, y_{\pi^e} > 0, \quad l^d = y/x.$$

The resulting dynamics are then given by the following equations:

$$\begin{aligned}
\hat{\omega} &= -\beta_a(U_c - \bar{U}_c) && (6.169)\\
\hat{m} &= \Delta\mu - ((\omega^*(V) - \omega)/\omega + \pi^e + \beta_a(U_c - \bar{U}_c)) && (6.170)\\
\dot{\pi}^e &= \beta_{\pi_1^e}((\omega^*(V) - \omega)/\omega + \pi^e + \beta_a(U_c - \bar{U}_c)) && (6.171)
\end{aligned}$$

with $U_c = y/y^p$ and $V = l^d/l_o = y/(xl_o)$.

Proposition 6.17

Assume that the function $y = y(\omega, m, \pi^e)$ defined above fulfills $y_o = y(\omega_o, m_o, \pi^e_o)$ with respect to the steady state values defined in proposition 6.16. Assume furthermore that the now constant value of l is given by the steady state value l_o calculated in proposition 6.16. Then:

1. *There is* a unique interior steady–state solution *of the dynamics (6.169) – (6.171) which is a subset of the steady state values determined in proposition 6.16.*

2. *This steady state is locally asymptotically stable if $l^d_\omega = y_\omega/x > 0$ holds true and if price adjustment speed β_p is chosen sufficiently large and the speed of adjustment of inflationary expectations β_{π^e} sufficiently low.*

3. *The steady state loses its stability by way of a Hopf bifurcation if in the situation considered in assertion 2. price adjustment speed is decreased to a sufficient extent or inflationary expectations are adjusted sufficiently fast.*

4. *In the case $l^d_\omega < 0$ holds, the role of the speed of adjustment of the price level is the reverse of the situations just considered.*

Proof: Assertion 1 is an obvious consequence of the steady state calculations provided in proposition 6.16 while the remaining stability assertions are a routine exercise in view of the many similar situations already considered in this book. ■

6.5 Summary

In this chapter various aspects of imperfect competition have been included into the KMG framework. After reformulating it in discrete time in section 6.2 and extending it with regard to an endogenization of the NAIRU, implying hysteresis in the dynamics, its former wage-price- sector has been replaced in section 6.3 by the two key elements of the basic imperfect competition model of Carlin and Soskice (1990), i.e. the so-called bargained-real-wage curve and the price-determined-real-wage curve. With the help of some simplifying assumptions the resulting model could, in a next step, be reduced to a 2 D subdynamics, whose stability properties could be considerably improved by the additional assumption of a kinked Phillips-curve. After allowing again for sluggish adjustments of output and the workforce of firms, a 4 D system emerged, which again turned out to be stable for low adjustment speeds, a result, that was then shown to hold also for the original 6 D model in the case of a low accelerator and a high adjustment speed of sales expectations. In the next section, 6.4, the assumption of a linear production function is replaced by a substitutional one with the consequence of a now fluctuating wage share. After considering the changes caused by this, a further modification of firms' pricing behavior has been considered in form of profit share targets in the tradition of Rowthorn (1980). In a final subsection the consequences of a variable markup factor, depending on the rate of capacity utilization, have been analyzed.

Up to this point, imperfect competition on the goods market and on the labor market have been introduced into the KMG model in a variety of ways, thereby capturing important features of actual market economies. Further steps in this direction might include other deviations from perfect markets. In this context one might think of various forms of credit rationing arising from incomplete information. Thus, moral hazard and adverse selection effects could be integrated into an appropriately modified KMG framework with consequences reaching from capital accumulation to government policy issues. This, however, is left to future research and we now turn to part III of the book where the KMG growth model is considerably reformulated and extended towards a continuous time macroeconometric model of a small open economy.

Part III

The Perspective: Theoretical Aspects of Modern Macroeconometric Model Building

Part III of the book provides an important perspective for our future work, since it attempts to show in detail that there is now available a close relationship or link between theoretical structural macrodynamics and applied macroeconometric model building. There are model types that either rely on labor market disequilibrium solely (AS-AD approaches) or allow for both labor and goods market disequilibria.

In this last part of the book we start from the other side and make use of the integrated structures of structural macroeconometric models. We want to find out where the structure of our working model and its extensions should find further improvement and extension. To solve this task is considerably easier today than it was in the sixties and seventies when structural macroeconometric models were very popular. The large models of early Keynesian type tended to be presented in a way that could not easily transferred to theoretical core representations. The models lacked a growth perspective and steady state reference situations and were also biased towards a detailed treatment of quantity relationships while price, wage and interest rate dynamics were not considered in an equally detailed way. Since then the situation has however changed significantly and presentations of structural macroeconometric models now tend to be small scale, are assuming intertemporally optimizing behavior of economic agents, include more details on stock and flow constraints, are more explicit in the way they allow for disequilibrium adjustment processes and attempt to include long-run and in particular steady state considerations, see sections 7.10 and 9.8 for more details.

As this book has shown so far we have available now, on the one hand, high order disequilibrium growth theories with detailed treatments of labor and goods market adjustment processes, and, on the other hand, better and more complete representations of the core structure of applied macrodynamic models to which the high order theoretical dynamics can be compared and which should lead to further structural improvements in both approaches. To show how this task can be approached is the purpose of this part III of the book.

In chapter 7 we therefore start from a very detailed presentation of a prototype modern macroeconometric model, provided in Powell and Murphy (1997), and transform this presentation into the continuous time structure of our theoretical disequilibrium growth models. We suppress econometric details but spell out all stock and flow budget equations in order to have all feedback relationships under explicit control. We first provide the accounting framework in section 7.2, then go on to fill this framework with behavioral assumptions concerning two types of households, firms and the government in sections 7.3 - 7.5 with a separate treatment of price and quantity adjustments and of asset markets in sections 7.6, 7.7, however. The sections 7.3 to 7.7 also carefully compare this significant extension of our disequilibrium growth model to the disequilibrium model presented by Powell and Murphy (1997). In section 7.10, we consider the currently widely used alternative to disequilibrium macroeconometric model building, the McKibbin and Sachs (1991) model for the US economy, which is of the AS-AD type and thus not as large scale as the Powell and Murphy (1997) approach with its labor and goods market disequilibrium scenarios.

The purpose of chapter 8 then is to show, in sections 8.2 and 8.3, that our theoretical growth dynamics of chapter 7 exhibits a meaningful intensive form or state variable representation, from which the equations for steady state calculations are obtained in section 8.4. The obtained 39D dynamics and steady state expressions are however too complicated still to allow for analytical or numerical investigation at the present stage. We therefore introduce in section 8.5 simplifying assumptions that allow to reduce our model to a 22 dimensional dynamics in section 8.6. A more thorough treatment of the steady state is then given in sections 8.6 - 8.7. The general finding is, however, that a generic treatment of the type we have performed in parts I and II of the book should be possible, but that at present only subsystems of the full dynamics could be investigated in order to gain first insights into the analytical and numerical features of such a high order dynamics.

It is the purpose of chapter 9 to introduce such further simplification and to show what types of theoretical and numerical investigations are then possible on the dynamics of the general macro model of chapters 7 and 8. Yet, this model is still of dimension 18. These 18D core dynamics are derived in sections 9.2 and 9.3 now with an explicit presentation of the laws of motion, in section 9.3, as well as a uniquely determined interior steady state solution of the 18D dynamics in section 9.4. An important way of analyzing these 18 D dynamics is given by the so-called switch off / on methodology which studies by way of appropriate assumption subsystems of the full dynamics and their partial feedback mechanisms and then recombines the partial dynamics again in order to investigate the interaction of the important feedback chains present in the 18D core dynamics. This method is demonstrated on the 9D level analytically as well as numerically in section 9.5. Section 9.6 adds in this way policy issues and section 9.7 reintegrates the asset market dynamics of the full 18D structure.

Our investigations of the core 18D dynamics is closed with brief numerical investigations of the full dynamics in section 9.8. We employ eigenvalue diagrams by which the stabilizing or destabilizing role of the partial macroeconomic feedback mechanisms can be investigated. Those feedback mechanisms can be tested as to their relevance in the full dynamics. The general finding here is that partial analysis often allow a good guess on what will happen in the full dynamics if the adjustment speeds of the price level, the wage level, quantities, expectations, and asset price are increased. The prominent feedback mechanisms represented by the Keynes-effect, Mundell-effect, Rose-effect, Metzler-effect and more, thus shape the presently considered 18D dynamics in important ways that are generally not considered in applied work and that lack any elaborate analysis in the theoretical literature on macrodynamics.

We close this chapter, in section 9.9, with a detailed consideration of the structure of the Fair model for the US economy which, as we shall see, provides another very important example for the application of a high order disequilibrium growth approach, concerning labor as well as product markets. This closing section shows that there remains much to done, but that there is a promising perspective, in the comparison of high order models of growth in disequilibrium and applied disequilibrium growth analysis, which may improve both macrodynamic theory as well as macroeconometric structural model building.

Chapter 7

Applied Disequilibrium Growth Theory

7.1 Introduction

In this chapter we extend the hierarchical structured continuous-time models of Keynesian monetary growth, introduced with increasing dimension in Chiarella and Flaschel (1999a,d) for the closed and the open economy, into the direction of the macroeconometric Murphy model for the Australian economy, i.e., toward an empirically motivated modeling of a small open economy with a Keynesian short- and medium-run, but with also classical and monetarist features and adjustment processes in the medium- as well as in the long-run behavior of the economy.[1] The Murphy model, see Powell and Murphy (1997) for its detailed description, and our theoretical reformulation of it for the case of fixed proportions in production in Chiarella and Flaschel (1999e,f), therefore blends demand and supply side approaches into an integrated and coherent whole with a – from a theoretical point of view – very detailed description of the structure of a small open economy, like Australia.

In the present chapter we build on and modify our reformulation of the Murphy model in Chiarella and Flaschel (1999e,f), which in some components was still very different from the Murphy model, by replacing fixed proportions in production with neoclassical smooth input and output substitution, by allowing for wealth and interest income effects in consumption demand and by allowing for some flexibility in the world market prices for the imports and the exports of the considered economy. It is our aim to show that this makes the dynamics (and the description of its temporary equilibrium positions) of the considered economy much more involved, without however altering the general philosophy underlying this model of Keynesian disequilibrium growth with neoclassical medium run and long run supply side influences.

Further modifications concern the money market where we no longer assume a Taylor type interest rate policy rule as in Chiarella and Flaschel (1999e), there based on a complete neglect of cash balances, but return to the traditional description of money market equilibrium (by way of an LM curve) as in Powell and Murphy (1997). However, we have

[1]This chapter is based on the material presented in Chiarella, Flaschel, Groh, Köper and Semmler (1999a).

to extend the there employed money demand function of Cagan type to the two household types (workers and pure asset holders) assumed in our approach, but will still neglect money holdings of firms and of the government. This change of the model (away from a Taylor rule) induces a number of further changes in the model's structure which will be explained when the model's equations are introduced in section 7.3.

An important change, besides the complications now involved in the production decision of firms, concern the consumption behavior of workers and asset holders where we now assume, based on intertemporal considerations, for both types of households a life cycle approach, and thus introduce wealth besides disposable income as a determinant of their total consumption. These changes make the dynamical structure of the model much more involved, since they imply that personal wealth allocation feeds back into the goods market and thus into the core dynamics of the model, as discussed in Chiarella and Flaschel (1999f) and Chiarella, Flaschel and Zhu (1999a). The dynamics of these models are thus extended towards much longer feedback chains and are also augmented by important further state variables which increase their dimension significantly.

Still further changes concern the formulation of a price index formula which now includes housing rents and which makes the money wage Phillips curve more complicated in its appearance. Altogether the model will therefore and on the one hand depart further from the possibility of an analytical treatment, but will, on the other hand, move closer to the structure of the original Murphy model.

The present chapter approaches the investigation of such a model type still from the macrotheoretic perspective developed and employed in Chiarella and Flaschel (1999a-g), see also Chiarella, Flaschel and Zhu (1999a,b), and thus mirrors the approach chosen in Powell and Murphy (1997) only to some degree. We will derive in subsequent chapters complete intensive form representations and also complete steady state descriptions of the model considered in this chapter in structural form (extensive level form) solely. Yet in chapter 8 we will here only derive an 18D core dynamics of the model of chapter 7 which allows for numerical investigations at the present stage of model formulation, thereby continuing the discussion of section 3.4.3, and which also allows its further decomposition into still smaller subdynamics as they were to some extent discussed in part I of this book, see chapter 9. We will there study the model with respect to the partial stabilizing or destabilizing feedback chains it still contains on this 18D level. We plan to further investigate their working in the full 18D model and also in much more general cases (22D to 39D) from the numerical point of view, in particular as in Barnett and He (1998) for the case of a continuous time model for the UK. We will add further extrinsic nonlinearities to this model type if global economic boundedness is not obtained by the basically intrinsic nonlinearities it already contains. All this however refers to future work which is so far only partly finished and which should significantly increase our understanding on the working of the feedback mechanism as they are present in structural macroeconometric models for the Australian economy (the here considered Murphy model) as well as many others, as for example in the Fair model for the US economy, see Fair (1984, 1994) for a detailed discussion which shows the close relationship between the Fair and the Murphy approach to labor and goods market disequilibrium dynamics (though the former model type does not yet include factor growth and technological change and thus fully developed steady state reference path solutions.

We have added to the structural form of the Murphy model a complete set of fully specified budget equations for all sectors (including two types of households in addition) and thereby take account of all feedback structures, in particular with respect to asset accumulation, implied by such budget restrictions. Furthermore all equations are specified in a consistent way from the perspective of dimensional analysis and are nevertheless chosen as linear as possible in this continuous-time reformulation of the Murphy model. This allows for a discussion of intrinsic (natural) nonlinearities first, besides the empirically motivated nonlinearities present in production, through smooth input and output substitution, and in Cagan type money demand function to be removed from the model only in its intensive form investigation in chapter 8. In the present book no attempts are made to design further nonlinearities that may keep the economy viable should it depart too much from the steady state in its naturally nonlinear design, see chapter 3 for brief discussions of such an addition of extrinsic (behavioral) nonlinearities later on. As stated we shall however rely in this theoretical reconsideration of the Murphy model on a neoclassical production function (with smooth substitution between three factors of production and two outputs), which in fact introduces a fairly complex nonlinear subsystem on the production side of the economy, but which can nevertheless be interpreted as in the linear case of fixed proportions in production treated in Chiarella and Flaschel (1999e,f), i.e., varying rates of capacity utilization of the capital stock will also be present in the present approach to applied disequilibrium growth theory.

On the one hand, this choice of a starting point for the analysis of the dynamic properties of small structural macroeconometric models of open economies (with about one hundred equations) thus allows us, on the one hand, to study the implications of its intrinsic or 'natural' nonlinearities first, as they derive from unavoidable growth rate formulations, products or quotients of state variables, but also from standard nonlinearities in production and in the description of the money market. We have already seen analytically in part I and II, and shall find this here again to hold true numerically, that viability or boundedness of the dynamics, and in particular convergence to the steady state, will often depend on the assumption of sufficiently low adjustment speeds for quantities, prices and expectations, augmented now also by sufficiently high substitution elasticities in production, while local and even global stability will normally get lost if the adjustment speed of certain quantities, prices and the expectational mechanisms are chosen sufficiently high.

On the other hand, our approach allows us to introduce further extrinsic nonlinearities into the assumed technological or behavioral relationships in a systematic way later on, as a (theoretically reflected) response of the economy to the specific instabilities that are observed in the working of the basic form of the model, often already known from partial dynamic macro-models. For example, a kink in the money wage Phillips curve, as discussed in chapters 2 and 3, which reflects the institutional fact that money wages may rise quickly in the boom but will only fall slowly – if at all – in the depression, is often already sufficient to avoid the inflationary instability that derives in such models from the existence of so-called Mundell effects, which are generally neglected in the theoretical debate on Phillips-curves, inflation and stagflation.

We therefore will attempt in the chapters of part III, and in future work, to slowly proceed to a detailed and systematic theoretical and numerical analysis of the dynamic features (attractors, transients, steady states, etc.) of complete and coherently formulated structural macroeconometric models, including applications to actual economies, a theoretical discussion which so far has basically been lacking in the literature[2] We believe that this type of investigation (and more) is urgently needed with respect to applied macroeconomic model building, in particular since detailed numerical investigations are generally not possible by means of the simulation software available for prominent examples of structural macroeconometric model building for the USA (Fair), Germany (Westphal), Australia (Murphy) and other countries.

Since this chapter builds to some extent on the extensive form disequilibrium model structure considered in Chiarella and Flaschel (1999e), by modifying certain module descriptions in it, we refer the reader to this work for further detailed comments that apply to such modeling in general. In the next section we however provide as in Chiarella and Flaschel (1999e) an overview on the structure of the real and the financial part of the model, characterizing the sectors, markets and activities that will be included into our following model building, in both table form and from the viewpoint of the system of national accounts, thereby providing a detailed introduction into the notation that is used in the following. In sections 3 - 10 we then present the structural equations of the model (in their extensive form) by way of an appropriate subdivision into important modules that build up the model. Section 11 finally gives an outlook on what can be done with this model type when it is reduced from extensive form to per unit of capital expressions, and thus to intensive form, i.e., to the laws of motion for the state variables of the model (supplemented by definitional and structural equations needed for a full description of the model in per unit of capital terms), a form of the model that we shall exploit in the following chapters only on the basis of simplifying assumptions that allow in particular for numerical investigations and subsystem analysis at the present stage of the investigation.

We have already observed close relationships between the theoretical KMG approach of Chiarella and Flaschel (1999e,f), and its various extensions, and the Murphy model for the Australian economy in this earlier work. We now move much closer in this chapter to the structure of the Murphy model of the Australian economy by allowing for smooth factor and output substitution in production in particular, the basis of the 'neoclassical heart' of the Murphy model. We show that this addition (and also the now included wealth effects and further more or less secondary ones) will not modify significantly the qualitative structure of the KMG approach to disequilibrium growth with its Keynesian short- and medium-run with over- or underutilized labor and capital and its classical and monetarist features in the medium- and the long-run, despite the fact that the presentation in Powell and Murphy (1997) seems to be on the surface very different from ours as far as the production block of the considered economy is concerned. We shall see in fact that this is only a difference in presentation, but not really a difference in substance. Of course, adding more flexibility in production and more interdependence in other parts of the economy will change its quantitative features in more or less important ways, and also allows for new questions such as whether labor usage can be substituted for energy consumption in production in the medium- and the long-run by lowering for example payroll taxes and by increasing taxes on imported energy commodities. This and other topics will be treated in future work to be built on the present part of the book.

---

[2]See however Barnett and He (1998) for an interesting approach to the analysis of macroeconometric models from the theoretical perspective.

7.2 A general framework for modeling disequilibrium growth

In the following we provide a survey of the structure of the economy to be modeled in this chapter that is closely related – but in significant other ways not identical – to the description of the Australian economy given in Powell and Murphy (1997). The aim of the present chapter is to present an integrated first order continuous time model of disequilibrium growth, which in its general form gives rise to an autonomous system of 39 differential equations, see also Chiarella, Flaschel, Groh, Köper and Semmler (1999b), still from the theoretical perspective, where all sectors are fully specified with respect to their behavior and their budget constraints. This is still done from the viewpoint of integrated theoretical models of disequilibrium growth we discussed in part I and II, thereby providing a bridge between the KMG type monetary growth models of these parts and the Powell and Murphy (1997) approach. Whenever needed from the theoretical perspective we therefore deviate from the applied framework given in Powell and Murphy (1997). We will comment on the differences between their discrete time macroeconometric model and the continuous time model of this chapter briefly in sections where we present the structural form of our model.

The purpose of the present section is to provide the reader with a short but complete guide to the modeled economy. In subsection 2.1 we discuss the basics of the economy's structure and we supply in subsection 2.2 a complete national accounting system for the framework (including the notation) on which the model is to be built in the next section. These various views on the framework used will include some repetitions which however may help in the understanding of what is to be modeled in the next section.

7.2.1 The assumed structure of the economy

To provide a survey on the economy's structure we pick up the often utilized separation of the economy into two parts: On the one hand the real part concerning goods and labor markets, and on the other hand the financial part concerning money and other financial assets. For convenience we employ a tabular representation.[3]

We begin with the real part of economy in table 7.1. The columns of the table refer to the different goods in our model: labor, non traded goods, exports, imports and dwellings. The first four rows refer to the considered sectors: two types of households (asset holders and workers), firms, and the government (including the monetary authority). We distinguish between workers and asset holders to model the role of income distribution explicitly, and this not only by way of a time dependent aggregate consumption function as in Powell and Murphy (1997), and will study the implications of this aspect of our model carefully in future work to be based on this chapter. Furthermore, assuming for the time being only two types of households is clearly best done in the way here considered, since these are the two fundamental activities (supplying work or credit) in which households can be engaged in capitalistic market economies. Of course, intermediate types of behavior must be introduced later on, but will in fact then only mean that the number of household types must be increased beyond 2.

[3]See also the appendix for the employed notation.

	Labor	Non traded Goods	Exports	Imports	Dwellings
Workers	$L = \alpha_l L_1$	C_w^g	–	–	C_w^h
Asset holders	–	C_c, I_h	–	–	C_h^s, I_h
Firms	L_f^d, L_f^w	$Y^p, Y, I, \mathcal{I}$	X^a	J^a	–
Government	L_g^d	G	–	–	–
Prices	w, w^b, w^u, w^r	$p_v = (1+\tau_v)p_y$	$p_x = ep_x^*$	$p_m = (1+\tau_m)ep_m^*$	p_h, p_y
Expectations	$\pi = \hat{p}_v^e$	$\pi = \hat{p}_v^e$	–	–	$\pi = \hat{p}_v^e$
Stocks	L_1	K, N	–	–	K_h
Growth	$\hat{L}_1 = n$	$\hat{K} = I/K - \delta$ $\dot{N} = Y - Y^d$	–	–	$\hat{K}_h = I_h/K_h - \delta_h$

Table 7.1: The real part of the economy.

Other important items of this table are the goods' prices and their expected values (their expected rates of change) as well as the real stocks of the economy and their rates of growth. Note that the foreign countries do not appear explicitly in the table. But by allowing for exports and imports it is clear that imports for the home country reappear as exports for the foreign countries and vice versa. So we have to introduce prices for those goods that are sold and purchased abroad: p_x^* denotes the foreign price (in US \$) for the exported good of the domestic economy and p_m^* denotes the price (in US \$) that firms have to pay for the imported commodity they use in their production activity. Prices in domestic currency are denoted by ep_x^* and $e(1+\tau_m)p_m^*$ where e denotes the nominal exchange rate (\$A/\$) and τ_m the taxation rate on imported commodities (here there are no taxes with respect to exports).

Only workers supply labor. The amount of their labor supply L depends on the number of workers in working age L_1 and the participation rate α_l. Therefore the dimension of the supplied labor L is a number of persons. In contrast to this the dimension of L_f^d, the labor time demanded by firms per week is measured in hours. This latter expression is used for modeling over– and under–utilization of the labor force L_f^w employed in the firms' sector. To relate the supply of workers and the demand of labor time we thus consider the link to the workforce of firms L_f^w, the number of persons that are employed by firms. By assuming a normal work time (of say 35 hours per week) for a working person then provides the connection between L_f^w, a stock variable, and L_f^d, a flow variable by which over- and undertime work can be measured. The column of labor lacks an entry in the row of asset holders because asset holder do not supply labor nor do they have a demand for it. The government needs labor L_g^d to provide public goods. But in contrast to firms we assume that there is no need for over– or under–utilization of the workforce in the government sector, since there is no demand constraint for the supply of public services.

There is a set of prices for labor: w is the wage that workers get for a time unit of labor. However, w is not the amount that firms or the public sector have to pay for a unit of labor, because they have to pay the payroll taxes in addition. The wage including payroll tax is denoted by w^b. The income of unemployed and workers beyond working age can also be viewed as a kind of wage and has thus also been included into the column representing the labor market. They are denoted by w^u and w^r. Expectations about wage changes are based for simplicity on the expected growth rate $\hat{p}_v^e$ of prices p_v. The growth rate of the stock of workers of working age is assumed to be a constant: n (which also applies to the growth rate of the number of young persons, under 16, and the number of retired workers).

The non traded good serves for the workers and the asset holders as a consumption good, in the amounts C_w^g and C_c, respectively. For the latter it also serves as investment good for the supply of dwelling services. The firms' sector is related to the domestic good in two ways. It produces the quantity Y of the non–traded good, restricted by the full capacity output of firms, Y^p. Secondly the firms use the domestic good for inventory investments ($\mathcal{I}$ denotes the amount of planned inventory investments) as well as for gross business fixed capital investments I. The government uses the domestic good for public consumption. The prices for the non–traded good can be denoted inclusive or exclusive of the value added tax, by p_v and p_y, respectively, and inflationary expectations refer to the expected growth rate of consumer prices p_v. Stocks of the domestic good are held only by the firms' sector. The fixed business capital stock is K and the actual level of inventories N. The growth rates of these magnitudes are provided by $\hat{K} = \dot{K}/K = I/K - \delta$, with δ as the rate of depreciation, and $\hat{N} = \dot{N}/N$.

The exported good X is the second output good of the firms. It cannot be sold on the domestic market. We assume, that unlimited amounts of this good, produced by our small open economy, can be sold to foreign countries at a price p_x that depends on the price abroad and the exchange rate. The imported good J^a is only for the firms to use. They need it as an input factor for production. Its domestic price depends on the exchange rate e the world market price p_m^* and the rate of import taxation τ_m.

Asset holders supply the dwelling services C_h^s. For simplicity we assume that only workers demand dwelling services C_w^h, while asset owners can consume the domestically produced good in the form of houses if they desire to do so. The domestic good also serves for gross investments into dwellings I_h made by asset owners. So we have to consider two prices: p_h, the rent for dwelling services and p_y, the price for a unit of investment into dwellings (which is not subject to value added tax). Again the expectations about these prices are based on their expected growth rates (which is the same for the consumer as well as producer price level, since there is a constant percentage of value added tax added to producer prices). The capital stock in the housing sector is K_h and its growth rate $I_h/K_h - \delta_h$ depends on gross investment and depreciation.

Now we have to consider the financial part of the economy. The rows of table 7.2 give all financial assets considered in our model. They consist of money, short–term bonds, long–term bonds equities and foreign bonds. The first four rows show, how the assumed sectors of the economy interact on all these asset markets. Note that only flows are considered in these rows.

The first row has only two entries. We assume that the only way workers do in fact participate in the assets markets is by holding money and saving deposits (short-term bonds) and so only changes in their stock of money $\dot{M}_w$ and saving deposits $\dot{B}_w$ is of interest here. In contrast to this the households of asset holders can spread their financial surplus to all kinds of assets: money, bonds (short and long term as well as foreign long term bonds), and equities. The latter are issued by the firms' sector and provide the only way of financing the deficits firms are facing. Bonds are issued only by the government and the same holds true for money which is issued by the monetary authority via open market operations.

	Money	Short-term Bonds	Long-term Bonds	Equities	Foreign Bonds
Workers	$\dot{M}_w$	$\dot{B}_w$	–	–	–
Asset holders	$\dot{M}_c$	$\dot{B}_c$	$\dot{B}_1^l$	$\dot{E}$	$\dot{B}_2^l$
Firms	–	–	–	$\dot{E}$	–
Government	$\dot{M}$ $[\dot{R}]$	$\dot{B}$	$\dot{B}^l$	–	–
Prices	1	1 $[r]$	$p_b = 1/r_l$	p_e	$ep_b^* = e \cdot 1/r_l^*$
Expectations	–	–	$\pi_b = \hat{p}_b^e$	$\pi_e = \hat{p}_e^e$	$\epsilon = \hat{e}^e$
Stocks	$M = M_w + M_c, R$	$B = B_w + B_c$	B^l, B_1^l	E	B_2^l
Growth	$\hat{M}, \hat{R}$	$\hat{B}$	$\hat{B}^l, \hat{B}_1^l$	$\hat{E}$	$\hat{B}_2^l$

Table 7.2: The financial part of the economy.

The price of short term bonds is unity and the corresponding interest rate is r. The price of long term bond is $1/r_l$ and the interest consists of the annual payment of one dollar (i.e. the case of consols or perpetuities). The stock of foreign reserves R of the central bank represents another important stock of money, which however will not be subject to endogenous changes as the model is formulated in the present chapter, where the budget equations of the private sector will always imply (despite a temporarily given nominal exchange rate e) equilibrium on the market for foreign exchange. Of course, this does not exclude the possibility that the central bank adopts an active exchange rate policy in the case it is dissatisfied with the evolution of the exchange rate as it may be implied by the dynamics of the model. Note here finally that $\dot{B}^l - \dot{B}_1^l$ gives the amount of newly issued domestic bonds sold to the world market, with $\dot{B}_1^l$ (indexed by 1) going to domestic residents, while $\dot{B}_2^{l*}$, indexed by 2, is the amount of foreign long-term debt currently purchased by domestic residents.

7.2.2 The structure from the viewpoint of national accounting

In order to provide the reader with a short but complete overview of the sectors and their activities, we supply now a closed national accounting system for the whole economy. It shows the interactions between the sectors in our model and helps to check the formal correctness of the system. Note that all amounts are valued in domestic currency, to be represented by Australian dollars ($A).

The firms' sector

Production Account of Firms:

Uses	Resources
Imports $ep_m^* J^a$	Consumption $p_v C_w^g$ (workers)
Depreciation $p_y \delta K$	Consumption $p_v C_c$ (asset holders)
Value Added Taxes $\tau_v p_y (C_w^g + C_c + G)$	Consumption $p_v G$(*government*)
Taxes on imports $\tau_m e p_m^* J^a$	Exports $p_x X^a$
Wages (excluding payroll taxes) wL_f^d	Gross Investment $p_y I$ (of firms)
Payroll Taxes $\tau_p w L_f^d$	Durables (Dwellings) $p_y I_h$ (sold to asset holders)
Profits $\Pi = \rho^e p_y K + p_y \mathcal{I} = \rho^a p_y K + p_y \dot{N}$	Inventory Investment $p_y \dot{N}$ (of firms)

The firms produce two kinds of output, the export good which only is tradeable on the world market and the domestic good which can only be sold in the domestic economy. The domestic good serves as the consumption good for the asset holders, the workforce, and the government. It can also be used for investments in inventories, in business fixed capital and in housing. Firms use three kinds of inputs for their production: imports, capital, and labor. Imports and labor have to be bought on their markets at prices including import and payroll taxes. The capital stock in the firms' sector depreciates by a given depreciation rate δ. The value added taxes, which only apply to trade in consumer goods, appear on the left side of the production account, because they have to be paid to the government. The balance is the profit of the firms' sector which can be viewed from an ex-ante perspective (as expected profit and intended inventory investment) as well as from an ex-post perspective (as realized profit plus actual inventory investment).

We note that profits are not subject to any direct tax. By assumption expected profits $\rho^e p_y K$ (with ρ^e being the expected profit rate) are either used to pay dividends to asset holders (which are subject to capital income taxation) or used for planned inventory investments. One can see this in the income account. Note that there are no subsidies paid to the firms' sector.

Income Account of Firms:

Uses	Resources
Dividends $\rho^e p_y K$	Profits Π
Savings $S_f^n = p_y \mathcal{I}$	

The accumulation account displays investments in business fixed capital and in inventories, representing the only stocks which can be accumulated by firms. There is therefore no possibility of accumulation of financial stocks, i.e., no holding of money and bonds by firms. Investments that generally will exceed the savings and the depreciation funds of firms generate a financial deficit in this sector. Note that all investment occurs at producer prices p_y.

Accumulation Account of Firms:

Uses	Resources
Gross Investment $p_y I$	Depreciation $p_y \delta K$
Inventory Investment $p_y \dot{N}$	Savings S_f^n
	Financial Deficit FD

The financial deficit must be financed by selling new equities. This assumption is not very realistic, but is used for reasons of simplicity for the time being. It will be reconsidered in future reformulations of the model of this chapter.

Financial Account of Firms:

Uses	Resources
Financial Deficit FD	Equity Financing $p_e \dot{E}$

Asset holders

While firms produce and sell two types of goods (Y, X), the sector of asset holders sells dwelling services to workers (who do not own houses by themselves in the present framework). Hence there is a production account for this sector as well.

Production Account of Households (Asset Owners/Housing Investment):

Uses	Resources
Depreciation $p_y \delta_h K_h$	Rent $p_h C_w^h$
Earnings Π_h	

The income of this sector consists of interest payments (long and short term bonds, the former also from abroad), dividends from the firms sector, and the profits from selling dwelling services. This income is diminished by capital income taxation at the rate τ_c and spent on domestic goods (consumption proper and housing). The remaining amount represents the savings of this sector.

Income Account of Households (Asset Owners):

Uses	Resources
Tax payment $\tau_c r B$	Interest payment rB (short-term bonds)
Tax payment $\tau_c B_1^l$	Interest payment B_1^l (long-term bonds)
Taxes $\tau_c(p_h C_w^h - p_y \delta_h K_h)$	Interest payment $e(1-\tau_c^*)B_2^l$ (from abroad)
Tax payment $\tau_c \rho^e p_y K$	Dividend payment $\rho^e p_y K$ (of firms)
Consumption $p_v C_c$	Earnings Π_h (from rent)
Savings S_c^n	

The savings S_c^n, together with the depreciation of the housing capital stock, is split into gross investment in housing and the financial surplus in the sector of asset holders.

Accumulation Account of Households (Asset Owners):

Uses	Resources
Gross Investment $p_y I_h$	Depreciation $p_y \delta_h K_h$
Financial Surplus FS	Savings S_c^n

The financial surplus is distributed to all financial assets contained in our model.

Financial Account of Households (Asset Owners):

Uses	Resources
Money $\dot{M}_c$	Financial Surplus FS
Short-term bonds $\dot{B}_c$	
Long-term bonds $\dot{B}_1^l/r_l$	
Foreign Bonds $e\dot{B}_2^l/r_l^*$	
Equities $p_e\dot{E}$	

Households (workers)

This sector produces nothing at all, but only supplies the labor services to firms. Therefore the production account remains empty. The income of workers includes wages, unemployment benefits, and pensions. It is used for tax payments and consumption. The remaining item, savings of workers, are not used for any type of real investment, but are held in two specific financial assets only: Money and saving-deposits (short-term bonds). Note that we apply the participation rate of workers in the working age (16 to 65) also to the calculation of pension payments to the retired worker L_2 who therefore only get pension payments in an amount that is scaled down by this participation rate.

Production Account of Households (Workers):

Uses	Resources
–	–

Income Account of Households (Workers):

Uses	Resources
Taxes $\tau_w[wL^d + w^u(L - L^w) + w^r\alpha_l L_2]$	Wages $wL^d = wL_f^d + wL_g^d$
Consumption $p_v C_w^g + p_h C_w^h$	Unemployment benefits $w^u(L - L^w)$
Savings S_w^n	Pensions $w^r\alpha_l L_2$

Accumulation Account of Households (Workers):

Uses	Resources
Financial Surplus FS	Savings S_w^n

Financial Account of Households (Workers):

Uses	Resources
Money accumulation $\dot{M}_w$	
Bond accumulation $\dot{B}_w$	Financial Surplus FS

Fiscal and monetary authorities

The government sector's production takes up the costless provision of public goods which is considered as identical to the self consumption of the government. To provide the economy with these public goods the government has to buy the goods G on the domestic market and pay wages to the workers it employs for this purpose ($L_g^w = L_g^h$). There is no over- or under-time work in the public sector.

Production Account of Fiscal and Monetary Authorities:

Uses	Resources
Government expenditure for goods $p_v G$	Costless Provision of
Salaries $w^b L_g^d = (1+\tau_p) w L_g^d$	public goods = self consumption

The only sources of income for the government are the various taxes. They are used for interest payments, pensions, unemployment benefits and salaries as well as public consumption. The balance of this account are the savings of the government. Mostly these savings are negative hence there is in general a financial deficit present in the accumulation account, rather than a financial surplus.

Income Account of Fiscal and Monetary Authorities:

Uses	Resources
Interest payment rB	Wage income taxes $\tau_w[wL^d + w^u(L-L^w) + w^r \alpha_l L_2]$
Interest payment $B^l = B_1^l + B_1^{l*}$	Profit and interest taxes $\tau_c \rho^e p_y K + \tau_c rB + \tau_c B_1^l + \tau_c B_1^{l*}$
Pensions $w^r \alpha_l L_2$	Rent income taxes $\tau_c(p_h C_w^h - p_y \delta_h K_h)$
Unemployment benefits $w^u(L-L^w)$	Payroll taxes $\tau_n w L_f^d + \tau_n w L_g^d$
Self consumption $p_v G + w^b L_g^d$	Value added tax $\tau_v p_y (C_w^g + C_c + G)$
Savings S_g^n	Import taxes $\tau_m e p_m^* J^a$

Accumulation Account of Fiscal and Monetary Authorities:

Uses	Resources
	Savings S_g^n
	Financial Deficit FD

In the financial account of the government one can see the sources, from which the deficit is financed: by issuing new money or new bonds (short- and long-term). Another item of this financial account may be given by changes in the stock of foreign reserves R. Such changes become necessary and have to be considered when interventions in the market for foreign exchange, in order to influence the exchange rate e appear desirable to the monetary authority. In the present form the model will however imply $\dot{R} = 0$ on the basis of the savings decisions made by households, firms and the government.

Financial Account of Fiscal and Monetary Authorities:

Uses	Resources
Reserve changes $e\dot{R}$	Money supply changes $\dot{M} = \dot{M}_c + \dot{M}_w$
Financial deficit FD	Short-term debt $\dot{B}$
	Long-term debt $\dot{B}^l/r_l = \dot{B}_1^l/r_l + \dot{B}_1^{l*}/r_l$

International relations

The balance of payments contains all transactions with the foreign countries. It shows the amounts of goods, interest payments (on the basis of capital services), and flows of capital, in \$A, that cross the borders at the considered point in time.

Balance of Payments:

Debit	Credit
Imports $ep_m^* J^a$	Exports $ep_x^* X^a$
Factor Income to abroad $(1-\tau_c)B_1^{l*}$	Factor Income from Abroad $e(1-\tau_c^*)B_2^l$
Capital Exports $e\dot{B}_2^l/r_l^*$	Capital Imports $\dot{B}_1^{l*}/r_l$
Changes in reserves $e\dot{R}$	

7.2.3 Aggregate concepts from the system of national accounts

The national accounting system presented above leads us to the following definitions of national products of the GDP, NDP, and NDP at factor costs.[4]

Gross Domestic Product (GDP):

$$p_y\delta K + p_y\delta_h K_h + \tau_v(C_w^g + C_c + G) + \tau_m e p_m^* J^a + w^b L_f^d + \Pi + \Pi_h =$$
$$p_v(C_w^g + C_c + G) + p_x X^a - e p_m^* J^a + p_y I + p_y I_h + p_y \dot{N} + p_h C_w^h$$

There are no wage payments that cross the border, or related types of transfer payments, i.e., only the trade account is involved in the presentation of the equation that represents Gross Domestic Product. The measure of GDP (in current prices) is thus based on adding up the products sold by firms, but taking here account only of net exports $p_x X^a - e p_m^* J^a$, plus actual inventory changes plus the nominal value of the dwelling services sold on the housing market. Deducting from this magnitude total depreciation (of the capital stock and the stock of houses), value added tax, import taxes and total wages (paid by the firms and the government) leaves as residual the profits that accrue to firms and asset holders (from the housing sector) including however the value of the inventory changes that firms had to face.

Net Domestic Product at market prices is obtained from the above presentation of GDP by deducting the depreciation items from both sides of its above presentation which gives:[5]

Net Domestic Product at market prices (NDP):

$$\tau_v(C_w^g + C_c + G) + \tau_m e p_m^* J^a + w^b L_f^d + \Pi + \Pi_h =$$
$$p_v(C_w^g + C_c + G) + (p_x X^a - e p_m^* J^a) + p_y(I - \delta K) + p_y(I_h - \delta_h K_h) + p_y \dot{N} + p_h C_w^h$$

Net Domestic Product at factor costs flows from NDP at market prices when product taxes (value added taxes and import taxes) are removed from the two expression that have formed NDP at market prices.[6]

Net Domestic Product at factor costs (NDP_f):

$$w^b L_f^d + \Pi + \Pi_h =$$
$$p_y(C_w^g + C_c + G) + (p_x X^a - p_m J^a) + p_y(I - \delta K) + p_y(I_h - \delta_h K_h) + p_y \dot{N} + p_h C_w^h$$

On the basis of the presentations of the usage (sinks) of the nominal savings of the four sectors considered in our model, provided in the above accounting framework for households, firms and the government, one gets for aggregate savings $S^n = S_w^n + S_c^n + S_f^n + S_g^n$ the usual equality with total investment and the balance of the capital account:

$$\begin{aligned} S^n &= S_w^n + S_c^n + S_f^n + S_g^n = I^{na} + [e\dot{B}_2^l / r_l^* - (\dot{B}^l - \dot{B}_1^l)/r_l] \quad \text{with} \\ I^{na} &= p_e \dot{E} + p_y \mathcal{I} + p_y(I_h - \delta_h K_h) = p_y(I - \delta K) + p_y \dot{N} + p_y(I_h - \delta_h K_h) \end{aligned}$$

[4] GNP=GDP + $e(1-\tau_c^*)B_2^l - (1-\tau_c)(B^l - B_1^l)$.

[5] NNP=NDP + $e(1-\tau_c^*)B_2^l - (1-\tau_c)(B^l - B_1^l)$.

[6] National Income=$NDP_f + e(1-\tau_c^*)B_2^l - (1-\tau_c)(B^l - B_1^l)$.

as one identity that relates nominal savings to nominal actual investment and – in this case – net capital exports (we stress again that there are no reserve changes of the monetary authorities in the present model).

Approaching aggregate nominal savings from the definition of the various savings components (from the viewpoint of their sources) on the other hand gives rise to:

$$\begin{aligned} S^n &= S_w^n + S_c^n + S_f^n + S_g^n = I^{na} + [p_x X^a - ep_m^* J^a] + [e(1-\tau_c^*)B_2^l - (1-\tau_c)(B^l - B_1^l)] \\ I^{na} &= p_y(I - \delta K) + p_y \dot{N} + p_y(I_h - \delta_h K_h) \end{aligned}$$

i.e., aggregate nominal savings equals aggregate nominal actual investment plus nominal net exports plus the international nominal net transfers of interest payments.

To prove this statement, we start from aggregate nominal savings as given by the following expressions:

$$\begin{aligned} & Y_w^{Dn} - p_v C_w^g - p_h C_w^h && \text{(workers)} \\ + \; & Y_c^{Dn} - p_v C_c && \text{(asset holders)} \\ + \; & p_y \mathcal{I} && \text{(firms)} \\ + \; & T^n - w^u(L - L^w) - w^r L_2 - (rB + B^l) - (G^n + w^b L_g^d) && \text{(government)} \end{aligned}$$

which gives rise to

$$\begin{aligned} & wL^d + w^u(L - L^w) + w^r L_2 - p_v C_w^g - p_h C_w^h \\ + \; & \rho^e p_y K + rB + B_1^l + p_h C_w^h - p_y \delta_h K_h + e(1-\tau_c^*)B_2^l - p_v C_c \\ + \; & p_y \mathcal{I} + \tau_m e p_m^* J^a + \tau_c(B^l - B_1^l) \\ + \; & \tau_p w L^d + \tau_v p_y (Y^d - I - I_h - R_h) - w^u(L - L^w) - w^r L_2 - (rB + B^l) - (G^n + w^b L_g^d) \end{aligned}$$

which gives

$$\begin{aligned} & w^b L^d - p_v C_w^g \\ + \; & \rho^e p_y K + rB + B_1^l - p_y \delta_h K_h + e(1-\tau_c^*)B_2^l - p_v C_c \\ + \; & p_y \mathcal{I} + \tau_m e p_m^* J^a + \tau_c(B^l - B_1^l) \\ + \; & \tau_v p_y (C_w^g + C_c + G) - (rB + B^l) - (G^n + w^b L_g^d) \\ = \; & w^b L_f^d - p_y C_w^g + \rho^e p_y K - (1-\tau_c)(B^l - B_1^l) - p_y \delta_h K_h + e(1-\tau_c^*)B_2^l - p_y C_c \\ + \; & p_y \mathcal{I} + \tau_m e p_m^* J^a - p_y G \\ = \; & p_y(Y^e - \delta K) + p_x X^a - e p_m^* J^a - (p_y C_w + p_y C_c^g + p_y G) \\ - \; & (1-\tau_c)(B^l - B_1^l) + e(1-\tau_c^*)B_2^l - p_y \delta_h K_h + p_y \mathcal{I} \\ = \; & p_y(Y - Y^d) + p_y Y^d - (p_y C_w^g + p_y C_c + p_y G) - p_y \delta K + p_x X^a - e p_m^* J^a \\ + \; & e(1-\tau_c^*)B_2^l - (B^l - B_1^l) - p_y \delta_h K_h \\ = \; & p_y \dot{N} + p_y(I - \delta K) + p_y(I_h - \delta_h K_h) \\ + \; & p_x X^a - e p_m^* J^a + e(1-\tau_c^*)B_2^l - (1-\tau_c)(B^l - B_1^l) \end{aligned}$$

Note here that $B^l - B_1^l = B_1^{l*}$ and that $Y^d = C_w^g + C_c + I + I_h + G$.

This proves the asserted identity from the viewpoint of the definitions of nominal savings. Note here that $B^l - B_1^l = B_1^{l*}$ holds by definition for the international allocation of domestic long-term bonds and that aggregate goods demand is defined by the expression: $Y^d = C_w + C_c + I + I_h + G$.

Note furthermore, as an important result of the proof just given, that there is no need for the monetary authority to intervene in the foreign exchange market, since the balance of payments will always be balanced in the considered economy due to the budget restrictions that hold for our four domestic agents, despite a temporarily given exchange rate e, which is here compatible with a self regulating market for foreign exchange.

Having presented the model from the ex post point of view by means of structured tables and the system of national accounts we now turn to the structural form of the model and present in the following section its technological foundations, its behavioral relationships, various definitions and the budget equations of the four agents of the domestic economy, and finally also its laws of motion for quantities, prices and expectations.

7.3 Households

We now start with the structural form of the continuous time disequilibrium (CTD) growth model that is the subject of this chapter and that extends considerably the KMG growth model of the preceding parts and also the fixed proportions reference Murphy type model of the companion book by Chiarella and Flaschel (1999e), by including substitution of three inputs and two outputs as characteristics of the production possibilities of firms, by including money and cash management, and by including wealth effects on consumption. This increases the empirical relevance of the model but also the complexity of the feedback structure characterizing the overall dynamics of the model.

Module 1. of the model provides some definitions of rates of return, of nominal wealth of workers and asset holders, of wages including payroll taxes, prices including value added tax and of pension rates and unemployment benefits to be used in various places of the model. In equation (7.1) we in particular define the currently *expected rate* of profit ρ^e based on the sales expectations of firms (as far as the domestically produced good is concerned) and on actual exports, imports and the actual employment of the workforce of the firms (and in a similar way the normal rate of return – based on normal rates of capacity utilization, in an environment where, as we shall see, smooth factor substitution in production is present). While equation (7.2) describes the *actual* rate of return ρ^a, based on actual sales of the firms, equation (7.4) defines the rate of return of capital in the housing sector, ρ^h. Equation (7.5) gives the definition of the average *real* rate of interest of long-term bonds, taking into account the long-run rate of inflation, π^l. These definitions are basically the same as those underlying module 1 in Chiarella and Flaschel (1999e), but they are here in particular applied to smooth factor and output substitution in the production technology of the firms and to a different structure and allocation of wealth between the two groups of households considered.

1. Definitions (Rates of Return, Nominal Wealth, Wages and Prices):

$$\rho^e = \frac{p_y(Y^e - \delta K) + p_x X^a - w^b L_f^d - p_m J^a}{p_y K} \quad [\dot{\rho}^{av} = \alpha_\rho(\rho^e - \rho^{av})] \tag{7.1}$$

$$\rho^a = \frac{p_y(Y^d - \delta K) + p_x X^a - w^b L_f^d - p_m J^a}{p_y K} \tag{7.2}$$

$$Y^n = \bar{U}_c Y^p \quad \text{(normal capacity utilization)} \tag{7.3}$$

$$\rho_h = \frac{p_h C_w^h - p_y \delta_h K_h}{p_y K_h} \quad [\dot{\rho}_h^{av} = \alpha_{\rho_h}(\rho_h - \rho_h^{av})] \tag{7.4}$$

$$r^r = (1-\tau_c) r_l^{av} - \pi^l \tag{7.5}$$

$$r_l = 1/p_b \quad [\dot{r}_l^{av} = \alpha_{r_l}(r_l - r_l^{av})] \tag{7.6}$$

$$W_w^n = M_w + B_w \tag{7.7}$$

$$W_c^n = M_c + B_c + B_1^l/r_l + eB_2^l/r_l^* + p_e E + p_y K_h \tag{7.8}$$

$$w^b = (1+\tau_n) w \tag{7.9}$$

$$w^r = \alpha^r w \tag{7.10}$$

$$w^u = \alpha^u w \tag{7.11}$$

$$p_v = (1+\tau_v) p_y. \tag{7.12}$$

In brackets, we have added to the above definitions of actual or expected short-run rates of return $\rho^a, \rho^e, \rho_h, r_l$ within firms, in the housing sector, and on long-term bonds, three adjustment laws for average concepts of these rates of return, that is for the average rate of profit ρ^{av} (expected to hold over the medium run) in contrast to the rate of profit ρ^e that is expected for this year, for the average rate of return ρ_h^{av} on housing investment expected over a medium run horizon and for the average rate of interest r_l^{av} on long-term bonds (with price $p_b = 1/r_l$), again formulated as a particular type of weighted average of actual interest rates on long-term bonds (due to the chosen formulae with exponentially declining weights). All these lags serve to make the response of real investments less immediate to changes in the current rates of return which is probably typical for the sector of real capital holdings. We furthermore provide a definition for the required rate of return which serves as a measuring rod for the rates that direct investment into real capital or dwellings.

The above list of definitions furthermore shows normal output Y^n (in its relation to normal capacity usage) (eqn. (7.3)), nominal wealth of workers and asset owners (eqns. (7.7) and (7.8)), the various concepts of wages used in our model (including payroll taxes, representing pensions, unemployment benefits) (eqns. (7.10) – (7.11)) and finally consumer price level p_v, including value added taxes, (7.12).

Powell and Murphy's (1997, p.291ff.) list of consolidated equations exhibits with respect to this module in eqn. 32 the definition of gross operating surplus, see also their p.233, which is identical to the numerator in our definition of the expected profit rate ρ^e of firms. In eqn. 29 it provides the definition of wages including payroll taxes, w^b as defined above. In the equation for fixed business investment they use a rate r_B^{ALR}, see eqn. 44 in their consolidated list and their pages 171, 248, in the place of our rate ρ^l, which is following the rate ρ^e with some time delay. They define the rate r_B^{ALR} to be the gross rate of return that would be *realized on business fixed investment (before depreciation is deducted and inclusive of the risk premium required for equity investment) if all prices (including the wage rate) were frozen indefinitely at their current values and they relate this rate to the real rental price of capital r_B^{LR}/p_Y. It appears that this definition of gross return is closer to our definitions of the rates ρ^e, ρ^a than to the rate ρ^{av} that we will use in our investment function.*

There is no equation for the actual gross rate of return of housing investment in the consolidated list of equations, which is however provided on p. 145 of their book. This rate differs from our rate ρ_h (which is net of depreciation) in that we neglect taxes on rental services and maintenance costs (as measured by their term β_2^{05}). Furthermore we have set the parameter β_1^{05} equal to one and have thus identified housing supply with the stock of housing that is supplied for rental services. On this basis we however distinguish occupancy rates C_w^h from corresponding supply and will enter this discrepancy as a demand pull term into the housing investment equation as well as into the dynamics of rental prices. Note here also that the rate of return on housing services must then be based on rented units C_w^h and not on the amount of housing services C_h^s that is offered on the market.

The required real rate of return r^r of the above module is basically of the same type as the one defined in eqn. 52 of the consolidated list of Powell and Murphy (1997), see also their page 52. These authors however use an estimated average inflation rate $\tilde{\xi}_{10}$ based on model-consistent expectations over a time horizon of ten years (coupled with a ten year nominal interest rate on government bonds) in the place of our medium-run concept of expected inflation π^l. We furthermore do not make use of the average interest rates on outstanding foreign and domestic debt, the eqns. 54 and 55 in the consolidated list of Powell and Murphy (1997), see also their page 229, in the calculation of private sector property income, but simply make use here of the two actual rates r^l, r^{l*} in their place when calculating the interest rate income received by asset holders at each moment of time. Eqn. 88 of their list simply provides a symbol for interest rate differential used to capture the influence of tight monetary policy on the real investment of firms and asset holders which is used in explicit form in our following model. Finally the measure of nominal wealth used by Powell and Murphy (1997) is not contained in their consolidated list, but can be found on p.120 of their book. It differs from the measure defined in our module 1 insofar as private sector debt to foreigners contracted in two ways is allowed for as well as real stock owned by foreigners. In the place of equities Powell and Murphy (1997, p.120) immediately use the current value of the capital stock owned by the private sector and they also include inventories into the definition of such measures of the value of the stock of firms.

Their concept of private wealth (coupled with a life cycle hypothesis of a single representative consumer) is thus somewhat different from the one we employ in the above module 1. We will not include here valuations of the capital stock (that includes inventories[7]), which in our model are only present for the domestically marketed good, but will use the issued equities explicitly instead and will pay no attention to indebtedness of the private sector to foreigners, but use public indebtness instead, and consider also purchases of foreign bonds by domestic residents.

Module 2 provides the equations that concern the household sector where, as in Chiarella and Flaschel (1999e), two types of households are distinguished. The most important distinction from the treatment in Chiarella and Flaschel (1999e) is that we now apply

[7] And the windfall profits that may occur when there are unplanned inventory changes.

the life cycle hypothesis in order to determine total consumption expenditures of workers (and of asset holders), which includes wealth effects into workers' consumption decision. Total consumption for workers is then divided again into consumption proper and housing services, in a way that corresponds to the assumption of a Cobb-Douglas utility function and utility maximization as discussed in Powell and Murphy (1997).

2a. Households (Workforce):

$$
\begin{aligned}
Y_w^{Dn} &= (1-\tau_w)[wL^d + w^u(L-L^w) + w^r\alpha_l L_2] + (1-\tau_c)rB_w && (7.13)\\
L^w &= L_f^w + L_g^w && (7.14)\\
L^d &= L_f^d + L_g^d = L_f^d + L_g^w && (7.15)\\
C_w^{on} &= c_{w_1}Y_w^{Dn} + c_{w_2}W_w^n, \quad W_w^n = M_w + B_w && (7.16)\\
C_w^{og} &= \alpha_w C_w^{on}/p_v && (7.17)\\
C_w^{oh} &= (1-\alpha_w)C_w^{on}/p_h && (7.18)\\
\hat{C}_w^g &= \alpha_1^w(C_w^{og}/C_w^g - 1) + \alpha_2^w(V-\bar{V}) + \gamma && (7.19)\\
\hat{C}_w^h &= \alpha_1^w(C_w^{oh}/C_w^h - 1) + \alpha_2^w(V-\bar{V}) + \gamma && (7.20)\\
M_w^d &= p_v k C_w^g \exp(-\alpha_r(1-\tau_c)r), \quad B_w^d = W_w^n - M_w^d && (7.21)\\
S_w^n &= Y_w^{Dn} - (p_v C_w^g + p_h C_w^h) = \dot{W}_w^n = \dot{M}_w + \dot{B}_w && (7.22)\\
\hat{M}_w &= \mu + \frac{M_c}{M}(\hat{C}_w^g - \hat{C}_c), \quad \dot{B}_w = S_w^n - \dot{M}_w, \ \mu = \hat{M} && (7.23)\\
\hat{L}_1 &= \hat{L}_2 = \hat{L}_0 = n \qquad (L_o(0), L_1(0), L_2(0) \quad \text{given}) && (7.24)\\
\dot{n} &= \beta_n(\tilde{n} - n), \quad \tilde{n} = \tilde{n}(V, \bar{V}) && (7.25)\\
L &= \alpha_l L_1 && (7.26)\\
M_w(0) &= p_v(0)kC_w(0)\exp(-\alpha_r(1-\tau_c)r(0)) && (7.27)
\end{aligned}
$$

Income of workers consists of the various sources of wage income and wage-like transfers as in the reference model in Chiarella and Flaschel (1999e), and again the interest payments on the short-term bonds held by this group of households as described by eqn. (7.13). We are now assuming that workers accumulate wealth in the form of money (checking deposits) as well as in the form of saving deposits (short-term bonds). We here choose this extended approach to workers' wealth accumulation, since we want to treat money and monetary policy differently from Chiarella and Flaschel (1999e) and more as in Powell and Murphy (1997), in order to show to the reader how a different route with respect to asset accumulation and monetary policy can be formulated and justified (as compared to Chiarella and Flaschel (1999e)).

The next difference, as compared to the reference model of the companion book by Chiarella and Flaschel (1999e), represented by eqn. (7.16), is that we now base workers' consumption function on a simple linear life cycle approach which adds workers' wealth as an argument and determinant of their total consumption in nominal terms (but not yet the rate of interest, however measured). Desired nominal consumption of goods ($p_v C_w^{og}$) and of housing services ($p_h C_w^{oh}$) is assumed to be a constant fraction of total desired nominal consumption (C_w^{on}). Equations (7.17) and (7.18) provide expressions for the real optimal consumption plans of goods and housing services by dividing these expressions through

p_v, p_h, respectively. According to equation (7.19) and (7.20) actual consumption adjusts to these desired magnitudes with a time delay as in the model we considered in Chiarella and Flaschel (1999e).

Based on the nominal value of goods consumption of workers (excluding the consumption of housing services for the time being) we define their money demand function in the usual way by a Cagan type transactions demand for money function, which is given by equation (7.23). This narrow definition of the transactions of workers (and later on asset holders), that must be backed up by money holdings, is chosen here in order to get rid of distributional effects of money holdings and money accumulation in a simple, coherent and easy to follow way. Of course, more general reasons for money holdings must be integrated later on, but will not provide a real difficulty once the principles of a coherent allocation of money holdings, here still of households only, have been understood.

By contrast, in the Murphy model, there is only one aggregate demand function for money holdings (also of Cagan type), as is customary in (empirical) treatments of the money market, which is based on a broad measure of the commodity transactions that occur in an economy, including investment and government purchases of the domestic commodity (financial transactions are altogether neglected). Yet, all money is held in the (representative) household sector of the Murphy model and not by firms (the investors) and by the government. We do not think that this is convincing from the theoretical point of view and thus have gone to the other extreme of assuming (as in the Murphy model) that all money is held in the household sector and there, in contrast to the Murphy model, for transaction purposes in the domestic goods market solely (leaving the treatment of the sector of housing services, of firms and of government money holdings for later extensions of this approach).

We obtain the demand of workers for short-term bonds via their wealth constraint $W_w^n = M_w + B_w \equiv M_w^d + B_w^d$ and will later on show that adjustments of the nominal rate of interest will not only imply that private households taken together voluntarily hold (as is standard) the stock of money in existence at the equilibrium rate of interest rate that results, but that this is also true for the stock of money held by workers and asset holders separately, and this at the equilibrium rate of interest that is established by the market.

The flow of savings finally is directed towards an increase in money holdings and interest bearing short-term bond holdings (saving deposits) of workers as described by equation (7.22). We here assume that the new money supply is allocated to the two types of households of our model in proportions that will just correspond to the new transactions demand caused by their change in the consumption of C_w^g as determined by equation (7.19). By implication this will allow workers (and asset holders) to just be content with their new money holdings in view of their revised transactions in domestically produced commodities at new prices p_v if the nominal rate of interest adjusts to clear the overall money market. The distribution of new money supply between workers and asset holders is therefore here assumed to be of a neutral type, a type which allows us to concentrate on the money market as a whole without accompanying (discontinuous) redistribution of money and short-term bonds between workers and asset holders at each moment in time.[8]

[8]Such a distributional rule is implicitly present in most presentations of the money market, which generally focus on household behavior as a whole.

Due to the form of money market equilibrium we shall obtain later on, it will therefore be shown that there is no readjustment needed in the holding of money between our two groups of households caused by the inflow of new money due to the money supply rule assumed for the monetary authority. The addition of new bonds to the workers' portfolio is then determined by their nominal savings subtracting from them the inflow of new money as determined in equation (7.23). All other components of this module of the model are as in Chiarella and Flaschel (1999e) and thus do not need detailed explanation here. We have added however as a final equation to block 2a of the model that workers were content with their actual money holdings at the point in time 0 from where we start our dynamic investigations.

Finally, the growth rate of the different parts of the population are given by equation (7.24). This common growth rate n furthermore changes in time according to equation (7.25), i.e. it depends on the difference between its actual level and a reference value $\tilde{n}$, which again is a function of the employment rate V and its natural level $\bar{V}$. Equation (7.26) concerns the participation rate of the work force. We stress that this participation rate α_l of workers of age between 15 and 65 (L_1) is again a given magnitude here, and that this rate must be applied to the retired people (L_2) as well in order to determine the amount of pension payments by transfers from the government. This is not so in the Murphy model where the participation rate is an endogenous component of a much richer demographic module than is present here. However, there is implied a budget constraint for workers in the Murphy model which appears to be quite complicated in such an advanced formulation of the various components and vintages of the working population.

Therefore only the life cycle approach of consumption behavior has been taken from the Murphy model, with an explicit treatment of income distribution between two types of households now (but a uniform treatment of retired people). Income distribution is only captured by a trend term in the single consumption function considered in Powell and Murphy (1997). The present model is therefore sometimes more explicit and detailed than the Murphy model and sometimes more restrictive, due to the need to specify all income and asset flows in the economy in a coherent way if consistency requirements such as a full set of budget restrictions are taken into account.

Powell and Murphy's (1997, p.291ff.) list of consolidated equations, as already stated, contain this module 2a of our model in form of a representative consumer (and thus in aggregated form regarding the next module of our model), but occasionally refer to the role of income distribution which they represent as a time trend in the equation they provide for optimal consumption on their page 117. We will include a consumer price index in the following as in their eqns. 19, 21 (see also their pages 132/3) in the calculation of the real consumption of workers, so that their consumption of housing service then forms an exponentially weighted average with the consumer price of the goods marketed domestically, also to be applied in the money wage Phillips curve as the cost-push expression (in a purely adaptive way in the Murphy model). With respect to the dynamic adjustment of consumption plans we use somewhat different functional forms than Powell and Murphy (1997, p.121), a difference that should not be too important in a comparative evaluation of these two approaches. Their inclusion of (real) interest rate effects may however strengthen the nominal instability that we will investigate in future reconsiderations of the present model, i.e., of the so-called Mundell effect of inflationary expectations. Note here also that the rate of employment enters this adjustment equation in derivative form in the Murphy model. Eqn. 3 (see also their p.112) of their consolidated list provides a long expression for labor force participation which is constant in our formulation of the model, in order to avoid the complicated calculation of total unemployment benefits and also of total rents that go to retired workers. With respect to the treatment of labor supply the Murphy model is thus much more advanced than our approach, but also much more complicated as far as a proper (still lacking) treatment of the budget equations of all worker households is concerned. We neglect their logistic trend term in the propensity to consume dwelling services, i.e., their eqn. 20 (see also p.126) and also apply a different approach to the endogeneity of the natural rate of growth of the working population, their eqn. 94 (discussed on their page 140). Furthermore, the number of unemployed people is not adjusted by a weight that accounts for the difference of two unemployment rate measures.

Wage income Y_L is defined on page 117 in Powell and Murphy and its consists of the wages of the employed (after taxes) plus unemployment benefits plus rent payment and also plus further transfers that are not considered in our model (in particular to families with children). It is further modified by taking account of certain lump sum taxes and of transfers from overseas to this sector of the economy. This extends our above definition of worker households' income to some extent, but is not basically different from it. Note also that the Murphy model does not relate unemployment benefits and rent payments to the time profile of the actual participation of potential workers in this social insurance system. As in our model, the Murphy model distinguishes between private and public employment, but it does not explicitly consider over- and undertime work of the employed, though the effects that we will describe in this matter are basically present in the employment equation and the money wage dynamics, to be considered later on.

We observe again that the demand C_w^h for housing services is identified with the supply for these services in Powell and Murphy (1997, p.128), so that the above module contains two more equations in this respect as compared to the Murphy model. There is no separate savings decision S_w^n of workers in the Murphy model and the issue and absorption of new assets is determined in their model basically from the supply side and is thus similar to the treatment in the model of this chapter.

Finally, we have only a very simple demographic module in the sector of worker households, where we assume that all age groups of workers grow with the same rate (made endogenous by assuming an appropriate type of migration) and also that the participation rate of the people in the potential workforce stays constant in time (see chapter 6 in Powell and Murphy (1997) for details on this matter).

The life cycle hypothesis is also used to describe the consumption plans of asset holders which therefore are no longer growing at a constant rate as it was assumed in Chiarella and Flaschel (1999e).

2b. Households (Asset-Holders):

$$\begin{aligned} Y_c^{Dn} &= (1-\tau_c)[\rho^e p_y K + rB_c + B_1^l + p_h C_w^h - p_y \delta_h K_h] \\ &+ e(1-\tau_c^*)B_2^l && (7.28) \\ C_c^{on} &= c_{c_1} Y_c^{Dn} + c_{c_2} W_c^n, && (7.29) \\ W_c^n &= M_c + B_c + p_b B_1^l + p_e E + e p_b^* B_2^l + p_y K_h, \quad p_b^* = 1/r_l^* && (7.30) \end{aligned}$$

$$
\begin{aligned}
C_c^o &= C_c^{on}/p_v & (7.31)\\
\hat{C}_c &= \alpha_1^c(C_c^o/C_c - 1) + \alpha_2^c(r_l^{av} - r_l) - \alpha_3^c(r + \xi - r_l) + \gamma & (7.32)\\
M_c^d &= p_v k C_c \exp(-\alpha_r(1-\tau_c)r), \quad B_c^d = M_c + B_c - M_c^d & (7.33)\\
S_c^n &= Y_c^{Dn} - p_v C_c & (7.34)\\
&= \dot{M}_c + \dot{B}_c + \dot{B}_1^l/r_l + e\dot{B}_2^l/r_l^* + p_e\dot{E} + p_y(I_h - \delta_h K_h) & (7.35)\\
\hat{M}_c &= \mu + \frac{M_w}{M}(\hat{C}_c - \hat{C}_w^g), \quad \dot{B}_c = \dot{B} - \dot{B}_w, \ \mu = \hat{M} & (7.36)\\
M_c(0) &= p_v(0)kC_c(0)\exp(-\alpha_r(1-\tau_c)r(0)). & (7.37)
\end{aligned}
$$

There is no change here, compared to Chiarella and Flaschel (1999e), with respect to the definition of disposable income of asset holders Y_c^{Dn} which derives from various sources of interest and profit (eqn. (7.28)). Asset holders consume the domestic good as consumptions goods proper as well as in the form of new houses and thus have only to be modeled with respect to such total consumption plans here. There is thus no need for an aggregate price index to measure the living costs of asset owners (as it will be necessary in the treatment of money wage changes of workers in module 5b). According to equation (7.29) consumption behavior is here also based on a simple life cycle theory of consumption, instead of being characterized by a constant trend as in Chiarella and Flaschel (1999e). As in the preceding module of the model we assume here too that actual consumption C_c follows desired consumption C_c^o with a time delay that is governed by the discrepancy between these two magnitudes, by the deviation of some average concept of the rate of return on long-term bonds (see module 6 in this section) from the current nominal rate of return on these bonds (a discrepancy which, if positive, stimulates the actual consumption of asset holders, see also Powell and Murphy (1997) in this regard) and by the discrepancy that exists between the short-term rate of interest (augmented by a risk and liquidity premium) and the current nominal rate of return on long-term bonds, which can be considered as a measure for the tightness of monetary policy. The functional dependence of the rate of change of actual consumption on these magnitudes is given by equation (7.32).

The savings decision of asset holders as described by equation (7.34) and (7.35) is modeled as in Chiarella and Flaschel (1999e), but now includes the absorption of the new money as a further asset and in a proportion that determines – as already explained in the comments on module 2a – the relative distribution of money between asset holders and workers in such a way that the new money supply will result in interest rate changes that do not redistribute money holdings between workers and asset holders as far as the establishment of stock equilibrium is concerned. Note here that we have assumed some sort of Walras' law of stocks as far as the two perfectly liquid assets, money and short-term bonds, are concerned. Not only workers, but also asset holders would reallocate their liquid wealth in each moment of time according to the transaction needs they face in each period which implies $B_c^d = M_c + B_c - M_c^d$ and which implies furthermore that the money market will be in equilibrium if and only if the market for short-term bonds is balanced as far as initial stocks are concerned.

We have assumed, in equations (7.23) and (7.34), that the stock of money of workers and asset holders grow according to:

$$\hat{M}_w = \hat{M} + \frac{M_c}{M}(\hat{C}_w^g - \hat{C}_c),$$

$$\hat{M}_c = \hat{M} + \frac{M_w}{M}(\hat{C}_c - \hat{C}^g_w).$$

From these two rules we first of all get:

$$\begin{aligned} & \frac{M_w}{M}\hat{M}_w + \frac{M_c}{M}\hat{M}_c \\ = & \frac{M_w}{M}(\hat{M} + \frac{M_c}{M}(\hat{C}^g_w - \hat{C}_c)) + \frac{M_c}{M}(\hat{M} + \frac{M_w}{M}(\hat{C}_c - \hat{C}^g_w)) \\ = & \frac{M_w}{M}\hat{M} + \frac{M_c}{M}\hat{M} = \hat{M}, \end{aligned}$$

i.e.,

$$\dot{M}_w + \dot{M}_c = \dot{M}.$$

Thus the assumed growth rules for $\dot{M}_w$ and $\dot{M}_c$ ensure that the new money supply $\dot{M}$ is exactly allocated to the money holdings of the two households. This in a way, as we shall see, that needs no further reallocation in view of future consumption of workers and asset holders by way of their transactions demands and the future money market equilibrium.

Furthermore, these two rules for the allocation of new money between workers and asset holders also imply:

$$\begin{aligned} \hat{M}_c - \hat{M}_w &= \hat{M} + \frac{M_w}{M}(\hat{C}_c - \hat{C}^g_w) - (\hat{M} + \frac{M_c}{M}(\hat{C}^g_w - \hat{C}_c)) \\ &= (\frac{M_w}{M} + + \frac{M_c}{M})(\hat{C}_c - \hat{C}^g_w) = \hat{C}_c - \hat{C}^g_w \end{aligned}$$

which gives

$$\hat{C}_c - \hat{M}_c = \hat{C}^g_w - \hat{M}_w. \tag{7.38}$$

The change in the nominal rate of interest the workers would require in order that their stock of money remains in equilibrium through the addition to it implied by (7.23) is given by:

$$\dot{r}_w - \frac{\hat{p}_v + \hat{C}^g_w - \hat{M}_w}{\alpha_r(1-\tau_c)} \tag{7.39}$$

This equation is obtained by differentiating workers' money demand function with respect to time (by means of the usual growth rate formulae). Similarly the asset holders, in order that their money holdings stay in equilibrium, would require that the nominal interest rate changes according to:

$$\dot{r}_c = \frac{\hat{p}_v + \hat{C}_c - \hat{M}_c}{\alpha_r(1-\tau_c)}. \tag{7.40}$$

By substituting (7.38) into (7.40) we see that $\dot{r}_c = \dot{r}_w$. The two interest rate changes $\dot{r}_w, \dot{r}_c$ necessary for partial transactions balances equilibrium of workers and asset holders, respectively, are thus equal to each other, The common rate that they both equal should be $\dot{r}$, if the money market is to remain in equilibrium. That this is indeed the case as can be seen from the following calculations. First we note from (7.23) and (7.33) that $M = p_v k(C_c + C_w^g)\exp(-\alpha_r(1-\tau_c)r)$ from which by time differentiation we get

$$\begin{aligned}
\dot{r} &= \frac{\hat{p}_v + (\widehat{C_w^g + C_c}) - \hat{M}}{\alpha_r(1-\tau_c)} \\
&= \frac{C_w^g}{C_w^g + C_c}\frac{\hat{p}_v + \hat{C}_w^g - \hat{M}}{\alpha_r(1-\tau_c)} + \frac{C_c}{C_w^g + C_c}\frac{\hat{p}_v + \hat{C}_c - \hat{M}}{\alpha_r(1-\tau_c)} \\
&= \frac{C_w^g}{C_w^g + C_c}\dot{r}_w + \frac{C_c}{C_w^g + C_c}\dot{r}_c \\
&= \dot{r}_w, \quad \text{since} \quad \dot{r}_c = \dot{r}_w \\
&= \dot{r}_c, \quad \text{since} \quad \dot{r}_w = \dot{r}_c.
\end{aligned}$$

The uniform change $\dot{r}$ in the nominal interest rate will preserve money market equilibrium through time, in such a way that both groups of households will just hold the stock of money they are instantaneously accumulating.

In the course of time prices, quantities and interest rates that concern the money market will all change in different ways, but the change in money supply will happen in such a way that there is only need for interest change given by

$$\dot{r} = \frac{\hat{p}_v + (\widehat{C_w^g + C_c}) - \hat{M}}{\alpha_r(1-\tau_c)}$$

in order to imply stock equilibria for money holdings for both types of households as well as in the aggregate. Note here, that this leaves open the question how the needed allocation of new money supply between workers and asset holders is actually performed, since new money enters the economy via open (and sometimes also foreign market) operations. Some sort of neutralizing policy is therefore needed in order to guarantee that the new supply of money in fact concerns the saving decisions of workers and asset holders in the way it is described in modules 2a and 2b.

The above interest rate reaction function in fact is replacing the interest rate policy rule of Taylor type we have used in Chiarella and Flaschel (1999e). It is now an implication of the policy rule for the money supply we shall introduce in module 4 of section 7.5 and the dynamic laws assumed for prices and consumption behavior in the domestic goods market and thus much more roundabout than the direct steering of the short term rate of interest assumed in Chiarella and Flaschel (1999e).

Since workers and asset holders will voluntarily hold their accumulated stock of money through time they will do the same with respect to the holdings of their stock of short-term bonds, since reallocations of financial assets at each moment in time concerns only the perfectly liquid ones. Supply side considerations therefore drive the stock of money in the aggregate as well as in detail, while the new supply of short-term bonds $\dot{B}$ is allocated as to first satisfy workers' demand with only the remainder going to asset holders. All other domestic financial assets (long-term bonds and equities) are absorbed by asset holders to the extent they are supplied by the government and the firms while the remainder of the savings decision of asset holders concerns investment in housing and foreign long-term bonds where the latter are demanded as a residual in the foreign bond market and supplied there without limits. This group of households thus accepts the new supply of equities and of domestic long-term bonds that the firms and the government place on the domestic market and adjusts their demand and purchase (or sale) of foreign long-term bonds such that the intended investments in dwellings can be realized.

In the present chapter we therefore still consider an economy where the allocation of domestic financial assets is basically supply side driven (up to investment in houses), where the demand for newly issued short-term bonds implied by the savings decision of workers is served first, and where asset holders adjust their demand for foreign bonds in such a way that their budget (or savings) constraint is satisfied. Financial markets are therefore still very supply side determined as far as quantities actually traded are concerned and are based on an explicit, detailed, but also very specific allocation of newly issued assets throughout the economy. Asset price dynamics, by contrast, does not take account of such distribution of assets in the economy, but simply assumes certain laws of motion based on rate of return differentials as we shall see in module 6 of the model. This is a necessary procedure in models where no full portfolio approach to asset demands is specified, where adjustment rules for asset prices are assumed in the place of equilibrium relationships, and where nevertheless the budget restriction of all agents are considered, so that the accumulation of wealth can and must be traced explicitly. Note finally that (here as in the case of workers) the rate of interest plays no role in the determination of the optimal consumption plans of asset holders.

The housing sector is treated, as in Chiarella and Flaschel (1999e), as part of the household sector (as part of the savings and investment decision of asset holders). There is still no explicit resale market for dwellings, and thus no trade in used houses between our two groups of households. Investment in dwellings and the supply of housing services is under the control of asset-owners, while the production of dwellings is part of the production of firms of the domestic (non traded) commodity. In sum there is thus no real change in our description of the housing sector, where rents remain to be driven by cost push terms that are based on the price of domestically produced commodities solely (with no reference to the price index that applies to workers consumption decision).

2c. Housing (Housing Supply, Rent and Investment in Dwellings):

$$C_h^s = K_h \quad [C_w^h \text{ see 2a.}] \tag{7.41}$$

$$g_h^d = (I_h/K_h)^d$$
$$= \alpha_1^h((1-\tau_c)\rho_h^{av} - r^r) + \alpha_2^h(r_l - (r+\xi)) + \alpha_3^h(\frac{C_w^h}{C_h^s} - \bar{U}_h) + \gamma + \delta_h \tag{7.42}$$

$$\dot{\rho}_h^{av} = \alpha_{\rho_h}(\rho_h - \rho_h^{av}) \tag{7.43}$$

$$\dot{g}_h = \beta_{gh}(g_h^d - g_h), \; g_h = I_h/K_h \tag{7.44}$$

$$\hat{p}_h = \beta_{ph}(\frac{C_w^h}{C_h^s} - \bar{U}_h) + \kappa_h\hat{p}_v + (1-\kappa_h)\pi^l \tag{7.45}$$

$$\hat{K}_h = I_h/K_h - \delta_h. \tag{7.46}$$

Note that housing demand is always satisfied (as is goods demand) in this Keynesian approach to the short-run. Note also, that in the steady state there holds that individual consumption of housing services (per head) grows with the rate $\gamma - n$. By and large the housing sector is formulated as in the Murphy model. There, however, this sector is not related to activities between two types of households (as in the present approach), due to the representative household assumption implicitly made in Powell and Murphy (1997).

Powell and Murphy's (1997, p.291ff.) list of consolidated equations exhibits with respect to this module in their eqn. 53 the definition of private property income, see also their p.233. With respect to this equation and the whole approach chosen by Powell and Murphy (1997) we neglect in this section all investment of foreigners into the domestic capital stock (and also all public investment as a separate item in this regard).

We also will not consider private debt to foreigners here, although our model would allow for such a possibility. We distinguish however explicitly between short-term bonds and long-term bonds in the budget equations of asset owners and the government, a distinction that is not so obvious in the equations, such as the one under consideration, that are used in the Murphy model. Furthermore we have domestic private holdings of foreign long-term bonds, and thus a positive entry in the income account of asset holders in the place of their indebtedness to the foreign sector which appears as a negative entry in Powell and Murphy (1997, p. 233).[9] *In sum Powell and Murphy's treatment of property income may be the more appropriate one for the consideration of actual economies like Australia*[10] *and is thus to be approached in future elaborations of our theoretical model of a small open economy.*

We have already commented on a uniform treatment of consumption behavior in the preceding subsection and only note here that the above module chooses a particular simple approach in this respect as far as asset holders are concerned. Private savings S_c^n *(or* $S_c^n + S_w^n$*) are not treated explicitly in Powell and Murphy (1997), but only appear in the form of asset accumulation equations. At present it is not clear to us whether these asset accumulation equations can be consistently checked by means of the private savings that are implied by the income and the consumption equations of the Murphy model. Note also again that saving decisions of our pure asset holders concern the issue of new equities and residually the purchase of foreign bonds (if their savings exceeds their domestic wealth accumulation).*

Equations 76 and 77 of the consolidated list of equations of the Murphy model, see also their pages 260 and 261, describe the accumulation identity for private debt to foreigners (in two types of currency there) as they derive from actions of the government which we provide indirectly via the saving decisions of asset holders (and which is denoted only in the foreign currency). In the Murphy model there is instead a rigid allocation rule assumed with respect to the denomination of such private debt (so that only part of it is subject to exchange rate revaluations). Eqn. 73, see Powell and Murphy (1997, p.257), describes foreign owned fixed business investment as a fixed proportion of overall private business fixed investment, the latter of which is treated in the next module of our model while the former is simply lacking in our model.

Housing is treated separately in Powell and Murphy (1997, Chs. 8,9), but is integrated here into the above module of the behavior of asset holders. As in the Murphy model we have

[9] Our model will give rise to such an item if $\dot{B}_2^l$ turns out to be negative in which case domestic wealth allocation of asset owners is financed to some extent by reductions in their foreign bond holdings or by foreign debt if there are no such bond holdings. Our model therefore in principle allows for foreign indebtness of the private sector (in which case the capital account will exhibit only negative entries).

[10] Their use of average rates of return in the calculation of actual returns, however, is somewhat problematic from the purely theoretical point of view and its use of consistent budget equations.

strict proportionality between the stock of houses and the supply of rental services, the eqn. 22 of their consolidated list (and see also their p.138). The accumulation equation 79 is a direct definitional consequence of the description of housing investment (to be considered next) and is of course the same in their and our model. The dwelling investment equation 7 of their list (discussed on their p.144) exhibits a strong influence of past rates of housing investment on current housing investment which we represent in our formulation of this equation as a lagged response of actual rates of investment to the desired one. All further discussion of this investment equation therefore now refers to this desired accumulation rate for housing investment. As in the Murphy model we have the influence of the rate of return of housing services and its deviation from the required return on the rate of housing investment, where we make use of an average concept ρ_h^l *in the place of their actual rate of return and use a rate of inflation that is expected to hold over the medium run in the place of their use of model consistent expectations.*

In the place of the impact of the rate of employment on the housing investment decision we use the rate of utilization of the housing stock that is offered for rent, but as they do we use the differential between the short- and the long-term rate of interest in order to give expression to the tightness of monetary policy and its impact on housing investment. There is furthermore trend growth in our model as in the Murphy model, but not the constant coefficients $\alpha_0^{05}, \alpha_*^{05}$ *that they discuss in detail in their chapter 9. We bypass their equation 2 of the consolidated list, see also their p.129, since this equation is difficult to justify as an equilibrium price of rental services ,which is used in the equation 1 of their list (see also p.130) describing the price dynamics of housing services. This equation is basically based on past values for actual and the just mentioned equilibrium prices of housing services and is replaced in our model by a simple demand pressure cost-push approach to the rate of inflation concerning rental prices.*

7.4 Firms

In module 3. we describe the sector of firms as given by the following set of equations.

3*a*. Firms (Technology, Production, Employment and Investment):

$$T(Y,X) = F(K, \exp(n_l t)L^d, J^d), \quad \text{the production technology of firms} \tag{7.47}$$

Firms' optimization problem in face of given demand:

$$\max_{X,J^d,L^d} [\frac{p_x}{p_y}X - \frac{p_m}{p_y}J^d - \frac{w^b}{p_y}L^d] \tag{7.48}$$

$$\text{s.t.} \quad T(Y,X) = F(K, \exp(n_l t)L^d, J^d), \ Y \text{ given,}$$

yields:

$$X^o/K = x^o(\frac{p_x}{p_y}, \frac{p_m}{p_y}, \frac{w^b}{p_y}, Y/K) \tag{7.49}$$

$$L_f^{do}/K = l_f^{do}(\frac{p_x}{p_y}, \frac{p_m}{p_y}, \frac{w^b}{p_y}, Y/K) \quad \text{not needed in the following} \tag{7.50}$$

$$J^{do}/K = j^{do}(\frac{p_x}{p_y}, \frac{p_m}{p_y}, \frac{w^b}{p_y}, Y/K) \tag{7.51}$$

Firms' optimization problem to obtain potential output:

$$\max_{Y,X,J^d,L^d} [Y + \frac{p_x}{p_y} X - \frac{p_m}{p_y} J^d - \frac{w^b}{p_y} L^d] \tag{7.52}$$

$$\text{s.t.} \quad T(Y,X) = F(K, \exp(n_l t)L^d, J^d)$$

yields:

$$Y^p/K = y^p(\frac{p_x}{p_y}, \frac{p_m}{p_y}, \frac{w^b}{p_y}) \tag{7.53}$$

$$X^p/K = x^p(\frac{p_x}{p_y}, \frac{p_m}{p_y}, \frac{w^b}{p_y}) \quad \text{not needed in the following,} \tag{7.54}$$

$$L_f^{dp}/K = l_f^{dp}(\frac{p_x}{p_y}, \frac{p_m}{p_y}, \frac{w^b}{p_y}) \quad \text{not needed in the following,} \tag{7.55}$$

$$J^{dp}/K = j^{dp}(\frac{p_x}{p_y}, \frac{p_m}{p_y}, \frac{w^b}{p_y}) \quad \text{not needed in the following.} \tag{7.56}$$

$$\dot{n}_l = \beta_{n_l}(\tilde{n}_l - n_l), \quad \tilde{n}_l = \tilde{n}_l(g_k) \tag{7.57}$$

$$U_c = Y/Y^p \tag{7.58}$$

$$\hat{J}^a = \alpha_1^j(J^{do}/J^a - 1) + \alpha_2^j(U_c - \bar{U}_c) + \gamma \tag{7.59}$$

$$\hat{X}^a = \alpha_1^x(X^o/X^a - 1) + \alpha_2^x(U_c - \bar{U}_c) + \gamma \tag{7.60}$$

$$T(Y, X^a) = F(K, \exp(n_l t)L_f^d, J^a) \to L_f^d \tag{7.61}$$

$$\dot{L}_f^w = \beta_l(L_f^d - L_f^w) + (\gamma - n_l)L_f^w \tag{7.62}$$

$$g_k^d = (I/K)^d$$

$$= \alpha_1^k((1-\tau_c)\rho^{av} - r^r)) + \alpha_2^k(r_l - (r + \xi)) + \alpha_3^k(U_c - \bar{U}_c) + \gamma + \delta \tag{7.63}$$

$$\dot{g}_k = \alpha_{gk}(g_k^d - g_k), \; g_k = I/K \tag{7.64}$$

$$\dot{\rho}^{av} = \alpha_\rho(\rho^e - \rho^{av}) \tag{7.65}$$

$$Y_f = Y - Y^e = \mathcal{I} \tag{7.66}$$

$$S_f^n = p_y Y_f \tag{7.67}$$

$$S_f^n + p_e\dot{E} = p_y(I - \delta K) + p_y\dot{N} \tag{7.68}$$

$$I^a = I + \dot{N} \tag{7.69}$$

$$\hat{K} = I/K - \delta = g_k - \delta. \tag{7.70}$$

Firms now operate with a neoclassical production technology, again with three inputs (labor L^d, imports J^d and capital K) and two outputs (domestically traded commodities Y and exports X). Inputs are combined by way of the gross output function F and provide a productive capacity level $\mathcal{Y} = F(K, \exp(n_l t)L^d, J^d)$ on the basis of which a transformation function then describes how this productive capacity $\mathcal{Y}$ is used to produce domestically traded goods Y and exports X. These functions have the usual concavity properties which guarantee that the two maximization problems considered above have a unique solution for the data on which they are based (homogeneity of degree one is of course also assumed).

The first maximization problem is the one the firms must solve in the face of a given (expected) aggregate demand Y^e for domestic goods (leading to production plans $Y = Y^e + \mathcal{I}$), also facing given prices for their export commodities, p_x, and their import demand, p_m (both measured in the domestic currency, and including import taxation), and for their labor input, w^b, that is gross wages including payroll taxes. Furthermore, the price for domestic output that firms are currently charging is temporarily given by p_y, while its rate of change will be explained in module 5b below. Based on these data, the optimizing response of firms is to maximize the gap between export proceeds and the costs of the two variable inputs, imports and employment of the employed labor force, the unique solution of which is described in abstract terms in equations (7.49) –(7.51). Note that the optimal response only depends on the output capital ratio Y/K if homogeneity of degree one prevails. These equations describe the optimal responses of firms that are constrained by (their point expectations of) a Keynesian aggregate demand schedule (to be provided below) and by the input and output prices that currently prevail.

The second maximization problem describes the supply-side decision of the firms, i.e., what they would produce and demand for given input and output prices were there no demand constraint on the domestic market for goods. The solution to this problem is described in abstract terms by equations (7.53)–(7.56). This solution is used in a particular way in the Murphy model as a moving target that determines the pricing and the investment decisions of firms. To see how this corresponds to the description of firms' behavior developed in Chiarella and Flaschel (1999e) we observe first of all that firms are never constrained on import and export markets. There they simply act as price takers who buy and sell there whatever they intend to. In particular the export decision is therefore of secondary importance for firms in the sense that they always operate 'at full capacity' in this market.

This is different on the market for domestic, non-traded goods where they would like to produce the amount Y^p, but are faced with an expected sales constraint Y^e on the basis of which they produce $Y = Y^e + \mathcal{I}$ as in Chiarella and Flaschel (1999e). The rate $U_c = Y/Y^p$ thus measures the extent to which firms are constrained on this market and can be called as in Chiarella and Flaschel (1999e) the rate of capacity utilization of firms, which now however refers to economic constraints and not simply to technological constraints that are absolutely binding as in Chiarella and Flaschel (1999e). Indeed it is quite possible that firms temporarily produce at levels where $U_c > 1$ holds, where thus marginal costs exceed marginal revenue, e.g., in the case where they want to defend their market share by serving customers at prices were there are indeed marginal losses. Despite joint production (for domestic purposes and exports) we therefore think that firms will use only a one-dimensional expression U_c to measure the discrepancy between actual performance and their targeted performance, on the basis of which they will revise their pricing and their investment decision.

Powell and Murphy (1997) use a different measure for this performance which they call the medium-run equilibrium price for the domestic good p_y^{MR}. In order to derive this price level they use duality theory, the unit-cost function dual, and other concepts from the profit-maximizing theory of the firm. We shall provide here a short description of their and a comparison with our type of approach to the optimal targets used by firms in order to adjust their pricing and investment decisions in view of these targets.[11]

Using the functional expression (7.53) the price p_y^{MR} can be easily determined from it, as it simply is the price level where the actual production level would be profit maximizing: $Y/K = y^p(\frac{p_x}{p_y^{MR}}, \frac{p_m}{p_y^{MR}}, \frac{w^b}{p_y^{MR}})$. This simply inverts this partial supply relationship between

[11]See Chiarella, Flaschel, Groh, Köper and Semmler (1999b) for a detailed derivation of these optimality considerations of firms in the case of CES / CET production technologies.

desired output and output price, which is possible since the $Y^p/K = y^p(\frac{p_x}{p_y}, \frac{p_m}{p_y}, \frac{w^b}{p_y})$ is an increasing function of p_y for given prices p_x, p_m, w^b. In Powell and Murphy (1997) firms move their prices p_y towards their target prices p_y^{MR} and increase (or decrease) their investment per unit of capital for $p_y > p_y^{MR}$ (for $p_y < p_y^{MR}$). It is surely possible to motivate this type of behavior on the basis of price and cost considerations alone. Yet, as there is a strictly increasing relationship between output Y and prices p_y^{MR} for any given set of actually prevailing input and output prices, w^b, p_m, p_x, p_y, we may simply substitute the above approach to pricing and investment decisions of firms by saying that firms will raise (or lower) their prices (ceteris paribus) when capacity utilization Y/Y^p, as measured above, is above the norm $\bar{U}_c(< 1!)$ (below it) and will also realize more (less) investment in such a case. Using our measure of capacity utilization in the place of the medium run target prices of the Murphy model is, on the one hand, easier to understand in its implications for pricing and investment and it, on the other hand, also explains why Powell and Murphy (1997, p.220) face difficulties with their steady state calculations which there do not lead to the condition $p_y = p_y^{MR}$, because it is quite natural to assume that $\bar{U}_c < 1$ holds for the benchmark level of capacity utilization which separates expansionary from contractionary situations, as we have already done it in Chiarella and Flaschel (1999e) (and will do so here as well).

The maximizing procedure (7.49) –(7.51) states what firms would like to do in the situation they are currently in, while (7.53) – (7.56) only serves to measure potential output Y^p with which firms compare their current output level. Powell and Murphy (1997) however add also delayed adjustments to the short-run import and export targets of firms, as we described it in (7.59), (7.60), which show the actual growth rates of imports and exports. Powell and Murphy (1997) furthermore use an independent employment function of firms (with no distinction between inside and outside employment) which however will generally imply that they will not produce efficiently by staying on their production functions. We instead again assume – as in Chiarella and Flaschel (1999e) – that the employment decision of firms is efficient and thus get the actual employment of the employed workers from equation (7.61) residually on the basis of given Y, X^a, J^a, K. Note that we have assumed as in Chiarella and Flaschel (1999e) that there is Harrod neutral technological progress at a rate n_l which is endogenous and depends on the rate of gross investment per unit of capital g_k.

The remaining equations of this module are formulated as in Chiarella and Flaschel (1999e) and concern the hiring and firing policy of the firms (eqn. (7.62)), desired and actual rates of investment (g_k^d and g_k) (which now incorporate an extended concept for the required rate of return, see module 1) (eqn. (7.63) and (7.64)) and the financing of the investment. The latter is defined by equation (7.68), which states that net investment in fixed capital $p_y(I - \delta K)$ and the actual change in inventory $p_y\dot{N}$ is financed partly by the savings of the firm (S_f^n) and the emission of new equities ($p_e\dot{E}$). Actual total investment I^a is then given by equation (7.69). Equations (7.66) and (7.67) define planned inventory investment $\mathcal{I}$ and the saving decision S_f^n of the firms. The actual growth rate of the capital stock is finally given by equation (7.70). The pricing decision of firms is described in module 5b of the model below.

The great innovation in this module of the model – the neoclassical heart of the model as Powell and Murphy (1997) call it – concern the integration of smooth factor and output substitution into the approach of Chiarella and Flaschel (1999e) and the new measurement of potential output and the rate of capacity utilization needed for such an extension. It is easily possible to add further characteristics of the business cycle to the investment decision of firms, for example a derivative control term (accelerator term) like $\dot{U}_c$ which describes the direction into which the economy tends. This is done in Powell and Murphy (1997) in a particular way, but is neglected here for reasons of simplicity.

Powell and Murphy's (1997, p.291ff.) list of consolidated equations appears to be - on the surface – in this sector very different from the equations that we employ above for the description of the behavior of firms, due to their use of cost-duals for their nested CES technology descriptions with smooth factor (labor, imports, and capital) and smooth output substitution (domestically marketed commodities and exports, to be subdivided later on in addition) in the place of our quantity imbalances shown in the above module, i.e., due to their reliance on medium run price concepts in the place of our measure of capacity utilization for domestically produced goods. This use of price duals, the 'neoclassical' heart of the Murphy model, see their page 149, is in fact intimately related to our use of demand determined deviations from the normal capacity utilization of firms, which shows that the employed price duals can indeed be reinterpreted from a Keynesian perspective. Eqns. 33 – 39 of the consolidated list of equations of the Murphy model thus appear in a different way here, but play a similar role as in our current representation of the enterprise production block with quantity imbalances in the place of price imbalances. The same applies to the eqns. 40, 41 and 100 which thus also reappear in different form in the formulation of the model of this chapter.

Eqn. 12 of the consolidated list of the Murphy model is the business sector employment equation, see also p.186 in Powell and Murphy (1997). In our reading of this equation, it is based on various measures of the capacity utilization of firms and the development of medium run employment, but not on an efficient use of labor as it is determined by means of the assumed production technology and the state of effective demand on the domestically marketed goods as in the module of the firm of the present model. We have therefore proposed above that firms employ labor in an efficient way and thus determine employment on the basis of the data that exist at each moment in time for the capital stock, for imports and exports and for domestic output, while the rate of capacity utilization will only appear in the investment and pricing behavior of firms in an obvious way.

The eqn. 15 of the consolidated list of the Powell and Murphy model, see also page 182 in their book, is basically the same as ours if we interpret their measure $\frac{p_Y^{MR}}{p_Y}$ *as measure for the rate of capacity utilization of firms as already proposed, since the profitability differential with respect to the required rate of returns is the same as in the housing investment equation and thus subject to the same comments there made and since the tightness of monetary policy is also expressed in their impact on investment in the way we explained it already for housing investment. As in the Murphy model there is endogenous trend growth in our fixed business investment equation. There is however an additional term b in Murphy's investment equation which refers to changes in the business cycle and which could be built into our investment equation by assuming that investment not only depends on the level of capacity utilization but also on its time rate of change, that is on a proportional and a derivative control in this respect. This is a meaningful extension of the determinants of investment behavior which however will not be integrated into our present model. As in the case of housing we distinguish the desired rate of investment (whose determinants have just been discussed) from the actual one, and use a feedback loop from desired to actual investment in the place of the influence of past investment decision on the current ones in the equation that is used in the Murphy model.*

We do not allow for a capital stock outside the enterprise sector and thus do not need eqn. 31 of the consolidated list of the Murphy model, see also their p.226, as well as the eqns. 27, 62 and 84 from this list which also concern public enterprise fixed business investment and which therefore are not present in our model. There remains from the list of the 100 eqns. of the Murphy model the accumulation identity for the capital stock of firms which as in our model is demand determined (eqn. 86 and p.262 for the Murphy model, and eqn. 95, see also p.140 in Powell and Murphy (1997)) which provides the description of endogenous Harrod neutral technical change which differs formally from our approach to an endogenous rate of technical progress, but which is nevertheless similar in spirit to it.

3*b*. Firms (Exports and Imports):

$$\begin{aligned}
p_m &= (1+\tau_m)ep_m^* && (7.71)\\
\hat{J}^a &= \alpha_1^j(J^{do}/J^a-1)+\alpha_2^j(U_c-\bar{U}_c)+\gamma && (7.72)\\
\hat{X}^a &= \alpha_1^x(X^o/X^a-1)+\alpha_2^x(U_c-\bar{U}_c)+\gamma && (7.73)\\
X_c^a &= \alpha_x X^a && (7.74)\\
X_o^a &= (1-\alpha_x)X^a && (7.75)\\
p_{xc} &= ep_{xc}^*\alpha_0^c(X_c^a/X_c^*)^{\alpha_1^c} && (7.76)\\
p_{xo} &= ep_{xo}^*\alpha_0^o(X_o^a/X_o^*)^{\alpha_1^o} && (7.77)\\
p_x &= \alpha_x p_{xc}+(1-\alpha_x)p_{xo} \quad (p_xX^a=p_{xc}X_c^a+p_{xo}X_o^a). && (7.78)
\end{aligned}$$

The first equation of this module is as in Chiarella and Flaschel (1999e) and says that import prices p_m are obtained from the world market and thus need only to be transformed to domestic currency expressions by means of the exchange rate e (they again include an import tax rate τ_m). Actual imports and exports are as determined in module 3a. Exports are divided in Powell and Murphy (1997) into commodity and other exports in a linear fashion, a procedure which we do follow here. Next, Powell and Powell (1997) allow for effects of Australian exports on their respective prices as described by equations (7.76), (7.77) which state that relative supplies have impact on the price of commodity exports and other exports with elasticity terms α_1^c, α_1^o. Finally the aggregate price index for exports is provided which due to the linear relationship between these two types of exports is also given by a linear expression in this case. Powell and Murphy (1997) assume the existence of inventories in the export good sector which are however neglected here, based on the assumption of price taking behavior of firms as far as international markets are concerned. Note also that there is no role for the PPP theorem in the considered situation since exports and imports are of quite different type and since the main product of the country is not traded internationally.

Powell and Murphy's (1997, p.291ff.) list of consolidated equations contain a detailed presentation of import and export relationships, including two types of exports (in fixed proportions to each other however), inventories in exported commodities, lagged adjustment of imports and exports in view of desired medium run values, price reactions on the world markets with respect to price taking Australian export and import decisions, the use of price indices and an equation concerning import duties, see the eqns. 8, 9, 11, 13, 16, 17, 23, 25, 28, 30, 42, 43 and 82 of the consolidated list of equations in Powell and Murphy (1997). It is obvious that our above module on the exports and imports of firms is to some extent close to this approach to internationally traded goods for the Australian economy.

7.5 Government and the monetary authority

In module 4. we describe the government sector of the economy in a way that allows for government debt in the steady state and for a monetary policy that fixes the growth rate of the money supply in a specific way. We thus depart from the use of the interest rate policy rule of the central bank we used in Chiarella and Flaschel (1999e) and take a more orthodox view here that believes that the monetary authority can control the money supply process and steer in this indirect way the short-term rate of interest. This change in policy description corresponds to Powell and Murphy's (1997) use of a stable money demand function of Cagan type[12] that we will also use (in a specific way) in the description of the government module shown below.

4. Government (Fiscal and Monetary Authority):

$$
\begin{aligned}
T^n &= \tau_w Y_w^{Dn} + \tau_p w L^d + \tau_v p_y (C_w^g + C_c + G) \\
&+ \tau_c [\rho^e p_y K + rB + B^l + p_h C_w^h - p_y \delta_h K_h] \\
&+ \tau_m e p_m^* J^a && (7.79) \\
G^n &= g p_v Y^e, \quad g = \text{const.} && (7.80) \\
L_g^d &= L_g^w = \alpha_g (G^n / p_v) / \exp(n_l t) && (7.81) \\
\hat{M} &= \mu = \bar{\pi} + \gamma + \beta_{\mu_1}(\bar{\pi} - \hat{p}_v) + \beta_{\mu_2}(\bar{U}_c - U_c) + \beta_{\mu_3}(r - r_o) && (7.82) \\
d &= \frac{B + B^l / r_l}{p_v Y^e} && (7.83) \\
\hat{\tau}_w &= \alpha_{\tau_{w1}}(d/\bar{d} - 1) + \alpha_{\tau_{w2}} \hat{d} && (7.84) \\
\hat{\tau}_m &= \alpha_{\tau_m} \frac{p_x X^a - p_m J^a}{p_x X^a} && (7.85) \\
\dot{B} &= \alpha_b^g (G^n + rB + B^l + w^u(L - L^w) + w^r \alpha_l L_2 + w^b L_g^d \\
&- T^n - \dot{M}) && (7.86) \\
\dot{B}^l / r_l &= (1 - \alpha_b^g)(G^n + rB + B^l + w^u(L - L^w) + w^r \alpha_l L_2 + w^b L_g^d \\
&- T^n - \dot{M}) && (7.87) \\
S_g^n &= T^n - w^u(L - L^w) - w^r \alpha_l L_2 - (rB + B^l) - (G^n + w^b L_g^d) && (7.88) \\
\dot{B}_1^l &= \alpha_{b1}^g \dot{B}^l && (7.89) \\
\dot{B}_1^{l*} &= (1 - \alpha_{b1}^g) \dot{B}^l && (7.90)
\end{aligned}
$$

We have no taxation of financial wealth, no taxation of firms and no taxation of exports, just as in Chiarella and Flaschel (1999e). By contrast, taxation concerns here only disposable

[12] They however assume that the growth rate of the money supply is strictly exogenous.

income Y_w^{Dn} of workers, payroll taxes, taxation of private and public consumption, of capital income and imports, as shown by equation (7.79). Equation (7.80) and (7.81) describe government consumption G^n and the employment in the government sector; note, that here is no distinction between the employed L_g^w and the employment of the employed L_g^d as in the firms' sector. According to equation (7.82) money is now held as an asset, and there are now open market operations of the central bank as a consequence of the assumed money supply policy in the place of the interest rate policy of Chiarella and Flaschel (1999e), which makes the growth rate of the money supply an endogenous variable of the model depending on reactions of the monetary authority to a certain inflation differential, the degree of capacity utilization of firms and the deviation of short-term interest from its steady state value. There are however still no foreign market interventions of the central bank, since we have as in Chiarella and Flaschel (1999e,f) that the capital account just balances the current account under the assumed asset flows and their embedding into consistent budget equations, without need for intervention of the monetary authority despite a temporarily given nominal rate of exchange. As stated we have, however, a domestic money supply rule which determines the growth rate of the money supply with reference to a target rate of inflation $\bar{\pi}$, but lets money supply grow faster when there is less inflation (in p_v) than is targeted, when the economy is operating at subnormal rates of capacity utilization and when the short term rate of interest is above the steady state rate. The opposite holds of course in the opposite situations, while also mixed possibilities may arise where the direction of the growth rate of the money supply is dependent on the strength and sign of the various items. The novel thing in comparison to Chiarella and Flaschel (1999e) thus is that money is now held for transaction purposes and as component of private wealth (by workers and asset holders) and that its supply is perfectly controlled by the government in a specific way.

Equation (7.84) (in connection with (7.83)) defines the rate of change of the income tax for workers, which reacts in a specific way to the government's debt ratio d. The dynamics of the tax on imports is given by equation (7.85). The following three equations describe the rate of change of short-term and long-term bonds as well as government's savings S_g^n according to its budget constraints. Note again that we follow Powell and Murphy (1997) in that government bonds are issued in rigid proportions as short-term and long-term bonds and the later in rigid proportions to domestic and foreign asset holders. This is a consequence, and a disadvantage, of the lack of a complete explicit modeling of portfolio decisions of asset holders.

Powell and Murphy's (1997, p.291ff.) list of consolidated equations does not contain the equation that describes government revenue, which however is presented on p.233 in Powell and Murphy (1997). This revenue is composed of wage income taxation, the taxes (at a different rate) that stem from property income, some sort of lump-sum taxation that is proportional to nominal GDP, value added taxes paid on the consumption of households, import duties, payroll taxes on the private sectors wage bill, taxes on housing rental services and gross operating surplus from public enterprises. In our model we do not have public investment and therefore no such profit incomes of the government, and no lump-sum taxes and taxes on housing services (apart from taxes on the profit that derives from them). Instead we also have taxes unemployment benefits, rents of retired persons (to the extent they are actually paid), payroll taxes on all employment and value added taxes on all consumption. Recall in this respect also that our definition of property income is different from the one given in Powell and Murphy (1997) as was explained in the description of the module of asset holders.

Government expenditure, eqn. 66 of the consolidated list (see also p.233 in Powell and Murphy (1997)), consequently only concern wage payments net of payroll taxes, corrected by a term that corresponds to enterprise activities of the government (not present in our model), public consumption (and investment, not present in our model) at producer's prices, inventory investment (not present in our model), nominal transfers to the old, the unemployed and for children (not present in our model), and further transfers to the whole population (not present in our model), all of course calculated net of wage taxation. Remaining terms then concern foreign aid (not present in our model), interest rate payments on government debt (only denominated in domestic currency in our model and at actual rates in the place of the average one of the Murphy model). All these expressions and concepts concern the equations 66, 63 and 64 of the consolidated list of their model and they are also built on the eqns. 58 – 61 of this list which define the aggregate value of interest-bearing debt of the public sector and its allocation to the domestic and the foreign economy, similar to the way we have done this in the above module of the government sector of our model. The same holds true for the accumulation identities of government debt which are definitional in essence, see eqns. 78 and 83 of their consolidated list.

There is an equation in this list, eqn. 65 (see also their p.237), which represents an adjusted ratio of transfer payments to the after-tax wage rate, which is not present in our approach as is eqn. 69 which represents some average tax rate concept as far as wage taxation is concerned (integrating an exogenous component of wage taxation that is not present in our model).

The final equation of the government block is eqn. 68 of the consolidated list (see also their page 236), which concerns the wage taxation rate. As in our approach this tax reaction is based on a proportional and a derivative term as far as a particular type of measurement of total government debt is concerned and also on a historical value of the endogenous part of wage taxation. This extra component as well as an exogenous component of wage taxation are neglected in our present reformulation of the Murphy model.

Our treatment of government expenditures on domestic goods makes them dependent on expected sales just as the choice of government employment, while Powell and Murphy (1997) seem to treat them as exogenously determined. Further differences lie in the import taxation rule which is in our model intended to give rise to balanced trade in the steady state. Finally, government savings and the allocation of government debt have already been discussed above.

7.6 Quantity and price adjustment

Next, module 5a of the model basically describes the inventory adjustment process for the non traded good of firms. Module 5b thereafter describes the nominal price adjustments in the goods and the labor market.

5a. Quantity Adjustments in the Production of the Domestic Good:

$$Y^e \neq Y^d = C_w^g + C_c + I + I_h + G \tag{7.91}$$

$$S^n = S_p^n + S_f^n + S_g^n = I^{na} + NCX^n = I^{na} + NX^n + NFX^n \tag{7.92}$$

$$I^{na} = p_y(I - \delta K) + p_y(I_h - \delta_h K) + p_y \dot{N} \tag{7.93}$$

$$N^d = \beta_{n^d} Y^e \tag{7.94}$$

$$\mathcal{I} = \beta_n(N^d - N) + \gamma N^d \tag{7.95}$$

$$Y = Y^e + \mathcal{I} \tag{7.96}$$

$$\dot{Y}^e = \beta_{y^e}(Y^d - Y^e) + \gamma Y^e \tag{7.97}$$

$$\dot{N} = Y - Y^d. \tag{7.98}$$

There is no real change in the module 5a as compared to its formulation in Chiarella and Flaschel (1999e). Equation (7.91) shows the components of aggregate demand Y^d, which has to be distinguished from the sales expectations Y^e of the firms. The next equation describes the uses of national savings, i.e. total net investment I^{na} (which is defined in equation (7.93)), net exports NX^n and net factor export payments NFX^n. Equations (7.94)–(7.96) give the definitions of the desired inventory stock N^d of the firms, their planned investment in inventories $\mathcal{I}$ and output Y of the domestic good. Finally, the actual rate of change of the inventories $\dot{N}$ (in contrast to the planned one $\mathcal{I}$) is given by equation (7.98) as the difference between output Y and actual demand Y^d. We note, that Powell and Murphy (1997) assume that sales expectations are always correct which in our view is not the really general situation in a Keynes-Metzler formulation of the short-run behavior of firms.

Powell and Murphy's (1997, p.291ff.) list of consolidated equations is in this case basically identical to our treatment of inventories of the domestically marketed commodity, up to the fact that we allow for disappointed sales expectations and thus for a truly Metzlerian inventory adjustment process and neglect other inventory activities of firms or of the government. There are three accounting identities used for sales, GDP and GNE in the Murphy model, see the eqns. 26, 96 and 97 of the consolidated list of equations of this model. The sales composition equation for the domestic good, see their page 224, contains as additional items with respect to our formulation of it, purchases for housing maintenance and public investment, which are both missing in our model. We stress again that these sales are correctly perceived by firms in the Murphy model so that there is no adjustment mechanism needed for sales expectations. GNE is defined as eqn. 97 of the consolidated list and consists of sales of the domestic good and of inventories of this good, valued at producer prices, the nominal value of the supplied rental services net of maintenance costs, inventories in export commodities, gross wages in the government sector (net of payroll taxes) and value added tax on the consumption goods supplied to the household sector. Gross domestic product is then defined, in eqn. 96 (see also the page 260), by adding net exports to GNE. The GNE concept is used in defining money demand in the Murphy model and the GDP concept appears in the description of the balance of payments, both still to be discussed in the modules that follow below.

The remaining equations describe domestic production, see eqn. 81 in their consolidated list, as in our model as the sum of (expected) sales plus voluntary inventory changes, determine planned and actual domestic inventory investment somewhat differently from our formulation, see equation 10 in the consolidated list, by referring to trend growth (as we do) but also by including a time trend component and import considerations. The similarity to our approach becomes more obvious on the pages 216/7 in Powell and Murphy (1997) where the derivation of this inventory adjustment equation is explained in some detail. In our model we neglect the term which formulates a partial proportionality of planned inventories with excess import supply. The equation 81 of the consolidated list of the Murphy model for the actual change in inventories is of course only a definitional matter. Note here again that there is no difference between desired and actual stocks of inventories in the Murphy model.

Next we have the module which basically describes wage and price adjustment on the basis of the described disequilibria on the market for labor and for goods and in view of the various measures of cost-push variety that exist in our economy.

5*b*. Wage-Price Adjustment Equations, Expectations:

$$\begin{aligned}
\hat{w}^b &= \hat{w} = \beta_{w_1}(V - \bar{V}) + \beta_{w_2}(V_f^w - 1) \\
&+ \kappa_w(\hat{p}_c + n_l) + (1-\kappa_w)(\pi_c^l + \tilde{n}_l) && (7.99)\\
\hat{p}_c &= \alpha_w \hat{p}_y + (1-\alpha_w)\hat{p}_h \quad [p_c = p_v^{a_w} p_h^{1-a_w}, \text{ see (7.16), (7.17) of mod. 2a.}] && (7.100)\\
\hat{p}_v &= \hat{p}_y = \beta_p(U_c - \bar{U}_c) + \kappa_p(\hat{w}^b - n_l) + (1-\kappa_p)\pi_c^l && (7.101)\\
\dot{\pi}^l &= \beta_{\pi^l}(\alpha_{\pi^l}(\hat{p}_v - \pi^l) + (1-\alpha_{\pi^l})(\bar{\pi} - \pi^l)) && (7.102)\\
\pi_c^l &= \alpha_w \pi^l + (1-\alpha_w)\pi_h^l, && (7.103)\\
\dot{\pi}_h^l &= \beta_{\pi_h^l}(\hat{p}_h - \pi_h^l) && (7.104)\\
L^w &= L_f^w + L_g^w = L_f^w + L_g^d && (7.105)\\
V &= L^w/L = V_f + V_g = L_f^w/L + L_g^w/L && (7.106)\\
V_f^w &= L_f^d/L_f^w, \qquad [V_g^w = L_g^d/L_g^w = 1] && (7.107)\\
\dot{\bar{V}} &= \beta_{\bar{v}}(V - \bar{V}) && (7.108)
\end{aligned}$$

Equation (7.99), which describes the dynamic of gross money wages w^b, is basically of the same form as in Chiarella and Flaschel (1999e), up to the use of the rate of inflation $\hat{p}_c$ of consumer prices (as defined by equation (7.100)) and its expected average over the medium-run, π_c^l, which represent the true cost-push terms in workers wage considerations and are thus now used in the place of solely the inflation rate for the domestically produced good and its expected medium-run average. The same holds true for equation (7.101), which gives the price inflation of the domestic good, $\hat{p}_v$, which is the same for producer's as well as consumer prices (including value added tax), and which reads as in Chiarella and Flaschel (1999e), up to the assumption that producers now expect the rate π_c^l as expected cost-push terms or medium-run average wage inflation. They therefore believe that wage formation is basically determined by cost-push considerations in its medium-run average behavior (corresponding to $\beta_{w_1}, \beta_{w_2} = 0, \kappa_w = 0$ as far as medium-run averages are concerned, see Fair (1997a,b) on empirical estimates of this type).

The formula for expected average inflation of the domestic good again employs backward and forward looking components as shown by equation (7.102). The backward looking part, on the one hand, is here simply given by adaptively formed expectations (in the place of a more complicated formula using past observations of price inflation). The forward looking component, on the other hand, is simply based on the target $\bar{\pi}$ that the central bank attempts to realize for the domestic rate of commodity price inflation. As in Chiarella and Flaschel (1999e) we assume that average expected inflation π^l over the medium-run is some average of the backward-looking time series approach and the forward looking (theory based) measure with weight α_{π^l} that is here constant in time. Note that we have assumed in block 4. of the model that the central bank attempts to move the rate of growth μ of the money supply towards $\bar{\pi} + \gamma$.

Having determined π^l it is easy to present the growth rate for the consumer-price index of worker households if it is for simplicity assumed that expectations of the medium-run average of the price inflation $\hat{p}_h$ for housing services follow the actual development in these prices with a time delay (in an adaptive fashion) (eqn. (7.104)). Due to our formula for the consumer price index we then get that the rate of inflation of this index, π_c^l, expected to hold over the medium run is the weighted average of the two rates π^l, π_h^l with the weights taken from the corresponding price index formula, as shown by equation (7.103).

The remaining equations of this block of the model are basically definitional ones and they are of the same type as those used in Chiarella and Flaschel (1999e) for this purpose. Note, that we have here an endogenous natural rate of employment $\bar{V}$ according to equation (7.108).

Why is there more refined expectation formation with respect the domestically produced good than with respect to the price of housing services as is assumed in the above approach to wage-price dynamics? The justification for this is that the expected average behavior of the rate of inflation of the domestically produced commodity enters the required rate of return used by investors in their fixed business and housing investment decisions. There is therefore more effort made in the estimation of the medium run average of the rate of inflation of domestic goods produced by firms (which do not produce housing services) and bought by workers and asset holders for their total consumption (consumption proper and houses) and their total investment in housing. By contrast, there is no need to apply the price index p_c to the decision making of firms and asset holders as far as their estimation of real magnitudes is concerned.

Note finally that we do not yet include import price inflation (caused by varying e or τ_m) into the price Phillips curve of the present approach to disequilibrium growth. This is partly due to the fact that both imports and exports of firms vary uniformly with the exchange rate and partly due to our focus on the output-employment-capital-utilization relationship as far as domestically marketed commodities are concerned. Import price inflation may however be an important cost-push term and thus should be included into later reformulations of the model.

Powell and Murphy's (1997, p.291ff.) list of consolidated equations contains with respect to the module of the present section only two equations, eqns. 4 and 14, that are discussed in Powell and Murphy (1997) on pages 107 and 219 respectively. Eqn. 4 is the money wage Phillips curve where adaptively formed inflationary expectations are already inserted in the usual way of an augmented Phillips curve of the monetarist type (with unity coefficient). This equation is nonlinear (strictly convex) in the rate of unemployment and it exhibits the rate of change of the rate of employment as a derivative control term (as in the original Phillips approach) which is implied in our model by the assumptions made on insider employment and the employment policy of the firm with respect to the over- or underemployment of their insiders. The other equation, the price dynamics for the domestically marketed good, is primarily based on the concept of medium run target prices p_Y^{MR} *of firms as they derive from the nested CES technology used in Powell and Murphy (1997). These prices are determined such that the current output becomes an optimal output of firms and have already been related to capacity utilization calculations in such a setup in module 3a of this chapter. Murphy's domestic inflation equation thereby basically reduces to an equation where inflation is driven by capacity utilization considerations of firms augmented by a cost-push term that is based on the rate of change of* p_Y^{MR}*, which may be related to the rate of change of capacity utilization as far as our own approach is concerned. There is also a constant term in this equation which in our reformulation of it will imply that the rate of inflation will rise before full capacity utilization is achieved and which therefore need not create the problems that are observed in Powell and Murphy (1997, p.220) in this respect (since it simply defines the desired rate of capacity utilization which is thus now less than one, see also Chiarella and Flaschel (1999a, Ch.5) in this regard).*

In the place of our concept of capacity utilization Powell and Murphy (1997) use a certain output capital ratio b, see the eqn. 99 in the consolidated list, to introduce accelerator relationships into the investment behavior of firms, but not into the pricing behavior of them as it has just been discussed. The eqn. 49 of their list finally introduces the symbol ξ *to denote the actual rate of inflation which in the form of model consistent expectations is used in investment equations but not in the price-wage dynamics. With regard to such expectations and the adaptive ones employed in the money wage equation, we therefore have formulated in our wage price dynamics an intermediate situation which is based on forward and backward looking expectations, but not either only 'rational' or purely adaptive ones. Note also that our wage and price dynamics is based on two Phillips curves of the demand pressure - cost push variety.*

Note finally that our model assumes that the NAIRU level of the rate of employment is determined endogenously in the place of the exogenous determination of the this rate in Powell and Murphy (1997, pp.106/7), estimated as approximately 8% in their treatment of the labor market.

The sixth module lists the equilibrium conditions for liquid assets and the price adjustment equations we assume to hold for the other financial assets we have allowed for in this model: long-term domestic and long-term foreign bonds and equities as claims to the capital stock of the firms'. We here follow Powell and Murphy (1997) in that we only present the equilibrium condition on the money market (in the form it is used in the Murphy model) which in contrast to the corresponding treatment of the monetary policy in the model of Chiarella and Flaschel (1999e) now is present as a market and cleared through an instantaneously adjusting short-term rate of interest in the usual way. All other equations of the following module concern asset price and interest rate dynamics (and expectations about them) and can be justified by referring to the Murphy model where however all following speeds of adjustment are chosen equal to infinity, giving rise to model-consistent or rational expectations and the jump variable technique that is then conventionally used to overcome the saddlepoint instability problems of such situations. By contrast, we assume in the following block that all such adjustment speeds may be very large but remain finite and have to deal instead with the problem of determining bounds for the resulting dynamics which then is generally locally explosive around the steady state solution of the model.

7.7 Asset market dynamics

Asset markets, in contrast to their treatment in parts I and II, are now treated in a way that departs from the perfect substitutability assumptions there used, by replacing the exact interest rate parity conditions by a somewhat delayed adjustment towards the establishment of such conditions and by replacing the assumption of a uniform prevalence of myopic perfect foresight of capital gains by heterogeneous expectations, which are only partly of the myopic perfect foresight variety and partly, with respect to less informed agents, of a backward looking type, here modeled by adaptive expectations for reasons of simplicity (in the place of more powerful univariate time series methods). Furthermore, there is now a certain hierarchy present in the interdependence of expected rates of returns on financial assets. We in fact assume that short-term interest rates (determined through money market equilibrium) drive the long-term rate on consols, which in turn (including expected capital gains) in the basis for adjustments of expected returns on equities and foreign bonds and thus of the share price and the rate of exchange, based on temporarily given capital gain expectations and a given foreign rate of interest. Should the central bank allow for steady state inflation, by setting its inflationary target $\bar{\pi}$ to a positive value, we assume in addition that asset price dynamics reflects this target as a trend term added to the dynamics of long-term bond prices, share prices and the Dornbusch type exchange rate dynamics.[13]

6. Money Market Equilibrium, Asset-Price and Interest-Rate Adjustments:

$$
\begin{aligned}
M &= M^d = M_w^d + M_c^d && (7.109)\\
&= p_v k C_w^g \exp(-\alpha_r(1-\tau_c)r) + p_v k C_c \exp(-\alpha_r(1-\tau_c)r) && (7.110)\\
M+B &= M_w + B_w + M_c + B_c = M_w^d + B_w^d + M_c^d + B_c^d && (7.111)\\
\hat{p}_b &= \beta_{p_b}[(1-\tau_c)r_l + \pi_b - ((1-\tau_c)r + \xi)] + \bar{\pi}, \quad p_b = 1/r_l && (7.112)\\
\hat{p}_e &= \beta_{p_e}[(\frac{(1-\tau_c)\rho^e p_y K}{p_e E} + \pi_e) - ((1-\tau_c)r_l + \pi_b)] + \bar{\pi} && (7.113)\\
\hat{e} &= \beta_e[(1-\tau_c^*)r_l^* + \epsilon - ((1-\tau_c)r_l + \pi_b)] + \bar{\pi} && (7.114)\\
\dot{\pi}_{bs} &= \beta_{\pi_{bs}}(\hat{p}_b - \pi_{bs}), \qquad p_b = 1/r_l && (7.115)\\
\pi_{bc} &= \hat{p}_b && (7.116)\\
\pi_b &= \alpha_s \pi_{bs} + (1-\alpha_s)\pi_{bc} && (7.117)
\end{aligned}
$$

[13]See Flaschel and Köper (1999) for the introduction of a Tobin type portfolio approach into models of KMG type, that integrates the behavior of financial markets as considered in Franke and Semmler (1999) with the dynamics of the real part of the economy. The above kind of asset price dynamics is investigated in a simple Blanchard (1981) type framework in Chiarella, Semmler and Mittnik (1998) from the theoretical, the numerical and the empirical perspective.

$$\dot{\pi}_{es} = \beta_{\pi_{es}}(\hat{p}_e - \pi_{es}) \tag{7.118}$$
$$\pi_{ec} = \hat{p}_e \tag{7.119}$$
$$\pi_e = \alpha_s \pi_{es} + (1-\alpha_s)\pi_{ec} \tag{7.120}$$
$$\dot{\epsilon}_s = \beta_{\epsilon_s}(\hat{e} - \epsilon_s) \tag{7.121}$$
$$\epsilon_c = \hat{e} \tag{7.122}$$
$$\epsilon = \alpha_s \epsilon_s + (1-\alpha_s)\epsilon_c \tag{7.123}$$
$$\dot{r}_l^{av} = \beta_{av}(r_l - r_l^{av}) \tag{7.124}$$

Assuming as in the Murphy model conventional money market equilibrium (here with differentiated money demand functions and with short-term bond market equilibrium as an equivalent to money market equilibrium) and assuming an instantaneously adjusting short-term rate of interest has a variety of questionable features which should be compared as to their importance and relevance with the problems of the alternative treatment of money and monetary policy we have presented in Chiarella and Flaschel (1999e). As our model is formulated now, the short-term rate of interest is the only price variable of the model that can adjust with infinite speed. Next, there is the problem of measuring the volume of transactions that is relevant for the formation of money demand. Here typically all financial transactions are plainly ignored in the literature and all real transactions are lumped together and measured by a proxy of aggregate demand though money holdings generally only occur in the household sector. In equation (7.110) we have departed from this tradition slightly by basing (interest sensitive) transactions demand for money on the two actual consumption decisions of workers and asset holders, but not on other transactions (investment decisions, government expenditures), since there is no money demand of firms and no money demand of the government here (as is generally, but only implicitly assumed in treatments of aggregate money demand, which – as already stated – abstract from all financial transactions already).

We state without further consideration, see the calculations following module 2b. in this regard, that the above determination of the interest rate r and its rate of change $\dot{r}$, obtained by differentiating this equilibrium condition with respect to time, just implies that the new supply of money $\dot{M}$ is just absorbed by workers and asset holders in the way it is described in the section on their behavior, so that aggregate money market equilibrium automatically supplies the neutral distribution of money we have analyzed in modules 2a. and 2b. and thereafter. This holds true despite the fact that the variable $\dot{r}$ does not appear in the individual demands for extra transaction balances.

Note again that the new supply of long-term bonds (as distributed by the government) is just absorbed by asset holders as are the equities of firms. There are thus no constraints to this supply in the present model. Note also that we only postulate in the same way as in Chiarella and Flaschel (1999e) certain laws of motion for asset prices (interest rates) and expectations about their rate of change (see equations (7.112)–(7.124)) and do not treat portfolio decisions of asset holders explicitly. There are generally no uniform (expected) returns on assets, but only somewhat delayed asset price reactions on the basis of perceived rate of return differentials. Note finally that we now make use of an average concept r_l^{av} with respect to the long-term interest rate, r_l, too, which has also been used in module 1 to define the medium-term required rate of interest, with which other medium term averages representing the various rates of return of the model are to be compared in the housing and the capital stock investment decisions of the two investors of the model, asset holders and firms.

Powell and Murphy's (1997, p.291ff.) list of consolidated equations is very brief with respect to the representation of this module. We have a conventional (Cagan) form of money demand function, eqn. 18 of the consolidated list, which is based on gross national expenditure (GNE), which give eqn. 97 of the consolidated list. This function can be explicitly solved for the short-term rate of interest since it is linear in logarithms and it provides an interest rate steering condition that is based on the ratio between money supply and GNE solely. There is thus stock market equilibrium assumed with respect of the usual representation of the LM curve and liquidity preference theory, as in the presently considered model. In eqn. 57 of their consolidated list, Powell and Murphy (1997) furthermore provide the definition of the growth rate of the money supply which is exogenous to the Murphy model. Finally, in view of our above module 6, describing the dynamics of the asset prices, Powell and Murphy (1997) assume in their consolidated list in eqns. 45, 50, 51, see also their pages 250, 178, 246, that long-term domestic bonds are perfect substitutes of short term domestic bonds as are long-term foreign bonds which together with the assumption of model consistent expectations (also for the rate of inflation that is used by investors) provides them with an equation for the term structure of interest rates and the uncovered interest rate parity condition. We have assumed in our module 6. that asset prices do not immediately adjust to these two types of conditions and that there are heterogeneous expectations of asset holders with respect to asset returns. In the limit, where all the adjustment speeds that are involved in our module are set equal to infinity we would however obtain the rational expectations solution of equilibrated asset markets used in the Murphy model, but would then either have to apply the conventional jump variable technique of the rational expectations approaches or study the limit process just mentioned in its definitely very complicated details.

7.8 The foreign sector

Module 7. describes various items that appear in the balance of payments Z, such as nominal net exports NX^n and nominal net capital exports NCX^n. Concerning nominal net interest payments,[14] which need not cross borders and thus need not appear as an item in the current account, we have in fact assumed that they do cross borders. They are fully present in the calculation of the disposable income of wealth owners and also in the current account of the balance of payments Z. We stress that the balance of payments must be balanced in our model due to the assumptions made on the absorption of assets by the private sector of the economy. There is thus no need (though maybe in some cases nevertheless the obligation) for the central bank to intervene in the market for foreign exchange, despite a temporarily given rate of exchange e, see section 2 for a detailed proof of this assertion. Equations (7.125)–(7.128) now give the definitions of nominal net exports NX^n, net nominal factor export payments NFX^n, net nominal capital exports NCX^n and the balance of payments Z in the framework of the present model.

7. Balance of Payments:

$$NX^n = EX^n - IM^n = ep_x^* X^a - ep_m^* J^a \tag{7.125}$$

[14]Which are normally interpreted as net 'factor' exports NFX^n.

$$
\begin{aligned}
NFX^n &= e(1-\tau_c^*)B_2^l - (1-\tau_c)B_1^{l*} && (7.126)\\
NCX^n &= e\dot{B}_2^l/r_l^* - \dot{B}_1^{l*}/r_l && (7.127)\\
Z &= NX^n + NFX^n - NCX^n = 0. && (7.128)
\end{aligned}
$$

Powell and Murphy's (1997, p.291ff.) list of consolidated equations contains the balance of payments description as equation 74, see also their page 258, and it is based on a more diversified list of interest payments and other transfers besides the trade account as far as the current account is concerned, including equity investment returns (where equities are represented by the capital stock items owned by foreigners) as profit payments based on the gross operating surpluses of firms. The capital account on the other hand exhibits New Borrowing Overseas (NBO) and equity investment inflow, represented as net investment in the domestic capital stock. There is also a balancing item ABL in this equation, which may be due to various statistical discrepancies, but also contain elements of foreign exchange market operations of the central bank as they occur in actual economies. A question we have with respect to this representation of the balance of payments is to what extent the average rates of return there used are consistent with the assumption of rational expectations and asset market equilibrium rates of interest considered in the preceding module of our model. We do not have international trade in equities in our model yet, and thus can ignore this item in the balance of payments as well as eqn. 75 of the consolidated list of the Murphy model which provides the accumulation identity for foreign owned business fixed capital.

Module 8. finally provides the data needed from the 'foreign' economy in the simplest form possible. It is assumed that the modeling of the foreign economy is based on the principles we used for the description of the domestic economy, but based on steady state values throughout, that is it is assumed in particular as inflation-free, exhibits a constant rate of growth and a given nominal rate of interest on long-term bonds. Note that we assume $\tau_c = \tau_c^*$ for reasons of notational simplicity. Assuming constant foreign prices for the internationally traded goods implies for reasons of consistency, and in particular for the steady state calculations of the following chapter, that the inflationary target of the monetary authority, $\bar{\pi}$, should be set equal to zero which it is assumed to be from now on.

8. Foreign Country Data:

$$
\begin{aligned}
r_l^* &= const. && (7.129)\\
\tau_c^* &= \tau_c && (7.130)\\
\hat{p}_m^* &= 0 && (7.131)\\
\hat{p}_{xc}^* &= 0 && (7.132)\\
\hat{p}_{xo}^* &= 0 && (7.133)\\
\hat{X}_c^* &= \gamma && (7.134)\\
\hat{X}_o^* &= \gamma && (7.135)
\end{aligned}
$$

all fixed at their steady state values

Powell and Murphy's (1997, p.291ff.) list of consolidated equations here finally contain the given short- and long-term interest rates of the world market, see eqns. 70 and 71 of their consolidated list, which are determined as a weighted average of the respective rates for the

US, Japan, Germany and the UK. We consider in our model the rest of the world as one country and thus do not have to use such average concepts in our model. Furthermore, as we allow only for international trade of long-term bonds for the moment we only use the foreign long-term rate of interest as a datum for our model and do not consider its relationship to the short-term foreign rate (which in fact is the rate that appears in the uncovered interest rate parity condition of the Murphy model), while their long-term foreign rate appears in the form of a moving average in the calculations that concern their representation of the balance of payments.

There are various exchange rate identities in the Murphy model, see the eqns. 46, 47, 48, and 72 which all boil down to one exchange rate e in the model of this chapter. Finally, there is the definition of the given foreign rate of inflation (which in this case is not a weighted average of the countries that are confronted with the Australian economy) in the formulation of the Murphy model. We do not really consider in this chapter and in fact do not investigate in the subsequent chapters inflation in the world economy, as well as persistent inflation in the domestic economy, but simply assume given US-dollar world prices for export and import commodities and an inflation target of zero for the domestic monetary authority.

7.9 A summing up

This closes the description of the extensive or structural form of the CTD growth model here proposed as a theoretical reflection of the structure of the Murphy model (and its detailed comparison with the structure of this latter model for the Australian economy) by which we extended the less advanced predecessor disequilibrium growth model of Chiarella and Flaschel (1999e) in significant ways (including in particular now substitution in production for inputs and outputs and wealth effects in consumption). We stress once again that the short-run of the model is Keynesian throughout which means that supply bottlenecks can either be avoided through appropriate buffers or have still to be added for larger deviations of the economy from its steady state behavior as in chapter 5.

Summarizing the comparison with the Murphy model of Powell and Murphy (1997) we can state both models basically differ in the range of assets they allow in the financial part of the economy where we in addition use a disequilibrium approach to asset market dynamics and expectations. The Murphy model here rests on rate of return parity conditions coupled with rational expectations of investors, both with respect to financial as well as real investment, which represents a limit case of the approach we have adopted in this chapter. It may be that this limit case of perfect substitutability appears to be the only truly convincing case for the reader from the purely theoretical perspective for modeling asset market dynamics, as long as an explicit modeling of stocks demanded and supplied as in Tobin's (1969) portfolio approach with imperfect substitutability between assets is avoided. In our view this would imply that the asset market module of our model must be replaced by a full portfolio approach where asset prices clear asset markets in later reformulations of the model as it is presented in Franke and Semmler (1999), in particular if the demand side on asset markets is to be modeled explicitly and behaves in a less tranquil way as is here still the case.

Another important difference is given by the treatment of production and the optimizing behavior of firms as far as formal descriptions are concerned. Powell and Murphy (1997) have to solve an eight dimensional nonlinear equation system in their treatment of the objectives of firms on the background of their nested CES-technology in order to derive medium run target level of firms in particular with respect the pricing of the domestically produced commodity, while we employ only certain optimal quantity targets throughout (for potential output, exports and imports) which influence the pricing and the investment decision of firms on a subsequent stage. We have argued however that the approach chosen for the Murphy model, its so-called neoclassical heart, can be reinterpreted in terms of demand determined deviations from quantity targets that are used by firms in the model presented in this chapter. There are also many further, but generally minor differences to the Murphy model which will not be repeated here. Despite all this we would nevertheless claim at the present stage of the investigation that the model of this chapter and the Murphy model are definitely very similar in spirit, though of course still different in purpose and with respect to the weights these two model types give to theoretical and applied considerations.

The figure 7.1 summarizes again the theoretical aspects and feedback chains that are now present in this largely extended approach to disequilibrium growth theory of this chapter. It shows that we now have reached a stage with a very advanced modeling of Keynesian IS-LM growth (with a Metzlerian description of goods-market disequilibrium and the output adjustment processes this implies), with a fairly developed wage-price module (as the supply side of the model) and also the inclusion of various feedback policy rules (also including a GBR with many aspects of actual government expenditures and their financing).

We stress that all of the shown feedback mechanisms are now in principle present in our extended dynamical model, in difference to the more basic representation of the Murphy model in Chiarella and Flaschel (1999c). As always we have the stabilizing Keynes-effect of comovements between the price level and the nominal rate of interest. We have in addition now the stabilizing Pigou effect (real balance effect) and further accompanying wealth effects through the life cycle hypothesis now assumed to apply to the consumption behavior of workers and asset holders. These two effects are however the only ones which unambiguously give rise to the possibility that price deflation (based on wage deflation) will improve economic activity, by their increasing directly or indirectly the investment demand of firms and the consumption demand of the two considered types of households.

As in the basic KMG model and its extensions we have, from a partial perspective, that either wage or price flexibility is destabilizing (adverse real wage Rose type adjustment possibilities), that inflationary expectations are destabilizing when they are adjusted with sufficient speed (real rate of interest or Mundell effects) and that inventory adjustments may bear the germ of instability when they are exercised with sufficient speed (Metzler type accelerator effects). Harrodian fixed business investment accelerator effects will be added as further destabilizing accelerator mechanisms if such investment responds not only to the level of capacity utilization, as is currently assumed, but also in the way of a derivative control, to its rate of change. These possibly destabilizing mechanisms concern the interaction of labor and goods markets, the wage price spiral, and quantity and price dynamics internal to the market for goods.

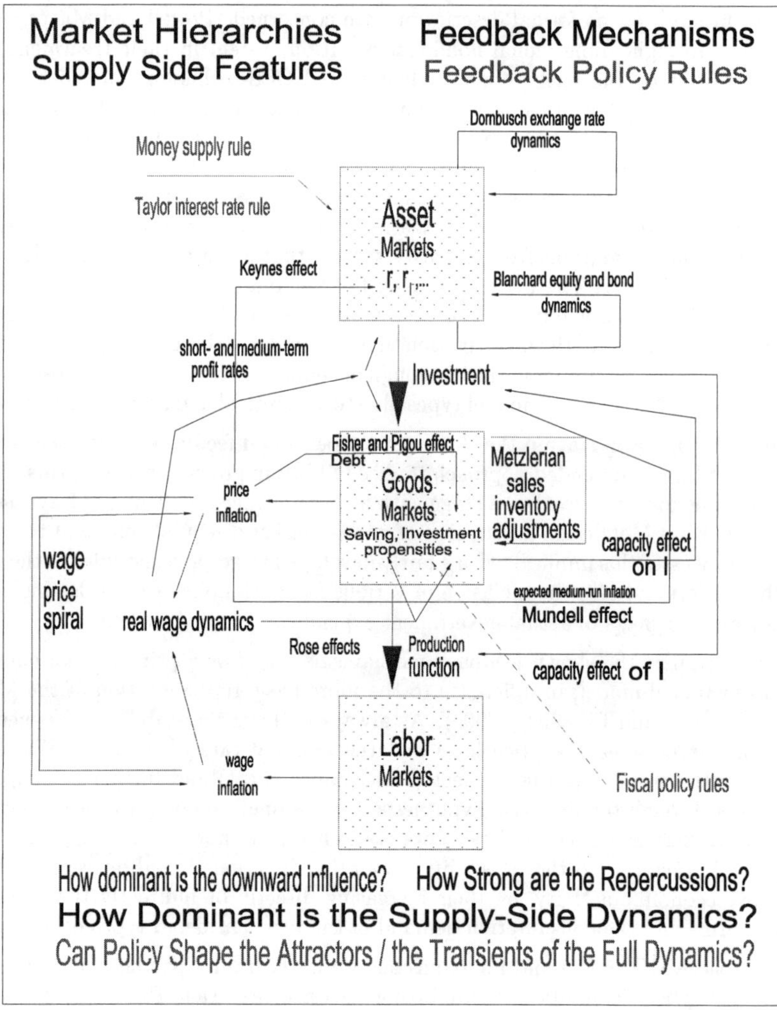

Figure 7.1:
The Keynesian downward causal nexus, the added feedback structure, the wage-price supply side dynamics and policy feedback rules of the advanced modeling of disequilibrium growth theory.

There is now also the possibility for a destabilizing Fisher debt effect, in the case where $B_w < 0$ holds, and where we thus have lending of the amount $B_c - B$ of asset holders to workers (the former then hold all short term government debt in particular). Deflation is in such a situation dangerous for economic stability, if consumption of debtors (workers) reacts more strongly than the consumption of creditors (asset holders) with respect to increases in their real interest and debt burden, which of course improves the real interest and wealth position of asset holders and thus their consumption, but probably not by so much that depressing effect on the consumption of workers is overcome. We do not yet have loans of firms from asset holders or banks as they were considered in section 2.3.2 included into the present general framework which however is easily done, see Chiarella, Flaschel and Semmler (1999), and which then would add debt deflation effects via the investment channel, where declining nominal revenues and profitability would then occur simultaneously with given or even increasing nominal volumes of interest payments and debt burdens, again leading to further declines of economic activity through multiplier effects and thus to a further strengthening of the deflationary spiral that is already in operation.

There are finally the centrifugal forces on the markets for long-term bonds, equities and foreign currency, since we have on all these markets that the expectations of increasing capital gains improve the position of the asset on which these expectations are formed giving rise to further actual capital gains on these assets and thus by way an immediate self-reference to further increases in expected capital gains. These forces are clearly visible through our assumption of a somewhat delayed adjustment of asset price and the exchange rate, and also their expected changes, to rate of return differentials between long-term domestic and foreign bonds and also equities which generalize the Dornbusch (1976) approach to exchange rate dynamics and the Blanchard (1981) approach to bond and shares price dynamics.

There is thus now a rich interaction of stabilizing and destabilizing partial feedback chains involved in the present approach to disequilibrium, growth and labor market dynamics which will be studied in chapter 9 to some extent with respect to their dominance and shaping of the overall outcome from various numerical perspectives. By and large, however, the large dynamic model of this part of the book must be left for future research, concerning the implications of the laws of motion and their steady state solutions described in subsequent chapters on the general level as well as important special cases of it. This even more applies to the consideration of fiscal and monetary policy rules to be designed in view of the destabilizing feedback chains in order to diminish or even remove their cumulative tendencies from the dynamics of the model.

However, we have also to stress that the asset market component represents in its present form still the weakest module of the model. This is so, since we so far have modeled only the interaction of various rates of return (actual and expected ones) with the dynamics of asset prices in a hierarchical and thus special manner and since we have assumed that the new supply of financial assets just flows into the economy without any explicit influence of these flows (and the related stocks) on the dynamics of asset prices. Surely, financial markets behave in a much more complicated way and show also much richer financing relationships, even on the macroeconomic level, than we have included them at present into our model. For example, as was shown above, one needs loans of asset holders or banks to worker households or firms in order to model the destabilizing Fisher deflation effect and thus needs further financing instruments in the latter case for such a macrodynamics. One needs international trade in equities if firm takeovers are to be included as an investment strategy of large corporations, other international capital movements and so on.

Despite this, the model is nevertheless already capable of showing on an advanced level how strong the influences of the supply side and of income distribution dynamics are, in particular in the shaping of the long run dynamical features of the model, of showing how many of the most important feedback mechanisms interact which each other and how feedback policy rules may change the course of the economy, however not yet in a way that shows explicitly the reaction of the private sector to the working of these policy rules as it would be demanded by the Lucas (1976) critique of structural macroeconometric model building.

Summing up, we have introduced in this chapter a very general theoretical reformulation of the Murphy model of the Australian economy, but here developed as high order continuous time dynamics, partly based on the experience gained with lower dimensional models of the KMG type in earlier work by Chiarella and Flaschel (1999a-d). We have also employed a variety of simplifications and reformulations of the a Powell and Murphy (1997) approach which improved the compact formulation of the model of the present chapter with its already very complex nonlinear relationships, in particular in production and in wealth allocation. In the next chapter 8 we will derive the 39D intensive or state variable form and the steady state of the dynamics here presented on the extensive level and will subsequently introduce specializing assumptions which will allow us to reduce their dimension to 22, which is still a large system with highly nonlinear subsystems in production and wealth allocation. These 22D dynamics be further reduced to an 18D core dynamics by removing the complex nonlinearities caused by smooth input and output substitution and wealth feedback effects and will then allow us to run first simulation studies for this general type of disequilibrium growth dynamics.

7.10 Macroeconometric model building of the AS-AD type: A brief comparison

In section 2.1, we have quoted Barro with respect to the opinion that there are two types of internally consistent monetary macrodynamic models available now, the market-clearing approach and the non-market-clearing approach, the latter being represented by the IS-LM model and its dynamic extensions which allow for sluggish wages as well as sluggish prices and, due to this, for under- or over-utilized labor as well capital. We have represented the market-clearing model as limit case of the working model of our book in chapter 4. We have also made the non-market clearing version of KMG growth, with its labor and goods market disequilibrium adjustment processes, more complete with respect to the possibility of supply bottlenecks and aspects of imperfect competition and the endogeneity of the NAIRU they can give rise to. These disequilibrium growth models are still of the IS-LM type, though 'IS' is now represented by IS-disequilibrium adjustment of Metzlerian type where sluggish quantity adjustment occurs in combination with sluggish price adjustment of the PC type.

There are numerous treatments and extensions of the market clearing approach for example in RBC and endogenous growth models which we did not reconsider extensively in our book, see Romer (1996) and Barro and Sala-i-Martin (1995) for example. There are rarely integrated treatments of monetary growth with labor and goods market disequilibrium, which in the present book are built on work of Flaschel (1993), Flaschel, Franke and Semmler (1997) and Chiarella and Flaschel (1999), expanding in particular the working model of the latter book towards Non-Walrasian and New Keynesian types of analysis and also towards an inclusion of endogenous growth coupled with smooth factor substitution.

The present work therefore continued into the direction of building an internally consistent model of labor and goods market dynamics in disequilibrium in order to make it comparable with the achievements that have been made in the area of the market clearing approach. There is however a further popular approach to monetary growth that is situated in the middle between the pure market clearing approach and the (with respect to real markets) pure non market clearing approach, the well known AS-AD growth model. This approach has been investigated extensively in Flaschel (1993), Flaschel, Franke and Semmler (1997) and Chiarella and Flaschel (1999).

We do not go here again into the details of the AS-AD approach to monetary growth once again, but refer the reader, up to the following few observations, to these earlier works in this respect, in particular to chapter 5 in the latter work. Let us first briefly enumerate some characteristics of the AS-AD approach which in sum give rise to an internal inconsistency of this approach. Weaknesses and inconsistencies of the AS-AD model are as follows:

1. Firms appear to be quantity takers and price takers at one and the same time, since there is a Keynesian demand constraint on the market for goods and at the same time profit maximizing employment (and output) on the market for labor.

2. These two characteristics may be justified to some extent by explaining the side by side occurrence of these two characteristics from the usual Keynesian perspective, augmented by the statement that firms are forced by competition to set prices equal to marginal wage costs and thus behave in a way such that the rules of perfect competition prevail.

3. If it is admitted that labor markets can be in disequilibrium in such a framework, one should go one step further and also allow for firms and the goods market to be in disequilibrium, in the IS sense if one only assumes disequilibrium in the use of the productive capacity of firms on the basis of temporarily given prices or in the Metzlerian sense if IS disequilibrium or erroneous inventory adjustment is considered.

4. If disequilibrium in the goods market is allowed for, the question of how prices are determined is raised anew and should not lead us back simply to marginal wage cost pricing in a truly Keynesian demand constrained goods market and its quantity adjustment processes.

We have considered in this respect simple PC approaches to the price level dynamics in the KMG approach and also models of imperfect competition in chapter 6. By way of summary we would therefore state that model builders should choose between a proper Keynesian approach to labor and goods markets dynamics and a proper Walrasian approach to these two markets, but not a problematic hybrid construction based on two very different paradigms of how market economies work (the possibility of disequilibrium in one, but not in the other market and the in behavior of firms). Yet, it is exactly this latter choice that is generally made when non-market clearing approaches are discussed on the textbook level and in the research literature. This also holds for the design of macroeconometric models of output, inflation and growth, to be considered below, which are called Computational General Equilibrium models (CGE) in applied modeling work, see McKibbin and Sachs (1991, pp.42/3) for example.

There has recently, and not for the first time, been another debate on the meaning and consistency of AS-AD and IS-LM analysis, the prototype models generally believed to represent Keynesian statics and dynamics in particular on the textbook level, but also in research papers, as in Sargent (1987), who in a particularly striking way shows how AS(-AD) can dominate IS-LM when it comes to considerations of medium- and long-run nature. Contributions were among others by Barens (1997), Barro (1994), Bhaduri, Laski and Riese (1998), Colander (1993, 1995), Clower (1996), Dutt and Skott (1996), Fields and Hart (1996) and Neville and Rao (1996), see Barens (1998) for a recent survey on this work. Before we come to applications of the AS-AD growth approach to actual economies, here the US economy as modeled by McKibbin and Sachs (1991) and Laxton et al. (1998), we want to state with respect to this debate the following few further remarks on Keynesian models of monetary growth.

We will not go into the details of the discussion of the above quoted work, however, but simply observe that our working KMG model can be of great help in evaluating this debate, since it provides as limit case IS-LM growth modeling, if adjustment of sales expectations is infinite ($\beta_{y^e} = \infty$) and if there is no desire to hold or adjust inventories ($\beta_{n^d} = \beta_n = 0$). We have found in Chiarella and Flaschel (1999, Chs. 4,6) that the consideration of this limit of KMG growth makes things more complicated than the use of sluggish quantity adjustment on the market for goods, since three equilibrium situations of sometimes problematic nature are then to be investigated if income distribution interacts with IS-LM equilibrium formation. Admitting disequilibria instead can therefore be less complicated, since feedback chains do not interact instantaneously, but work through laws of motion in the course of time.

Next, AS-AD growth can be obtained as limit from the IS-LM growth model as presented in Chiarella and Flaschel (1999, Ch.4/5), by replacing fixed proportions in production through smooth factor substitution and by assuming the further limit of an infinite adjustment speed of the price level ($\beta_p = \infty \quad U_c = 1$). Chiarella and Flaschel show in these chapters that this limit case is even more problematic than the preceding one, with respect to interpretations and analytical features, see also Flaschel (1993) and Flaschel, Franke and Semmler (1997) in this regard, and might be characterized as done above as mixing Keynesian and Walrasian features into an incoherent whole.

The recent work on AS-AD and IS-LM, quoted above, offers various pros and cons for these prototype models of the literature on Keynesian statics, but can, in our view, not really come to a definite conclusion unless the disequilibrium (and growth) situation that surrounds these concepts of temporary equilibrium are worked out in their details, as proposed in Chiarella and Flaschel (1999) and in part I of the present book. Making the analysis more general thus indeed helps to penetrate the situation where quantities and prices act with infinite speed and where non-causal equilibrium relationships have replaced the causal relationships of the underlying laws of motion. In addition, having assumed equilibrium on so many ways, based on infinite adjustment speeds and competitive pricing rules, should then induce the desire, as of classical economists, to assume infinite adjustment speed of wages as well which then implies the market clearing approach of our chapter 4 (and its myopic perfect foresight assumptions when expectations are also adjusted with infinite speed).

By contrast we would stick to finite adjustment speeds, at least as far as labor and goods market behavior is concerned, and thus would recommend to transfer the whole debate on AS-AD and IS-LM to this more general model type and the consistency (or if found: inconsistency) of the various assumptions there made, and of course their empirical relevance to be contrasted with the relevance of assuming infinite adjustment speeds. Note here that our approach also works in the case of fixed proportions of production, as any truly general approach should, while AS-AD depends on the use neoclassical production functions. Note also that the role of varying price, wage or quantity flexibility in stabilizing or destabilizing the economy, a discussion that started with Tobin's (1975) contribution, can only be meaningfully approached in a framework where such flexibilities can be varied, as in the KMG model of this book.[15]

Problematic and, at least in the case of destabilizing flexibilities: discontinuous, limit situations should therefore give way to work on refining the KMG approach, as we have undertaken it here in part II of the book.

On the basis of what has just been formulated we want to discuss in the remainder of this section now two prominent modern macroeconometric models that stress global linkages, economic interdependence and policy, coordinations, in the world economy. These model types are the MSG2 model for the world economy by McKibbin and Sachs (1991) and the Multimod Mark III model of the IMF as presented in Laxton et al. (1998). We will here basically discuss in some detail the MSG2 model and will only briefly comment on the IMF model, since the latter is very similar in its philosophy to the MSG2 approach, though with more stress on steady state reference solutions and less emphasis on issues of fiscal and monetary policy.

The dynamic 'general equilibrium' MSG2 model of the world economy by McKibbin and Sachs grew out of earlier work by the authors, the MSG1 model, which was based on a model of two country interaction of Mundell-Fleming type, exhibiting an IS-LM block, a static wage price block (including price expectations) and the UIP condition. Intertemporal linkages, in particular the dynamics of the government budget constraint and of the net foreign asset position were added later as well as wealth effects, rational expectations and also more details on the supply side of the economy. On this basis the MSG2 model was then formulated where the intertemporal budget constraint for the government as well as the international asset position of the country are supposed to hold.

MSG2 combines Keynesian demand side and classical supply side features. Demand equations are a combination of intertemporal optimizing behavior and liquidity constrained behavior. Wage price dynamics are basically due to a money wage Phillips curve, coupled with marginal cost pricing rules. Stock accumulation is basically considered for capital,

[15]See also Bhaduri, Laski and Riese (1998) in this regard, who however do not go far enough, since they stop their dynamic analysis with the dynamic multiplier in place of a proper quantity adjustment that also takes account of induced inventory changes. Note also that their price adjustment rule, as in Powell and Murphy (1997), makes use of a delayed adjustment towards competitive (or imperfectly competitive) marginal cost pricing, which according to this chapter can be reinterpreted in terms of quantities and capacity utilization rates.

government debt and net external debt and interacts with forward looking expectations. Finally, it is assumed that high international capital mobility prevails and that therefore UIP conditions characterize the accumulation of interest bearing financial assets. The model is based on microeconomic foundations as far as consumption and investment behavior is concerned, but it also allows for deviations from the fully optimizing behavior of economic agents. There is Harrod neutral technical change of an exogenously given rate.

> As with any modeling project that purports to describe reality, some trade-offs between theoretical rigor and empirical regularities are inevitable. (McKibbin and Sachs, 1991, p.42).

Note that in their model there is only one representative household, in the place of the four household types present in our CTD growth dynamics. This representative household decides over an infinite horizon on the aggregate consumption path and thus on savings and wealth accumulation by maximizing an intertemporal utility function subject to a wealth constraint, which includes human capital besides various financial assets. Since the model allows for unemployment, consumption is constrained by actual labor income and not by the desired one. This implies that the whole future of the labor market, where employment is always determined by the decision of firms, affects the consumption of the representative consumer and that also the calculation of human wealth is subject to these perfectly foreseen labor market conditions.

With reference to empirical evidence, McKibbin and Sachs, however, assume that consumption is only partially determined by intertemporal consumption smoothing and partially along simpler Keynesian lines by current disposable income. This adds a second household type to the model, which is interpreted as liquidity constrained worker households, which however would demand the use of disposable labor income in the place of disposable total income. Due to a special choice of the utility function for the first type of household, the authors then finally arrive at an aggregate consumption function that is linear in actual wealth and current disposable income and thus qualitatively of the same type as we have used it in the household sector of our economy. Indeed, when it comes to their empirical specifications, where consumption spending depends on income and assets, there is no difference as to what we would obtain as empirical specification in our model. The important novelty of their microfounded approach is however that human capital is taken into account and added to financial wealth in the consumption and savings decision, a variable that (as well as its law of motion) is still lacking in our CTD growth dynamics.

Nevertheless, we would like to point out that the solution of constrained maximization problems may be of help in finding convincing functional forms for aggregate consumption behavior, but that the final empirical specification of this type of theorizing is not really a surprise for the ad hoc macroeconomist and its perspective of integrated macrodynamic model building. Already in earlier macro models such empirical specifications have been employed. Consumption is further disaggregated in McKibbin and Sachs, in a way that is comparable, but not identical, to the disaggregation procedures applied to our CTD model. It is also akin to the approach presented in Powell and Murphy (1997). Flows of newly issued assets (by firms and the government) are just accepted by households and absorbed into their portfolio of asset, just as in our CTD growth model, but here on the basis of the general prevalence of UIP conditions. We note that the array of financial assets differs from the one we have chosen to consider.

In the next section of chapter 3, McKibbin and Sachs (1991) are concerned with the factor input and output decision of firms which is here jointly determined with their investment decision from an intertemporal after tax profit maximization problem that involves cost of adjustment of the capital stock as in Lucas (1967). As in Powell and Murphy (1997) there is a nested production technology, yet here of simple Cobb-Douglas type. Capital stock growth is always driven by net investment demand, so that only the Keynesian regime prevails as far as goods market equilibrium is concerned. With respect to the representation of such and other details of the model of McKibbin and Sachs one should note in addition that everything is already expressed per unit of labor (measured in efficiency units) in a way that cannot always easily related to the original extensive form level.

It is assumed that firms are always in equilibrium, on their supply schedule if their behavior is (illegitimately) reinterpreted as price taking, profit-maximizing behavior in this Keynesian setup of the market for goods (where savings decisions have to be coordinated with investment decisions by adjusting the level of output). Therefore. this situation is coupled with marginal productivity rules as far as labor and imports are concerned or with a marginal cost pricing rule as far as wages are concerned, see also p.39 in McKibbin and Sachs (1991), and still with a cost-minimizing input choice regarding imports, everything interpreted relative to a given volume of outputs due to demand constraints on the market for goods. As we have already argued above, such a mixture of Keynesian and Walrasian behavioral assumptions is inconsistent and unsatisfactory, also from the point of view that capital is always fully employed, while labor is not during the business cycle. Following Powell and Murphy (1997) one should allow for a delayed adjustment of output prices to such competitive conditions as the pricing policy of firms or, as we have reformulated the Powell and Murphy approach, a delayed pricing response of firms in the light of their rate of capacity utilization which is defined as the ratio of actual output to profit maximizing output, see section 7.5 in this regard. Output pricing is thus, in correspondence to the Keynesian situation of demand rationed firms, subject to certain imperfections and impacted by certain medium run targets of firms. This puts firms off their aggregate supply schedule in the short-run and also allows to decouple their investment behavior from the short-run production and pricing decision.[16]

Investment may however still be determined through the cost of adjustment model of capital stock formation and therefore be related to Tobin's marginal q as in McKibbin and Sachs (1991, p.52), see also Hayashi (1982). On the basis of this article by Hayashi (1982) the authors add current profits as determinant of current investment behavior for empirical realism, again motivated by certain liquidity constraints for some firms. We would make investment basically dependent on profitability differentials, that may be related to Tobin's average q, see Sargent (1987) in this regard, and also on current capacity utilization and a measure for the tightness of monetary policy. Making investment directly dependent on Tobin's average or marginal q would demand that the law of motion of this variable has to be added always to the real dynamics of the model, see the following chapters 8 and 9 as far as the average q is concerned.

[16]Note here also that the employment policy of firms may deviate from marginal productivity rules, even if the choice of over- or under-time work is dependent on them. Empirically it is highly implausible that labor is hired up to the point at which marginal productivity equals the real wage as far a outside labor recruitment is concerned.

Next, concerning the wage dynamics, McKibbin and Sachs (1991, p.53) make use of a standard PC approach that explains the money wage growth rate as in Phillips (1958), yet coupled here with simple forward and backward looking expectations of the consumer price level, very akin to what we have proposed in various places of this book. As in our approach to disequilibrium growth labor is inelastically supplied on the external labor market, but there is no additional employment rate within firms nor are their derivative or integral controls in the money wage PC as discussed in chapter 2 of our book. In sum, the wage price module of the McKibbin and Sachs (1991) MSG2 model is basically of the form as discussed in Sargent (1987, Ch.5) in the context of a textbook model of AS-AD growth and thus subject to the critique presented at the beginning of the present section. Interesting however is the application of a weighted average of forward and backward looking expectations of price inflation and also the choice of other wage adjustment rules for countries other than the USA.

Concerning the government budget constraint at each moment in time, McKibbin and Sachs (1991, p.54) only consider bond financing of the government deficit (which may be justified on empirical grounds) and assume in addition a transversality condition to hold and thus an intertemporal budget constraint to hold for the behavior of the government. They also employ a tax policy rule where there are given rates of wage and capital income taxation as in our CTD growth model and where there is additional shift term in tax collection that responds to increases in interest payments and falls entirely on wage income. We have assumed instead in section 7.5 that the wage tax rate is altered into the direction of achieving a certain target level for the government debt to GDP ratio and thus have circumvented a discussion of the need for intertemporal budget constraints in a way that is not unrelated to the tax policy rule used in McKibbin and Sachs (1991).

Money demand is explained in McKibbin and Sachs (1991, pp.55,213) by assuming that it is a factor of production and by specifying the money demand function in the standard way making as dependent on the output of firms and the short-term nominal rate of interest. Asset markets are treated separately from money demand and assumed to be perfectly integrated so that there are no interest rate differentials in the world economy, including gains from depreciation or other capital gains. The situation assumed is thus a limit case of our modeling of asset markets in section 7.7 where imperfect capital mobility is also considered, however in a still preliminary way we must admit.

The model of McKibbin and Sachs (1991) is closed by assuming that prices are fully flexible and clear the goods market and that nominal short-term interest does the same for the money market. We have already discussed the problems related to the first assumption from the theoretical point of view as well as from the perspective of empirical relevance. In our view there must be a second PC, one for the domestic goods market, that is built in a similar way as the wage PC on demand pressure, now in the market for goods, and cost-push concerning money wage and expected medium run inflation. This is the most basic critique of the McKibbin and Sachs (1991) MSG2 model which incorporates a degree of price level flexibility that is implausible from the empirical point of view, since quantities normally adjust faster than prices at least in industrialized countries, and which is also problematic from the theoretical perspective, since AS-AD is not the proper basis of Keynesian static and dynamic analysis as we hope to have shown in Chiarella and Flaschel (1999) and the first two parts of this book.

Rose effects are not fully present in the McKibbin and Sachs approach, as there is no distinction between rates of capacity utilization for the stock of labor and the stock of capital, since capital is always fully utilized in this approach. Furthermore, income distribution only plays a role in investment behavior and not in consumption behavior which, if at all, only allows price flexibility, but not wage flexibility, to be destabilizing (the orthodox case). Price flexibility is however set equal to infinity and thus removed from sight anyhow. Mundell effects are not directly involved, since investment and consumption do not depend on the real rate of interest, though however the q-concept of investment and the human capital concept used in the consumption function depend on this rate, but are treated by the jump variable technique in any case. Finally, Metzler inventory adjustment, or other possibly destabilizing accelerator mechanisms, are totally missing in this AS-AD approach. Instead, Keynes-, Pigou and wealth effects appear in the usual way through the formulation of money demand and of consumption demand and thus can exercise their stabilizing influence in conjunction with the stabilizing role of the jump variable technique used to remove saddlepoint instability from asset markets and investment behavior. As in chapter 4 we therefore see that there is a huge difference between our labor market dynamics and disequilibrium growth modeling and the McKibbin and Sachs (1991) model with disequilibrium solely in the labor market.

Disregarding these problematic feature of the McKibbin and Sachs (1991) MSG2 model we have learnt from it that a law of motion for Tobin's q coupled with an investment function that partly depends of it may be an alternative to the investment theory presented in section 7.4 and that human capital formation, including its law of motion, may represent a sensible addition to the life cycle hypotheses used in section 7.3. Further reflections of our CTD growth dynamics may concern the degree of disaggregation of the commodities traded in the world, where McKibbin and Sachs (1991) differentiate according to the structure existing in current international trade, and the price indices that are to based on such a differentiated world production structure (and the different wage negotiation schemes that may prevail in the world economy). In most other respects there are significant similarities between our approach and the approach of McKibbin and Sachs (1991), perhaps with the difference that we are more detailed in presenting the structure of a single small open economy, while McKibbin and Sachs (1991) are more interested in creating a global presentation of the world economy.

The basic difference, however, remains and is of fundamental theoretical as well as empirical nature, namely the question of whether a detailed KMG growth dynamics with sluggish wage, price and quantity dynamics (including in each case expectations) of a dynamics of AS-AD growth type is better suited for building macroeconometric models of the industrialized economies operating in the world economy. This concludes our brief comparison of the MSG2 model of McKibbin and Sachs with our reformulation of the disequilibrium growth model by Powell and Murphy (1997). Our CTD growth model allows for interior steady state solutions which are uniquely determined at least under certain assumptions on the generally 39D dynamics in intensive form. This feature is not treated as an important one in the McKibbin - Sachs approach who do not go into the details of steady world wide growth even if only as a reference path for the actual dynamics that is generate by the model.

This situation is changed when the IMF model as represented in Laxton et al. (1998) is considered which is basically of the same type as the MSG2 model. The steady state solution there serves several purposes, in particular as an interpretive device, for the construction of control solutions and also to obtain terminal conditions for the rational expectations saddle point methodology that is there applied. We have stressed in particular in chapter 3 of the book that obtaining steady state solutions is an important consistency test for the construction of CTD growth model which allows to check the assumptions that are needed in order to obtain balanced growth in detailed models of disequilibrium growth, of KMG or AS-AD type. Having found the conditions for economically meaningful steady state solutions guarantees that there is a point of rest of the dynamics whose stability properties can then be investigated with respect to the general prejudice that asymptotic stability should apply in one way or another. Of course, actual applications of these model types to particular episodes of the evolution of market economies may refer to assumptions, demographic or other, that prevent that the dynamics in intensive form can find a point of rest which however is more a problem for the AS-AD rational expectations growth dynamics than it would be for the CTD KMG growth models we have considered in this book, since there is no need in our model types to supply terminal conditions for the forward solution of the model.

Apart from its stress on steady state reference solutions the IMF model, Multimod Mark III, is very similar to the MSG2 model in its fundamental structural components, with more stress on the inflation-unemployment nexus which is here of the traditional across markets type already, with a life cycle approach as in Blanchard (1985) that distinguishes cases of small open economies from those of closed ones, and again a discussion of liquidity constraints, with a marginal q approach to business fixed investment that is again modified to some extent to take account empirically motivated considerations and with a brief discussion of international trade linkages. We do not go into a discussion of this variant of AS-AD growth any more, but again only note that the inclusion of sluggish price and quantity adjustment on the market for goods (and sluggish employment adjustment on the market for labor), as in our CTD growth dynamics of chapters 5 to 7, would contribute to the relevance of the model framework in view of actual characteristics of business fluctuations in developed market economies, independently from any desire to use optimizing frameworks in the determination of consumption as well as investment behavior (where of course labor and goods market disequilibrium situations have to be taken account of then).

7.11 Appendix A: Notation

The following list of symbols contains only domestic variables and parameters. Foreign magnitudes are defined analogously and are indicated by an asterisk ($*$). To ease verbal descriptions we shall consider in the following the 'Australian Dollar' as the domestic currency (A$) and the 'US Dollar' ($) as a representation of the foreign currency (currencies).

A. Statically or dynamically endogenous variables:

Y	Output of the domestic good
Y^d	Aggregate demand for the domestic good
Y^p	Potential output of the domestic good
Y^n	Normal output of the domestic good
Y^e	Expected sales for the domestic good
Y_w^{Dn}, Y_c^{Dn}	Nominal disposable income of workers and asset-holders
U_c	Rate of capacity utilization of firms

L	Labor supply
L_1	Population aged 16 – 65
L_2	Population aged 66 – ...
L_0	Population aged 0 – 14
L^d	Total employment of the employed
$L_f^d(L_f^{do}, L_f^{dp})$	Total actual (desired, potential) employment of the work force of firms
$L_g^d = L_g^w$	Total government employment (= public work force)
L_f^w	Work force of firms
L^w	Total active work force
V_f^w	Employment rate of those employed in the private sector
α_l	Participation rate of the potential work force
$V = L^d/L$	Rate of employment ($\bar{V}$ the employment–complement of the NAIRU)
C_w^{on}	Total nominal equilibrium consumption of workers
$C_w^g(C_w^{og})$	Real (equilibrium) goods consumption of workers
$C_w^h(C_w^{oh})$	Real (equilibrium) dwelling services consumption of workers
C_c^{on}	Total nominal equilibrium consumption of asset holders
$C_c(C_c^o)$	Real (equilibrium) goods consumption of asset owners
$C = C_w + C_c$	Total goods consumption
C_h^s	Supply of dwelling services
I	Gross business fixed investment
I_h	Gross fixed housing investment
$I^a(I^{na})$	Gross (net) actual total investment
$\mathcal{I}$	Planned inventory investment
N	Actual inventories
N^d	Desired inventories
r	Nominal short-term rate of interest (price of bonds $p_b = 1$)
r_l^{av}	Average rate of interest of long-term bonds
r^l	Nominal long-term rate of interest (price of bonds $p_b = 1/r^l$)
$\pi_b = \hat{p}_b^e$	expected appreciation in the price of long-term domestic bonds
ρ^r	Required rate of interest
p_e	Price of equities
$\pi_e = \hat{p}_e^e$	expected appreciation in the price of equities
$S^n = S_p^n + S_f^n + S_g^n$	Total nominal savings
$S_p^n = S_w^n + S_c^n$	Nominal savings of households
S_f^n	Nominal savings of firms ($= p_y Y_f$, the income of firms)
S_g^n	Government nominal savings
S_w^n	Nominal savings of workers
S_c^n	Nominal savings of asset owners
$T^n(T)$	Nominal (real) taxes
G	Real government expenditure
Π	Nominal profits of firms
Π_h	Nominal earnings in the housing sector
ρ^e	Expected short-run rate of profit of firms
ρ^a	Actual short-run rate of profit of firms
ρ^n	Normal operation rate of profit of firms
ρ^{av}	Average rate of profit of firms
ρ^l	Expected long-run rate of profit of firms
ρ_h	Actual rate of return for housing services
ρ_h^{av}	Average rate of return for housing services
ρ_h^l	Expected long-run rate of return for housing services
K	Capital stock
K_h	Capital stock in the housing sector
w^b	Nominal wages including payroll tax
w	Nominal wages before taxes
w^u	Unemployment benefit per unemployed
w^r	Pension rate

p_v	Price level of domestic goods including value added tax
p_y	Price level of domestic goods net of value added tax
p_x	Price level of export goods in domestic currency
p_{xc}	Price level of commodity exports
p_{xo}	Price level of other exports
p_m	Price level of import goods in domestic currency including taxation
p_h	Rent per unit of dwelling
$\pi^l = \hat{p}_v^e$	Expected rate of inflation
π_c^l	Expected growth rate of the consumer price index of worker households
π_h^l	Expected growth rate of the price of housing services
e	Exchange rate (units of domestic currency per unit of foreign currency: A\$/\$)
$\epsilon = \hat{e}^e$	Expected rate of change of the exchange rate
B	Stock of domestic short-term bonds (index d: stock demand)
B_w	Short-term debt held by workers
B_c	Short-term debt held by asset owners
B^l	Stock of domestic long-term bonds, of which B_1^l are held by domestic asset-holders (index d: demand) and B_1^{l*} by foreigners (index d: demand)
B_2^l	Foreign bonds held by domestic asset-holders (index d: demand)
M	Money supply
M_w	Money holdings of workers
M_c	Money holdings of asset holders
M_w^d	Money demand of workers
M_c^d	Money demand of asset holders
M^d	Total money demand
$\mu = \hat{M}$	Growth rate of the money supply
R	Stock of foreign reserves of the central bank
E	Equities (index d: demand)
W^n, W	Nominal and real domestic wealth
n	Natural growth rate of the labor force (adjustment towards $\tilde{n}$)
n_l	Rate of Harrod neutral technical change (adjustment towards $\tilde{n}_l$)
τ_m	Tax rates on imported commodities
$X^a(X^o, X^p)$	Actual (desired, potential) Exports
X_c	Commodity exports
X_o	Other exports
$J^a(J^{do}, J^{dp})$	Actual (desired, potential) Imports
$NX^n = p_x X - e p_m^* J^d$	Net exports in terms of the domestic currency
NFX^n	Net nominal factor export payments (in A\$)
NCX^n	Net nominal capital exports (in A\$)
τ_w	tax rate on wages, pensions and unemployment benefits
t^n	total taxes per value unit of capital
g_k^d, g_k	Desired and actual rate of growth of the capital stock K
g_h^d, g_h	Desired and actual rate of growth of the housing capital stock K_h
d	Actual public debt / output ratio

B. Parameters of the model

δ	Depreciation rate of the capital stock of firms
δ_h	Depreciation rate in the housing sector
α_i^j	All α-expressions (behavioral or other parameters)
β_x	All β-expressions (adjustment speeds)
γ	Steady growth rate in the rest of the world
$\bar{U}_c$	Normal rate of capacity utilization of firms
$\bar{U}_h$	Normal rate of capacity utilization in housing
κ_w, κ_p	Weights of short– and long–run inflation ($\kappa_w \kappa_p \neq 1$)

κ	$= (1 - \kappa_w \kappa_p)^{-1}$
$\bar{d}$	Desired public debt / output ratio
ξ	Risk and liquidity premium of long-term over short-term debt
τ_c	Tax rate on profit, rent and interest
τ_v	Value added tax rate
τ_p	Payroll tax
c_{w1}	Propensity to consume goods of workers (out of income)
c_{w2}	Propensity to consume goods of workers (out of wealth)
c_{c1}	Propensity to consume goods of asset holders (out of income)
c_{c2}	Propensity to consume goods of asset holders (out of wealth)
k	Parameter concerning the transaction demand for money
$\rho_1, \rho_2, a_1, b_1, a_2, b_2$	Coefficients of the nested CES-production function
ρ_3, a_3, b_3	Coefficients of the CET-transformation technology

C. Further notation

$\dot{x}$	Time derivative of a variable x
$\widehat{x}$	Growth rate of x
x^a	Actual value of x
$r_o, etc.$	Steady state values
$y = Y/K, etc.$	Real variables in intensive form
$m = M/(p_v K), etc.$	Nominal variables in intensive form
$\nu = N/K$	Inventory-capital ratio
GBR	Government Budget Restraint

7.12 Appendix B: Representing technology by nested CES / CET production functions

We briefly provide in this appendix intensive form expressions for the equations in block 3a of section 4 for the case of a nested CES / CET production technology which describe the short-run profit maximizing behavior of demand constrained firms and their profit maximizing output and input target levels (which they use for pricing and investment decisions) similar to Powell and Murphy's (1997) presentation of the production block of their model.

Powell and Murphy (1997, Ch.10) assume as technological basis of their model of the Australian economy that capital K and labor L^d are combined via a CES production function to deliver an intermediate output potential Y_1 which then is used on the basis of a further CES technology assumption together with imported commodities J^d to provide the output potential Y_2 on the basis of which firms can decide to produce combinations of the domestic and the exported commodity, Y, X by means of a CET transformation technology. In extensive form we therefore have as technological description for the economy:

$$\begin{aligned} Y_1 &= [a_1 K^{-\rho_1} + b_1(\exp(n_l t) L_f^d)^{-\rho_1}]^{-1/\rho_1}, \quad \rho_1 > -1 \\ Y_2 &= [a_2 Y_1^{-\rho_2} + b_2 (J^d)^{-\rho_2}]^{-1/\rho_2}, \quad \rho_2 > -1 \\ Y_2 &= [a_3 Y^{-\rho_3} + b_3 X^{-\rho_3}]^{-1/\rho_3}, \quad \rho_3 < -1 \end{aligned}$$

which are related to our use of general production potential functions F and transformation technologies T, see block 3a. of the model, as follows:

$$F(K, \exp(n_l t) L_f^d, J^d) = [a_2([a_1 K^{-\rho_1} + b_1(\exp(n_l t) L_f^d)^{-\rho_1}]^{-1/\rho_1})^{-\rho_2} + b_2 (J^d)^{-\rho_2}]^{-1/\rho_2} =$$

$$T(Y,X) = [a_3Y^{-\rho_3} + b_3X^{-\rho_3}]^{-1/\rho_3}.$$

Note that we have Harrod neutral technological change present as far the labor input is concerned, which will give rise to labor measures in efficiency units in intensive form representations of this technology. The above functions exhibit a constant elasticity of substitution between inputs or outputs, measured by $\sigma_i = \frac{1}{1+\rho_i}, i = 1,2,3$. Note that ρ_3 has to be assumed to be smaller than -1 in order to provide a concave transformation curve as they are usually assumed to underlie the output decisions of joint production technologies in the case of substitution on the advanced textbook level.[17] As far as input substitution is concerned we have the case of fixed proportions in production as a limit case when ρ_i approaches infinity, and the case of a Cobb-Douglas production function when ρ_i approaches zero, separating the case of inelastic from elastic input substitution.

In intensive form, where everything is measured per unit of capital K, and in efficiency units (denoted by the index e) as far as labor and wages are concerned, the above technological assumptions are represented by the following three equations:

$$\begin{aligned} y_1 &= [a_1 + b_1(l_f^{de})^{-\rho_1}]^{-1/\rho_1}, \quad \rho_1 > -1 \\ y_2 &= [a_2y_1^{-\rho_2} + b_2(j^d)^{-\rho_2}]^{-1/\rho_2}, \quad \rho_2 > -1 \\ y_2 &= [a_3y^{-\rho_3} + b_3x^{-\rho_3}]^{-1/\rho_3}, \quad \rho_3 < -1. \end{aligned}$$

where as usual expressions measured per unit of capital are denoted by lowercase letters.

In the case of a demand constrained firm, where $y = Y/K$ is a given magnitude from the viewpoint of firms, one can derive from these equations the following representation of its technological underpinnings:

$$\begin{aligned} y_1 &= f^1(l_f^{de}) = [a_1 + b_1(l_f^{de})^{-\rho_1}]^{-1/\rho_1}, \quad \rho_1 > -1 \\ y_2 &= f^2(y_1, j^d) = [a_2y_1^{-\rho_2} + b_2(j^d)^{-\rho_2}]^{-1/\rho_2}, \quad \rho_2 > -1 \\ x &= f^3(y_2, y)) = [(y_2^{-\rho_3} - a_3y^{-\rho_3})/b_3]^{-1/\rho_3}. \end{aligned}$$

In symbolic form we thus get as representation of production in this case a function of the type:

$$x = f(l_f^{de}, j^d, y) = f^3(f^2(f^1(l_f^{de}), j^d), y)$$

by inserting the expressions obtained for y_1, y_2 into the x function successively. To do this explicitly is however of not much help in the analysis to be based on this production function, since it leads us to a formula that is more complicated to read than the list of expressions that constitute it:

$$x = [(([a_2[[a_1 + b_1(l_f^{de})^{-\rho_1}]^{-1/\rho_1}]^{-\rho_2} + b_2(j^d)^{-\rho_2}]^{-1/\rho_2}]^{-\rho_3} - a_3y^{-\rho_3})/b_3]^{-1/\rho_3}.$$

The demand constrained firm chooses, according to section 4, here transferred to intensive form expressions, the input ratios l_f^{de}, j^d for labor and imports and the output ratio x

[17] A particular simple case is given by $\rho = -2$ which provides as output transformation function the 'ellipsoid' type shapes $[a_3Y^2 + b_3X^2]^{1/2}$, while the similar looking function $[a_3Y^{1/2} + b_3X^{1/2}]^2$ still provides isoquants that are of a strictly convex shape.

for exports not only in a technologically efficient way (according to the shown production functions), but also by maximizing profits in this constrained situation, i.e.

$$\max_{x,j^d,l_f^{de}} [\frac{p_x}{p_y}x - \frac{p_m}{p_y}j^d - \frac{w^{be}}{p_y}l_f^{de}] \quad \text{s.t. } x = f(l_f^{de}, j^d, y), \quad y \text{ being given}$$

which provides uniquely determined values for these input and output variables denoted by l_f^{do}, j^{do}, x^o, on the extensive form level however as far as 3a. in section 4 is concerned. The optimality conditions read in this case:

$$\begin{aligned} \frac{p_x}{p_y} f_1(l_f^{de}, j^d, y) &= \frac{w^{be}}{p_y} \\ \frac{p_x}{p_y} f_2(l_f^{de}, j^d, y) &= \frac{p_m}{p_y} \end{aligned}$$

plus of course the representation of the employed technology

$$x = f(l_f^{de}, j^d, y)$$

which provides three equations in the three unknowns l_f^{de}, j^d, x that can, in the given situation, be uniquely and meaningfully solved for the optimal responses l_f^{do}, j^{do}, x^o of the demand constrained firm. In these equations subscripts denote partial derivatives which in the case of f^1 is also the total derivative of course. Of course, as shown, these optimal values are functions of the parameters that the firms face in their profit maximizing decision, which are: $y, \frac{w^{be}}{p_y}, \frac{p_m}{p_y}, \frac{p_x}{p_y}$. These functions have to be solved explicitly when numerical applications and investigations of the model are intended, see Chiarella, Flaschel and Zhu (1998c) for the details.

Neglecting the demand constraint y in the profit maximizing behavior of firms, which make their decision on y also a profit maximizing one, we get the target values that firms use when deciding on their pricing policy and their desired investment per unit of capital, see again section 4 for the details. This profit maximization exercise provides now optimal input ratios $l_f^{pe}, j^{dp}, x^p, y^p$ for labor and imports and for domestic and exported output x per unit of capital, that are considered as the potential or desired ratios of the firms. Hence we now have

$$\max_{l_f^{de},j^d,y,x} [\frac{p_x}{p_y}x + y - \frac{p_m}{p_y}j^d - \frac{w^{be}}{p_y}l_f^{de}] \quad \text{s.t. } x = f(l_f^{de}, j^d, y)$$

which provides uniquely determined values for these input and output variables denoted by $l_f^{pe}, j^{dp}, y^p, x^p$, that have to transferred back to extensive from in order to get the expressions shown in block 3a. of section 4. The optimality conditions read in this case:

$$\begin{aligned} \frac{p_x}{p_y} f_1(l_f^{pe}, j^{dp}, y^p) &= \frac{w^{be}}{p_y} \\ \frac{p_x}{p_y} f_2(l_f^{pe}, j^{dp}, y^p) &= \frac{p_m}{p_y} \\ \frac{p_x}{p_y} f_3(l_f^{pe}, j^{dp}, y^p) &= -1 \end{aligned}$$

plus of course again

$$x^p = f(l_f^{pe}, j^{dp}, y^p)$$

which now provides four equations in the four unknowns $l_f^{pe}, j^{dp}, y^p, x^p$ that can, in the given situation, be uniquely and meaningfully solved for the medium run target ratios $l_f^{pe}, j^{dp}, y^p, x^p$ of firms.

We note that the functional shape of the relationship between the optimal responses of firms, as far as employment and imports and the ratio w^{be}/p_m is concerned is the same as the one described for the demand constrained firm above. The remaining equations for the unconstrained maximization problem however differ from the preceding optimization problem, but do, by way of proper reformulation of the optimality conditions, allow for a successive solution for the values of l_f^{pe}, j^{dp}, y^p and x^p.

Chapter 8

Intensive Forms and Steady State Calculations

8.1 Introduction

In this chapter we derive and discuss the 39D intensive (state variable) form of the general structural model of disequilibrium growth we have introduced and discussed on its extensive form level in chapter 7.[1] We will represent the resulting 39D dimensional dynamical system, obtained from this extensive form of the model, from various perspectives, providing compact intensive form representations of the real and the financial sector of this economy in table form, in form of a system of national accounts, and in laws of motion form, and will furthermore discuss the contents of the obtained laws of motion on their intensive form level to some extent. Presenting the system from these various perspectives serves again the purpose of making the reader acquainted with the notation and the relationships that apply on the intensive form level of the model. We hope that this increases the readability of the laws of motion for quantities (including rates of growth), for prices (including wages, asset prices, and expectations), financial asset accumulation and feedback fiscal and monetary policy rules presented and discussed in section 3 of chapter 8.

Section 4 then provides the equations for the interior steady state solution of these dynamics and shows in particular that this steady state is now determined by a large set of simultaneous nonlinear equations that cannot be solved in the recursive fashion as in the case of fixed proportions in production (and no wealth effects) considered in Chiarella and Flaschel (1999e-g). In particular, supply side and demand side influences now interact also in the long-run of the model, as represented by its steady state. The present model therefore overcomes the one-sidedness of many similar model types as to the role of supply in forming the steady state solution of monetary growth dynamics. The complications now present are basically due to our assumption of a neoclassical production function with smooth input and output substitution., in particular since we allow (as in Powell and Murphy (1997)) for three inputs (capital, imported commodities and labor) and two outputs (domestically traded goods and exported commodities), in the place of a production function of this type with only fixed input-output ratios as in Chiarella and Flaschel (1999e-g). This production

[1]This chapter is based on the material presented in Chiarella, Flaschel, Groh, Köper and Semmler (1999b).

structure is augmented by the additional assumption that exports and imports adjust to their optimal values (for firms that are demand restricted on the domestic market, but not on the world markets) with some time delay that depends on the rate of capacity utilization for the domestic product of firms.

The present chapter basically prepares the ground for subsequent more manageable formulations of the model in intensive form and serves the purpose of showing the complexity of the achieved level of generality (which is also inherent in the Murphy model) and the way the model should be treated on the intensive form level, once the core case of it to be investigated in chapter 9, see also Chiarella, Flaschel and Zhu (1999c), has been thoroughly investigated and understood. These simpler situations are not always convincing from the economic perspective, but are really necessary in order to provide a starting point for the analysis of applied complex macrodynamic model building where mathematical structure and details are for the present stage of the investigation still such that a systematic exploration of the dynamics of the model is within reach and can be approached.

Let us close these introductory observations by returning to the contents of figure 7.1 of the preceding chapter which serves as a guide to all subsequent analyses of the disequilibrium growth approach which is considered in its generality on intensive form level in the following sections. Figure 7.1 shows the various points we want to stress here in different shading, presenting in the middle portion as starting point (or prejudice) the basic market hierarchy of Keynes' (1936) General Theory as we interpret it. This view claims that asset markets dominate (in a casino like fashion) the outcome in the real markets basically through the investment decision of firms that is here considered to depend on financial markets and the structure of nominal interest rates they generate, but does not yet exercise a feedback influence on them. Effective demand (with a Metzlerian feedback mechanism included) that derives from this investment decision determines the outcome on the market for goods which is therefore purely demand determined. Finally, at the lowest stage of the hierarchy, there come the labor markets which just have to accept the amount of employment that is generated by (expected) goods demand and the technology with which firms produce their demand determined supply of goods (including intended inventory changes).

This 'prejudice' on the fundamental macroeconomic forces that may (or may not) shape the temporary equilibrium position of the economy represents in our view a method of thinking that allows one to approach the full situation in a systematic hierarchically ordered way that does not just state that everything depends on everything else as far as financial decisions and quantity and price determination are concerned. Of course, it has to address the question of what kind of feedback mechanisms have to be added to this picture (and which ones may be left aside due to their minor importance) and in what way they will alter the temporary equilibrium position (or its evolution in time) as determined by the fundamental 'causal nexus' shown in the middle section in figure 7.1. Therefore, the proposed feedback mechanisms (or repercussions) have to be discussed as to their importance for full employment positions or (if they work with a delay) as to their role as stabilizing or destabilizing mechanism in the evolution of the temporary equilibrium positions of the economy.

Of course, there may be feedback mechanisms of great importance that are still missing in figure 7.1. An example for this is given by the Fisher debt effect relating firms with households or banks which is still missing in our model due to its limited set of asset markets and the financial decisions made on this basis by the firms. Note however that we have a Fisher debt effect in the present model as far as the sector of households is concerned where we can have the situation that workers with a high marginal propensity to consume become debtors to asset holders (with a low or zero marginal propensity to consume) which in this way implies that consumption will be depressed in deflationary periods and accelerated in periods of inflation. By contrast, it may be questioned whether for example the Keynes short-term interest rate effect on investment or the Pigou effect on consumption demand are really of importance in the picture of the real and financial interaction shown in figure 7.1. There are also feedback mechanisms that are internal to the asset markets and that may create cumulative processes in them that are to be bounded by certain switches in expectational regimes later on.

An important controversial aspect of figure 7.1 is given by its presentation of supply side influences bottom - left in figure 7.1. In our view this is basically the question of the wage price interaction or spiral (including expectations) which should be approached from the viewpoint of a separate treatment of Phillips curves, one for the nominal wage and one for the price level. Such an approach allows the analysis to escape from the narrow perspective of the monetarist type of a unique augmented price-inflation, labor market based Phillips curve which does not really allow for the discussion of wage price spirals as it is needed in a full approach to disequilibrium growth where both labor and capital will in general be over- or underutilized. Such a view on the working of the wage price mechanism, which allows for a sluggish adjustment of both of these nominal magnitudes, will include Rose (1967) effects into the interaction of the goods and the labor markets, which generally imply that either wage or price flexibility will lead to instability in the process that is usually considered as the medium run of macrodynamic model building.

Finally figure 7.1 shows top-left and bottom-right certain policy feedback rules which are interacting with the dynamics of the private sector. Such rules are present in the approach investigated in the chapters 7 and 8, but are not yet at the center of interest in the present stage of the investigation. The final aim is of course to understand the working of such fiscal or monetary policy rules. This demands however a well established analysis of the working of the private sector of the economy which will by and large still be out of reach, up to certain numerical investigations of an 18D core dynamics of the model, as far as the present book is concerned. At the bottom of figure 7.1 we see in this regard a summary of the main questions that should find some answer in the course of the investigations of this general approach to disequilibrium growth. First, we have the question to what extent the asset markets dominate the outcome of the real / financial interaction, which is here still of a very particular type and thus demands further extensions of the model if the dynamics of asset prices is to be linked more closely to the stocks supplied and demanded on these markets. Secondly, there is the question as to what the various feedback mechanisms shown above add to the real / financial interaction and to what extent they will contribute to or undermine, when working together, the local stability of the balanced growth solution(s) of the model. Thirdly, the dynamics of income distribution, as it finds expression in the wage price spiral, has to be investigated, in particular in its role of shaping the long-run outcome of this model which has a strictly Keynesian short-run outcome. Finally again, the perspective of our approach is of course to contribute to the analysis of policy issues which, due to the fact that we want to treat medium and long run dynamics as well, is more oriented to the treatment of policy rules than to an investigation of the consequences of isolated fiscal or monetary shocks that occur only once in time. In the present chapter we only set the stage for such investigations, while subsequent work is needed, starting from special cases of the model as in Chiarella, Flaschel and Zhu (1999c) in the next chapter 9, in order to understand in a systematic way the implications that are contained in the chosen approach to disequilibrium growth.

8.2 The real and the financial structure of the economy

The following two tables provide a survey on the structure of the economy to be considered in the following sections and they do this directly on the intensive form level of the originally extensive structural model of disequilibrium growth introduced and discussed in chapter 7.[2] This chapter therefore continues the investigations begun there by showing that this model type has a well-defined intensive-form state variable (and steady state) representation which however is difficult to analyze in its present formulation and which therefore will be simplified in this and the subsequent chapter significantly in order to allow explicit steady state calculations and numerical applications that are much easier to program than the general case provided by chapter 7.

8.2.1 The real sector

Let us start with a presentation of the variables that comprise the real part of the economy to be considered and which are all recalculated here in per unit of capital form as far as the side of quantities and in per value unit of the capital stock as far as nominal magnitudes are concerned, plus in addition in efficiency units in the case of labor, and also in efficiency units in the case of wage rates, since these variables would exhibit a positive trend otherwise (as they rise with labor productivity on average). Price levels, however, are at present without trend in the considered dynamical model, since it has been assumed that the central bank follows a money supply policy rule with a zero target rate of inflation, which restricts the steady state solution for the rate of inflation to zero (in correspondence to what has been assumed for the world economy).

[2]In the case of problems in understanding the notations used and the contents they represents the reader should therefore go back to the original presentation of the model in chapter 7.

	Labor	Non traded Goods	Exports	Imports	Dwellings
Workers	$l^e = \alpha_l l_1^e$	c_w^g	–	–	c_w^h
Asset holders	–	c_c	–	–	c_h^s, g_h
Firms	l_f^{de}, l_f^{we}	$y^p, y, g_k, \mathcal{I}/K$	x^a	j^a	–
Government	$l_g^{de} = l_g^{we}$	$g^d = gy^e$	–		–
Prices	$w^e \quad [w^{be}, w^{re}, w^{ue}]$	$p_v = (1+\tau_v)p_y$	$p_x = ep_x^*$	$p_m =$ $(1+\tau_m)ep_m^*$	p_h, p_y
Expectations	$\pi_c = \hat{p}_c^e$	$\pi = \hat{p}_v^e$	–	–	$\pi_h = \hat{p}_h^e$
Stocks	$l_1^e[l_2^e, l_0^e]$	$\nu = N/K\ [K = 1]$	–	–	$c_h^s = k_h$
Growth	$\hat{L}_1 = n[= \hat{L}_2 = \hat{L}_0]$	$\hat{K} = g_k - \delta$ $\hat{N} = (y - y^d)/\nu$	–	–	$\hat{K}_h = g_h - \delta_h$

Table 8.1: The real part of the economy.
(Foreign country data: γ, p_x^*, p_m^*.)

Table 8.1 describes the real sector of the considered economy. We have a labor market, three commodity markets and the housing market. Domestic production $y = Y/K$, per unit of capital, concerns one good that is only domestically used (for all private consumption $c_w^g + c_c$, all investment $g_k, g_h, \mathcal{I}/K$, also into housing, and all government consumption $g^d = G/K = gy^e$ and which uses up all the imports j^a as intermediate goods) and one good that is only used for exports x^a, everything calculated per unit of capital K as symbolized by lowercase letters in the place of the originally uppercase ones. There is thus only a single commodity used in domestic absorption – up to the housing services c_w^h demanded by workers. We denote the demand for this domestically produced and absorbed commodity by $y^d (= Y^d/K)$.

The table exhibits again three domestic sectors: Households, firms and the government, but with heterogeneous agents in the household sector, workers and (pure) asset holders. The former supply their labor l^e (measured here in efficiency units per unit of capital: $l^e = \exp(n_l t)L^e/K$) at the gross wage level $w^{be} = \exp(-n_l t)w^b$ (which includes payroll taxes and is also calculated in efficiency units such that the wage sum is the same in natural as well as in efficiency units). The latter supply the housing services $c_h^s = K_h/K$ for the workers. Firms produce a non-traded domestic and an exported commodity and employ labor l_f^{we} (with varying rates of utilization l_f^{de}) and imports j^a (besides their capital stock K) for these purposes, and they invest into fixed business capital g_k (per unit of capital) and inventories $\mathcal{I}/K$, of course also per unit of capital. Government finally provides public consumption goods g^d, pays pensions w^{re} and unemployment benefits w^{ue} and also employs part of the workforce l_g^{de}. There is endogenous growth n of the potential labor force L_1, of the capital stock K, determined by $g_k - \delta$, and of the stock of housing K_h, determined by $g_h - \delta_h$, (supplied at price p_h for rental services) and actual change of inventories are given per unit of capital by $\nu = N/K$ and are to be distinguished from their desired rate of change $\mathcal{I}/K$.

8.2.2 The financial sector

Let us next consider the financial part of the economy. Note that all stock variables $B, B^l, ...$ (and their rates of change) that appear here are measured relative to the gross value of the capital stock $p_v K$, based on the consumer price level p_v (that includes value added tax). They are then denoted again by lowercase letters (and by ε in the case of equities E). Note also flow variables in intensive form are related to the growth rate of the extensive form analog by multiplying this rate with the stock value of this variable per value unit of the capital stock as shown in various places in the following table 8.2.

	Money	Short-term Bonds	Long-term Bonds	Equities	Foreign Bonds
Workers	$\hat{M}_w m_w[=\frac{\dot{M}_w}{p_v K}]$	$\hat{B}_w b_w[=\frac{\dot{B}_w}{p_v K}]$	–	–	–
Asset holders	$\hat{M}_c m_c[=\frac{\dot{M}_c}{p_v K}]$	$\hat{B}_c b_c[=\frac{\dot{B}_c}{p_v K}]$	$\hat{B}_1^l b_1^l[=\frac{\dot{B}_1^l}{p_v K}]$	$\hat{E}\varepsilon[=\frac{\dot{E}}{p_v K}]$	$\hat{B}_2^l b_2^l[=\frac{\dot{B}_2^l}{p_v K}]$
Firms	–	–	–	$\hat{E}\varepsilon[=\frac{\dot{E}}{p_v K}]$	–
Government	–	$\hat{B}b[=\frac{\dot{B}}{p_v K}]$	$\hat{B}^l b^l[=\frac{\dot{B}^l}{p_v K}]$	–	–
Prices	1	1 [r]	$p_b = 1/r^l$	p_e	$ep_b^* = e \cdot 1/r_l^*$
Expectations	–	–	$\pi_b = \hat{p}_b^e$	$\pi_e = \hat{p}_e^e$	$\epsilon = \hat{e}^e$
Stocks ($/p_v K$)	$m = m_w + m_c$	$b = b_w + b_c$	$b^l = b_1^l + b_1^{l*}$	ε	b_2^l
Growth	$\hat{M}, \hat{M}_w, \hat{M}_c$	$\hat{B}, \hat{B}_w, \hat{B}_c$	$\hat{B}^l, \hat{B}_1^l$	$\hat{E}$	$\hat{B}_2^l$

Table 8.2: The financial part of the economy.
(Foreign country data: $r_l^*, \tau_c^* = \tau_c$)

The first column in table 8.2 shows that we consider money holdings explicitly in the model of chapter 7, see Chiarella and Flaschel (1999e) for an alternative approach to monetary policy. There are thus five financial assets in our model that can be held by the (pure) asset owners and by the workers of our economy (as shown in the above table). As in the KMG model of monetary growth of closed and open economies of Chiarella and Flaschel (1999a-d) we here again have, in order to start with a simple representation of financial flows, that bonds are only issued by the government, that firms use only equity financing and pay out expected earnings as dividends, and that there exist also long-term bonds issued by the 'foreign government'. Financial flows between the sectors of our economy are therefore still somewhat narrowly defined. Note that we allow for savings out of wages (in a Kaldorian way) and that workers save only in the form of money or short-term debt (interest-bearing saving deposits[3], the latter held at the local branches of the central bank[4]). All other assets (plus the remainder of short-term debt) are exclusively held by the (pure) asset holders of our model. We stress again that this serves the purpose of simplifying the budget constraints of the agents and needs to be refined and extended in future reformulations of the model. This is the basic structure we assume for our economy which will be further characterized in the next subsection from the viewpoint of national accounting before we present and discuss the intensive form equations of the model of chapter 7.

8.2.3 National accounting

We shall consider in this subsection the production accounts, income accounts, accumulation accounts and financial accounts in integrated form for each of the four internal agents in our economy :[5] This representation of firms, asset holders, workers, and the government (including the monetary authority) – plus the balance of payments account – provide basic information on what is assumed for these four sectors and which of their activities are still excluded from the present framework of a small open economy.

The sector of firms

We start with the accounts of the firms – shown in table 8.3 – which organize production y (per unit of capital), employment l_f^{de}, in efficiency units, of their workforce l_f^{we} and gross business fixed investment g_k (per unit of capital) and which use only equities ε (per value unit of capital) as financing instrument (no debt in the form of bank loans or bonds issued by firms). There are value added taxes τ_v on consumption goods, import taxes τ_m and payroll taxes τ_p with respect to hours worked l_f^{de}, but no further taxation in the sector of firms and there are also no subsidies paid to this sector.

Firms build dwellings – which are of the same type as all other domestic (non-traded) production – and sell them to the asset holders (as investors) and thus have no own investment occurring in the housing sector. They sell consumption goods to workers, asset holders and the government, export goods to the world economy, organize fixed gross investments with respect to their capital stock (as well as voluntary inventory changes $\mathcal{I}/K$ with respect to finished goods) and experience involuntary inventory changes $\dot{N}/K = (y - y^d)/\nu$ (per unit of capital) due to the deviation of aggregate demand y^d from output y (which is based on expected sales y^e and planned inventories $\mathcal{I}/K$) (everything per unit of capital).

Firms use up all imports as intermediate goods which thereby become part of the unique homogeneous good that is produced for domestic purposes. They have replacement costs with respect to their capital stock, pay indirect taxes and wages including payroll taxes. Their

[3]Or fixprice bonds, which are perfectly liquid, while the other type of bonds: long-term bonds (here consols or perpetuities, held by asset holders) cannot be liquidated at a given price from the viewpoint of the sector of asset holders as a whole.

[4]Their purpose is to finance government expenditures with no explicit reserve requirements.

[5]The fifth agent, the foreign economy, is represented by the balance of payments at the end of this subsection and is confined to steady state behavior in the present form of the model. All demands of this foreign sector are indexed by $*$, while its supply of long-term bonds B_2 to domestic residents is indexed here by 2.

accounting profit is therefore equal to expected profits (based on sales expectations and paid out as dividend to equity owners) and retained profits (equal to planned inventories). As is obvious from the narrow income account of firms, firms thus only save an amount equal to their intended inventory changes. The accumulation account is self-explanatory as is the financial account which repeats our earlier statement that the financial deficit of firms is financed by the issuing of new equities solely.

Note that all investment is valued (and performed) net of value added tax and thus at producer prices p_y in the place of the consumer prices $p_v = (1 + \tau_v)p_y$. Indirect taxes (value added taxes)[6] thus only fall on consumption activities and not on gross investment of any kind, (i.e., here also not on housing investments and the inventory investment of firms). There are furthermore no direct (capital) taxes in the sector of firms, neither on property nor on profits, since our model will be formulated in such a way that all expected profits are distributed to asset holders and since there are no taxes on windfall profits (unexpected retained earnings – or losses – of firms that help to finance investment). Note however that the wages w^{be} (in efficiency units) paid by firms include payroll taxes $\tau_p w^e$ (for unemployment insurance, health and other social insurance, and retirement pensions) and that wage income w^e of workers is taxed at the rate τ_w in addition. Note finally that the accumulation account of firms is based on realized magnitudes and thus refers to their intended inventories $\mathcal{I}/K$ only indirectly (via the expected rate of profit ρ^e, to be distinguished from the actual rate of profit ρ^a, which includes windfall profits or losses, due to unfulfilled sales expectations y^e of firms, $\dot{N}/K = \hat{N}N/K, N/K = \nu$).

[6]There is however a tax on the imports made by the firms.

Uses	Resources
Imports $ep_m^* j^a/p_v$	Consumption c_w^g
Depreciation $\delta p_y/p_v$	Consumption c_c
Indirect Taxes $\tau_v(c_w^g + c_c + g^d)p_y/p_v + \tau_m ep_m^* j^a/p_v$	Consumption $g^d = gy^e$
Wages (including payroll taxes) $w^{be} l_f^{de}$	Exports $ep_x^* x^a/p_v$
	Gross Investment g_k/p_v
	Durables (Dwellings) $g_h k_h p_y/p_v$
Profits $\rho^e p_y/p_v + \mathcal{I}/K p_y/p_v = \rho^a p_y/p_v + \hat{N}\nu p_y/p_v$	Inventory Investment $\hat{N}\nu p_y/p_v$
Dividends $\rho^e p_y/p_v$	Profits $\rho^a p_y/p_v$
Savings $S_f^n/p_v K = p_y \mathcal{I}/p_v K$	
Gross Investment $g_k p_y/p_v$	Depreciation $\delta p_y/p_v$
Inventory Investment $\hat{N}\nu p_y/p_v$	Savings $S_f^n/p_v K$
	Financial Deficit $FD/p_v K$
Financial Deficit $FD/p_v K$	Equity Financing $p_e \hat{E}\varepsilon = p_e \dot{E}/p_v K$

Table 8.3: Production, income, accumulation and financial account of firms

Note with respect to the above that profit rates are calculated per net value of the capital stock $p_y K$, since there is no value added tax $\tau_v p_y$ on all purchases intended for investment purposes, while the relative variables and the intensive form of the model is calculated by definition per gross value of the capital stock $p_v K, p_v = (1+\tau_v)p_y$, which implies that the ratio p_y/p_v has to be used in various places in order to correct for such differences in the valuation of the capital stock. Note also that we do not always supply short-cut expressions for the intensive form variables in those cases, where such a lower case representation is not needed in the presentation of the laws of motion of the model in section 3. Note finally that we use ε in the place of e for denoting E/K since e is used to denote the nominal exchange rate of our model.

The sector of households: Asset holders

Turning next to the sector of asset-holders we already know that the investment in housing as well as the supply of housing services has been exclusively allocated to this sector. The production account, see table 8.4, in this regard shows the actual sale (not the potential sale) of housing services (= demand for housing services by assumption) which is divided into replacement costs and actual earnings or profits on the uses side of the production account.

Income of asset holders comes from various sources: interest payments on short- and long-term domestic bonds and on long-term foreign bonds (net of tax payments which must be paid abroad), dividend payments of firms (based on their expected profit) and profits from housing rents. All domestic profit income is subject to tax payments at the rate τ_c and after tax income by definition is divided into the consumption of domestic commodities (including houses, but not housing services) and the nominal savings of asset owners.

Uses	Resources
Depreciation $\delta_h k_h p_y/p_v$	Rent $p_h c_w^h/p_v$
Earnings $\Pi_h/p_v K$	
Tax payment $\tau_c r b_c$	Interest payment $r b_c$
Tax payment $\tau_c b_1^l$	Interest payment b_1^l
Taxes $\tau_c(p_h c_w^h/p_v - \delta_h k_h p_y/p_v)$	Interest payment $e(1-\tau_c^*)b_2^l$
Tax payment $\tau_c \rho^e p_y/p_v$	Dividend payment $\rho^e p_y/p_v$
Consumption c_c	Earnings $\Pi_h/p_v K$
Savings $S_c^n/p_v K$	
Gross Investment $g_h k_h p_y/p_v$	Depreciation $\delta_h k_h p_y/p_v$
Financial Surplus $FS/p_v K$	Savings $S_c^n/p_v K$
Money $\hat{M}_c m_c = \dot{M}_c/p_v K$	Financial Surplus $FS/p_v K$
Short-term bonds $\hat{B}_c b_c = \dot{B}_c/p_v K$	
Long-term bonds $p_b \hat{B}_1^l b_1^l = p_b \dot{B}_1^l/p_v K$	
Foreign Bonds $e p_b^* \hat{B}_2^l b_2^l = e p_b^* \dot{B}_2^l/p_v K$	
Equities $p_e \hat{E}\varepsilon = p_e \dot{E}/p_v K$	

Table 8.4: Production /income / accumulation and financial account of households (asset owners, including housing investment):

The accumulation account shows the sources for gross investment of asset-holders in the housing sector, namely depreciation and savings, the excess of which (over housing investment) is then invested into financial assets as shown in the financial account. Note here that short-term bonds are fixed price bonds $p_b = 1$ (which are perfectly liquid), while long-term bonds have the variable price[7] $p_b = 1/r^l$ (and fixed nominal interest payments of one unit of money per period) which shows that they are of the type of consols or perpetuities (the same holds true for imported foreign bonds, which are of long-term type solely).

The sector of households: Workers

The next set of accounts (see table 8.5), the ones of worker households, are fairly simple and easy to explain. First, there is no production account in this sector. Income of the members of the workforce, which may be employed, unemployed or retired, thus derives from wages, unemployment benefits or pension payments where $l^e = \alpha_l l_1^e$ denotes the total number of persons in the current workforce (l^{we} the part that is employed) and $\alpha_l l_2^e$ the number of retired people who have access to pension funds (α_l=const. is the participation rate of the potential workforce l_1^e). To this we have to add the interest income on saving deposits (short-term bonds) which is taxed at the general rate used for financial asset income. All wage type incomes are subject to taxation at the rate τ_w and are by definition divided into nominal consumption (consumption goods and housing services) and savings. Note here that the employment l^{de} of the employed l^{we} can differ from their normal employment which is measured by l^{we}, the number of persons that are employed (reduced to efficiency units and per unit of capital). Note also that wages w^e (in efficiency units) are calculated net of payroll taxes. We assume in the following that workers have a positive savings rate and that they hold their savings in the form of money and short-term bonds solely which is mirrored here in the accumulation and finance account in a straightforward way.

Uses	Resources
–	–
Taxes $\tau_w[w^e l^{de} + w^{ue}(l^e - l^{we}) + w^{re}\alpha_l l_2^e] + \tau_c r b_w$	Wages $w^e l^{de}$
Consumption $c_w^g + p_h c_w^h / p_v$	Unemployment benefits $w^{ue}(l^e - l^{we})$
–	Pensions $w^{re}\alpha_l l_2^e$
Savings $S_w^n / p_v K$	rb_w Interest payments
Financial Surplus $FS/p_v K$	Savings $S_w^n / p_v K$
Money accumulation $\hat{M}_w m_w = \dot{M}_w / p_v K$	Financial Surplus $FS/p_v K$
Short-term bond accumulation $\hat{B}_w b_w = \dot{B}_w / p_v K$	

Table 8.5: Production / income / accumulation and financial account of households (workers).

[7]They are thus not perfectly liquid, since there is no 'money back' guarantee here for the sector of asset owners as a whole.

The public sector: Government and monetary authority

Next there are the accounts of the fiscal and monetary authority (see table 8.6) which due to the many taxation schemes and transfer payments that are assumed are more voluminous than the preceding accounts – at least with respect to the income account. There is first however a fictitious production account where the supply of public goods is valued at production costs which consist of government expenditures for goods and labor.

Uses	Resources
Government expenditure for goods $g^d gy^e$	Costless Provision
Government expenditure for services $w^{be}l_g^{de}$	of public goods
Interest payment rb	Wage income taxation $\tau_w[w^e l^{de} + w^{ue}(l^e - l^{we}) + w^{re}\alpha_l l_2^e]$
Interest payment b^l	Profit and interest taxation $\tau_c[\rho^e p_y/p_v + rb + b^l]$
Pensions $w^{re}\alpha_l l_2^e$	Rent income taxation $\tau_c(p_h c_w^h/p_v K - \delta_h k_h p_y/p_v)$
Unemployment benefits $w^{ue}(l^e - l^{we})$	Payroll taxes $\tau_p w^e l^{de}$
Government consumption $g^d = gy^e$	Value added tax $\tau_v(c_w^g + c_c + g^d)p_y/p_v$
Salaries $w^{be}l_g^{de}$	Import taxes $\tau_m e p_m^* j^a/p_v$
Savings $S_g^n/p_v K$	
	Savings $S_g^n/p_v K$
	Financial Deficit $FD/p_v K$
Financial deficit $FD/p_v K$	Short-term debt $\hat{B}b = \dot{B}/p_v K$
	Long-term debt $p_b\hat{B}^l b^l = p_b\dot{B}^l/p_v K$
	Money $\hat{M}m = \dot{M}/p_v K$

Table 8.6: Production / income / accumulation and financial account of fiscal and monetary authorities:

The resources of government income consist of taxes on the various forms of workers' income (taxed at a uniform rate), of taxes on the various forms of profit, interest and rent income (again taxed at a uniform rate), payroll taxes, value added taxes and import taxes. Uses of this tax income of the government are interest payments, transfers to the unemployed and the retired persons and the costs of the mentioned government 'production'. In general all these uses of the tax income of the government will exceed its income so that there will result a negative amount of nominal savings S_g^n/p_vK which balances the income account of the government.

There is no accumulation of real assets in the government sector which means that we only have to look into the financial account of the government to see how the excess of government outlays over government revenue is financed through issuing money or short- or long-term debt. Note that there is now money as a financial asset in the economy that can be used by the government to finance its expenditures (if the central bank is willing to buy government bonds from the market at the corresponding amount).

The balance of payments

Let us finally describe the balance of payments of the economy under consideration. This is done from the viewpoint of the foreign sector which is thus a fifth agent of the economic structure considered in this paper. The description of the behavior of this agent will however be confined to steady state behavior in the present investigation of the structural equations of the model.

The balance of payments:

Uses	Resources
ep^*x^a/p_v	ep^*j^a/p_v
$e(1-\tau_c)b_2^l$	$(1-\tau_c)b_1^{l*}$
$\hat{B}_1^{l*}b_1^{l*}/r^l = \dot{B}_1^{l*}/(r^lp_vK)$	$e\hat{B}_2^lb_2^l/r^{l*} = e\dot{B}_2^l/(r^{l*}p_vK)$

Table 8.7: The foreign account

The balance of payments (see table 8.7) shows the trade account (exports x^a and imports j^a per unit of capital), the international component of interest payments (to foreigners and from abroad) that are all assumed to cross borders and the outflow and the inflow of new capital (long-term bonds).[8] Note that this account does not show any reserve changes of the central bank due to foreign exchange market operations. This is possible in the approach chosen in this paper, despite a temporarily given exchange rate e, since the supply of bonds of the government domestically and abroad of the equities of firms are channeled here into the savings decisions of households without readjustments, while the excess of domestic private savings is going into foreign bonds, which in turn implies that the balance of payments must be balanced without any intervention from the central bank, see chapter 7 for the details of this.

This concludes our intensive form description of the four accounts of the three typical sectors of a small open economy (here with heterogeneous agents in the household sector) plus a foreign sector that is here represented via the balance of payments solely.

[8] $\dot{B}_2^l$ is the amount of domestic bonds purchased by foreigners and $\dot{B}_1^{l*}$ is the amount of foreign bonds purchased by the domestic asset holders.

8.3 Intensive form of the implied 39D dynamics

Let us first of all state again that the intensive form model to be derived in this section is based on some minor simplifying set of assumptions of the general approach of chapter 7:

$$\bar{\pi} = 0, \alpha_x = 1, \alpha_0^c = 1, \alpha_1^c = 0 \quad \text{and} \quad \tilde{n} = \tilde{n}(V, \hat{V}) = \tilde{n}(V),$$

i.e., we abstract from steady state inflation, allow only for one exported commodity (with a given foreign price level) and assume that the growth rate of the labor force only depends on the actual rate of employment and not also on its time rate of change as it was assumed in chapter 7. These assumptions reduce the complexity of the dynamics to some extent, but will still not be sufficient to allow for intensive form and steady state equations that can be treated explicitly from an analytical point of view.

Since the inflation target of the central bank is a zero rate of inflation, we in fact will get in the next section that money supply μ will grow with the real rate γ in the steady state which furthermore implies that all price magnitudes (but not wage levels) will become stationary in the steady state and thus can be treated as state variables of the dynamical model to be presented in this section, and thus need not be reduced to relative forms (real balances and the like) in order to allow for expressions that are stationary in the steady state. This makes the laws of motion to be stated and investigated below much more transparent and easier to understand. Steady state inflation should however be allowed for in future extensions of our disequilibrium growth dynamics.

The first block of the laws of motion in intensive form of the disequilibrium growth dynamics introduced in chapter 7 to be presented below provides the price dynamics of the real part of the economy (including inflationary expectations):

1a. <u>Wage - Price Dynamics and Expectations:</u>

$$\begin{aligned}
\hat{w}^e &= \beta_{w_1}(V - \bar{V}) + \beta_{w_2}(l_f^{de}/l_f^{we} - 1) & (8.1)\\
&+ \kappa_w(\hat{p}_c + n_l) + (1 - \kappa_w)(\pi_c^l + \tilde{n}_l(g_k)) - n_l &\\
&\quad \text{with} \quad \hat{p}_c = \alpha_w \hat{p}_y + (1 - \alpha_w)\hat{p}_h \quad [p_c = p_v^{a_w} p_h^{1-a_w}] &\\
&\quad \text{with} \quad \pi_c^l = \alpha_w \pi^l + (1 - \alpha_w)\pi_h^l &\\
\hat{p}_y &= \beta_p(y/y^p - \bar{U}_c) + \kappa_p \hat{w}^e + (1 - \kappa_p)\pi_c^l & (8.2)\\
\hat{p}_h &= \beta_h\Big(\frac{c_w^h}{k_h} - \bar{U}_h\Big) + \kappa_h \hat{p}_y + (1 - \kappa_h)\pi^l & (8.3)\\
\dot{\pi}^l &= \beta_{\pi^l}(\alpha_{\pi^l}(\hat{p}_y - \pi^l) + (1 - \alpha_{\pi^l})(\bar{\pi} - \pi^l)), \quad \bar{\pi} = 0 & (8.4)\\
\dot{\pi}_h^l &= \beta_{\pi_h^l}(\hat{p}_h - \pi_h^l) & (8.5)
\end{aligned}$$

Due to our assumption of Harrod neutral technological change we have to express all state variables that refer to labor supply or demand in efficiency units which in the block of dynamical equations we have just presented applies to the economy wide rate of employment $V = l^{we}/l^e$ and to the rate of utilization $V_f^w = l_f^{de}/l_f^{we}$ of the workforce of firms.

Next we present the dynamics of asset prices and their expected rate of change which – up to the use of the new state variable $q = \frac{p_e E}{p_y K}$, representing Tobin's average q – is basically identical to their formulation in chapter 7 on the extensive form level. There is therefore not much difference between the extensive form and the intensive form of the model (also with respect to the above block 1.) which is basically due to the fact that we do not allow for steady state inflation in the presently considered intensive form of the model. Note, that equation (8.7) is easily derived by using the growth rate formulation $\hat{q} = \hat{p}_e + \hat{E} - \hat{p}_y - \hat{K}$ and inserting for $\hat{K}$ the term $(g_k - \delta)$ and for $\hat{E}$ the expression $[g_k - \delta + y - y^d - (\beta_n(\beta_{n^d} y^e - \nu) + \gamma\beta_{n^d} y^e)]/q$, where the numerator sums up the financial needs of the firms and the denominator $q = \frac{p_e E}{p_y K}$ translates this sum into the number of equities which have to be emitted for this purpose.

1b. Asset Price Dynamics and Expectations:

$$\hat{p}_b = \beta_{p_b}[(1-\tau_c)\frac{1}{p_b} + \pi_b - ((1-\tau_c)r + \xi)], \tag{8.6}$$

$$\hat{q} = \hat{p}_e - \hat{p}_y + [g_k - \delta + y - y^d - (\beta_n(\beta_{n^d} y^e - \nu) + \gamma\beta_{n^d} y^e)]/q - (g_k - \delta) \tag{8.7}$$

$$\hat{p}_e = \beta_{p_e}[(1-\tau_c)\rho^e/q + \pi_e - ((1-\tau_c)\frac{1}{p_b} + \pi_b)]$$

$$\hat{e} = \beta_e[(1-\tau_c^*)r_l^* + \epsilon - ((1-\tau_c)\frac{1}{p_b} + \pi_b)] \tag{8.8}$$

$$\dot{\pi}_{bs} = \beta_{\pi_{bs}}(\hat{p}_b - \pi_{bs}), \quad \pi_{bc} = \hat{p}_b, \quad \pi_b = \alpha_s\pi_{bs} + (1-\alpha_s)\pi_{bc} \tag{8.9}$$

$$\dot{\pi}_{es} = \beta_{\pi_{es}}(\hat{p}_e - \pi_{es}), \quad \pi_{ec} = \hat{p}_e, \quad \pi_e = \alpha_s\pi_{es} + (1-\alpha_s)\pi_{ec} \tag{8.10}$$

$$\dot{\epsilon}_s = \beta_{\epsilon_s}(\hat{e} - \epsilon_s), \quad \epsilon_c = \hat{e}, \quad \epsilon = \alpha_s\epsilon_s + (1-\alpha_s)\epsilon_c \tag{8.11}$$

The next block provides the laws of motion for quantities and sales expectations. Here, everything has to be calculated per unit of capital (and is then denoted by lowercase letters) in order to allow for stationary steady state values of the state variables to be employed. As a result the laws of motion look different from their extensive form equivalents, basically due to the fact however that the growth rate of the capital stock $g_k - \delta$ has to be deducted from all expressions in order to allow for per unit of capital state variables. Based on the existence of Harrod neutral technological change we have to express the state variable l_f^{we} in efficiency units (which however is easily done on the basis of the formula $\hat{l}_f^{we} = \beta_l(V_f^w - 1) + \gamma - (g_k - \delta)$ due to the definition $l_f^{we} = L_f^w \exp(n_l t)/K$. Note furthermore, that although equation (8.17) seems to suggest some kind of path dependence of the steady state rate of employment $\bar{V}$, the latter will nevertheless be determined uniquely, given the parameters of the whole model (especially the external growth rate γ, compare the corresponding calculations in section 4). The main reason for this can be seen in the fact, that the growth rate of the labor force in the steady state, $\tilde{n}$, is a function of $\bar{V}$.

2. Quantity Dynamics and Expectations:

$$\dot{y}^e = \beta_{y^e}(y^d - y^e) + (\gamma - (g_k - \delta))y^e \tag{8.12}$$

$$\dot{\nu} = y - y^d - (g_k - \delta)\nu \tag{8.13}$$

$$\hat{c}_w^g = \alpha_1^w(c_w^{go}/c_w^g - 1) + \alpha_2^w(V - \bar{V}) + \gamma - (g_k - \delta) \tag{8.14}$$

$$\hat{c}_w^h = \alpha_1^h(c_w^{ho}/c_w^h - 1) + \alpha_2^h(V - \bar{V}) + \gamma - (g_k - \delta) \tag{8.15}$$

$$\dot{l}_f^{we} = \beta_l(l_f^{de} - l_f^{we}) + [\gamma - (g_k - \delta)]l_f^{we} \tag{8.16}$$

$$\begin{aligned}
\dot{\bar{V}} &= \beta_{\bar{v}}(V - \bar{V}) && (8.17)\\
\hat{j}^a &= \alpha_1^j(j^{do}/j^a - 1) + \alpha_2^j(y/y^p - \bar{U}_c) + \gamma - (g_k - \delta) && (8.18)\\
\hat{x}^a &= \alpha_1^x(x^o/x^a - 1) + \alpha_2^x(y/y^p - \bar{U}_c) + \gamma - (g_k - \delta). && (8.19)
\end{aligned}$$

Next we supply the laws of motion for rates of return, rates of interest (medium run averages) and tax rates. All dynamical laws considered in this block are easily obtained from their extensive form equivalents.

3. Medium-run Rates of Return and Tax Rate Dynamics:

$$\begin{aligned}
\dot{\rho}^{av} &= \alpha_\rho(\rho^e - \rho^{av}) && (8.20)\\
\dot{\rho}_h^{av} &= \alpha_{\rho_h}(\rho_h - \rho_h^{av}) && (8.21)\\
\dot{r}_l^{av} &= \beta_{av}(r_l - r_l^{av}) && (8.22)\\
\hat{\tau}_w &= \alpha_{\tau_{w1}}(\frac{b + b^l/r_l}{y^e \bar{d}} - 1) + \alpha_{\tau_{w2}}\hat{d} && (8.23)\\
\hat{\tau}_m &= \alpha_{\tau_m}\frac{p_x x^a - p_m j^a}{p_x x^a}. && (8.24)
\end{aligned}$$

Next we get the growth laws of our intensive form model which do not differ very much from their extensive form expressions in chapter 7, since the growth rate of the capital stock $\hat{K} = g_k - \delta$ has only to be deducted in order to arrive at the expressions for l^e, k_h. Recall however that labor intensity l^e is measured in efficiency units (due to our assumption of Harrod neutral technological change), i.e., its numerator includes the fact that the productivity of labor is growing at the rate n_l. Note also that the formula for labor supply growth (for the rate n) has been simplified by excluding the influence of the rate of change of the employment rate on this rate of growth.

4. Growth Dynamics:

$$\begin{aligned}
\dot{n} &= \beta_n(\tilde{n}(V) - n) && (8.25)\\
\dot{n}_l &= \beta_{n_l}(\tilde{n}_l(g_k) - n_l) && (8.26)\\
\hat{l}^e &= n + n_l - (g_k - \delta) && (8.27)\\
\hat{k}_h &= g_h - \delta_h - (g_k - \delta) && (8.28)\\
\dot{g}_k &= \alpha_k(g_k^d - g_k) && (8.29)\\
\dot{g}_h &= \alpha_h(g_h^d - g_h). && (8.30)
\end{aligned}$$

Due to the existence of wealth effects in consumption all items of wealth accumulation of workers (money and saving deposits) do now count for the evolution of the economy and thus will all be relevant for the real part of the given disequilibrium growth dynamics. Furthermore, due the advanced form of the government budget constraint employed in the present model the laws of financial asset accumulation form the most involved part of the considered dynamics.

5. <u>The Dynamics of Financial Assets Supply:</u>

$$
\begin{aligned}
\hat{m}_w &= \mu + \frac{m_c}{m}(\hat{c}_w^g - \hat{c}_c) - \hat{p}_y - (g_k - \delta) && (8.31)\\
\hat{m}_c &= \mu + \frac{m_w}{m}(\hat{c}_c - \hat{c}_w^g) - \hat{p}_y - (g_k - \delta) \\
\hat{m} &= \mu - \hat{p}_y - (g_k - \delta) && (8.32)\\
\dot{b} &= \alpha_b^g[gy^e + rb + b^l + (w^{ue}/p_v)(l^e - l^{we}) + (w^{re}/p_v)\alpha_l l_2^e + (w^{be}/p_v)l_g^{de} \\
&- \ t^n - \mu m] - (\hat{p}_y + g_k - \delta)b && (8.33)\\
\dot{b}_w &= y_w^D - (c_w^g + p_h c_w^h/p_v) - (\mu m_w + \frac{m_c}{m}(\hat{c}_c - \hat{c}_w^g)m_w) - (\hat{p}_y + g_k - \delta)b_w && (8.34)\\
\dot{b}_c &= \dot{b} - \dot{b}_w \\
\dot{b}^l &= r_l(1 - \alpha_b^g)[gy^e + rb + b^l + (w^{ue}/p_v)(l^e - l^{we}) + (w^{re}/p_v)\alpha_l l_2^e + (w^{be}/p_v)l_g^{de} \\
&- \ t^n - \mu m] - (\hat{p}_y + g_k - \delta)b^l && (8.35)\\
\dot{b}_1^l &= r_l\alpha_{b1}^g(1 - \alpha_b^g)[gy^e + rb + b^l + (w^{ue}/p_v)(l^e - l^{we}) + (w^{re}/p_v)\alpha_l l_2^e + (w^{be}/p_v)l_g^{de} \\
&- \ t^n - \mu m] - (\hat{p}_y + g_k - \delta)b_1^l && (8.36)\\
\dot{b}_1^{l*} &= r_l(1 - \alpha_{b1}^g)(1 - \alpha_b^g)[gy^e + rb + b^l \\
&+ \ (w^{ue}/p_v)(l^e - l^{we}) + (w^{re}/p_v)\alpha_l l_2^e + (w^{be}/p_v)l_g^{de} \\
&- \ t^n - \mu m] - (\hat{p}_y + g_k - \delta)b_1^{l*} && (8.37)\\
\dot{b}_2^l &= \dot{B}_2^l/(p_v K) - (\hat{p}_y + g_k - \delta)b_2^l \quad \text{with} && (8.38)\\
&\frac{\dot{B}_2^l}{p_v K} = \frac{r_l^*}{e}[y_c^D - c_c - \frac{\dot{M}_c}{p_v K} - \frac{\dot{B}_c}{p_v K} - \frac{p_b \dot{B}_1^l}{p_v K} - \frac{p_e \dot{E}}{p_v K} - \frac{p_y}{p_v}(g_h - \delta_h k_h)] \\
&= \frac{r_l^*}{e}\{y_c^D - c_c - (\mu - \frac{m_w}{m}(\hat{c}_c - \hat{c}_w^g))m_c - (\alpha_b^g + (1 - \alpha_b^g)\alpha_{b1}^g) \\
&[gy^e + rb + b^l + (w^{ue}/p_v)(l^e - l^{we}) + (w^{re}/p_v)l_2^e + (w^{be}/p_v)l_g^{de} \\
&-t^n - \mu m] \\
&-(p_y/p_v)[g_k - \delta + y - y^d - (\beta_n(\beta_{n^d}y^e - \nu) + \gamma\beta_{n^d}y^e)] \\
&-(p_y/p_v)(g_h - \delta_h k_h)\}.
\end{aligned}
$$

These laws of motion of the state variables of the disequilibrium growth model in intensive form, in addition to what has already been added above, make use of the following definitional equations and equilibrium relationships that have to be all used when the representation of the dynamics as an autonomous system of nonlinear differential equations is considered.

The first block of the algebraic equations describes the components needed to complete KMG type goods market disequilibrium adjustment processes as far as the market for domestically traded commodities is concerned, and it also provides certain expressions for the price taking demand and supply of firms on import and export markets.[9]

[9]Note here that all demand and supply considerations of firms depend directly or indirectly, via the world market prices in terms of the domestic currency, on the nominal exchange rate which thus is also involved in the steady state calculations of the next section, see also Powell and Murphy (1997, p.169) in this regard.

1. Demand and Supply of Goods:

$$
\begin{aligned}
y^d &= c_w^g + c_c + g_k + g_h k_h + g y^e && (8.39)\\
y &= y^e + \beta_n(\beta_{n^d} y^e - \nu) + \gamma\beta_{n^d} y^e && (8.40)\\
y^p &= y^p(\frac{p_x}{p_y}, \frac{p_m}{p_y}, \frac{w^b}{p_y}) \quad \text{see the appendix to this section} && (8.41)\\
j^{do} &= j^{do}(\frac{p_x}{p_y}, \frac{p_m}{p_y}, \frac{w^b}{p_y}, y) \quad \text{see the appendix to this section} && (8.42)\\
x^o &= x^o(\frac{p_x}{p_y}, \frac{p_m}{p_y}, \frac{w^b}{p_y}, y) \quad \text{see the appendix to this section} && (8.43)\\
c_w^o &= c_{w_1} y_w^D + c_{w_2} w_w && (8.44)\\
c_w^{go} &= \alpha_w c_w^o && (8.45)\\
c_w^{ho} &= p_v(1-\alpha_w)c_w^o/p_h && (8.46)\\
c_c &= c_{c_1} y_c^D + c_{c_2} w_c. && (8.47)
\end{aligned}
$$

The next set of equations determines employment of the workforce of firms (per unit of capital and in efficiency units) as being efficiently chosen with respect to the given technology of firms, given that all other input and output decisions are already fixed by the firms and it also shows the employment decision of the government (where there is always a normal utilization of the labor force). These employment variables can be translated into rates of employment (as shown), and labor supply and retired person (measured in efficiency units and expressed per unit of capital) close this list of labor market characteristics.

2. Employment and Labor Supply:

$$
\begin{aligned}
T(y, x^a) &= F(1, l_f^{de}, j^a) \to l_f^{de} = f^{-1}(y, j^a, x^a), y = f(l_f^{de}, j^a, x^a) \quad \text{see app.x} && (8.48)\\
l_g^{de} &= l_g^{we} = \alpha_g g y^e, l^{de} = l_f^{de} + l_g^{de} && (8.49)\\
V &= (l_f^{we} + l_g^{we})/l^e = l^{we}/l^e && (8.50)\\
V_f^w &= l_f^{de}/l_f^{we} \quad (V_g^w = L_g^{de}/L_g^{we} = 1) && (8.51)\\
l_1^e &= l^e/\alpha_l && (8.52)\\
l_2^e &= (L_2(0)/L_1(0))l_1^e. && (8.53)
\end{aligned}
$$

Next we present the desired growth rates of the capital stock of firms and in the housing sector, needed for the adjustment of the actual rates of growth chosen by firms and asset holders on this basis. We also add here the money supply rule of the central bank that relates the growth rate μ of this money supply to certain imbalances of the economy.

3. Growth Rates (Real and Nominal):

$$
\begin{aligned}
g_k^d &= \alpha_1^k((1-\tau_c)\rho^{av} - r^r)) + \alpha_2^k(r_l - (r-\xi)) + \alpha_3^k(y/y^p - \bar{U}_c) + \gamma + \delta && (8.54)\\
g_h^d &= \alpha_1^h((1-\tau_c)\rho_h^{av} - r^r) + \alpha_2^h(r_l - (r-\xi)) + \alpha_3^h(\frac{c_w^h}{k_h} - \bar{U}_h) + \gamma + \delta_h && (8.55)\\
\mu &= \bar{\pi} + \gamma + \beta_{\mu_1}(\bar{\pi} - \hat{p}_v) + \beta_{\mu_2}(\bar{U}_c - y/y^p) + \beta_{\mu_3}(r - r_o), \quad \bar{\pi} = 0. && (8.56)
\end{aligned}
$$

The needed expressions for the rates of return and of interest to be employed in various places are given next. Note that the short-term rate of interest is here determined by solving the loglinear money market equilibrium condition (based on a Cagan type money demand function). We also show the law of motion for the short run rate of interest which, as shown, represents an equilibrium variable of the model.

4. Rates of Return:

$$\rho^e = y^e - \delta + (p_x/p_y)x^a - (w^{be}/p_y)l_f^{de} - (p_m/p_y)j^a \tag{8.57}$$

$$r^r = (1-\tau_c)r_l^{av} - \pi^l \tag{8.58}$$

$$\rho_h = (p_h/p_y)c_w^h/k_h - \delta_h \tag{8.59}$$

$$r = \frac{\ln h + \ln y^e - \ln m}{\alpha_r(1-\tau_c)} \qquad [\dot{r} = \frac{\hat{c}_c - \hat{m}_c}{\alpha_r(1-\tau_c)} = \frac{\hat{c}_w^g - \hat{m}_w}{\alpha_r(1-\tau_c)}]. \tag{8.60}$$

The next block provides expressions for the various prices of exported and imported commodities, for the three types of wage measures that supplement the gross wages that are paid to workers and finally consumer prices which represent producer prices augmented by value added tax. For convenience we also repeat the definition of the consumer price index that applies to workers' households.

5. Prices:

$$p_x = ep_x^* \tag{8.61}$$

$$p_m = (1+\tau_m)ep_m^* \tag{8.62}$$

$$w^{be} = (1+\tau_p)w^e \tag{8.63}$$

$$w^{ue} = \alpha^u w^e \tag{8.64}$$

$$w^{re} = \alpha^r w^e \tag{8.65}$$

$$p_v = (1+\tau_v)p_y \tag{8.66}$$

$$p_c = p_v^{a_w} p_h^{1-a_w}. \tag{8.67}$$

The final block of the equations that underlie our dynamic model provides the definitions of real disposable incomes (per unit of capital) for workers and asset holders, defines the real wealth concepts (per unit of capital) that apply to these two types of households, gives the expression for government debt per unit of (expected) demand and finally defines real taxes per unit of capital.

6. Government Characteristics, Disposable Income and Wealth:

$$y_w^D = (1-\tau_w)[w^e l^{de} + w^{ue}(l^e - l^{we}) + w^{re} l_2^e]/p_v + (1-\tau_c)rb_w \tag{8.68}$$

$$\begin{aligned} y_c^D &= (1-\tau_c)[\rho^e(p_y/p_v) + rb + b_1^l + (p_h/p_v)c_w^h - (p_y/p_v)\delta_h k_h] \\ &+ e(1-\tau_c)b_2^l \end{aligned} \tag{8.69}$$

$$w_w = m_w + b_w \tag{8.70}$$

$$w_c = m_c + b_c + b_1^l/r_l + eb_2^l/r_l^* + q + (p_y/p_v)k_h \tag{8.71}$$

$$d = \frac{b + b^l/r_l}{y^e} \tag{8.72}$$

$$\begin{aligned} t^n &= \tau_w[w^e l^{de} + w^{ue}(l^e - l^{we}) + w^{re} l_2^e]/p_v + \tau_p(w^e/p_v)l^{de} + \tau_v(p_y/p_v)(y^d - g_k - g_h k_h) \\ &+ \tau_c[\rho^e(p_y/p_v) + rb + b^l + (p_h/p_v)c_w^h - (p_y/p_v)\delta_h k_h)] + \tau_m e(p_m^*/p_v)j^a \end{aligned} \tag{8.73}$$

This closes the description of the employed disequilibrium growth model on the intensive level. The following appendix adds to this description explicit calculations of the optimal decisions of firms based on a nested CES / CET production technology which are needed whenever numerical investigations of the considered model are intended.

Appendix: Nested CES / CET production functions

We again briefly provide in this appendix intensive form expressions for the production block of the model for the case of a nested CES / CET production technology to describe the short-run profit maximizing behavior of demand constrained firms and their profit maximizing output and input target levels (which they use for pricing and investment decisions).

Powell and Murphy (1997, Ch.10) assume as technological basis of their model of the Australian economy that capital K and labor L^d are combined via a CES production function to deliver an intermediate output potential Y_1 which then is used on the basis of a further CES technology assumption together with imported commodities J^d to provide the output potential Y_2 on the basis of which firms can decide to produce combinations of the domestic and the exported commodity, Y, X by means of a CET transformation technology. In intensive form, where everything is measured per unit of capital K, and in the case of labor in efficiency units (denoted by the index e), their technological assumptions are represented by the following three equations:

$$\begin{aligned} y_1 &= [a_1 + b_1(l_f^{de})^{-\rho_1}]^{-1/\rho_1}, \quad \rho_1 > -1 \\ y_2 &= [a_2 y_1^{-\rho_2} + b_2(j^d)^{-\rho_2}]^{-1/\rho_2}, \quad \rho_2 > -1 \\ y_2 &= [a_3 y^{-\rho_3} + b_3 x^{-\rho_3}]^{-1/\rho_3}, \quad \rho_3 < -1. \end{aligned}$$

with expressions measured per unit of capital again denoted by lowercase letters.

In the case of a demand constrained firm, where $y = Y/K$ is a given magnitude from the viewpoint of firms, one can derive from these equations the following representation of its technological underpinnings:

$$\begin{aligned} y_1 &= f^1(l_f^{de}) = [a_1 + b_1(l_f^{de})^{-\rho_1}]^{-1/\rho_1}, \quad \rho_1 > -1 \\ y_2 &= f^2(y_1, j^d) = [a_2 y_1^{-\rho_2} + b_2(j^d)^{-\rho_2}]^{-1/\rho_2}, \quad \rho_2 > -1 \\ x &= f^3(y_2, y)) = [(y_2^{-\rho_3} - a_3 y^{-\rho_3})/b_3]^{-1/\rho_3}. \end{aligned}$$

In symbolic form we thus get as representation of production in this case a function of the type:

$$x = f(l_f^{de}, j^d, y) = f^3(f^2(f^1(l_f^{de}), j^d), y)$$

by inserting the expressions obtained for y_1, y_2 into the x function successively. The demand constrained firm chooses, in intensive form expressions, the input ratios l_f^{de}, j^d for labor and imports and the output ratio x for exports not only in a technologically efficient way (according to the shown production functions), but also by maximizing profits in this constrained situation

$$\max_{x, j^d, l_f^{de}} \left[\frac{p_x}{p_y}x - \frac{p_m}{p_y}j^d - \frac{w^{be}}{p_y}l_f^{de}\right] \quad \text{s.t. } x = f(l_f^{de}, j^d, y), \quad y \text{ being given}$$

which provides uniquely determined values for these input and output variables denoted by l_f^{do}, j^{do}, x^o. The optimality conditions read in this case:

$$\begin{aligned}\frac{p_x}{p_y} f_1(l_f^{de}, j^d, y) &= \frac{w^{be}}{p_y} \\ \frac{p_x}{p_y} f_2(l_f^{de}, j^d, y) &= \frac{p_m}{p_y}\end{aligned}$$

plus of course the representation of the employed technology

$$x = f(l_f^{de}, j^d, y)$$

which provides three equations in the three unknowns l_f^{de}, j^d, x that can, in the given situation, be uniquely and meaningfully solved for the optimal responses l_f^{do}, j^{do}, x^o of the demand constrained firm. In these equations subscripts denote partial derivatives which in the case of f^1 is also the total derivative of course. Of course, as shown, these optimal values are functions of the parameters that the firms face in their profit maximizing decision, which are: $y, \frac{w^{be}}{p_y}, \frac{p_m}{p_y}, \frac{p_x}{p_y}$. These functions have to be solved explicitly when numerical applications and investigations of the model are intended, see Chiarella, Flaschel and Zhu (1999c) for the details.

Neglecting the demand constraint y in the profit maximizing behavior of firms, which make their decision on y also a profit maximizing one, we get the target values that firms use when deciding on their pricing policy and their desired investment per unit of capital. This profit maximizing exercise provides now optimal input ratios $l_f^{pe}, j^{dp}, x^p, y^p$ for labor and imports and for domestic and exported output x per unit of capital, that are considered as the potential or desired ratios of the firms. Hence we now have

$$\max_{l_f^{de}, j^d, y, x} [\frac{p_x}{p_y} x + y - \frac{p_m}{p_y} j^d - \frac{w^{be}}{p_y} l_f^{de}] \quad \text{s.t. } x = f(l_f^{de}, j^d, y)$$

which provides uniquely determined values for these input and output variables denoted by $l_f^{pe}, j^{dp}, y^p, x^p$. The optimality conditions read in this case:

$$\begin{aligned}\frac{p_x}{p_y} f_1(l_f^{pe}, j^{dp}, y^p) &= \frac{w^{be}}{p_y} \\ \frac{p_x}{p_y} f_2(l_f^{pe}, j^{dp}, y^p) &= \frac{p_m}{p_y} \\ \frac{p_x}{p_y} f_3(l_f^{pe}, j^{dp}, y^p) &= -1\end{aligned}$$

plus of course again

$$x^p = f(l_f^{pe}, j^{dp}, y^p)$$

which now provides four equations in the four unknowns $l_f^{pe}, j^{dp}, y^p, x^p$ that can, in the given situation, be uniquely and meaningfully solved for the medium run target ratios $l_f^{pe}, j^{dp}, y^p, x^p$ of firms.

We note that the functional shape of the relationship between the optimal responses of firms, as far as employment and imports and the ratio w^{be}/p_m are concerned is the same as the one described for the demand constrained firm above. The remaining equations for the unconstrained maximization problem however differ from the preceding optimization problem, but do, by way of proper reformulation of the optimality conditions, allow for a successive solution for the values of l_f^{pe}, j^{dp}, y^p and x^p.

8.4 Steady state calculations

Let us state again the assumptions made in the derivation of the intensive form of the model presented in the last section:

$$\bar{\pi} = 0, \alpha_x = 1, \alpha_0^c = 1, \alpha_1^c = 0 \quad \text{and} \quad \tilde{n} = \tilde{n}(V, \hat{V}) = \tilde{n}(V),$$

i.e., we have abstracted from steady state inflation, allow only for one exported commodity (with a given foreign price level) and assume that the growth rate of the labor force only depends on the actual rate of employment and not also on its time rate of change. In addition we now also assume that the consumption of asset holders c_c is a given magnitude (and thus no longer determined by life cycle considerations).[10] This helps to simplify the equations for the steady state solution somewhat and will allow us to determine the characteristics that apply to workers independently of (and prior to) those of asset holders[11] if the rate of import taxation is chosen in a particular way as we will argue below. To simplify notation we also assume for the liquidity premium applied to long-term debt $\xi = 0$.

In this section of the chapter we however are only capable of presenting the equations that will determine the balanced growth path or steady state solution of our model. As we shall see there is now full interdependence between these equations, due to the production functions now assumed to hold in our three input – two output world, which therefore no longer allows for the recursive solution of the fixed proportions case, as in Chiarella and Flaschel (1999e). The present calculation of steady state values is thus much more involved due to the profit-maximizing behavior of firms.[12]

The first set of steady state conditions presented below concerns the growth rates of our small open economy which are easily obtained from the assumption of steady growth in the rest of the world.

$$\gamma = g_k - \delta = g_k^d - \delta \quad \rightarrow g_k = g_k^d = \gamma - \delta \tag{8.74}$$

$$\gamma = g_h - \delta_h = g_h^d - \delta_h \quad \rightarrow g_h = g_h^d = \gamma - \delta_h \tag{8.75}$$

$$\gamma = \tilde{n}(\bar{V}) + \tilde{n}_l(g_k) = \tilde{n}(\bar{V}) + \tilde{n}_l(\gamma + \delta) \quad \rightarrow \bar{V} \rightarrow n = \tilde{n}, n_l = \tilde{n}_l. \tag{8.76}$$

[10]This simplification may be justified by the observation that the assumption of only two polar types of heterogeneous agents suggests this further discrimination between their typical attitudes.

[11]Their complicated composition of wealth does then not influence aggregate demand and the equilibrium to be derived for the market for goods below.

[12]Note here that we neglect as alternative steady state positions all zeros which can be obtained mathematically from the growth law formulations that our model employs. Note also again that the steady state depends parametrically on the initial conditions for $\frac{L_2(0)}{L_1(0)}, p_v, \frac{C_c(0)}{L_1(0)}$ that characterize the initial composition of the labor force, the initial output price level (including value added taxes) and a relative expression for the consumption of asset owners.

These equations state that capital (and thus also output) will grow with the external rate γ, to which also the natural rate of growth adjusts. This means that the steady state value of the rate of employment $\bar{V}(=V)$ has to adjust such that $\gamma = \tilde{n}(\bar{V}) + \tilde{n}_l(g_k)$ holds. This determines a unique NAIRE (rate of employment) $\bar{V} = V$ for the long-run of the model under suitable – but simple – assumptions on the function $\tilde{n}$.

The next set of steady state conditions concerns expected inflation (for all prices that exist in our model, except wage rates) and also the various rates of interest and profit of our model:

$$\hat{p}_v = \hat{p}_y = \hat{p}_h = \hat{p}_c = \hat{p}_e = \hat{p}_b = \hat{e} = \hat{p}_m = \hat{p}_x = \bar{\pi} = 0 \tag{8.77}$$

$$\pi^l = \pi^l_h = \pi^l_c = \pi_{bs} = \pi_b = \pi_{es} = \pi_e = \epsilon_s = \epsilon = \bar{\pi} = 0 \tag{8.78}$$

$$r^l = 1/p_b = r^r/(1-\tau_c) = r = \rho^e = \rho_h = r^*_l \tag{8.79}$$

$$\mu = \gamma. \tag{8.80}$$

These conditions state that there is no steady state inflation and thus no nonzero expectations of it, which is due to the form of the interest rate policy rule chosen by the central bank. Furthermore, all (expected) rates of return (also the average concept used in various places) are equalized in the steady state and are determined by the world rate of interest on long-term bonds r^*_l. Note however that all nominal wage magnitudes are increasing at the constant rate n_l in the steady state and thus have to be expressed in efficiency units in order to allow for stationarity in the steady state.

The next block concerns the steady state determination of various supply side quantities. We stress that the supply side conditions now form a nonlinear system of ten equations in eleven unknowns $(\frac{w^{be}}{p_y}, l^{we}_f, x^o, j^{do}, y^e, y, y^p, p_m, p_x, e, \tau_m)$ that will only be solved uniquely (under the usual strict concavity / convexity conditions on joint production technologies) if the nominal exchange rate e is considered as given (which it is not, see its steady state equation below). The following equation system therefore cannot be solved independently of the rest of the steady state variables as in the case of fixed proportions in production considered in Chiarella and Flaschel (1999c g). We thus get that the supply side steady state variables not only depend on the world rate of interest r^*_l, but also – via the exchange rate – on the demand side of the model. This means that the 'long run' of the model is no longer purely supply side determined, but that also parameters of the demand side will influence its position via adjustment (substitution) of inputs and outputs. Note finally that import taxation is determined in such a way that the trade account is always balanced in the steady state, when net exports are defined in terms that include import taxation (due to the import taxation rule that is adopted by the government).

$$r^*_l = y^e - \delta - \frac{w^{be}}{p_y} l^{we}_f \tag{8.81}$$

$$x^a = x^o = x^o(w^{be}/p_y, p_m/p_y, p_x/p_y, y), \quad \text{see the preceding appendix} \tag{8.82}$$

$$j^a = j^{do} = j^{do}(w^{be}/p_y, p_m/p_y, p_x/p_y, y), \quad \text{see the preceding appendix} \tag{8.83}$$

$$y^e = \frac{y}{1+\gamma\beta_{n^d}} \tag{8.84}$$

$$y = y^p \bar{U}_c \tag{8.85}$$

$$y^p = y^p(w^{be}/p_y, p_m/p_y, p_x/p_y), \quad \text{see the preceding appendix} \tag{8.86}$$

$$
\begin{aligned}
T(y, x^o) &= F(1, j^{do}, l_f^{we}), \quad l_f^{de} = l_f^{we}, \quad \text{see the preceding appendix} && (8.87)\\
\tau_m &= \frac{p_x^* x^o - p_m^* j^{do}}{p_m^* j^{do}} && (8.88)\\
p_m &= (1+\tau_m) e p_m^* && (8.89)\\
p_x &= e p_x^*. && (8.90)
\end{aligned}
$$

The above equations for exports x^a and imports j^a show their dependencies on relative prices and on output per unit of capital only in symbolic form (as they are caused by the demand-constrained profit maximization program of firms assumed to underlie the short-run behavior of firms in chapter 7. These equations have to be solved explicitly by assuming a nested CES / CET technology in numerical simulations of the dynamics. Employment l_f^{we} finally is determined via the production function in an efficient way based on the other input and output decisions of firms which however interact with their employment decision in the steady state.

From these equations one easily also gets the following set of steady state values of the remaining employment relationships:

$$
\begin{aligned}
l_g^{de} &= l_g^{we} = \alpha_g g y^e && (8.91)\\
l^{we} &= l^{de} = l_f^{we} + l_g^{we} && (8.92)\\
l^e &= l^{de}/\bar{V} \quad [V = \bar{V}],\ l_1^e = l^e/\alpha_l,\ l_2^e = (L_2(0), L_1(0)) l_1^e. && (8.93)
\end{aligned}
$$

Further steady state relationships obtained from the above description of the supply side of the economy are the following:

$$
\begin{aligned}
y^d &= y^e && (8.94)\\
\nu &= \beta_{n^d} y^e && (8.95)\\
d &= (b + b_l/r_l^*)/y^e = \bar{d}. && (8.96)
\end{aligned}
$$

They state that aggregate demand has to adjust to the conditions found to hold on the supply side in the steady state (where they are independent of the exchange rate e), and that the level of steady state inventories can also be calculated on this basis, and that total government debt is exogenously fixed by the government in the steady state.

By using the distribution laws for government bonds we furthermore get for the distribution of domestic bonds:

$$
\begin{aligned}
b &= \alpha_b^g \bar{d} y^e && (8.97)\\
b^l &= r_l^*(1-\alpha_b^g)\bar{d} y^e && (8.98)\\
b_1^l &= r_l^*(1-\alpha_b^g)\alpha_{b1}^g \bar{d} y^e && (8.99)\\
b_2^l &= r_l^*(1-\alpha_b^g)(1-\alpha_{b1}^g)\bar{d} y^e && (8.100)
\end{aligned}
$$

where nothing is known yet about the size of the remaining item b_1^{l*} since we will generally not have that the capital account and the interest transfer account are both balanced in the steady state.

Next, one can determine the following nominal steady state expressions on the basis of a given price level p_v. The indeterminacy of the price level of domestically produced goods has to be resolved later on by supplying a nominal value for the money stock (relative to the capital stock $M(0)/K(0)$) which by a quantity type relationship, see eqn. (8.130), will then allow the determination of absolute price levels.

$$\begin{aligned} p_v &= \text{a given parameter for the time being} && (8.101)\\ p_y &= p_v/(1+\tau_v) && (8.102)\\ w^{be} & \; via \;\; r_l^* = y^e - \delta - \frac{w^{be}}{p_y} l_f^{we}: \quad w^{be} = \frac{y^e - \delta - r_l^*}{l_f^{we}} p_y && (8.103)\\ w^e &= w^{be}/(1+\tau_p),\; w^{ue} = \alpha^u w^e,\; w^{re} = \alpha^r w^e && (8.104)\\ p_b &= 1/r_l^* && (8.105)\\ q &= 1, \quad \text{by solving equation (8.7) for } \hat{q} = 0. && (8.106) \end{aligned}$$

From the definition of q, the last equation implies that we have $p_e E = p_y K$ in the steady state. The equations $c_h^d = \bar{U}_h k_h$ and $r_l^* = p_h c_h^d/(p_y k_h) - \delta_h$ next imply for the housing sector as equation for the price of housing services:

$$\frac{p_h}{p_y} = \frac{r_l^* + \delta_h}{\bar{U}_h}$$

which also allows us to determine the price level of rents.

The equation for the determination of gross wages in efficiency units holds since we have balanced trade in the steady state (including import taxation, see the above), and thus no influence of the international trade in goods on the rate of profit in the steady state. Note here that net real wages ω^e (excluding payroll taxes, but before wage taxation), measured by in terms of consumer prices p_v and efficiency units, are given by

$$\omega^e = \frac{w^e}{p_v} \frac{y^e - \delta - r_l^*}{l_y y} \frac{1}{(1+\tau_v)(1+\tau_p)}$$

and thus can be calculated independently of the – for the moment still undetermined – nominal price level p_v. This observation also applies to all other real magnitudes implying that there will be no real effects of monetary shocks; see the following determination of the consumer price level p_v. Thus, though the model does not dichotomize in any obvious way we will have long run neutrality of money as far as steady state values are concerned.

The next set of steady state values concerns the characteristics of the worker households as far as their income, their wealth and their spending conditions are concerned, i.e., we now consider the determination of the following nine variables:

$$y_w^D, w_w, c_w^g, c_w^h, c^o = c_w^g + c_w^h p_h/p_v, m_w, b_w, \tau_w, k_h.$$

Note that the steady state value of the housing stock – owned by asset holders – is involved in the calculation of steady state spending habits of workers. These variables are to be obtained from the following nine steady state conditions:

$$\begin{aligned} y_w^D &= (1-\tau_w)[w^e l^{de} + w^{ue}(l^e - l^{we}) + w^{re} l_2^e]/p_v + (1-\tau_c) r_l^* b_w && (8.107)\\ y_w^D &= c^o + \gamma w_w && (8.108)\\ c^o &= c_w^g + c_w^h p_h/p_v = c_{w_1} y_w^D + c_{w_2} w_w && (8.109) \end{aligned}$$

$$
\begin{aligned}
c_w^g &= \alpha_w c^o && (8.110)\\
c_w^h &= (1-\alpha_w)c^o p_v/p_h && (8.111)\\
w_w &= m_w + b_w && (8.112)\\
m_w &= k c_w^g \exp(-\alpha_r(1-\tau_c)r_l^*) && (8.113)\\
y^e &= c_w^g + \gamma + \delta + (\gamma+\delta_h)k_h + gy^e && (8.114)\\
k_h &= c_w^h/\bar{U}_h. && (8.115)
\end{aligned}
$$

These equations describe disposable income of workers from the side of resources and uses, present their spending habits on the basis of their life cycle characterization, define workers' wealth, determine their money demand , consider goods market equilibrium in the steady state and finally provide the steady state relationship between housing services demand and supply.

Inserting the life cycle hypothesis $c^o = c_{w_1}y_w^D + c_{w_2}w_w$ into the uses equation of disposable income gives rise to:

$$y_w^D = c_{w_1}y_w^D + c_{w_2}w_w + \gamma w_w$$

which gives the following strict proportionality between income and wealth of workers:

$$y_w^D = \frac{c_{w_2}+\gamma}{1-c_{w_1}}w_w$$

This proportionality gives rise to further proportionalities of the kind:

$$c^o = (c_{w_1}\frac{c_{w_2}+\gamma}{1-c_{w_1}} + c_{w_2})w_w,\, c_w^g = \alpha_w c^o,\, c_w^h = (1-\alpha_w)c^o(1-\tau_v)p_y/p_h,\, c_w^h = k_h\bar{U}_h$$

which shows that all these items are strictly proportional to real wealth per unit of capital w_w. Inserting the foregoing expressions into the goods market equilibrium condition then yields:

$$
\begin{aligned}
y^e &= \alpha_w(c_{w_1}\frac{c_{w_2}+\gamma}{1-c_{w_1}} + c_{w_2})w_w + \gamma + \delta\\
&+ (\gamma+\delta_h)[(1-\alpha_w)(c_{w_1}\frac{c_{w_2}+\gamma}{1-c_{w_1}} + c_{w_2})/\bar{U}_h]w_w + gy^e
\end{aligned}
$$

which finally gives ($\alpha_w < 1$):

$$
\begin{aligned}
w_w &= \frac{(1-g)y^e - (\gamma+\delta)}{\alpha_w(c_{w_1}\frac{c_{w_2}+\gamma}{1-c_{w_1}} + c_{w_2}) + (\gamma+\delta_h)[(1-\alpha_w)(c_{w_1}\frac{c_{w_2}+\gamma}{1-c_{w_1}} + c_{w_2})/\bar{U}_h]} && (8.116)\\
y_w^D &= \frac{c_{w_2}+\gamma}{1-c_{w_1}}w_w && (8.117)\\
c_w^g &= \alpha_w c^o = \alpha_w(c_{w_1}\frac{c_{w_2}+\gamma}{1-c_{w_1}} + c_{w_2})w_w && (8.118)\\
c_w^h &= (1-\alpha_w)(c_{w_1}\frac{c_{w_2}+\gamma}{1-c_{w_1}} + c_{w_2})w_w(1-\tau_v)p_y/p_h && (8.119)\\
k_h &= c_w^h/\bar{U}_h && (8.120)\\
m_w &= k c_w^g \exp(-\alpha_r(1-\tau_c)r_l^*) && (8.121)\\
b_w &= w_w - m_w && (8.122)\\
\tau_w &= 1 - \frac{y_w^D - (1-\tau_c)r_l^* b_w}{[w^e l^{de} + w^{ue}(l^e - l^{we}) + w^{re}l_2^e]/p_v}. && (8.123)
\end{aligned}
$$

Next we consider the equations concerning the steady state values of income, wealth and spending characteristics of the pure asset holders. We stress that this subsequent treatment of asset holders' characteristics is only possible due to our assumption that the steady state value of their consumption is a given magnitude c_c as in Chiarella and Flaschel (1999f,g) (which may or may not be equal to zero).

$$\begin{aligned}
y_c^D &= (1-\tau_c)[\rho^e(p_y/p_v) + rb_c + b_1^l + \rho_h(p_y/p_v)k_h + eb_2^l] && (8.124)\\
y_c^D &= c_c + \gamma w_c && (8.125)\\
w_c &= m_c + b_c + b_1^l/r_l^* + eb_2^l/r_l^* + q + (p_y/p_v)k_h, \quad q = 1 && (8.126)\\
b_c &= b - b_w && (8.127)\\
m_c &= kc_c \exp(-\alpha_r(1-\tau_c)r_l^*), \qquad m = m_w + m_c && (8.128)
\end{aligned}$$

Inserting the expression for w_c into (8.125), the uses of interest income, gives, when equating the resulting equation with the equation (8.124), the sources of asset holders' income:

$$\begin{aligned}
& c_c + \gamma[m_c + b_c + b_1^l/r_l^* + eb_2^l/r_l^* + 1 + (p_y/p_v)k_h] \\
= \; & (1-\tau_c)[\rho^e(p_y/p_v) + rb_c + b_1^l + \rho_h(p_y/p_v)k_h + eb_2^l]
\end{aligned}$$

from which we get (assuming $\gamma > (1-\tau_c)r_l^*$ in order to ensure economical meaningfulness):

$$\begin{aligned}
[\gamma/r_l^* - (1-\tau_c)]eb_2^l &= -c_c - \gamma[m_c + b_c + b_1^l/r_l^* + 1 + (p_y/p_v)k_h] \\
&+ \; (1-\tau_c)[\rho^e(p_y/p_v) + rb_c + b_1^l + \rho_h(p_y/p_v)k_h]
\end{aligned}$$

which finally gives as the steady state equation of foreign assets held by domestic asset holders (in terms of the domestic currency):

$$eb_2^l = \frac{(1-\tau_c)[\rho^e\frac{p_y}{p_v} + rb_c + b_1^l + \rho_h\frac{p_y}{p_v}k_h] - c_c - \gamma[m_c + b_c + b_1^l/r_l^* + 1 + \frac{p_y}{p_v}k_h]}{\gamma/r_l^* - (1-\tau_c)} \qquad (8.129)$$

Inserting this latter expression into the equations (8.124), (8.125) for disposable income and wealth (8.126) of the asset holders then provides us with the steady state values of these two magnitudes (independently of whether the side of uses or resources of income is used for this purpose).

There remains to be determined the values for the nominal exchange rate e and thereby the expression for b_2^l – and finally the absolute level of consumer prices p_v, which then implies absolute levels for the other commodity prices as well.

The theory of the steady state value of the nominal exchange rate is a complicated one in the present context where there is no adjustment of export and import prices on the world market due to changing export and import demand of the domestic economy. Exchange rate revaluations in the steady state work through the GBR and thus have to be determined from it in the following way:

$$\begin{aligned}
0 &= gy^e + r_l^*b + b^l + (w^{ue}/p_v)(l^e - l^{we}) + (w^{re}/p_v)\alpha_l l_2^e + (w^{be}/p_v)l_g^{de} - t^n - \gamma m - \gamma\bar{d}y^e \\
t^n &= \tau_w[w^e l^{de} + w^{ue}(l^e - l^{we}) + w^{re}l_2^e]/p_v + \tau_p(w^e/p_v)l^{de} + \tau_v(p_y/p_v)(y^d - g_k - g_h k_h) \\
&+ \; \tau_c[r_l^*(p_y/p_v) + r_l^*\bar{d}y^e + (p_h/p_v)c_w^h - (p_y/p_v)\delta_h k_h)] + \tau_m e(p_m^*/p_v)j^a \\
&\quad \text{with} \quad \tau_m e(p_m^*/p_v)j^a = (ep_x^*x^a - ep_m^*j^a)/p_v.
\end{aligned}$$

From these two equations we get:

$$\begin{aligned}\gamma \bar{d} y^e &= gy^e + r_l^* b + b^l + (w^{ue}/p_v)(l^e - l^{we}) + (w^{re}/p_v)\alpha_l l_2^e + (w^{be}/p_v) l_g^{de} \\ &- [\tau_w [w^e l^{de} + w^{ue}(l^e - l^{we}) + w^{re} l_2^e]/p_v \\ &+ \tau_p (w^e/p_v) l^{de} + \tau_v (p_y/p_v)(y^d - (\gamma + \delta) - (\gamma + \delta_h) k_h) \\ &+ \tau_c [\rho^e (p_y/p_v) + r_l^* b + b^l + r_l^* (p_y/p_v) k_h] + (e p_x^* x^a - e p_m^* j^a)/p_v) - \gamma m]\end{aligned}$$

from which the steady state value of e can be obtained by solving this linear equation for the value of e.

We stress that neither the trade account (before import taxation) nor the interest rate transfer account nor the capital account must be balanced in the steady state. This is basically due to the two taxation rules (for imports and wages) that are in use by the government in our model. Note again that the equation for the nominal exchange rate feeds back into the rest of the equations for the steady state through the behavior of firms and the supply side of the economy, which thus implies that nearly all of the steady state equations must be solved simultaneously. This implies a considerable degree of complexity for the computation of the steady state which must be reduced by appropriate assumptions in order to obtain some initial results on steady state behavior as we shall show below.

Finally the level of nominal magnitudes (up to wage levels which are rising in the steady state) are determined from

$$m = k(c_w^g + c_c) \exp(-\alpha_r (1 - \tau_c) r_l^*)$$

by supplying an initial condition for the nominal value of the stock of money relative to the capital stock: $M(0)/K(0)$ and by taking note of the definition of real balances $m = M/p_v K$ which gives:

$$p_v = (M(0)/K(0))/[k(c_w^g + c_c) \exp(-\alpha_r (1 - \tau_c) r_l^*)]. \tag{8.130}$$

This closes the set of equations that have to be used for the calculation of interior steady state solutions of the disequilibrium growth model in the intensive form presented in the preceding section. It is obvious by now that the existence (and uniqueness) of such steady state solutions is not at all an easy question which calls for the consideration of special cases first in order to approach the general case in a systematic way. This task will be approached in Chiarella, Flaschel, Groh, Köper and Semmler (1999b), while we have to be content in the present paper with the above description of the steady state equations to be solved in cases of increasing generality.

We observe that the steady state has neither been shown to exist so far in any economically meaningful way, nor is it obviously uniquely determined on the basis of the discussion so far. Furthermore, the present set of steady state equations does not dichotomize with respect to the treatment of the nominal variables, but it seems to allow for neutrality of monetary shocks due to the formulae so far established. There thus remains the task of providing assumptions under which these questions can be treated in a less roundabout way, in an attempt to first consider simpler situations to learn about the complexities of the general case in a systematic way. This task will be solved in subsequent papers, see Chiarella, Flaschel and Zhu (1999c) in particular (see also the following section).

Summarizing the preceding discussion, we see that the steady state of the considered economy heavily depends on the data assumed to apply to the rest of the world and that the steady values of domestic output, exports, imports, employment, private wealth, the wage taxation rate and in particular the exchange rate are complicated functions of the parameters and various other steady state solutions of the dynamics. We stress, see again the preceding section, that the external growth rate γ determines the NAIRE (rate of employment) via

$$\gamma = \tilde{n}(\bar{V}) + \tilde{n}_l(\gamma + \delta)$$

which for example implies that an increase in γ will increase this NAIRE rate of employment $\bar{V}$ (if $\tilde{n}' > 0, \tilde{n}_l \in (0,1)$ holds).

As this section furthermore suggests there will be neutrality of money in the long-run, meaning the steady state path(s) of the economy, since all prices in the real part of the economy have to be increased by the same percentage as the money supply in order to arrive at a new steady state situation. However, as has been made clear in the preceding subsection, neutrality of money supply shocks does not derive in the present model from a dichotomy in its structure and thus cannot be obtained in a recursive fashion. Furthermore the superneutrality of money cannot yet be a question in the present approach since the rate of growth of the money supply is simply given by the real rate of growth, as the model is not yet formulated in a way that allows the consideration of steady state inflation. The Tobin and Anti-Tobin effects of the literature on models of monetary growth cannot thus be an issue at the present stage of model formulation.

A further important problem for which the model is not yet in a suitable shape to address the question of whether an increase in the price of energy and a decrease in the gross wage rate (brought about by an increase of import taxation and a decrease of payroll taxes for example) will reduce energy consumption per unit of capital and increase employment (per unit of capital) and may thus be of a desirable nature. Again we have used import taxation in a specific way that on the one hand allows us to simplify the calculation of steady states, but on the other hand prevents us from considering this question in the present state of the model. Despite the generality that is achieved in the present form of the model there are thus important macroeconomic problems for which it does not yet provide an answer.

Instead of expanding the chosen approach into such directions we will however simplify it further in subsequent sections in order to allow its analytical and numerical treatment to some extent on this stage of the investigation and to learn in this way some basic features of the approach chosen in Chiarella and Flaschel (1999e-g) when substitution in production, wealth effect in consumption and questions of cash management are included into the framework considered there. These simplifications will be achieved by setting the parameter α_{τ_m} equal to infinity, which implies that import taxation always equalizes the value of imports with the value of exports as far as the cash flow of firms is concerned.

Profits of firms are therefore independent of their input and output decisions as far as traded commodities are concerned which however has the problematic implication that firms would tend to increase imports towards infinity and to decrease exports to zero in order to get higher and higher profits, by substituting imports for labor and the non traded commodity for the exported one. Additional assumptions are therefore needed in order to prevent such an extreme outcome from the profit maximizing behavior of firms. In Chiarella, Flaschel and Zhu (1999c) this will be achieved by assuming a particular rationing scheme of domestic firms on the world market which allows them to import at most $\bar{j}$ commodities per unit of capital and forces them to export at least the amount $\bar{x}$ per unit of capital. This fixes the decisions of firms on the world markets and thus also fixes (via the assumed technology) their employment decision when they are constrained by goods demand on the market for domestic goods (as it is assumed in our approach to disequilibrium growth). However unconstrained profit-maximizing output is not yet a given magnitude in the presently considered situation, but has to be determined via the gross real wage rate from the FOC equality with the marginal product of labor. These supply side consideration therefore show that this part of the model is again reduced to the much simpler analysis of smooth factor substitution defined and investigated in an IS-LM framework in Chiarella and Flaschel (1999a).

Such a procedure, which basically removes the endogenous consideration of international trade from the model, will be used as the starting point of our analysis of the case of substitution, wealth effects and cash management in Chiarella, Flaschel and Zhu (1999c) and will there give rise to a 22 dimensional dynamical model with a uniquely defined interior steady state solution that in its structure is not too far away from the 18D case of fixed proportions in production investigated in Chiarella, Flaschel, and Zhu (1999a,b).

8.5 Simplifying assumptions

In this section we present the assumptions underlying the derivation of the laws of motion in the next section and our subsequent simplified steady state calculations, which in sum provides us with an important special 22D dynamics of the general 39D dynamical model introduced in the preceding sections and which will serve here as the core dynamics for the case of substitution in production, wealth effects in consumption and the explicit considerations of money holdings. This special case is obtained basically via one crucial assumption on import taxation which allows us to simplify the profit maximizing behavioral rules for firms considerably and one also crucial simplification concerning the calculation of the price level that guides the wage bargain.

Let us first of all state the assumptions already made in the derivation of a general intensive form presentation and steady state configuration of the preceding sections. These assumptions were:

$$\bar{\pi} = 0, c_c = const, \alpha_x = 1, \alpha_0^c = 1, \alpha_1^c = 0$$

i.e., we have abstracted there from steady state inflation, have assumed a given level of asset holder consumption per unit of capital, have allowed for only one exported commodity (with a given foreign price level) and have also assumed a given foreign price level for the imported commodity.

In addition to this we now also assume that the import taxation rate is given by (see the following for the explanation of the symbols $\bar{x}, \bar{j}$):

$$\tau_m = \frac{p_x^* x^o - p_m^* j^{do}}{p_m^* j^{do}} = \frac{p_x^* \bar{x} - p_m^* \bar{j}}{p_m^* \bar{j}} > 0$$

even in the short-run (and thus also in the long run), which can be achieved by setting the parameter α_{τ_m} of the model of chapter 7 equal to infinity. This equality states that the import costs of firms are always equal to their proceeds from exports and it implies that there is no need to consider these two expressions as far as the sector of firms and their profit maximizing behavior is concerned. This helps to simplify the following calculations of laws of motion and steady states significantly, as a comparison with the general approach presented in chapter 7 immediately shows. Note also that import and export prices in terms of the domestic currency unit continue to be given by:

$$p_m = (1 + \tau_m)ep_m^*, \qquad p_x = ep_x^*$$

but that only $\tau_m ep_m^* \bar{j}$ will be of relevance in the following as an entry in the government budget equation, which therefore depends on the nominal rate of exchange and the above expression for τ_m that can now be treated as a parameter of the model.

Profits of firms are therefore now independent of their input and output decisions as far as traded commodities are concerned. This however has the problematic implication that firms would tend to increase their imports towards infinity and decrease their exports towards zero allowing them to get higher and higher profits, by substituting imports for labor and the non traded commodity for the exported one. Additional assumptions are therefore needed in order to prevent such an extreme outcome of the profit maximizing behavior of firms. This is here achieved by assuming in addition to the above a particular rationing scheme of domestic firms on the world market which allows them to import at most $\bar{j}$ commodities per unit of capital and forces them to export at least the amount $\bar{x}$ per unit of capital. This will fix the decisions of firms on the world markets to these bounds (via their profit maximizing behavior) and thus also fixes (via the assumed production technology features) their employment decision when they are constrained by demand on the market for domestic goods (as it is assumed in this approach to disequilibrium growth). However, unconstrained profit-maximizing output is not yet a given magnitude in the presently considered situation, but will be determined via the FOC equality of the gross real wage rate with the marginal product of labor in the following in the short-run as well as in the long-run (steady state) of the economy. Such supply side consideration indicate that this part of the model is now reduced to the much simpler analysis of smooth factor substitution with one output and only capital and labor as inputs, already employed and investigated in a temporary equilibrium IS-LM framework in Chiarella and Flaschel (1999a).

Such a procedure, which basically removes the endogenous consideration of international trade from the model, will be used as the starting point of our following analysis of the case of substitution, wealth effects and cash management and will there give rise to only a 22 dimensional dynamical model with a uniquely defined interior steady state solution that in its overall structure, but not in its mathematical complexity, is not too far away from the 18D case of fixed proportions in production investigated in Chiarella, Flaschel, and Zhu (1999a,b) to be investigated in the following chapter, but through the above 'simple' assumptions now relatively far away from the general approach adopted in chapter 7.[13]

Due to the above additional assumptions, the equations for the supply side of the economy, concerning laws of motion and steady state positions, are now independent of the demand

[13]Note here that we neglect as alternative steady state positions all zeros which can be obtained mathematically from the growth law formulations that our model employs. Note also the steady state depends parametrically on the initial conditions for $\frac{L_2(0)}{L_1(0)}$ that characterize the initial composition of the labor force.

conditions of our economy, which will also allow us to determine the characteristics that apply to workers independently of (and prior to) those of asset holders.[14] To simplify notation we also assume for the liquidity premium applied to long-term debt $\xi = 0$.

Note finally that all lagged adjustments of the consumption of goods and housing services and of investment towards their desired values (and of course also of imports and exports) are removed from the present version of the model, that Tobin's q is not involved in the core dynamics here to be considered (and that $\alpha_{\tau_{w2}}$ will be set equal to zero in the consideration of the intensive form of the model in the next section). Furthermore rates of 'natural' growth and employment $n = \tilde{n}, n_l = \tilde{n}_l, \bar{V}$ are now given magnitudes, the former equal to γ in sum: $\gamma = n + n_l$. These are all assumption that are needed to discuss the basic dynamical version of the model and the uniquely determined interior steady state solution.

8.6 Intensive form of the implied 22D dynamics

Let us now present the dynamical equations of the model in intensive form on the basis of the simplifying assumptions made in the preceding section. We thus will remove in particular from the presentation of the intensive form dynamics considered so far all delayed adjustments of consumption and investment plans towards their desired values in order to get as starting point a set of dynamical laws that is of as low dimension as possible and nevertheless still in the spirit of the integrated disequilibrium growth model with substitution in production and wealth effects in consumption we have introduced in chapter 7. Note again that all adjustments assumed there for natural rates of growth and employment (including Harrod neutral technological change) are suppressed in the following basic version of this model.

Since the inflation target of the central bank is a zero rate of inflation, we still have that money supply μ will grow with the real rate γ in the steady state which furthermore implies that all price magnitudes (but not wage levels) will become stationary in the steady state and thus can be treated as state variables of the dynamical model to be presented in this section. They thus need not be reduced to relative forms which makes their laws of motion much more transparent and easier to understand.

Before presenting the model we briefly list for its better understanding the 22D state variables it exhibits and also the variables that are defined via various algebraic relationships. The state variables of our dynamics are given by:

w^e = the nominal wage net of payroll taxes

p_y = the goods price level net of value added taxes

p_h = the price of housing services

p_b = the price of long-term bonds

π^l = the expected rate of inflation for p_y

π^l_h = the expected rate of inflation for p_h

π_{bs} = the growth rate of $p_b$expected by the 'lazy' agents

[14] Whose complicated composition of wealth does then not influence aggregate demand and the equilibrium to be derived for the market for goods below.

$$
\begin{array}{rcl}
e &=& \text{the rate of exchange} \\
\epsilon_s &=& \text{the growth rate of } e \text{ expected by the 'lazy' agents} \\
y^e &=& \text{the sales expectations of firms} \\
\nu &=& \text{the inventory capital ratio} \\
l_f^{we} &=& \text{the workforce employed by firms} \\
l^e &=& \text{the full employment labor intensity} \\
\rho^{av} &=& \text{the medium run rate of profit of firms} \\
\rho_h^{av} &=& \text{the medium run rate of profit in housing} \\
r_l^{av} &=& \text{the medium run rate of interest on long term bonds} \\
\tau_w &=& \text{the wage tax rate} \\
k_h &=& \text{the stock of houses} \\
m &=& \text{the real balances of the economy} \\
b &=& \text{the stock of short term bonds} \\
b_w &=& \text{the stock of short term bonds owned by workers} \\
b^l &=& \text{the stock of long term bonds}
\end{array}
$$

The first block of the laws of motion in intensive form of the disequilibrium growth dynamics presented below provides the price dynamics of the real part of the economy (including inflationary expectations):

1a. Wage - Price Dynamics and Expectations (Original Form):

$$
\begin{array}{rcl}
\hat{w}^e &=& \beta_{w_1}(V - \bar{V}) + \beta_{w_2}(l_f^{de}/l_f^{we} - 1) \\
&+& \kappa_w(\hat{p}_c + n_l) + (1 - \kappa_w)(\pi_c^l + n_l) - n_l \\
&& \text{with} \quad \hat{p}_c = \alpha_w \hat{p}_y + (1 - \alpha_w)\hat{p}_h, \quad \text{and} \\
&& \text{with} \quad \pi_c^l = \alpha_w \pi^l + (1 - \alpha_w)\pi_h^l \\
\hat{p}_y &=& \beta_p(y/y^p - \bar{U}_c) + \kappa_p \hat{w}^e + (1 - \kappa_p)\pi_c^l \\
\hat{p}_h &=& \beta_h(\dfrac{c_w^h}{k_h} - \bar{U}_h) + \kappa_h \hat{p}_y + (1 - \kappa_h)\pi^l \\
\dot{\pi}^l &=& \beta_{\pi^l}(\alpha_{\pi^l}(\hat{p}_y - \pi^l) + (1 - \alpha_{\pi^l})(\bar{\pi} - \pi^l)), \quad \bar{\pi} = 0 \\
\dot{\pi}_h^l &=& \beta_{\pi_h^l}(\hat{p}_h - \pi_h^l).
\end{array}
$$

Due to our assumption of Harrod neutral technological change we have to express all state variables that refer to labor supply or demand in efficiency units which in the block of dynamical equations we have just presented concerns the definition of the economy wide rate of employment $V = l^{we}/l^e$ and to the rate of utilization $V_f^w = l_f^{de}/l_f^{we}$ of the workforce of firms.

From the foregoing formulation we find that $\hat{w}^e, \hat{p}_y, \hat{p}_h$ are to be determined by the matrix equation in the next representation of block 1a.

1*a*. Wage - Price Dynamics and Expectations (Intermediate Reformulation):

$$\begin{pmatrix} 1 & -\kappa_w\alpha_w & -\kappa_w(1-\alpha_w) \\ -\kappa_p & 1 & 0 \\ 0 & -\kappa_h & 1 \end{pmatrix} \begin{pmatrix} \hat{w}^e \\ \hat{p}_y \\ \hat{p}_h \end{pmatrix} = \begin{pmatrix} \beta_{w_1}(V-\bar{V}) + \beta_{w_2}(l_f^{de}/l_f^{we}-1) + (1-\kappa_w)\pi_c^l \\ \beta_p(y/y^p - \bar{U}_c) + (1-\kappa_p)\pi_c^l \\ \beta_h(c_w^h/k_h - \bar{U}_h) + (1-\kappa_h)\pi^l \end{pmatrix}$$

$$\dot{\pi}^l = \beta_{\pi^l}(\alpha_{\pi^l}(\hat{p}_y - \pi^l) + (1-\alpha_{\pi^l})(\bar{\pi} - \pi^l)), \quad \bar{\pi} = 0$$
$$\dot{\pi}_h^l = \beta_{\pi_h^l}(\hat{p}_h - \pi_h^l)$$

As shown the first three equations of block 1a. are now represented as a linear equation system in the three unknowns $\hat{w}^e, \hat{p}_y, \hat{p}_h$ that can be uniquely solved when $\Delta = 1-\alpha_w\kappa_w\kappa_p-(1-\alpha_w)\kappa_w\kappa_p\kappa_h \neq 0$ holds true and then gives rise to the following reduced form expressions for the wage and price level dynamics (the latter for domestic commodities and housing services):

1*a*. Wage - Price Dynamics and Expectations (Reduced Form):

$$\begin{aligned} \hat{w}^e &= \frac{1}{\Delta}[\beta_{w_1}(V-\bar{V}) + \beta_{w_2}(l_f^{de}/l_f^{we}-1) + \{(1-\alpha_w)\kappa_w\kappa_h + \alpha_w\kappa_w\}\beta_p(y/y^p - \bar{U}_c) \\ &+ (1-\alpha_w)\kappa_w\beta_h(\frac{c_w^h}{k_h} - \bar{U}_h) + (1-\kappa_w)\pi_c^l \\ &+ \{(1-\alpha_w)\kappa_w\kappa_h + \alpha_w\kappa_w\}(1-\kappa_p)\pi_c^l + (1-\alpha_w)\kappa_w(1-\kappa_h)\pi^l] \end{aligned} \tag{8.131}$$

$$\begin{aligned} \hat{p}_y &= \frac{1}{\Delta}[\kappa_p(\beta_{w_1}(V-\bar{V}) + \beta_{w_2}(l_f^{de}/l_f^{we}-1)) + \beta_p(y/y^p - \bar{U}_c) \\ &+ (1-\alpha_w)\kappa_w\kappa_p\beta_h(\frac{c_w^h}{k_h} - \bar{U}_h) \\ &+ \kappa_p(1-\kappa_w)\pi_c^l + (1-\kappa_p)\pi_c^l + (1-\alpha_w)\kappa_w\kappa_p(1-\kappa_h)\pi^l] \end{aligned} \tag{8.132}$$

$$\begin{aligned} \hat{p}_h &= \frac{1}{\Delta}[\kappa_p\kappa_h(\beta_{w_1}(V-\bar{V}) + \beta_{w_2}(l_f^{de}/l_f^{we}-1)) + \kappa_h\beta_p(y/y^p - \bar{U}_c) \\ &+ (1-\alpha_w\kappa_w\kappa_p)\beta_h(\frac{c_w^h}{k_h} - \bar{U}_h) \\ &+ \kappa_p\kappa_h(1-\kappa_w)\pi_c^l + \kappa_h(1-\kappa_p)\pi_c^l + (1-\alpha_w\kappa_w\kappa_p)(1-\kappa_h)\pi^l] \end{aligned} \tag{8.133}$$

$$\dot{\pi}^l = \beta_{\pi^l}(\alpha_{\pi^l}(\hat{p}_y - \pi^l) + (1-\alpha_{\pi^l})(\bar{\pi} - \pi^l)), \quad \bar{\pi} = 0 \tag{8.134}$$

$$\dot{\pi}_h^l = \beta_{\pi_h^l}(\hat{p}_h - \pi_h^l) \tag{8.135}$$

The first three equations need to be used at various places in the model in order to remove derivative expressions from the right hand sides of the equations.

In the following investigations the model could be simplified considerably if a special case of this block 1a. of the dynamics is assumed, given by the parameter choice $\alpha_w = 1$ (to be coupled with π^l in the place π_c^l of course) as far as price indices are concerned. Note however that this does not mean that there is no demand for housing services, but only that price indices are made somewhat simpler than in the full model, i.e., we of course retain $\alpha_w < 1$ in the allocation of workers' nominal consumption demand between consumption goods proper and housing services. This makes the price dynamics significantly less intertwined and gives rise to the following special case of the equations (8.131) – (8.135):

1a. Wage - Price Dynamics and Expectations (Simplified Form):

$$\begin{aligned}
\hat{w}^e - \pi^l &= \frac{1}{1-\kappa_w\kappa_p}[\beta_{w_1}(V-\bar{V}) + \beta_{w_2}(l_f^{de}/l_f^{we} - 1) + \kappa_w\beta_p(y/y^p - \bar{U}_c)] \\
\hat{p}_y - \pi^l &= \frac{1}{1-\kappa_w\kappa_p}[\beta_p(y/y^p - \bar{U}_c) + \kappa_p\{\beta_{w_1}(V-\bar{V}) + \beta_{w_2}(l_f^{de}/l_f^{we} - 1)\}] \\
\hat{p}_h &= \beta_h(\frac{c_w^h}{k_h} - \bar{U}_h) + \kappa_h\hat{p}_y + (1-\kappa_h)\pi^l \\
\dot{\pi}^l &= \beta_{\pi^l}(\alpha_{\pi^l}(\hat{p}_y - \pi^l) + (1-\alpha_{\pi^l})(\bar{\pi} - \pi^l)), \quad \bar{\pi} = 0 \\
\dot{\pi}_h^l &= \beta_{\pi_h^l}(\hat{p}_h - \pi_h^l).
\end{aligned}$$

Next we present the dynamics of asset prices and their expected rate of change which, since the state variable $q = \frac{p_e E}{p_y K}$ (representing Tobin's average q), is nowhere needed in the remainder of the dynamics, can now be reduced to a consideration of the dynamics of domestic long-term bond prices p_b and the nominal exchange rate e (assuming however that the eliminated state variables remain economically meaningful during the evolution of the core dynamics of the model). Note that we have removed here any explicit representation of the perfect foresight expectations of the 'clever' agents in the sector of asset holders.

1b. Asset Price Dynamics and Expectations:

$$\hat{p}_b = \frac{\beta_{p_b}}{1-\beta_{p_b}(1-\alpha_s)}[(1-\tau_c)r_l + \alpha_s\pi_{bs} - (1-\tau_c)r], \quad r_l = 1/p_b \tag{8.136}$$

$$\dot{\pi}_{bs} = \beta_{\pi_{bs}}(\hat{p}_b - \pi_{bs}) \tag{8.137}$$

$$\hat{e} = \frac{\beta_e}{1-\beta_e(1-\alpha_s)}[(1-\tau_c)r_l^* + \alpha_s\epsilon_s - ((1-\tau_c)r_l + \pi_{bs})], \quad r_l = 1/p_b \tag{8.138}$$

$$\dot{\epsilon}_s = \beta_{\epsilon_s}(\hat{e} - \epsilon_s). \tag{8.139}$$

The next block provides the laws of motion for quantities and sales expectations. Here, everything is calculated per unit of capital in order to allow for stationary steady state values of the state variables. Note that there is no longer a delayed adjustment of the consumption plans of workers (with respect to domestic output and housing services) and that the NAIRE rate of employment has now become a parameter of the model.

2. Quantity Dynamics and Expectations:

$$\dot{y}^e = \beta_{y^e}(y^d - y^e) + (\gamma - (g_k - \delta))y^e \tag{8.140}$$

$$\dot{\nu} = y - y^d - (g_k - \delta)\nu \tag{8.141}$$

$$\dot{l}_f^{we} = \beta_l(l_f^{de} - l_f^{we}) + [\gamma - (g_k - \delta)]l_f^{we}. \tag{8.142}$$

Next we supply the laws of motion for rates of return, rates of interest (medium run averages) and the wage tax rate. Note that there is no longer a dynamic adjustment of the tax rate on imports, which adjusts here with infinite speed to a level that balances import costs with export proceeds and that the parameter $\alpha_{\tau_{w2}}$ has been set equal to zero in equation (8.146):

3. Medium-run Rates of Return, and the Wage Taxation Rate:

$$\dot{\rho}^{av} = \alpha_\rho(\rho^e - \rho^{av}) \tag{8.143}$$

$$\dot{\rho}_h^{av} = \alpha_{\rho_h}(\rho_h - \rho_h^{av}) \tag{8.144}$$

$$\dot{r}_l^{av} = \beta_{av}(r_l - r_l^{av}) \tag{8.145}$$

$$\hat{\tau}_w = \alpha_{\tau_{w1}}(\frac{b + b^l/r_l}{y^e \bar{d}} - 1). \tag{8.146}$$

Next we have the remaining growth laws of our intensive form model which now only concern the law of motion of full employment labor intensity and of the housing capital stock per unit of the business fixed investment capital stock. Note that labor intensity l^e is measured in efficiency units (due to our assumption of Harrod neutral technological change), i.e., its numerator includes the fact that the productivity of labor is growing at the now given rate n_l ($n + n_l = \gamma$, and $\bar{V}$ now also a given magnitude).

4. Growth Dynamics:

$$\hat{l}^e = \gamma - (g_k - \delta) \tag{8.147}$$

$$\hat{k}_h = g_h - \delta_h - (g_k - \delta). \tag{8.148}$$

Due to the existence of wealth effects in the consumption function of workers all items of their wealth accumulation (here only money and saving deposits) do affect the evolution of the economy and thus will all be relevant now for the real part of the given disequilibrium growth dynamics in contrast to the models we have used in the case of fixed proportions in production. Note that, due the advanced form of government budget constraint employed in this model type, the laws of financial asset accumulation form the most involved part of the considered dynamics.

5. The Dynamics of Financial Assets Supply:

$$\hat{m} = \mu - \hat{p}_y - (g_k - \delta) \tag{8.149}$$

$$\begin{aligned} \dot{b} &= \alpha_b^g[gy^e + rb + b^l + (w^{ue}/p_v)(l^e - l^{we}) + (w^{re}/p_v)\alpha_l l_2^e + (w^{be}/p_v)l_g^{de} \\ &\quad - t^n - \mu m] - (\hat{p}_y + g_k - \delta)b \end{aligned} \tag{8.150}$$

$$\dot{b}_w = y_w^D - (c_w^g + p_h c_w^h/p_v) - \mu m_w - (\hat{p}_y + g_k - \delta)b_w \tag{8.151}$$

$$\begin{aligned} \dot{b}^l &= r_l(1 - \alpha_b^g)[gy^e + rb + b^l + (w^{ue}/p_v)(l^e - l^{we}) + (w^{re}/p_v)\alpha_l l_2^e + (w^{be}/p_v)l_g^{de} \\ &\quad - t^n - \mu m] - (\hat{p}_y + g_k - \delta)b^l. \end{aligned} \tag{8.152}$$

These laws of motion of the state variables of the core dynamics of our disequilibrium growth model make use of the following definitional equations and equilibrium relationships that have to be inserted into them when the representation of the dynamics as an autonomous system of nonlinear differential equations is approached.

The list of algebraically determined variables to be used in the above dynamical laws and their state variables is the following one:

y^d = aggregate demand

y = domestic output of firms

$$
\begin{aligned}
y^p &= \text{potential output} \\
c_w^o &= \text{total consumption of workers} \\
c_w^g &= \text{consumption of workers of the domestic commodity} \\
c_w^h &= \text{consumption of housing services by workers} \\
l_f^{pe} &= \text{potential employment of firms} \\
l_f^{de} &= \text{actual employment of the workforce of the firms} \\
l_g^{de} &= \text{actual employment of the workforce of the government} \quad (= l_g^{we}) \\
l^{we} &= \text{the employed part of the workforce} \quad (l^{we} = l_f^{we} + l_g^{we}) \\
l^{de} &= \text{actual employment of the employed workforce} \\
l_1^e &= \text{the workforce of the economy (including the unemployed)} \\
l_2^e &= \text{the retired workforce of the economy} \\
V &= \text{the overall rate of employment} \\
V_f^w &= \text{the rate of employment of the workforce of firms} \\
g_k &= \text{the gross rate of growth of the capital stock of firms} \\
g_h &= \text{the gross rate of growth of the capital stock in housing} \\
\mu &= \text{the rate of growth of money supply} \\
\rho^e &= \text{the expected rate of profit of firms} \\
\rho^r &= \text{the required real rate of return} \\
\rho_h &= \text{the rate of return in the housing sector} \\
r &= \text{the short term rate of interest} \\
r_l &= \text{the long term rate of interest} \quad (= 1/p_b) \\
r^r &= \text{the required rate of return} \quad (= r_l - \pi^l) \\
w^{be} &= \text{gross wages including payroll taxes} \\
w^{ue} &= \text{unemployment benefits} \\
w^{re} &= \text{wage income of retired workers} \\
p_v &= \text{the price level of domestic goods including value added tax} \\
p_c &= \text{the consumer price index (for workers consumption)} \\
y_w^D &= \text{disposable income of workers} \\
m_w &= \text{real balances of workers} \\
w_w &= \text{real wealth of workers} \\
d &= \text{the debt sales ratio of the government} \\
t^n &= \text{aggregate taxes}
\end{aligned}
$$

The first block of the algebraic equations describes the components needed to complete the Keynes-Metzler type goods market disequilibrium adjustment processes as far as the market for domestically traded commodities is concerned. Note here that equation (8.156) makes use of the function f defined in equation (8.155) and has to be solved first, before the solution to equation (8.155) can be obtained

1. Demand and Supply of Goods:

$$y^d = c_w^g + c_c + g_k + g_h k_h + g y^e \tag{8.153}$$

$$
\begin{aligned}
y &= y^e + \beta_n(\beta_{n^d} y^e - \nu) + \gamma\beta_{n^d} y^e && (8.154)\\
T(y^p, \bar{x}) &= F(1, l_f^{pe}, \bar{j}) \to y^p = f(l_f^{pe}, \bar{j}, \bar{x}), && (8.155)\\
&\quad \text{see eqn. (8.186) in the appendix to this section} \\
w^{be}/p_y &= f_1(l_f^{pe}, \bar{j}, \bar{x}) \to l_f^{pe} = f_1^{-1}(w^{be}/p_y, \bar{j}, \bar{x}), && (8.156)\\
&\quad \text{see eqn. (8.185) in the appendix to this section} \\
c_w^o &= c_{w_1} y_w^D + c_{w_2} w_w && (8.157)\\
c_w^g &= \alpha_w c_w^o, \quad \alpha_w \in (0,1) && (8.158)\\
c_w^h &= p_v(1-\alpha_w)c_w^o/p_h. && (8.159)
\end{aligned}
$$

The following set of equations determine employment of the workforce of firms (per unit of capital and in efficiency units) as being efficiently chosen with respect to the given technology of firms, given that all other input and output decisions are already fixed for the firms and it also shows the employment decision of the government (where there is always a normal utilization of the labor force). These employment variables can be translated into rates of employment (as shown). Labor supply and retired persons (measured in efficiency units and expressed per unit of capital) close this list of labor market characteristics.

2. Employment and Labor Supply:

$$
\begin{aligned}
T(y, \bar{x}) &= F(1, l_f^{de}, \bar{j}) \to y = f(l_f^{de},, \bar{j}, \bar{x}) \to l_f^{de} = f^{-1}(y, \bar{j}, \bar{x}) \neq l_f^{we} && (8.160)\\
&\quad \text{see eqn. (8.184) in the appendix to this section} \\
l_g^{de} &= l_g^{we} = \alpha_g g y^e && (8.161)\\
l^{de} &= l_f^{de} + l_g^{de} && (8.162)\\
V &= l^{we}/l^e = (l_f^{we} + l_g^{we})/l^e && (8.163)\\
V_f^w &= l_f^{de}/l_f^{we} \quad (V_g^w = L_g^{de}/L_g^{we} = 1) && (8.164)\\
l_1^e &= l^e/\alpha_l && (8.165)\\
l_2^e &= (L_2(0)/L_1(0))l_1^e. && (8.166)
\end{aligned}
$$

Next we present the desired growth rates of the capital stock of firms and in the housing sector, equal to the actual rates of growth chosen by firms and asset holders in the present version of the model, and we also show the money supply rule assumed to underlie the behavior of the central bank of the model.

3. Growth Rates (Real and Nominal):

$$
\begin{aligned}
g_k &= \alpha_1^k((1-\tau_c)\rho^{av} - r^r)) + \alpha_2^k(r_l - r) + \alpha_3^k(y/y^p - \bar{U}_c) + \gamma + \delta && (8.167)\\
g_h &= \alpha_1^h((1-\tau_c)\rho_h^{av} - r^r) + \alpha_2^h(r_l - r) + \alpha_3^h(\frac{c_w^h}{k_h} - \bar{U}_h) + \gamma + \delta_h && (8.168)\\
\mu &= \bar{\pi} + \gamma + \beta_{\mu_1}(\bar{\pi} - \hat{p}_v) + \beta_{\mu_2}(\bar{U}_c - y/y^p) + \beta_{\mu_3}(r - r_l^*), \quad \bar{\pi} = 0 && (8.169)
\end{aligned}
$$

The needed expressions for the rates of return and of interest to be employed in various places in the dynamics are given next. Note that the short-term rate of interest is here determined by solving the loglinear money market equilibrium condition (based on a Cagan type money demand function) on the basis of a temporarily given level of real balances per unit of capital, m; k the given income velocity of money.

$$\text{4. }\underline{\text{Rates of Return:}}$$

$$\rho^e = y^e - \delta - (w^{be}/p_y)l_f^{de} \quad (8.170)$$

$$r^r = (1-\tau_c)r_l^{av} - \pi^l \quad (8.171)$$

$$\rho_h = (p_h/p_y)c_w^h/k_h - \delta_h \quad (8.172)$$

$$r = \frac{\ln k + \ln(c_w^g + c_c) - \ln m}{\alpha_r(1-\tau_c)} \quad (8.173)$$

The next block provides expressions for the three types of wage measures that supplement the treatment of gross wages paid to workers (concerning payroll taxes, retired persons and the unemployed) and it also supplies expressions for the consumer price level of domestically produced goods (producer prices augmented by value added tax) and for the consumer price index that applies to workers' households.

$$\text{5. }\underline{\text{Prices:}}$$

$$w^{be} = (1+\tau_p)w^e \quad (8.174)$$

$$w^{ue} = \alpha^u w^e \quad (8.175)$$

$$w^{re} = \alpha^r w^e \quad (8.176)$$

$$p_v = (1+\tau_v)p_y \quad (8.177)$$

$$p_c = p_v^{a_w} p_h^{1-a_w}. \quad (8.178)$$

The final block of the equations that underlie our dynamic model provides the definitions of real disposable income (per unit of capital) for workers, provides the expression for the real balance that are held by them (and by asset holders), defines the real wealth of worker households (per unit of capital), defines the ratio of government debt per unit of (expected) demand and finally defines real taxes per unit of capital.

$$\text{6. }\underline{\text{Government Characteristics, Money Holdings, Disposable Income and Wealth:}}$$

$$y_w^D = (1-\tau_w)[w^e l^{de} + w^{ue}(l^e - l^{we}) + w^{re} l_2^e]/p_v + (1-\tau_c)rb_w \quad (8.179)$$

$$m_w = kc_w^g \exp(-\alpha_r(1-\tau_c)r), \qquad m_c = kc_c \exp(-\alpha_r(1-\tau_c)r) \quad (8.180)$$

$$w_w = m_w + b_w \quad (8.181)$$

$$d = \frac{b + b^l/r_l}{y^e} \quad (8.182)$$

$$\begin{aligned} t^n &= \tau_w[w^e l^{de} + w^{ue}(l^e - l^{we}) + w^{re} l_2^e]/p_v + \tau_p(w^e/p_v)l^{de} + \tau_v(p_y/p_v)(y^d - g_k - g_h k_h) \\ &+ \tau_c[\rho^e(p_y/p_v) + rb + b^l + (p_h/p_v)c_w^h - (p_y/p_v)\delta_h k_h)] + \tau_m e(p_m^*/p_v)\bar{j} \quad (8.183) \end{aligned}$$

$$\text{with } \tau_m e(p_m^*/p_v)\bar{j} = \frac{ep_x^*\bar{x} - ep_m^*\bar{j}}{p_v}.$$

This ends the description of the intensive form of the 22D dynamics that we have obtained as a special case of the general disequilibrium growth dynamics of chapter 7. These dynamics will be further simplified and investigated from the numerical point of view in chapter 9 of the book.

Appendix: CES / CET production functions for the simplified dynamics

We briefly provide in this appendix basic expressions for explicit forms of the equations (8.155), (8.156), (8.160) for the case of a nested CES / CET technology of firms. Applied to the special situation considered in this section ($x = \bar{x}, j^d = \bar{j}$) we get from the equations of the appendix to chapter 7 the following intensive form simplifications:[15]

$$\begin{aligned}
y_1 &= f^1(l_f^{de}) = [a_1 + b_1(l_f^{de})^{-\rho_1}]^{-1/\rho_1}, \quad \rho_1 > -1 \\
y_2 &= f^2(y_1, \bar{j}) = [a_2 y_1^{-\rho_2} + b_2 \bar{j}^{-\rho_2}]^{-1/\rho_2}, \quad \rho_2 > -1 \\
y_2 &= [a_3 y^{-\rho_3} + b_3 \bar{x}^{-\rho_3}]^{-1/\rho_3}, \quad \rho_3 < -1
\end{aligned}$$

The last equation can be solved for the level of domestic output per unit of capital y which gives:

$$y = f^3(y_2, \bar{x}) = [(y_2^{-\rho_3} - b_3 \bar{x}^{-\rho_3})/a_3]^{-1/\rho_3}$$

Due to the special assumptions made we therefore get as production technology a function of the type:

$$y = f(l_f^{de}, \bar{j}, \bar{x}) = f^3(f^2(f^1(l_f^{de}), \bar{j}), \bar{x})$$

by inserting the expressions obtained for y_1, y_2 into the y function successively. To do this explicitly is however of not much help in the analysis to be based on this production function, since it leads us to an unwieldy formula that is more complicated to read than the list of expressions that constitute it, viz:

$$y = f(l_f^{de}, \bar{j}, \bar{x}) = [([[a_2[[a_1 + b_1(l_f^{de})^{-\rho_1}]^{-1/\rho_1}]^{-\rho_2} + b_2 \bar{j}^{-\rho_2}]^{-1/\rho_2}]^{-\rho_3} - b_3 \bar{x}^{-\rho_3})/a_3]^{-1/\rho_3}.$$

In view of the above, the equations (8.155), (8.156), (8.160) can now be rewritten as follows:[16]

$$\begin{aligned}
y &= f(l_f^{de}, \bar{j}, \bar{x}) = f^3(f^2(f^1(l_f^{de}), \bar{j}), \bar{x}) \\
y^p &= f(l_f^{pe}, \bar{j}, \bar{x}) = f^3(f^2(f^1(l_f^{pe}), \bar{j}), \bar{x}) \\
\frac{w^{be}}{p_y} &= f_1(l_f^{pe}, \bar{j}, \bar{x}) = f_1^3(f^2(f^1(l_f^{pe}), \bar{j}), \bar{x}) \cdot f_1^2(f^1(l_f^{pe}), \bar{j}) \cdot f_1^1(l_f^{pe})
\end{aligned}$$

In these equations subscripts denote partial derivatives which in the case of f^1 is also the total derivative of course.

[15] Note that because of these assumptions the optimization problem faced by demand and supply constrained firms becomes degenerate.

[16] Note that the second and third of the following conditions arise by solving the firms' unconstrained optimization problem in the current context.

For the rate of profit ρ^e we in addition have ($\neq r_l^*$ now):

$$\rho^e = \frac{f(l_f^{de}, \bar{j}, \bar{x})}{1+\gamma\beta_{n^d}} - \delta - \frac{w^{be}}{p_y} l_f^{de}$$

Note here that $\frac{w^{be}}{p_y}$ is now resultant from two state variables of the model, i.e., it is a given magnitude in each moment of time (whose change is then obtained by the two laws of motion for w^{be} and p_y). A similar observation applies to the variable y which is given in each moment of time by a linear combination of the state variables y^e and ν, as shown by the algebraic equations of the model. The order of derivation in the solution of the production block of the economy is thus given by the following sequence of equations:

$$y = f(l_f^{de}, \bar{j}, \bar{x}) = f^3(f^2(f^1(l_f^{de}), \bar{j}), \bar{x}) :\to l_f^{de} \quad (8.184)$$

$$\frac{w^{be}}{p_y} = f_1(l_f^{pe}, \bar{j}, \bar{x}) = f_1^3(f^2(f^1(l_f^{pe}), \bar{j}), \bar{x}) \cdot f_1^2(f^1(l_f^{pe}), \bar{j}) \cdot f_1^1(l_f^{pe}) :\to l_f^{pe} \quad (8.185)$$

$$y^p = f(l_f^{pe}, \bar{j}, \bar{x}) = f^3(f^2(f^1(l_f^{pe}), \bar{j}), \bar{x}) \quad (8.186)$$

These equations have to be solved in this way during each iteration of the laws of motion of the model.

8.7 The steady state solution of the 22D dynamics

In this section we derive the equations for the interior steady state values of the dynamics considered in the preceding section as they can be obtained on the basis of the assumptions of section 8.5. Recall that the list of state variables is given as follows and note that we do not only present the steady state values of this set of state variables, but also further ones that are of importance for the economic understanding of the considered dynamics.

w^e = the nominal wage net of payroll taxes
p_y = the goods price level net of value added taxes
p_h = the price of housing services
p_b = the price of long-term bonds
π^l = the expected rate of inflation for p_y
π_h^l = the expected rate of inflation for p_h
π_{bs} = the growth rate of $p_b$expected by the 'lazy' agents
e = the rate of exchange
ϵ_s = the growth rate of e expected by the 'lazy' agents
y^e = the sales expectations of firms
ν = the inventory capital ratio
l_f^{we} = the workforce employed by firms
l^e = the full employment labor intensity
ρ^{av} = the medium run rate of profit of firms

$$\begin{aligned}
\rho_h^{av} &= \text{the medium run rate of profit in housing} \\
r_l^{av} &= \text{the medium run rate of interest on long term bonds} \\
\tau_w &= \text{the wage tax rate} \\
k_h &= \text{the stock of houses} \\
m &= \text{the real balances of the economy} \\
b &= \text{the stock of short term bonds} \\
b_w &= \text{the stock of short term bonds owned by workers} \\
b^l &= \text{the stock of long term bonds}
\end{aligned}$$

The first set of steady state conditions presented below concerns the growth rates of capital stocks of our small open economy which are determined in a straightforward manner from the assumption of steady growth in the rest of the world.

$$g_k = \gamma + \delta \tag{8.187}$$
$$g_h = \gamma + \delta_h. \tag{8.188}$$

The next set of steady state conditions concerns expected inflation (for all prices that exist in our model, except wage rates) and also the various rates of interest and profit, plus the steady growth rate of the money supply μ:

$$\pi^l = \pi_h^l = \pi_c^l = \pi_{bs} = \pi_b = \pi_{es} = \pi_e = \epsilon_s = \epsilon = \bar{\pi} = 0 \tag{8.189}$$
$$r_l = 1/p_b = r^r/(1-\tau_c) = r = \rho^e = \rho_h = \rho^{av} = \rho_h^{av} = r_l^{av} = r_l^* \tag{8.190}$$
$$\mu = \gamma. \tag{8.191}$$

These conditions state that there is no steady state inflation due to the monetary policy that is adopted by the central bank and thus all expectations concerning price level changes are given by zero. Furthermore, all (expected) rates of return (also the average concept used in various places) are equalized in the steady state and are determined by the world rate of interest on long-term bonds r_l^*. Note however that all nominal wage magnitudes are increasing at the constant rate n_l in the steady state and thus have to be expressed in efficiency units in order to allow for stationarity in the steady state. Note that the variables $\pi^l, \pi_h^l, \pi_{bs}, \epsilon_s, p_b, \rho^{av}, \rho_h^{av}, r_l^{av}$ will be used as state variables in the representation of the intensive form of the dynamics in the next section.

The next block concerns the steady state determination of various supply side quantities. We stress that the supply side conditions (see below) turn out to form a nonlinear system of six equations in the six unknowns $(\frac{w^{be}}{p_y}, l_f^{we}, y^e, y, l_f^{pe}, y^p)$ that can here be solved in a unique and basically simple way (under the usual strict concavity / convexity (and homogeneity) conditions on production and transformation technologies) in a way that is completely independent from all other steady state calculations. We thus obtain in the assumed 22D special case of the general 39D model that the supply side steady state variables only depend on the world rate of interest r_l^*, and no longer, via the exchange rate, on the demand side of the model. This indeed means that the 'long run' of the model is purely supply side determined in the considered situation (as far as domestic conditions are concerned). This situation will be described by a system of six nonlinear equations below. The details of a

CES / CET solution to this nonlinear system of algebraic equations, based on production and transformation functions, are given in the appendix to this section.

Using, as in Chiarella, Flaschel, Groh, Köper and Semmler (1999a,b),[17] the representation $T(\cdot,\cdot)$ to denote the output transformation function and $F(\cdot,\cdot,\cdot)$ to denote the underlying output capacity generating production function, we have that output y and employed workforce $l_f^{we}(= l_f^{de}$ in the steady state), both in per unit of capital terms, are related by

$$T(y,\bar{x}) \quad = \quad F(1,l_f^{we},\bar{\jmath})$$

from which we obtain (for invertible T):

$$y \quad = \quad f(l_f^{we},\bar{\jmath},\bar{x}). \tag{8.192}$$

The same production relationship holds between potential output y^p and potential employment l_f^{pe}, viz.:

$$y^p \quad = \quad f(l_f^{pe},\bar{\jmath},\bar{x}). \tag{8.193}$$

Since block 1a. of the dynamics presented in the preceding section implies that all excess demand in the labor and the goods market must be equal to zero in the steady state, the steady state actual output and potential output (per unit of capital) are related by:

$$y \quad = \quad y^p\bar{U}_c \tag{8.194}$$

whilst the steady state of the quantity dynamics gives for expected sales (equal to actual demand now)

$$y^e \quad = \quad \frac{y}{1+\gamma\beta_{n^d}}. \tag{8.195}$$

From the marginal productivity relationship between real gross wages and potential employment we next get:

$$w^{be}/p_y \quad = \quad f_1(l_f^{pe},\bar{\jmath},\bar{x}), \tag{8.196}$$

where f_1 denotes the partial derivative of the function f defined above. Finally, rates of return are equalized in the steady state giving rise to

$$r_l^* \quad = \quad y^e-\delta-\frac{w^{be}}{p_y}l_f^{we}, \tag{8.197}$$

which is a condition that relates actual to potential employment and output decisions.

As we stated above, equations (8.192) – (8.197) indeed form a system of six nonlinear equations in the six unknowns $\boxed{\frac{w^{be}}{p_y},l_f^{we},y^e,y,l_f^{pe},y^p}$ which under the usual concavity / convexity conditions on T and F will have a uniquely determined economically meaningful solutions. In the case that T and F are given by CET / CES functions this system of

[17]See also Powell and Murphy (1997) for a detailed presentation of such a production block for the economy.

six equations and its unique solution is described in more detail in the appendix to this section.

The above equations for potential output based on potential employment per unit of capital (where real wages w^{be}/p_y are equal to the marginal product of labor $F_2(1, l_f^{pe}, \bar{j})$) shows their dependence on real wages (and on the profit maximizing border solution for exports $\bar{x}$ and imports $\bar{j}$ per unit of capital) in symbolic form only. These equations can be presented more explicitly by assuming a nested CES / CET technology, see the appendix to this section. Note that the actual steady state labor demand of firms is obtained from the given technology once the level of actual output y has been determined from the potential level y^p by means of the normal rate of capacity utilization $\bar{U}_c$ and is thus also subject to unconstrained profit maximization (in the steady state) up to the fact that $\bar{U}_c < 1$ creates a gap between the normal and the full usage of potential or profit-maximizing capacity utilization. [18] Note also that the variable y^e for expected sales is a state variables of the intensive form of the dynamics, but is here to be combined with the supply side of the model in order to get a solution for potential and actual supply in the steady state.

From these equations one easily also gets the following set of steady state values of further employment relationships:

$$l_g^{de} = l_g^{we} = \alpha_g g y^e \tag{8.198}$$
$$l^{we} = l^{de} = l_f^{we} + l_g^{we} \tag{8.199}$$
$$l^e = l^{de}/\bar{V} \quad [V = l^{we}/l^e = \bar{V}],\ l_1^e = l^e/\alpha_l,\ l_2^e = (L_2(0)L_1(0))l_1^e. \tag{8.200}$$

Further steady state relationships obtained from the above description of the supply side of the economy are the following:

$$y^d = y^e \tag{8.201}$$
$$\nu = \beta_{n^d} y^e \tag{8.202}$$
$$d = (b + b_l/r_l^*)/y^e = \bar{d}. \tag{8.203}$$

They state that aggregate demand has to adjust to the conditions found to hold on the supply side in the steady state, that the level of steady state inventories can also be calculated on this basis, and that total government debt is exogenously fixed by the government in the steady state. Note that the variables l^e, ν are used as state variables in the intensive form of the dynamics in the next section.

By using the distribution laws for government bonds we furthermore get for the distribution of domestic bonds:

$$b = \alpha_b^g \bar{d} y^e \tag{8.204}$$
$$b^l = r_l^*(1 - \alpha_b^g)\bar{d} y^e \tag{8.205}$$
$$b_1^l = r_l^*(1 - \alpha_b^g)\alpha_{b1}^g \bar{d} y^e \tag{8.206}$$
$$b_2^l = r_l^*(1 - \alpha_b^g)(1 - \alpha_{b1}^g)\bar{d} y^e \tag{8.207}$$

[18] Powell and Murphy (1997) indeed find for the steady state of their applied model that $\bar{U}_c < 1$ holds true, as can be seen from their p.220 when their price formulae are expressed in terms of quantities as described in chapter 7 of this book.

where nothing is known yet about the size of the remaining item b_1^{l*} since we will generally not have that the capital account and the interest transfer account are both balanced in the steady state.

Next, one can determine the following nominal steady state expressions on the basis of a given price level p_v. The indeterminacy of the general price level of domestically produced goods has to be resolved later on by supplying a nominal value for the money stock which by a quantity type relationship will then allow the determination of absolute price levels. Thus

$$p_v = \text{momentarily given, see below} \quad (8.208)$$

$$p_y = p_v/(1+\tau_v) \quad (8.209)$$

$$w^{be} = \frac{y^e - \delta - r_l^*}{l_f^{we}} p_y \quad (8.210)$$

$$w^e = w^{be}/(1+\tau_p), \; w^{ue} = \alpha^u w^e, \; w^{re} = \alpha^r w^e \quad (8.211)$$

$$p_b = 1/r_l^* \quad (8.212)$$

$$q = 1. \quad (8.213)$$

The equations $c_h^d = \bar{U}_h k_h$ and $r_l^* = p_h c_h^d/(p_y k_h) - \delta_h$ next imply for the housing sector as equation for the price of housing services:

$$p_h = p_y \frac{r_l^* + \delta_h}{\bar{U}_h}$$

which thus gives the price level of rents in addition to the above nominal magnitudes. The variables p_y, w^e, p_h are used as state variables in the intensive form of the dynamics provided in the next section.

The next set of steady state values concerns the characteristics of the worker households, i.e., the following eight variables:[19]

$$\boxed{w_w, y_w^D, c_w^g, c_w^h, m_w, b_w, k_h, \tau_w.}$$

The equations that determine these magnitudes are the following. Note that $\alpha_w < 1$ has been assumed throughout, see the block 1. of the algebraic equations. Note also that the steady state value of the housing stock and of the wage income taxation rate is implied by steady state characteristics of worker households as they are here presented.

$$w_w = \frac{(1-g)y^e - (\gamma+\delta)}{\alpha_w(c_{w_1}\frac{c_{w_2}+\gamma}{1-c_{w_1}} + c_{w_2}) + (\gamma+\delta_h)[(1-\alpha_w)(c_{w_1}\frac{c_{w_2}+\gamma}{1-c_{w_1}} + c_{w_2})/\bar{U}_h]} \quad (8.214)$$

$$y_w^D = \frac{c_{w_2}+\gamma}{1-c_{w_1}} w_w \quad (8.215)$$

$$c_w^g = \alpha_w(c_{w_1}\frac{c_{w_2}+\gamma}{1-c_{w_1}} + c_{w_2})w_w \quad (8.216)$$

[19] $c^o = c_w^g + c_w^h p_h/p_v$.

$$
\begin{aligned}
c_w^h &= (1-\alpha_w)(c_{w_1}\frac{c_{w_2}+\gamma}{1-c_{w_1}}+c_{w_2})w_w(1+\tau_v)p_y/p_h && (8.217)\\
m_w &= kc_w^g\exp(-\alpha_r(1-\tau_c)r_l^*) && (8.218)\\
b_w &= w_w-m_w && (8.219)\\
k_h &= c_w^h/\bar{U}_h && (8.220)\\
\tau_w &= 1-\frac{y_w^D-(1-\tau_c)r_l^*b_w}{[w^el^{de}+w^{ue}(l^e-l^{we})+w^{re}l_2^e]/p_v}. && (8.221)
\end{aligned}
$$

The variables b_w, k_h, τ_w are used as state variables in the intensive form of the dynamics in the next section. Note that the steady state of τ_w is less than 1 if $\gamma > (1-\tau_c)r_l^*$ holds, but may become negative if there is excessive debt financing by the government. The parameters of the model have therefore to be chosen such that a positive steady value of τ_w is assured in real applications of the model.

Next we provide the equations concerning the steady state values of income, wealth and of the spending characteristics of the pure asset holders (assuming $\gamma > (1-\tau_c)r_l^*$ in order to ensure economical meaningfulness). We stress that this subsequent treatment of asset holders' characteristics is only possible due to our assumption that the steady state value of their consumption is a given magnitude c_c.

$$
\begin{aligned}
b_c &= b-b_w\\
m_c &= kc_c\exp(-\alpha_r(1-\tau_c)r_l^*)\\
m &= m_w+m_c\\
eb_2^l &= \frac{(1-\tau_c)[r_l^*\frac{p_y}{p_v}+r_l^*b_c+b_1^l+r_l^*\frac{p_y}{p_v}k_h]-c_c-\gamma[m_c+b_c+b_1^l/r_l^*+1+\frac{p_y}{p_v}k_h]}{\gamma/r_l^*-(1-\tau_c)}\\
y_c^D &= (1-\tau_c)[r_l^*(p_y/p_v)+r_l^*b_c+b_1^l+r_l^*(p_y/p_v)k_h+eb_2^l]\\
w_c &= m_c+b_c+b_1^l/r_l^*+eb_2^l/r_l^*+q+(p_y/p_v)k_h, \quad q=1.
\end{aligned}
$$

There remains to be determined the values for the nominal exchange rate e – and on this basis – the expression for b_2^l and finally the absolute level of consumer prices p_v, which then implies absolute levels for the other commodity prices as well.

The theory of the steady state value of the nominal exchange rate is a complicated one in the present context where there is no adjustment of export and import prices on the world market due to changing export and import demand of the domestic economy. Exchange rate revaluations in the steady state work through the GBR and are thus determined from it in the following way:

$$
\begin{aligned}
\{\tau_mp_m^*\bar{j}\}e &= -(\gamma-(1-\tau_c)r_l^*)\bar{d}p_vy^e+\gamma p_vm\\
&- \tau_ww^el_f^{de}-\tau_c[r_l^*p_y+r_l^*p_yk_h]\\
&- \tau_pw^el_f^{de}-\tau_vp_y(y^d-(\gamma+\delta)-(\gamma+\delta_h)k_h)\\
&+ (gp_vy^e+(1-\tau_w)w^{ue}(l^e-l^{we})+(1-\tau_w)w^{re}\alpha_ll_2^e+w^el_g^{we}) \qquad \text{with}\\
\tau_mp_m^*\bar{j} &= p_x^*\bar{x}-p_m^*\bar{j}>0.
\end{aligned}
$$

We stress that in particular the parameters characterizing government expenditures and government debt have to chosen appropriately in order to ensure a positive value for the exchange rate e and that neither the trade account (before import taxation) nor the interest rate transfer account nor the capital account must be balanced in the steady state. This is basically due to the two taxation rules (for imports and wage labor) that are used by the government in our model. Note also that the equation for the nominal exchange rate no longer feeds back into the rest of the steady state equations. This implies a considerable degree of simplicity for the computation of the steady state as compared to the general model considered in chapter 7.

Finally the level of nominal magnitudes (up to wage levels which are rising in the steady state) are determined from

$$m = k(c_w^g + c_c)\exp(-\alpha_r(1-\tau_c)r_l^*)$$

by supplying an initial condition for the nominal value of the stock of money: $M(0)/K(0)$ relative to the capital stock and by taking note of the definition of real balances $m = M/p_v K$ which gives:

$$p_v = (M(0)/K(0))/[k(c_w^g + c_c)\exp(-\alpha_r(1-\tau_c)r_l^*)]. \qquad (8.222)$$

This closes the set of equations that have to be used for the calculation of the interior steady state solution of the disequilibrium growth model of chapter 7 under the simplifying assumptions made. It is obvious by now that the proof of existence and uniqueness of such steady state solutions is now an easier task which no longer demands the solution of large nonlinear equation systems. Note that parameters have to chosen in size such that all expressions are meaningful from an economic perspective. This in particular means that c_{w_1} should be less than 1, γ larger than $(1-\tau_c)r_l^*$ and that $(1-g)y^e - (\gamma+\delta)$ should be positive. Those assumptions are both meaningful and pose no significant restriction of generality. Note that b_w need not be positive, but will, if negative, simply mean that worker households are indebted to asset holders which then are creditors of both the government and workers. We stress without further proof that the described steady state solution is uniquely determined, that there is a long-run dichotomy present in it as far as the determination of nominal magnitudes is concerned (implying that 'money is neutral' as far as steady state comparisons are concerned (but that superneutrality cannot yet be considered as there always holds $\mu = \gamma$ in the present approach) and that not all comparative exercises are an easy matter, since in particular the supply side demands further consideration even in this simplified setup (see the appendix to this section below).

Appendix: Nested CES / CET production functions. Steady state calculations.

We provide in this appendix explicit expressions for nonlinear system of six equations (8.192) – (8.197) for the case of a nested CES / CET technology of firms which have to be employed in the steady reference path of the numerical simulations of the 22D dynamics. In extensive form we have as technological description for the economy, in the steady state where $L^d = L^w$ holds:

$$\begin{aligned} Y_1 &= [a_1 K^{-\rho_1} + b_1(\exp(n_l t)L_f^w)^{-\rho_1}]^{-1/\rho_1}, \quad \rho_1 > -1 \\ Y_2 &= [a_2 Y_1^{-\rho_2} + b_2(J^d)^{-\rho_2}]^{-1/\rho_2}, \quad \rho_2 > -1 \\ Y_2 &= [a_3 Y^{-\rho_3} + b_3 X^{-\rho_3}]^{-1/\rho_3}, \quad \rho_3 < -1 \end{aligned}$$

In intensive form these expressions are represented by the following three equations ($l_f^{de} = l_f^{we}$ in the steady state):

$$\begin{aligned} y_1 &= [a_1 + b_1(l_f^{we})^{-\rho_1}]^{-1/\rho_1}, \quad \rho_1 > -1 \\ y_2 &= [a_2 y_1^{-\rho_2} + b_2(j^d)^{-\rho_2}]^{-1/\rho_2}, \quad \rho_2 > -1 \\ y_2 &= [a_3 y^{-\rho_3} + b_3 x^{-\rho_3}]^{-1/\rho_3}, \quad \rho_3 < -1 \end{aligned}$$

where as usual expressions measured per unit of capital are now used in the place of level magnitudes considered beforehand.

Applied to the special situation considered in this section ($x = \bar{x}, j^d = \bar{j}$) we get from these equations:

$$\begin{aligned} y_1 &= f^1(l_f^{we}) = [a_1 + b_1(l_f^{we})^{-\rho_1}]^{-1/\rho_1}, \quad \rho_1 > -1 \\ y_2 &= f^2(y_1, \bar{j}) = [a_2 y_1^{-\rho_2} + b_2 \bar{j}^{-\rho_2}]^{-1/\rho_2}, \quad \rho_2 > -1 \\ y_2 &= [a_3 y^{-\rho_3} + b_3 \bar{x}^{-\rho_3}]^{-1/\rho_3}, \quad \rho_3 < -1. \end{aligned}$$

The last equation can be solved for the level of domestic output per unit of capital y, which gives:

$$y = f^3(y_2, \bar{x}) = [(y_2^{-\rho_3} - b_3 \bar{x}^{-\rho_3})/a_3]^{-1/\rho_3}.$$

Due to the special assumptions made in this section we therefore get as production technology the function:

$$y = f(l_f^{we}, \bar{j}, \bar{x}) = f^3(f^2(f^1(l_f^{we}), \bar{j}), \bar{x}) \tag{8.223}$$

which determines actual output y as the result of the application of l_f^{we}, the normal employment of the workforce employed by firms. Thus we arrive at the CET / CES version of equation (8.192). The same production technology relates potential output y^p to potential employment l_f^{pe} of firms:

$$y^p = f(l_f^{pe}, \bar{j}, \bar{x}) = f^3(f^2(f^1(l_f^{pe}), \bar{j}), \bar{x}) \tag{8.224}$$

whereby we arrive at the CET / CES version of equation (8.193).

We note that an explicit representation of these composed functional forms would leads us to expressions of the type

$$y = [(([a_2[[a_1 + b_1(l_f^{we})^{-\rho_1}]^{-1/\rho_1}]^{-\rho_2} + b_2 \bar{j}^{-\rho_2}]^{-1/\rho_2}]^{-\rho_3} - b_3 \bar{x}^{-\rho_3})/a_3]^{-1/\rho_3}$$

which indicates the complexity involved in this type of production technology with smooth input and output substitution.

Next, the marginal productivity determination of potential employment (8.196) reads in the present special case of a CET / CES technology:

$$\frac{w^{be}}{p_y} = f_1(l_f^{pe}, \bar{j}, \bar{x}) = f_1^3(f^2(f^1(l_f^{pe}), \bar{j}), \bar{x}) \cdot f_1^2(f^1(l_f^{pe}), \bar{j}) \cdot f_1^1(l_f^{pe}) \tag{8.225}$$

In these equations subscripts denote partial derivatives which in the case of f^1 is also the total derivative of course. This formula for potential employment provides us with an even more complicated expression for one of the six equations involved in the description of the supply side of the economy.

Substituting (8.195) into (8.197), and making use of (8.223), next provides us with

$$r_l^* = \frac{f(l_f^{we}, \bar{\jmath}, \bar{x})}{1+\gamma\beta_{n^d}} - \delta - \frac{w^{be}}{p_y} l_f^{we}. \tag{8.226}$$

Substituting (8.196) into this last equation then yields:

$$r_l^* = \frac{f(l_f^{we}, \bar{\jmath}, \bar{x})}{1+\gamma\beta_{n^d}} - \delta - f_1(l_f^{pe}, \bar{\jmath}, \bar{x}) l_f^{we}. \tag{8.227}$$

By inverting (8.224) we have

$$l_f^{pe} = f^{-1}(y^p, \bar{\jmath}, \bar{x}) \tag{8.228}$$

where we denote by f^{-1} the inverse of the function $f : l_f^{pe} \to y^p$ (treating $\bar{\jmath}, \bar{x}$ as parameters). Substituting (8.228) into (8.227) and making use of (8.194) we finally obtain:

$$r_l^* = \frac{f(l_f^{we}, \bar{\jmath}, \bar{x})}{1+\gamma\beta_{n^d}} - \delta - f_1(f^{-1}(y/\bar{U}_c, \bar{\jmath}, \bar{x}), \bar{\jmath}, \bar{x}) l_f^{we} \tag{8.229}$$

which is a relationship between l_f^{we} and y. But the production function (8.223) provides another such relationship, which upon substitution into (8.229) yields:

$$\boxed{r_l^* = \frac{f(l_f^{we}, \bar{\jmath}, \bar{x})}{1+\gamma\beta_{n^d}} - \delta - f_1(f^{-1}(f(l_f^{we}, \bar{\jmath}, \bar{x})/\bar{U}_c, \bar{\jmath}, \bar{x}), \bar{\jmath}, \bar{x}) l_f^{we}.} \tag{8.230}$$

We thus finally have one single nonlinear equation in the unknown $\boxed{l_f^{we}}$ which when solved provides the steady state value for this variable. Equation (8.223) then provides us with the steady state value for $\boxed{y}$ while the one for $\boxed{y^p}$ is then obtained from (8.194) and the one for $\boxed{y^e}$ from equation (8.195). Next the steady state value for $\boxed{l_f^{pe}}$ is obtained from equation (8.228), and thus also provides us with the steady state value for the remaining unknown $\boxed{\frac{w^{be}}{p_y}}$ by means of equation (8.225). This closes the description of the computation of the steady state solution of the production block of the economy in the case of a particular type of a nested CET / CES technology. All other steady state values are then determined in the way shown in the main part of this section.

8.8 Concluding observations

We have presented in section 8.2 the accounting framework of the general CTD growth model of chapter 7 on the intensive form level in order to introduce the notation and the definitions that have to used on this level and also in order to provide a compact framework that should be helpful in understanding the laws of motion of the considered economy that have to be derived on this level in order to allow for stationarity and steady state analysis. Section 8.3 then showed that these implied dynamics are of dimension 39 indeed quite complicated and involved even without steady state inflation and other (minor) simplifications in the state variable representation now achieved. This observation also applies to the steady state characteristics of these 39D dynamics which are of a form that no explicit solution to the steady state equations presented in section 8.4 could be provided there.

Yet, to know the assumptions under which a general CTD growth will exhibit a uniquely determined[20] and economically meaningful steady state reference path is important, since this represents a consistency check for the model in the sense that the situation where it allows for steady state solutions is controlled by the model builder, even if the then necessary assumptions will not be used when the model is empirically estimated and applied. Furthermore, only the existence of such steady state solution allows for the situation of point attractors as they are usually assumed to underlie the deterministic part of structural macroeconometric models. The importance of steady state analysis is now also more and more acknowledged in applied macrodynamic model building, as for example the Murphy and the IMF Multimod Mark III models show, see Powell and Murphy (1997) and Laxton et al. (1998), and this also in theoretical reflections of such applied work, see Whitley (1994, Ch.5) and Deleau, Le Van and Malgrange (1990).

We therefore have added further simplifying assumptions to the model of section 8.3 (and chapter 7) in section 8.5 which, on the one hand, simplified the state variable presentation of the dynamics considerably (to only 22 laws of motion), and which, on the other hand, did not remove too much structure from the original dynamics, by retaining the 'neoclassical heart' of the Murphy model in the production block and the fairly complicated wealth effect structure in particular. This intensive form of the model was presented in section 8.6. The interior steady solution of these dynamics could then be determined explicitly in section 7. We thereby arrived at a compact presentation of our CTD growth dynamics with substitution and wealth effects that besides 22 laws of motion employed two nonlinear equation systems, a six dimensional one for the production block of the economy and an eight dimensional one for worker households characterizing in particular their wealth, disposable income, consumption and the wage taxation rate. A similar system was avoided for the other household type, the asset holders, by fixing their consumption per unit of capital to a given parameter, on the basis of the argument that consumption is not an important issue in this part of the household sector with its still simple and stylized two polar types of households.

Yet, also the 22D dynamics is difficult to handle, also from the numerical perspective, where the nested three CES /CET production function have to used with specific parameter choices, since two large nonlinear systems of algebraic equations have to be solved at each iteration step. In order to get first insights into the feedback structure of such, from the mathematical point of view large, dynamical systems we will therefore simplify the dynamics still further in the next chapter 9 in order to allow, on the one hand, for first numerical investigations of such systems and in order to provide a bridge to the theoretical KMG approach we have investigated in detail in parts I and II of this book. To allow for such a possibility we have in fact to remove smooth input and output substitution from the

[20]As long as no extrinsic, behavioral and technological relationships are assumed to supplement the model far off the steady state.

production block of the model (by using fixed proportions in their place) and also the wealth effects from workers' consumption which removes the two nonlinear equation systems from the state variable presentation of the dynamics, making it basically a linear structure as far as behavior is concerned which only exhibits a variety of intrinsic nonlinearities due to certain products and ratios on the right hand side of the 18 laws of motion that then still apply. As we shall see in the next chapter, the interior steady state solution of the dynamics can then be calculated explicitly and be used as starting situation for numerical simulations (which displace the system from this steady state through policy, demand or supply side shocks at point $t = 1$.)

Chapter 9

Ways Ahead: Analyzing Structural Macroeconometric Model Building

9.1 Introduction

In this chapter we consider the general CTD growth model of chapters 7 and 8 on a level that allows for a compact presentation of a type of core dynamics of the general 39D system which is basically linear in the assumed behavior of the economy, but is nevertheless intrinsically nonlinear due to interdependence of the remaining 18 state variables in the form of products, ratios, the occurrence of growth rate equations and the like.[1] In this form the laws of motion of the economy are easily understood with respect to their meaning and they provide a picture of an economy evolving in disequilibrium where quantities, prices, expectations, stocks and flows, in particular factor endowments, a housing sector, the government budget constraint, asset markets, and various fiscal and monetary policy all interact with each other, yet still without substitution between capital, labor, imports as well as domestic and exported commodities and also without wealth effects in consumption. Section 9.2 lists the changes that allow to reduce the model of chapter 7 to a 18 D system whose laws of motion and steady state analysis are provided in section 9.3 and 9.4, respectively.

These 18D core dynamics can be treated analytically by the various possibilities of decomposing them further into real, nominal, financial and policy subsystems which can also be linked again in various ways as we shall exemplify it in section 9.5. This helps to understand the dynamics of the full 18D system which later is briefly investigated in section 9.8. Before, however, various monetary and fiscal policy issues are investigated in section 9.6. Section 9.7 then considers the inclusion of asset price dynamics. Such analytical and numerical investigations must suffice here for demonstrating the power of subsystem analysis and the switch off / on methodology underlying it in the investigation of larger dynamical system with an applied perspective. Much more time and effort must however be spent in order to really get hold of the dynamical possibilities of such intrinsically nonlinear systems which attempt to incorporate enough detail for applicable macroeconomic model building (with for example enough heterogeneity with respect to household types and expectation

[1] This chapter is based on the material provided in Chiarella and Flaschel (1999f,g,h), Chiarella, Flaschel and Zhu (1999a,b,c).

formation, stock / flow interactions of more or less advanced type and enough detail with respect to policy issues that are currently considered important).

The main purpose of this final chapter of the book is therefore to show the ways in which small macroeconometric, but at the same time large macrodynamic systems can be treated analytically as well as numerically such that their relationship to the hierarchy of integrated theoretical macrodynamical models developed in Chiarella and Flaschel (1999b,e), here continued in part I and II of the book, can be seen and evaluated with respect to the potential for future research on macroeconometric model building. Section 9.9, finally, considers the Fair model for the US economy and compares some of its main assumptions with the structures of our model developed in this book.

9.2 Further simplifying assumptions

In this section we reformulate the extensive form equations of the CTD growth model introduced in chapter 7 and considered in intensive form from various perspectives such that an explicit dynamical system of dimension 18 results and a number of explicit algebraic equations that have to be inserted into the dynamical equations in order to get an autonomous nonlinear system of differential equation from that in the next section of this chapter. The present reformulation of the model of chapter 7 is furthermore based on the experience gained in Chiarella and Flaschel (1999a,d) in the modeling of integrated Keynes-Metzler-Goodwin models of monetary growth for closed as well as open economies, whereby certain features of this dynamical system approach to growth and fluctuations are shown to apply also to the 18D dynamics that is the focus of interest of this chapter 9.

Our interest in this section is not such much to be close to the dynamical structure and implications of the Murphy model, but to formulate and to investigate, in a first extensive approximation of this 100 equations approach to macroeconometric model building, a set of more or less prominent feedback structures of macrodynamic theory it basically contains and the role they play for stability analysis, and this, as stated, in an integrated macrotheoretic monetary growth framework as in parts I and II of this book that in its generality is however much closer to this type of macroeconometric model building and thus theoretically more complex to analyze. This section therefore attempts to build a bridge between empirically motivated work on structural model building (where there generally is no analysis of the mechanism that are hidden in the formulated structure) and theoretical investigations of reasonably large representation of concrete economies, where the interest is to see what the steady state of such economies will look like in all of its details and what stabilizing (or destabilizing) effects are present around it (or have to be added far off the steady state in order to ensure the boundedness of the considered dynamics).

Block 1. describes the changes that have been adopted with respect to the sector of firms as compared to the model of chapter 7.

1. Firms:

$$Y = Y^e + \mathcal{I}, \quad Y^e \neq Y^d = C_w + C_c + I + I_h + G \tag{9.1}$$

$$Y^p = y^p K, \quad y^p = const \tag{9.2}$$

$$
\begin{aligned}
J^d &= j_y Y, \quad j_y = const && (9.3)\\
X &= x_y Y, \quad x_y = const && (9.4)\\
L^d_f &= l_y \exp(-n_l t) Y, \quad l_y = const && (9.5)\\
U_c &= Y/Y^p, \quad V_f = L^w_f/L, \quad V^w_f = L^d_f/L^w_f, && (9.6)\\
p_m &= (1+\tau_m) e p^*_m && (9.7)\\
p_x &= e p^*_x. && (9.8)
\end{aligned}
$$

Equation (9.1) describes in the usual way the production plans of firms Y which are based on expected sales Y^e, generally different from actual demand Y^d, and on intended inventory changes $\mathcal{I}$. Equations (9.3) – (9.5) provide on this basis the import demand equation, J^d, the export supply equation X and the employment decision of firms, L^d, with respect to the workforce L^w they currently employ by means of fixed proportions between these inputs and outputs and the actual production level Y, and subject to Harrod neutral technical change in the case of labor. The neoclassical production function with smooth factor and output substitution that related the input and output decisions of firms in chapter 7 and 8 is therefore now replaced by a simple fixed proportions technology which in addition also provides us with a simple measure for potential output $Y^p$by means of equation (9.2). We thus now have simple linear relationships in the production block of the economy, though with the same set of input and output commodities, which allow for simple and straightforward measures of the rate of capacity utilization U_c and of the external labor market rate as well as of the internal rate of employment of firms, V_f, V^w_f. Finally, equations (9.7), (9.8) now simply provide the domestic prices p_m, p_x of import and export commodities which are based on given world market prices and a fluctuating rate of exchange e. There is thus no substitution possibility in supply and demand for the traded commodities which can obtained from or sold on the world market in any desired amount, due to our small open economy assumption.

The next change in the model of chapter 7 concerns the worker households, where we define their disposable income as chapter 7, but where we now assume that their nominal consumption plans (concerning consumption proper and housing services) depend only on (all types of) after tax wage payments, but not on the interest payments these households receive from their accumulated short-term bonds (demand deposits) and also not on the level of nominal wealth defined by the number of short-term bonds held by the workers.

2a. Households (Workforce):

$$
\begin{aligned}
Y^{Dn}_w &= (1-\tau_w)[wL^d + w^u(L-L^w) + w^r \alpha_l L_2] + (1-\tau_c) r B_w \\
&= Y^{Dn}_{w1} + (1-\tau_c) r B_w && (9.9)\\
C^{on}_w &= c_1(1-\tau_w)[wL^d + w^u(L-L^w) + w^r \alpha_l L_2], \quad C^o_w = C^{on}_w/p_v && (9.10)\\
p_h C^{do}_h &= c_2(1-\tau_w)[wL^d + w^u(L-L^w) + w^r \alpha_l L_2]. && (9.11)
\end{aligned}
$$

Note that there are no longer any money holdings of worker households which also applies to the following sector of asset holders, a new instance of the model that will be explained in relation to the government sector below.

2b. Households (Asset-Holders):

$$Y_c^{Dn} = (1-\tau_c)[\rho^e p_y K + rB_c + B_1^l + p_h C_h^d - p_y \delta_h K_h)] + e(1-\tau_c^*)B_2^l \quad (9.12)$$

$$\hat{C}_c = \gamma. \quad (9.13)$$

Disposable income of asset holders is also unchanged as compared to chapter 7 and its here immediately supplemented with the assumption that the consumption of asset holders simply grows at a constant rate (the world growth rate), since this type of consumption is not considered important for in the type of dynamics of the core 18D model to be derived and investigated in this chapter.[2]

Concerning the fiscal and monetary authority we have only one change in their behavior. The central bank is now pursuing an interest rate policy rule $\dot{r}$, according to which the short-term interest rate is changed in an upward direction when inflationary pressure is above the target $\bar{\pi}$ of the monetary authority or when capacity utilization is above the norm. Furthermore, the central bank aims at moving the nominal rate of interest r towards the world interest rate r_l^* if inflation and demand pressure on the market for goods are of neglectable order. Of course all these targets and intermediate targets interact with each other in many different way depending on the state of the business cycle and the magnitude of the adjustment speeds assigned by the central bank to their various targets.

4. Government (Fiscal and Monetary Authority):

$$\dot{r} = -\beta_{r_1}(r - r_l^*) + \beta_{r_2}(\hat{p}_v - \bar{\pi}) + \beta_{r_3}(U_c - \bar{U}_c) \quad (9.14)$$

$$\dot{B} + \dot{B}^l/r^l = p_v G + rB + B^l + w^u(L - L^w) + w^r \alpha_l L_2 + w^b L_g^d) - T^n. \quad (9.15)$$

The second equation in block 4 is the GBR which shows that there is non money financing of government debt. Money supply is of course endogenous in the present approach to monetary policy and interest rate targeting. It is moreover assumed that money is solely held and advanced for transaction purposes by the various branches of the central bank (or the banking sector) and that all saving or deficit financing is made through interest bearing bonds or equities. Budget equations are therefore satisfied each day by means of interest bearing assets (saving deposits of short-term fixed price bonds in particular), so that any sort of cash management is performed by the banking sector solely.[3] Note that we do not show the various types of tax payments in this reformulation of the model explicitly, but abbreviate their sum by T^n for notational simplicity.

Summing up, we have changed the model of chapters 7, 8 basically in the following way:

- by assuming fixed proportions in production in the place of smooth input (capital, labor and imports) and output substitution (domestic goods and exported commodities),

- by suppressing wealth and interest rate effects in households' consumption demand, and less importantly

[2]This assumption will be further modified and simplified when the 18D core dynamics is introduced.

[3]See Chiarella and Flaschel (1999f) for the details of such an approach which neglects cash management and uses a Taylor type interest rate policy rule in the place of a money supply rule.

- by switching from money supply targeting to interest rate targeting which makes the 'price level' indeterminate as we shall see in the following discussion of this simplified approach.

This dynamical model is investigated in detail in Chiarella and Flaschel (1999f,g) on the extensive as well as on the intensive level where it gives rise to a 34D dynamical system still, in particular due to the many delayed adjustment processes that are still contained in it. Therefore some further assumption on this model are needed and introduced in the next section in order to obtain a core 18D dynamical system from which we can start the numerical investigations of the various feedback mechanisms still involved in these reduced dynamics.

9.3 The 18D core dynamics of the model

In order to get (as a starting point for future research and later dynamical investigations of the general CTG growth model in subsequent publications) a dynamical system that is, on the one hand, as close as possible in spirit to the one of the general model of chapter 7 and, on the other hand, as low dimensional as possible, we consider in this section a further simplified structure for the CTD growth dynamics presented in the preceding section which reduces its 34D representation, see Chiarella and Flaschel (1999g), to the 18D core dynamics presented in the next section. This reformulation makes use of the assumptions $C_c = 0$, i.e., abstracts from consumption of asset holders (to simplify slightly the calculation of the interior steady state of the model in section 9.4), and it removes furthermore certain lags from the considered dynamics, which gives the dynamic model an outlook that is not too far away from the theoretical models introduced and analyzed in Chiarella and Flaschel (1998a, Ch.7, 1998b, Ch.3). Furthermore, the natural rate of growth, of Harrod neutral technological change, and of employment are assumed as constant in the following. Finally, the tax policy parameter $\alpha_{\tau_{w1}}$ is set equal to zero, implying that there is only a proportional influence of government debt on the wage taxation rate (and no longer an additional derivative one).

9.3.1 The laws of motion

We present in this subsection the laws of motion of the reduced dynamics which are subdivided into quantity dynamics, price dynamics, growth dynamics, asset market dynamics and three dynamic fiscal policy rules. The first subdynamics 1. basically represents the Metzlerian inventory adjustment process which when operated in isolation leads to instability for sufficiently high inventory adjustment speeds β_n when coupled with a sufficiently fast revisions of sales expectations, due to static equation that relates output decisions with inventory adjustments, see eqn. (9.36).

1. The Quantity Dynamics:

$$\dot{y}^e = \beta_{y^e}(y^d - y^e) + (\gamma - (g_k^d - \delta))y^e \tag{9.16}$$

$$\dot{\nu} = y - y^d - (g_k^d - \delta)\nu \tag{9.17}$$

$$\dot{l}_f^{we} = \beta_l(l_f^{de} - \bar{V}_f^w l_f^{we}) + [\gamma - (g_k^d - \delta)]l_f^{we}. \tag{9.18}$$

In the quantity dynamics we have removed the adjustment equations for the actual consumption of workers (for goods and housing services) and have thus replaced these consumption plans by the desired consumption targets which are now immediately realized (without any lag). Furthermore, the NAIRU rate of employment, $\bar{V}$, is no longer considered as endogenously determined, but now a parameter of the model. There remain the equations for the adjustment of sales expectations, for inventories and for the workforce employed by firms which is the Metzler inventory adjustment mechanism augmented by an employment policy rule of firms.

2. The Price Dynamics:

$$\hat{w}^e = \beta_{w_1}(l^{we}/l^e - \bar{V}) + \beta_{w_2}(l_f^{de}/l_f^{we} - \bar{V}_w^f) + \kappa_w \hat{p}_y + (1-\kappa_w)\pi^l \tag{9.19}$$

$$\hat{p}_y = \beta_p(y/y^p - \bar{U}_c) + \kappa_p \hat{w}^e + (1-\kappa_p)\pi^l \tag{9.20}$$

$$\dot{\pi}^l = \beta_{\pi^l}(\alpha_{\pi^l}(\hat{p}_y - \pi^l) + (1-\alpha_{\pi^l})(0-\pi^l)) \tag{9.21}$$

$$\hat{p}_h = \beta_h(\frac{c_h^{do}}{k_h} - \bar{U}_h) + \kappa_h \hat{p}_y + (1-\kappa_h)\pi^l. \tag{9.22}$$

There is no direct change of the dynamics with respect to the various types of price adjustment rules of the model, on the market for labor, goods and housing services (including the expectations formation mechanism for medium run inflation rate of the domestically produced good), but an indirect on due to the following assumptions on natural growth and employment (which are now considered as given: $\gamma = n + n_l = \tilde{n} + \tilde{n}_l, \bar{V}$ all constant). We thus basically have the two Phillips curves already discussed in detail in part I of the book, augmented by heterogeneous inflationary expectations over the medium run as usual, and a further Phillips curve for the price dynamics of housing services. This subdynamics includes, on the one hand, the Rose effects, which imply normal or adverse real wage adjustments depending on propensities to consume and to invest and on the relative adjustment speed of prices vs. nominal wages. On the other hand, this subsystem gives rise to destabilizing Mundell - effects, due to the interaction of the real rate of interest in the investment function with the expected rate of inflation when the latter is adjusted with sufficient speed. This activity accelerating process is now also present, in a more indirect way, in the housing sector, since economic activity also depends on housing investment of asset holders and thus on the required real rate of return ρ^r as one of the determinants of this investment behavior. There are thus two possible sources for instability present in t he price block of the economy, while the following growth equations do not carry any of the feedback mechanism that are the focus of this book.

3. The Growth Dynamics:

$$\hat{l}^e = \gamma - (g_k^d - \delta) \tag{9.23}$$

$$\hat{k}_h = g_h^d - \delta_h - (g_k^d - \delta). \tag{9.24}$$

In block 3 we have assumed that the natural rates of growth and of technical change, n, n_l, are given exogenously and equal in sum to γ, the given world rate of growth. Furthermore actual accumulation rates are assumed to be adjusted with infinite speed to their desired targets and thus are no longer represented as lagged adjustment rules. We have furthermore removed from this block 3 of the dynamics the adjustment equations for the rates of return ρ^l, ρ^l_h by assuming that these rates are adjusted with infinite speed to their short-run equivalents, now used in the corresponding behavioral equations in their place. We have as usual the growth law for full employment labor intensity (measured in efficiency units) and the growth law for the stock of houses, of course both laws per unit of the capital stock of firms.

Next, we present the set of equations that represent the dynamics of asset accumulation and asset prices that are needed for the analysis of the real part of the dynamics of the model:

4. Asset Market Dynamics:

$$\begin{aligned}
\dot{b} &= \alpha_b^g[(gy^e + rb + b^l \\
&- t^w - t^c + (w^{ue}/p_v)(l^e - l^{we}) + (w^{re}/p_v)\alpha_l l_2^e + (w^{be}/p_v)l_g^{de}] \\
&- (\hat{p}_y + g_k^d - \delta)b \qquad (9.25)\\
\dot{b}^l &= r^l(1-\alpha_b^g)[gy^e + rb + b^l \\
&- t^w - t^c + (w^{ue}/p_v)(l^e - l^{we}) + (w^{re}/p_v)\alpha_l l_2^e + (w^{be}/p_v)l_g^{de}] \\
&- (\hat{p}_y + g_k^d - \delta)b^l \qquad (9.26)\\
\hat{p}_b &= \frac{\beta_{p_b}}{1-\beta_{p_b}(1-\alpha_s)}[(1-\tau_c)r_l + \alpha_s\pi_{bs} - ((1-\tau_c)r)] + \bar{\pi}, \quad r_l = \frac{1}{p_b} \qquad (9.27)\\
\dot{\pi}_{bs} &= \beta_{\pi_{bs}}(\hat{p}_b - \pi_{bs}), \qquad \pi_b = \alpha_s\pi_{bs} + (1-\alpha_s)\hat{p}_b \\
\hat{e} &= \frac{\beta_e}{1-\beta_e(1-\alpha_s)}[(1-\tau_c)r_l^* + \alpha_s\epsilon_s - ((1-\tau_c)r^l + \pi_b)] + \bar{\pi} \qquad (9.28)\\
\dot{\epsilon}_s &= \beta_{\epsilon_s}(\ddot{e} - \epsilon_s). \qquad (9.29)
\end{aligned}$$

The price adjustment rules in block 4 concern the nominal value of long-term bonds p_b and the nominal exchange rate e and they are of the type discussed in chapter 7 and again based (as explained in chapter 7) on heterogeneous expectations of the pure wealth owners of this model. Note that we will set the inflation target $\bar{\pi}$ of the central bank equal to zero in the following. Note also that – as in the larger models – the dynamics of equity prices and of Tobin's q are not needed in the investigation of the core dynamics of the model, since they do not feed back into the real part of the dynamics. In contrast to equities the bond dynamics (short- and long-term) will feed back into the real part of the economy, due to the wage tax policy adopted by the government, see block 5. There is no change here with respect to the division of the government deficit into short- and long-term financing, but, as explained in the preceding section, there is no longer a money-financing of government debt as far as the aspect of pure cash (and thus cash management for transaction purposes) is concerned.

As the above asset price adjustment equations show there is a positive self-reference or feedback mechanism between expected capital gains and actual capital gains for long-term bonds and between expected currency depreciation and actual currency depreciation. due to the agents that form backward looking expectations, which need not be of the simple adaptive type here assumed. These self-references add explosiveness to the vicinity of the steady state which may be tamed far off the steady state if it is assumed that adjustment speeds of the adaptively formed expectations slow down to a sufficient degree for large deviations between the relevant rates of returns that drive asset prices. Block 4. also provides the two bond accumulation equations as they flow from the government budget restraint. At current not much is known as to their (de-)stabilizing potential which has to be investigated in conjunction with debt and wage taxation rule shown in block 5 of the dynamics.

Next, the dynamic policy rules are presented which are basically the same as in the larger dynamics. Note however that we have removed the derivative term from the right hand side of the wage tax rate dynamics.

5. The Feedback Policy Rules:

$$\dot{r} = -\beta_{r_1}(r - r_l^*) + \beta_{r_2}(\hat{p}_y - 0) + \beta_{r_3}(y/y^p - \bar{U}_c) \tag{9.30}$$

$$\hat{\tau}_w = \alpha_{\tau_{w1}}(d/\bar{d} - 1), \quad d = \frac{b + b^l/r^l}{y^e} \tag{9.31}$$

$$\hat{\tau}_m = \alpha_{\tau_m}\frac{p_x x - p_m j^d}{p_x x}. \tag{9.32}$$

These subdynamics basically provide the stabilizing potential of the Keynes-effect which is here present in the form of an interest rate policy that directly moves the short-term nominal rate of interest in ways opposite to inflationary pressure and demand pressure as measured by the capacity utilization rate of firms.

Summing up we thus have arrived at a 18D dynamical system by setting certain adjustment speeds equal to infinity or equal to zero, by cutting certain feedback effects of the individual distribution of bonds on aggregate demand (due to the fact that now $C_c = 0$ holds and that workers save all their interest income) and on the government budget equation (the latter as in the larger dynamics), and by assuming constant natural growth as well as employment rates. Note that the housing sector feeds back into this core dynamics of the model through the investment demand for dwellings (on the market for domestic goods) of the wealth owners and through its rate of return which is in particular determined through the law of motion for the rent price for housing services.

9.3.2 Static relationships

As abbreviations and static relationships we are left with the following reduced and modified list of equations underlying the 18D dynamical system of the preceding subsection.

1. Output and Demand:

$$y^d = c_w^o + g_k^d + g_h^d k_h + g y^e, \tag{9.33}$$

$$c_w^o = c_1 y_{w1}^D \tag{9.34}$$

$$c_h^{do} = p_v c_2 y_{w1}^D / p_h \tag{9.35}$$

$$y = y^e + \beta_n(\beta_{n^d} y^e - \nu) + \gamma\beta_{n^d} y^e \tag{9.36}$$

$$x = x_y y \tag{9.37}$$

$$j^d = j_y y \tag{9.38}$$

2. Employment and Labor Supply:

$$
\begin{aligned}
l_f^{de} &= l_y y && (9.39)\\
l_g^{de} &= l_g^{we} = \alpha_g g y^e && (9.40)\\
l^{de} &= l_f^{de} + l_g^{de} && (9.41)\\
l^{we} &= l_f^{we} + l_g^{we} && (9.42)\\
l_2^e &= (L_2(0)/L_1(0))l_1^e = (L_2(0)/L_1(0))l^e/\alpha_l && (9.43)
\end{aligned}
$$

3. Growth Rates of the Capital Stocks of Firms and Asset Owners:

$$
\begin{aligned}
g_k^d &= \alpha_1^k((1-\tau_c)\rho^e - \rho^r)) + \alpha_2^k(r^l - r) + \alpha_3^k(y/y^p - \bar{U}_c) + \gamma + \delta && (9.44)\\
g_h^d &= \alpha_1^h((1-\tau_c)\rho_h - \rho^r) + \alpha_2^h(r^l - r) + \alpha_3^h(\frac{c_h^{do}}{k_h} - \bar{U}_h) + \gamma + \delta_h && (9.45)
\end{aligned}
$$

4. Rates of Return:

$$
\begin{aligned}
\rho^e &= y^e - \delta + (p_x/p_y)x - (w^{be}/p_y)l_f^{de} - (p_m/p_y)j^d && (9.46)\\
\rho^r &= (1-\tau_c)r^l - \pi^l && (9.47)\\
\rho_h &= (p_h/p_y)c_h^{do}/k_h - \delta_h && (9.48)
\end{aligned}
$$

5. Prices, Wages and Transfers:

$$
\begin{aligned}
p_x &= ep_x^* && (9.49)\\
p_m &= (1+\tau_m)ep_m^* && (9.50)\\
w^{be} &= (1+\tau_p)w^e && (9.51)\\
w^{ue} &= \alpha^u w^e && (9.52)\\
w^{re} &= \alpha^r w^e && (9.53)\\
p_v &= (1+\tau_v)p_y && (9.54)
\end{aligned}
$$

6. Disposable Income of workers and Taxes per Value Unit of Capital:

$$
\begin{aligned}
y_{w1}^D &= (1-\tau_w)[w^e l^{de} + w^{ue}(l^e - l^{we}) + w^{re}\alpha_l l_2^e]/p_v && (9.55)\\
y_w^D &= y_{w1}^D + (1-\tau_c)rb_w && (9.56)\\
t^w &= \tau_w[w^e l^{de} + w^{ue}(l^e - l^{we}) + w^{re}\alpha_l l_2^e]/p_v + \tau_p(w^e/p_v)l^{de} \\
&+ \tau_v(p_y/p_v)(y^d - g_k^d - g_h^d k_h) + \tau_m e p_m^* j^d/p_v && (9.57)\\
t^c &= \tau_c[\rho^e(p_y/p_v) + rb + b^l + (p_h/p_v)c_h^d - (p_y/p_v)\delta_h k_h)]. && (9.58)
\end{aligned}
$$

These equations basically reflect in their new expression the assumption of fixed proportions in production, the absence of adjustment lags for desired consumption and investment plans as well as medium run concepts of rates of return, the neglect of wealth effects and interest rate effects in the consumption demand of workers. Though basically linear, these equations, as well as the laws of motion, nevertheless contain some multiplicative expressions and ratios of state variables. Most of these nonlinearities cannot be removed from the representation of the dynamics by an appropriate choice of state variables, as for example rb and c_h^{do}/k_h, while others. generally price ratios, can be removed in this way.

9.4 Steady state analysis

In this section we show that there is an, up to the level of nominal variables, uniquely determined economically meaningful balanced growth path or steady state solution of our model of the preceding section which provides a useful reference point for the dynamical evolutions implied by the model, which may or may not converge to this steady state solution, not even if long-run moving averages are used in the place of the temporary positions the economy will run through.

9.4.1 Steady state equations

The calculation of the interior, economically meaningful, steady state solution[4] of the 18D model (which up to the level of nominal magnitudes for wages and goods prices is uniquely determined) is in many respects simple due to the given growth rate of the world economy and the given interest rate (on consols) abroad. Note that we only consider expressions for the total supply of domestic bonds in the following, and not their distribution at home and abroad which can be easily obtained from the savings decisions of workers and pure asset owners. we stress that nominal magnitudes are no longer uniquely determined, there is no longer an LM curve in the model and thus no longer a force that might restrict the evolution of these magnitudes (driven by demand and cost pressure items) in the long run.

The first set of steady state conditions presented below concerns the growth rates of our small open economy:

$$\gamma = g_k^d - \delta \quad \to g_k^d = \gamma - \delta \tag{9.59}$$

$$\gamma = g_h^d - \delta_h \quad \to g_h^d = \gamma - \delta_h. \tag{9.60}$$

These equations state that capital (and thus also output) will grow with the external rate γ, which is equal to the sum of the given growth rate of the labor force and the rate of technical change by assumption.

The next set of steady state conditions concerns inflation and expected inflation (for all prices that exist in our model, except wage rates) and also the various rates of interest and profit of our model:

$$\hat{p}_v = \hat{p}_y = \hat{p}_h = \pi^l = \pi_{bs} = \pi_b = \pi_{es} = \pi_e = \epsilon_s = \epsilon = 0 \tag{9.61}$$

$$r_l^* = r^l = 1/p_b = \rho^r = r \tag{9.62}$$

$$r_l^* = \rho^e = \rho_h. \tag{9.63}$$

These conditions state that there is no steady state inflation and thus no nonzero expectations of it, which is due to our assumption on the interest rate policy rule of the central bank. Furthermore, all (expected) rates of return are equalized in the steady state and determined by the world rate of interest on long-term bonds r_l^*.

[4]We neglect as alternative steady state positions all zeros which can be obtained mathematically from the growth law formulations that our model employs. Note also the steady state depends parametrically on the initial conditions for $\frac{L_2(0)}{L_1(0)}, p_v, \frac{C_c(0)}{L_1(0)}$ that characterize the initial composition of the labor force, the initial output price level (including value added taxes) and a relative expression for the consumption of asset owners.

The next block concerns the steady state determination of various quantities, of the steady state ratio of government debt to aggregate demand and of the tax rate on imports:

$$
\begin{aligned}
y &= y^p \bar{U}_c, \quad c_h^d = k_h \bar{U}_h && (9.64)\\
l_f^{de} &= l_f^{we} = l_y y && (9.65)\\
l_g^{de} &= l_g^{we} = \alpha_g g y^e && (9.66)\\
l^{we} &= l^{de} = l_f^{we} + l_g^{we} && (9.67)\\
l^e &= l^{de}/\bar{V} \quad [V = \bar{V}],\ l_1^e = l^e/\alpha_l,\ l_2^e = (L_2(0), L_1(0)) l_1^e && (9.68)\\
x &= x_y y, \quad j^d = j_y y && (9.69)\\
d &= (b + b_l/r_l^*)/y^e = \bar{d} && (9.70)\\
\tau_m &= \frac{p_x^* x - p_m^* j^d}{p_m^* j^d}. && (9.71)
\end{aligned}
$$

These equations still depend on the steady state value of y^e – which will be given below – and they definitely reveal certain supply side influences on the steady behavior of our economy.

Further steady state relationships on the side of quantities are:

$$
\begin{aligned}
y^e &= \frac{y}{1 + \gamma \beta_{n^d}} && (9.72)\\
y^d &= y^e, \quad \nu = \beta_{n^d} y^e && (9.73)\\
c_w^o &= = c_1 y_{w1}^D, \quad c_h^{do} = c_2 p_v y_{w1}^D / p_h && (9.74)\\
y_{w1}^D &= (1 - \tau_w)[w^e l^{de} + w^{ue}(l^e - l^{we}) + w^{re} \alpha_l l_2^e]/p_v. && (9.75)
\end{aligned}
$$

By using the distribution laws for government bonds we furthermore get:

$$
\begin{aligned}
b &= \alpha_b^g \bar{d} y^e && (9.76)\\
b_l &= r_l^*(1 - \alpha_b^g) \bar{d} y^e && (9.77)
\end{aligned}
$$

from which the individual distribution of bonds can be derived if desired.

Next, one can determine the following nominal steady state expressions on the basis of an (arbitrarily) given price level p_v. This indeterminacy of the general price level of domestically produced goods is due to the fact that the central bank has adopted an interest rate policy rule and allows for intraday deviations from the budget constraints of the two types of households, the firms and the government and that therefore, in our present model, money is not held as cash balance by the agents of our economy.

$$
\begin{aligned}
p_v &= \text{a given parameter} && (9.78)\\
p_y &= p_v/(1 + \tau_v) && (9.79)\\
w^{be} & \ via \ r_l^* = y^e - \delta - \frac{w^{be}}{p_y} l_f^{de}, \quad w^{be} = \frac{y^e - \delta - r_l^*}{l_y y} \frac{p_v}{1 + \tau_v} && (9.80)\\
w^e &= w^{be}/(1 + \tau_p),\ w^{ue} = \alpha^u w^e,\ w^{re} = \alpha^r w^e. && (9.81)
\end{aligned}
$$

The equation for the determination of gross wages in efficiency units holds since we have balanced trade in the steady state (see the above), and thus no influence of the international trade in goods on the rate of profit in the steady state. Note here that net real wages ω^e (excluding payroll taxes, but before wage taxation), measured by in terms of consumer prices p_v and efficiency units, are given by

$$\omega^e = \frac{w^e}{p_v}\frac{y^e - \delta - r_l^*}{l_y y}\frac{1}{(1+\tau_v)(1+\tau_p)}$$

and thus do not depend on the arbitrarily determined nominal price level p_v. This observation also applies to all other real magnitudes implying that there are no real effects of shocks that may lead to a different consumer price level p_v in the long-run.

The equations $c_h^d = \bar{U}_h k_h$ and $r_l^* = p_h c_h^d/(p_y k_h) - \delta_h$, on the one hand, and

$$\begin{aligned} c_2 y_{w1}^D &= p_h c_h^d / p_v \\ y^e &= c_1 y_{w1}^D + \gamma + \delta + (\gamma + \delta_h) k_h + g y^e, \end{aligned}$$

on the other hand,[5] allow us now to first determine the ratio p_h/p_y and then k_h, y_{w1}^D, and τ_w as follows:

$$p_h/p_y = (r_l^* + \delta_h)/\bar{U}_h \quad (9.82)$$

$$k_h = \frac{y^e(1-g) - \gamma - \delta}{c_1(r_l^* + \delta_h)/(c_2(1+\tau_v)) + \gamma + \delta_h} \quad (9.83)$$

$$y_{w1}^D = p_h \bar{U}_h k_h / (c_2 p_v) \quad (9.84)$$

$$\tau_w = 1 - \frac{y_{w1}^D}{[w^e l^{de} + w^{ue}(l^e - l^{we}) + w^{re}\alpha_l l_2^e]/p_v} \quad (9.85)$$

Note also that this determination of y_{w1}^D and k_h must be used above for the determination of consumption plans per unit of capital.

There remains the determination of the steady state value of the exchange rate e,[6] since the price of long term bonds $p_b = 1/r_l^*$ has already been determined and since the price of equities does not matter in the core dynamics of the model.[7] The calculation of the steady state exchange rate is economically seen complex, but mathematically still simple. Mathematically seen it is provided by the following implicit equations for the variables t^w, e on the basis of the expression for t^c shown below:

$$\begin{aligned} 0 &= g y^e + rb + b^l - t^w - t^c + [w^{ue}(l^e - l^{we}) + w^{re}\alpha_l l_2^e + w^{be} l_g^{de}]/p_v - \gamma b/\alpha_b^g \\ 0 &= \tau_w y_{w1}^D/(1-\tau_w) + \tau_p (w^e/p_v) l^{de} + \tau_v (p_y/p_v)(y^d - g_k^d - g_h^d k_h) + \tau_m e p_m^* j^d / p_v - t^w \end{aligned}$$

where

$$\begin{aligned} t^c &= \tau_c[\rho^e(p_y/p_v) + rb + b^l + (p_h/p_v)c_h^d - (p_y/p_v)\delta_h k_h] \\ &= \tau_c[(\rho^e + r_l^* k_h)/(1+\tau_v) + rb + b^l] \end{aligned}$$

---

[5] Where the last one stands for goods-market equilibrium in the steady state

[6] Which in turn determines the prices p_x, p_m.

[7] The same holds true for the disposable income of asset holders y_c^D.

which give rise to:

$$t^w = gy^e + rb + b^l - t^c + [w^{ue}(l^e - l^{we}) + w^{re}\alpha_l l_2^e + w^{be}l_g^{de}]/p_v - \gamma b/\alpha_b^g \quad (9.86)$$

$$e = \frac{t^w - [\tau_w y_{w1}^D/(1-\tau_w) + \tau_p(w^e/p_v)l^{de} + \tau_v(p_y/p_v)(y^d - g_k^d - g_h^d k_h)]}{\tau_m p_m^* j^d/p_v}. \quad (9.87)$$

We see that the long-run rate of exchange is neither determined in the market for goods, nor through the trade balance nor by international capital flows, but is a complicated expression of many parameters and steady state values of the model and is in particular heavily dependent on the form of the GBR and its components.

9.4.2 Steady state comparisons

Summarizing, we see that the steady state of the considered economy heavily depends on the data assumed to apply to the rest of the world (generally in a fairly straightforward and simple way) and that the steady values of the wage taxation rate and in particular the exchange rate are complicated functions of the parameters and various other steady state solutions of the dynamics. Furthermore, since the steady rate of profit ρ^e and thus also the real wage rate $\omega^e = w^e/p_v$, see the above expression for it, is determined through the foreign rate of interest,[8] we get for the real wage ω^{ne} (after taxes, at consumer prices and in efficiency units) the expression:

$$\omega^{ne} = (1-\tau_w)\omega^e = \frac{1-\tau_w}{(1+\tau_v)(1+\tau_p)} \frac{y^e - \delta - r_l^*}{l_y y}$$

which implies that all increases in the three tax rates shown (sales value taxes, payroll taxes and (endogenously determined) wage income taxes) fall on the real wages of workers (measured here by the consumer price of domestic goods solely). There is however also an influence of the value added tax on overall interest rate income per value unit of capital, besides of course a dependence of this income on the capital taxation rate τ_c.

Output levels (per unit of capital) and also steady employment (per unit of capital and measured in efficiency units) are basically determined through supply side considerations (technology and desired rates of capacity utilization), but the latter also depend on government expenditures per unit of capital and thus will be changing with this ratio.

The preceding subsection has shown that there is no inflation occurring in the 18D dynamics as far as goods and asset prices are concerned. It is of course important to also consider economies with (moderate) steady state price inflation, in the place of stationary price levels determined in the preceding subsection, in particular if there is no productivity growth and if there is the institutional constraint that the nominal wage level cannot fall, since we would then get a continuum of steady state solutions by such a modification of the money wage Phillips curve in the case where there is no steady state inflation, see Chiarella, Flaschel and Zhu (1998b) for the introduction and investigation of such 'kinks' in money wage Phillips curves. The extension of the dynamics to the inclusion of steady state price inflation is however not yet considered in the present approach to disequilibrium growth –

[8]Since output and sales per unit of capital are predetermined through tax independent supply side features and the world growth rate.

which allows us the determination of steady levels of goods and asset prices (and also of wages (when measured in efficiency units).

Just as rates of growth, the steady levels of interest rates and profit rates are all fixed and given through the external rate of interest r_l^* so that there is no possibility that the considered country may exhibit an extraordinary level of profitability in the steady state (but possibly in its long-run average behavior if there are attractors of the dynamics that are not 'well situated' with respect to the point of rest of the dynamics.

9.5 Subsystem analysis and switch off/on methodology: Some examples

In this section we consider the dynamics of the real part of the economy on various levels of generality, in separation from the financial markets as well as from policy issues. These aspects of the full 18D dynamics will be added again in subsequent sections of this chapter. We start with the full 9D version of these real dynamics (which includes the nominal dynamics of wages and prices and expectations about their rate of change).

9.5.1 The 9D real part of the economy

We separate the real part of the dynamics, i.e., labor and goods markets, from the rest of model by making the following assumptions:

$$\begin{aligned} \tau_m &= \frac{p_x^* x - p_m^* j^d}{p_m^* j^d} = \frac{p_x^* x_y - p_m^* j_y}{p_m^* j_y}, \quad \text{also in the short-run,} \\ \alpha_{\tau_{w1}} &= 0: \quad \tau_w = \text{const. at its steady state value,} \\ \beta_{p_b} &= \beta_{\pi_{bs}} = \beta_e = \beta_{\epsilon_s} = 0: \quad p_b, e = \text{const. at their steady state values,} \\ \beta_{r_1} &= \beta_{r_2} = \beta_{r_3} = 0: \quad r = \text{const. at its steady state value.} \end{aligned}$$

The first assumption must be guaranteed via an appropriate choice of the four parameters that govern the equation relating to it. The second assumption says that government does not care about the evolution of its debt position and keeps the rate of wage taxation fixed at its steady state value. The third excludes asset price dynamics and freezes asset prices and the nominal exchange rate at their steady state position. Finally, the last assumption does the same for the short-term nominal rate of interest by an appropriate action of the monetary authority.

Using as abbreviation:

$$\Delta\hat{p}_y = \hat{p}_y - \pi^l = \kappa[\kappa_p(\beta_{w_1}(l^{we}/l^e - \bar{V}) + \beta_{w_2}(l_f^{de}/l_f^{we} - 1)) + \beta_p(y/y^p - \bar{U}_c)]$$

with $\kappa = 1/(1-\kappa_w\kappa_p)$, the 18 laws of motion of the economic dynamics around the steady state solution can be reduced on the basis of the above assumptions to:

$$\dot{y}^e = \beta_{y^e}(y^d - y^e) + (\gamma - (g_k^d - \delta))y^e \tag{9.88}$$

$$\dot{\nu} = y - y^d - (g_k^d - \delta)\nu \tag{9.89}$$

$$\dot{l}_f^{we} = \beta_l(l_f^{de} - l_f^{we}) + [\gamma - (g_k^d - \delta)]l_f^{we} \tag{9.90}$$
$$\hat{l}^e = \gamma - (g_k^d - \delta) \tag{9.91}$$
$$\hat{w}^e = \pi^l + \kappa[\beta_{w_1}(l^{we}/l^e - \bar{V}) + \beta_{w_2}(l_f^{de}/l_f^{we} - 1) + \kappa_w\beta_p(y/y^p - \bar{U}_c)] \tag{9.92}$$
$$\hat{p}_y = \pi^l + \Delta\hat{p}_y \tag{9.93}$$
$$\dot{\pi}^l = \beta_{\pi^l}(\alpha_{\pi^l}\Delta\hat{p}_y + (1 - \alpha_{\pi^l})(0 - \pi^l)) \tag{9.94}$$
$$\hat{p}_h = \beta_h(\frac{c_h^o}{k_h} - \bar{U}_h) + \kappa_h\Delta\hat{p}_y + \pi^l \tag{9.95}$$
$$\hat{k}_h = g_h^d - \delta_h - (g_k^d - \delta) \tag{9.96}$$

with the following supplementary definitions and abbreviations:

$$\begin{aligned}
y^d &= c_g^o + g_k^d + g_h^d k_h + g y^e \\
y &= y^e + \beta_n(\beta_{n^d} y^e - \nu) + \gamma\beta_{n^d} y^e \\
l_f^{de} &= l_y y \\
l_g^{de} &= l_g^{we} = \alpha_g g y^e \\
l^{de} &= l_f^{de} + l_g^{de} \\
l^{we} &= l_f^{we} + l_g^{we} \\
c_g^o &= c_1(1 - \tau_w)y_{w1} \\
c_h^o &= (1 + \tau_v)p_y c_2(1 - \tau_w)y_{w1}/p_h \\
y_{w1} &= w^e[l^{de} + \alpha^u(l^e - l^{we}) + \alpha^r\frac{L_2(0)}{L_1(0)}l^e]/[(1 + \tau_v)p_y] \\
g_k^d &= \alpha_1^k((1 - \tau_c)\rho^e - ((1 - \tau_c)r_l^* - \pi^l)) + \alpha_3^k(y/y^p - \bar{U}_c) + \gamma + \delta \\
\rho^e &= y^e - \delta - ((1 + \tau_p)w^e/p_y)l_f^{de} \\
g_h^d &= \alpha_1^h((1 - \tau_c)\frac{(p_h/p_y)c_h^o}{k_h} - \delta_h - ((1 - \tau_c)r_l^* - \pi^l)) + \alpha_3^h(\frac{c_h^o}{k_h} - \bar{U}_h) + \gamma + \delta_h.
\end{aligned}$$

Inserting these equations into the above laws of motion gives a system of nine autonomous differential equations in the 9 state variables shown above. Note that we have to supply again as initial conditions the relative magnitudes $\frac{L_2(0)}{L_1(0)}$ in order to get a complete characterization of this 9D dynamics.

By standard arguments it is again shown that the law of motion for real wages reads:

$$\hat{\omega}^e = \kappa[(1 - \kappa_p)(\beta_{w_1}(l^{we}/l^e - \bar{V}) + \beta_{w_2}(l_f^{de}/l_f^{we} - 1)) - (1 - \kappa_w)\beta_p(y/y^p - \bar{U}_c)].$$

Inspecting the above static relationship then shows that – ignoring the housing sector[9] – it is only the expected inflation rate that brings about an influence of the nominal magnitudes on the real magnitudes of this real part of the economy. Therefore, if inflationary expectations are stationary, we can decouple the real dynamics of the real part of the economy from the nominal dynamics in this subsystem as will be shown in more detail below.

Solving for the interior steady state or point of rest of these dynamics is performed in the following way. Equations (9.91), (9.96) imply that $g_k^d = \gamma + \delta, g_h^d = \gamma + \delta_h$ must hold in the steady state. The remaining adjustment equations for quantities then imply:

[9] Which however can also be reformulated in terms of real magnitudes

$y^d = y^e, y = y^d + \gamma\nu, l_f^{de} = l_f^{we}$. Setting equation (9.94) equal to zero implies furthermore: $\Delta\hat{p}_y = \frac{1-\alpha_{\pi^l}}{\alpha_{\pi^l}}\pi^l$ which when inserted into (9.93), set equal to zero, implies that π^l must be zero. Equations (9.92), (9.93), set equal to zero, then imply two equations in the unknowns $l^{we}/l^e - \bar{V}, y/y^p - \bar{U}_c$, which are linearly independent of each other and which therefore imply $l^{we}/l^e = \bar{V}, y = y^p\bar{U}_c$. This provides us with the steady state value of y and therefore also with the ones for $l_f^{we}, l_g^{we}, l^{we}$, since we have according to the above $y = y^e + \gamma\nu, y = y^e + \beta_n(\beta_{n^d}y^e - \nu) + \gamma\beta_{n^d}y^e$ and thus $y^e = \frac{y^p\bar{U}_c}{1+\gamma\beta_{n^d}}, \nu = \beta_{n^d}y^e$. The equation $l^{we}/l^e = \bar{V}$ then provides us with the steady state value of l^e.

Due to what has been shown for y we get from the equation for g_k^d the equality $\rho^e = r_l^*$ and thus as real wage $\omega^e = w^e/p_y$ since all other expressions that define the rate of profit ρ^e have already been determined. Inserting this real wage into the definition of y_{w1} then provides us with the steady state value of this part of workers' income, since again all other steady state expressions that form this expression have already been determined. From this income expression we immediately get c_g^o and thus from goods market equilibrium

$$y^d = y^e = c_g^o + \gamma + \delta + (\gamma + \delta_h)k_h + gy^e$$

the steady state value of k_h. Equation (9.95), set equal to zero, next implies that $c^o = k_h\bar{U}_h$ must hold true, which finally implies via the investment function in the housing sector:

$$(p_h/p_y)c_h^o/k_h - \delta_h - r_l^* = 0$$

and provides us with the steady state value of p_h/p_y.

This is however all that can be deduced for the steady state positions of this economy, since the above system of differential equations and its static definitional equations do all only depend on the relative prices $\omega^e = w^e/p_y, \phi = p_h/p_y$ and thus do not imply anything for the absolute levels of the prices shown in these expressions. Introducing the laws of motion for $\omega^e = w^e/p_y, \phi = p_h/p_y$ given by

$$\hat{\omega}^e = \hat{w}^e - \hat{p}_y, \quad \hat{\phi} = \hat{p}_h - \hat{p}_y$$

by inserting the above nominal laws of motion into these dynamical equations would indeed reduce the above dynamical system two a system with dimension 8, with the law of motion for $\hat{p}_y$ as an appended dynamics that does not feed back into the now truly real part of the economy.

The steady state of the dynamics of this section is therefore only uniquely determined up to the level of p_y which can be preset to any positive value. From the above we also conclude that the determinant of the Jacobian J of the dynamics at the steady state must be zero (the matrix J has rank 8), which in addition implies that the system is subject to hysteresis in that all of its nominal price magnitudes depend on historical conditions and the shocks the system is subject to. Finally, we conjecture, on the basis of the knowledge on the dynamics of related, but smaller dynamical models considered in Chiarella and Flaschel (1998a,b), see also part I of this book, that the steady state of the dynamics will be asymptotically stable for low adjustment speeds of prices, low adjustment speeds of inventories and a fast sales expectations mechanism, but that such stability will get lost (via Hopf-bifurcations, implying the birth or death of periodic orbits at the Hopf bifurcation point) as the speed of adjustment of the slow variables is increased.

9.5.2 A 5D KMG type subdynamics

The 9D dynamics can be reduced to a 7D dynamical system by excluding the housing sector from consideration by way of the following assumptions: $c_2 = 0, g_h^d = 0, \beta_h = 0, k_h(0) = 0$. They imply that the ratio k_h stays at zero, that equations where divisions through k_h occur are suppressed and that the then still given, but purely formal evolution of the price level p_h does not matter for the rest of the dynamics. Due to $c_2 = 0$ there is then of course also no demand for housing services. It is likely for the present formulation of the dynamics that the housing sector is not of central importance for the overall dynamical features of the full 18D or real 9D dynamics as far as interesting feedback mechanisms are concerned. This however is in part due to the approach chosen for it in the present formulation of the model and may be different if other formulations of housing investment and housing services are attempted.

The 7D dynamics can be reduced to a 5D dynamical system, in fact the most basic integrated dynamics of our 18D system, and to be called the Keynes-Metzler-Goodwin (KMG) model in the following, when it is assumed in addition that $\beta_{\pi^l} = 0, \kappa_w = 1$ holds true. This 5D system can, as we already know, be reformulated in real terms as follows:

$$
\begin{aligned}
\hat{\omega}^e &= \beta_{w_1}(l^{we}/l^e - \bar{V}) + \beta_{w_2}(l_f^{de}/l_f^{we} - 1) \\
\hat{l}^e &= -[\alpha_1^k(1-\tau_c)(y^e - \delta - (1+\tau_p)\omega^e l_f^{de} - r_l^*) + \alpha_3^k(y/y^p - \bar{U}_c)] \\
\dot{l}_f^{we} &= \beta_l(l_f^{de} - l_f^{we}) - [\alpha_1^k(1-\tau_c)(y^e - \delta - (1+\tau_p)\omega^e l_f^{de} - r_l^*) + \alpha_3^k(y/y^p - \bar{U}_c)]l_f^{we} \\
\dot{y}^e &= \beta_{y^e}(y^d - y^e) - [\alpha_1^k(1-\tau_c)(y^e - \delta - (1+\tau_p)\omega^e l_f^{de} - r_l^*) \\
&+ \alpha_3^k(y/y^p - \bar{U}_c)]y^e \\
\dot{\nu} &= y - y^d - [\alpha_1^k(1-\tau_c)(y^e - \delta - (1+\tau_p)\omega^e l_f^{de} - r_l^*) + \alpha_3^k(y/y^p - \bar{U}_c) + \gamma]\nu
\end{aligned}
$$

with the following supplementary definitions

$$
\begin{aligned}
y^d &= c_1(1-\tau_w)y_{w1} + \alpha_1^k(1-\tau_c)(y^e - \delta - (1+\tau_p)\omega^e l_f^{de} - r_l^*) + \alpha_3^k(\frac{y}{y^p} - \bar{U}_c) + \delta + \gamma + gy^e \\
y &= y^e + \beta_n(\beta_{n^d}y^e - \nu) + \gamma\beta_{n^d}y^e \\
l_f^{de} &= l_y y \\
l_g^{de} &= l_g^{we} = \alpha_g g y^e \\
l^{de} &= l_f^{de} + l_g^{de} \\
l^{we} &= l_f^{we} + l_g^{we} \\
y_{w1} &= \omega^e[l^{de} + \alpha^u(l^e - l^{we}) + \alpha^r \frac{L_2(0)}{L_1(0)} l^e]/(1+\tau_v).
\end{aligned}
$$

These subdynamics consist of a Goodwin (1967) type accumulation and income distribution mechanism, coupled with a Keynesian goods market demand block that is here based on sluggish quantity adjustment as in Metzler (1941). This KMG model therefore represents a very basic way of marrying the Goodwin growth cycle idea (with also inside labor) with the Keynesian problem of deficient aggregate demand on the market for goods and a sluggish quantity adjustment of Metzlerian type, due to the fact that the nominal rate of interest is still a given magnitude in these subdynamics (no Keynes-effects are present). Note that this interaction of the dynamics of income distribution and growth with sluggish quantity adjustment on the market for goods now also contains a sluggish employment adjustment policy of firms which adds more realism to the Goodwin growth cycle mechanism.

The steady state values of the state variables of the above dynamics are given by:

$$\begin{aligned} y^e &= \frac{y^p \bar{U}_c}{1+\gamma\beta_{n^d}} \\ \nu &= \beta_{n^d} y^e \\ l_f^{we} &= l_y y^p \bar{U}_c \quad [l^{we} = l_f^{we} + \alpha_g g y^e] \\ l^e &= (l_f^{we} + \alpha_g g y^e)/\bar{V} \\ \omega^e &= \frac{y^e - \delta - r_l^*}{l_f^{we}(1+\tau_p)}. \end{aligned}$$

We add that the tax parameter τ_w cannot be chosen arbitrarily for the above 5D dynamical system, but is determined by steady state goods market equilibrium as follows:

$$\begin{aligned} y_{w1} &= \omega^e[l^{we} + \alpha^u(l^e - l^{we}) + \alpha^r L_2(0)/L_1(0)l^e]/(1+\tau_v) \\ c_g^o &= y^e - (\gamma+\delta) - gy^e \\ \tau_w &= 1 - \frac{c_g^o}{c_1 y_{w1}} \end{aligned}$$

in order to allow for an interior steady state position of the 5D dynamical system.

With respect to this lowest dimensional situation we now start our numerical investigations of the 18D dynamics. The figures 9.1 show the 5D dynamics for very low adjustment speeds of quantities and thus a very sluggish Keynes-Metzler block and medium sized adjustment speeds of prices in which case the dynamics are converging to the steady state in a nearly monotonically way. Note here that there has been a large shock to sales expectations at time $t = 1$ which basically causes one long cycle during which inventories are accumulated and then decumulated to a considerable degree and with a long phase. This simulation and various other ones of this type showed that there is considerable difference to the stability properties of the seemingly closely related dynamical models of KMG type considered in part I of the book. This is in particular true with respect to the occurrence of instability which is here happening much more often (when the speed of adjustment of inventories and sales expectations are increased).

The figures 9.2 show the dynamics for higher speeds of adjustments of quantities, but with otherwise unchanged parameters. It is visible that the increase in the adjustment speed of sales expectations and inventories adds considerably to the size and the extent of the fluctuations around the steady state that now occur. This indicates, as also further simulations have shown, that the Metzler quantity adjustment process may destabilize the model when realistic magnitudes for the two involved adjustment parameters are assumed (both larger than 0.5).

The increase in cyclical fluctuations is clearly visible in figures 9.2, though the business cycle shown will die out eventually. Increasing speeds of quantity adjustments still further then seems to give rise to explosive cycles, i.e., the loss of asymptotic stability does here generally not give rise to stable limit cycle situations or more complex attractors. These therefore at best seem to exist for very limited intervals of the parameters that are here modified. It appears that the nonlinearities of the 5D dynamics, which are all intrinsic in nature, are still too weak to bound the dynamics globally once the steady state has become a repeller.

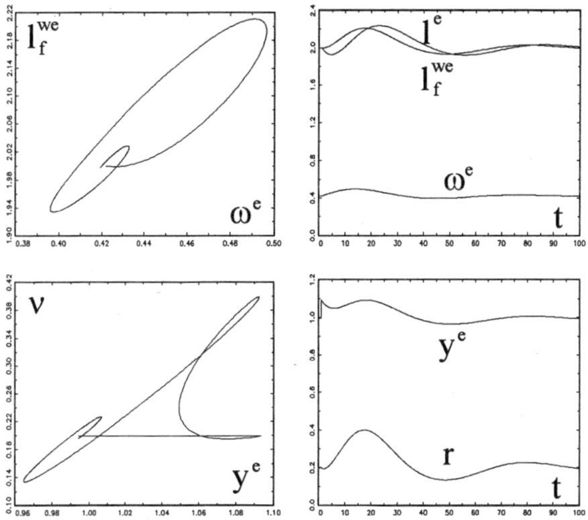

Figure 9.1:
Simulating the 5D dynamics for very low adjustment speeds of quantities.[10]

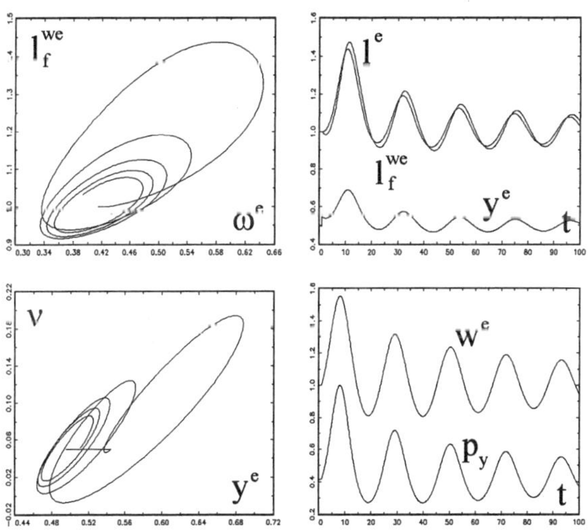

Figure 9.2:
5D dynamics with still moderate quantity adjustment speeds ($\beta_n = \beta_{y^e} = 0.3$).

[10]The parameters of this simulation run are the following ones: $\beta_{w_1} = 1.5; \beta_{w_2} = 0.5; \beta_n = 0.1; \beta_{n^d} = 0.1; \beta_{y^e} = 0.1; \beta_l = 0.2; \alpha_g = 0; \alpha_u = 0; \alpha_r = 0; \alpha_{k_1} = 0.5; \alpha_{k_3} = 0.2; L_1(0) = 20000; L_2(0) = 5000; \bar{U}_c = 1; l_y = 2; \bar{V} = 1; c_1 = 0.9; r_l^* = 0.03; \delta = 0.05; \tau_p = 0; g = 0.5; \tau_v = 0; \gamma = 0.1; y^p = 5.$

9.5.3 The 5D dynamics with a housing sector

Next we add the housing sector to the 5D dynamics and consider the 7D dynamics that are generated thereby. As the figure 9.3 exemplifies this need not add stability to the situation considered in figure 9.2 in contrast to what one could expect from an isolated discussion of the housing sector as in Chiarella and Flaschel (1998h).

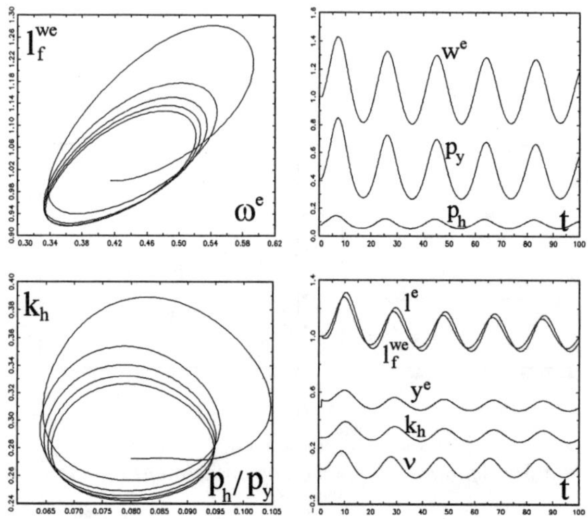

Figure 9.3:
The 5D dynamics with the addition of a housing sector.

We have chosen here a very high adjustment speed for the price of housing services which to some extent contributes to the stability of the motion that is still shown. Also, the former propensity to consume domestic goods has now been split in its size between goods and housing services. Broadly speaking the appearance of the fluctuations is of the same type as those shown in figure 9.2, though there are now considerable fluctuations in the stock of housing and the relative price of dwelling services which interact with each other in an overshooting fashion as it is known from the Goodwin growth cycle model. In all our simulations so far – and also in the following – there is a long phase length of the cycles that are shown (exceeding twenty years), in line with what is known for the Goodwin (1967) growth cycle model and its modifications.

9.5.4 The 5D dynamics with Rose goods-market effects

As an alternative we next consider the KMG 5D dynamics augmented by the Rose (adverse or normal) real wage effect which integrates goods market dynamics into the subdynamics of income distribution and growth (but not yet the Mundell effect of inflationary expectations which would add their law of motion to the 5D dynamics and also the dynamics of the price level p_y). This is done by assuming on the one hand $\kappa_w < 1$, but leaving on the other hand inflationary expectations at their steady state value by still assuming $\beta_{\pi^l} = 0$, and of course by suppressing again the fluctuations in the housing sector. As may be expected as one among two possible outcomes from the isolated 1D discussion of the Rose effect in part I of the book, we see in the simulation in figure 9.4 – in comparison to figure 9.2 – that the addition of these subdynamics makes the motion around the steady state of the model more stable in the present case, suggesting that price flexibility here adds stability to the dynamics considered so far. We have assumed here that price adjust with speed $\beta_p = 0.5$ now which implies that price adjustment now appears with negative weight in the dynamics of the real wage in the usual way. Note also that the fluctuations are insofar asymmetric as booms are now more pronounced in amplitude and in length than depressions.

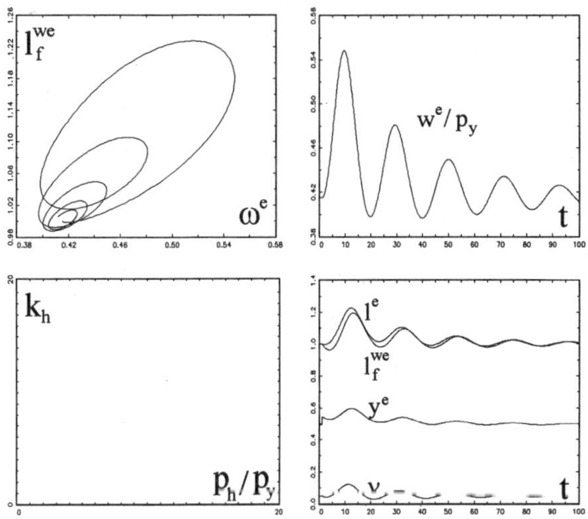

Figure 9.4:
The 5D dynamics with the addition of the Rose price inflation effect.

9.5.5 Nominal dynamics in the real part of the economy

We have to stress at the present stage of the investigation that the addition of Mundell effects, i.e., positive feedback mechanisms between actual and expected inflation via investment depending on real rate of interest expectations ($\beta_{\pi^l} > 0$ now) is generally problematic as this effect seems to imply not only additional cyclical explosiveness to the plots so far shown, but also leads to saddlepoint situations in the sense of a superimposed positive or negative trend around which the cycles occur (and this also in real magnitudes which therefore fluctuate around a path that is diverging from the steady state). From a local point of view – which only involves intrinsic nonlinearities – the Mundell inflationary positive feedback mechanism thus provides no reasonable time series and phase plots at this stage of the investigation, also in cases where the adjustment speed of inflationary expectations is as low as 0.02.

The intuitive explanation for this is however not too difficult if one observes that the trend in the real magnitudes away from their steady state values is – when observed – accompanied by a monotonic divergence of inflationary expectations away from their steady state level 0. Adding the Mundell effect of inflationary expectations as sixth law of motion (and price inflation as an appended seventh law) to the real 5D dynamics in fact means that one adds a positive nominal feedback mechanism without any other nominal feedback mechanism that can keep this mechanism bounded, since nominal interest rates are still fixed at their steady state values. In particular in the situation depicted in figure 9.4 we have that there is strong positive impact effect of expected inflation rate π_l on the term $\Delta\hat{p}_y$ that in turn drives expected inflation as one can see from (9.88) – (9.94). There is thus a significant positive entry J_{77} in the Jacobian matrix J of the 7D dynamics, with inflationary expectations describing now the seventh law of motion, see again (9.88) – (9.94). Hence, it is at least plausible that inflation can easily generate a cumulative process in prices as well as in the level of economic activity in such a situation (by its positive impact on the rate of investment) which is nowhere checked, e.g., by a Keynes-effect of rising nominal interest rates which could bring this cumulative process to a turning point by its own effects on economic activity. This is easily obtained from the 2D model of the interaction of the Keynes- and the Mundell-effect considered in chapters 2 and 6, but is much more complicated to analyze in the 6D situation (neglecting the law of motion for the price level) here under consideration.[11] We conjecture that the considered 7D dynamics will provide reasonable time series (with no cumulative tendencies in the real magnitudes) when combined with the interest rate policy rule of the central bank, since this adds a stabilizing feedback to the economy when inflation and expected inflation depart too much from their steady state values.

9.5.6 The integrated real dynamics of the economy

Next we investigate the 9D union of the two situations, the inclusion of a housing sector and the Rose real wage effect, considered in figures 9.3 and 9.4 and get again that the housing sector does not add stability to the implosive situation given in figure 9.4. Due to what has been observed in the preceding section we still ignore the Mundell real rate of interest effect of inflationary expectations in the simulation studies presented in figures 9.5, but have now of course the interaction of Metzler inventory accelerator and the Rose real wage effects through the assumed quantity and price adjustment behavior. The role of the Mundell effect will be investigated later on when the Keynes-effect is introduced into the dynamics in section 9.7 via the Taylor nominal interest rate policy rule of the full 18D dynamics. The trajectories and time series of figure 9.5 show a situation of slow convergence back to the steady state after an initial shock of sales expectations at time $t = 1$, with cyclically overshooting patterns between the stock labor intensity of firms and the real wage, both measured in efficiency units, and the housing stocks per unit of capital and the the real renting price of housing services.

[11] We stress here again that the evolution of p_y does not influence any of the other laws of motion if nominal wage dynamics is reformulated as real wage dynamics:

$$\hat{\omega}^e = \kappa[(1-\kappa_p)(\beta_{w_1}(l^{we}/l^e - \bar{V}) + \beta_{w_2}(l_f^{de}/l_f^{we} - 1) - (1-\kappa_w)\beta_p(y/y^p - \bar{U}_c)].$$

The 5D real part of the economy (and the evolution of inflationary expectations) then depend on the evolution of this real wage, but nowhere on the evolution of the price level itself, which in particular means that the dynamical system based on the state variables $y^e, \nu, l_f^{we}, l^e, \omega^e, p_y, \pi_l$ has a vanishing sixth column in its Jacobian at the steady state.

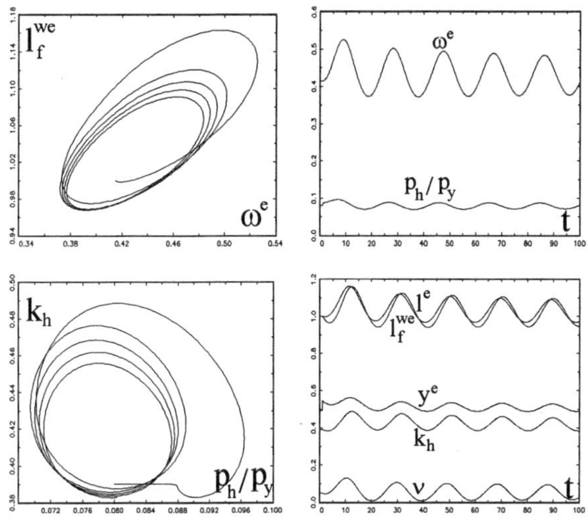

Figure 9.5:
The unified 9D dynamics without the Mundell effect.

The parameters of this simulation run are the following ones:

$\beta_{w_1} = 1.5$	$\beta_{w_2} = 0.5$	$\beta_p = 0.5$	$\beta_{\pi^l} = 0$	$\beta_{p_b} = 0$	$\beta_{\pi_{bs}} = 0$	$\beta_c = 0$	$\beta_\epsilon = 0$
$\beta_n = 0.3$	$\beta_{n^d} = 0.1$	$\beta_{y^e} = 0.3$	$\beta_h = 20$	$\beta_l = 0.2$	$\beta_{r_1} = 0$	$\beta_{r_2} = 0$	$\beta_{r_3} = 0$
$\alpha_{\pi^l} = 0.5$	$\alpha_s = 1$	$\alpha_{h_1} = 0.5$	$\alpha_{h_2} = 0.2$	$\alpha_{h_3} = 0.5$	$\alpha_{k_1} = 0.5$	$\alpha_{k_2} = 0$	$\alpha_{k_3} = 0.2$
$\alpha_{\tau_w} = 0$	$\alpha_{\tau_m} = 0$	$\alpha_g = 0$	$\alpha_b^g = 0.5$	$\alpha_u = 0$	$\alpha_r = 0$	$L_1(0) = 20000$	$L_2(0) = 5000$
$\kappa_p = 0.5$	$\kappa_w = 0.5$	$\kappa_h = 0.5$	$\bar{U}_c = 1$	$\bar{U}_h = 1$	$\bar{V} = 1$	$\bar{d} = 0.6$	$g = 0.5$
$p_m^* = 1$	$p_x^* = 1$	$r_l^* = 0.03$	$\delta = 0.05$	$\delta_h = 0.05$	$\tau_c = 0.5$	$\tau_v = 0$	$\tau_p = 0$
$\gamma = 0.1$	$c_1 = 0.5$	$c_2 = 0.4$	$l_y = 2$	$x_y = 0.2$	$j_y = 0.1$	$y^p = 0.5$	$p_v = 1$

Table 9.1: The parameters corresponding to figure 9.5.

Finally we add more structure to the tax and employment decision of the government and see in the next figure 9.6 that this does not alter the preceding numerical example very much.

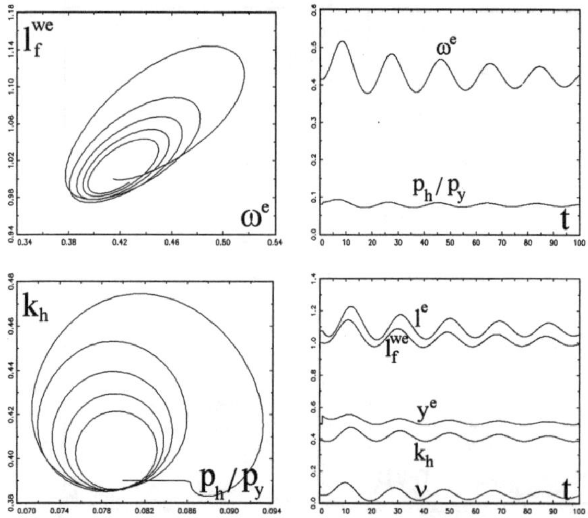

Figure 9.6:
The unified 9D dynamics with a complete set of exogenous government taxes
$(\alpha_g = 0.3; \alpha_u = 0.6; \alpha_r = 0.7; \tau_p = 0.2; \tau_v = 0.15)$.

9.6 Adding policy issues to the real dynamics

9.6.1 Interest rate policy rules

In this and the following sections we relax the assumptions made in the preceding section step by step towards a reestablishment of the full 18D dynamics of section 9.3 and 9.4. In order to do this in a systematic way we at first allow for the interest policy rule of the central bank in the setup considered in the preceding subsection.

$$\dot{r} = -\beta_{r_1}(r - r_l^*) + \beta_{r_2}(\Delta\hat{p}_y + \pi^l) + \beta_{r_3}(y/y^p - \bar{U}_c).$$

This brings back the negative effects of the short-term rate of interest on fixed business and housing investment, at present only compared with a given rate of interest on long-term bonds r_l^* through the α_2 terms in the two investment functions. We now consider here a situation where the Mundell effect is at work (i.e., at least a 7D dynamics) and where the system would experience breakdown if the interest rate policy would be switched off as we have seen in the preceding subsection (even for very sluggish adjustments of inflationary expectations). By having this policy rule present, we get that a positive and increasing rate of inflation is counteracted, since the interest rate policy rule will work against economic expansion and further increases in the rate of inflation and expectations about it in such cases. This policy indeed does significantly reduce the extent of nominal instability inherent in the real part of private sector of the economy, since it works against the Mundell-effect of a positive feedback structure between the expected and the actual rate of inflation, which we found to be very destabilizing and problematic in the observations made in the last subsection.

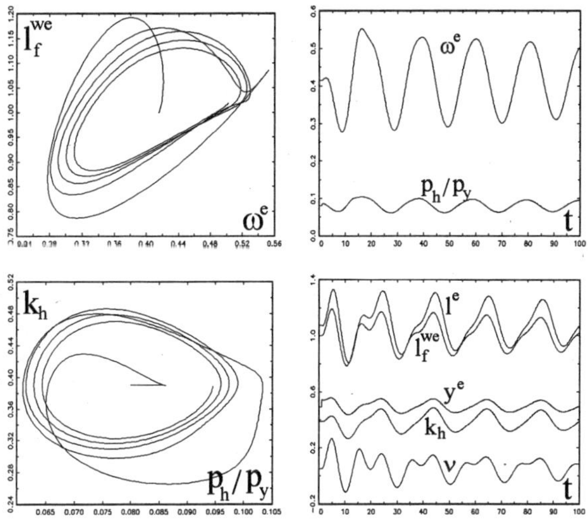

Figure 9.7:
The unified 9D dynamics with the Taylor rule switched on.

The β-parameters of this simulation run of a 10D dynamics are the following ones:

$\beta_{w_1} = 1.5$	$\beta_{w_2} = 0.5$	$\beta_p = 0.5$	$\beta_{\pi^l} = 0.3$	$\beta_{p_b} = 0$	$\beta_{\pi_{bs}} = 0$	$\beta_{\theta} = 0$	$\beta_{\epsilon} = 0$
$\beta_n = 0.3$	$\beta_{n^d} = 0.1$	$\beta_{y^e} = 0.3$	$\beta_h = 20$	$\beta_l = 0.2$	$\beta_{r_1} = 0.1$	$\beta_{r_2} = 1$	$\beta_{r_3} = 0.5$

Table 9.2: The parameters corresponding to figure 9.7 (all others as in figure 9.6).

We stress, but do not prove this here that a Taylor rule of the type:

$$r = \pi^e + \beta_{r_1}(\pi^e - \bar{\pi}) + \beta_{r_2}(l^{we}/l^e - \bar{V}), \qquad \beta_{r_1}, \beta_{r_2} > 0.$$

would be even more successful in fighting the explosiveness caused by the Mundell effect. This rule states that the central bank sets the expected real rate of interest according to the discrepancy that exists between the expected rate of inflation π^e and the target rate $\bar{\pi}$ of the central bank and the deviation of the actual rate of employment from the NAIRE-rate and this in such a way that interest rates counteract to what is observed as high or low economic activity and inflation.[12] This rule is not based on a dynamic law, but concerns levels and thus reduces the dimension of the system of differential equations considered by one. In addition it directly attempts to steer the expected real rate of interest and thus appears to be more powerful as it immediately attacks the source of the Mundell effect, and is not only a counteraction to it via the Keynes-effect.

[12]See Flaschel and Groh (1998) for a further discussion of the properties of this monetary policy rule.

9.6.2 Fiscal policy rules

We have so far ignored the role of the government budget constraint, since it did not exercise any influence on the real dynamics of the model as considered in the preceding subsections. This is however problematic, since the accumulation of government debt may follow an explosive path in the background of the dynamics that is to be explicitly considered and may be of a kind which would not be tolerated by the present or a subsequent government. We therefore have to consider the evolution of government debt explicitly and will do this of course subject to the hopefully stabilizing influence that may come from the assumed adjustment in the wage taxation rate in the pursuit of a given ratio of government debt per unit of an appropriate index for the social product, of the type shown below:

$$\begin{aligned}
\dot{b} &= \alpha_b^g[(1-\tau_c)(r_l^*b+b^l)-\tau_w c^1+c^2]-\gamma b\\
\dot{b}^l &= r_l^*(1-\alpha_b^g)[(1-\tau_c)(r_l^*b+b^l)-\tau_w c^1+c^2]-\gamma b^l\\
\hat{\tau}_w &= \alpha_{\tau_{w1}}(\frac{b+b^l/r_l^*}{y^e\bar{d}}-1)
\end{aligned}$$

where the $c^1 > 0, c^2$ are however no longer given magnitudes, as in the partial model considered in Chiarella and Flaschel (1998h). The above shown bond dynamics therefore has to be integrated again into the dynamics of the real part of the economy as shown in section 9.3 of this paper.

This is a decisive extension of the dynamics of the model, since it brings back into the considered dynamics the complicated evolution of short and long term bonds per unit of capital, b, b^l, together with the law of motion of the taxation rate τ_w.

Let us however first consider an example of the 5D core dynamics with damped fluctuations and reveal what happens to government debt in the background of this dynamics when government does not attempt to steer debt to a target ratio as assumed in our general 18D model. The following simulation is based on a contractionary shock applied to ye accompanied by a favorable shock to government debt which puts its initial level to one half of the desired target (in addition we assume that all government debt is in short-term bonds for the moment). Government will therefore initially reduce wage taxation and thereby create scope for more government debt.

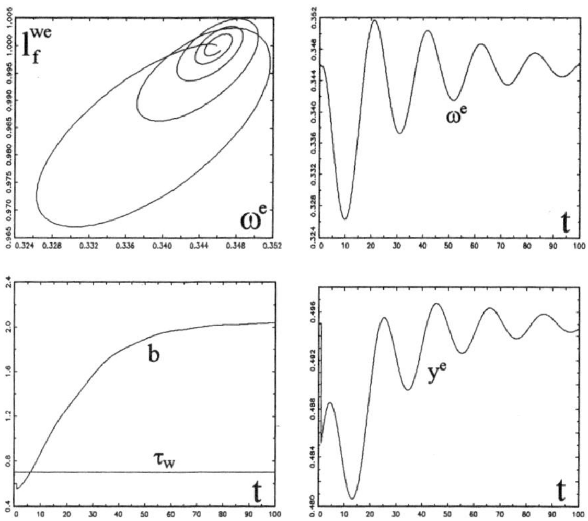

Figure 9.8a:
The 5D dynamics and its implications for government debt.

The parameters of this simulation run are the following ones:

$\beta_{w_1} = 1.5$	$\beta_{w_2} = 0.5$	$\beta_p = 0.5$	$\beta_{\pi^l} = 0$	$\beta_{p_b} = 0$	$\beta_{\pi_{bs}} = 0$	$\beta_e = 0$	$\beta_\epsilon = 0$
$\beta_n = 0.3$	$\beta_{n^d} = 0.1$	$\beta_{y^e} = 0.3$	$\beta_h = 0$	$\beta_l = 0.2$	$\beta_{r_1} = 0$	$\beta_{r_2} = 0$	$\beta_{r_3} = 0$
$\alpha_{\pi^l} = 1$	$\alpha_s = 1$	$\alpha_{h_1} = 0$	$\alpha_{h_2} = 0$	$\alpha_{h_3} = 0$	$\alpha_{k_1} = 0.5$	$\alpha_{k_2} = 0$	$\alpha_{k_3} = 0.2$
$\alpha_{\tau_w} = 0$	$\alpha_{\tau_m} = 0$	$\alpha_g = 0.2$	$\alpha_b^g = 1$	$\alpha_u = 0.5$	$\alpha_r = 0.6$	$L_1(0) = 20000$	$L_2(0) = 5000$
$\kappa_p = 0.5$	$\kappa_w = 0.5$	$\kappa_h = 0.5$	$\bar{U}_c = 1$	$\bar{U}_h = 1$	$\bar{V} = 1$	$\bar{d} = 0.6$	$g = 0.5$
$p_m^* = 1$	$p_x^* = 1$	$r_l^* = 0.03$	$\delta = 0.05$	$\delta_h = 0.05$	$\tau_c = 0.5$	$\tau_v = 0.15$	$\tau_p = 0.2$
$\gamma = 0.1$	$c_1 = 0.9$	$c_2 = 0$	$l_y = 2$	$x_y = 0.2$	$j_y = 0.1$	$y^p = 0.5$	$p_v = 1$

Table 9.3: The parameters corresponding to figure 9.8a.

As we can see from figure 9.8a the government debt ratio will at first increase rapidly, crossing soon the 60 percent line we have assumed as target for the current government and then converge to a ratio of about 200 percent. Due to the fact that wage taxation does nor react to this evolution of government debt we have that the fluctuations in the real part of the economy are completely decoupled from the GBR and its implications for government debt.

Next we add an extremely slow response of the wage tax rate τ_w to the evolution of the government debt ratio d. As can be seen from the figure 9.8b this implies a dramatic worsening of the situation considered in the preceding figure 9.8a concerning the evolution of government debt as well as the dynamics of the real part of the economy which is now influenced through the evolution of this debt. Note also that the tiny variation in the tax rate is not visible in figure 9.8b (bottom left) due to the scale that applies to the vertical axis there.

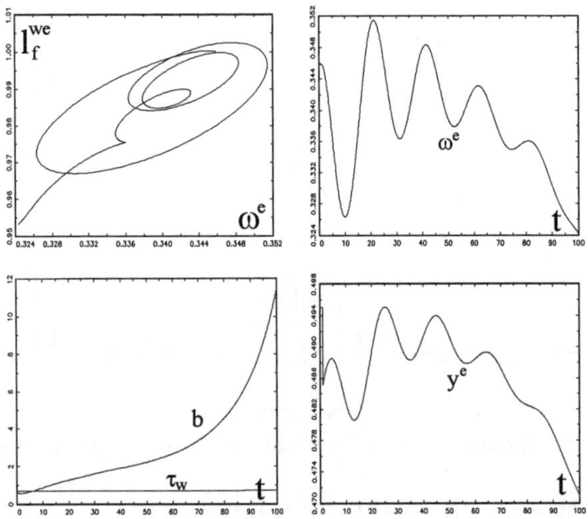

Figure 9.8b:
The 5D dynamics with weak responses of the wage tax rate ($\alpha_{\tau_w} = 0.0005$).

Next we ask whether the shown situation can be improved by the interest rate policy rule which as we know tends to add stability to the dynamics. The next figure 9.8c indeed shows that this is the case, though – as other simulations have shown — the power of this policy rule will be limited, in particular when the speed of adjustment of the tax rate is increased.

Employing the wage income taxation rule in the place of the interest rate policy rule is thus not stabilizing in the 5D setup in contrast to what might be expected from such a rule according to the comments made in Murphy and Powell (1997). This seems to be due (even in the case where government debt converges toward the target ratio) to the cumulative effect the evolution of government debt has on the change in the wage taxation rate (which makes things worse instead of better).

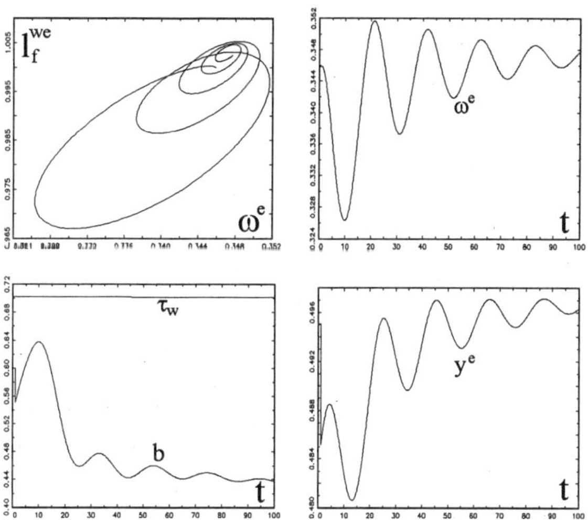

Figure 9.8c:
The 5D dynamics with weak responses of the wage tax rate plus a stabilizing interest rate policy rule ($\beta_{r_2} = \beta_{r_3} = 0.5$).

Quite the contrary to what we expect on the basis of Chiarella and Flaschel (1998h) and its treatment of the GBR even small positive parameters α_{τ_w} contribute significantly to the instability of the steady state and are therefore problematic. This may also be due to the complicated government bond feedback mechanism which so far did not influence the dynamics shown and which may not have the properties expected for its working in Powell and Murphy (1997). The evolution of the government debt based on our complicated formulation of the GBR is however always there and must be integrated into full dynamics at some stage of the investigation. The question can then only be whether its evolution is helpful ore problematic in its consequences for the whole system when the taxation rule is switched on with the aim to stabilize government debt at a certain target ratio.

9.6.3 Fiscal and monetary policy rules in interaction

The next and final figure 9.8d of this section show the joint working of the tax policy rule and the interest rate policy rule for a parameter constellation where we get limit cycle behavior for the full 9D real part of the dynamics. This figure therefore provides an example where the private sector of the economy is showing fluctuations of an economically reasonable type. Note with respect to the fiscal policy rule that we still have to assume a very small parameter α_{τ_w} in order to get the boundedness of the dynamics. Note also that we have added this fiscal policy to the case of a stabilizing monetary policy rule considered in figure 9.7. Note finally that inventories become negative in the present simulation run which may be interpreted as an accumulation of orders until production and inventories are back to satisfying levels.

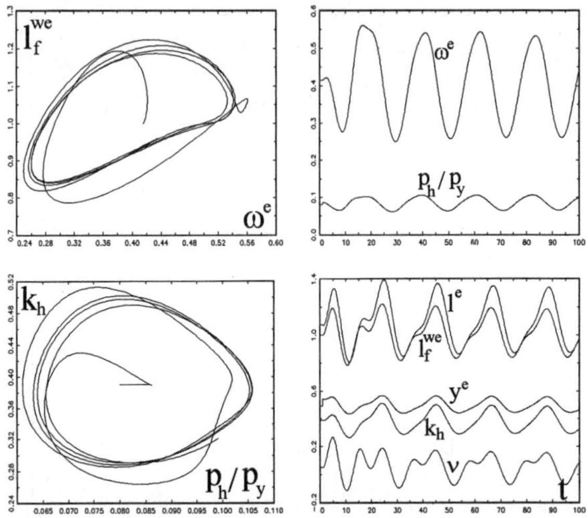

Figure 9.8d:
The unified 9D dynamics with monetary and fiscal policy rules in operation.

The parameters of this simulation run are the following ones:

$\beta_{w_1} = 1.5$	$\beta_{w_2} = 0.5$	$\beta_p = 0.5$	$\beta_{\pi^l} = 0.3$	$\beta_{p_b} = 0$	$\beta_{\pi_{bs}} = 0$	$\beta_e = 0$	$\beta_\epsilon = 0$
$\beta_n = 0.3$	$\beta_{n^d} = 0.1$	$\beta_{y^e} = 0.3$	$\beta_h = 20$	$\beta_l = 0.2$	$\beta_{r_1} = 0.1$	$\beta_{r_2} = 1$	$\beta_{r_3} = 0.5$
$\alpha_{\pi^l} = 0.5$	$\alpha_s = 1$	$\alpha_{h_1} = 0.5$	$\alpha_{h_2} = 0.2$	$\alpha_{h_3} = 0.5$	$\alpha_{k_1} = 0.5$	$\alpha_{k_2} = 0.5$	$\alpha_{k_3} = 0.2$
$\alpha_{\tau_w} = 0.003$	$\alpha_{\tau_m} = 0$	$\alpha_g = 0.3$	$\alpha_b^g = 0.5$	$\alpha_u = 0.6$	$\alpha_r = 0.7$	$L_1(0) = 20000$	$L_2(0) = 5000$
$\kappa_p = 0.5$	$\kappa_w = 0.5$	$\kappa_h = 0.5$	$\bar{U}_c = 1$	$\bar{U}_h = 1$	$\bar{V} = 1$	$\bar{d} = 0.6$	$g = 0.5$
$p_m^* = 1$	$p_x^* = 1$	$r_l^* = 0.03$	$\delta = 0.05$	$\delta_h = 0.05$	$\tau_c = 0.5$	$\tau_v = 05$	$\tau_p = 0$
$\gamma = 0.1$	$c_1 = 0.5$	$c_2 = 0.4$	$l_y = 2$	$x_y = 0.2$	$j_y = 0.1$	$y^p = 0.5$	$p_v = 1$

Table 9.4: The parameters corresponding to figure 9.8d.

We close this section on the real part of the 18D dynamics of this chapter by the observation that all findings of this section are still of a very preliminary nature and have to be supplemented by many further and more systematic explorations of these subdynamics in order to get more understanding of the theory of business fluctuations they imply for empirically plausible ranges of its set of parameters.

9.7 Adding asset price dynamics to the real dynamics

So far asset price adjustment speeds have been set zero throughout and expected capital gains also stayed at zero, due to the lack of inflationary forces in the steady state and since also all adjustment speeds of expectations concerning the asset markets have been set equal to zero. We now go on to asset market dynamics in isolation, starting with long-term bonds and adding exchange rate dynamics thereafter, before we come to the investigation of the impact of asset markets on real activity and thereafter to real-financial interactions. We stress again that the obtained results are of a very preliminary, purely illustrative nature for the switch off/on methodology that is the focus of interest in this chapter. They should be supplemented by more systematic numerical and analytical studies of this type in future work on the 18D core dynamics that is here investigated.

9.7.1 Independent bond market dynamics and the real economy

This extension of the real dynamics adds first of all and most importantly long-term interest rate movements to them (expected and actual long term bond price dynamics) through their influence on the investment in fixed capital and housing and thus on aggregate demand and the output of firms. We therefore now integrate into the real dynamics the two dynamic equations:[13]

$$\begin{aligned}\hat{p}_b &= \frac{\beta_{p_b}}{1-\beta_{p_b}(1-\alpha_s)}[(1-\tau_c)\frac{1}{p_b}+\alpha_s\pi_{bs}-(1-\tau_c)r]\\ \dot{\pi}_{bs} &= \beta_{\pi_{bs}}(\hat{p}_b-\pi_{bs})\end{aligned}$$

and their two (opposing) effects on the two types of investment just considered, via profitability differentials, here shown for fixed business investment $(1-\tau_c)\rho^e-((1-\tau_c)r_l-\pi^l)$, $r_l=1/p_b$, and via the interest rate spread r_l-r. This extension generally adds instability to the real dynamics, since it represents a positive feedback loop between the expected and the actual increase in the growth rate of long-term bond prices, if the adaptive component in the expectations mechanism works with sufficient strength. We stress that these asset market dynamics are independent of the movements in the real part of the economy as long as the central bank keeps the short-term rate of interest fixed to its steady state value, in which case there is only a one way route leading from the market for long-term bonds to the real part of the economy.

9.7.2 Adding exchange rate dynamics to the bond market dynamics

A similar observation does not so obviously hold, if we allow the exchange rate e to influence the evolution of the real part of the dynamics, by removing the assumption that the rate of import taxation is always set such that the trade account of firms is balanced (when measured in domestic prices). In this latter case, the expected rate of profit of firms does not depend on their exports and imports levels and thus on exchange rate changes. As long

[13]The fraction in front of the first equation as usual assumed as being positive.

as there are no wealth effects in the model and as long as the individual allocation of bonds on the various sectors does not matter, there is indeed only this one channel through which the nominal exchange rate can influence the real economy (besides of course through the GBR which includes the tax income of the government deriving from import taxation, but which does not play a role for the real part of the model unless wage taxation is responsive to the evolution of government debt (as we have discussed it in the preceding section). To have this influence of the exchange rate we thus have to extend the 9D real dynamics by the following three laws of motion:[14]

$$\begin{aligned}
\hat{\tau}_m &= \alpha_{\tau_m}\frac{p_x^* x - (1+\tau_m)p_m^* j^d}{p_x^* x}, \\
\hat{e} &= \frac{\beta_e}{1-\beta_e(1-\alpha_s)}[(1-\tau_c)r_l^* + \alpha_s\epsilon_s - ((1-\tau_c)\frac{1}{p_b} + \pi_b)], \\
\dot{\epsilon}_s &= \beta_{\epsilon_s}(\hat{e} - \epsilon_s).
\end{aligned}$$

The exchange rate dynamics is more difficult to analyze, since their two laws of motion need the influence of the bond dynamics in order to be meaningful. Otherwise these two laws of motion would imply monotonic implosion or explosion of exchange rate expectations and the actual exchange rate depending on whether the adjustment speed of the exchange rate is smaller or larger than one (for $\alpha_s = 1$). The financial dynamics is therefore in this respect immediately of dimension 5 and it also needs input from the real dynamics to get the effects from the exchange rate e on bond prices p_b and thus an interdependent dynamics and not one of the appended monotonic form just discussed. Yet, the effect of changes in e via the rate of profit ρ^e of firms and the investment decisions that are based on it, needs a long way in order to reach the market for long term bonds. Changes in investment lead to changes in aggregate goods demand and thus to changes in sales expectations and actual output. This leads to changes in capacity utilization of firms and domestic price inflation which – if and only if monetary policy responds to them – are transferred to changes in the short-term rate of interest and thus to changes in the long-term rate of interest. In this way there is a feedback of a change in the exchange rate on its rate of change which has to be analyzed if the full 18D dynamics are investigated.

Taken together the above two extensions which integrate the financial dynamics with the real dynamics will lead us to a 14D dynamics of the real financial interaction, but with no feedbacks from government policy and the GBR yet. This system will be investigated numerically on various levels of generality, i.e., by means of appropriate subcases, in this section.

Clearly the bond dynamics is the more important one from among these two possibilities of making the real dynamics dependent on what happens in the financial part of the economy. We will therefore investigate next how independent monotonic or cyclical movements in long-term bond prices act by themselves (with no coupling with the exchange rate dynamics) on the real part of the dynamics and how they can be bounded in an economically sensible way in the case where their steady state solution is surrounded by centrifugal forces. We shall show here, as already discussed in Chiarella and Flaschel (1998h), that locally explosive asset market dynamics can give rise to limit or even limit limit cycle behavior (relaxation oscillations) in the bond market and thus to more or less fast, persistent

[14]Where the first one is independent of the changes of the exchange rate.

fluctuations in the long-term rate of interest and expectations about its rate of change. This result is of interest in its own rights, but of course also important when studying its consequences for the economy as a whole, without (or with) feedback from the real side on the financial markets.

Arriving at such a situation thus provides an interesting intermediate step in the analysis of the full 18D dynamics, since we can study here the role of fluctuations in long-term interest rates (and the exchange rate) on the real dynamics in isolation before it comes to a real-financial interaction of these two fundamental modules of our model. The obtained result can be usefully contrasted with the one way investigation of the real-financial interaction of Franke and Semmler (1999), who study the behavior of a fully specified set of asset markets in its dependence on a given wave form of the business cycle in the real sector, whereas this section considers how the opposite situation can be investigated as a natural subcase of our general model of the real-financial interaction, where asset market fluctuations only work on the functioning of the goods and the labor markets of the economy.

9.7.3 Asset markets and real markets: One way routes and interactions

We now apply these observations to the numerical investigation of a 5D real dynamics (the KMG core dynamics of this chapter) augmented by the 2D dynamics in long-term bond prices and interest rates and their impact on the real part of the economy. We start this with an exploration of a situation where bond price dynamics are still convergent and where there is thus no need for thresholds far off the steady state.

The plots shown in figure 9.9 show that the isolated bond price dynamics are based on the situation of a stable focus (bottom right). This long swing in the bond market is transferred to the real sector as described above. It superimposes this long swing on the shorter fluctuations of the real sector giving rise to more advanced types of fluctuations than we have seen so far. Of course, one would expect the opposite to the above shown situation, short cycles in the asset market and longer cycles in the real part of the model. One task should therefore be to find out when this may happen. We stress that the exchange rate dynamics is also switched on in the present simulation but that it does not influence the real economy since the expected rate of profit of firms does not yet depend on it and since there is no influence of the GBR in the presently considered case.

From the parameter set belonging to figure 9.9 we see that the adjustment of bond price expectations is still very slow, in order to obtain a convergent adjustment in the market for long-term bonds. In the opposite case of explosive bond market dynamics one has of course to add some limiting mechanism to these dynamics, in order to get a meaningfully bounded situation. We have described in Chiarella and Flaschel (1998h), see also section 2.2 of part I of this book, how this can be done and pointed to limit or limit limit cycles that may be generated in this way.

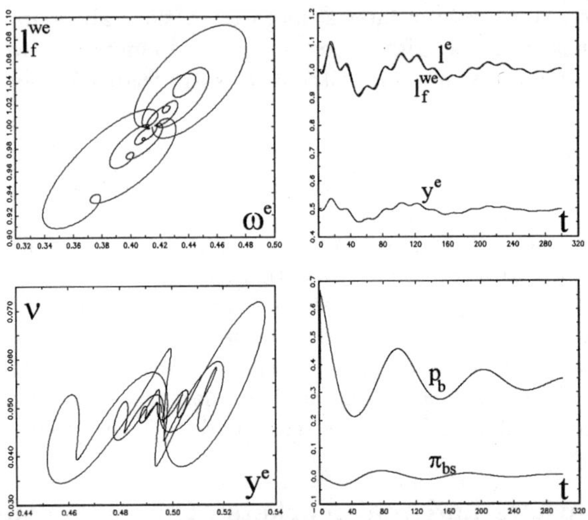

Figure 9.9:
Simulating the 5D dynamics with fluctuating prices of long-term bonds.

The parameters of this simulation run are the following ones:

$\beta_{w_1} = 1.5$	$\beta_{w_2} = 0.5$	$\beta_p = 0$	$\beta_{\pi^l} = 0$	$\beta_{p_b} = 1.2$	$\beta_{\pi_{bs}} = 1$	$\beta_e = 0.5$	$\beta_\epsilon = 0.5$
$\beta_n = 0.3$	$\beta_{n^d} = 0.1$	$\beta_{y^e} = 0.3$	$\beta_h = 0$	$\beta_l = 0.2$	$\beta_{r_1} = 0$	$\beta_{r_2} = 0$	$\beta_{r_3} = 0$
$\alpha_{\pi^l} = 1$	$\alpha_s = 1$	$\alpha_{h_1} = 0$	$\alpha_{h_2} = 0$	$\alpha_{h_3} = 0$	$\alpha_{k_1} = 0.5$	$\alpha_{k_2} = 0$	$\alpha_{k_3} = 0.2$
$\alpha_{\tau_w} = 0$	$\alpha_{\tau_m} = 0$	$\alpha_g = 0$	$\alpha_b^g = 0.5$	$\alpha_u = 0$	$\alpha_r = 0$	$L_1(0) = 20000$	$L_2(0) = 5000$
$\kappa_p = 0.5$	$\kappa_w = 1$	$\kappa_h = 0.5$	$\bar{U}_c = 1$	$\bar{U}_h = 1$	$\bar{V} = 1$	$\bar{d} = 0.6$	$g = 0.5$
$p_m^* = 1$	$p_x^* = 1$	$r_l^* = 0.03$	$\delta = 0.05$	$\delta_h = 0.05$	$\tau_c = 0.5$	$\tau_v = 05$	$\tau_p = 0$
$\gamma = 0.1$	$c_1 = 0.9$	$c_2 = 0$	$l_y = 2$	$x_y = 0.2$	$j_y = 0.1$	$y^p = 0.5$	$p_v = 1$

Table 9.5: The parameters corresponding to figure 9.9.

The next set of plots in figure 9.10 shows such a situation where again a slow limit cycle mechanism in the asset markets is added to the real dynamics giving rise now to persistent fluctuations, with two different period lengths, in the real sector as well. The situation without the influence of the bond market is presented in the figure 9.11 showing damped fluctuations leading back to the original steady state position.

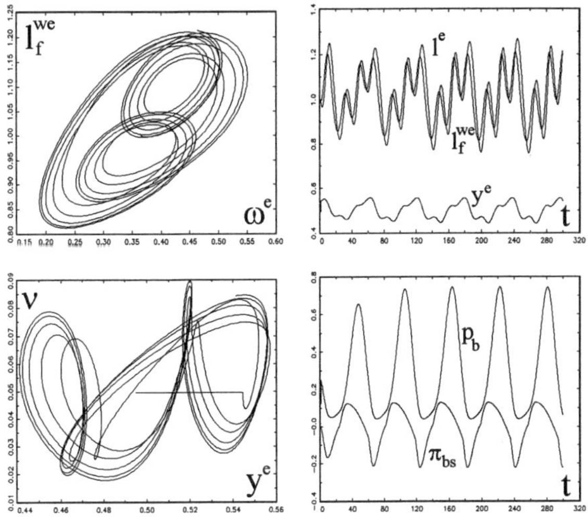

Figure 9.10:
The 5D dynamics with fluctuating bond prices and threshold behavior.

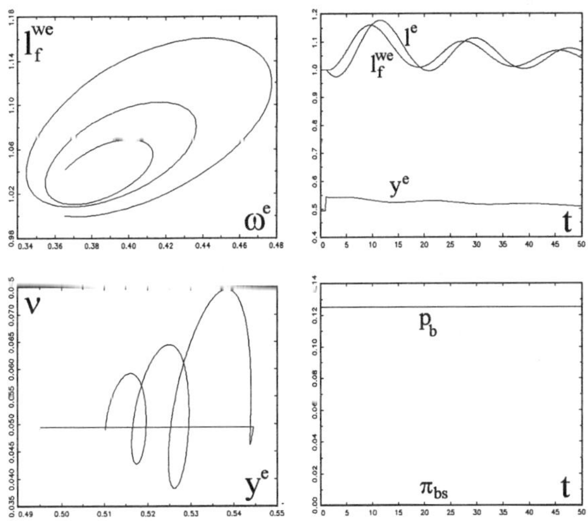

Figure 9.11:
The 5D dynamics without influence from asset markets.

We stress with respect to the simulations shown in figure 9.10 that they are based on the 5D dynamics with which we began the numerical investigations of the 18D dynamics in this section. There are thus no housing activities involved, no Rose or Mundell effects at work and no policy rules implemented in the dynamics shown. Yet. we have assumed here more rapid bond price adjustment, leading to instability close to the steady state, which is tamed through threshold behavior, i.e., more sluggish adjustment of bond price far off the steady state which bounds the local explosiveness of the system.

The figure 9.11 shows how these dynamics look like if the above dependence on oscillations in the market for long-term bonds is removed from them. As we can see they are then much less cyclical than in the case of their dependence on bond price dynamics. This closes our considerations of the basic case of a one-sided analysis of the real-financial interaction of lowest dimension 7D.

Let us consider next the integrated financial market interaction (between domestic and foreign bonds and their expected rates of return) which are of the following final form:

$$\begin{aligned}
\hat{p}_b &= \beta_{p_b}[(1-\tau_c)\frac{1}{p_b} + \pi_{bs} - (1-\tau_c)r_l^* - \beta_r(e-e_o)], \\
\dot{\pi}_{bs} &= \beta_{\pi_{bs}}(\hat{p}_b - \pi_{bs}), \\
\hat{e} &= \beta_e[(1-\tau_c)r_l^* + \epsilon_s - ((1-\tau_c)\frac{1}{p_b} + \pi_{bs})], \\
\dot{\epsilon}_s &= \beta_{\epsilon_s}(\hat{e} - \epsilon_s).
\end{aligned}$$

We conjecture that this system, with appropriate nonlinearities added, will give rise to two coupled relaxation oscillations of the type we have introduced them in Chiarella and Flaschel (1998h) for the bond dynamics. It is therefore to be expected that the fluctuations in financial markets and their impact on the real part of the economy will become significantly more complicated in such situations of coupled (relaxation) oscillations and their effect on the real part of the economy without or with feedback on the financial sector via the interest rate policy rule of the central bank.

9.8 Numerical investigations of the full 18D dynamics

We base our subsequent numerical investigation of the 18D core model of section 9.3 on the following compact representation of its 18 laws of motion (adjusted in presentation to programming needs) and the, up to the level of nominal magnitudes, unique interior steady state that this dynamical model exhibits. We consider the 18 steady state values of the model first. All these values should have an index 'o' (denoting their steady state character) when used for programming purposes. To not overload the notation here we do not add this index to following list of steady state values. Note again that all steady state values are expressed in per unit of capital form and if necessary in efficiency units.

$$y^e = \frac{y^p\bar{U}_c}{1+\gamma\beta_{n^d}}, \quad [y = y^p\bar{U}_c] \tag{9.97}$$

$$\nu = \beta_{n^d}y^e \tag{9.98}$$

$$l_f^{we} = l_f^{de} = l_y y^p\bar{U}_c \quad [\text{total employment: } l^{we} = l_f^{we} + l_g^{we}, l_g^{we} = \alpha_g g y^e] \tag{9.99}$$

$$l^e = (l_f^{we} + \alpha_g g y^e)/\bar{V} \tag{9.100}$$

$$p_y = \frac{p_v}{1+\tau_v}, \quad [p_v \quad \text{arbitrarily given}] \tag{9.101}$$

$$w^e = \frac{\omega^{be}p_y}{1+\tau_p}, \quad [\omega^{be} = \frac{w^e}{p_y} = \frac{y^e - \delta - r_l^*}{l_f^{we}}] \tag{9.102}$$

$$\pi^l = 0 \tag{9.103}$$

$$p_h = p_y(r_l^* + \delta_h)/\bar{U}_h \tag{9.104}$$

$$k_h = \frac{c_2(y^e(1-g) - (\gamma+\delta))}{c_1(r_l^* + \delta_h)/(1+\tau_v) + (\gamma+\delta_h)c_2} \tag{9.105}$$

$$b = \alpha_b^g \bar{d} y^e \tag{9.106}$$

$$b_l = r_l^*(1-\alpha_b^g)\bar{d}y^e \tag{9.107}$$

$$p_b = 1/r_l^* \tag{9.108}$$

$$\pi_{bs} = 0 \tag{9.109}$$

$$\epsilon_s = 0 \tag{9.110}$$

$$r = r_l^* \quad [=\rho^e] \tag{9.111}$$

$$\tau_m = \frac{p_x^* x_y - p_m^* j_y}{p_m^* j_y} \tag{9.112}$$

$$\tau_w = 1 - \frac{p_h \bar{U}_h k_h}{c_2(1+\tau_v)p_y y_{w1}} \tag{9.113}$$

$$e = \frac{s_o - [\tau_w y_{w1} + \frac{\tau_p}{1+\tau_v}\frac{w^e}{p_y} l^{we} + \frac{\tau_v}{1+\tau_v}(y^e - (\gamma+\delta) - (\gamma+\delta_h)k_h)]}{\tau_m p_m^* j_y y/((1+\tau_v)p_y)}. \tag{9.114}$$

With respect to the last two of the above equations, for the taxation rate τ_w and for the rate of exchange e of the model, we have to apply (besides the definitions of y, l^{we}, and ω^{be}, see the above) the further defining expressions:

$$\begin{aligned}
c_h^o &= \bar{U}_h k_h \\
t_o^c &= \tau_c[r_l^*/(1+\tau_v) + rb + b^l + (p_h/p_y)c_h^o/(1+\tau_v) - \delta_h k_h/(1+\tau_v)] \\
s_o &= gy^e + rb + b^l - t_o^c + \frac{w^e}{(1+\tau_v)p_y}[\alpha^u(l^e - l^{we}) + \alpha^r L_2(0)/L_1(0)l^e] \\
&+ (1+\tau_p)\frac{w^e}{(1+\tau_v)p_y}\alpha_g g y^e - \frac{\gamma b}{\alpha_b^g} \\
y_{w1} &= w^e[l^{we} + \alpha^u(l^e - l^{we}) + \alpha^r L_2(0)/L_1(0)l^e]/((1+\tau_v)p_y)
\end{aligned}$$

in order to have a determination of the steady state that is complete.

Note that the value of the exchange rate e will be indeterminate when we have $\tau_m = 0$ in the steady state in which case the above formula for e cannot be applied. Note furthermore that the parameters of the model have to be chosen such that k_h, τ_w, e are positive in the steady state.[15] Note finally that the parameter α_s must always be larger than $1 - 1/\beta_x$ for $x = p_b, e, p^e$ in order to guarantee that asset price react in a normal way in their adjustment to interest rate differentials, due the modification of the parameter in front of these differentials the removal of the explicit representation of myopic perfect foresight from the laws of motion of long-term bond prices and nominal exchange rates implies.

Equation (9.97) gives (the steady state solution of) expected sales per unit of capital K (and also output per K) and eqn. (9.98) provides on this basis the steady inventory-capital ratio N/K. Eqn. (9.99) provides the amount of workforce per K employed by the firms which in the steady state is equal to the hours worked by this workforce (assuming that

[15]There are further simple restrictions on the parameters of the model due to the economic meaning of the variables employed.

the normal working day or week is represented by 1). It also shows total employment per K where account is taken of the employment in the government sector in addition. Eqn. (9.100) is the full employment labor intensity (in the steady state). Eqn. (9.101) provides the price level (net of value added tax) and eqn. (9.102) gives the wage level (net of payroll taxes) on the basis of the steady state value for the real wage ω^{be}. The steady state value of the inflation rate expected to hold over the medium run is zero, in eqn. (9.103), since the inflationary target of the central bank is zero in the present formulation of the model.

Next we have the price level for housing rents (in eqn. (9.104)) and the stock of houses per unit of the capital stock K (in eqn. (9.105)). There follows the steady state value of $b = B/(p_v K)$ as well as the one for long-term domestic bonds in eqns. (9.106), (9.107) . The price of these bonds is given by the given price $1/r_l^*$ of foreign long-term bonds in the steady state, see eqn. (9.108) . Since there is no steady state inflation there is no change in the expected price of long-term bonds and also no change in the expected exchange rate where we both have rational expectations in the long-run, see eqns. (9.109), (9.110). The steady state value of the short term rate of interest settles at its long-run equivalent as there is no risk or liquidity premium allowed for in the 18D version of the general model, see (9.111) . Import taxes τ_m just balance the trade balance in the steady state, see eqn. (9.112) , while the wage tax rate τ_w must be calculated from gross steady wage income y_{w1} and the marginal propensity to spend this income for housing services, see eqn. (9.113). Eqn. (9.114), finally, is the most complicated one and it provides the steady state value of the rate of exchange which depends on nearly all of the parameters of the model, due to the definitional terms shown that have still be inserted into the expression for e shown into the eqn. (9.114).

This closes the description of the interior steady state solution of out dynamical model. Next we present the 18 laws of motion of our dynamical system which of course make use of the same state variables we have just discussed with respect to steady state determination.

Making use of the formula:

$$\Delta\hat{p}_y = \hat{p}_y - \pi^l = \kappa[\kappa_p(\beta_{w_1}(V-\bar{V}) + \beta_{w_2}(l_f^{de}/l_f^{we}-1)) + \beta_p(y/y^p - \bar{U}_c)],$$

with $\kappa = 1/(1-\kappa_w\kappa_p)$, for the deviation of the actual inflation rate from the expected one, the laws of motion around the above steady state solutions of the dynamics read as follows:

$$\dot{y}^e = \beta_{y^e}(y^d - y^e) + (\gamma - (g_k^d - \delta))y^e \tag{9.115}$$

$$\dot{\nu} = y - y^d - (g_k^d - \delta)\nu \tag{9.116}$$

$$\dot{l}_f^{we} = \beta_l(l_f^{de} - l_f^{we}) + [\gamma - (g_k^d - \delta)]l_f^{we} \tag{9.117}$$

$$\hat{l}^e = \gamma - (g_k^d - \delta) \tag{9.118}$$

$$\hat{w}^e = \pi^l + \kappa[\beta_{w_1}(l^{we}/l^e - \bar{V}) + \beta_{w_2}(l_f^{de}/l_f^{we} - 1) + \kappa_w\beta_p(y/y^p - \bar{U}_c)] \tag{9.119}$$

$$\hat{p}_y = \pi^l + \kappa[\kappa_p(\beta_{w_1}(l^{we}/l^e - \bar{V}) + \beta_{w_2}(l_f^{de}/l_f^{we} - 1)) + \beta_p(y/y^p - \bar{U}_c)] \tag{9.120}$$

$$\dot{\pi}^l = \beta_{\pi^l}(\alpha_{\pi^l}\Delta\hat{p}_y + (1-\alpha_{\pi^l})(0-\pi^l)) \tag{9.121}$$

$$\hat{p}_h = \beta_h(\frac{c_h^o}{k_h} - \bar{U}_h) + \kappa_h\Delta\hat{p}_y + \pi^l \tag{9.122}$$

$$\hat{k}_h = g_h^d - \delta_h - (g_k^d - \delta) \tag{9.123}$$

$$\dot{b} = \alpha_b^g[gy^e + rb + b^l - t^a - t^c + g^a] - (\Delta\hat{p}_y + \pi^l + g_k^d - \delta)b \tag{9.124}$$

$$\dot{b}^l = (1-\alpha_b^g)/p_b[gy^e + rb + b^l - t^a - t^c + g^a] - (\Delta\hat{p}_y + \pi^l + g_k^d - \delta)b^l \tag{9.125}$$

$$\hat{p}_b = \frac{\beta_{p_b}}{1-\beta_{p_b}(1-\alpha_s)}[(1-\tau_c)r_l + \alpha_s \pi_{bs} - (1-\tau_c)r], \quad r_l = 1/p_b \tag{9.126}$$

$$\dot{\pi}_{bs} = \beta_{\pi_{bs}}(\hat{p}_b - \pi_{bs}) \tag{9.127}$$

$$\dot{r} = -\beta_{r_1}(r - r_l^*) + \beta_{r_2}(\Delta\hat{p}_y + \pi^l) + \beta_{r_3}(y/y^p - \bar{U}_c) \tag{9.128}$$

$$\hat{\tau}_m = \alpha_{\tau_m}\frac{p_x^* x - (1+\tau_m)p_m^* j^d}{p_x^* x}, \quad x = x_y y, j^d = j_y y \tag{9.129}$$

$$\hat{\tau}_w = \alpha_{\tau_{w1}}(\frac{d}{\bar{d}} - 1), \quad d = \frac{b + p_b b^l}{y^e} \tag{9.130}$$

$$\hat{e} = \frac{\beta_e}{1-\beta_e(1-\alpha_s)}[(1-\tau_c)r_l^* + \alpha_s\epsilon_s - ((1-\tau_c)r_l + \pi_b)], \quad r_l = 1/p_b \tag{9.131}$$

$$\dot{\epsilon}_s = \beta_{\epsilon_s}(\hat{e} - \epsilon_s). \tag{9.132}$$

These laws of motion make use of the following supplementary definitions and abbreviations:

$$\begin{aligned}
y &= y^e + \beta_n(\beta_{n^d}y^e - \nu) + \gamma\beta_{n^d}y^e \\
l_f^{de} &= l_y y \\
l_g^{de} &= l_g^{we} = \alpha_g g y^e \\
l^{de} &= l_f^{de} + l_g^{de} \\
l^{we} &= l_f^{we} + l_g^{we} \\
y_{w1} &= w^e[l^{de} + \alpha^u(l^e - l^{we}) + \alpha^r\frac{L_2(0)}{L_1(0)}l^e]/[(1+\tau_v)p_y] \\
c_g^o &= c_1(1-\tau_w)y_{w1} \\
c_h^o &= (1+\tau_v)p_y c_2(1-\tau_w)y_{w1}/p_h \\
\rho^e &= y^e - \delta + (ep_x^*/p_y)x_y y - ((1+\tau_p)w^e/p_y)l_f^{de} - ((1+\tau_m)ep_m^*/p_y)j_y y \\
g_k^d &= \alpha_1^k((1-\tau_c)\rho^e - ((1-\tau_c)r_l - \pi^l)) + \alpha_2^k(r_l - r) \\
&+ \alpha_3^k(y/y^p - \bar{U}_c) + \gamma + \delta, \quad r_l = 1/p_b \\
g_h^d &= \alpha_1^h((1-\tau_c)((p_h/p_y)c_h^o/k_h - \delta_h) - ((1-\tau_c)r_l - \pi^l)) + \alpha_2^h(r_l - r) \\
&+ \alpha_3^h(\frac{c_h^o}{k_h} - \bar{U}_h) + \gamma + \delta_h, \quad r_l = 1/p_b \\
y^d &= c_g^o + g_k^d + g_h^d k_h + g y^e \\
\pi_b &= \alpha_s\pi_{bs} + (1-\alpha_s)\hat{p}_b \\
g^a &= w^e[\alpha^u(l^e - l^{we}) + \alpha^r\frac{L_2(0)}{L_1(0)}l^e + (1+\tau_p)l_g^{de}]/(1+\tau_v)p_y \\
t^a &= \tau_w w^e[l^{de} + \alpha^u(l^e - l^{we}) + \alpha^r\frac{L_2(0)}{L_1(0)}l^e]/((1+\tau_v)p_y) + \tau_p w^e l^{de}/((1+\tau_v)p_y)) \\
&+ \frac{\tau_v}{1+\tau_v}(y^d - g_k^d - g_h^d k_h) + \tau_m e p_m^* j_y y/((1+\tau_v)p_y) \\
t^c &= \tau_c[\rho^e/(1+\tau_v) + rb + b^l + (p_h/p_y)c_h^o/(1+\tau_v) - \delta_h k_h/(1+\tau_v)].
\end{aligned}$$

Inserting these equations into the above 18 laws of motion gives an explicit system of eighteen autonomous nonlinear differential equations in the 18 state variables (9.115) - (9.132) shown above. Note that we have to supply as initial conditions the relative magnitude

$\frac{L_2(0)}{L_1(0)}$ in order to get a complete characterization of the dynamics and that the evolution of price levels is subject to hysteresis, since it depends on historical conditions due to our assumptions on costless cash balances for the behavior of the four agents of the model.

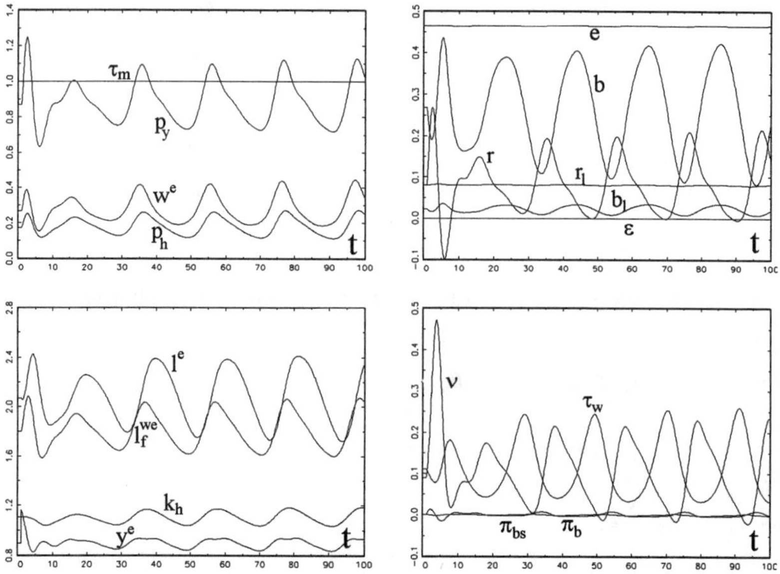

Figure 9.12:
Convergence to a limit cycle for the full 18D dynamics.

The parameters of this simulation run are the following ones:

$\beta_{w_1} = 0.4$	$\beta_{w_2} = 1$	$\beta_p = 0.7$	$\beta_{\pi^l} = 0.5$	$\beta_{p_b} = 0.1$	$\beta_{\pi_{bs}} = 0.1$	$\beta_e = 0.1$	$\beta_\epsilon = 0.1$
$\beta_n = 0.2$	$\beta_{n^d} = 0.1$	$\beta_{y^e} = 1$	$\beta_h = 0.8$	$\beta_l = 0.5$	$\beta_{r_1} = 0.1$	$\beta_{r_2} = 0.5$	$\beta_{r_3} = 0.1$
$\alpha_{\pi^l} = 0.1$	$\alpha_s = 0.5$	$\alpha_{h_1} = 0.1$	$\alpha_{h_2} = 0.5$	$\alpha_{h_3} = 0.1$	$\alpha_{k_1} = 0.1$	$\alpha_{k_2} = 0.5$	$\alpha_{k_3} = 0.1$
$\alpha_{\tau_w} = 0.5$	$\alpha_{\tau_m} = 0.5$	$\alpha_g = 0.2$	$\alpha_b^g = 0.5$	$\alpha_u = 0.5$	$\alpha_r = 0.5$	$L_1(0) = 20000$	$L_2(0) = 5000$
$\kappa_p = 0.5$	$\kappa_w = 0.5$	$\kappa_h = 0.5$	$\bar{U}_c = 0.9$	$\bar{U}_h = 0.9$	$\bar{V} = 0.9$	$\bar{d} = 0.6$	$g = 0.33$
$p_m^* = 1$	$p_x^* = 1$	$r_l^* = 0.08$	$\delta = 0.1$	$\delta_h = 0.1$	$\tau_c = 0.5$	$\tau_v = 0.15$	$\tau_p = 0.3$
$\gamma = 0.06$	$c_1 = 0.5$	$c_2 = 0.33$	$l_y = 2$	$x_y = 0.2$	$j_y = 0.1$	$y^p = 1$	$p_v = 1$

Table 9.6: The parameters corresponding to figure 9.12.

We have so far discussed in chapter 9 various possibilities for a systematic approach towards an investigation of the numerical properties of the full 18D dynamics by means of appropriate subdynamics of them. We now approach the analysis of the simultaneous interaction of all the feedback mechanism of the 18D model, interacting in chapter 7 on a very general level, but now restricted to the above 18 state variables. Note therefore again that there are some feedback mechanisms of the general framework that are not contained in the presently considered dynamics (namely the Fisher debt effect, based on different consumption propensities of creditors and debtors) and the Pigou real balances effect (which would introduce wealth as an argument into the consumption functions of the model). The question of course again is whether the remaining feedback mechanisms uniformly increase or decrease the local stability features of the 18D dynamics around the steady state (leading towards convergence to or divergence away from NAIRU 'full' employment positions) when their relative strength is increased and by how much the downward causal nexus shown in the middle of figure 7.1 or the supply side real wage dynamics shown on its right hand side dominate the dynamics in the medium and longer run.

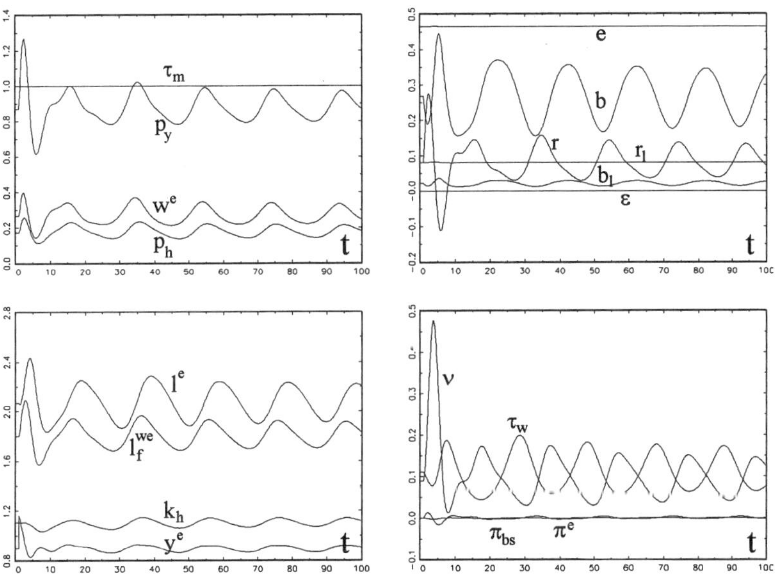

Figure 9.13:
Shrinking limit cycles when the parameter β_{w_2} is increased.

Let us first continue our numerical investigations of the preceding sections by showing a situation where all equations of the 18D system interact with each other, but where adjustment speeds in the asset markets, concerning asset revaluations (long-term bonds, exchange rate) and expectations on their rate of change, are still low so that there is not much movement present in this part of the model. Larger fluctuations, which are of a simple limit cycle type, therefore basically concern the interaction of prices and quantities on the real markets, as the figure 9.12 shows.

The simulation of the full 18d dynamics in figure 9.12 provides a first impression of a type of persistent economic fluctuations (here in fact a fairly simple limit cycle) as it may be generated by the intrinsic nonlinearities characterizing the dynamics. Of course, there can exist supply bottlenecks in the case of larger fluctuations, as discussed in chapter 5, which must be taken into account in the formulation of the dynamics if certain thresholds are passed, but which are ignored in the present chapter.

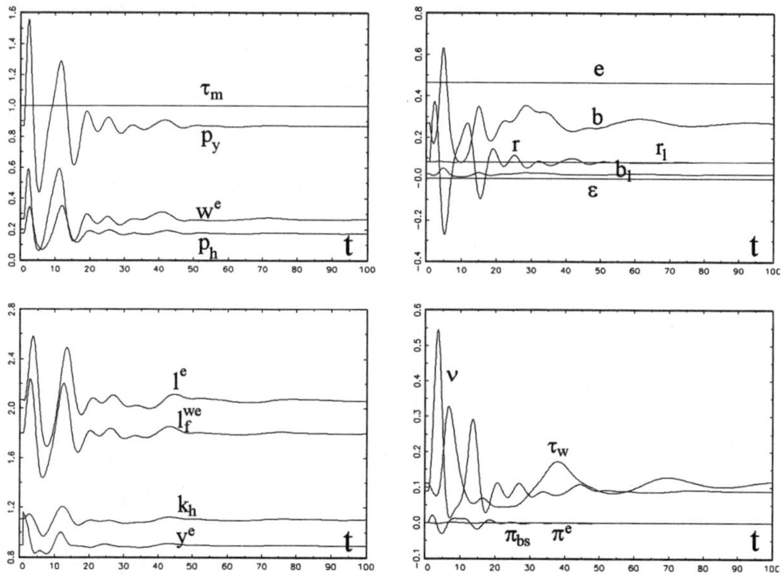

Figure 9.14: Establishment of a point attractor as the parameter β_{w_2} is further increased (to the value 3).

Table 9.6 shows that parameters that were critical with respect to the dynamic behavior of certain subdynamics, like the speed of adjustment for the wage taxation rate τ_w, need no longer be restricted to small values in order to get a meaningful dynamic evolution. However, the table also shows that asset prices are still very sluggishly adjusted with respect to the relevant interest rate differentials, which leaves for future research to investigate in more detail what thresholds to these dynamics must be used in order to get bounded or viable dynamics also for larger adjustment speeds of asset prices and capital gain expectations around the steady state of the dynamics. Note also that rates of growth and of interest are now chosen in a more plausible range than was the case in some of the subdynamics considered in the preceding sections. The simulation 9.12 and further ones (not shown) suggest that the full dynamics behaves more smoothly with respect to parameter changes than the various subdynamics we have investigated beforehand.

Increasing the parameter β_{w_2} to 1.14, the adjustment speed of nominal wages due to the employment rate of inside workers, stabilizes the dynamics further in the sense of making the limit cycle shown in figure 9.13 a smaller one. In fact, further increases of this parameter will remove the limit cycle totally and will create the situation of an asymptotically stable steady state or point attractor, as shown in figure 9.14. This indicates that a supercritical Hopf bifurcation is occurring from stable limit cycles back to convergence to the steady state as the parameter β_{w_2} beyond 1.14. This situation will be confirmed by a subsequent eigenvalue diagram calculation. We note finally here that the situation considered in figure 9.13 is in fact the same as the ones investigated in figures 3.15, 3.16 which show 2D phase plots of the limit cycle, here considered by means of time series representations. Note in this regard also that the wage rate shown in figures 3.15, 3.16 is measured in efficiency units and thus can decline in spite of the there considered situation of a kink in the money wage Phillips curve that does no allow for a fall in nominal wages. We will return to the situation of a kinked wage Phillips curve at the end of this section.

We note with respect to figure 9.13 that there is a long transient behavior shown in this figure with irregular fluctuations and varying cycle lengths of the time series of the 18 state variables that are shown. Note however that is partly caused by the enormous shock that is here applied (a thirty percent increases in sales expectations).

In the situation shown in figure 9.14 we may increases the adjustment parameters on the asset markets, $\beta_{p_b}, \beta_{\pi_{bs}}, \beta_e, \beta_\epsilon$ up to 0.6 and will find that fluctuations will now occur in the corresponding state variables (still of a minor degree), but quite astonishingly accompanied by a further increase in stability, i.e., by a more rapid convergence to the steady state. Asset prices and capital gain expectations do thus not always destabilize the dynamics when their corresponding adjustment speeds are increased. This may be due to the Taylor rule, the steering of the short-term rate of interest by the central bank, which may move the term structure of returns on assets in a way that increases the stability of the steady state.

However, if the four parameter just considered are all in fact increased to 0.6 and if we change the portion α_{π^l} of people which form adaptive price inflation expectations from 0.1 to 0.5 the fluctuations of the economy, and also the transient behavior, are significantly changed as the figure 9.15 shows.

These fluctuations still converge to a limit cycle which however is only revealed when the economy is simulated over a much longer time horizon than is here shown (100 years).

Next we come to the calculation of eigenvalue diagrams for speeds of adjustment and important other parameters characterizing fiscal or monetary policy and the behavior of the private sector of the economy. These eigenvalue diagrams show the maximum real part of the eighteen eigenvalues of the 18D core dynamics and they are based on the parameter values given in table 9.6, with $\beta_{w_2} = 1.14$ however. Note that due to the indeterminacy of the level of nominal magnitudes one eigenvalue must always be zero in these 18D dynamics, in distinction to the dynamics we have considered in chapters 7 and 8. Therefore, local asymptotic stability of the remaining variables is given when we see a horizontal portion (at zero) in the eigenvalue diagrams shown below. The degree of asymptotic stability therefore cannot be seen from the depicted eigenvalue diagrams, but only the points where stability gets lost, presumably by way of a Hopf-bifurcation.

The eigenvalue diagrams shown in figure 9.16 are remarkable in that they in a very straightforward way confirm what intuition from the partial 1D or 2d perspective would suggest, despite the fact that the partial stability analysis is often quite easy to understand since destabilizing feedback mechanism very often sit there in the trace of the Jacobian of the dynamics at the steady state while they are distributed in the full 18D Jacobian in a very uninformative way at first glance. We thus get that the system very often behaves in a very simple way though it integrates Rose type price adjustment, Metzler type quantity adjustment, Goodwin type growth cycles, a housing sector related to the Goodwin - Rose approach to the employment cycle, the dynamics of the government budget constraint, asset market dynamics of Dornbusch type, and monetary and fiscal policy rules.

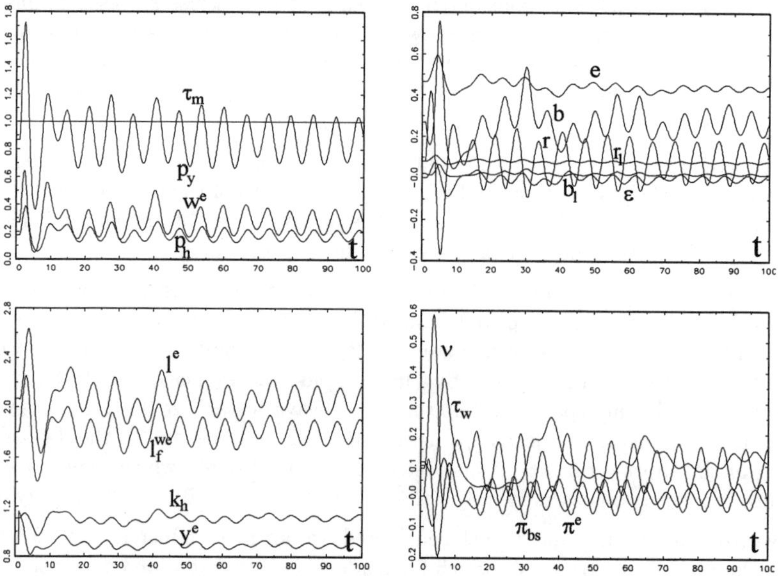

Figure 9.15:
A more dominant role for price inflation and adaptive expectations.

Inspecting the parameter set, underlying these eigenvalue diagrams, which is given by table 9.6, with β_{w_2} equal to 1.14, as for figures 3.15, 3.16, 9.13, first of all shows that wage flexibility (on the outside labor market) should be destabilizing and price flexibility on the market for goods should be stabilizing, since broadly speaking aggregate demand y^d depends positively on the real wage, due to very low marginal propensities to invest as far as profitability component of investment behavior is concerned. These two diagrams therefore concern what has been called Rose effects in this book. Indeed, this is what is shown in the first two diagrams in figure 9.16 over the range $(0,1)$ in the case of the parameter β_{w_1} and the range $(0,2)$ in the case of β_p. The Hopf-bifurcation value for these two parameter values, where stability gets lost, is slightly below respectively above the parameter values $\beta_{w_1} = 1.14$ and $\beta_p = 0.7$ since the parameter values of figure 9.13 already provide a stable limit cycle around an unstable steady state.

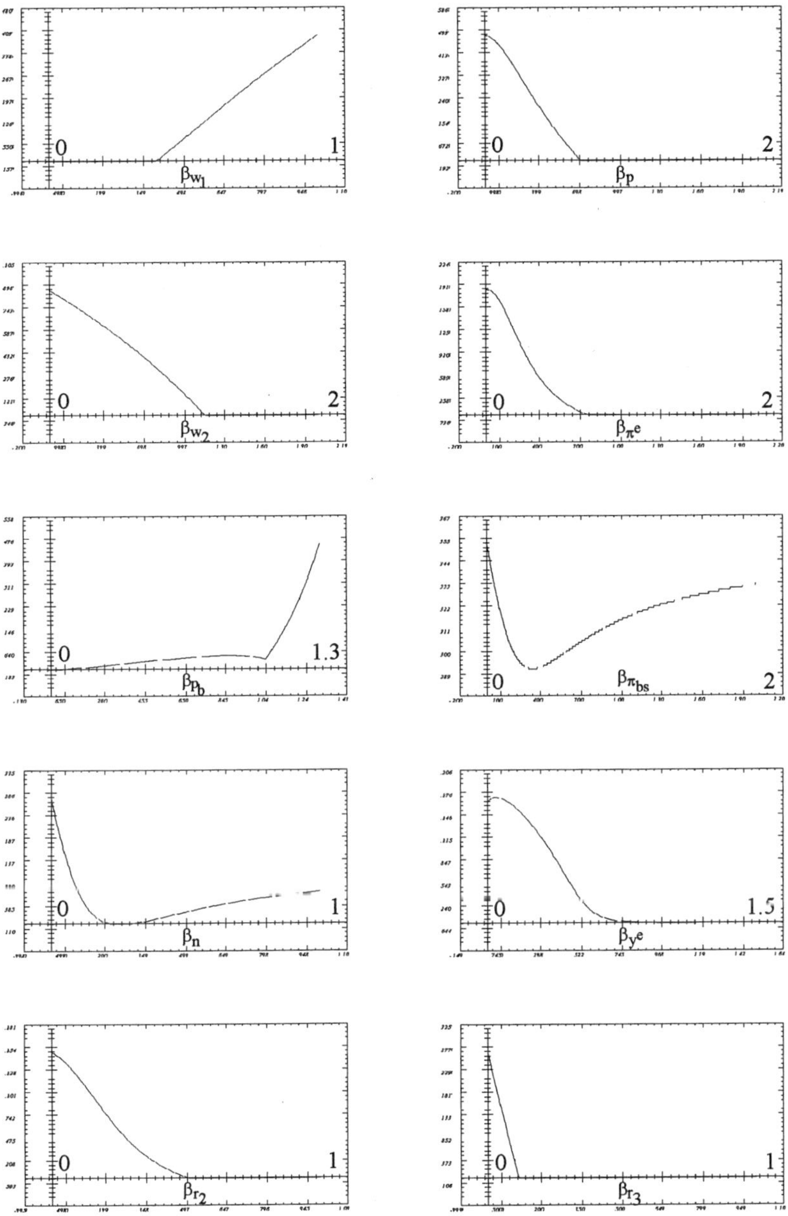

Figure 9.16:
Eigenvalue calculations for adjustment speed parameters.

In the second row of figure 9.16 we see again what has already been demonstrated in relation to figures 9.12, 9.13, namely that larger flexibility of the money wage with respect to the employment rate within firms is stabilizing, in correspondence with what has already been shown in proposition 4.20 for a 3D classical dynamics without any Keynesian features. We also see in this row that increasing flexibility of adaptively formed inflationary expectations is stabilizing, which stands in striking contrast with what we know about the role of Mundell effects from the smaller KMG models considered in this book. It is however easy to understand why this adverse situation is given here. The parameter characterizing the portion of adaptively behaving persons is, as table 9.6, shows in the present situation equal to $\alpha_{\pi^l} = 0.1$ which means that the other, regressive, component of inflationary expectations is the dominant one which is stabilizing, see equation (9.121). Increasing the parameter α_{π^l} to its extreme 1 indeed reverts this situation and gives for the β_{π^l} eigenvalue diagram the same form as for the β_{w_1} diagram and thus implies that the Mundell effect is working as usually in a destabilizing way when the adaptive expectations of price inflation become faster.

The third row in figure 9.16 shows very low bond price adjustment speeds turn the stable limit cycle situation given by the base parameter set into convergence to the steady state, while an increase has only moderate effect on instability for a while, until a point is reached (approximately $\beta_{p_b} = 1$) where instability increases significantly with the parameter β_{p_b}. Modifying the speed of adjustment $\beta_{\pi_{bs}}$ of the adaptive part of expectations formation in the market for long-term bonds, on the other hand, provides no way of obtaining stability in the present situation, i.e., the limit cycle will not shrink to zero in this case for either high or low values of this expectational parameter. similar conclusions hold in the case of exchange rate dynamics, where however a small middle range of adjustment speeds for the exchange rate provides local asymptotic stability, while the system becomes unstable again for very low adjustment speeds of exchange rate dynamics. Asset markets thus behave by and large as expected for isolated changes towards higher adjustment speeds of prices and expectations. Note here however that we have found in connection with figure 9.14 that a simultaneous increase in the for speeds of adjustment here involve could improve the rate of convergence of the dynamics.

Turning to the fourth row of figure 9.16 we see that there is a small range for inventory adjustment speeds β_n where local asymptotic stability is given, while there is instability below and above this range. Not only do faster inventory adjustments destroy stability, as expected from the 2D presentation of the Metzler dynamics in chapter 2, but also very slow adjustments of inventories now. The finding for sales expectations, β_{y^e}, is as expected from the 2D situation, i.e., the stable limit cycle situation underlying the parameters of table 9.6 is turned into local asymptotic stability when the parameter β_{y^e} is increased, since the marginal propensity to spend is broadly speaking smaller than one in the considered situation and the dynamic multiplier process, here in expected sales, therefore stabilizing.

Finally, the interest rate policy rule works as it is expected to work. Increasing inflation or activity levels here lead to increasing short-term nominal interest rates and this counteracts the increases in inflation and economic activity. Increasing the adjustment speeds with which the central bank reacts to inflation or economic activity changes thus leads to local asymptotic stability and makes the stable limit cycle around the then unstable steady state again disappear. We furthermore not, but do not demonstrate this here increasing adjustment speed β_h of the price level for housing services (from a certain point onwards) will destabilize the economy, as will increasing adjustment speeds in the employment policy of firms, β_l. However, in both cases, this will also occur if these adjustment speeds are decreased to a sufficient degree which again means that there is only a certain corridor for which in can be expected in the present situation that convergence to the steady state is assured.

Our next set of eigenvalue diagrams concerns important policy parameters of the 18D core model.

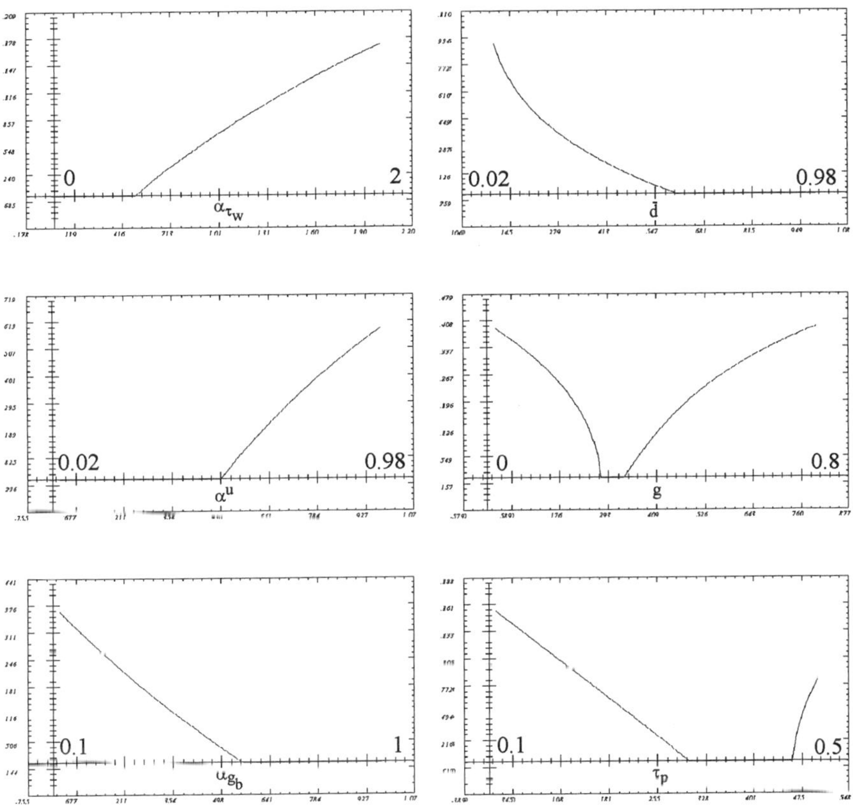

Figure 3.17:
Eigenvalue calculations for policy parameters.

In the first row of figure 9.17 we see that an increase of the adjustment speed of the wage taxation rate in order to approach a target level of 60 percent for the debt to expected sales ratio is destabilizing further when started from the reference case of the limit cycle situation in figure 9.13, while a decrease of this speed will produce convergence to the steady state. By contrast, increasing the targeted debt to expected sales ratio $\bar{d}$ removes the limit cycle and leads to asymptotic stability. the presently considered case therefore leads to the remarkable conclusion that the Maastricht criterion for the ratio $\bar{d}$ should be relaxed and

/ or the speed of adjustment towards this ratio be reduced if asymptotic stability of the steady state is a desired objective

The second row of diagrams in figure 9.17 show to the left that (further) increases in the percentage of unemployment benefits, and also pension payments (not shown), as compared to the limit cycle reference situation tend to be destabilizing, while reductions in both of these ratios bring asymptotic stability and thus convergence to the steady state of the dynamics. To the right this row provides the eigenvalue diagram for the percentage of government expenditures per unit of (expected) sales, which shows that there is a small corridor for this ratio below the reference situation where local asymptotic stability of the steady state is given. Variations in this expenditure ratio therefore generally do not add much to the stability features of the reference situation.

Finally, in the last row of eigenvalue diagrams, we consider to the left the shift in debt financing of government expenditures away from short-term bonds towards long-term bonds and find that this is stabilizing in the current situation. By contrast, in the diagram bottom right, we see again that there is a range of parameter values for the payroll-tax parameter τ_p, and similarly increase in capital income taxes τ_c and value added taxes τ_v, to the right of the reference situation where convergence to the steady state is obtained, i.e., increasing payroll taxes in the reference situation will produce asymptotic stability, while decreases from there will be destabilizing. Payroll tax increases are therefore only in a limited way comparable to increases in the adjustment speed of nominal wages with respect to the external labor market and thus must be considered as an independent event from the proposal that the (downward) adjustment speed of nominal wages should be increased somewhat.

Note that we here only consider stability issues, and not how steady state values themselves may be changed through those of the here considered parameters that do not concern adjustment speeds, which do not affect steady state positions. Such steady state comparisons have to use the set of steady state values presented at the beginning of this section. Note also that the stability assertions made are generally not confined to very limited basins around the steady state, but can in most cases be tested by means of considerable shocks out of the steady state. Yet, as figure 3.15 has shown there are limits to the size of the shocks, there for labor intensity l^e and wages in efficiency units w^e, beyond which the system will become mathematically and thus in particular economically non-viable (with also an intermediate range of shocks where the system, in the reference limit cycle situation, converges back to this limit cycle, but in way that violates economic side conditions at some point in time.

We note that the parameter values α_{τ_m} and α_l, the speed of adjustment of import taxation and the participation rate of the labor forces, do not influence, when changed, the eigenvalues of the Jacobian of the dynamics at the steady state, and that variations in the ratio of heterogeneity in capital gains expectations on the asset markets do not produce asymptotic stability in the presently considered situation. Not unexpected there is a band of intermediate ranges for the marginal propensities of workers to consume goods and housing services (below the reference ratio) where convergence is established, but low as well as high values of these ratios between zero and one do not produce such results. Note here that both ratios may exceed 1 in sum and thus give rise to unstable multiplier dynamics and also to the possibility of debt deflation since workers then become debtors of asset holders in and around the steady state. Finally, and also not demonstrated by an explicit presentation such a numerical result, we have that a portion of adaptively formed expectations, α_{pi^l}, that lies between 0.12 and 0.84 provides convergence instead of the limit cycle situation shown for the value $\alpha_{pi^l} = 0.1$.

In the last set of eigenvalue diagrams we consider further important parameters of the 18d core dynamics, characterizing business fixed investment, labor productivity, external growth and the external labor market.

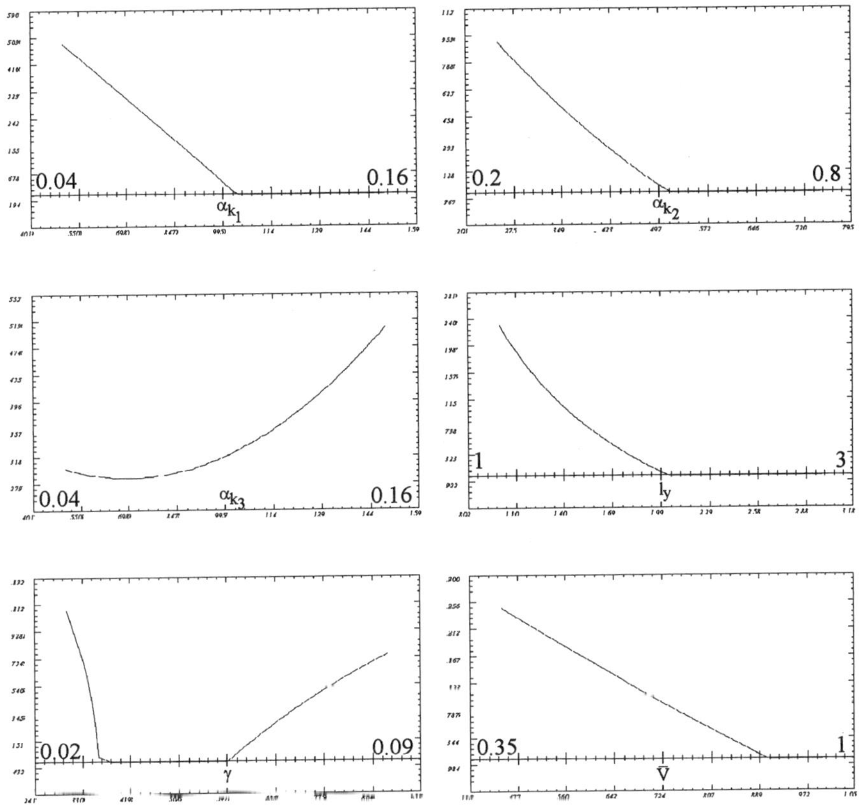

Figure 9.18:
Eigenvalue calculations for investment, growth, the NAIRU and labor productivity.

The first row in these diagrams in figure 9.18 show that increased sensitivity with respect to both the profit / required interest differential and the sensitivity towards the term structure of interest rates increase the stability of the steady state as far as convergence towards it is concerned. The same however does not hold true for the impact of capacity utilization rates on the rate of investment which when varied does not create situations of local asymptotic stability (see second row to the left). On the right hand side of the second row we consider the ratio l_y, the labor coefficient which is the inverse of labor productivity. Increasing this ratio adds convergence to the dynamics, a thing one would have expect for the reciprocal ratio, the labor productivity of the economy. At the bottom left of figure 9.18 we consider the growth rate of the world economy which when lowered, starting from the reference situation of figure 6.13, adds asymptotic stability to the dynamical system, unless it becomes to close to zero. Finally, a higher NAIRU level for the employment rate, $\bar{V}$, equal to 0.9 in the reference situation, produces convergence ,that is a smaller corridor for nominal wage increases on the external labor market adds to the stability of the economy, see the diagram bottom right. the same holds true for the NAIRU rate for capacity utilization of firms as well as for housing services (not shown).

All these stability investigations are of great importance since in particular in macroeconometric work convergence back to the steady state, if not enforced by the so-called jump variable technique, is a basic requirement in these types of approaches, not however in the present modeling framework. Nevertheless, adjustment speeds are difficult to estimate with respect to their most plausible range, and are therefore to be studied intensively in their role of creating or destroying convergence. As the figures of this section show the outcome for our 18D core dynamics, though basically only a single example into this direction, looks quite reasonable compared to the discussion of the basic feedback mechanism of such a model type that we have conducted on various levels of generality in part I and II of the book.

9.9 The Fair model for the US economy

Introduction

We have briefly discussed in section 7.10 macroeconometric models that are, in their basic structure, of Keynesian AS-AD growth type, there however based to a considerable degree on intertemporal aspects and model-consistent expectations in addition, specifically the MSG2 model as documented in McKibbin and Sachs (1991) and the Multimod Mark III model of the IMF as documented in Laxton et al. (1998). These model types are interesting in their attempt to build modern macroeconometric models on a fairly small set of core static and dynamic behavioral and technical equations (including budget constraints) which are to a large extent firmly rooted in modern macrodynamic theorizing and its stress on intertemporal budget constraints and rational expectations. Based on empirical observations there are however also components of the structural equations of these models which are of a more traditional type and which thus represent a compromise between purely theoretical model foundations and those which are believed to represent some macro constraints on economic behavior, which are not so easily microfounded as the purely theoretical ones.

Applied work of this type needs such compromises and we would suggest here indeed that a further empirical evidence should be taken account by such model types, besides the acceptance that labor markets and wage formation are to be treated as a disequilibrium phenomena by way of various types of money wage PC's and the NAIRU concept as benchmark for the measurement of labor market disequilibrium. Our suggestion here is, not unexpectedly, that the goods market should be treated in a similar way, giving rise to a second type of PC as discussed in various places in this book with respect to the many possibilities that are at present available for the specification of aggregate price Phillips curves.

Wage levels and price levels are both to be treated as sluggishly adjusting magnitudes on the macro-level and are to be related to demand pressure variables on the market for labor and goods, respectively, which may be of proportional, derivative and / or integral type as discussed in section 3.4 of this book. Furthermore, there generally exists over- or under-time work in the economy with respect to the workforce 'inventory' of firms which will induce firms to adjust their workforce in the light of such internal employment observations with some time delay in one way or another. This can be considered as a quantity adjustment process on the labor market, that supplements and also influences the price adjustment process on this market. Similarly, there is not only sluggish price adjustment on the market for goods, but also quantity adjustment, which we have formalized in the present book as a Metzler type inventory adjustment process.

AS-AD growth dynamics has taken one step away from pure market clearing approaches and should in our view also take the next step and allow for disequilibrium adjustment processes also on the market for goods, even if these are significantly faster than the ones on the market for labor.

The proper choice is between pure market clearing approaches and those which allow for both sluggish wage and price adjustment, since the intermediate AS-AD case represents a theoretically inconsistent or at least problematic mixture of Keynesian and Walrasian theory. We have shown in chapter 7 that the Murphy model as presented in Powell and Murphy (1997) avoids AS-AD growth dynamics in a specific way, by allowing for sluggish adjustment of actual prices towards competitive ones. They have argued that this adjustment can be reinterpreted as adjustment that is guided by capacity considerations of firms and capacity utilization rates that fluctuate over the business cycle.

A prominent example in the literature on large, not small, economies, as in the case of the Murphy model, which moreover makes immediately use of capacity utilization rates for both labor and capital in the easily understood case of fixed proportions in production of a type we have investigated in this chapter, is given by the work of Ray Fair which has started with short-run modeling in the early seventies and has been further developed up to the present in a series of book publications, see in particular Fair (1971), Fair (1974), Fair (1976), Fair (1984), Fair (1994). Fair's work, even in its most recent form, allows for disequilibrium in both the labor and the goods market and for inventory adjustment processes in the latter market in particular and is therefore much closer in the spirit of what we have tried to model from the theoretical perspective in chapter 7 than the AS-AD models of the US economy considered in section 7.10. It is therefore suitable to compare the approach chosen and developed over the last three decades by Fair for the representation of the US economy with the theoretical framework we have introduced and investigated in this part of the book in order to discuss how those approaches might be further developed in future research.

General observations

In the following we will basically use Fair's (1994) representation of his approach to structural macroeconometric model building, and occasionally also his earlier work Fair (1984), in order to discuss his work in comparison to what we have done in chapters 7, 8 and 9. Fair (1994, Preface) characterizes the aim of his book as a 'rallying cry for the Cowles Commission approach', which was the dominant methodology in structural macroeconometric model building up to the sixties and which he feels too many academic researchers have abandoned in the seventies. Fair (1994, pp.1/2) gives two reasons for the decline of the Cowles Commission approach in academic research, one given by the commercialization of such macroeconomic models (of which the Murphy model in fact represents one example) and one based on the consequences of the Lucas (1976) critique of such model building. yet, he believes, and we agree with this opinion, that the subject of the Cowles Commission approach is still the best way to learn about the economy. Based on Chiarella and Flaschel (1999) and on what we have shown in this book, we further justify this believe by the claim that it is indeed now possible to build models of growth with disequilibrium in both the labor and the goods market in a hierarchical manner such that each subsequent model type improves one or more central weaknesses of the preceding model type, at first up to the point where the working KMG model of Chiarella and Flaschel (1999, Ch.6) has been obtained and then going further from this working model to the inclusion of substitution, endogenous technical change, supply side bottlenecks and market imperfections as far as part II of the present book is concerned and then finally to the theoretically large, but empirically small CTD growth model of chapter 7. There is work in progress that systematically extends the theoretical models here considered in part II towards the inclusion of portfolio theory, more refined investment behavior, issues of fiscal and monetary policy rules and more which attempts to provide further systematic bridges between what we have done here in part II and part III and which will also improve the economic structure discussed in chapter 7, for example with respect to a proper treatment of asset markets in the context of KMG growth. We therefore would stress that much remains to be done, in particular from the theoretical perspective, in providing structural macroeconometric models that are understood in their interacting feedback mechanisms and in their transmission of fiscal and monetary policy actions, that are thoroughly investigated from the numerical point of view with respect to attractors and transients in the many ways we have discussed this in this book and that are successfully applied to small, large and interacting economies.

Going from empirical work to theoretical work on structural macroeconometric model building and vice versa has become much easier and much more interesting today, as in particular the present book should demonstrate, since theoretical CTD models, for examples, are becoming larger through integration and extension, without becoming too complex to be analyzed and since applied models are now much better represented in their core structure, their identities and their steady state implications than was the case when the Cowles Commission approach dominated academic research in this area.

The Cowles Commission approach is, as to its formal aspects, briefly discussed in Fair (1994, Ch.1.2) and it is compared to the RBC approach and the New Keynesian approach in subsequent sections. We would agree here with his critique of the first type of approach that it may simply not be sensible to estimate deep (individual) parameters from aggregate data and that therefore the empirical content of the first of these alternative approaches to macrodynamics is and will remain poor and with respect to the second approach that it has not provided a big picture yet, as the one we have provided in chapters 5 and 6. Furthermore, our chapter 4 has shown that RBC approaches aim at a small scale model with intertemporal optimization of agents and only a few stylized macroeconomic relationships. RBC models are then matched with the data with respect to the first and second moments. From the econometric point of view Fair criticizes the RBC literature as well as the New Keynesians:

> ... The RBC literature should entertain the possibility of testing models based on estimating deep structural parameters against models based on estimating approximations of decision equations. Also, the tests should be more than just observing whether a computed path mimics the actual path in a few ways. The new Keynesian literature should entertain the possibility of putting its various ideas together to specify, estimate, and test structural macroeconometric models. Finally, both literatures ought to consider bigger models.
> ... Fair (1994, p.16).

Fair (1994, Ch.2) only briefly considers the theory underlying his macroeconometric model, before he starts the transition from theory to empirical specifications, and refers the reader to his earlier work, in particular Fair (1974/84) for more details on the theoretical approach chosen by him. Three basic ingredients are stressed by him at the start of his theoretical considerations, solid microfoundations, disequilibrium in some markets, and accounting for all balance-sheets and flow of funds constraints.

> The existence of excess supply in the labor market is a justification for including income as an explanatory variable in the consumption function, and the existence of excess supply in the goods market is a justification for the existence of unemployment. (Fair, 1994, p.17)

Our book represents the same corner stones as Fair's macroeconometric work, in particular disequilibrium both in the market for labor and for goods coupled with both price and quantity adjustment processes, with under- and over-utilization of both factors of production, and a fully specified set of budget equations for both stocks and flows. Microfoundations are more stressed in Fair's work than in our approach, though they are implicitly (through the literature on such structural relationships) present in various of the behavioral equations we assumed in chapter 7, see also our chapter 6 as far as wage and price formation processes are concerned, a subject that is related to work by Phelps and others in Fair (1994, Ch.2). We have however also stressed in section 7.10 that intertemporal aspects concerning consumption and investment behavior are still somewhat neglected or hidden in our approach to disequilibrium growth which therefore could be improved here along lines discussed in Fair (1984, 1994) or in McKibbin and Sachs (1991) and Laxton et al. (1998). On the other hand, we have included the important topic of the role of income distribution in economic dynamics and thus heterogeneity in the household sector and also heterogeneous expectations formation and more.

Theoretical background

Discussing theoretical aspects in Fair (1994, Ch.2) basically means that the determining variables, that influence the decision variables of households, firms and the government, are presented and discussed with respect to their relationship to the variables they determine. In the case of household behavior (worker households) the multiperiod optimization problem is sketched which is also subject to reoptimization (the dual decision hypothesis) if a labor constraint becomes binding. In the case of firms production, employment, wage and price and investment decisions are all treated by way of a joint maximization problem with the possibility of excess labor and excess capacity with respect to the factors actually employed by firms explicitly stressed, a situation which closely corresponds to what we have formulated in our basic model. There, however, investment decisions, pricing decisions, and output and employment decision are formulated independently from each other, a situation that is also to some extent present in Fair's (1994) approach when he derives the equations to be estimated, see his page 107. He assumes that the pricing decision precedes the production decision which is followed by the investment and employment decision followed finally by the wage rate decision, a sequence of events that differs from our modeling of the sector of firms. Despite this, however, the sector of firms of subsection 2.1.3 in Fair (1994) and here in subsections 7.4 and 7.6 are very close in spirit to each other. Finally, Fair (1994) considers banking and government behavior where the use of policy reaction functions and the importance of the government budget constraint is stressed.

Commenting on the complete model, see Fair (1994, Ch.2.15), it is noteworthy that the Keynes and the Pigou, or more generally, wealth effect are stressed in their role of stabilizing the economy, but that none of the possibly destabilizing feedback mechanism, we have discussed in various places in this book, are mentioned. In our view, this is severe gap in the understanding of the working of macroeconometric models that has to be closed in future reconsiderations of these types of models. Observed disequilibria are related to expectational errors in Fair (1994, Ch.2.1.5) and also to nominal rigidities to some extent. It is stressed finally that there is no stable Okun's law and no stable across markets Phillips curve, a finding which our model of chapters 7 - 9 could and in various also did support due to its independent definitions of the rate of employment of labor and capital, V, U_c, on the one hand, and due to its use of two PC's in the place of only one, on the other hand.

Theory in Fair (1994) is thus basically selecting the range of decision and determining variables that have to be used when model specification is approached in the final form of the model which is the traditional role of theory in macroeconometric model building. We would add to this here, that theory should also provide a complete continuous (or discrete) time structure of the model, including all budget constraints, all basic forms of behavioral and technological relationships and also steady state reference path calculations on the basis of appropriate assumptions as we have done it here in continuous time in chapters 7 and 8. Note here that we have chosen functional forms as linear as possible and have postponed the introduction of behavioral linearities for later investigations when specific reasons can be given that certain large fluctuations can be tamed by specifically specified behavioral nonlinearities. However, chapter 5 has shown already, following the French school of modeling disequilibrium growth, that supply side bottlenecks may arise, even in largely Keynesian growth dynamics, which may demand the use of certain inequalities, such as nonnegative inventories, in order to restrict the economy to economically sensible situations.

Fair (1994, Ch.2.2) then immediately discusses two country approaches (instead of the small country approach of our chapters 7 – 9) and the trade, price, interest rate and exchange rate links they exhibit. The consideration of these model types is the subject of Chiarella and Flaschel (1999e) and thus not further pursued here. Though only briefly considered, the above suggests that there are not only close links between the integrated labor market dynamics and goods market disequilibrium adjustment processes investigated in the present book (where financial markets are also present in the form of a delayed adjustment to interest rate parity conditions) and the Murphy model as discussed in chapter 7, but also to Fair's vision of the working of advanced market economies which deserve closer investigation in future research. This should help to improve theoretical model formulations as well as applied structural model buildings and also the understanding of the dynamics generated by these model types. Fair stresses decision problems and their approximations when going to estimate such interacting decisions, while we would add the aspect that such considerations should also lead to model formulations that can be investigated from the theoretical point of view and improved in the hierarchical manner we have done this in Chiarella and Flaschel (1999) and in the present book. The subject of part III is therefore situated somewhat in between Fair's characterization of theory and his applied work, where stochastic simulation, multiplier determination and their standard errors and related issues are then approached.[16]

The transition from theory to empirical specification

An important next step in Fair's (1994) methodology of providing and testing macroeconometric models, see his Ch.3, is given by the transition from theory to empirical modeling specifications. Topics here are the availability of data, the problem of unobservable variables, the use of stochastic equations, of lags and, of course, variable construction. He observes, in Fair (1984), that the relationship between theory and empirical specification is usually not very tight, a situation which we believe can be improved by the approach we have chosen in part III of this book. Variable construction in particular concerns overtime work, housing, inventories, excess capital and labor including measures for potential output and labor market tightness of various sorts, and more, which all represent variables that are also present in our theoretical approach to macroeconometric model building. There are thus many common elements of part III of our book and the Fair approach, even on the level of the choice of the relevant variables that guide economic behavior.

The next step then however is the choice of aggregate behavioral relationships (in our approach) and the empirical specification of such relationships (in Fair's approach). We stress here that both approaches treat the aggregation problem only in an intuitive way, since for example the numerous possibilities for pricing behavior with their many details are simply transferred to macroeconomic equations such that only the most important variables that theory suggests are represented systematically. Macroeconomic work with an applied perspective has no other choice at present, since it must suppress detail in order to arrive at structural equations whose interaction can be studied with respect to the interacting feedback mechanisms they give rise to. Economics after all is first of all about interdependence of markets and sectors, in macro of a fully specified set of possible markets and sectors, and the study of such interdependence must proceed even if structural details may still be subject to continual improvements, or even radical reformulations.

The stochastic equations of the Fair model

We now come to the stochastic equations that are actually used in the Fair (1994, Ch.5) US-model. We will not go through all of these equations systematically, in particular not in the complete form they are represented in appendix A of Fair's book, but will again only stress the instances where there are important similarities or differences in the approach presented in Fair (1994, 1984) and here in chapters 7 – 9. Note however that Fair's model is not presented on the intensive form level and not subject to steady state considerations as our theoretical macroeconometric model in chapters 8 and 9, see also Powell and

[16]Compare also again our methodological consideration of chapter 3.

Murphy (1997), and thus can be compared only as far as the original or extensive form of structural equations is concerned (neglecting the use of logarithms of empirically specified macromodels, which would be categorized as the addition of extrinsic nonlinearities in the methodology of this book). In the place of considering appropriate relative variables that are capable of becoming stationary in the long run[17] use is made in Fair's approach of time trends that are meant to capture the effects of variables not explicitly shown in the employed structural equations. Of course, we will neglect all econometric details that are used when going from theory to empirical specifications since our comparison will be on the level presented and discussed in chapter 7.

Household expenditures in Fair's (1984, 1994) US-model concern services, non-durables, durables and residential investment. Up to durables (apart from housing), we employ the same distinction in our CTD growth model of chapter 7 in a specific way, since we have non-durables as well as the market for housing services and also housing investment, but in a framework of heterogeneous households types that allows us to treat questions of income distribution and also of debt deflation as far as debt between different types of consumers is concerned. Fair states instead that the distinction between labor and non labor income is not of great importance and employs instead three age variables and thus gives more attention to demographic issues, also concerning labor supply, just as in the approach presented in Powell and Murphy (1997). Fair's consideration of durables introduces aspects of consumer choice that are also reflected in our CTD growth model, regarding the use of lagged dependent variables, which in our approach also appear in the form of a lagged adjustment towards target values of consumption and housing investment. There are wealth effects in consumption and the distinction between short- and long-term interest rates is important, but the use of nominal interest rates in the place of real ones is stated to be supported by the facts. He distinguishes the Keynesian from the 'classical' case on the labor market which in his approach distinguish loose from tight labor markets and thus broadly speaking low rates of capacity utilization (where there is also a 'discouraged worker' effect) from high ones.

Though his approach does throws doubts on the empirical relevance of Rose effects and the role of income distribution as well as of Mundell effects and the role of inflationary expectations in consumption (and later in investment), there are many similarities between his and our approach which suggest that both can gain from each other in future more detailed comparisons and integrations of them. Note however that residential investment, though part of the household sector as in our model, is not subject to rate of return comparison as in our approach. Note also that the price of houses and the price of housing services is not explicitly discussed in Fair's (1984, 1994) presentations of the econometric model he employs.

Money demand is of the usual form of a Cagan money demand function in Fair (1994, Ch.5.3), as in our approach, but it is disaggregated there into one for households, one for firms and a currency demand equation. Again there is an adjustment of actual towards desired values, which is, based on empirical observations, formulated in nominal terms. Money is therefore treated in more detail by Fair, while we have chosen with respect to our two households approach that money is distributed between them in a way such that only the aggregate relationships matters for the evolution of the short-run ate of interest.

[17]Note however that household demand is discussed in per capita terms.

The main firm sector equations are the following ones. There is a price level PC which is first discussed in two forms, a level form (which was related to a derivative control mechanism in chapter 2) and a growth rate form which is the conventional form based on a proportional control mechanism. There is also a more general equation that encloses both possibilities. Fair makes use of demand pressure and cost-push variables in these equations, concerning the market for goods and wages, respectively and he also adds the price of imports as another expression of the cost-push variety. He finds that the level equation is supported by the data. This raises of course again the question what this equation will look like if the economy is close to the steady state (where nominal rates of change of the price level and of efficiency wages are close to each other), see here section 2.4, and what a modeler should do if he attempts to build a theoretical macroeconometric model on such an observation where he wants to show the existence of a steady state reference path as in our chapters 8 and 9.

Actual production is decided in Fair (1994, p.111) in close correspondence to what we have assumed for the interaction of output, demand, desired and actual inventory changes, though – as in Powell and Murphy (1997) – the process of sales expectation formation is down played and resulting errors in production plans by Fair. Fair in particular finds that production smoothing relative to sales actually occurs contrary to what has been maintained by Blinder and others. The production technology has already been described as being of the fixed proportions type in the chapter on variable construction in Fair (1994).

Fixed investment of firms is considered next and at first postulated to depend proportionally on capacity utilization and output changes, i.e., on derivative control expression that introduce Harrodian accelerator aspects into the goods market adjustment process which we have completely neglected in chapter 7. Instead, we have employed in chapter 7 profitability relative to the real rate of interest on long-term bonds in addition which to some extent is also added in Fair (1994) to his investment equation later on. There is again adjustment towards desired values in his and our approach. In sum we find here that his approach appears to support quantity adjustment over profitability considerations while we treat them (without any empirical measurement) on an equal footing for the moment.

The employment policy of firms, concerning number of jobs and overtime hours, as well as the wage payments related to this distinction is closely related to what we have formulated in chapter 7 in this respect and provides interesting details to the comments we have made in chapter 7 on this issue. This subject again provides an example of fruitful penetration of purified theoretical presentations of such empirical relationships and actually estimated equations where adjustments towards available data have to be made. Concerning the money wage PC we have already discussed Fair's procedure in section 2.4 and found that another restriction has to be imposed here on coefficients, not only to ensure a meaningful real wage equation, but also to ensure the possibility of steady growth in our model economy. Astonishing remains Fair's finding that labor market imbalances do not play a role in his level form of a money wage PC, which is supported by estimates of the KMG approach with its to rates of growth PC's for prices as well as wages in Flaschel, Gong and Semmler (1999), but which is not yet really supported by theoretical reflections of labor market dynamics.[18] Further work here seems to be necessary in order to decide on such an issue of considerable importance.

Further issues concerning the firms sector that are discussed in Fair (1994, Ch.5) are the issue of dividends paid, which is also of great importance in our discussion of budget constraints of firms and the two household types considered, valuation of inventories, to which we pay no particular attention and capital consumption where in particular the role of tax law changes are discussed by Fair.

Concerning financial sector equations Fair considers bank borrowing from the FED, which is not present in our CTD growth model, since there is not yet a commercial banking sector in it, which may be a serious omission. Concerning moreover the bond rate and the mortgage rate (not present in our model), Fair (1994, p.125) refers to the expectations theory of the term structure of interest rates and then chooses that these are indeed determined according to the expectations theory, 'where the current and past values of the short term interest rate (the three month bill rate, RS) are used as proxies for expected future values.' There is finally a discussion of changes in the market value of stocks, which in theory should be a function of changes in expected future after tax cash flow and interest rates, and which is reduced in Fair's estimated equation to changes in the current bond rate and the after tax cash flow. Such pragmatic solutions to the estimation of unobserved variables suggest that our treatment of asset markets with their delayed response to interest rate differentials, in particular in reference to the bond rate, may also be a sensible first step to the treatment of asset markets in theoretical macroeconometric model building, until better solution, for example suggest by portfolio approaches and delayed adjustment mechanisms based on them, become available.

In the remainder of chapter 5, Fair (1994) discusses the import equation used by his econometric model which provides an interesting alternative to the ones used by Powell and Murphy (1997) and in our chapter 7. Next, there follows a policy reaction function concerning the three month treasury bill rate, which we have added to the model in chapter 9 in place of the money supply rule employed in chapter 7. Note that this implies that money demand determines money supply which thus reformulates the use of money demand functions introduce earlier. Finally, interest payments of firms and the government give rise to detailed considerations on how to deal with these issues in view of the many details that here exist in reality. We have so far only considered equity financing of firms, but have made as in Fair (1994) the distinction between short-term and long-term government bonds, with respect to which the considerations of Fair may become of importance in future refinements and applications of our CTD growth dynamics.

There are a number of findings on the empirical relevance of certain determining variables, concerning in particular the discouraged worker effect, the excess labor for the employment policy of firms and the excess capital variable for their investment decision and again the level form of price and wage equations. The findings that he stresses there are interesting, also from the theoretical point of view, and must be considered further in future work. Our main objective in this presentation of the econometric equations of the Fair model was to show that there are many interesting relationships between his and our approach

[18]See however chapter 6 for a theoretical modification of our KMG growth dynamics which moves closer to Fair's understanding of goods and labor market dynamics and an endogenous determination of the labor market NAIRU this may entail.

of this part of the book, which surely deserve closer inspection in our future work on macroeconometric model building. The gap between theoretical and applied work in this area is surely becoming smaller and this provides the hope that macroeconometric models of the future will have a detailed and coherent theoretical representation (including theoretical and numerical analysis), for example in the form of CTD growth modeling, and a detailed empirical reflection and specification with respect to the condensed theoretical representation that will allow to go back and forth between better and better theoretical and empirical model construction. Theory will in particular gain from this interaction by getting ideas on parameter sizes, multiplier sizes etc., which may help to narrow down the implications of models of CTD growth for local stability, more complicated attractors, transients and the degree comovements of important time series that are generated by such models.

Estimating, testing and analysis of properties
Since the focus in part III of the book is theoretical and numerical analysis of theoretical counter pieces to actually applied models, like the Fair model for the US and the Murphy model for Australia, we cannot contribute here anything to the discussion in Fair how single equations and complete models are estimated and tested. This will however be relevant when the CTD growth dynamics of this part of the book would itself be estimated, like for example the basic working KMG model, transferred to discrete format as in chapter 6, has been estimated and applied in Flaschel, Gong and Semmler (1999). The properties Fair (1994, Ch.10) is analyzing concern the computation of multipliers and their standard error, based on deterministic and stochastic simulation, the discussion of the sources and form of economic fluctuations, optimal policy issues and other policy experiments including sensitivity analysis and also counter factual multiplier experiments.

On the theoretical level that has been reached with our CTD growth dynamics in the intensive form of chapters 8 and 9, a first step is to study the comparative dynamics of its steady state solutions, on the general level, for the core dynamics and maybe also to reflect the whole structure again from the perspective of other steady state analysis of the literature in order to find out where our CTD dynamics can be further improved, especially regarding international trade, price, interest and exchange rate links.

Next there should be a thorough analysis of the local dynamics around the relevant steady state solution, at first on the level of the various subdynamics, for example the ones whose analysis we have begun in the present chapter 9, and later also for the 18D core dynamics and even further back to the general dynamics of chapter 8. The basic tool here is the eigenvalue analysis we have used in chapter 9, continued by calculations of Hopf bifurcation (and other) curves and the types of Hopf bifurcations that occur, as exemplified in chapter 3 of the book, also including the calculation of basins of attraction for the attracting limit cycles (and also the point attractors). Should the intrinsic nonlinearities already be sufficient to generate more complicated attractors than just points and or limit cycles, there should of course follow calculations of the shape of these attractors, of the way they are generated by parameter changes, for example though a series of period doublings, of the transients towards these attractors, of bifurcation diagrams, Liapunov coefficients in order to show the degree of complexity of such attractors and more.

If however parameter changes, in general parameter increases as we know form our medium sized KMG growth models of parts I and II, will lead to economically meaningful values along the trajectories of the dynamics, or even to explosiveness and breakdown of the economy, we have to investigate further such situations. We have to find out which of the partial feedback chains that have been one of the important topics of this book, might be responsible for such an outcome and how extrinsic (behavioral or technological) nonlinearities, also with respect to adjustment speeds far off the steady state, can be found that in an economically meaningful way restrict the dynamics to economically meaningful ranges of the phase space, creating not only boundedness of the dynamics, but also their viability in the sense that also convergence to zero values is avoided. We have discussed such extrinsic nonlinearities only in three respects in this book, concerning the money wage PC and the possibility of an institutional kink that restricts wages from falling faster than a predetermined rate,[19] concerning the adjustment of inventories (see chapter 2) and concerning the actual mobility of capital and in this way the adjustment speed of the exchange rate (see chapter 3). The study of extrinsic nonlinearities is thus still in its infancy as far as the models considered in this book are concerned, and must thus be left here for future research.

This brief list on theoretical analysis of CTD growth models with an applied background shows that models studied in Fair (1994) and in the present work are still fairly apart from each other. From the theoretical point of view, one should be prepared to find any sort attracting sets in such high dimensional macrodynamical models, in particular if extrinsic nonlinearities are used in order to limit explosive of collapsing behavior. Whether such a wealth of attractors is also possible for economically or even empirically acceptable parameter sizes is another issue, that should be investigated in a next step. As chapter 3 has shown adjustment speeds may simply be implausibly high in order to get period doubling sequences towards complex dynamics. But this remains a matter of investigation, since it is not at all clear at the moment what the dynamic complexities of high order growth dynamics may be. One may of course hope that the jump variable technique can always be issued in order to simply suppress mathematical complexities that happen off the stable manifold. This however, though superficially not always of this type, is basically a local perspective and thus not really applicable if the forces that shape the course of the economy have nothing to do with its properties in the neighborhood of the steady state.

When attracting sets have been determined and classified, there remain of course the questions concerning the size of basin of attraction, the length of the transient towards such attracting sets, the sensitivity of attractors with respect to parameter changes and more. Therefore, even on the theoretical level, there are a host of topics that have to be investigated in order to understand the working of such model types, quite independently of the topics that will in addition arise when the issues treated in Fair's analysis of macroeconometric models are approached. We expect that there will be a fruitful interaction between these two ways of analysis in the future, based on theoretical representations of macroeconometric models (learned to some extent from actual macroeconometric model building) as well as on factual structural model building (which may find improvement from CTD growth theory due to the fact that the latter is complete with respect to budget restrictions and steady state calculations in particular).

Compared to the Murphy model for the Australian economy, as documented in Powell and Murphy (1997), Fair's approach to macroeconometric model building is much broader in

[19] Which may be zero, see chapter 2, 6 for a discussion of such nonlinearities.

scope, not only because he models a large in the place of a small economy, but also due to his multicountry approach, which like the models of McKibbin and Sachs and the IMF tend to stress global linkages concerning, trade, pricing, interest rates and nominal exchange rates. In our view these models, to the extent the allow for goods market besides labor market disequilibrium as in Fair (1984, 1994), would gain from allowing for heterogeneous agents in the household sector and a detailed treatment of property income besides wage income, (not just overlapping generations) and heterogeneous expectations formation (not just rational expectations in the single markets),[20] sluggish quantity as well as employment adjustments with respect product and manpower inventories, investment behavior that integrates profitability measures with accelerator mechanisms, a more fully developed wage price sector as we have treated it in section 2.4, where the weight of traditional proportional control against the relevance of derivative or integral control has still to be discussed, and also the treatment of Phillips curves in other sectors of the economy (like the housing sector). Finally, static or dynamic portfolio approaches based on imperfect asset substitution should be used on the theoretical level first, see Franke and Semmler (1999), Köper and Flaschel (1999) for example, before it is decided which (delayed) interest rates adjustment rules should be used in their place should the data demand for such approximations.

9.10 Conclusions and outlook

In our book we have reviewed a macroeconomic modeling paradigm of Keynesian tradition. We have presented a reasonable working model which allows disequilibria in the goods and labor market, includes growth and permits fairly detailed modeling and studying of the labor market and Phillips-curves dynamics which pertain to wage and price dynamics.

Our basic working model, elaborated in part I of the book, is in part II confronted with three currently in macroeconomics widely employed paradigms: (1) the general equilibrium flex-price approach, (2) the traditional Keynesian fix-price approach and (3) the New Keynesian view that imperfections in product and labor markets lead to macroeconomic imbalances for protracted periods. Further, in part III, we have employed our working model as a benchmark model to evaluate currently widely employed macroeconometric models both of large scale as well as small scale types. On the other hand, having attempted to provide a foundation of macroeconomic model building of Keynesian type in previous work and in the current book, further work needs to be undertaken to provide tools and to give answers to ever emerging and evolving macroeconomic issues.

Extensions of our basic modeling framework need to deal more with problems of open economies in particular international trade and capital flows under pegged or flexible exchange rate regimes. Here indeed new macrodynamic issues will arise. Macrotheory, for example, is challenged to understand the dynamics of sudden reversal of capital flows generating large swings in exchange rates and asset prices and possibly large output losses as result of currency crisis as for example documented in the financial crisis of Asia in the years 1997 – 1998. Macroeconomics need an understanding of how currency and financial shocks are transmitted through the financial markets to large output fluctuations. In this context also a better understanding of debt-deflation mechanisms might be useful.

[20]See also Fair (1984, Ch.4.1.3.) in this regard.

A further understanding is needed of what the forces of long run growth are. There are numerous contributions from modern endogenous growth theory and extended empirical work on this matter but macroeconomics from a Keynesian perspective - although we have dealt with this topic in our book - is still facing challenging issues as concerns the forces of endogenous growth and their effect on income distribution and employment prospects in advanced market economies. In fact, as many growth theorists have recently argued: growth is all that matters in particular with respect to employment prospects.

Moreover, labor market issues are very challenging nowadays in Europe for macroeconomists if they do not want to leave explanations of causes of persistence of unemployment solely to microtheorists. Formally, a reformulation of the two different variants of Phillips-curve dynamics, the wage and price Phillips-curves and the role of proportional, derivative or integral control in shaping disequilibrium adjustment processes in the labor market as well as the problem of time varying NAIRU needs to be studied. There have been long term changes in the relation of unemployment and the wage-price dynamics for the U.S. as well Europe which need to be better understood. Too much theoretical work on the "natural" rate of unemployment by microeconomists is divorced from macroeconomics and too much microeconometric work seems in search of a broader framework for interpretation. Joint work effort is needed by micro, macro and labor economists to better integrate theoretical and empirical work on the determination of unemployment, moving "natural" rates – if there are such – and Phillips-curves.

As we have stressed, we do think intertemporal optimizing behavior of agents, intertemporal budget constraints, and rational behavior are important as benchmarks to give investment and consumption functions as well as government behavior a better foundation. Yet, we need to allow for models with less perfections in markets, information and transaction cost, liquidity constrained agents and for dynamic models with heterogeneous agents and path dependency. Also, expectations dynamics, as Sargent (1998) has recently pointed out, should be formulated by allowing for an expectations formation based on adaptive learning of agents. More macro modeling along those lines is necessary. By following Keynesian traditions but partially picking up on those themes, we have attempted to demonstrate in this book – and this seems to us essential in macroeconomics– that there are, given that markets are out of equilibrium most of the time, adjustment and feedback mechanisms that only can be studied from a macroeconomic perspective.

Finally, we want to note that we have left aside fiscal and monetary policy issues. We have only included simple policy rules in our model. Modern macroeconomics needs to understand what the short, medium and long run effects of fiscal and monetary policy rules are and what the dynamics are that they set in motion. These have become and will remain major issues not only in the economic controversies over the effect of monetary and fiscal policies since Friedman's contributions in the 1960s but in particular in connection with the creation of the European Monetary Union. Major issues here are; for example: to what extent can fiscal and monetary instruments be used for employment and economic growth, what are the feedback effects of debt deflation and of zero bounds on interest rates, how will a major financial crisis, if occurring again, affect the EMU and is the European Central Bank equipped to deal with it? All these issues, and more, need to be addressed in the future by macroeconomists.

References

AGHION, P. and P. HOWITT (1998): *Endogenous Growth Theory.* Cambridge, MA: MIT Press.

AKERLOF, G.A. and J. YELLEN (1985): A Near-Rational Model of the Business Cycle with Wage and Price Inertia. *Quarterly Journal of Economics*, 100, supp., 823 – 838.

ALLEN, C. and S. HALL (1997): *Macroeconomic Modelling in a Changing World.* New York: John Wiley & Sons.

BARENS, I. (1997): What went wrong with IS-LM / AS-AD analysis - and why? *Eastern Economic Journal*, 23, 89 – 99.

BARENS, I. (1998): Makroökonomische Lehrbücher im Elch-Test. Einige Anmerkungen zur jüngsten Debatte über die (In)Konsistenz von IS-LM / AS-AD Modellen. TU Darmstadt: mimeo.

BARNETT, W., G. GANDOLFO and C. HILLINGER (1996): *Dynamic Disequilibrium Modeling: Theory and Applications.* Cambridgo, UK: Cambridge University Press.

BARNETT, W. and Y. HE (1998): Bifurcations in continuous-time macroeconomic systems. Washington University in St. Louis: Mimeo.

BARRO, R. (ed.) (1989): *Modern Business Cycle Theory.* Cambridge, MA: Harvard University Press.

BARRO, R. (1994): The Aggregate-Supply Aggregate-Demand Model. *Eastern Economic Journal*, 20, 1 – 6.

BARRO, R. and V. GRILLI (1994): *European Macroeconomics.* London: Macmillan.

BARRO, R. and H. GROSSMAN (1971): A General Disequilibrium Model of Income and Employment. *American Economic Review*, 61, 82 – 93.

BARRO, R. and X. SALA-I-MARTIN (1995): *Economic Growth.* New York: McGraw Hill.

BENASSY, J.-P. (1977): On Quantity Signals and the Foundations of Effective Demand Theory. *Scandinavian Journal of Economics*, 79, 147 – 168.

BENASSY, J.-P. (1984a): A Non-Walrasian Model of the Business cycle. *Journal of Economic Behaviour and Organization*, 5, 77 – 89.

BENASSY. J.-P., (1984b), *The Economics of Market Disequilibrium.* New York: Academic Press.

BENASSY, J.-P. (1986): *Macroeconomics. An Introduction to the Non-Walrasian Approach.* New York: Academic Press.

BENASSY, J.-P. (1993): Nonclearing Markets: Microeconomic Concepts and Macroeconomic Applications. *Journal of Economic Literature*, XXXI, 732 – 761.

BENASSY, J.-P. (1995): Classical and Keynesian features in macroeconomic models with imperfect competition. In: H.-D. Dixon and N. Rankin (eds.): *The New Macroeconomics.* Cambridge: Cambridge University Press.

BENHABIB, J. and T. MIYAO (1981): Some New Results on the Dynamics of the Generalized Tobin Model. *International Economic Review*, 22, 589 – 596.

BHADURI, A., K. LASKI and M. RIESE (1998): Effective demand versus profit maximization in aggregate demand / supply analysis from a dynamic perspective. Working paper: The Vienna Institute for Comparative Economic Studies.

BERGSTROM, A.R. (1996): Survey of continuous time econometrics. In: W. Barnett, W., G. Gandolfo and C. Hillinger: *Dynamic Disequilibrium Modeling: Theory and Applications.* Cambridge, UK: Cambridge University Press.

BERGSTROM, A.R., K.B. NOWMAN and S. WANDASIEWICZ (1994): Monetary and fiscal policy in a second-order continuous time macroeconometric model of the United Kingdom. *Journal of Economic Dynamics and Control,* 18, 731 – 761.

BLANCHARD, O. (1979): Backward and Forward Solutions for Economies with Rational Expectations. *American Economic Review*, 69, 114 – 118.

BLANCHARD, O. (1981): Output, the stock market, and interest rates. *American Economic Review*, 71, 132 – 143.

BLANCHARD, O. (1985): Debt, deficits, and finite horizons. *Journal of Political Economy*, 93, 223 – 247.

BLANCHARD, O. (1997a): *Macroeconomics.* Upper Saddle River: Prentice Hall.

BLANCHARD, O. (1997b): Is there a core of usable macroeconomics. *American Economic Review. Papers and Proceedings*, 87, 244 – 246.

BLANCHARD, O. and S. FISCHER (1989): *Lectures in Macroeconomics.* Cambridge: The MIT Press.

BLANCHARD, O. and C. M. KAHN (1980): The Solution of Linear Difference Models Under Rational Expectations. *Econometrica*, 48, 1305 – 1311.

BLANCHARD, O. and L.F. KATZ (1997): What we know and do not know about the natural rate of unemployment. *Journal of Economic Perspectives*, 11, 51 – 72.

BLANCHARD, O. and N. KIYOTAKI (1987): Monopolistic Competition and the Effects of Aggregate Demand. *American Economic Review*, 77, 647 – 666.

BLANCHARD, O. and L.H. SUMMERS (1986): Hysteresis and the European Unemployment Problem. *NBER Macroeconomics Annual*, Cambridge, MA: MIT Press.

BLANCHFLOWER, D.G. and A.J. OSWALD (1994): *The Wage Curve.* Cambridge, MA: The MIT Press.

BROCK, W.A. (1974): Money and Growth: The Case of Long-Run Perfect Foresight. *International Economic Review*, 15, 750 – 777.

CARLIN, W. and D. SOSKICE (1990): *Macroeconomics and the Wage Bargain.* Oxford: Oxford University Press.

CHANG, W. W. and D. J. SMYTH (1971): The Existence and Persistence of Cycles in a Non-Linear Model: Kaldor's 1940 Model Re-examined. *Review of Economic Studies*, 38, 37 – 46.

CHIARELLA, C. (1986): Perfect foresight models and the dynamic instability problem from a higher viewpoint. *Economic Modelling*, 4, 283 – 292.

CHIARELLA, C. (1990a): *The Elements of a Nonlinear Theory of Economic Dynamics.* Berlin: Springer Verlag.

CHIARELLA, C. (1990b): Excessive exchange rate variability; a possible explanation using nonlinear economic dynamics. *European Journal of Political Economy*, 6, 315 – 352.

CHIARELLA, C. (1991): The bifurcation of probability distributions in a non-linear rational expectations model of a monetary economy. *European Journal of Political Economy*, 7, 65 – 78.

CHIARELLA, C. (1992a): Monetary and fiscal policy under nonlinear exchange rate dynamics. In: G. Feichtinger (ed.): *Dynamic Economic Models and Optimal Control.* North-Holland, 527 – 546.

CHIARELLA, C. (1992b): A new approach to the saddlepoint problem in a discrete-time non-linear perfect foresight monetary model. *Economic and Financial Computing*, 2, 39 – 52.

CHIARELLA, C. and P. FLASCHEL (1995): Keynesian monetary growth dynamics. The missing prototype. In: J. Flemmig (ed.): *Moderne Makroökonomik. Eine kritische Bestandsaufnahme.* Metropolis-Verlag, 345 – 411.

CHIARELLA, C. and P. FLASCHEL (1996a): Real and monetary cycles in models of Keynes-Wicksell type. *Journal of Economic Behavior and Organisation*, 30, 327 – 351.

CHIARELLA, C. and P. FLASCHEL (1996b): An integrative approach to prototype 2D-macromodels of growth-, price- and inventory dynamics. *Chaos, Solitons & Fractals*, 7, 2105 – 2133.

CHIARELLA, C. and P. FLASCHEL (1998): The dynamics of 'natural' rates of growth and employment. *Macroeconomic Dynamics*, 2, 345 – 368.

CHIARELLA, C. and P. FLASCHEL (1999a): The emergence of complex dynamics in a "naturally" nonlinear integrated Keynesian model of monetary growth. In: W.A. Barnett, C. Chiarella, S. Keen, R. Marks, and H. Schnabl (eds.): *Commerce, Complexity and Evolution: Topics in Economics, Finance, Marketing and Management.* Proceedings of the Twelfth International Symposium in Economic Theory and Econometrics. Cambridge: Cambridge University Press.

CHIARELLA, C. and P. FLASCHEL (1999b): *The Dynamics of Keynesian Monetary Growth: Macro Foundations.* To appear: Cambridge University Press.

CHIARELLA, C. and P. FLASCHEL (1999c): Keynesian monetary growth in open economies. *Annals of Operations Research*, 89, 35-59.

CHIARELLA, C. and P. FLASCHEL (1999d): 'High order' disequilibrium growth dynamics: Theoretical aspects and numerical features. To appear: *Journal of Economic Dynamics and Control.*

CHIARELLA, C. and P. FLASCHEL (1999e): *Open Economy Disequilibrium Growth Theory.* To appear: Springer Verlag.

CHIARELLA, C. and P. FLASCHEL (1999f): Towards Applied Disequilibrium Growth Theory: I. The starting model. UTS Sydney: Discussion Paper.

CHIARELLA, C. and P. FLASCHEL (1999g): Towards Applied Disequilibrium Growth Theory: II. Intensive form and steady state analysis of the model. UTS Sydney: Discussion Paper.

CHIARELLA, C. and P. FLASCHEL (1999h): Towards Applied Disequilibrium Growth Theory: III. Basic partial feedback structures and stability issues. UTS Sydney: Discussion Paper.

CHIARELLA, C. and P. FLASCHEL (1999i): Towards Applied Disequilibrium Growth Theory: IX. Global boundedness in the case of substitution. UTS Sydney: Discussion Paper.

CHIARELLA, C. and P. FLASCHEL (1999j): Applying disequilibrium growth theory. I. Investment, debt and debt deflation. University of Bielefeld: Discussion paper.

CHIARELLA, C. and P. FLASCHEL (1999k): Numerical analysis of debt deflation in a general model of disequilibrium growth. University of Bielefeld: Discussion paper.

CHIARELLA, C. and P. FLASCHEL (1999l): Applying disequilibrium growth theory. II. Housing, debt and debt deflation. University of Bielefeld: Discussion paper.

CHIARELLA, C., P. FLASCHEL, G. GROH, C. KÖPER and W. SEMMLER (1999a): Towards Applied Disequilibrium Growth Theory: VI. Substitution, money-holdings, wealth-effects and other extensions. UTS Sydney: Discussion Paper.

CHIARELLA, C., P. FLASCHEL, G. GROH, C. KÖPER and W. SEMMLER (1999b): Towards Applied Disequilibrium Growth Theory: VII. Intensive form and steady state analysis in the case of substitution. UTS Sydney: Discussion Paper.

CHIARELLA, C., P. FLASCHEL, G. GROH and W. SEMMLER (1999): AS-AD disequilibrium dynamics and economic growth. University of Bielefeld: Mimeo.

CHIARELLA, C., P. FLASCHEL and A. KHOMIN (1999a): *Numerical Simulation of Integrated Macrodynamic Systems*, Software and Manual (16bit version). Sydney: UTS, School of Finance and Economics.

CHIARELLA, C., P. FLASCHEL and A. KHOMIN (1999b): *Numerical Simulation of High Order Macrodynamic Systems*, Software and Manual (32bit version). Sydney: UTS, School of Finance and Economics.

CHIARELLA, C., P. FLASCHEL and P. ZHU (1999a): Towards Applied Disequilibrium Growth Theory: IV. Numerical investigations of the core 18D model. UTS Sydney: Discussion Paper.

CHIARELLA, C., P. FLASCHEL and P. ZHU (1999b): Towards Applied Disequilibrium Growth Theory: V. Global considerations. UTS Sydney: Discussion Paper.

CHIARELLA, C., P. FLASCHEL and P. ZHU (1999c): Towards Applied Disequilibrium Growth Theory: VIII. Numerical analysis in the case of substitution. UTS Sydney: Discussion Paper.

CHIARELLA, C. and A. KHOMIN (1999c): How to jump in the Dornbusch model. UTS Sydney, School of Finance and Economics: Working paper.

CHIARELLA, C., W. SEMMLER and S. MITTNIK (1998): Stock market, interest rate and output: A model and estimation for US time series data. University of Bielefeld: Discussion paper.

CLOWER, R. (1965): The Keynesian Counter-Revolution: A Theoretical Appraisal. In: F.H. Hahn and F.P.R. Brechling (eds.): *The Theory of Interest Rates.* London: Macmillan, 103 – 125.

CLOWER, R. (1996): On truth in teaching macroeconomics. In: D. Vaz and K. Velupillai (eds.): *Inflation, Institutions and Information. Essays in Honour of Axel Leijonhufvud.* London: Macmillan, 35 – 61.

COLANDER, D. (1993): Truth in teaching macroeconomics. In: Colander, D. and R. Brenner (eds.): *Educating Economists.* Ann Arbor: University of Michigan Press.

COLANDER, D. (1995): The stories we tell: A reconsideration of AS / AD analysis. *Journal of Economic Perspectives*, 9, 169 – 188.

COOLEY, T. (ed.) (1995): *Frontiers of Business Cycle Research.* Princeton, NJ: Princeton University Press.

CROSS, R.B. (1987): Hysteresis and instability in the natural rate of unemployment. *Scandinavian Journal of Economics*, 89, 71 – 89.

CROSS, R.B. (ed.) (1995): *The Natural Rate of Unemployment.* Cambridge, UK: Cambridge University Press.

DANA, R.A. and P. MALGRANGE (1984): The Dynamics of a Discrete Version of a Growth Cycle Model. In: J. Ancot (ed.): *Analyzing the Structure of Macromodels.* The Hague: Nijhoff Publishing.

D'ASPREMONT, C., R. DOS SANTOS FERREIRA and L.-A. GÉRARD-VARET (1989): Unemployment in an Extended Cournot Oligopoly Model. *Oxford Economic Papers*, 41, 490 – 505.

D'ASPREMONT, C., R. DOS SANTOS FERREIRA and L.-A. GÉRARD-VARET (1990): On Monopolistic Competition and Involuntary Unemployment. *Quarterly Journal of Economics*, 105, 895 – 919.

D'ASPREMONT, C., R. DOS SANTOS FERREIRA and L.-A. GÉRARD-VARET (1991): Imperfect Competition, Rational Expectations and Unemployment. In: W. A. Barnett et al. (eds.): *Equilibrium Theory and Applications: Proceedings of the sixth international symposium in economic theory and econometrics.* Cambridge: Cambridge University Press, 353 – 381.

D'ASPREMONT, C., R. DOS SANTOS FERREIRA and L.-A. GÉRARD-VARET (1995): Market power, coordination failures and endogenous fluctuations. In: H.-D. Dixon and N. Rankin (eds.): *The New Macroeconomics.* Cambridge: Cambridge University Press.

DEHEZ, P. (1985): Monopolistic Equilibrium and Involuntary Unemployment. *Journal of Economic Theory*, 36(1), 160 – 165.

DELEAU, M., C. LE VAN and P. MALGRANGE (1990): The long run of macroeconometric models. In: P. Champsaur et al.: *Essays in Honour of Edmond Malinvaud. Vol. 2: Macroeconomics.* Cambridge, MA: The MIT Press.

DESAI, M. (1973): Growth cycles and inflation in a model of the class struggle. *Journal of Economic Theory*, 6, 527 – 45.

DESAI, M. (1984): An econometric model of the share of wages in national income: UK 1855 - 1965. In: R.M. Goodwin et al. (eds.): *Nonlinear Models of Fluctuating Growth.* Heidelberg: Springer, 253 – 277.

DESAI, M. and A. SHAH (1981): Growth Cycles with Induced Technical Change. *The Economic Journal*, 91, 1006 – 1010.

DEVEREUX, M.B., HEAD, A.C. and B.J. LAPHAM (1993): Monopolistic competition, technology shocks, and aggregate fluctuations. *Economics Letters*, 41, 57 – 61.

DIXIT, A. and J. STIGLITZ (1977): Monopolistic Competition and Optimum Product Diversity. *American Economic Review*, 67, 297 – 308.

DIXON, H.D. (1987): A simple model of imperfect competition with Walrasian features. *Oxford Economic Papers*, 39, 134 – 160.

DIXON, H.D: and N. RANKIN (eds.) (1995): *The New Macroeconomics. Imperfect Markets and Policy Effectiveness.* Cambridge, UK: Cambridge University Press.

DOMAR, E.D. (1946): Capital expansion, rate of growth, and employment. *Econometrica*, 14, 137 – 147.

DORNBUSCH, R. (1976): Expectations and Exchange Rate Dynamics. *Journal of Political Economy*, 84, 1161 – 1176.

DORNBUSCH, R. and S. Fischer (1994/96): *Macroeconomics.* New York: McGraw-Hill (6/7th edition).

DUTT, A. and P. SKOTT (1996): Keynesian theory and the aggregate supply / aggregate demand framework. A defense. *Eastern Economic Journal*, 22, 313 – 30.

EICHENBAUM, M. (1997): Some thoughts on practical stabilization policy. *American Economic Review. Papers and Proceedings*, 87, 236 – 239.

EVANS, M.K. (1969), *Macroeconomic Activity.* New York: Harper & Row.

FAIR, R. (1971): *A Short-Run Forecasting Model of the United States Economy.* Lexington, MA: D.C. Heath.

FAIR, R. (1974): *A Model of Macroeconomic Activity. Vol. I: The Theoretical Model.* Cambridge, MA: Ballinger.

FAIR, R. (1976): *A Model of Macroeconomic Activity. Vol. II: The Empirical Model.* Cambridge, MA: Ballinger.

FAIR, R. (1984), *Specification, Estimation, and Analysis of Macroeconomic Models.* Cambridge: Harvard University Press.

FAIR, R. (1994): *Testing Macroeconometric Models.* Cambridge, MA: Harvard University Press.

FAIR, R. (1997a): Testing the NAIRU model for the United States. Yale University: Mimeo.

FAIR, R. (1997b): Testing the NAIRU model for 27 countries. Yale University: Mimeo.

FEICHTINGER, G. and R.F. HARTL (1986): *Optimale Kontrolle ökonomischer Prozesse.* Berlin/New York: de Gruyter.

FIELDS, T.W. and W.R. HART (1996): The AS-AD Model in Introductory Macroeconomics Texts: Theory Gone Awry. In: N. Aslanbeigui and M.I. Naples (eds.): *Rethinking Economic Principles. Critical Essays on Introductory Textbooks.* Burr Ridge, IL: Richard D. Irwin.

FISHER, I. (1933): The debt-deflation theory of great depressions. *Econometrica*, 1, 337 – 57.

FLASCHEL, P. (1984a): Some stability properties of Goodwin's growth cycle model. *Zeitschrift für Nationalökonomie*, 44, 63 – 69.

FLASCHEL, P. (1984b): The inflation-based "natural" rate of unemployment and the conflict over income distribution. In: R.M. Goodwin et al. (eds.): *Nonlinear Models of Fluctuating Growth.* Berlin et al.: Springer Verlag, 103 – 126.

FLASCHEL, P. (1991): Stability - independent of economic structure? A prototype analysis. *Structural Change and Economic Dynamics*, 2, 9 – 35.

FLASCHEL, P. (1992): A Keynes-Wicksell model of the 'growth cycle'. The myopic perfect foresight case. In: G. Feichtinger (ed.): *Dynamic Economic Models and Optimal Control. Proceedings of the Fourth Viennese Workshop on Dynamic Economic Models and Optimal Control.* Amsterdam: North Holland, 467 – 489.

FLASCHEL, P. (1993): *Macrodynamics. Income Distribution, Effective Demand and Cyclical Growth.* Frankfurt/M.: Verlag Peter Lang.

FLASCHEL, P. (1994a): Keynes-Friedman and Keynes-Marx models of monetary growth. *Ricerche Economiche*, 48, 45 – 70.

FLASCHEL, P. (1994b): The stability of models of monetary growth with adaptive or perfect expectations. In: W. Semmler (ed.): *Business Cycles: Theory and Empirical Methods.* Dordrecht, The Netherlands: Kluwer Academic Publishers, 197 – 229.

FLASCHEL, P. (1994c): A Harrodian knife-edge theorem for the wage-price sector? *Metroeconomica*, 45, 266 – 278.

FLASCHEL, P. (1995): Cooperation vs. solidarity in a complete version of the classical growth cycle. In: A. Riedl, G. Winckler and A. Wörgötter (eds.): *Macroeconomic Policy Games.* Physica-Verlag, 57 – 85.

FLASCHEL, P. (1999a): On the dominance of the Keynesian regime in disequilibrium growth theory. A note. To appear: *Journal of Economics.*

FLASCHEL, P. (1999b): Disequilibrium growth theory with insider - outsider effects. To appear: *Structural Change and Economic Dynamics.*

FLASCHEL, P. (1999c): Viability and corridor stability in Keynesian supply driven growth. To appear: Metroeconomica.

FLASCHEL, P. (1999d): Keynes-Marx and Keynes-Wicksell models of monetary growth. A framework for future analysis. To appear: *Review of Political Economy.*

FLASCHEL, P. and R. FRANKE (1996): Wage flexibility and the stability arguments of the Neoclassical Synthesis. *Metroeconomica*, 47, 1 – 18.

FLASCHEL, P. and R. FRANKE (1998): An old-Keynesian note on destabilizing price flexibility. To appear: *Review of Political Economy.*

FLASCHEL, P., FRANKE, R. and W. SEMMLER (1997): *Dynamic Macroeconomics: Instability, Fluctuations and Growth in Monetary Economies.* Cambridge, MA: The MIT Press.

FLASCHEL, P., GONG, G. and W. SEMMLER (1999): A Keynesian based econometric framework for studying monetary policy rules. University of Bielefeld: Discussion paper.

FLASCHEL, P. and G. GROH (1995): The Classical growth cycle: Reformulation, simulation and some facts. *Economic Notes*, 24, 293 – 326.

FLASCHEL, P. and G. GROH (1996a): *Keynesianische Makroökonomik. Unterbeschäftigung, Inflation und Wachstum.* Heidelberg: Springer.

FLASCHEL, P. and G. GROH (1996b): The stabilizing potential of policy rules in Keynesian monetary growth dynamics. *Systems Analysis – Modelling – Simulation*, 23, 39 – 72.

FLASCHEL, P. and G. GROH (1998): Textbook Stagflation Theory and Beyond. University of Bielefeld: Discussion Paper.

FLASCHEL, P., G. GROH and W. SEMMLER (1999): Investment of firms in capital and productivity growth. A macrodynamic analysis. University of Bielefeld: Discussion paper.

FLASCHEL, P. and C. Köper (1999): Real-financial interaction: A Keynes-Metzler-Goodwin portfolio approach. University of Bielefeld: Discussion paper.

FLASCHEL, P. and M. Krüger (1984): A model of cyclical growth using an endogenous aspiration factor. *Ricerche Economiche*, 38, 588 – 612.

FLASCHEL, P. and M. Krüger (1988): *Recent Approaches to Economic Dynamics.* Frankfurt/M.: Verlag Peter Lang.

FLASCHEL, P. and R. PICARD (1986): Problems concerning the dynamic analysis of a Keynesian model with perfect foresight. In: W. Semmler (ed.): *Competition, Instability, and Non-linear Cycles.* Berlin: Springer, 269 – 288.

FLASCHEL, P. and R. SETHI (1996): Classical dynamics in a general model of Keynes-Wicksell type. *Structural Change and Economic Dynamics*, 7, 401 – 428.

FLASCHEL, P. and R. SETHI (1999): The stability of models of monetary growth: Implications of nonlinearity. *Economic Modelling*, 16, 221 – 233.

FRANKE, R. (1992): Stable, Unstable, and Cyclical Behaviour in a Keynes-Wicksell Monetary Growth Model. *Oxford Economic Papers*, 44, 242 – 256.

FRANKE, R. (1996): A Metzlerian model of inventory growth cycles. *Structural Change and Economic Dynamics*, 7, 243 – 262.

FRANKE, R. and T. LUX (1993): Adaptive expectations and perfect foresight in a nonlinear Metzler model of the inventory cycle. *The Scandinavian Journal of Economics*, 95, 355 – 363.

FRANKE, R. and W. SEMMLER (1999): Bond rate, loan rate and Tobin's q in a temporary equilibrium model of the financial sector. To appear: Metroeconomica.

FRANKEL, J. A. and K. FROOT (1987): Using Survey Data to Test Standard Propositions Regarding Exchange Rate Expectations. *American Economic Review*, 77, 133 – 153.

FRANKEL, J. A. and FROOT, K. (1990): Chartists, Fundamentalists and Trading in the Foreign Exchange Market. *American Economic Review*, 80, 181 – 185.

FRIEDMAN, M. (1970): A Theoretical Framework for Monetary Analysis. *Journal of Political Economy*, 78, 193 – 238.

FRIEDMAN, M. (1971): A Monetary Theory of Nominal Income. *Journal of Political Economy*, 79, 323 – 337.

GALÍ, J. (1994a): Monopolistic Competition, endogenous markups, and growth. *European Economic Review*, 38, 748 – 756.

GALÍ, J. (1994b): Monopolistic Competition, Business Cycles, and the Composition of Aggregate Demand. *Journal of Economic Theory*, 63, 73 – 96.

GARRATT, A., LEE, K., PESERAN, M. and Y. SHIN (1998): A long-run structural macroeconometric model of the UK. Cambridge, UK: Mimeo.

GEORGE, D. A. R. and L. T. OXLEY (1985): Structural Stability and Model Design. *Economic Modelling*, 2, 307 – 316.

GONG, G., FLASCHEL, P. and W. SEMMLER (1999): A macroeconometric study on the labor market and monetary policy. Germany and the EMU. University of Bielefeld: Mimeo.

GOODWIN, R.M. (1951), The Non-linear Accelerator and the Persistence of Business Cycles. *Econometrica* 19, 1 – 17.

GOODWIN, R.M. (1967): A growth cycle. In: C.H. Feinstein (ed.): *Socialism, Capitalism and Economic Growth.* Cambridge: Cambridge University Press, 54 – 58.

GORDON, R. (1997): The time-varying NAIRU and its implications for economic policy. *Journal of Economic Perspectives*, 11, 11 – 32.

GRAY, M. and S. TURNOVSKY, S. (1979): The stability of exchange rate dynamics under myopic perfect foresight. *International Economic Review*, 20, 641 – 660.

GROTH, C. (1992): Keynesian-Monetarist dynamics and the corridor: A note. University of Copenhagen, Mimeo.

GROTH, C. (1993): Some unfamiliar dynamics of a familiar macro model. *Journal of Economics*, 58, 293 – 305.

HAIRAULT, J.-O. and F. PORTIER (1993): Money, New Keynesian macroeconomics and the business cycle. *European Economic Review*, 37, 1533 – 1568.

HARROD, R. (1939): An essay in dynamic economic theory. *The Economic Journal*, 49, 14 – 33.

HART, O.D. (1982): A Model of Imperfect Competition with Keynesian Features. *Quarterly Journal of Economics*, 97, 109 – 138.

HAYASHI, F. (1982): Tobin's marginal and average *q*. A neoclassical interpretation. *Econometrica*, 50, 213 – 24.

HEAP, H.S. (1980): Choosing the wrong natural rate: Accelerating inflation or decelerating employment and growth. *Economic Journal*, 90, 611 – 20.

HÉNIN, P.-Y. and P. MICHEL: (1982) *Croissance et Accumulation en Deséquilibre.* Paris: Economica.

HICKS, J. (1950): *A Contribution to the Theory of the Trade Cycle.* Oxford: Oxford University Press.

HIRSCH, M. AND S. SMALE (1974): *Differential Equations, Dynamical Systems and Linear Algebra.* London: Academic Press.

HORNSTEIN, A. (1993): Monopolistic competition, increasing returns to scale, and the importance of productivity shocks. *Journal of Monetary Economics*, 31, 299 – 316.

JONES, H.G. (1975): *An Introduction to Modern Theories of Economic Growth.* London: Thomas Nelson & Sons.

KALDOR, N. (1940): A model of the trade cycle. *Economic Journal*, 50, 78 – 92.

KALECKI, M. (1935): A macro-dynamic theory of business cycles. *Econometrica*, 3, 327 – 44.

KEEN, S. (1999): The nonlinear economics of debt deflation. In: W.A. Barnett, C. Chiarella, S. Keen, R. Marks, and H. Schnabl (eds.): *Commerce, Complexity and Evolution: Topics in Economics, Finance, Marketing and Management.* Proceedings of the Twelfth International Symposium in Economic Theory and Econometrics. Cambridge: Cambridge University Press.

KEYNES, J.M. (1936): *The General Theory of Employment, Interest and Money.* New York: Macmillan.

KLUNDERT, T. VAN DE and A. VAN SCHAIK (1990): Unemployment persistence and the loss of productive capacity: A Keynesian approach. *Journal of Macroeconomics*, 12, 363 – 380.

KUH, E. (1967): A productivity theory of the wage levels – An alternative to the Phillips curve. *Review of Economic Studies*, 34, 333 – 360.

KYDLAND, F. E. AND E. F. PRESCOTT (1982): Time to Build and Aggregate Fluctuation. *Econometrica*, 50, 1345 – 1370.

LAXTON, D., D. ROSE and D. TAMBAKIS (1997): The U.S. Phillips curve: The case for asymmetry. Mimeo.

LAXTON, D., P. ISARD, H. FARUQUEE, E. PRASAD and B. TURTELBOOM (1998): *MULTIMOD Mark III. The core dynamic and steady-state models.* Washington, DC: International Monetary Fund.

LAYARD, R., S. NICKELL and R. JACKMAN (1991): *Unemployment. Macroeconomic performance and the labor market.* Oxford: Oxford University Press.

LINDBECK, A. and D.J. SNOWER (1989): *The Insider-Outsider Theory of Employment and Unemployment.* Cambridge, MA: The MIT Press.

LONG, J.B. and PLOSSER (1983): Real Business Cycles. *Journal of Political Economy*, 91, 39 – 69.

LORENZ, H.W. and G. GABISCH (1989): *Business Cycle Theory: A Survey of Methods and Concepts.* Berlin: Springer, 2nd ed.

LUCAS, R.E. (1976): Econometric Policy Evaluation: A Critique. In: K. Brunner and A. Meltzer (eds.): *The Phillips Curve and Labor Markets.* Amsterdam and New York: North Holland.

LUCAS, R.E.(1988): On the mechanics of economic development. *Journal of Monetary Economics*, 22, 3 – 42.

LUCAS, R.E. and L.A. RAPPING (1969): Real Wages, Employment, and Inflation. *Journal of Political Economy*, 77, 1969, 721 – 754.

LUX, T. (1993): A note on the stability of endogenous cycles in Diamond's model of search and barter. *Journal of Economics*, 56, 185 – 196.

LUX, T. (1995): Corridor stability in the Dendrinos model of regional factor movements. *Geographical Analysis*, 27, 360 – 368.

MALINVAUD, E. (1977): *The Theory of Unemployment Reconsidered.* Oxford: Basil Blackwell.

MALINVAUD, E. (1980): *Profitability and Unemployment.* Cambridge: Cambridge University Press.

MALINVAUD, E. (1984): *Mass Unemployment.* Oxford: Basil Blackwell.

MANKIW, N.G. (1985): Small Menu Costs and Large Business Cycles: A Macroeconomic Model of Monopoly. *Quarterly Journal of Economics*, 100, 529 – 537.

MANKIW, N.G. and P.M. Romer (eds.) (1991): *New Keynesian Economics,* Vol. I,II. Cambridge, MA: MIT Press.

MANKIW, N. G., P.M. ROMER and D. N. WEIL (1992): A Contribution to the Empirics of Economic Growth. *The Quarterly Journal of Economics*, 107, 407 – 437.

MATTHEWS, R.C.O. (1970): *The Trade Cycle.* Cambridge: Cambridge University Press.

MCCALLUM, B.T. (1996): Neoclassical v. endogenous growth analysis: An overview. *Federal Reserve Bank of Richmond: Economic Quarterly*, 1996, 82, 41 – 71.

MCDONALD, I.M. AND R.M. SOLOW (1981): *Wage Bargain and Employment. American Economic Review*, 71, 896 – 908.

MCKIBBIN, W. and J. SACHS (1991): *Global Linkages. Macroeconomic Interdependence and Cooperation in the World Economy.* Washington, D.C.: The Brookings Institution.

METZLER, L. A. (1941): The nature and stability of inventory cycles. *Review of Economic Statistics*, 23, 113 – 129.

MURPHY, K.M. and R. TOPEL (1997): Unemployment and nonemployment. *American Economic Review. Papers and Proceedings*, 87, 295 – 300.

NELSON, C.R. and C.I. PLOSSER (1982): Trends and random walks in macroeconomic time series: Some evidence and implications. *Journal of Monetary Economics*, 10, 139 – 162.

NEVILLE, J. and B. RAO (1996): The use and abuse of aggregate demand and supply functions. *The Manchester School*, LXIV, 189 – 207.

OKUN, A.M. (1970): *The Political Economy of Prosperity.* Washington, D.C.: The Brookings Institution.

ORPHANIDES, A. and R. SOLOW (1990): Money, inflation and growth. In: B. Friedman and F. Hahn (eds.): *Handbook of Monetary Economics.* Amsterdam: North Holland, 223 – 261.

OXLEY, L. and D. A. R. GEORGE (1994): Linear Saddlepoint Dynamics 'On Their Head'. The Scientific Content of the New Orthodoxy in Macrodynamics. *European Journal of Political Economy*, 10, 389 – 400.

PARKER, T.S. and L.O. CHUA (1989): *Practical Numerical Algorithms for Chaotic Systems.* Berlin: Springer Verlag.

PARKIN, M. (1986): The Output-Inflation Tradeoff When Prices Are Costly to Change. *Journal of Political Economy*, 94, 200 – 224.

PHELPS, E. and G. ZOEGA (1997): The rise and downward trend of the natural rate. *American Economic Review. Papers and Proceedings*, 87, 283 – 289.

PHILLIPS, A.W. (1954): Stabilisation Policy in a Closed Economy. *The Economic Journal*, 64, 290 – 323.

PHILLIPS, A.W. (1958): The relation between unemployment and the rate of change of money wage rates in the United Kingdom, 1861 – 1957. *Economica*, 25, 283 – 299.

PICARD, P. (1983): Inflation and growth in a disequilibrium macroeconomic model. *Journal of Economic Theory*, 30, 266 – 295.

PISSARIDES, C. AND G. MORTENSEN (1997): Theories of Unemployment. in: J.B. Taylor and M. Woodford (eds.): *Handbook of Macroeconomics.* Amsterdam: North-Holland, forthcoming 1999.

POSTON, T. and I. STEWART (1978): *Catastrophe Theory and its Applications.* Boston: Pitman.

POWELL, A. and C. MURPHY (1997): *Inside a Modern Macroeconometric Model. A Guide to the Murphy Model.* Heidelberg: Springer.

ROBERTS, J.M. (1997): *The wage curve and the Phillips curve.* Washington: Board of Governors of the Federal Reserve System, mimeo.

ROMER, P.M. (1986): Increasing returns and long-run growth. *Journal of Political Economy*, 94, 1002 – 37.

ROMER, P.M. (1990): Endogenous Technological Change. *Journal of Political Economy*, 98, 71 – 102.

ROMER, D. (1996): *Advanced Macroeconomics.* New York: McGraw-Hill Companies.

ROSE, H. (1967): On the non-linear theory of the employment cycle. *Review of Economic Studies*, 34, 153 – 173.

ROSE, H. (1990): *Macroeconomic Dynamics. A Marshallian Synthesis.* Cambridge, MA: Basil Blackwell.

ROTEMBERG, J.J. (1987): The New Keynesian Microfoundations. In: S. Fischer (ed.): *NBER macroeconomics annual.* Cambridge: NBER and MIT Press.

ROTEMBERG, J.J. and M. WOODFORD (1992): Oligopolistic Pricing and the Effects of Aggregate Demand on Economic Activity. *Journal of Political Economy*, 100, 1153 – 1207.

ROTEMBERG, J.J. and M. WOODFORD (1993): Dynamic General Equilibrium Models with Imperfectly Competitive Product Markets. In: T.F. Cooley (ed.): *Frontiers in Business Cycle Research.* Princeton: Princeton University Press.

ROWTHORN, B. (1980): *Capitalism, Conflict and Inflation.* London: Lawrence and Wishart.

SAMUELSON, P. (1939): Interactions between the multiplier analysis and the principle of acceleration. *Review of Economic Statistics*, 21, 75 – 78.

SARGENT, T. (1973): Interest rates and prices in the long run: A study of the Gibson paradox. *Journal of Money, Credit, and Banking*, 5,385 – 449.

SARGENT, T. (1987): *Macroeconomic Theory.* New York: Academic Press.

SARGENT, T. (1993): *Bounded Rationality in Macroeconomics.* Oxford: Oxford University Press.

SARGENT, T. (1998): *The Conquest of American Inflation.* Princeton, N.J.: Princeton University Press

SARGENT, T. and N. WALLACE (1973): The Stability of Models of Money and Growth with Perfect Foresight. *Econometrica*, 41, 1043 – 1048.

SCHNEIDER, J. and T. ZIESEMER (1994): What's new and what's old in new growth theory: Endogenous technology, microfoundation and growth rate predictions - A critical overview. Maastricht Economic Research Institute on Innovation and Technology. Discussion paper.

SEMMLER, W. and M. SIEVEKING (1997): The use of vector field analysis for studying debt dynamics. University of Bielefeld: Discussion paper.

SHAPIRO, C. and J. STIGLITZ (1984): Equilibrium Unemployment as a Worker Discipline Device. *American Economic Review*, 74, 433 – 444.

SILVESTRE, J. (1990): There May Be Unemployment when the Labour Market is Competitive and the Output Market is Not. *The Economic Journal*, 100, 899 – 913.

SILVESTRE, J. (1993): The Market-Power Foundations of Macroeconomic Policy. *Journal of Economic Literature*, XXXI, 105 – 141.

SILVESTRE, J. (1995): Market Power in Macroeconomic Models: New Developments. *Annales d'Économie et de Statistique*, 37/38, 319 – 356.

SKOTT, P. (1991): Cyclical Growth in a Kaldorian model. In: E.J. Nell and W. Semmler (eds.): *Nicholas Kaldor and Mainstream Economics.* London: Macmillan, 379 – 394.

SOLOW, R. (1990): Goodwin's growth cycle: Reminiscence and rumination. In: K. Velupillai (ed.): *Nonlinear and Multisectoral Macrodynamics.* London: Macmillan, 31 – 41.

SOLOW, R. and J. STIGLITZ (1968): Output, employment and wages in the short-run. *Quarterly Journal of Economics*, 82, 537 – 560.

STAIGER, D., STOCK J.H. and M.W. WATSON (1997): The NAIRU, unemployment and monetary policy. *Journal of Economic Perspectives*, 11, 33 – 50.

STIGLITZ, J. (1997): Reflections on the natural rate hypothesis. *Journal of Economic Perspectives*, 11, 3 – 10.

STOCK J.H. and M.W. WATSON (1997): Business cycle fluctuations in U.S. macroeconometric time series. Harvard / Princeton University: Mimeo.

STROGATZ, S. H. (1994): *Nonlinear Dynamics and Chaos.* New York: Addison-Wesley.

SUMMERS, L. (1990): *Understanding Unemployment.* Cambridge, MA: The MIT Press.

TIROLE, J. (1988): *The Theory of Industrial Organization.* Cambridge, MA/London: The MIT Press.

TOBIN, J. (1969): A General Equilibrium Approach to Monetary Theory. *Journal of Money, Credit and Banking*, 1, 15 – 29.

TOBIN, J. (1975): Keynesian models of recession and depression. *American Economic Review*, 65, 195 – 202.

TOBIN, J. (1992): An Old Keynesian counterattacks. *Eastern Economic Journal*, 18, 387 – 400.

TOBIN, J. (1993): Price flexibility and output stability. *Journal of Economic Perspectives*, 18, 387 – 400.

TOBIN, J. (1994): Price flexibility and output stability. An Old Keynesian view. In: W. Semmler (ed.): *Business Cycles: Theory and Empirical methods.* Boston: Kluwer Academic Publishers, 165 – 195.

TURNOVSKY, S.J. (1977): *Macroeconomic Analysis and Stabilization Policies.* Cambridge: Cambridge University Press.

TURNOVSKY, S. J. (1995): *Methods of Macroeconomic Dynamics.* Cambridge, MA: The MIT Press.

UZAWA, H. (1965): Optimum technical change in an aggregative model of economic growth. *International Economic Review*, 6, 18 – 31.

VARIAN, H. R. (1979): Catastrophe Theory and Business Cycle. *Economic Inquiry*, 17, 14 – 28.

WEITZMAN, M.L. (1985): The Simple Macroeconomics of Profit Sharing. *American Economic Review*, 75, 937 – 953.

WHITLEY, J. (1994): *A Course in Macroeconomic Modelling and Forecasting.* New York: Harvester / Wheatsheaf.

WIGGINS, S. (1990): *Introduction to Applied Nonlinear Dynamical Systems and Chaos.* Heidelberg: Springer Verlag.

Druck: Strauss Offsetdruck, Mörlenbach
Verarbeitung: Schäffer, Grünstadt